July 4–6, 2012
Berlin, Germany

Association for
Computing Machinery

Advancing Computing as a Science & Profession

EuroITV'12

Proceedings of the 10th European Conference on
Interactive TV and Video

Sponsored by:

FOKUS Fraunhofer

In-cooperation with:

ACM SIGCHI, ACM SIGMM and ACM SIGWEB

Advancing Computing as a Science & Profession

The Association for Computing Machinery
2 Penn Plaza, Suite 701
New York, New York 10121-0701

Notice to Past Authors of ACM-Published Articles

ACM intends to create a complete electronic archive of all articles and/or other material previously published by ACM. If you have written a work that has been previously published by ACM in any journal or conference proceedings prior to 1978, or any SIG Newsletter at any time, and you do NOT want this work to appear in the ACM Digital Library, please inform permissions@acm.org, stating the title of the work, the author(s), and where and when published.

ISBN: 978-1-4503-1107-6

Additional copies may be ordered prepaid from:

ACM Order Department
PO Box 30777
New York, NY 10087-0777, USA

Phone: 1-800-342-6626 (USA and Canada)
+1-212-626-0500 (Global)
Fax: +1-212-944-1318
E-mail: acmhelp@acm.org
Hours of Operation: 8:30 am – 4:30 pm ET

Printed in the USA

Chairs' Welcome

It is our great pleasure to welcome you to the *2012 European Interactive TV conference – EuroITV'12*. This year's conference marks the 10th anniversary of our community. The conference continues its tradition of being the premier forum for researchers and practitioners in the area of interactive TV and video to share their insights on systems and enabling technologies, human computer interaction as well as media and economic studies.

EuroITV'12 provides researchers and practitioners a unique interdisciplinary venue to share and learn from each others' perspectives. This year, the theme of the conference - *Bridging People, Places and Platforms* - aimed at eliciting contributions that cover the increasingly diverse and heterogeneous infrastructure, services, applications and concepts that make up the experience of interacting with audio-visual content. We hope you will find them interesting and help you identify new directions for future research and development.

The call for papers attracted 91 full and short paper submissions from Asia, Australia, Europe, and the Americas. The program committee accepted 31 papers that cover a variety of topics, including *cross-platform experiences, leveraging social networks, novel gesture based interaction techniques, accessibility, media consumption, content production and delivery optimization.* In addition, the program includes keynote speeches by Janet Murray (Georgia Tech) on Emerging Storytelling Structures and Olga Khroustaleva & Tom Broxton (YouTube) on supporting the ecosystem of YouTube. We hope that these proceedings will serve as a valuable reference for researchers and practitioners in the area of interactive multimedia consumption.

We extend our gratitude to all members of the organizing committee, the steering committee and our host FOKUS Fraunhofer who made this event possible. We thank Kenneth Cruz for his support on the ACM DL inclusion and Lisa Tolles at Sheridan Printing Company for taking good care of processing the papers and providing the proceedings in a timely manner.

Putting together *EuroITV'12* was a genuine team effort spanning six continents and many time zones. We first thank the authors for providing the content of the program. We are also grateful to the program committee, who worked very hard to review papers and provide feedback for authors, and to the track chairs for their dedicated work and meta-reviews. Finally, we thank our sponsors Fraunhofer and DFG, our (in-)cooperation partners the ACM SIGs (SIGCHI, SIGWEB, SIGMM) and interactiondesign.org, and our media partners informitv and Beuth University Berlin.

We hope that you will find this program interesting and thought provoking and that the conference will provide you with a valuable opportunity to share ideas with other researchers and practitioners from institutions and companies from around the world.

Stefan Arbanowski & Stephan Steglich
EuroITV'12 General Chairs
Fraunhofer FOKUS, Berlin, Germany

Hendrik Knoche[1] & Jan Hess[2]
EuroITV'12 Program Chairs
[1] EPFL, Switzerland
[2] University of Siegen, Germany

Table of Contents

Session 4: Second Screens I

Session Chair: Regina Bernhaupt *(Ruwido)*

Session 5: New Perspectives

Session Chair: David Geerts *(K.U. Leuven)*

Session 6: Mobile Perspectives

Session Chair: Michael Darnell *(Microsoft TV)*

Session 7: Social – Bridging People

Session Chair: Pablo Cesar *(CWI)*

Session 8: Second Screen II – Bridging Platforms

Session Chair: Marianna Obrist *(University of Newcastle)*

Session 9: Bridging Topics

Session Chair: Jorge Abreu *(Universidade de Aveiro)*

2012 EuroITV, Bridging People, Places & Platforms

General Chairs:	Stefan Arbanowski, Fraunhofer *(Fraunhofer FOKUS, Germany)* Stephan Steglich, Fraunhofer *(Fraunhofer FOKUS, Germany)*
Program Chairs:	Hendrik Knoche *(EPFL, Switzerland)* Jan Hess *(University of Siegen, Germany)*
Tutorial & Workshop Chairs:	Maria da Graça Pimentel *(Universidade de São Paulo, Brazil)* Regina Bernhaupt *(Ruwido, Austria)*
Doctoral Consortium Chairs:	Marianna Obrist *(University of Newcastle, UK)* George Lekakos *(Athens University of Economics and Business, Greece)*
Demonstration Chairs:	Jean-Claude Dufourd *(France Telecom, France)* Lyndon Nixon *(STI, Austria)*
iTV in Industry:	Patrick Huber *(Sky Germany)*
Grand Challenge Chairs:	Artur Lugmayr *(Tampere University of Technology, Finland)* Milena Szafir *(Manifesto 21.TV, Brazil)*
Track Chairs:	David A. Shamma *(Yahoo! Research, USA)* Teresa Chambel *(Universidade de Lisboa, Portugal)* Florian 'Floyd' Mueller *(RMIT University, Australia)* Gunnar Stevens *(University of Siegen, Germany)* Célia Quico *(Universidade Lusófona de Humanidades e Tecnologias, Portugal)* Filomena Papa *(Fondazione Ugo Bordoni, Roma, Italy)*
Sponsor Chairs:	Oliver Friedrich *(Deutsche Telekom/T-Systems, Germany)* Shelley Buchinger *(University of Vienna, Austria)* Ajit Jaokar *(Futuretext, UK)*
Publicity Chairs:	David Geerts *(CUO, IBBT / K.U. Leuven, Belgium)* Robert Seeliger *(Fraunhofer FOKUS, Berlin, Germany)*
Local Chair:	Robert Kleinfeld *(Fraunhofer FOKUS, Berlin, Germany)*

Reviewers:

Jorge Abreu
Pedro Almeida
Anne Aula
Frank Bentley
Petter Bae Brandtzæg
Regina Bernhaupt
Michael Bove
Dan Brickley
Shelley Buchinger
Steffen Budweg
Pablo Cesar
Teresa Chambel
Konstantinos Chorianopoulos
Matt Cooper
Cédric Courtois
Maria Da Graça Pimentel
Jorge de Abreu
Lieven De Marez
Sergio Denicoli
Carlos Duarte
Luiz Fernando Gomes Soares
Oliver Friedrich
David Geerts
Alberto Gil-Solla
Richard Griffiths
Gustavo Gonzalez-Sanchez
Rudinei Goularte
Mark Guelbahar
Nuno Guimarães
Gunnar Harboe
Henry Holtzman
Alejandro Jaimes
Geert-Jan Houben
Iris Jennes
Jens Jensen
Hendrik Knoche
Marie José Monpetit
Omar Niamut
Amela Karahasanovic
Ian Kegel
Rodrigo Laiola Guimarães
George Lekakos
Bram Lievens
Stefano Livi
Martin Lopez-Nores
João Magalhães
Reed Martin
Oscar Martinez-Bonastre
Judith Masthoff
Maja Matijasevic
Thomas Mirlacher
Lyndon Nixon
Marianna Obrist
Corinna Ogonowski
Margherita Pagani
Isabella Palombini
Jose Pazos-Arias
Chengyuan Peng
Jo Pierson
Fernando Ramos
Mark Rice
Bartolomeo Sapio
David A. Shamma
Mijke Slot
Mark Springett
Roberto Suarez
Manfred Tscheligi
Alexandros Tsiaousis
Pauliina Tuomi
Tomaz Turk
Chris Van Aart
Wendy Van den Broeck
Paula Viana
Nairon S. Viana
Petri Vuorimaa
Zhiwen Yu

Additional Reviewers:

Marco de Sa
Francisco Javier
Burón Fernández
Rong Hu
Johanna Meurer

EuroITV 2012 Sponsors & Supporters

Sponsors:

In cooperation with:

Supporters:

informitv

Transcending Transmedia: Emerging Story Telling Structures for the Emerging Convergence Platforms

Janet H. Murray
Georgia Tech
Digital Media Program
Atlanta, GA 30308 USA
+1 404 894 6202
jmurray@gatech.edu

ABSTRACT

Although the current paradigm for expanded participatory storytellling is the "transmedia" exploitation of the same storyworld on multiple platforms, it can be more productive to think of the digital medium as a single platform, combining all the functionalities we now associate with networked computers, game consoles, and conventionally delivered episodic television to enhance the traditional strengths and cultural functions of television. By looking at the how the four affordances of the digital medium – the procedural, participatory, encyclopedic, and spatial – apply to three core characteristics of television – moving images, sustained storytelling, and individual viewing in the presence of a mass audience -- we can identify areas of emerging conventions and widening opportunity for design innovation

Categories and Subject Descriptors

H.5.2 [**Information Interfaces and Presentation**]: User Interfaces - *Prototyping, Interaction styles, Graphical User Interfaces.*

Keywords

Interactive Television, Transmedia, Hyperserial

1. INTRODUCTION

In 2003 Henry Jenkins coined the term "transmedia storytelling" to describe a framework that he predicted would become the norm as the Pokemon generation came of age:

> By design, Pokemon unfolds across games, television programs, films, and books, with no media privileged over any other. For our generation, the hour-long ensemble-based, serialized drama was the pinnacle of sophisticated storytelling, but for the next generation, it is going to seem, well, less than child's play. Younger consumers have become information hunters and gatherers, taking pleasure in tracking down character backgrounds and plot points and making connections between different texts within the same franchise. [7]

Jenkins argued for "a model of co-creation not adaptation" similar to the way that the *Star Wars* series had added detail to a single consistent fantasy world by extending it beyond the films to print, TV, and videogames [7]. In 2006 he praised the *Matrix* producers for releasing a game that was supplementary in this way and identified this strategy as exemplary of "convergence culture" in which old and new media forms were increasingly intertwined but still distinct from one another [8]. Most recently, Jenkins has had to distinguish his vision from other claims on the "transmedia" buzzword (as it has become within the entertainment industry), such as "transmedia branding." For Jenkins, transmedia storytelling always extends rather than merely adapts an existing story, by serving one or more of these functions: offering backstory, maps of the world, multiple character's perspectives on the action, or by deepening audience engagement [9].

Jenkins distinguishes the transmedia model in this way from earlier franchising, which we can think of as the Mickey Mouse Lunchbox model. A lunchbox does not extend the story of Mickey Mouse or offer any additional insight into his motivations. It does increase audience attachment to the familiar figure, and it also commodifies that attachment by taking the character out of the fictional sphere and into the world of branding. He also distinguishes it from the "Digital Revolution model" in which old media displaces new media [8] [9].

In 1997 I included a chapter on "Digital TV" in a book on the future of narrative [11]. I was not proposing a "Digital Revolution" model of displacement, but I was predicting that the arrival of anew medium of representation would result in new narrative forms. I offered the term "hyperserial" to describe the kind of storytelling that I expected to be fostered by the movement of television to digital delivery and the advent of the web [11]. Observing that "the Internet is beginning to function as an alternate broadcasting system" as "the computer, television, and telephone are becoming a single home appliance." I noted the early stages of what is now called "social media" as "viewers populate hundreds of computer chat rooms and newsgoups, often logging on ... while watching the show in order to share their responses with fellow audience members." I predicted that this demand for participatory engagement would increase, and over the next decade it did just that as broadband coverage increased and more and more people became accustomed to watching TV while simultaneously online, first with their desktops and laptops, and then with their mobile devices.

In 1997 I thought that "the first steps toward a new *hyperserial* format would be the close integration of a digital archive such as a Web site, with a broadcast television program." I described the kinds of items that such a website might contain – diaries, personal possessions of fictional characters, explorable space that paralleled the sets of the television show—and I also predicted the increasing demand of fans for more participatory access to the story world. Like Henry Jenkins in his description of transmedia, I saw the value

EuroITV'12, July 4–6, 2012, Berlin, Germany.

of this web-based material as providing an extension of the story world:

> By filling in the holes in the dramatic narrative, holes that prevent viewers from fully believing in the characters, and by presenting situations that do not resolve themselves within the rhythms of series television, the hyperserial archive could extend melodramatic broadcast drama into a more complex narrative world.

I predicted as well that the bridge to this kind of storytelling would be the availability of complete seasons of television shows in digital form, which unlike the then standard of VCR tape, "would be searchable by content" so that viewers could call up a favorite scene or follow a single thread. [11]

The extensive fan involvement with the television series *Lost* (2004-2010) and the subsequent extension of the story into official websites and games, is a good model of the "transmedia" and "hyperserial" form, and gives ample examples of successful and unsuccessful storytelling strategies. The mysterious supernatural plot elements fostered a community of speculation, giving occupation to the "hunters and gatherers" that Jenkins described, and the encyclopedic detail of the proliferating characters, with their elaborate backstories, mysterious powers, and intertwined relationships led to the creation of an online fan-produced encyclopedia. *Lost* benefitted from the immersion phenomena I have called "the collective creation of belief" as viewers tried to make sense of elements that the writers often did not understand themselves, and in doing so reinforced the illusion of hidden depths. *Lost* also exemplified an important design challenge for "transmedia" in the dissatisfaction fans expressed at the poor imitation of the original cast in the videogame, and confusions it created over which non-broadcast story elements were "canonical" and part of the central storyworld and which were just throw-away riffs on similar situations.

Both *Hamlet on the Holodeck* and Henry Jenkins' seminal essay use the novels of William Faulkner as a reference point. Faulkner created a fictional county with characters who recurred and were seen from different angles and at different life stages across his many novels and short stories. Jenkins points to Faulkner and Tolkein as engaging in "world-creation." This perspective is consonant with the increasing emphasis in narratology [6] and game studies [10] on the creation of narrative not only as a sequence of events but as a richly imagined, concretely specified "story world." One useful way of thinking about a "canonical" design space that transcends any single media format and is consistent across it is to think of it not as a single "story" but as a "story world." Faulkner's Yoknapatapha County, Tolkein's Middle Earth, George Lucas' Star Wars universe are all self-consistent fictional worlds in which characters and events are kept consistent across multiple books (for the first two) and multiple media formats (for Lucas). Each fictional instance adds something to the story, deepening the experience of the other elements.

There are at least three key differences between earlier story franchises, and the more recent transmedia activity. However, often these differences do not go as far as my own or Jenkins' hopes for hyperserial/transmedia storytelling. First of all, current transmedia usually goes beyond the "lunch box" model of characters as decorative commodities. Web games, however, may still reflect a limited decorative approach, merely "skinning" a cliché'd game format with images loosely drawn from the television show, just as Mickey Mouse might appear on special editions of familiar board games, or popular superheroes on arcade platform games. Fans now expect to see not just repetition of the familiar story elements, but an elaboration with additional information, such as an on-line blog kept by one of the wives on the HBO show *Big Love*, or a spoof website for the Dunder Miflin paper firm that is the setting for *The Office.* But often this elaboration is thin and not as richly authored, not as dramatic, revealing, or funny as the base series.

Secondly, the current transmedia proliferation is usually simultaneous with the release of the primary, often episodic story content. In the older model, a fan might go to the movie when it is released and then months or years later go to the theme park ride based on the movie. Now viewers can tune into the TV show while downloading the social network or game or informational application that accompanies it. For example, cable subscribers to HBO can view its fantasy series, *Game of Thrones,* which is based on a series of novels with based on Tolkien-like world-creation, over the internet on HBO Go which provides annotations synchronized with the video feed. *Frontline* and the web-based video productions of the New York Times, provide similar synchronization of primary documents with video. For the fictional worlds, however, the synchronized material in some "companion apps" can be distracting trivia questions, or, in the case of *Game of Thrones,* it does not provide enough information to bring a new viewer up to speed on the highly complex story world.

Thirdly, as predicted by Jenkins' emphasis on fan creativity, the current transmedia landscape includes an active two-way channel between the creators of the fictional world and the viewers. For example, Graham Yost , the creator of Justified, has said that the writers decided to make Winona, the lover and ex-wife of the hero, Raylan, pregnant after reading online that fans thought she might be pregnant because of a scene in which Raylan tenderly touches her belly while discussing an encounter with a pregnant criminal. As the blogosphere and twitter feeds of active viewers converges with professional commentary and official postings, fans, critics, and writers find themselves in an ongoing conversation in which each group is very much aware of the other's presence. Fans are aware that the writers are reading their words just as the writers are aware that the fans are critically viewing their stories and scanning their blog posts for inside information. And critics are often caught in between, subject to energetic responses from the fan community while functioning as professionals in relationship to the producers.

So I agree with Henry Jenkins that there is a noticeable difference in media expression from the earlier franchise and adaptation model, that we can recognize as "transmedia." And I recognize that much of this activity corresponds to strategies that I predicted under the rubric of "hyperserial." But I take issue with the term because it is additive. Just as "photoplay," an early term for movies, captures the now outdated sense that a dramatic film was merely a photographed play, "transmedia" suggests that television is a fixed entity separate from videogames and websites and will always remain so. You do not have to subscribe to the Digital Revolution Model, as Jenkins calls it, find this Static Media Model (as I would call it) problematic.

Television has changed in important ways over the past 15 years because of the growth of digital modes of inscription and transmission. Television content is now detached from temporal presentation, networks, and from standard broadcast or cable/satellite delivery. Most of my students do not own a television set, but they watch television programs regularly on computers or mobile devices. Television series are increasingly conceptualized (as I predicted they would be) in year-long arcs because digital formats – DVDs, DVRs, streaming video, on-demand archives – are making them available to viewers as multi-episode and even multi-season units.

Convergence is usually seen as an opportunity for two new kinds of electronic participation. The first can be thought of as "Jennifer Anniston's Sweater" since it has been invoked at least from the time of the popularity of *Friends*, as associating a "buy" button with the enticing clothing and furniture and other products that are associated with the charisma of beloved and familiar TV characters. The second is often called "discovery" – the establishment of the equivalent of the TV program guide for the new multi-channel and multi-source environment – an electronic program guide that would cover YouTube and Hulu and Netflix as well as tonight's local and national and international offerings. But the buy button and the search utility are extraneous to the central activity of immersive viewing. The more interesting question for designers is to ask how television viewing itself will change as the full affordances of computation become available within the same platform.

2. Expanding TV with Digital Affordances

Instead of choosing between the Static Media Model and the Digital Revolution Model, we can look at how television might continue to change as producers and viewers take advantage of digital affordances. I have argued elsewhere [11] [16] that everything made of bits is a single medium, with four characteristic affordances: the procedural, participatory, encyclopedic, and spatial. Television is currently transmitted and stored in digital form and is delivered on the same screen and often through the same device that provides access to videogames and websites. If we step back from the current uncertain marketplace in which multiple vendors are vying to distribute and display television content, we can see the possibility of a future environment of true convergence in which everything we can do on a computer or a game console can also be done in the context of television viewing.

In trying to anticipate what we will make of such an environment we can start by identifying the core human purposes and pleasures of television that have nothing to do with whether or not networks, cable companies, or equipment manufacturers will profit from it. What makes a piece of media into television? It is not whether it is put on the air by NBC or HBO or BBC or delivered by Comcast or Direct TV or B Sky B. Television entails moving images, sustained story-telling with fictional or non-fictional characters and situations, and the opportunity for viewing at home alone while simultaneously sharing the experience with a mass audience. So the opportunities for design innovation lie at the intersection of these three characteristics of television with the four affordances of the digital medium.

2.1 High Resolution Interactivity

Television is recognizable as a stream of moving images appearing on some screen in our homes. We can imagine many enhancements of those images, from the underutilized 3D sets released with viewing glasses, to the creation of holographic projections. The more visually dense the information we transmit the more television becomes available as a window into immersive environments, both real and fantastic. This new visual platform has produced experimentation with ambient video, which does not require active or continuous viewership but which reward attention, according to Jim Bizzocchi who creates ambient video installations of scenes in the Rocky Mountains that change slowly [1].

Part of the power of television as a mass entertainment form is its role as a visual/auditory recorder of unfolding events whose outcome is unknown – such as political elections or athletic contests. The incorporation of computational affordances into televised sports events can lead to new participatory forms, such as an enhancement of the popular practice of "Fantasy Football" in which players compete with imaginary teams made up of players strategically chosen from multiple real teams. The imaginary league plays games in which player performance is determined by how well the actual player scores. Sports channels already provide enhanced broadcasts with access to statistics and replays. A truly digital television environment could build on existing conventions for showing simultaneous action from multiple locations, such as the webcast of the concurrent Olympic games or the broadcast (in Europe) of concurrent championship tennis matches. Fantasy football players could receive highlights of multiple games showing just the plays involving the players on their roster, linked to automatically updated score cards that reflected real-time play.

Story-telling by aggregation from multiple sources would also be useful for making sense of submissions of citizen journalists or eyewitness accounts captured on mobile video. Political demonstrations, insurrections, natural disasters, and other events that take place over a broad geographical area could be presented with recordings synchronized by time and place to provide multiple points of view. The coverage of the Japanese earthquake in documentaries made by Fuji Television [4] and NHK [19] are good models of how simulation, geographic information, and integration of surveillance camera sources from multiple angles can make an overwhelming story understandable, and can provide overviews and zoomed-in detail. So are the participatory structures created by a European research group for integrating and navigating home videos of the same high school performance taken by multiple official and family recorders [3]. With more innovation in technical transmission, metadata standardization, and conventions of presentation and navigation, such composite reports could be more easily compiled. Producers could be given greater editorial control over a wider range of video contributions, and viewers could be given navigation tools that would allow them to access deeper layers of information without confusion.

The new larger home video screens with higher resolution (and perhaps with 3D images) present new opportunities for augmenting the immediacy of the fictional world. Game consoles are increasingly gesture-driven, and though this technology is still relatively large-grained, it shows some promise for involving viewers with a sense of their own presence within a fictional landscape. For example, my eTV group created a prototype with Intel Research that drew on the television show *Supernatural,* which has a ghost-hunting, horror adventure format. Using the kinect as the interface, we replicated a common situation from the series, of a vulnerable person trapped in a spooky place and menaced by a ghost. Creating this prototype raised a number of design questions including how we could script the interactor to know what to do without explicit coaching. One of the most promising approaches was having a character hold out her hand, which immediately prompted the gesture of stretching out a hand toward the screen. By mapping this transparent gesture to a significant narrative event – it puts the interactor in the power of the ghost – we created an opportunity for dramatic agency within the story world without disrupting any of the canonical elements of the world. Our aim was to create the experience of "active creation of belief" [7]. in which interaction reinforces immersion because the procedural world responds appropriately to the participatory action.

Greater integration of affordances like gestural input that are now associated with game consoles, could also give viewers the ability to navigate moving image content in a more fluid way. For examples we might point at an area of a picture, such as coverage of a crowd scene to create a zoomed-in view with more detail and a change in audio focus, so that we could now hear dialog that was obscure before. Or we could point to character in order to hear their inner thoughts or to a document in order to have it delivered to a secondary screen, like a tablet computer. Extending hands and pointing are just two examples of gestural approaches to interaction that the increasingly large, high resolution digital home screens could make practical by bringing the viewer into a more immediate and more detailed landscape

2.2 Immersive Story Worlds

The story world of *Lost* was filled with mysterious elements that hinted at a deeper backstory, enticing fans into online discussions and searches for additional content. But it was not explicitly designed to support the "hunters and gatherers" of the fan community. If a television serial was created from the outset to induce the same level of fan engagement it could make use of procedural affordances to set up opportunities to hunt and gather directly within the program's moving images. One example of how this might work is a prototype that my eTV group did in collaboration with the AFI Digital Content Lab for a Cartoon Network program and the Sony Playstation. Our premise was that a children's television show, Ben Ten, would be delivered on the game console through a broadband rather than cable feed, allowing the viewer to watch it with the game controller in hand, ready for interaction. Our design goal was to create a game that would reinforce immersion in the story world rather than distract from it, and so we devised a system for flashing the image of an item that would appear within the cartoon for a brief period of time, challenging the viewer to click on it and thereby capture it. The captured objects were collected during the show and used afterwards in a mobile platform game. Our belief was that the more the producers of a show can invent game properties for the items that mirror the use of the item within the program, the more the viewer will feel reinforced in their belief in the depth of the fictional world. We also demonstrated the same system using content from *Lost,* showing how an intrinsically mysterious item like the hatch or a character's tattoo could be collected in order to unlock additional information. [14]

Reality shows with mystery components, also lend themselves to elaboration through synchronous, integrated interaction. For example, in a prototype that we created of an ABC series called Celebrity Mole, viewers were allowed to flag sequences in order to construct arguments about who they think is the "mole" or secret saboteur of the group [13]. As fan engagement grows, it will become important for producers to provide a way for them to play back short sequences from a program, aggregate them into their own compilations, and share them with one another without violating copyright. A tool that worked off a standardized notation for time code to provide this functionality so that fan-edited sequences could be played back within viewer forums drawing on licensed content delivered with proprietary restrictions (e.g. advertising, streaming, low resolution, etc.) set by the producers. Without this kind of a tool, the conversation between producers, critics, and viewers could turn more adversarial.

We can expect story-telling and story interfaces to co-evolve over the next decades as writers take advantage of the sustained attention of viewers to plot elements that last over dozens of hours of exposition and to larger casts of characters. Multi-sequential viewing may become the norm as segmentation within and across episodes with appropriate metadata and navigational interfaces allow viewers to follow subplots, choosing to re-view portions of multiple episodes and to follow some story threads more closely than others [17] [18]. Viewers may also be given the opportunity of watching the same event repeatedly through the eyes (that is, perhaps with different camera angles or access to interior monolog or whispered dialog) of multiple characters. Taking advantage of spatial navigation, viewers may be able to follow characters when they exit from one scene, in stories that have simultaneous events [12].

2.3 Viewer Participation

Television is unique in its intimacy and collectivity. We watch alone and we watch with a mass audience. It is simultaneously a solitary and a shared experience. We have only begun to take advantage of the opportunities for making viewers more aware of others watching at a distance [1]. Most of the efforts so far have been through the use of existing social media, by having actors or viewers tweet during a broadcast. This method may increase excitement, but it undermines the fictional premise, breaking the fourth wall of the drama by destroying the illusion that the world of the show is a self-contained reality. Watching the inane comments of other viewers proliferate in a twitter feed or – worst case – scroll across the bottom third of a TV screen can undermine one's pleasure in a program. Yet there is an excitement in sharing an unfolding dramatic event with others.

Designers can scaffold participation by funneling it into prescribed channels that are expressive but impersonal. For example, in the Celebrity Mole project, Shelley Palmer, one of the collaborators in the group, came up with the concept of the Mole-o-Meter, which registered the votes of people in the viewing audience for who they guessed the mole to be. The tally would necessarily change with unfolding events and potentially suspicious behavior by different members of the group.

A prototype the our group created for a set-top interaction environment created by Scientific Atlanta (now part of Cisco) created an "Avatar Theater" for collective viewing, with specific interaction icons associated with the scheduled content. For example, for a live broadcast of Obama's inaugural message the team prepared flags with symbols that represented anticipated themes such as a picture of John Kennedy, a peace symbol, and a picture of Martin Luther King. Avatars that loosely resembled group members were placed in front of the display at the bottom of the screen, somewhat in the manner of Mystery Science Theater. Clicking on a flag classed one's own avatar to turn toward the front and wave it. There were also icons of Elephants and Donkeys to represent affiliation with the Republican and Democratic parties, and virtual tomatoes for throwing at the screen to express partisan disapproval. Another interface for the Avatar Theater was built for the comic cult film Airplane. Here we created party-themed elements like confetti for use during the dance numbers. The pre-scripting of specific gestures made active communication simple, providing a satisfying and non-distracting collective context for viewing these events. [15]

The possibility of convening an audience for collective viewing raises a host of design issues. How big an audience is appropriate? How much control will viewers want over who is present and how visible attendees are to one another? How would we integrate personal image and voice streams associated with sound or video calls? Where do we place images or avatars of attendees so that they do not distract from the screen? How do we signal availability for collective viewing? Existing social networks like Facebook and Twitter are currently providing a means of exploring these issues, but they may turn out to be too loosely connected to the shows. Dedicated apps for tablet second screens may provide more specific formats for interaction, reflecting differences in genre and theme.

3. CONCLUSION

Since so many of the developments that I predicted in 1997 have occurred I am encouraged to continue to take the long view of media innovation. The current "transmedia" era is one of additive exploration, of spreading a story across devices and platforms in ways that sometimes enhance immersion in a consistent story world, but often provide little more than prolonged brand contact. The next stage of digital convergence will bring more integrated devices and more powerful interactivity to the home entertainment screen, breaking the isolation of television from other forms of digital entertainment and information like games and websites. Looking at the core elements of television that we can expect to last – moving images, sustained storytelling, home viewership in the presence of a mass audience – and the procedural, participatory, encyclopedic, and spatial affordances of the underlying digital medium - we can see many underexplored design opportunities for enriching story immersion. When we reject the Static Media Model that assumes that television will remain forever segregated from game platforms, and the Digital Revolution Model that assumes the disappearance of familiar, non-interactive television formats, we can find a fruitful middle ground on which to experiment with design innovations. When we start with the core pleasures of television and core affordances of the digital medium, we may still find it hard to estimate the pace of change, but we can be much more certain of that the direction of change will continue to be toward more meaningful interactivity and deeper narrative immersion.

4. ACKNOWLEDGMENTS

I am grateful to Sergio Goldenberg, Kartik Agarwal, Paul Clifton, and all the other members of the eTV group.

5. REFERENCES

[1] BASAPUR, S., HARBOE, G., MANDALIA, H., NOVAK, A., VUONG, V. AND METCALF, C. 2011. Field trial of a dual device user experience for iTV. In *Proceedings of the 9th international interactive conference on Interactive television* (EuroITV '11). ACM, New York, NY, USA, 127-136. DOI=10.1145/2000119.2000145 http://doi.acm.org/10.1145/2000119.2000145

[2] BIZZOCCHI, J. 2004. Video as ambience: reception and aesthetics of flat-screen video display. *Crossings: Electronic Journal of Art and Technology.*

[3] CESAR, P., BULTERMAN D.C.A., JANSEN A. J. 2008. Usages of the Secondary Screen in an Interactive Television Environment: Control, Enrich, Share, and Transfer Television Content. In *Proceedings of the 6th European conference on Changing Television Environments* (EUROITV '08), Manfred Tscheligi, Marianna Obrist, and Artur Lugmayr, Eds. Springer-Verlag, Berlin, Heidelberg, 168-177. DOI=10.1007/978-3-540-69478-6_22 http://dx.doi.org/10.1007/978-3-540-69478-6_22

[4] FUJI Television 2011. The Untold Story of the Tsunami in Japan.

[5] HBO GO, 2011. Game of Thrones Interactive Experience. http://www.hbo.com/game-of-thrones/about/video/hbo-go-interactive-experience.html

[6] HERMAN, D. 2004. Story Logic: Problems and Possibilities of Narrative. University of Nebraska Press.

[7] JENKINS, H. (January 15, 2003). "Transmedia Storytelling." *Technology Review*, MIT.

[8] JENKINS, H. (2006). *Convergence Culture: Where Old and New Media Collide.* New York: New York University Press.

[9] JENKINS, H. (August 1, 2011). Transmedia 202: Further Reflections, on *Confessions of an Aca-Fan: The Official Weblog of Henry Jenkins,* http://henryjenkins.org/2011/08/defining_transmedia_further_re.html

[10] JULES, J. 2011. Half-Real: Video Games between Real Rules and Fictional Worlds. MIT Press. MURRAY, J. 1998. Building Coherent Plots in Interactive Fiction. IEEE Intelligent Systems, Nov./Dec. 1998

[11] MURRAY, J.H. 1997. Hamlet on the Holodeck: The Future of Narrative in Cyberspace. Free Press, New York.

[12] MURRAY, J.H. 1998. Building Coherent Plots in Interactive Fiction, *IEEE Intelligent Systems,* Nov./Dec. 1998.

[13] MURRAY J. H., COGSWELL, D., BAGGA, C. CLARKE, Z. , ERDOGAN, E., PHALAKE, S. ROSS, A. 2005. Enhanced TV: Celebrity Mole Prototype. ETV LAB, Georgia Tech, documentation available at http://etv.gatech.edu/projects/celebrity-mole/

[14] MURRAY, J.H., GOLDENBERG, S., AMSBARY, P., BHILAVDIKAR, R., DONNELLY, J., LAUSIER, A., TEAGUE, J., PATE, M. 2007. Sync Game Prototype. ETV Lab, Georgia Tech, documentation available at http://etv.gatech.edu/projects/syncgame/

[15] MURRAY, J. H, GOLDENBERG, S., BARNWELL, PRADHAN, N, SCHWEIZER, B. 2009. Avatar Theater Project, ETV Lab Georgia Tech, documentation available at http://etv.gatech.edu/projects/avatar-theater

[16] MURRAY, J.H. 2011. Inventing the Medium: Principles of Interaction Design as a Cultural Practice. MIT Press.

[17] MURRAY, J.H., GOLDENBERG, S., AGARWAL, et al. 2011. StoryLines: an approach to navigating multisequential news and entertainment in a multiscreen framework. In *Proceedings of the 8th International Conference on Advances in Computer Entertainment Technology* (ACE '11), Teresa Romão, Nuno Correia, Masahiko Inami, Hirokasu Kato, Rui Prada, Tsutomu Terada, Eduardo Dias, and Teresa Chambel, Eds. ACM, New York, NY, USA, Article 92, 2 pages. DOI=10.1145/2071423.2071533 http://doi.acm.org/10.1145/2071423.2071533

[18] MURRAY, J.H., GOLDENBERG, S., AGARWAL, K, et. al 2012. Story-Map: iPad Companion for Long Form TV Narrative, *Proceedings of the 10th International Conference on Interactive Television (EuroiTV 2012).*

[19] NHK Television (Japan Broadcasting Company) 2011. Surviving the Tsunami

Supporting an Ecosystem: From the Biting Baby to the Old Spice Man

Olga Khroustaleva
YouTube
901 Cherry Ave.
San Bruno, CA. USA
okhroust@google.com

Tom Broxton
YouTube
901 Cherry Ave.
San Bruno, CA. USA
+1 650 201 4697
tbroxton@google.com

ABSTRACT

As YouTube evolves we look at how content creators thrive within the ecosystem, what motivates them, and how they get the best results. We also investigate how patterns of media consumption change in an engagement-driven environment, built upon a mix of existing and web-original content, available across platforms and devices.

These changes in creator and viewer expectations prompt video advertisers to rethink what effectiveness means in this new space, where a biting baby can get more attention than a high-cost video. How do lessons learned through years of TV and display advertising and research translate to the paradigm of active social engagement?

Categories and Subject Descriptors

H.5.1 [**Information Systems**]: Multimedia Information Systems – *video.*

General Terms

Design, Experimentation, Human Factors

Keywords

Interactive, user experience, design, video, YouTube, advertisers, attention, content, creator, devices, ecosystem, effectiveness, engagement, media, music, platforms, research, social, tv, user-generated

EuroITV'12, July 4–6, 2012, Berlin, Germany.
ACM 978-1-4503-1107-6/12/07.

Socio-spatial Context and the Habit-Goal Interface in Audiovisual Media Consumption: An Inter-paradigmatic Approach

Cédric Courtois
IBBT-MICT-Ghent University
Korte Meer 7-9-11
BE-9000 Gent
+32 9 264 91 54
cedric.courtois@ugent.be

Julie Van Lier
Ghent University
Korte Meer 7-9-11
BE-9000 Gent
+32 9 264 91 54
julievanlier@gmail.com

ABSTRACT

This article addresses the role of socio-spatial context on audiovisual media consumption by adopting a multi-paradigmatic approach that combines the Theory of Media Attendance, a socio-cognitive interpretation of Uses & Gratifications and Domestication Theory. We propose a framework that inquires *(RQ 1)* how goals and habits interface with each other as explanatory factors of consumption and *(RQ 2)* how the role of socio-spatial cues can be understood. Survey results show that different socio-spatial settings are associated with distinct explanations by goals and habits. Moreover, follow-up interviews indicate that these differences are best understood when framed in everyday life family dynamics.

Categories and Subject Descriptors

J.4 [**Social And Behavioral Sciences**]: Sociology

General Terms

Management, Human Factors, Theory.

Keywords

Inter-paradigmatic research, audiovisual media consumption, socio-spatial context, domestication theory

1. INTRODUCTION

As a consequence of convergence, audiovisual media are ever so pervasive in a multitude of social and spatial contexts. Nowadays, various (portable) devices furnish the consumption of audiovisual materials through a wide range of channels and in a myriad of social and physical spaces. At the same time, patterns of individualization persist to emerge [1]. This further pressures the once so rigid scheme of the nuclear family gathering around the living room television set. In this article, we focus on the socio-spatial context of audiovisual media consumption and how this affects the interplay of two major factors known to explain that consumption. First, we take into account intentional motivations or goals, which links smoothly with the traditional Uses & Gratifications paradigm [2]. Second, we draw upon the psychological habit construct that, however largely ignored by media studies, reflects the non-intentional substrate of our behavior [3]. More specifically, we first question whether distinct patterns of socio-spatial context affect the habit-goal interface of audiovisual consumption. Second, we aim to understand these relations by drawing upon Domestication Theory [4]. This social-constructivist perspective explicitly addresses the formation of media consumption routines.

Hence, in this article we first concentrate on the habit-goal interface in media studies by discussing the Theory of Media Attendance, which entails a socio-cognitive interpretation of Uses & Gratifications [5]. Second, we engage in a theoretical comparison between the Theory of Media Attendance and Domestication, which eventually accumulates in an integrated methodological framework that extends over both perspectives' native research methods. Finally, we discuss the results in terms of the proposed research questions and assess their theoretical and methodological implications.

1.1 The habit-goal interface

The reason why people use media has always been a central theme in media studies, with Uses & Gratifications (U&G) as perhaps one of the most attractive and prominent paradigms for empirical research [6]. Developed during the second half of the previous century, it steadily evolved from merely descriptive research into a more concrete phase of operationalization. Up until today, U&G draws upon its original assumptions of an active audience that is conscientiously aware of its needs and rationally selects the best means to gratify these needs from a range of alternatives, including various media [7]. In empirical research, this has led to a broad variety of data-driven typologies of gratifications that are considered to explain why media are used. In a subsequent phase, theories were built and explanatory models were tested [8]. The most remarkable attempts draw upon social-psychological reasoning, considering U&G as an expectancy-value process [8-10]. However, although enticing, this perspective does not fend off the major criticisms that exist up until today. That is the inevitable take on the ultimately rational individual who is perfectly aware of his or her own mental state. This does not comply with the observation that most of our behavior is habitual. More specifically, habitual behavior lacks awareness, is difficult to control and is prone to cognitive efficiency [3]. Moreover, research has shown that the effects of previous frequency, attitude and intention on behavioral frequency tend to diminish when controlled for habit [11].

Still, media consumption should not be seen as solely explained by automaticity, nor is it the isolated result of cautious forethought. In most cases, habits are actually residues of long-term repeated behavior, encouraged by underlying goals. Also, the causality can be reversed, as habits are informative of people's goals and lead people to contexts in which habitual behavior is prompted. Moreover, goals can interact with habits so that they are steadily preserved. Hence, models that propose to explain behavior need to incorporate both modes [12]. In media studies, this has been accomplished by the Theory of Media Attendance (TMA), which merges U&G with Social Cognitive Theory [5, 13]. The latter theory has its roots in Social Learning Theory [14, 15] and views behavior as a result of the triadic reciprocal relationship between individuals, their behavior and their environments. Multiple sources are identified to acquire behavioral patterns, which are exercised after forethought and are subject to self-regulation. People do not only learn through direct experience (enactive leaning), they also learn vicariously, by observing (non-human) models. At the onset of behavior, we assess our efficacy to attain favorable outcomes that reflect six categories of incentive motivators (novel, self-reactive, social, status, monetary and activity). In fact, in the model of media attendance, ad hoc gratifications were replaced by these theoretically embedded incentives. A brief literature review revealed that four major incentive categories are commonly covered by U&G typologies: activity (≈ entertainment), social (≈ interaction), novel (≈ information) and self-reactive (≈ escapism) [5]. In practice, these motivators are operationalized as expected outcomes and serve as indicators for a second-order construct in the model of media attendance.

The operational model of media attendance has been applied to various media cases, ranging from the Internet [5, 13, 16], mobile phone adoption [17], and video gaming [18] to illegal music downloading [19]. In each situation, the combination of expected outcomes (goals) and habit strength has proven to explain a substantial amount of variance in the frequency of media consumption. This is a major merit that to our knowledge was unprecedented in gratifications research. Nevertheless, some scholars recognized the importance of habit quite early. For example, Rubin [20] incorporated habit in a television viewing typology, yet treating it as a gratification like any other. Later on, he made a distinction between instrumental and more ritualistic gratifications, like relaxation and passing time [21]. Still, we hold the position that every outcome is prone to automaticity. Moreover, Rubin persisted to consider these types of gratifications as part of an active process.

1.2 The importance of socio-spatial context

As mentioned in the introduction, the fairly habitual behavior of audiovisual media consumption holds the potential of spreading to various social and physical spaces. Habits are typically formed by repeated behavior in a stable context, containing social, spatial and temporal cues. Habits can either be cued directly, as direct context-response relations or through motivation. In that case, rewards are conditioned onto context cues, later activating the motivation to get the initial reward [22]. Unstable contexts however contain *'shifts in the supporting environment* [that] *implicate alternate goals or challenge the smooth initiation, execution, and termination of practiced responses'* [23]. In such circumstances, it is very unlikely that habits are translated into actual behavior.

This raises questions about our audiovisual consumption today. When we look with hindsight, especially in post-war domestic geographies, it was habitually located in the shared space that is the living room [24]. Nowadays, in theory, we are able to consume wherever and with whoever. Consequently, some expand their consumption contexts even beyond traditional conceptions of the home, while others do not. However, we have no insight in the substrate of this potential diversity. To what extent is it due to explicit motivational factors or to extensions of existing habits? And in the latter case, it is possible that existing cues are generalized over contexts, or are new associations made? This ambivalence leads to a first research question:

- *RQ 1: How do goals and habits relate for different patterns of socio-spatial context of audiovisual media consumption?*

1.3 Understanding the socio-spatial

Although we argued that only very little research addresses the topic of media habits, this is not entirely true. For instance, Domestication Theory actually focuses on the appropriation of media technologies in everyday life routines [4, 25, 26]. This perspective has been especially influential in audience research, in a sense that it provoked what is referred to as the ethnographic turn in reception studies [27]. That is the acknowledgement that the sense-making process of media consumption extends beyond media texts as it also holds a material dimension. In other words, it broadened the research subject from what is on the screen to what is surrounding it. In brief, the domestication perspective posits that media technologies are first commodified by their producers. They are ascribed meanings through marketing communication that are then negotiated by consumers. This negotiation is not so much an individual process, as it must fit the moral economy of the home, reflecting the household's prevailing values, cognitions and aesthetic beliefs. This is often a difficult exercise prone to trial and error in granting the technology not only the appropriate physical space, but also in incorporating its use in consumers' everyday life routines. Simultaneously, through their use, the negotiated consumption meanings are further transferred into the public, so they confound with producers' meanings.

Actually, when we review the Domestication perspective, we see various similarities with Social Cognitive Theory's rationale as reflected in the Theory of Media Attendance (TMA). Both perspectives entail a social learning process that combines vicarious and enactive experiences. Moreover, they both seek to uncover how media are made meaningful by their consumers and how media consumption turns into a habit or routine. Nonetheless, despite a shared social-constructivist ontology, they strongly differ in their epistemological positions. Whereas the TMA takes an objective stance, pointing its arrows at explaining behavior in terms of causal relationships, Domestication adheres to a subjective position, aiming to understand media consumption as a social phenomenon best inquired from the inside. Also, in principle, their units of analysis diverge as TMA zooms in on the individual, while Domestication looks beyond and focuses on household dynamics. Nevertheless, from a pragmatic point of view, we strongly believe that both perspectives are compatible and add to each other. This sentiment is prudently shared by Schrøder [28] who applauds sensible inter-paradigmatic research between U&G and ethnographic audience research. He refers to the need of drawing maps on different scales, however warning for all too simplistic notions of triangulation in which methodological imperfections would cancel each other out. Hence, it is imperative to strive for a design that transcends the sum of its constituents.

Table 1: Measures means, standard deviations and Cronbach's α

Construct	Lean back viewing style			Lean forward viewing style		
	M	*SD*	α	*M*	*SD*	α
Expected outcomes						
Social	3.16	1.24	.79	2.93	1.34	.80
Novel	4.67	1.20	.79	4.89	1.35	.84
Self-Reactive	4.39	1.12	.70	3.30	1.15	.76
Activity	5.07	1.05	.82	3.77	1.33	.88
Habit strength	4.74	1.34	.88	3.43	1.31	.91
Consumption frequency	108.77	77.62	(r = .43)	24.95	34.10	(r = .70)

In this specific case, we firmly believe this is feasible. The first research question invites a systematic oversight of the habit-goal interface for different socio-spatial consumption patterns. An approach tailored onto the TMA renders a large map in the form of effects of habit and goals for different types of viewing environment. However, if we were to find that different socio-spatial contexts affect these relations, we would still be left in vain of what this might actually mean and how to understand it. This is where we believe the Domestication perspective with its strive for a rich, socially situated understanding of everyday life would make an indispensable contribution. More specifically, it offers the potential to provide with insight in the meaning of specific sets of socio-spatial cues. That is how and why they set off habits in the ecology of the home. Hence, we propose a second research question:

- *RQ 2: How can we understand the role of socio-spatial cues in the habit-goal interface?*

2. METHODOLOGY

In order to answer these two research questions, we implemented an integrated funnel approach. In a first phase, we devised a large-scale paper & pencil survey with operational measures drawn from the Theory of Media attendance. Moreover, as will be discussed in the measures section, we included a set of items inquiring how often respondents consume audiovisual media in what spatial and social environment. These variables were then subjected to a latent class analysis [29], rendering a number of distinct patterns of consumption environments. First of all, these patterns allowed a multi-sample analysis of the Model of Media Attendance. Secondly, the classes were used to sensibly recruit participants for a follow-up phase, consisting of domestic interviews. Chosen on the basis of very high to even absolute membership probabilities, the interviewees are treated as representatives for their respective classes. In the interview, we tapped into the meaning of the socio-spatial and how it allows the exercise of everyday media consumption routines.

Still, we first need to explicit our operationalization of audiovisual media consumption in today's increasingly converging media landscape. As put in the introduction, multiple devices furnish the consumption of audiovisual texts through various channels, while situated in a diversity of socio-spatial environments. Hence, we subscribe to an earlier empirically grounded recommendation for an agnostic approach towards media consumption [30], inciting to tap into the experience, independent of a specific type of device, content or socio-spatial context. However, this poses another problem concerning the differences in experience of for example quickly watching a short news clip on a laptop computer at a desk versus taking time and making yourself comfortable to watch a film or series on the very same device. We strongly believe it is a mistake to treat both viewing modes as chips from the same block. Therefore, based on literature on human-computer interaction [31, 32], we heuristically distinguish between a haphazard lean forward viewing style and a much more dedicated lean back viewing style. In the survey questionnaire, both viewing styles were aptly introduced and familiarized by a situational sketch.

2.1 Survey procedure and measures

The paper and pencil questionnaire was administered on a large quota sample, targeting three age cohorts: young adulthood (18-30y), middle adulthood (31-50y) and late adulthood (50y+), equally dispersed over gender. The data were gathered in the context of a research methodology seminar at a large Belgian university. This led to a total number of 1,559 valid responses (51% male, 49% female; M_{age} = 40.61, SD_{age} = 16.79). The following paragraphs enumerate the applied measures.

Socio-spatial viewing context entails nine dichotomous items inquiring whether a number of social contexts (e.g. alone, with partner) and spatial contexts (e.g. living room, bedroom, hobby room) are used at least once every two to three days. These variables are later on employed to form latent classes of socio-spatial viewing contexts.

The measures below, which make up the Model of Media Attendance, were gathered for lean back viewing as well as lean forward viewing. The constructs' means, standard deviations and measures of internal consistency (Cronbach's α) are summarized in Table 1.

Habit strength was assessed by Verplanken and Orbell's Self-Report Index of Habit Strength [33]. In line with current applications, items concerning past behavioral frequency were omitted [34]. The ten remaining items were rated on a seven-point Likert scale ranging from 'totally disagree' to 'totally agree'.

Expected outcomes were measured by twelve items drawn from previous research [13, 16]. The original items were slightly adapted to fit audiovisual consumption. The four most recurrent expected outcomes that match U&G research on television were retained [5]. Hence, novel, social, activity and self-reactive outcomes were assessed with seven-point Likert scales, ranging from 'very unlikely' to 'very likely'. The items and confirmatory factor analysis results are incorporated in the Appendix section.

Consumption frequency was measured by inquiring the hours and minutes spent on viewing moving images one and two days before the survey administration. This measure's metric was eventually converted to minutes.

2.2 Interview procedure and topics

The follow-up interviews were conducted with 28 participants recruited from the initial survey's respondent pool (18 females, 10 males, aged 18-63). Each interviewee counted as a

Table 2: Latent Class Analysis. Response probabilities, Wald statistics and variance explained.
*** $p < .05$, ** $p < .005$, *** $p < .001$**

p response *(at least every 2-3 days)*	**Class 1:** Unispace-social viewers	**Class 2:** Multispace-solo viewers	**Class 3:** Multispace-social/solo viewers	Wald	R^2
Alone	.65	.60	.93	29.02***	.09
Family, other generation	.40	.00	.38	4.52	.09
Partner	.77	.19	.60	79.86**	.18
Living Room	.99	.25	.94	56.91***	.56
Bedroom	.17	.37	.41	19.66**	.07
Kitchen	.16	.07	.19	9.69**	.01
Leisure Room	.04	.17	.47	38.52***	.23
Work/School	.07	.04	.38	51.13***	.17
Commuting (Public transport)	.00	.00	.05	3.47	.03

typical case for a specific socio-spatial context class. The semi-structured interviews took place in the participants' domestic environments and lasted about one hour. The participants were first asked to draw a ground plan of their house, labeling all the rooms and indicating device locations (Figure 1).

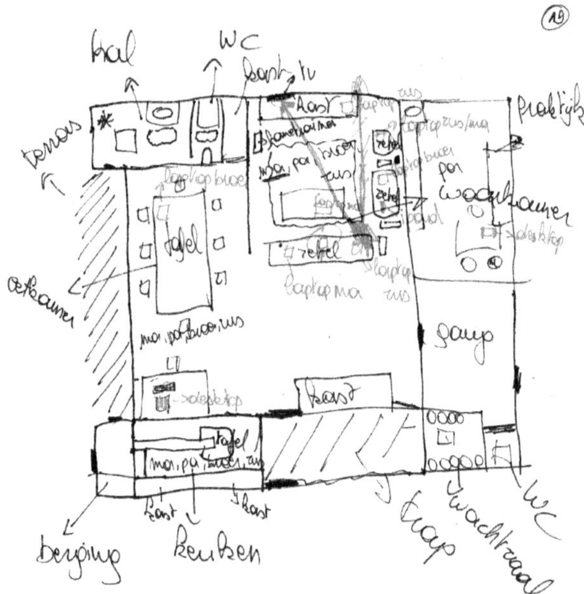

Figure 1: Example of a ground plan, drawn by one of the participants

It was also extended with non-domestic locations in which regular consumption takes place. The ground plan was then used to map social interactions and socio-spatial meanings. More specifically, the interviewees were invited to sketch a day in their life onto this map and talk about how audiovisual media consumption fits into that. This implicitly covers temporal context, which in practice strongly coincides with the socio-spatial. In the meanwhile, we tapped into notions of stable context cues and over-time changes in habits (e.g. by disruption or life events). The interviews were coded using a deductive coding scheme, based on the literature discussed in the introduction. In the analysis, patterns with class membership were actively sought, while pursuing a deepening account of the results that were drawn from the survey, discussed in the following sections.

3. RESULTS

3.1 Socio-spatial viewing classes

To distinguish between different socio-spatial context configurations, a latent class analysis is performed on a set of nine dichotomous indicator variables. A common strategy to discern the most suitable model is to iterate the analysis with an increasing number of classes until a satisfactory model fit is reached. In this case, a three-class model appears to be the most parsimonious solution ($L^2(1530) = 619.31$, $p = 1$). Table 2 summarizes the analysis' results.

The *unispace-social viewers* display high probabilities of engaging in social viewing, while mostly situated in the family living room. This is echoed by *multispace-solo/social viewers*, although they also have high chances of solitary viewing and viewing in a variety of locations in the home as well as beyond. Finally, the *multispace-solo viewers* tend to view in solitude, mostly situated in the bedroom, followed by the living room.

These results indicate a strong divergence in everyday socio-spatial configuration of audiovisual media consumption. Moreover, they are strongly associated with demographic variables such as age and gender (Table 3).

3.2 The habit-goal interface

To address the first research question, a structural equation model

Table 3: Latent viewing classes' demographic background $^{+}\chi^2(2) = 51.42, p < .001$ $^{++}\chi^2(4) = 200.69, p < .001$

	Class 1: Unispace-social viewers	**Class 2:** Multispace-solo viewers	**Class 3:** Multispace-social/solo viewers
Gender (%)$^{+}$			
Female, Male	56, 44	52, 48	35, 65
Age (years)			
Mdn	48	21	30
Age (cohort %)$^{++}$			
Young adulthood (18-30y)	22	65	50
Middle adulthood (31-50y)	39	19	34
Late adulthood (50y+)	39	16	16

Table 4: Summary of the multi-group analysis of the media attendance model.
+ Parameters estimates when constraining measurement weights and intercepts to equality for all three classes.
++ Model nested within constrained measurement model. * $p < .05$, ** $p < .005$, *** $p < .001$.

Path specifications	**Parameter estimates[+]**					
	Class 1: *Unispace-social viewers*		**Class 2:** *Multispace-solo viewers*		**Class 3:** *Multispace-solo/social viewers*	
	B	SE	B	SE	B	SE
Lean back viewing:						
Path A: Expected outcomes → Consumption	13.21***	*3.34*	21.85***	*4.85*	8.04*	*3.84*
Path B: Habit strength → Consumption	21.80***	*2.03*	13.58***	*2.23*	18.86***	*2.02*
Model with both paths constrained to equality:[++] (A=B)	$\Delta\chi^2 = 4.00$*		$\Delta\chi^2 = 2.03$		$\Delta\chi^2 = 5.27$*	
Lean forward viewing:						
Path A: Expected outcomes → Consumption	1.10	*.96*	2.95*	*1.43*	.13	*1.19*
Path B: Habit strength → Consumption	8.50***	*.62*	8.68***	*.89*	9.36***	*.62*
Model with both paths constrained to equality:[++] (A=B)	$\Delta\chi^2 = 39.15$***		$\Delta\chi^2 = 9.56$*		$\Delta\chi^2 = 37.10$***	

is specified for each viewing style, regressing consumption onto its respective expected outcomes and habit strength. The analyses were ran for all three distinguished subsamples, reaching a satisfactory overall goodness-of-fit of the lean back ($\chi^2(56)$ = 241.37, TLI = .92, CFI = .93, RMSEA = .05) and the lean forward constrained measurement models ($\chi^2(56)$ = 274.36, TLI = .91, CFI = .94, RMSEA = .05). Next, both paths towards consumption, situated in the structural model (A and B in Figure 2), were constrained to equality in order to identify the strongest explanatory factor.

Table 4 summarizes the analyses' results. It clearly shows that expected outcomes and habit strength are both strong explanatory factors of a comfortable, lean back consumption. Nonetheless, the strength of these effects varies between socio-spatial classes. The consumption of the two social viewing classes is mostly explained by habit strength, rather than expected outcomes. This suggests that for these classes, the consumption of audiovisual texts is something that is strongly embedded within everyday routines, while not so much inspired by individual deliberate considerations. For the multispace-solo viewers this is not quite the case, as both factors yield similar effects. Hence, its members' audiovisual consumption is equally driven by intentions and habit. Still, lean forward viewing is consistently explained by habit strength, whereas the effects of expected outcomes only yield a mildly significant effect for the multispace-solo viewers. In general, this finding tends to support the assumption associated with this viewing style, proposing it to be a less focussed, haphazard way of consuming audiovisual media.

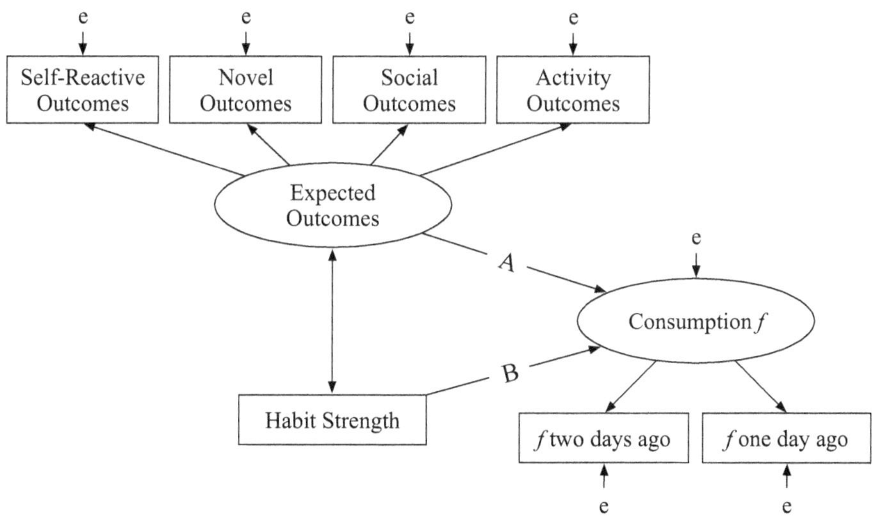

Figure 2: Specified structural equation model ran for both lean back and lean forward viewing styles

Although these results offer insight in what lies at the core of audiovisual media consumption, they immediately give rise to questions on how we can understand these relations and how they are rooted within everyday life. Therefore, in the following paragraphs, we provide a direct link with the subsequent domestic interviews that were performed with typical cases from each socio-spatial context class.

3.2.1 Class 1: Unispace-social viewers

In recapitulation, this class predominantly consists of somewhat elder people. Their consumption of audiovisual media happens in the living room, preferably with their partners and to a lesser extent with other family members. On a daily basis, over two hours are spent watching in a comfortable lean back manner, while about twenty minutes are allocated to lean forward viewing. Both behaviors are quite strongly explained by habit, whereas only lean back viewing is intentional.

In the interviews, we noticed that this class' participants maintain very rigid, traditional cognitive schemes of consumption geography. Their living room, where the bulk of lean back viewing is performed, is in all cases oriented towards a television set. When the participants were inquired about why they locate their consumption in that specific space, they find it rather difficult to explain. They attribute it to the fact that it has always been so and should not be put into question:

> Daniël (63, M): *Eventually, it's a habit you just took up. Why do we have a TV? You don't think about that. It's a habit that has been taught to you as a child, that you have to watch there* [the living room] *And so it was one of the first things we bought of the things that are present here.* [...] *Anyway, not in in the other rooms... they're not that cozy, because... because when you're there, you are isolated, unless you would tell the others to join you in that room. No, I don't feel the need to watch somewhere in complete isolation. That's mainly the reason why I feel no urge to have devices in the other rooms.*

The living room is consistently and spontaneously called a space to watch, indicating it to be a stable environment for consumption. In fact, when the habit would be disrupted, for instance by a broken device, it would be immediately replaced by a similar one. Moreover, as Daniël put it, the living room is unanimously considered a warm and cozy environment, equipped with comfortable furniture that affords to sit back or even lie down. Equally important is that living room consumption is actually heavily intertwined with the household's social dynamics. Watching television at night, after dinner, is considered a social lubricant that makes up a valuable part of family life. Other spaces, like bedrooms or kitchens, are deemed unsuitable because they are much more individualized and furnish other activities that are not compatible with this social character. Although some time is spent watching alone, other family members usually join them (although of course this also happens the other way round). Furthermore, as the participants from this class exercise hegemonic roles in the family's moral economy, they are able to steer its consumption. First of all, they exercise control over the remote control, either deciding what is watched or at least moderating the preceding family discussion. In fact, we encountered several instances in which such discussions were regarded beneficial in learning how to give and take. Second, the participants in this class play a decisive role in determining the amount, nature and place of technologies in the home. And third, they are able to engage in rule making. In fact, the parents we interviewed, especially those of younger children and teenagers, claim discomfort with the evasion of the living room, however not necessarily preventing it. For example, Helen's (42, F) television set is located in the living room. There is one that is used upstairs, yet only during ironing. As a mother of two, she actively prevents her boys from watching that set. When we asked her about her opinion on family viewing, she told us:

> Helen: *Yeah, that is the norm in society, that it is something you do together. In my case, watching alone would be bizarre. Anyway, it's a normal activity to do in company, like playing a game, that's something you don't do by yourself either. It is something you do with your family...*

On the contrary, lean forward viewing is accompanied with a shift in socio-spatial terms. It is often linked to other devices that are more spatially dispersed and that involve a more individualized approach. This experience is severely influenced by the lack in comfort, sitting alone on a chair, at a table or desk. This contrasts sharply with the comfortable situation previously described. Consequently, deliberate consumption is very rare and is limited to the few occasions in which other family members jointly occupy the primary set in the living room. More often, lean forward consumption is unplanned and is triggered by event-based onset stimuli such as e-mail links or events during web surfing. However, we do find traces of how people try to match the surroundings of both viewing styles, and even combine them. They do so for instance by locating the computer in the living room, so they would still be in the presence of family members, and even join in their activities from a distance.

3.2.2 Class 2: Multispace-solo viewers

This class is the youngest one with a median age of 20 years old. In comparison to other classes, they are much more likely to watch in the solitude of their bedrooms, away from a more socially oriented living room. On average, they consume 80 minutes per day in a lean back mode, while their lean forward consumption amounts to half an hour. The relations between the underlying factors of lean back viewing are interesting. In contrast with the other two classes, there is no significant difference between both explanatory paths. This implies that their lean back consumption is equally directed by intentions and habits. Still, the interviews allowed an understanding of this occurrence. It appears that these younger people strive for consumption autonomy, thus avoiding the living room, especially when there is ground for familial conflict. When they watch, they want to be able to make deliberate choices and keep away from disfavored social interaction. Still, they do cherish the living room and actually revert to it in particular situations in which they sense it adds value to the experience. This is articulated by Vera (21, F), who combines consumption in the living room, her own bedroom and her brother's bedroom:

> Vera: *The living room's major attractor is that it's homely; my parents watch here* [the living room]. *It is also something that is printed into us; it's a family value. Watching together with my* [younger] *brother, in his room is something recent, but then I'm in his personal space. I don't feel like an intruder, but it is a different feeling. I would never watch there without him. Here that's different because it's a shared space. Then again, with him it is different, a brother-sister thing, without the parents. Just the two of us, which gives me the feeling to be closer to him, to do the things he likes. Here, it's more general, depending on what everyone likes. In my own room, it's very personal, the things I want to see, the series I want to watch and of course also other stuff like my e-mail, Facebook,... things the other family members have no business with.*

In some cases, for instance when there is a joint preference for a certain program, the living room is valued as a social space. Yet even more important is that they too cherish the living room as a comfortable environment (e.g. warm, cozy sofa, ideal viewing position). Interestingly, this class' members put in quite some effort to replicate cues from this space into their own private spaces. In fact, they actively pursue to make a 'living room' for their own by incorporating a sofa, modifying their beds while watching and arrange their televisions or computers to get a similar viewing position.

Furthermore, the statistical analysis has shown that, next to habit strength, expected outcomes also explain variance in lean forward consumption. In fact, the interviews revealed a slightly different kind of interaction with lean back viewing. In the previous case, both were mostly separated. In contrast, this type of viewers often uses a computer for both consumption types, situated in the same room. Hence, there are notions of interaction for instance when coming across interesting content, that is actively previewed in a lean forward manner and then later on consumed in a lean back fashion. Still, the transition from one type to the other involves an active rearrangement of the affording device and its immediate surroundings. In other words, lean forward viewing serves as a motivated cue for lean back viewing.

3.2.3 Class 3: Multispace-social and solo viewers

Finally, the third class consists of people somewhat older than the one previously discussed. Their daily lean back consumption roughly amounts to two hours, while they allocate more than half an hour to lean forward viewing. The relations between the underlying factors closely resemble those of the first class we discussed. Nonetheless, they diverge strongly in the socio-spatial contexts of consumption. Drawing upon the interviews, it shows that this class, similar to the previous ones, experiences some tensions that require more dispersed viewing patterns. Still, there are accounts of individualized viewing without any specific need to do so. Although they too maintain the living room as a primary site of (social) consumption, they themselves tend to view in other rooms as well, be it to avoid tensions or not. The question is what separates them from the people in the first class. Whereas those were strongly tied to a joint experience, the participants from this class had a more balanced consumption. They hold tight to a socially oriented viewing, which is however combined with a more individualized consumption. IT-consultant Jasper (26, M) lives together with his girlfriend, in a house packed with multiple screens:

> Interviewer: *some people watch with their family, do you do that too?*
>
> Jasper: *No, not really. Yeah, there are some shows we watch together. Otherwise, we really enjoy being in separate places, to have 'me-time'. And that's something important for me, you know, I was brought up that way. I need some time to spend by myself. I think it's really important for people to have their own space, a personal space in the house.*

The origins of this behavior are manifold. One way to understand it is that similar meanings are attributed to various spaces. More specifically, cognitive schemes for certain spaces tend to overlap, for instance when the kitchen and the living room are perceived equal in terms of sites of family life, or viewing the bedroom as equally pleasant for quality time with a partner. In that case, audiovisual technologies have similar probabilities of entering that space or that kind of social interaction. This is a manifestation of stimulus generalization, in which cues in one space increasingly coincide with cues from another, supporting the same behavior. Moreover, the very same generalization accounts for non-domestic audiovisual consumption. For example, paramedic Victor (23, M) uses his laptop at the hospital's break-out room to fill his stand-by time. The living room-like environment makes him feel sufficiently comfortable to consume video over there.

However, we noted another interesting pattern. When we inquired about the occurrences that made them shift away from living room viewing, participants mentioned their consumption as teenagers. They reflect upon their autonomous use back then, having a television in the bedroom or some hobby space. Also, they touch upon their experiences as students, having a personal device in their student room in order not to disrupt their former media habits. As such, they learned a more individualized behavior that is much less contingent on social cues, causing an alteration of that habit. This is for instance the case for Erik (30, M). Before he had a television in his room as a teenager, he used to watch together with his family. From then on, his viewing individualized, through the already mentioned substitution of the 'living room experience' by arranging one of his own. Later, when he went to university, he had to have a set in his dorm too. Nowadays, he lives together with his girlfriend and although they watch together regularly, unlike his girlfriend he does not mind to go to another room to catch up with series episodes or watch sports on his own.

4. DISCUSSION

In our research we have found three distinct patterns of socio-spatial consumption contexts. Consumption in these environments is differentially explained by goal-directed expected outcomes and habits. The group of *unispace-social viewers* adheres to the traditional scheme of living room family viewing, which is strongly explained by habit. This is also the case for the *multispace-social/solo viewers* who demonstrate a complex configuration of numerous consumption environments, combining both individualized and joint experiences in multiple settings. Furthermore, we discovered a group of *multispace-solo viewers* who commute from the private bedroom to the living room, seeking an autonomous experience.

In elaborating on these effects, we discovered how routine patterns are best understood through the concept of the moral economy of the home. That is framing the household as a dynamic micro-economic entity in which values, cognitions and aesthetics are transferred between the constituent members from different generations. By combining this analytical framework with theoretical accounts of habit formation and execution processes drawn from social psychology, we were able to understand the habit-goal interface in audiovisual media consumption. More specifically, we discovered that the *unispace-social viewers* have no incentive to change their viewing patterns as they highly value family viewing and are able to exercise a more dominant role in promoting this kind of consumption. As such, they are inclined to perceive the living room as the one and only stable context. The *multispace-social/solo viewers* are however detached from this belief, displaying leniency towards more individualized viewing for themselves as well as the other family members. By means of the interviews, we were also able to trace the origins of this behavior and noticed that these viewers have a less compartmentalized conception of their homes and explicitly equate the meanings of several socio-spatial locations. Moreover, we came across notions of habit reconfiguration as a result of individualized viewing behavior as a teenager. This links in with the younger *multispace-solo viewers* who actively seek a disconnection from family viewing in order to make decisions of their own, which links in with earlier developmental-psychological theoretical and empirical accounts of teenage bedroom media consumption [35, 36]. However, they actively pursue to incorporate cues from the living room into their new consumption contexts, rendering it equally stable contexts in socio-spatial terms.

As such, this enables an understanding of today's changing (audiovisual) media consumption that appears to be intertwined with a generational shift. Whereas older generations have learned a strong association between the audiovisual and social viewing, younger generations have the opportunity to get used to a more individualized experience. This culminates in the teenage years, appearing to decline later on, yet leaving seemingly permanent traces.

5. CONCLUSION

In conclusion, this article sheds light on the origins of audiovisual media consumption. This is accomplished by a combination and integration of multiple theoretical accounts and their respective methodologies. Although Social Cognitive Theory and Domestication Theory diverge in their epistemological positions, we believe that by leaving each in its own right and by actively integrating its results, a more refined approach to the subject is rendered feasible. The large-scale questionnaire, based on operational quantitative measures derived from earlier work on the Theory of Media Attendance, has allowed us to sketch a broad map of the problematic, even allowing an explanation in statistical terms. Moreover, to our knowledge, this is the first research that looks for a way to detach U&G/TMA measures from a specific manifestation of device, content or socio-spatial context. We believe that in the age of convergence such an agnostic view is most productive when the aim is to grasp the broader picture, rather than focusing on one of its fragments and missing out on all the rest. Furthermore, by adding an in-depth qualitative layer guided by both Domestication and social-psychological concepts, we were able to obtain an understanding of the processes and dynamics that underlie these preliminary results. Hence, we want to make a case for more integrated accounts, both on the theoretical and methodological level. We hereby promote research that embraces a pragmatic stance towards different paradigms, looking for what unites, rather than for what divides.

Finally, we propose multiple venues for future research. On the one hand, the Model of Media Attendance, as we implemented it, could be applied to other kinds of media consumption and/or could be extended by various measures, depending on the research topic. On the other hand, different indicators could be used to group respondents into subsamples, enabling a different take on the multi-sample analysis as we performed it, for instance by tapping into the specific role of technology affordances or content preferences. Finally, the qualitative layer should be opened up to all kinds of traditions that embrace in-depth qualitative, or even ethnographic accounts of the social phenomenon of media consumption.

6. REFERENCES

[1] Bjur, J., Transforming Audiences: Patterns of individualization in television viewing. 2009, Göteborg: Livréna AB.

[2] Rubin, A.M., The Uses-and-Gratifications Perspective of Media Effect, in Media Effects: Advances in Theory and Research, J. Bryant and D. Zillman, Editors. 2002, Lawrence Erlbaum Associates: Mahwah.

[3] LaRose, R., The Problem of Media Habits. Communication Theory, 2010. 20(2): p. 194-222.

[4] Silverstone, R. and L. Haddon, Design and the domestication of information and communication technologies: technical change and everyday life, in Communication by Design, R. Mansell and R. Silverstone, Editors. 1996, Oxford University Press: Oxford.

[5] LaRose, R., D. Mastro, and M. Eastin, Understanding Internet Usage: A Social-Cognitive Approach to Uses and Gratifications. Social Science Computer Review, 2001. 19(4): p. 395-413.

[6] Ruggiero, T., Uses and Gratifications Theory in the 21st Century. Mass Communication & Society, 2000. 3(1): p. 3-37.

[7] Katz, E., J.G. Blumler, and M. Gurevitch, Utilization of Mass Communication by the Individual, in The Uses of Mass Communication, J.G. Blumler and E. Katz, Editors. 1974, Sage Publications: London.

[8] Palmgreen, P. and J.D. Rayburn, An Expectancy-Value Approach to Media Gratifications, in Media Gratifications Research: Current Perspectives. 1985, Sage Publications: London.

[9] Galloway, J.J. and F.L. Meek, Audience Uses and Gratifications: An Expectancy Model. Communication Research, 1981. 8(4): p. 435-449.

[10] Van Leuven, J., Expectancy Theory in Media and Message Selection. Communication Research, 1981. 8(4): p. 425-434.

[11] Verplanken, B., et al., Habit versus planned behaviour: A field experiment. British Journal of Social Psychology, 1998. 37(1): p. 111-138.

[12] Wood, W. and D. Neal, A New Look at Habits and the Habit-Goal Interface. Psychological Review, 2007. 114(4): p. 843-863.

[13] LaRose, R. and M. Eastin, A Social Cognitive Theory of Internet Uses and Gratifications: Toward a New Model of Media Attendance. Journal of Broadcasting & Electronic Media, 2004. 48(3): p. 358-377.

[14] Bandura, A., Self-Efficacy: The Exercise of Control. 1994, New York: Freeman.

[15] Bandura, A., A social cognitive theory. 1986, Englewood Cliffs: Prentice-Hall.

[16] Peters, O., et al., Explaining and analyzing audiences: A social cognitive approach to selectivity and media use. Communications, 2006. 31(3): p. 279-308.

[17] Peters, O., A Social Cognitive Perspective on Mobile Communication Technology Use and Adoption. Social Science Computer Review, 2009. 27(1): p. 76-95.

[18] Lee, D. and R. Larose, A Socio-Cognitive Model of Video Game Usage. Journal of Broadcasting & Electronic Media, 2007. 51(4): p. 632-650.

[19] LaRose, R. and J. Kim, Share, steal, or buy? A social cognitive perspective of music downloading. Cyberpsychology & Behavior, 2007. 10(2): p. 167-277.

[20] Rubin, A.M., Television uses and gratifications: The interactions of viewing patterns and motivations. Journal of Broadcasting, 1983. 27(1): p. 37-51.

[21] Rubin, A.M., Ritualized and Instrumental Television Viewing. Journal of Communication, 1984. 34(3): p. 67-77.

[22] Neal, D., W. Wood, and J. Quinn, Habits - A Repeat Performance. Current Directions in Psychological Science, 2006. 15(4): p. 198-202.

[23] Wood, W., J. Quinn, and D. Kashy, Habits in Everyday Life: Though, Emotion and Action. Journal of Personality and Social Psychology, 2002. 83(6): p. 1281-1297.

[24] Morley, D., Home Territories: Media, Mobility, and Identity. 2000, London: Routledge.

[25] Silverstone, R., Television and Everyday Life. 1994, London: Routledge.

[26] Haddon, L. and R. Silverstone, Information and Communication Technologies and Everyday Life: Individual and Social Dimensions, in The Information Society in

Europe, K. Ducatel, J. Webster, and W. Herrmann, Editors. 2000, Rowman & Littlefield Publishers: Lanham.

[27] Livingstone, S., The changing nature of audiences: From the mass audience to the interactive media user, ed. A. Valdivia. 2003, Oxford: Blackwell.

[28] Schrøder, K.C., The best of both worlds? Media audiences research between rival paradigms, in Rethinking the media audience: the new agenda, P. Alasuurari, Editor. 1999, Sage: London. p. 38-67.

[29] Vermunt, J.K. and J. Magidson. Latent Class Analysis. 2006; Available from: http://www.statisticalinnovations.com/articles/Latclass.pdf.

[30] Courtois, C., P. Verdegem, and L. De Marez. The Triple Articulation of Media Technologies in Audiovisual Media Consumption. Television and New Media, In Press.

[31] Ruy, H. and A. Wong, Perceived usefulness and performance of human-to-human communcations on television. Computers in Human Behavior, 2007. 24(4): p. 1364-1384.

[32] Tsekleves, E., et al., Entertainment Computing, 2011. 2(3): p. 151-161.

[33] Verplanken, B. and S. Orbell, Reflections on Past Behavior: A Self-Report Index of Habit Strength. Journal of Applied Social Psychology, 2006. 33(6): p. 1313-1330.

[34] Verplanken, B., Beyond Frequency: Habit as a Mental Construct. British Journal of Social Psychology, 2006. 45(3): p. 639-656.

[35] Courtois, C., et al., The Triple Articulation of Media Technologies in Teenagers' Media Consumption. New Media & Society, 2011.

[36] Livingstone, S., Young People and New Media. 2002, London: Sage.

Device Communication: A Multi-Modal Communication Platform for Internet Connected Televisions

James Cortez
Yahoo! Connected TV
Sunnyvale, CA USA
jecortez@yahoo-inc.com

David A. Shamma
Yahoo! Research
Santa Clara, CA USA
aymans@acm.org

Linghan Cai
Yahoo! Connected TV
Sunnyvale, CA USA
lcai@yahoo-inc.com

ABSTRACT

In this article, we describe Device Communication: a protocol and architecture to enable new TV viewing experiences driven by a sophisticated platform between the TV and modern tablets, mobile phones, and laptops. Beyond simple keyboard and remote control navigation, the device connectivity platform provides a channel for two-way, application-specific message passing over a new secure and open-sourced protocol over a local network. This platform is informed by current research, W3C reference specifications as well as advertiser and broadcaster requirements. We further describe its integration and deployment into a large, commercial Internet TV framework.

Categories and Subject Descriptors

H.4 [**Information Systems Applications**]: Miscellaneous; H.5.m [**Information Interfaces and Presentation**]: Miscellaneous; D.4.4 [**Operating Systems**]: Communications Management—*Message Sending, Communications Management*

General Terms

Human Factors, Design

Keywords

TV, devices, second screen, protocol, message-passing

1. INTRODUCTION

The television has become connected. In recent years, many TVs have gone online—wirelessly serving web videos, sports scores and social network status updates—and provided various microapp ecosystems. Unlike the smartphone and tablet experiences, TV has the benefit of being more immersive and cinematic; at the same time, TV's input modality is one of a few number buttons and a directional pad. This limitation is a burden on anyone trying to build rich cinematic Internet experiences to the TV; particularly when coupled with second screen devices. Towards this, many have devised second screen experiences, from basic remote control apps to popup video style information related to the show one is presumably watching. We propose a new extensible message passing interface for multi-modal experiences centering around the TV and mobile devices, such as smart phones and tablets.

While there have been a host of experiences and design considerations that suggest what a platform for TV plus secondary screens can do or should support [12, 2, 8, 18], the Application Programming Interfaces (APIs) in existing commercial TV systems remain, at best, sophisticated remote controls. Recently, the W3C has outlined a reference specification [11] for home networking and secondary screen interactions [25]. There is a disconnect of what research and standards say is needed and what can happen in a commercial system. The primary aim of this paper is to remove this disconnect through the real-world deployment of a secondary screen API, called Device Communication, built into a line of commercially available Internet connected TVs. This API is one that takes into consideration design implications from current research, requirements from reference specifications, and, additionally, needs of large publishers and advertisers.

Device Communication is a system of components and APIs that allows for multi-modal experiences through the Yahoo! Connected TV platform. Mobile, tablet, traditional desktops and laptops (client devices) are increasingly being used during the media watching experience. In order to capitalize on this trend, Device Communication aims to allow any network devices to interact with each other, using the television as both a server and a client. Using this system, new user experiences that bridge the shared TV screen and personal screen can be created for any device that has a home network connection. These experiences are not locked down and allow developers to create new flexible and innovative user experiences.

2. RELATED WORK

The idea of a secondary screen in an Interactive TV environment is not new and has been the focus of much research. Even without these systems being in place, several types of ad hoc experiences have been established, connecting people and devices through watching TV and using social networking [12]. For example, Basapur et al. [2] found people enjoy simple parallel experiences, ones with no actual linkage between the TV and the tablet device, as well as desired customization of certain push-feed social updates from the

EuroITV'12, July 4–6, 2012, Berlin, Germany.

Twitter [23] service. This finding is congruent with Mitchell et al.'s [15] earlier study on content navigation using social awareness which used only one screen. They found that *social closeness* can be used to affect the personalization of display content in social TV situations; while their study consisted largely of a single demographic, the need for social personalization was demonstrably evident.

Cesar, Bulterman, and Jansen [5] proposed four major usages of the TV and secondary screen combination: controlling, enriching, sharing, and transferring of television content. These areas can be non-exclusive as sharing is a form of enriching as well as transferring video to a new device can also be a type of enriching. Tsekleves, Whitham, Kondo and Hill [22] found similar usages. Additionally, they found network security to be a requirement as specified by many of their people in their study.

While there are several arguments for a global living room powered through social/interactive TV [16], little has been seen in its actual creation. Commercially, Internet TV devices and enhanced remotes are quite common: Apple TV has an iOS Remote app, Boxee has a QWERTY remote, Sony Playstation controllers that function as mouse pointers and, recently, XBox 360s added voice and gesture control using their Kinect module. In all of these cases, each remote is essentially a one way controller. Typically multiple controllers are not individually distinguished but a few researchers, namely Soares et al. [19], have developed protocols for multiple devices interacting with a single exhibition device (the TV); Soares et al. used a Nested Context Language [20] as a control model.

Outside of research, the "leading" industry standard for communication between networked devices in the home is Universal Plug and Play (UPnP) [24], or it is trademarked name Digital Living Network Alliance (DLNA) [9]. While it provides several mechanisms for communication between devices, it does not provide a method for sending messages to the application level. This deficiency coupled with lack of interoperability between manufactures, an undefined security model, and a lack of completely agreed upon APIs made it a poor choice for our requirements.

Finally, the W3C has a reference specification of what such a secondary screen API would require [11]. Much of this specification is geared towards TV on the Web and the Internet of Things [25], however, there are several key services which they suggest implementing such as service Discovery and Advertising, Control and Communication, and Security, which are applicable towards any Internet connected TV. They add additional requirements, such as migration (where a user can seamlessly move between devices and browsers) which is less universally applicable with regards to embedded home experiences.

3. DESIGN CONSIDERATIONS

The design considerations for such a second screen interface, be it a simple button remote or a rich interactive conduit, have factors beyond changing channels and beyond linking a web browser to the TV through a tablet computer. The TV, for better or worse, is a land of publishers and broadcasters who are looking to provide these large, cinematic, and personalized web experiences on an Internet connected TV, and they wish to do so at large scale. More so, they wish to have privileged access. Primarily, this is an argument against an open architecture. However, to the developers who are not advertisers and broadcasters, an open environment for rich second screen experiences on thousands of devices is an attraction. To this, a platform for second screen interactions for consumer electronics environment requires both a certain openness and some protections in addition to a new UI frameworks designed around the lean-back, 8-foot interactions commonly found in the living room.

With market concerns in mind, we identified four technical requirements when designing the Device Communication protocol:

1. Security
2. Real Time Events
3. Simplicity
4. Flexibility

Secured end-to-end communication ensures sensitive data, such as keystrokes, can be sent. If a user is going to need to login to an third party service, and the password is to be entered on the device and sent to the TV which authorizes a HTTP request, then all communication must be secured. The second requirement was to support real time events. Data must be able to be sent to the client devices in real time and vice versa. This means polling and cloud-based solutions were not an option. While many HTTP work around solutions are readily available, such as CometD [7], socket.io [21], and websockets [13], we require a solution which is be fast, responsive and lightweight. Similarly push solutions like XMPP [27] use verbose XML markup that require parsers with large memory footprints. Since TV's have slow processors and very little memory, a socket based protocol with a simple parsing grammar would be the more desirable. This will allow new developers to easily integrate into existing applications and quickly develop new experiences. Finally, the solution would require flexibility. The platform must allow communication between TV applications and client applications in a transparent manner in order to foster innovation beyond current use cases.

Several research studies [12, 17] have identified feature requirements for second screen experiences through detailed ethnographic studies. In particular, Hess et al. [12] ran a series of creative workshops to determine several concepts needed for social TV and second screens. Primarily they identified the following dimensions: social networks, integrated information, recommendation, and personalization. While most of these refer to application level concepts, their requirement for integrated information mandates rich communication capabilities between TVs and devices. In one of their examples, users wanted to have actions on the device affect on-TV notifications—in effect, passing the notification event to the other device. This consideration was fully accounted for when designing the Device Communication system.

4. IMPLEMENTATION

The first Device Communication prototype was a small experiment to interface a lightweight web server built into a TV engine. Many media center platforms have some form of web server available, XBMC Media Center [26] being the principal representative powering 7 platforms and over 25 commercial and free media center interfaces including

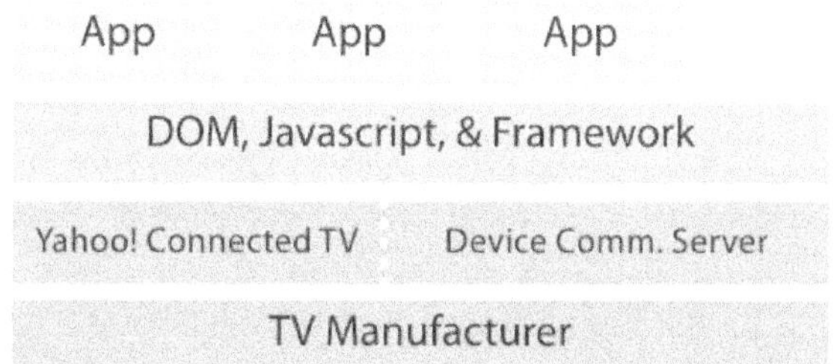

Figure 1: The overall TV software architecture contains the Device Communication component which sits next to an extensible application engine.

Boxee [3]. An advantage of using a web server is that no native clients have to be written for any particular device. Any device with a web browser could automatically be used to control the device by simply visiting a URL in a browser. However, this proved to be a disadvantage for several reasons. First, the communication in the prototype was based on HTTPS, which does not support statefull connections and server-to-client push messages. Second, a HTTPS server on a low-resource system can be very resource intensive. Primarily this is due to SSL requiring a key swap and verification for every new message. In our system, key swap is done at the start of the session; subsequent calls do not resend the key. A session will last as long as the app on the device is running. If the mobile device quits the app and restarts it, a new session will begin with a fresh key swap. The last major problem with HTTPS is establishing security. Most web browsers require the use of a Certificate Authority (CA) for certificate verification. Since the server is running within a local network, this made using a CA impossible and would lead to an unfavorable user experience. Removing the security requirement would allow for unacceptable security holes.

4.1 Device Communication Architecture

With the findings from the prototype, we began to build Device Communication using the Yahoo! Connected TV platform. This platform provides a JavaScript environment that manipulates a DOM structure. The platform then utilizes hardware accelerated graphics and video to render the user interface (UI) and uses Interactive Data Language (IDL) like definitions for new Javascript APIs which interact with the TV's subsystem, see Figure 1. A bridge compiler connectes internal objects from the Yahoo! Connected TV engine to Javascript. The bridge compiler generates code to deal with all the repetitive code that has to be normally written to marshal from JavaScript into the engine space.

Using the existing platform architecture and system interfaces, another service has been added to run along side the platform's engine. This service binds to the network interface on the device via standard Unix sockets and starts a server to handle all incoming messages. The Device Communication service in the engine is responsible for the authentication of new clients (detailed in section 4.4 Network Security) and routing of messages.

Information about authorized Device Communication clients such as name, security keys, and connection status are stored on the TV. Each client is assigned a unique identifier, which can be used to fetch various information about the client such as name, permissions and current connection status. The implementation of the Device Communication Engine service is also a dispatcher for incoming messages. It decides how messages are routed to TV application Javascript contexts, system services, or even other client applications.

4.2 Message Passing Interface

The key distinguishing feature of Device Communication is a rich message passing conduit. Message passing is divided into three types of messages:

1. Session Configuration
2. Publish/Subscribe
3. Remote Method Calls

Each message type deals with a different style or category of message. See Figure 2 for examples of each message type described.

4.2.1 Session Configuration Messages

Session Configuration messages encompass a small discrete set of commands that mainly deal with security and authorization. We will discuss these at further length in section 4.4 Network Security.

4.2.2 Publish/Subscribe Messages

Publish/Subscribe messages are for event based broadcast messages. Client devices can subscribe to certain data types and services. When messages are published from any device (including the TV), that message is broadcast to any clients that are listening to that message.

For example, a client application can subscribe to TV media player events such as play/pause states, time progress changes, and stream changes. When any of these states change, the client application is instantly notified and can update its visual state. On the other side, the client application can also publish changes, which will affect the streaming content on TV, such as advancing the stream to a desired time index or requesting playback of a video at a specific URI.

Each specific API that uses the publish/subscribe model is categorized into three sections: input, service, or widget. The *input* category holds all APIs that allow for generic user interaction across all applications such as navigation and keyboard handling. The *service* category contains the APIs that relate to specific services running on the TV, such as a media URI launcher and an automatic content recognition service. The final *widget* category allows messages to be sent directly from client applications to TV applications and vice-versa. The payload portion of the message is transparent to the engine and empowers the developer to design the data schema.

4.2.3 Remote Method Calling

As an alternative to the pub/sub broadcast model, Remote method calls for point-to-point message passing are also available. Remote method calls are designed to allow asyncronous single point-to-point call and response. The use of these calls are for requesting data that either does not change, or requires specific parameters to be sent in. An example use case is gathering a list of videos available from a certain application on the TV given a filter as a parameter

Publish Messages:

```
PUBLISH|<category>|<subject>|<data>|END
```

Example:

```
PUBLISH|INPUT|navigation|press_enter|END
```

Subscribe Messages:

```
SUBSCRIBE|<category>|<subject>|END}
```

Example:

```
SUBSCRIBE|SERVICE|medialaunch|END
```

Remote Calls:

```
CALL|<method_name>|<target>|<payload>|<call_id>|END
RETURN|<method_name>|<target>|<result>|<call_id>|END
```

Examples:

```
CALL|getVideoList|com.example.video|{''catId'':1}|6442|END
RETURN|getVideoList|com.example.video|[{''title'':''video1'',
                                         ''url'':''http://example.com/myvideo''}]|6442|END
```

Figure 2: The message passing interface (described in detail in section 4.2) provides three types of message primaries. Publish/Subscribe messages allow for event based broadcasts. Remote method calls allow point-to-point message passing. Session configuration messages (not depicted) are a small discrete set of commands dealing with security and authorization commands.

(for an example see Figure 2). Once the target processes the request, a response can be sent back in an asynchronous manner.

One requirement for remote method calls is that several calls to the same method should be able to be made at one time and responses to those calls should be able to match up to their responses, all while being asynchronous. To achieve this, the developer supplies a unique ID in the call that is also passed back in the return message. Using this ID, the developer can match specific calls with their responses.

4.3 Service Discovery

Discovery is a key piece of any system that wishes to allow users to connect to a server in a simple fashion. How do you discover and pair two or more devices automatically? While there are commercial solutions in place, automatic discovery is still an active area of research [6, 14, 1]. DNS Service Discovery (DNS-SD) [10] or Zeroconf [28] provides an adequate infrastructure discovering devices on a local network. However DNS-SD is not fully adequate as a single solution for discovery as some network configurations block some multicast packets. To remedy this, we implemented a mixed multi-tier system was created to allow for graceful degradation in service discovery, see Figure 3. The first choice in the multi-tier system is DNS-SD. The second uses a cloud-based web server as a simple hash lookup of an address. Finally, the third allows the user to manually enter a full IP address and port. Using a mixture of discovery and connection methods, any number of devices can be added to interact with the TV and each other, see Figure 4.

4.3.1 DNS-SD Discovery

The first and preferred tier uses DNS-SD. It is a system that allows services to announce themselves via multicast network packets. Using the standards set in place by the DNS-SD organizations, the Device Communication service

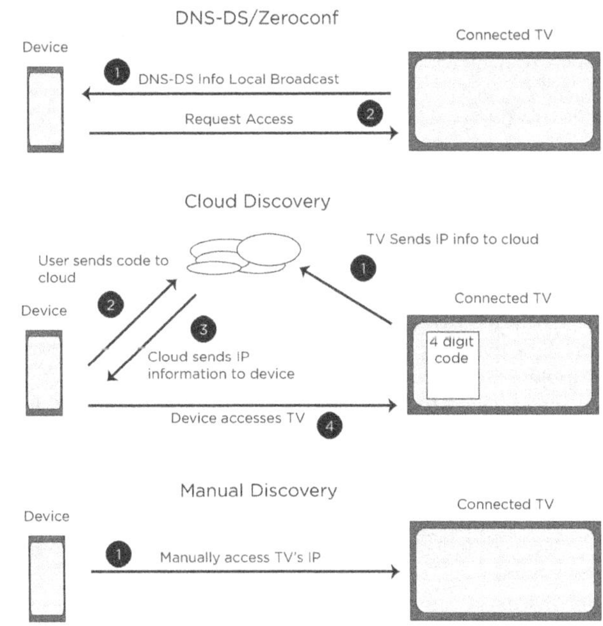

Figure 3: Three systems for device discovery. Top: DNS-DS/Zeroconf broadcasts connect information to the local subnet. Middle: A cloud web-service mediates the connection information. Bottom: A user manually enters all the required IP settings.

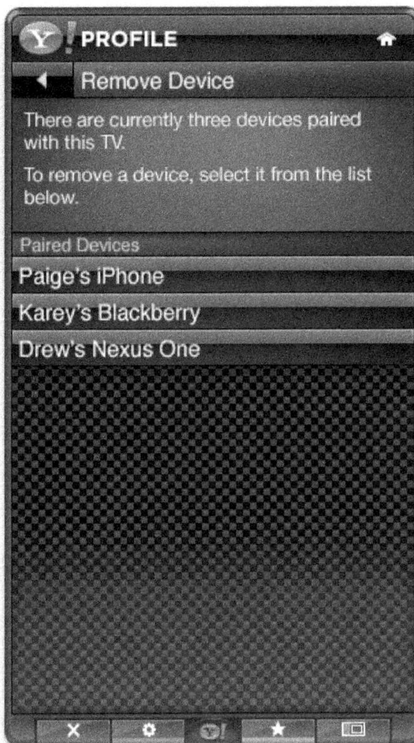

Figure 4: A screen shot of the device browser showing three paired devices.

running on the television announces its IP, port, and unique name on the network. Clients that are listening to these packets can then display user-friendly interfaces that do not require the user go through any additional steps to begin the connection process.

4.3.2 Cloud Based Web Service

The development attempt for the second tier was to create a redirect system using backend web servers hosted in the cloud. Using this system, the TV would register the current IP with the server, which would respond with a shortened URI to be displayed on screen. The client would then connect to this URI using a traditional browser, which would in turn open the native application on the device to handle the protocol. This approach was discarded due to inconsistencies with how browsers and operating systems (mobile or otherwise) registered new protocols and opened the applications. However, using a cloud based solution was not altogether abandoned.

The implementation of the second tier uses a web service in the cloud that simply stores IP and port addresses and returns a short four-digit code. The TV makes a request with its address and displays the resulting four-digit code on screen. The user then manually inputs this code into the client, which then makes a request to the web service to retrieve the correct address. Since the majority of addresses will be in a small block of IP addresses, the web service can be highly cached and be completely stored in memory which will greatly reduce retrieval latency from cloud based key-value storage solutions. Figure 5 shows the TV requesting the viewer to enter this four-digit code to pair the device.

4.3.3 Manual Entry

Manual entry is the final and last resort option built off the second tier. Here an IP address and port are displayed on the TV, which the user then has to input manually into the client to connect. While this is the simplest implementation, it is a high if not impassable barrier to entry for any nontechnical user. However, we allow this method for debugging, development, as well as for advanced users who may have more complicated home network routing.

4.4 Network Security

Although security is always a priority when building web applications, Device Communication could not use many of the traditional security mechanisms employed on the Internet. Traditional secure web (HTTPS) requires a Certificate Authority to verify an Internet host. In our case, the host is the TV on the local network, which is not traditionally verifiable. An important aspect of this system is the idea of a Certificate Authority, which is a trusted 3rd party that can verify that the keys sent are valid. These keys are validated by comparing the originating domain and a key stored by the Certificate Authority. Systems that do not use Certificate Authorities are vulnerable to a man-in-the-middle attack. This attack relays information to both clients with them knowing while inspecting the data for itself. Unfortunately, TVs do not have registered domains or static IPs and thus cannot use Certificate Authorities as the trust manager.

As an alternative, Device Communication was designed to use Secure Socket Layer (SSL) using a self-signed certificate, bypassing the need for a Certificate Authority. Instead, we verify that the user is physically able to see the TV display. As such, a guaranteed secure connections can be made. SSL is a system that uses asymmetric cryptography to secure messages between to points. During the initial connection process, public keys are swapped via the network connection and then are used to encrypt the data being sent. This data can only be decrypted if the receiver has the private key.

A key security model component for Device Communication is establishing that the user (and not a potential attacker) is able to see the TV display. If this viewership is verified, then the connection is deemed secure enough to continue. Figure 6 vizualizes the flow of the authorization scheme. To do this, the TV generates a self-signed certificate at first boot time to be used in the SSL key swap. After the "unsecure" SSL connection is made, a four-digit alphanumeric code is displayed on the TV screen, which the user manually inputs into the client device. The client device then uses SHA1-HMAC hash of this code and the public SSL certificate of the TV, which was received during the SSL handshake. The resulting hash is submitted back to the TV, which has done the same calculation and can verify the result.

After the signature is verified, an unique identifier (UUID) is generated by the TV and sent to the client for all subsequent connections. Since the key swap has already been done and the line of site has been established once, the client can use both the SSL keys and the assigned UUID reconnect to the device without having to go through the extra verification process.

The assumption behind this approach is that an attacker attempting to do a man-in-the-middle attack is not able to physically view the TV display and cannot correctly calculate the signature of both the TV's certificate and the

Figure 5: While watching a documentary, a user is connecting a device. They are prompted to enter a 4 digit code to authenticate the discovered device and create a secured connection. Post-authentication, application communication between the TV and device can occur.

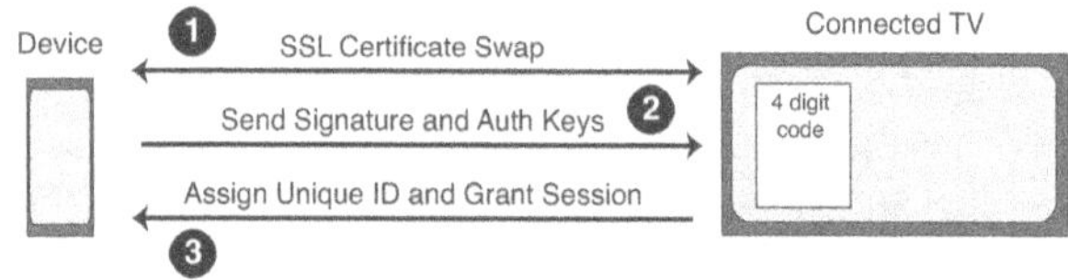

Figure 6: The TV Authentication flow requires an SSL key swap, and a unique code to disambiguate devices and add an added layer of security.

displayed code. In order to decrease the likelihood of an attacker guessing the code, the displayed code changes on every successful and unsuccessful signature generation. Using these security measures, developers are safe to send sensitive material such as keyboard strokes and application messages.

4.5 Client Access, Permissions, and Tracking

In order to maintain a secure and healthy application ecosystem, a requirement was made to allow a provider of Device Communication to unilaterally revoke application access to Device Communication API's for any reason, such as maliciousness or copyright infringement. On the flip side, this allows an implementor of Device Communication to allow certain APIs to be accessed by those who have entered into specific licensing agreements. Both use the same system for verification.

Before development begins on Device Communication, developers must first get issued developer credentials, typically an application ID and secret. This is commonly done through a developer portal. A combination of these issued keys is sent to the TV during the authorization process, before authorization is granted. The TV sends this key to a cloud-based web server, which verifies the key and returns a list of allowed API keys. This list of keys is moderated by a back-end administration tool that allows the addition and removal of certain permissions and entire applications.

5. EVALUATION AND DISCUSSION

Device Communication is a platform and method of providing a variety of second-screen experiences. Unlike other commercial device interactivity APIs, like those of Boxee [3] or Google TV [4], we had described and implemented a pure asynchronous API. This allows multiple messages to be sent concurrently as there is no single blocking socket, which makes for a more fluid second screen experience.

In the current production implementation of Device Communication on Yahoo! Connected TV, messages are parsed in the TCP stream's buffer, which is to say the system scans the incoming message and looks for the sentinel `|END` to mark the end. However, this sets a device dependent limitation, the TCP buffer length, on the message size. More so can cause problems if a client decides to flush the stream frequently. To remedy this, a content length header will be added to the message in future revisions, which removes both the dependence on the sentinel and the preset buffer size.

The W3C has released a specification of requirements for home networking scenarios [11] as part of a Web and TV initiative [25]. While our solution is not a web platform per se, the W3C Spec acts as a good set of guidelines. For example, Device Communication satisfies the specification's requirements for pairing and security. Most of the service discovery requirements is supported in our framework, however a few requirements, like application discovery, are not out-of scope for our solution and should either be handled by the backend application platform or are only applicable for web-based solutions.

5.1 URL Handling

One disadvantage of the Yahoo! Connected TV Platform is the inability to open URLs in a browser. However, most devices that have the ability to communicate using Device Communication also have a native browser (Mobile Safari, Google Chrome for Android, Firefox for Android, or Opera) that are designed for close user interaction. One API that is built into the Device Communication system allows for the TV to instruct the companion device to open pieces of media, such as a generic URL. However, once the URI is opened on the device, the resulting web application no longer has the ability to communicate with the TV.

We see two possible solutions for this hurdle. One solution would be to wrap a browser frame into an native app which can mediate the SSL connection between the TV and device. The app can then pull standard HTTP resources and coordinate between various web services and the TV by acting as a bridge. Another solution would be to use browser plugins or extensions to communicate over the arbitrary SSL socket. However, no current mobile browser supports this and the overhead of requiring a plugin install is too complex for the average user.

5.2 Content Awareness

Many commercially available TV systems, like Yahoo! Connected TV, have some ability to determine the content being displayed on the TV. This is also part of the W3C's requirements specification [11]. This style of broadcast interactivity allows Internet connected TVs to detect exactly what the user is currently watching regardless of source (antenna, cable, satellite, DVR, etc.) through audio fingerprinting. Using Device Communication, the current programming information, as well as its playback time, can be passed to client applications asynchronously via a publish/subscribe message for immersive experiences that relate to what the user is currently watching.

For example, if a person is watching the show *Mad Men* from American Movie Classics and the show has been detected by the content awareness system, a notification will be sent automatically via the active connection to the companion device via Device Communication. Using the data contained in the notification, more information about the episode, such as recaps or fun facts can be displayed and interacted with in real time. One interesting feature that can be built in conjunction would allow videos related to the current show to be selected on the companion device, then immediately played on the TV screen. Several second screen iPad apps, like TBS's *Big Bang Theory* app does this for live broadcasts but requires some manual synchronization by the user.

Further, using content detection systems, the TV can also detect commercials that are currently being shown on screen. Using previously connected companion applications, the TV can send requests to the user to download and install new client applications, or can redirect the user to an advertiser's web site. An example here would be, a commercial for a Ford car playing on screen. A prompt is subtly displayed on screen asking the user if they would like to find out more and explore the car on their companion device. Once the user interacts with the prompt, the companion device is directed to its own Application Store (Apple App Store, Android Market, etc.) so that the user can install the Ford app. This sort of experience can increase the advertiser's reach and extend the amount of time of user interaction with their product.

6. CONCLUSIONS

To build a comprehensive second-screen API, we have created a set of requirements based on current research, reference specifications, as well as advertiser and broadcaster needs. The implementation of the requirements has been successfully deployed to TV's running the Yahoo! Connected TV platform. Foremost, the Device Communication protocol commercial TV widget engine. The Device Communication API provides an asynchronous transport to support rich interactions and foster 3rd party development. While this architecture does not support integration into a HTML5 browser, it is a secure and flexible implementation built into a TV experience. Finally, the platform's client adaptors will be open sourced, thus allowing the platform's reuse in new domains.

7. ACKNOWLEDGMENTS

Thanks to Ryan Pressler, Grace Kim, Clark Jen, Atul Nayak, Kelly Ireland, and the rest of the Yahoo! Connected TV team for their efforts in designing and implementing this comprehensive API. Also thanks to Pablo Cesar and Elizabeth F. Churchill for their feedback for this article.

8. REFERENCES

[1] D. Balfanz, D. Smetters, P. Stewart, and H. Wong. Talking to strangers: Authentication in ad-hoc wireless networks. In *Proceedings of the Network and Distributed System Security Symposium*, NNDS '02, 2002.

[2] S. Basapur, G. Harboe, H. Mandalia, A. Novak, V. Vuong, and C. Metcalf. Field trial of a dual device user experience for itv. In *Proceedings of the 9th International Interactive Conference on Interactive Television*, EuroITV '11, pages 127–136, New York, NY, USA, 2011. ACM.

[3] Boxee. `http://boxee.org`, January 2012.

[4] Google TV. `http://www.google.com/tv`, January 2012.

[5] P. Cesar, D. C. Bulterman, and A. J. Jansen. Usages of the secondary screen in an interactive television environment: Control, enrich, share, and transfer television content. In *Proceedings of the 6th European conference on Changing Television Environments*, EUROITV '08, pages 168–177, Berlin, Heidelberg, 2008. Springer-Verlag.

[6] M. K. Chong and H. Gellersen. How users associate wireless devices. In *Proceedings of the 2011 annual conference on Human factors in computing systems*, CHI '11, pages 1909–1918, New York, NY, USA, 2011. ACM.

[7] Cometd bayeux ajax push. `http://cometd.org/`, December 2011.

[8] C. Concolato, J. Le Feuvre, and J.-C. Dufourd. Declarative interfaces for dynamic widgets communications. In *Proceedings of the 9th ACM symposium on Document engineering*, DocEng '09, pages 241–244, New York, NY, USA, 2009. ACM.

[9] Digital living network alliance (DLNA). http://www.dlna.org/, January 2012.

[10] DNS service discovery (DNS-SD). http://www.dns-sd.org/, January 2012.

[11] W. I. Group. Requirements for home networking scenarios. http://www.w3.org/TR/2011/NOTE-hnreq-20111201/, December 2011. Note 01.

[12] J. Hess, B. Ley, C. Ogonowski, L. Wan, and V. Wulf. Jumping between devices and services: towards an integrated concept for social TV. In *Proceedings of the 9th international interactive conference on Interactive television*, EuroITV '11, pages 11–20, New York, NY, USA, 2011. ACM.

[13] I. E. T. F. (IETF). The websocket protocol. http://tools.ietf.org/html/rfc6455, December 2011. ISSN: 2070-1721.

[14] C. Kray, D. Nesbitt, J. Dawson, and M. Rohs. User-defined gestures for connecting mobile phones, public displays, and tabletops. In *Proceedings of the 12th international conference on Human computer interaction with mobile devices and services*, MobileHCI '10, pages 239–248, New York, NY, USA, 2010. ACM.

[15] K. Mitchell, A. Jones, J. Ishmael, and N. J. Race. Social tv: toward content navigation using social awareness. In *Proceedings of the 8th international interactive conference on Interactive TV & Video*, EuroITV '10, pages 283–292, New York, NY, USA, 2010. ACM.

[16] M.-J. Montpetit, N. Klym, and T. Mirlacher. The future of iptv. *Multimedia Tools and Applications*, 53:519–532, 2011. 10.1007/s11042-010-0504-4.

[17] M. Obrist, C. Moser, D. Alliez, T. Holocher, and M. Tscheligi. Connecting tv & pc: an in-situ field evaluation of an unified electronic program guide concept. In *Proceedings of the seventh european conference on European interactive television conference*, EuroITV '09, pages 91–100, New York, NY, USA, 2009. ACM.

[18] M. Pirker, R. Bernhaupt, and T. Mirlacher. Investigating usability and user experience as possible entry barriers for touch interaction in the living room. In *Proceedings of the 8th international interactive conference on Interactive TV&Video*, EuroITV '10, pages 145–154, New York, NY, USA, 2010. ACM.

[19] L. F. G. Soares, R. M. Costa, M. F. Moreno, and M. F. Moreno. Multiple exhibition devices in dtv systems. In *Proceedings of the 17th ACM international conference on Multimedia*, MM '09, pages 281–290, New York, NY, USA, 2009. ACM.

[20] L. F. G. Soares and R. R. F. Nested Context Languages 3.0 Part 8 – NCL Digital TV Profiles. Technical Report MCC 35/06, Departamento de Informática da PUC-Rio, 2006. http://www.ncl.org.br/documentos/NCL3.0-DTV.pdf (Accessed January 2012).

[21] socket.io. http://socket.io/, December 2011.

[22] E. Tsekleves, R. Whitham, K. Kondo, and A. Hill. Bringing the television experience to other media in the home: an ethnographic study. In *Proceedings of the seventh european conference on European interactive television conference*, EuroITV '09, pages 201–210, New York, NY, USA, 2009. ACM.

[23] Twitter. http://www.twitter.com, Janurary 2012.

[24] UPnP specifications named international standard for device interoperability for ip-based network devices. http://www.upnp.org/news/documents/UPnPForum_02052009.pdf (Accessed January 2012), Feburary 2009.

[25] W3C. Web and tv. http://www.w3.org/standards/webofdevices/tv, December 2011.

[26] XBMC Media Center. http://xbmc.org, January 2012.

[27] Xmpp standards foundation. http://xmpp.org/, December 2011.

[28] Zero configuration networking (Zeroconf). http://www.zeroconf.org/, January 2012.

APPENDIX

A. OPEN SOURCE CLIENTS

Part of this work includes open sourced client adaptors for Java (Android) and ObjectiveC (iOS). The server side architecture is deeply integrated in a commercially available platform but could be more so easily replicated if one wanted to reuse this architecture. The release of these client adapters will be announced on the Yahoo! Connected TV website (http://connectedtv.yahoo.com Accessed 5/2012).

PalmRC: Imaginary Palm-based Remote Control for Eyes-free Television Interaction

Niloofar Dezfuli Mohammadreza Khalilbeigi Jochen Huber Florian Benjamin Müller
Max Mühlhäuser
Technische Universität Darmstadt
Hochschulstraße 10
64289 Darmstadt, Germany
{niloo, khalilbeigi, jhuber, müller, max} @tk.informatik.tu-darmstadt.de

ABSTRACT

User input on television (TV) typically requires a mediator device, such as a handheld remote control. While being a well-established interaction paradigm, a handheld device has serious drawbacks: it can be easily misplaced due to its mobility and in case of a touch screen interface, it also requires additional visual attention. Emerging interaction paradigms like 3D mid-air gestures using novel depth sensors, such as Microsoft's Kinect, aim at overcoming these limitations, but are known to be e.g. tiring.

In this paper, we propose to leverage the palm as an interactive surface for TV remote control. Our contribution is three-fold: (1) we explore the conceptual design space in an exploratory study. (2) Based upon these results, we investigate the effectiveness and accuracy of such an interface in a controlled experiment. And (3), we contribute PalmRC: an eyes-free, palm-surface-based TV remote control, which in turn is evaluated in an early user feedback session. Our results show that the palm has the potential to be leveraged for device-less and eyes-free TV remote interaction without any third-party mediator device.

Categories and Subject Descriptors

H5.2. [Information interfaces and presentation]: User Interface- Input devices and strategies.

General Terms

Design, Human Factors, Experimentations.

Keywords

Alternative Remote Control, TV, Device-less, Eyes-free, Omnipresent, Input, Direct Touch, Non-visual, Memory.

1. INTRODUCTION

User input on television is typically supported through remote controls. Common examples are conventional remotes with physical buttons or touch-based interfaces on smart phones. In effect, users are always required to utilize a particular *mediator device* to interact with the TVs. While this is a well-established interaction paradigm, it has various drawbacks. The device itself can be easily out of reach or misplaced [12]. Moreover, touch-

Figure 1. User taps on his non-dominant hand to operate the TV, while preserving his visual attention to the TV.

based interfaces on mobile devices [20] require a lot of attention as they provide visual feedback. This distracts the user, since she needs to switch her attention between the device and the content on the TV [14]. In summary, this increases the actual effort for controlling the TV and therefore may diminish the user experience while watching.

Researchers have been investigating other input modalities to control TV systems. Speech input [2, 6] and 3D mid-air gestures [12, 13] are two well-known approaches for device-less and eyes-free TV interaction [21]. However, these modalities still suffer from important drawbacks. Despite advantages of using natural language, the use of speech input is not always socially appropriate and the technology may fail to recognize commands in noisy environments. In addition, it is not well suited for common continuous interactions such as scrolling a channel list or adjusting the TV volume. As another approach, 3D gestures aim at overcoming these limitations, but are known to be e.g. tiring [12]. These drawbacks might explain why speech and 3D gestures as input modalities are still limited to lab environments and not yet widely deployed and included in home television environments.

In this work, we propose a novel approach to operate TVs. We leverage the non-dominant hand as an interactive input surface. Users can then operate the TV by interacting with the other hand's index finger (cf. Fig. 1). Therefore, the means to control a TV is naturally always available to viewers, without requiring any mediator device. Since humans are unconsciously aware of the relative position and orientation of one's own hands through proprioception [1], the palm can be appropriate for eyes-free interactions to operate the TV.

In this paper, we explore our concept in two studies. In the first study, being exploratory in nature, we aim at gaining insights into the conceptual space of palm-based remote controls. We particularly investigate different interaction styles and elicit implications on how to design such remote controls. Based on the results of this study, we designed a prototypical interface to conduct a controlled experiment. The major goal was to get a better understanding of the human capability of touching one's own palm without any visual attention. More precisely, the experiment aims at answering the following questions:

(1) How *precisely* can users touch their palm's salient regions (landmarks) without looking at them?

(2) How *effectively* can users select the target element of transferred on-screen user interface elements on their palm by pointing to the corresponding region on its surface without any visual attention?

The results of these studies gave us broad and deep insights into the conceptual design space. Building upon this, we designed and implemented PalmRC: an eyes-free, palm-surface-based TV remote control. Our prototype supports common tasks such as zapping through channels, menu navigation or social interaction between remote viewers. We evaluated PalmRC in early user feedback sessions.

The remainder of this paper is organized as follows. After reviewing related literature, we present the aforementioned studies and discuss the results. Then, we introduce PalmRC, interaction techniques and give a short technical overview. Finally, we report the results of our early user feedback sessions with PalmRC and conclude with an outlook upon future work.

2. RELATED WORK

While standard remote controls are still the most common interface for controlling TV systems at home, today's research is moving away from device-based interactions by observing and interpreting people's vocalization, movements and gestures with respect to the TV. In this section, we review research on device-less interaction with TVs and hand-based user interfaces. Our work is also inspired by prior work in the area of imaginary user interfaces, which we discuss at the end of this section.

2.1 Eyes-free and Device-less Interactions for Television Systems

Many studies investigated speech and 3D mid-air gestures input modalities to facilitate interaction with TV. Brutti et al. [2] presented a distant-talking interface for the interactive control of a TV set with multichannel acoustic data collection. Igarashi and Hughes [6] focused on direct control of interactive television by using non-verbal lower-level features of voice such as pith and volume. Although speech is a natural input modality, its usage is not always socially appropriate and the technology may fail to recognize commands in noisy environments.

Mäntyjärvi et al. [13] explored and generalized a possible set of gestures suitable for controlling home appliances such as a TV. They showed that 3D hand gestures lack an easy memorizable and universal vocabulary. Freeman and Weismann [12] have investigated how viewers can remotely control a television set by hand gestures without extensive user training and memorization. To do so, they provided visual feedback on the TV screen. This enabled users to move an on-screen pointer coupled to their hand to adjust various graphical controls. They reported that mid-air hand gestures are not appropriately recognizable for unpredictable scenes and suffer from scalability issues in group-watching experiences. In addition, their studies showed that people find mid-air gestures somewhat uncomfortable and tiring.

2.2 Hand-based Interactions

There are a number of wearable and mobile [7, 5, 9, 10] systems that leverage the surface of the hand and arm as always-available input systems.

KITTY [9] is a glove-type input device which covers parts of the hand with electronic contacts to enable touch event detection. An electric circuit is closed and a signal is generated upon closing of one finger-contact with one thumb-contact. This offers both speed and accuracy with a discrete signal input that is continuously ready and provides an ultra-portable solution for data input into portable computer systems. However, we focus on leveraging viewer's hand without any instrumentation such as gloves as this is not practical for TV rooms and also can mar the user experience while watching TV.

SixthSense [11] is a wearable camera-projector unit, which supports gestural manipulation of digital artifacts and augments physical surfaces with digital information. Moreover, it enables users to interact with the information projected on the surfaces in mobile contexts. While the system is superior to existing systems in terms of weight and size, the system uses color markers as artificial features that are placed on a user's fingertips to recognize hand gestures.

Skinput [8] presents a novel approach to recognize finger taps on the arm and hand by analyzing mechanical vibrations that propagates through the body. This is done using arrays of bio-acoustic sensors worn as an armband.

Brainy Hand [10] is another example of a wearable interaction device. It is equipped with a color camera, which captures an image of the user's hand to recognize its movements as input gestures. Since the digital data corresponding to each input gesture is projected as a picture onto the user's palm, it requires a lot of visual attention.

Recently, Harrison et al. presented OmniTouch [5], a wearable depth-sensing and projection prototype enabling multi-touch interaction by projecting on everyday surfaces such as a hand or an arm. They used depth sensing technology to track the hand and recognize whether a finger is hovering over or touched the hand surface. This work and the proposed algorithms inspired us when implementing the touch recognition on the hand surface.

The aforementioned research requires either a mediator instrument such as glove or visual attention to the input data. In contrast, we want to propose a device-less approach in which the visual attention can remain focused on the TV screen. To do this, we draw upon the concept of imaginary user interfaces. In this case, the actual interface elements are not projected onto the interactive surface (in our case the palm). They are just imagined by the user.

2.3 Imaginary User Interfaces

Imaginary interfaces, introduced as a new device-less interaction approach in [3], are based on a human's ability to map the spatial memory to physical surfaces. Here, no user interface is displayed on the surface but various sensing approaches are utilized to recognize on-surface interaction. Although, no information is projected on imaginary interfaces, the original concept requires users to look at their hands to define the origin of an imaginary space and attentively point and draw in the resulting physical space. Building on this work, Gustafson et al. designed an always-available imaginary phone [4], in which users can interact with their cell phone by recalling, mapping and touching different application icons on their hand attentively.

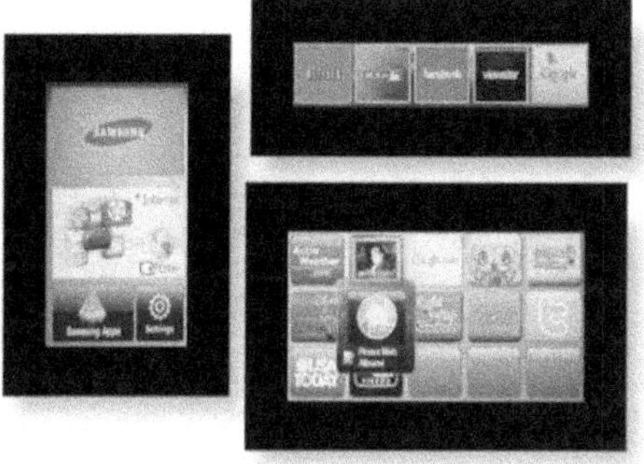

Figure 2. Example user interface screens of a Samsung TV used in the first study.

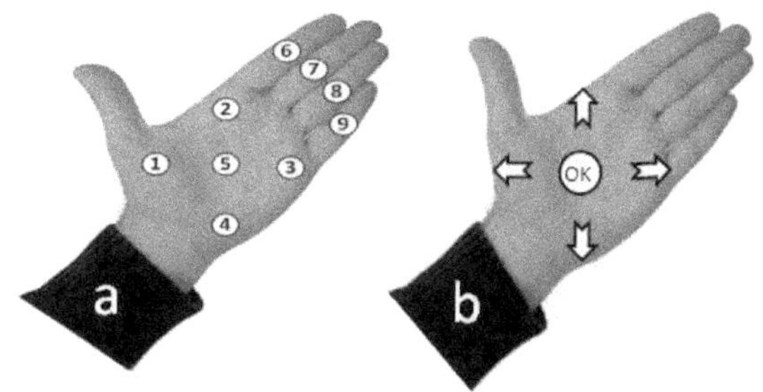

Figure 3. (a) The easily touchable landmarks on the hand. (b) Participants suggested linking the directional keys to the landmarks of the palm while holding the hand diagonally.

Although we aimed at designing interactions not requiring any visual attention to the hand, this prior work highly motivated our research agenda. We therefore combined the concept of proprioception with an imaginary user interface on a user's hand. In the following, we outline the design space and show how the hand surface can be leveraged for eyes-free interaction with television systems.

3. EXPLORATIVE STUDY

We conducted an exploratory study to empirically ground the requirements for designing an eyes-free, palm-based TV remote control. We were particularly interested to see how users would interact with their hand to perform a set of common interactions with TVs, while preserving their attention to the TV screen.

3.1 Design and Methodology

The study had a brainstorming character in which participants were asked to discuss high-level aspects of using the palm as a remote control (cf. Fig. 1). Initially, we asked about (1) how they would hold their hand and which side and parts of their hand would be suitable for interacting with the TV. Then, they were asked to particularly elaborate on (2) how they would transfer the remote control functions on their hand and (3) how they would interact with on-screen UI elements while mimicking their proposed interactions on their hand surface. To foster the discussion, we utilized and displayed some typical user interfaces of a Samsung Smart Internet TV on its screen and asked participants to show how they would interact with these elements using their hand. The user interface screens can be classified into three vertical, horizontal and whole screen grid-based menus (cf. Fig. 2).

We recruited 10 volunteer participants (3f, 7m). They were between 22-42 years old. All participants spent 2-3 hours in average per day watching TV. Each single-user session lasted about 1 hour. As data gathering methodologies, we videotaped the sessions and asked participants to think aloud. We then selected salient quotes and analyzed both quotes and videos using an iterative open, axial and selective coding approach [18]. For inter-coder independence, two coders coded the data separately.

3.2 Results

3.2.1 Using the Palm surface as a TV remote control

Generally, participants appreciated the idea of being able to use the palm surface for operating the TV. Unlike the one-hand usage of typical remote controls, all participants used their palmar (inner side) of the non-dominant hand as an input surface and interacted with the other hand's index finger similar to [5]. They said interacting with the palmar is not only more intuitive, but it also offers several salient regions (landmarks) to easily interact without any visual demand. P3 said *"I am able to* properly *touch any of my fingers as easy as* moving them." and P8 added *"I can touch four curved areas (convex) on my palm surface even in the darkness"*. Participants revealed nine landmarks on the palm surface, which they believed to be easily touchable without any visual demand based on the proprioceptive sense [1] (cf. Fig. 3a).

3.2.2 Mapping basic remote controls functionalities

Participants mentioned that they would only map frequently used functions to their palm such as navigation, selection, digits for direct switching between channels, volume adjustment, or play and pause. In addition, they offered to properly map these functionalities to the location of landmarks of the palm, since they can be easily hit without any visual attention. For example, participants stated that the mapping of directional keys could exactly match the four convex and one concave landmarks of the palm (cf. Fig. 3b).

In contrast, recalling and transferring digits (typical mapping of 3x3 buttons of digits from 1 to 9) to the palm was found to be very complex. P5 said *"Digits may have a conventional mapping but still they lack having a natural mapping and I would prefer to draw digits on my palm to change the channels"*. P7 added: *"Even if I could recall each digit position, I would not know where to map it on the palm surface as no landmarks afford their mapping"*.

Participants also commented, since no digital information is projected on the palm surface, the simplicity of the design of a palm-based remote control is crucial.

3.2.3 Interacting with on-screen UI content

Participants not only suggested 2D-touch gestures (e.g. swipe, scroll, and draw) on the palm, but they also proposed mapping UI elements displayed on the TV screen to the palm's surface. They then imagined triggering the target elements by pointing (tap, click) to the corresponding location on the palm surface. For this purpose, participants used three different hand orientations including diagonal, landscape and portrait (cf. Fig.4).

The diagonal orientation was stated as the most comfortable form of holding the hand as an interactive surface. The interactions requiring participants to map remote control functions to their palm (such as directional keys), as well as 2D-touch gestures, were mainly performed in diagonal orientation.

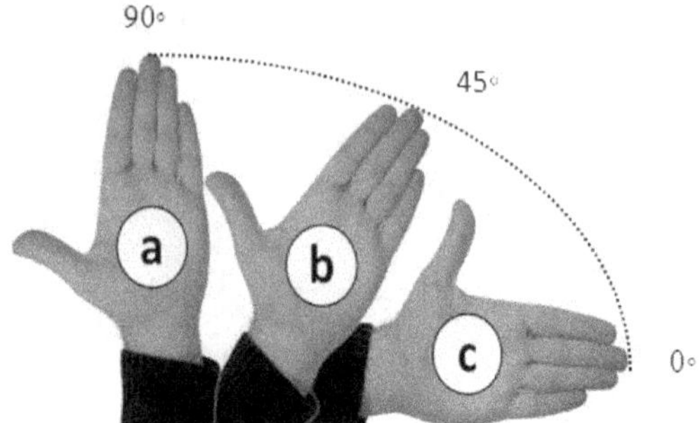

Figure 4. (a) Portrait: pointing toward TV. (b) Diagonal: 45° to user's body. (c) Landscape: parallel to body.

3.2.4 2D-touch gesture interaction on palm surface

Although a palm is not a flat planar surface, participants considered it as a concrete surface and proposed using 2D touch gestures on it while holding it in diagonal mode. This interaction technique was typically proposed for either efficiently browsing menus with a plethora of options, or mimicking digits on the palm surface for channel navigation, or even nonverbal communication between remote viewers; as P3 stated: *"I could for instance draw a smiley on my palm surface and send it to my online friends who are watching the same program"*.

3.2.5 Pointing on the palm surface

Participants suggested to transfer one-dimensional grid-based UI elements (e.g. list of applications or media player controls with three buttons including backward, pause and forward) onto the palm surface. While looking at the TV, participants first mapped the whole screen of the UI to the non-dominant hand surface and then selected/triggered UI elements by pointing to the corresponding location on the hand surface using the index finger of their dominant hand. Participants transferred the grid-based vertical and horizontal UI screens to their palm while holding it in portrait or landscape orientations respectively.

Participant's comments highlighted the fact that the design of TV UIs elements based on the location of the palm landmarks may improve the mapping. P4 stated: *"If a menu could have four options, I could easily touch my middle finger to select the second option"*. Discussion with participants revealed that hand-tailored TV UIs may decrease the cognitive effort of mapping these elements to the surface of palm and eventually results in more secured feeling of hitting appropriate location on the palm while looking at the TV.

3.3 Discussion

The results of this study empirically elicit implications for designing a palm-based remote control, which preserves a user's attention to the TV screen during interaction. We found 9 distinct landmarks on the palm surface which can be easily touched without visual attention. The main benefit of this is that it allows TV viewers to link the common functions of a remote control (e.g. directional keys) to these landmarks for eyes-free TV interaction.

Since no digital information is to be projected on the palm, participants also appreciated the way they can interact with the palm surface. Based on our observations, we believe that due to the similar form factor of the palm surface and the TV screen, participants could easily imagine the UI elements on TV screen to their palm surface and touch the corresponding location of the target elements. Considering the different orientations of the hand, the visualized interface elements on the TV screen can be tailored to the hand orientation. This enables users to easily switch between different menus based on the orientation of the hand.

Figure 5. Left: OptiTrack system. Right: the paper carton apparatus used in the controlled experiment.

The results discussed above, left us with two unexplored questions: (1) How *precisely* can users touch their palm's salient regions (landmarks) without looking at them? (2) How *effectively* can they select the target element of transferred on-screen user interface elements on their palm by pointing to the corresponding region on the palm surface without any visual attention?

4. CONTROLLED EXPERIMENT

We have formulated the aforementioned questions as hypotheses and verified them in a controlled experiment. The two questions map to the following two hypotheses:

H1: People can touch their palm landmarks precisely without looking at them (0.90 confidence level).

H2: When mapping on-screen UI elements to palm,

- **H2.1:** the effectiveness will decrease, the denser the UI elements are placed.
- **H2.2:** the effectiveness is independent of the UI elements' alignment; i.e. whether they are horizontally or vertically aligned.

Effectiveness here means, whether a participant successfully touches a mapped UI element on her palm.

4.1 Experiment Setup

We have conducted the experiment using an optical tracking system (OptiTrack[1] as shown in Fig. 5 left) to minimize any noise. We have designed a trackable paper carton apparatus, which the participants wore on the back of their non-dominant hand (cf. Fig 5 right). We have attached three retro-reflective markers as antennas to the paper carton. These markers are then tracked by the OptiTrack system with 6 IR-cameras and define a 3D plane that corresponds to the palm surface. This allowed us to reliably track the palm without covering the palm completely, e.g. using a glove. To allow for accurate touch input on the non-dominant hand, we have augmented the index finger of the dominant hand with another marker. A touch then is calculated by projecting the marker position on the hand plane and measuring the distance.

We recruited 15 participants (5f, 10m; 32 years of age in average, with near-to-perfect sight). The participants were introduced to the system upfront. Each single-user session lasted about 45 minutes.

4.2 Methodology

The experiment was subdivided into two parts according to our hypotheses. Each part was again subdivided into two tasks (cf. Fig. 6). The order of the presented targets within each task was completely counterbalanced. The system advanced to the next

[1] http://www.naturalpoint.com/optitrack/

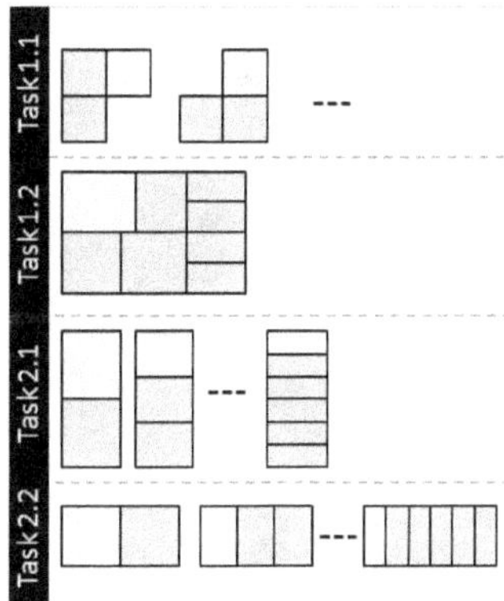

Figure 6. On-screen user interfaces of each task during the experiment.

target after each touch, regardless of whether the participant had successfully touched the target. We chose a within-subject design. We only repeated the trials in which the experimenter determined that participant looked at her palm.

Part 1: In the first part, participants were asked to touch landmarks without visual attention. Independent variable was the landmark location. Dependent variable was the success rate of a user touching the landmark on her palm. Task 1 was comprised of two sub-tasks.

- Task 1.1 required participants to map directional keys to their palm (see fig. 3.b), and navigate through a path of target items starting from the highlighted one (yellow box). For example, the first layout of task 1.1 in figure 5 required the participant to first touch left, then down. Participants had to touch 9 different landmarks.
- Task 1.2 required participants to map non-regular grids (see Fig. 6) to their palm surface and touch the highlighted position on their palm. Here, participants had to touch 8 different landmarks.

Part 2: In the second part, participants had to map and touch UI elements on their palm surface. Independent variable was the on-screen layout. Again, dependent variable was the success rate of a user touching the landmark corresponding to the UI element on her palm.

- Task 2.1 required participants to map vertical 1D regular grids to their palm surface and touch the highlighted position on their palm. Each user had to touch 20 different targets.
- Task 2.2 required participants to do the same with horizontal 1D regular grids, again for 20 different targets.

In order to determine boundaries for the number of targets in this task, we conducted a pilot study. We ask participants to target elements in various density levels starting from 2 adjacent targets in both horizontal and vertical orientations. We determined that participants were able to divide and eyes-freely touch the palm surface up to 6 locations at most. Therefore, the task started with 2 adjacent targets and stepwise became denser until 6 targets as depicted in Fig. 6, task 2.2.

4.3 Results

Each target was repeated 3 times, leading to a total of 2565 data points over all 15 participants: 15 * 3 * [9 (T1.1) + 8 (T1.2) + 20 (T2.1) + 20 (T2.2)]. We discarded 21 trials as outliers, since they were farther than 3 times the standard deviation away from the centroid. We normalized all hand sizes with the average index finger (7,31cm).

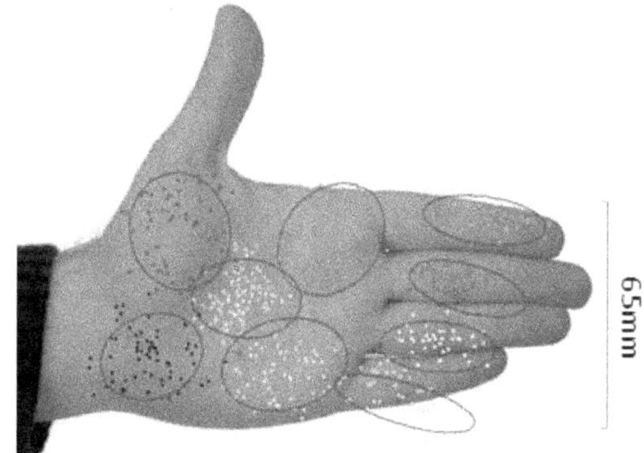

Figure 7. Distribution of raw data of all participants by 90% confidence ellipses.

Part 1: Figure 7 shows the distribution of the raw data for tasks 1.1 and 1.2 by 90% confidence ellipses. This illustrates the spatial precision of the touches with respect to the centroid of each landmark. To analyze targeting, we measured one overall systematic error (offset). On average, the diameter necessary to encompass 90% of all touches is 28mm (SD= 0.85).

The average effectiveness for each landmark is shown in figure 8. All of the palm landmarks were effectively touched with at least 94%. The finger landmarks were less effectively touched with as little as 53% for the pinky.

ANOVA tests revealed that the difference between palm and finger landmarks is statistically significant ($p<0.001$). Bonferroni post-hoc tests confirmed that this holds for all comparisons ($p<0.001$).

Part 2: The average effectiveness for the target elements is shown in Figure 9. The effectiveness decreased monotonically for more than 3 menu options. The average effectiveness is below 90% for more than 4 options and decreases below 50% for more than 5 options.

ANOVA with Bonferroni post-hoc tests revealed that these effects are statistically significant ($p<0.05$). The differences between horizontal and vertical alignments were not significant.

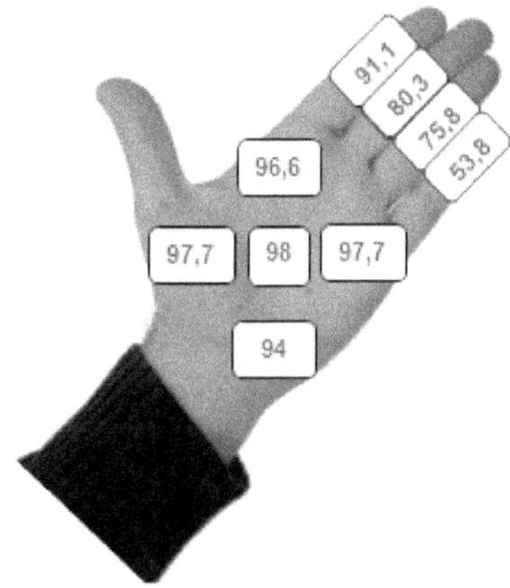

Figure 8. Average effectiveness percentage of targeting each landmark without visual demand.

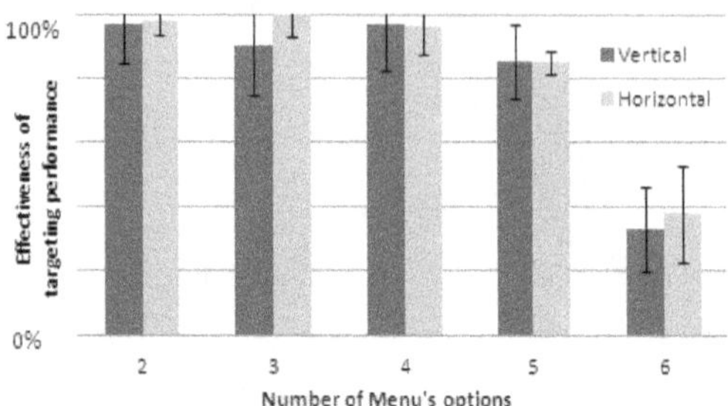

Figure 9. The average effectiveness of targeting vertical and horizontal grids with different equal-sized options.

4.4 Discussion

Based on the results of the studies, we showed that touching the 5 landmarks on the palm surface without any visual demand is highly effective. Moreover, it is precise enough to operate interfaces with target sizes of 28mm in diameter (H1).

This implies that future palm-based TV interfaces should not map functions to regions with a smaller diameter. Moreover, this shows that users can effectively map common functions of traditional remote controls such as navigational keys to the landmarks of a palm and touch them to operate a TV.

Our results provide evidence that people can reliably and effectively (>90%) map 1D grid-layout menus with up to 4 options to their palm surface (H2.1), independent of whether the menu is horizontally or vertically aligned (H2.2). For future palm-based TV interfaces, we envision this to be leveraged as region-based shortcuts. While the participants were not as effective when touching their fingers compared to their palm landmarks, they effectively targeted their index finger. This indicates that also the index finger could be used as an effective input source.

5. SUMMARY OF TWO STUDIES

The results of the studies show that:

- Users preferred to transfer typical remote control functionalities such as directional keys to the palm (inner side) of their non-dominant hands. We also found out that the palm offers nine salient regions (landmarks), which can be easily recognized and touched without requiring any visual attention.
- Users preferred 2D touch gestures such as swiping on the palm surface for efficient browsing of lists with so many options. Our findings also revealed that users utilized the palm surface as a canvas to draw short symbols such as digits or emoticons.
- The landmarks can be touched precisely enough for TV interaction if the size of targets is considered sufficiently large about 28mm (SD= 0.85) in diameter on the palm surface to encompass 90% of all touches.
- Users can reliably and effectively (>90%) map one-dimensional (1D) grid-layout menus with up to 4 options to their palm surface, independent of whether the menu is horizontally or vertically aligned.

The results discussed above show that users are able to use their palm to interact with TV without visual attention in two main ways: first, as a remote control with several functions (virtual buttons) that are linked to the landmarks and second, as an unique input surface which the television user interface is mapped to the entire surface of the palm. Our findings showed that under certain circumstances (28mm button size and 4 target options) the palm-based remote control is viable. Thus, frequently used functions can be ready at palm, virtually any time without need for an additional mediator device.

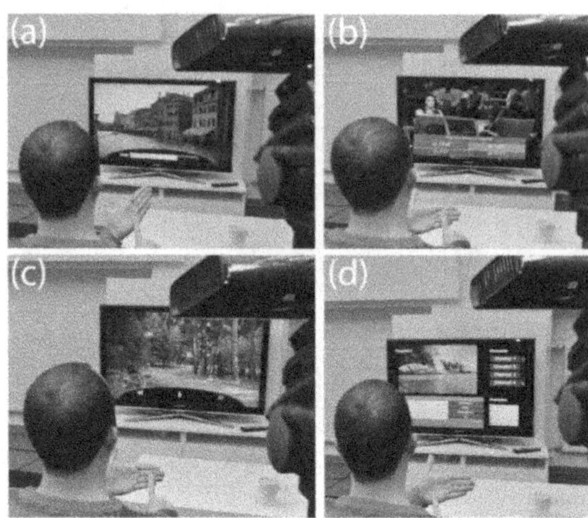

Figure 10. PalmRC system in different application scenarios.

Building upon these results, we developed a palm-based remote control called PalmRC along with two main interaction techniques. In addition, we implemented several applications to show the usefulness of PalmRC for varying interaction scenarios with TV systems.

6. PalmRC

PalmRC allows users to operate the TV using empty hands while focusing their visual attention on TV screen. The users interact by pointing and swiping on their non-dominant hand and the system enables the palm's surface to be capitalized as an input surface. The TV system receives touch positions and returns appropriate visual feedback on its screen. We developed interaction techniques to perform conventional TV interactions such as channel navigation in Electronic Program Guide (EPG), volume adjustment and direct interaction with menu options. PalmRC enables users to use their palm for various typical commands instead of retrieving a TV remote control.

Based on the orientation of the hand (see Fig. 4), the PalmRC supports two main interaction techniques (modes) that make use of pointing and 2D-touch gesturing on the palm surface:

6.1.1 Linking Functions to the palm's Landmark

Based on the results of the first study, the diagonal orientation of the non-dominant hand was found to be comfortable and resembles the style of holding a remote control in hand. Therefore, in this orientation, PalmRC links the common buttons of the remote control to the 9 landmarks of the palm. Users can trigger buttons by touching the corresponding locations on their palm.

We implemented this mode for directional keys and a confirmation/menu button (as the most frequent used buttons). These are in turn linked to the landmarks of the palm, as revealed in our studies respectively. This technique also allows for a natural spatial mapping between the buttons and the landmarks. Users can zap through the TV channel by tapping on the corresponding landmarks, which are mapped to the up or down keys. The volume can be adjusted similarly by touching the locations of the right and left keys (cf. Fig. 10-a). To open up the channel list or menu options users can touch the center of their palm surface. Similar to touch-enabled devices, swiping upwards

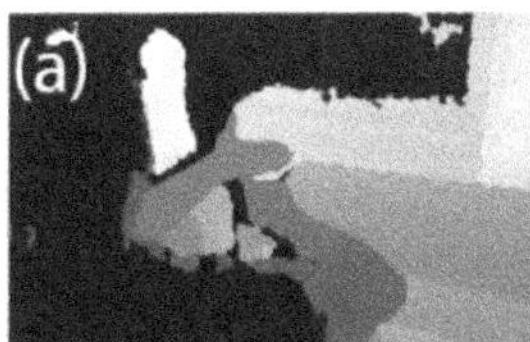

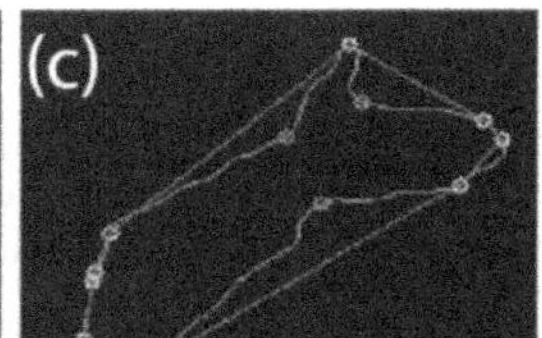

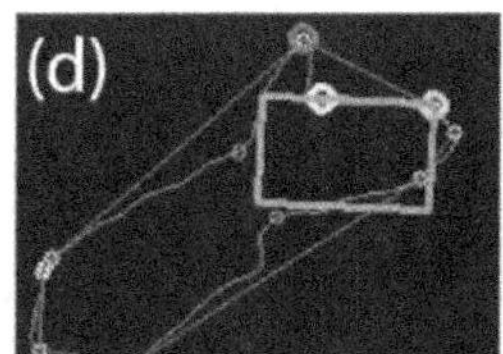

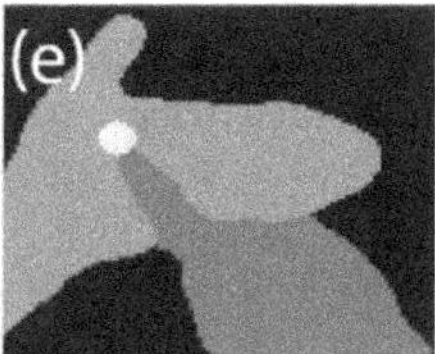

Figure 11. The process of recognizing a touch event in PalmRC: (a) original depth image, (b) subtracted background, (c) determining the contour of the reference hand and (d) its palm box, (e) and finally recognized touch on the surface.

or downwards on the palm surface allows for a fast browsing of the channel list. Users can also directly switch to another channel by drawing its number on the palm surface.

6.1.2 Direct Interacting with Interface Elements

By holding the hand in portrait or landscape mode, PalmRC maps the user interface screen to the entire palm surface. Then, users can touch the corresponding location of a target element on the palm. This interaction mode allows users to directly select a target on the TV screen.

We showcased this technique in a social interactive television interface, which incorporates common social features such as live chat (cf. Fig. 10-d). Once users hold their hands in landscape orientation, the communication mode will be activated and they can directly select and interact with one of the options. We also integrated this interaction technique in an application enabling remote viewers to answer questions of a quiz [15] by pointing to the appropriate location of their palm (cf. Fig. 10-b). The technique provides quick and immediate interactions with the social TV interface.

As another application example, while watching a movie or a program, users can hold their hands in landscape orientation. Thus, the media player menu including three options as backward, pause/play and forward appears on the TV screen. Then users can map it to the palm and touch the corresponding location of the desired option (cf. Fig. 10-c).

6.2 Technical Overview

Although the OptiTrack motion capture system used in the controlled study enabled us to precisely track the palm and recognize the touch position, it is not practical for TV room settings. As we reviewed in the related work section, there have been other sensing approaches such as using gloves [10], Skinput [9], depth cameras [6]. We chose to use a Microsoft Kinect [17] depth camera because it does not need any instrumentation on the hand of the viewers and also enables and supports recognizing touch and drag interactions [6, 5].

In PalmRC, we use the Kinect depth camera to track the non-dominant hand and recognize touch and dragging events with the index finger of the dominant hand. The built-in depth sensors recognize a user's hands in a minimum distance of ~50cm. Currently, we mount the depth camera on a tripod located at the back of a user's shoulder (cf. Fig. 10). We envision the future depth cameras to be small and precise enough to be either unobtrusively worn, or to be integrated into living room furniture. Touch events are recognized in a multistep process similar to [4]. The process is depicted in Fig. 11. In order to subtract the background, we first find the closest pixels in the raw image and remove all other relative depth values greater than 40cm. We classify the depth values of each hand by calculating the number of peaks in a histogram of all depth values (cf. Fig. 11-b). To track the non-dominant hand, we then calculate the contour and the convex hull of the hand including convexity defects (red points) and convexity start points (blue points) depicted in Fig. 11-c. The palm box is then calculated based on the prominent defect and the start point (illustrated with yellow and light-blue circles in Fig. 11 -d accordingly). To determine if and where the touch occurs, we compare the depth values of the finger tip with the surrounding values in the hand box. If the finger tip gets close enough to the reference hand, a touch event will be recognized. Due to the local noises and low-resolution of the Kinect depth camera, the precise end of finger tip is not fully recognizable. Similar to [4], we determine the touch location by offsetting a small vector in the direction of the finger (yellow circle in Fig. 11-e).

Although the tracking approach requires users to hold their thumb upright while using PalmRC, it robustly recognizes different orientation of the non-dominant hand. Future work is needed to improve the hand tracking and touch recognition so that users can arbitrary hold their hands.

7. EARLY USER FEEDBACK

In order to get initial user feedback on the interaction techniques, we conducted a focus group with 5 participants (26 years of age in average, all male and right handed with near-to-perfect sight). None of them had participated in our first studies. We were mainly interested in observing how they would use PalmRC, therefore allowing us to identify strengths and weaknesses of the overall system. Moreover, we wanted to get an initial impression on the usability of PalmRC. After a brief introduction to both, the concept and interaction techniques, the participants explored the interactions while thinking aloud.

The discussion with participants revealed that they found the concept of eyes-free palm-based remote control appealing. It received positive feedback for several reasons:

- Participants were able to quickly understand the interaction techniques. P5 stated that *"I don't need to think about how to interact or look for widgets on my palm"*.
- Participants found our concept very practical in terms of providing immediate shortcuts for TV interactions. P3 commented that *"This is great! I can turn the volume down quickly, for instance when my phone is ringing. And I don't need to look for the remote control everywhere, anymore"*.
- Three participants, who had used mid-air hand gestures before at home, compared the PalmRC interaction style with 3D mid-air gestures. They stated that they feel PalmRC interactions are less tiring. They added that these types of interactions seem to be more comfortable than 3D hand gestures since they are relaxing or even suitable in other body postures such as lying on the couch in front of the TV.

One participant was concerned with the two-handed usage of the system, in contrast to the one-handed usage of typical remote control. He commented: *"With my remote control at home, I can control the TV while I'm holding a glass with the other hand".* We believe that this issue will become less severe by extending the palm-based remote control to the surface of other parts of the body such as thigh, which affords one-handed interaction. Moreover, the Kinect depth camera has opened up new interactive experiences on any un-instrumented physical surface [5, 18, 19]. Future work should also investigate leveraging physical surfaces around users such as couch arms or tables as an input surface to operate TVs.

The discussion with participants also revealed that they were unsure about the effectiveness of transferring and interacting with more complicated UI elements on the TV such as an EPG. They emphasized that they would like to use PalmRC for sending frequent commands to operate the TV instead of a standard remote control.

8. CONCLUSION AND FUTURE WORK

In this paper, we explored the concept of leveraging the palm surface as an eyes-free remote control. Through an explorative study, we qualitatively gained insights into how people would use their palm as if it were a remote control. Results confirmed that users are able to touch several prominent regions of their palm without looking at them. In a controlled experiment, we quantitatively determined how precisely they could interact with these regions in an eyes-free manner. We also investigated the effectiveness of using the palm as an input surface for directly interacting with on-screen user interface elements. The findings showed that under certain circumstances (28mm button size and 4 target options) the palm-based remote control is viable.

Building upon the results, we introduced PalmRC as a prototypical realization of our concept. We designed two main interaction techniques and showcased them in different application scenarios. The early user feedback underlined the fact that PalmRC offers an always-available shortcut for performing frequently used interactions with TV systems without needing to find and retrieve any mediator.

Based on our results, we conclude that by leveraging different landmarks of the palm, users are able to perform precise interactions, while preserving their visual attention to the TV. Moreover, the palm surface is also appropriate for coarse gestures such as swiping. Initial results suggest that the interaction style of PalmRC is less tiring than mid-air gestures. However, more studies are needed to systematically compare both as device-less input modalities for television systems.

As a next step, we want to investigate more deeply how PalmRC can enrich the user experience while watching TV in real world settings. Finally, we will further explore the scalability of our concept to handle conflicts when people are watching TV together in co-located settings.

9. ACKNOWLEDGEMENT

This research was supported by the KCC (Korea Communications Commission), under the R&D program supervised by the KCA (Korea Communications Agency) "(KCA-2011-10035587/10921-03001)". We are grateful to Murat Özkorkmaz and Johann Raspasovic for their assistance.

10. REFERENCES

[1] Sherrington CS. On the proprioceptive system, especially in its reflex aspect. In *Brain* 1906.

[2] Brutti, A. and Cristoforetti, L. and Kellermann, W. and Marquardt, L. and Omologo, M. WOZ Acoustic Data Collection for Interactive TV. In *Language Resources and Evolutions* 2010, 205-219.

[3] Gustafson, S., Bierwirth, D., and Baudisch, P. Imaginary Interfaces: Spatial Interaction with Empty Hands and Without Visual Feedback. In *Proc.* UIST *2010*, 3-12.

[4] Gustafson, S., Holz, C., and Baudisch, P. Imaginary Phone: Learning Imaginary Interfaces by Transferring Spatial Memory from a Familiar Device. In *Proc.* UIST 2011, 283-292.

[5] Harrison, C., Benko, H., and Wilson, A. OmniTouch: wearable multitouch interaction everywhere. In *Proc.* UIST 2011, 441-450.

[6] Igrashi, T. Hughes, J.F., Voice as sound: using non-verbal voice input for interactive control . In *Proc.* UIST 2001, 10.1145.

[7] Kohli, L. and Whitton, M. The Haptic Hand: providing user interface feedback with the non-dominant hand in virtual environments. In *Proc.* GI 2005, 1–8.

[8] Harrison, C., Tan, D. and Morris, D. Skinput: appropriating the body as an input surface. In *Proc.* CHI 2010, 453–462.

[9] Kuester, F., Chen, M., Phair, M.E. and Mehring, C. Towards keyboard independent touch typing in VR. In *Proc.* VRST 2005, 86–95.

[10] Tamaki, E., Miyaki, T. and Rekimoto, J. Brainy Hand: an earworn hand gesture interaction device. In *Proc.* CHI Extended Abstracts 2009, 4255–4260.

[11] Mistry, P., Maes, P., and Chang, L. WUW - wear Ur world: a wearable gestural interface. In *Proc.* CHI Extended Abstracts 2009, 4111–4116.

[12] Freeman, W.T., Weissman, C.D. Television Control by Hand Gestures. In *Proc.* Intl Workshop on Automatic Face and Gesture Recognition 1995, 179-183.

[13] Mäntyjärvi, J., Kela, J., Korpipää, P., Kallio, S. Enabling fast and effortless customization in accelerometer based gesture interaction. In *Proc.* Mobile and ubiquitous multimedia 2004, 25-31.

[14] Weisz , J.D., Kiesler, S., Zhang, H., Ren, Y., Kraut R.E, Konstan, J.A. Watching together: integrating text chat with video. In *Proc.* CHI 2007, 877 886.

[15] Luyten, K., Thys, K., Huypens, S., Coninx, K. Telebuddies: social stitching with interactive television. In *Proc.* CHI Extended Abstracts 2006, 1049-154.

[16] Strauss, A., Corbin, J. Basics of Qualitative Research: Techniques and Procedures for Developing Grounded Theory. *Sage Publications*, 2008.

[17] Microsoft Kinect, http://www.xbox.com/kinect.

[18] Wilson, A.D. and Benko, H. Combining Multiple depth cameras and projectors for interactions on, above and between surfaces. In *Proc.* UIST 2010, 273-282.

[19] Wilson, A.D. Using a depth camera as a touch sensor. In *Proc.* ITS2010, 69-72.

[20] Robertson, S., C. Wharton, C., Ashworth, C., Franzke, M. Dual device user interface design: PDAs and interactive television. In *Proc.* CHI 1996, 79-86.

[21] Zimmermann, G., Nixon, T., Beard, M., Sitnik, E., LaPlant, B., Trewin, S., Laskowski, Sh. and Vanderheiden, G. Toward a unified universal remote console standard. In *Proc. CHI* Extended Abstracts 2003, 874-875.

Evaluating Performance and Acceptance of Older Adults Using Freehand Gestures for TV Menu Control

Jan Bobeth*, Susanne Schmehl*, Ernst Kruijff*, Stephanie Deutsch*, Manfred Tscheligi*†

*CURE – Center for Usability Research and Engineering
Modecenterstraße 17 / Objekt 2
1110 Wien, Austria

†ICT&S Center, University of Salzburg
Sigmund-Haffner-Gasse 18
5020 Salzburg, Austria

{bobeth, schmehl, kruijff, deutsch, tscheligi}@cure.at

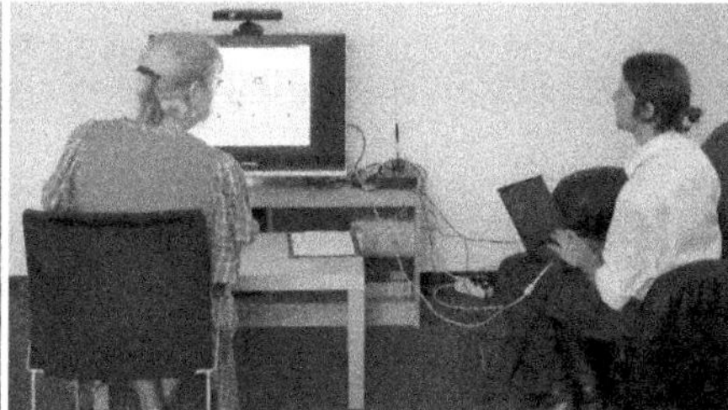

Figure 1: (a) Modified version of Box and Block Test (b) Participant controlling a TV menu using freehand gestures (c) Participant with supervisor

ABSTRACT

In this paper, we explore alternative TV menu control methods, focusing specifically on older users. We investigated performance and acceptance of freehand gestures by implementing several techniques and conducting a user study with 24 older adults. We expected that older adults would like gesture techniques as they are generally fun to use and easy to conduct. As a possible alternative to physical remote control, gesture techniques may also introduce some physical activity for older adults (positive health effects). In the user study, we compared four different kinds of freehand gesture interaction to control a corresponding TV menu, investigating specifically on abilities of older adults. Each of the interaction types was analysed regarding task completion time, error rate, usability and acceptance. Results showed that directly transferring tracked hand movements to control a cursor on a TV achieved the best performance and was preferred by the users. In general, the participating older adults showed a very positive attitude towards gesture-based interactions.

Categories and Subject Descriptors

H.5.2 [**Information Interfaces and Presentation**]: User Interfaces – *Ergonomics, Interaction styles.*

General Terms

Design, Experimentation, Human Factors, Verification

Keywords

TV control, freehand gestures, older adults

EuroITV'12, July 4-6, 2012, Berlin, Germany.

1. INTRODUCTION

Gestures can provide a very direct and natural way of interaction with a system. Over the last decade, gestures have earned increasing interest in research and industry, especially driven forward by a broad availability of gesture technology. As a result, a large number of studies have been performed to investigate the various factors affecting usable and useful deployment of gestures in 2D and 3D applications. Surprisingly, little research exists on how older adults could benefit from gesture-based interactions; regarding older adults performance and user acceptance factors are not well understood, in particular in reflection to specific needs and abilities. Research shows that ageing goes along with significant decline in cognitive, perceptual and motor abilities which not only leads to functional differences but also to differences in motivation [21]. As an example, to reduce perceptual and cognitive issues, it is better to raise illumination, contrast and font size as well as to reduce visual clutter and the used field of view in a user interface [26]. Extensive design guidelines are available in the mentioned literature. Within this paper, we primarily focus at motor issues. Motor issues of older adults include slower motion, less strength and less fine motor control (e.g. fatigue, tremble and additional sub-movements) [21]. Another aspect is a decreasing range of motion and grip force [2]. These issues may affect gestural interfaces for older users considerably: interactions with hand and arm need to be designed carefully, avoiding in particular fatigue and need of initiating fine motor control. Additionally, the body pose in which arm movements are conducted has an influence on the appearance of fatigue [17]. In direct relation, gestures may not be exhausting but a gestural interface always prompts little physical activity. It is noteworthy that activity is an often underestimated health aspect with potentially positive effects (e.g. [25]).

From a technological stance, some older adults tend to have more particular problems with the usage of new technology than younger ones because devices are not designed to accommodate special needs in terms of usability and accessibility. This may lead to a higher general rejection of modern ICT devices among older adults [8]. In contrast to computers, TVs are an accepted product and very popular among the majority of older adults. Simultaneously, industry and research try to enhance the functionality of TVs to multimedia and communication centres. As such, a wider functional spectrum becomes available that can theoretically also be accessed and controlled by older adults: some of the functionality, such as social media or casual games, may well fit within the interests of older users. Control-wise however, the usage of the remote control device is still cumbersome and rather complicated. Too many buttons, functions and menu levels are confusing and lead to non-use of certain functions, not only for older adults. Alternative approaches for controlling TV-based applications have been suggested and comprise simple remote devices, touch interactions, and gesturing. While even simple remote devices have the disadvantage that an object has to be grabbed first, freehand gestures can be conducted immediately. Freehand gestures have the advantage that the eyes can remain at the screen all the time. The higher efforts of visual accommodation [21] by switching between remote device and screen are omitted. Various gesture-based solutions have been proposed; however age-related impairments and the special needs of older adults and their effects on the performance have often not been taken into account.

To improve our understanding, we performed a user study with 24 older adults to particularly look at performance issues of several implemented freehand gesture techniques, as well as to study user acceptance. For evaluating the gestural interactions we selected four simple menu types: direct pointing using hand movement tracking, indirect pointing using static hand positions to control the cursor, directional gestures using hand strokes for a marking menu, and dial plate for a radial menu. In particular, we were interested to identify which kind of gesture control would be the fastest for selection tasks and produces little errors. Furthermore, we wanted to investigate if older adults accept gesture-based interactions by asking them about enjoyment, usability and behavioral intention. In order to control for any bias caused by constraints due to motor issues of hand and arm, the participants conducted a modified version of a standardized instrument for assessing gross motor skills, the Box and Block Test [18] and performed a motor self-assessment [27].

Our **contribution** aims at enhancing the understanding of performance and acceptance factors of older adults using gesture techniques. This paper shows that older adults aged around 70 years have no problems in using freehand gestures to interact with a TV. It seems that the involved gesture techniques did not contravene special needs of older adults. They enjoyed this new form of interaction and were overall positive. The direct transfer of tracked hand movements to control a cursor achieved overall the best performance and was ranked best by participants. Results show that older adults seem to be very open for new ways of controlling technical devices.

In the following sections, we review previous work, describe the four selected menu types including the tested prototype in more detail and report on the procedure of the user study and the results. We conclude with a discussion about implications for gestural interfaces for older adults and shortcomings of this study.

2. RELATED WORK

The usage of gestures for controlling interactive devices has been investigated extensively. Various taxonomies classifying the very different types of gestures have been presented and provide a good general overview of gesture issues. In the domain of human-computer interaction a basic classification distinguishing between static (postures) and dynamic gestures comes from Hummels and Stapers [9]. Karam and Schraefel [11] organized their research on gestures according to four categories: application domain, enabling technologies, system response and gesture style. According to this taxonomy our work applies in the desktop domain (TV), is enabled by remote sensing, feedback is visually displayed and control requires manipulative freehand gestures.

2.1 Gestures for TV and appliance control

Various directions focusing on gestural control of a TV have been explored. One possibility of using gestures for controlling a TV is to enhance the functionality of the usual remote device with sensing capabilities [12]. A similar idea is to use existing motion sensing devices like the Wiimote for interacting with a TV via gestures [4]. One of the earliest examples of dynamic hand gestures for TV control has been the work by Freeman and Weissman [6], following a mouse-cursor-like behavior on the screen, matching hand movements directly after an initial trigger command. Other researchers enhanced this approach by adapting the trigger and the execution command (e.g. [28]), as well as by introducing additional features like drag and drop functionality (e.g. [7]). Chen et al. surrendered the visible cursor and controlled TV channel and volume settings by moving the left or the right arm upwards or downwards [3]. Bailly et al. developed a visual tracking system distinguishing the amount of used fingers to trigger different interactions [1]. A more ubiquitous wearable system to control appliances like a TV is "Ubi-Finger" [30] which provides sensors attached to the hand and fingers to detect mainly postures. Instead of relying to a physical device Premaratne and Nguyen used a computer vision system able to interpret various static hand signs to interact with consumer appliances [23].

Specific menu control issues also need to be taken into account, reflecting in particular some of our implemented techniques. Instead of having an unconstrained cursor, radial menus leverage stroke gestures (marking menus) or circle gestures (ring menus) to fasten selection tasks. The marking menu [14] is a radial menu where the user's movement path starting from the menu's center by performing directional strokes is displayed as trail at the screen. The path is considered as selection and the corresponding menu element executed. This menu technique has been widely adopted in particular on desktop applications. The ring menu is a radial menu where the user either rotates the ring until the desired menu element matches the selection basket [16] or the user moves the selection basket itself along the ring [4].

2.2 Gestures and older adults

An important factor that has not been considered in gesture classification schemes so far concerns the needs and preferences of the user performing gestures. Especially for older users who have less experience with technology, the interaction via gestures provides chances and risks. High affordance of interaction possibilities is a very important attribute of easy-to-use interfaces. Therefore the gestures should rely on real-world metaphors [10]. Otherwise the visibility (and thus affordance) of the user interface is lost and - as Norman and Nielsen drastically formulated - we are back to the days of command-line interfaces [22]. However, gesture-based interfaces have the potential to ease the interaction of older adults with technical devices in a more natural way.

Current research on gesture-based interfaces for older adults deals mainly with touch interfaces. Research results indicate older adults with low or no computer skills report using touch screens easy and motivating [8]. Furthermore, older users tend to perform touch gestures as accurate as younger users but move slower [29].

It remains unclear, however, if these results can be transferred to freehand gestures. Another area of research focuses on the usage of gesture-based video games e.g. animating older adults to take part in social activities [19] or treating motor issues [25].

Gesture-based interfaces for older adults have also been realized with wearable sensor solutions. Yamamoto et al. [32] used a projector to display the user interface at an arbitrary surface, allowing older users to interact in a smart ambient environment. Lee et al. [15] suggested the usage of baby signs for controlling various appliances at home. Finally, Saleiro and Rodrigues developed a vision-based system where older adults use static freehand gestures to control a cursor indirectly [24]. To avoid extensive arm movements, they defined various hand signs that are translated to movement directions of the cursor.

3. EXPERIMENTAL DESIGN

This paper reports the main results from a study with older adults controlling a TV menu with gestures. The goal of this study was to compare four approaches of freehand gesturing for menu control when performed by older users, having their specific (motor) needs in mind. We focused mainly on performance and user acceptance factors, especially those related to user experience. So apart from measuring the objective values task completion time and error rate, we let participants assess their subjective user experience focusing on enjoyment, usability and behavioral intention, to measure acceptance.

3.1 Research questions

As basis for our study, we formulated the following two research questions, focusing on objective performance values and subjective acceptance factors during freehand gestural interaction:

Q1: *Which kind of gesture control is the fastest for selection tasks and produces a low error rate?*

We expected that the number of menu elements would affect the performance, assuming that the higher the number of elements, the lower the performance would be. Fine grain motor control impairments of the older and possible trembling of the hand would amplify this effect. We also thought that radial menus could be operated faster than the more linear grid menus like shown in [4], however, by costs of some additional errors. We consider error rates not higher than 5% as acceptable.

Q2: *Do older users accept freehand gesture-based interactions in terms of usability, enjoyment and behavioral intention and which kind of gesture control do older users prefer?*

We expected that direct pointing with hand movement tracking would receive the highest acceptance rate as it is a technique with direct similarity to the widely known practice of using a common computer mouse. In terms of enjoyment we expected positive ratings as gesture techniques are generally regarded to be fun and older persons seem to enjoy this form of interaction [19].

3.2 Implementation and apparatus

Alternative approaches for controlling a TV menu gain more importance due to changing use cases. The usage of arrow keys makes sense for classic TV watching scenarios as every press is associated with a channel switch. Zapping established as usual TV browsing use case. Although use cases differ, current interactive TV menus are mostly controlled via arrow keys as well. Usually the user of an interactive TV has a concrete task in mind e.g. to retrieve weather information. Freehand gestures are one modality to allow selections with one continuous interaction instead of various discrete ones with the arrow keys. So the goal was explicitly not to replace the arrow keys with accordant gestures but to apply different approaches for interaction. Having in mind physical constraints and inexperience of older adults with gesture controls, we chose the four menu types for this investigation. Other interesting approaches of freehand gesturing that require additional interactions to movements with one arm (such as rapMenu [20] or Finger-Count Menu [1]) have been discarded with regard to declining physical abilities of older adults (e.g. joint stiffness and problems with bimanual interactions [21]). In this study, participants only should move their dominant hand in front of the body for some seconds for all four approaches and for every task. For this reason we included the following four interaction techniques (see Figure 1b for more details):

(i) direct pointing using hand movement tracking,

(ii) indirect pointing using static hand positions to control the cursor,

(iii) directional gestures using hand strokes for a marking menu,

(iv) dial plate for a radial menu.

The prototypes were developed using Kinect for Windows SDK[1] to realize the tracking and Microsoft Expression Blend[2] for the creation of the user interface. The output device was a 32" Panasonic LCD TV with a refresh rate of 100 Hz. The control device was a common Lenovo X200 laptop with dual core 2.4GHz processor and 4GB RAM.

Every menu type has been implemented with a similar 2D user interface with four and with eight menu elements. The version with four elements picks up the four colorful interaction buttons of a standard TV remote control handset. The reason to investigate menus with eight elements in this study was to add variability as interactive TV provides an increasing amount of options. Table 1 introduces the utilized gesture-based user interfaces and provides screenshots of each menu type.

In order to concentrate only on the evaluation of the menu techniques we abandoned any technical problems with initiation and selection by making use of the Wizard of Oz technique [13]. In this study, the TV user interface of each menu type and visual feedback about the current hand position were presented to the users at the screen. However, the initiation of the gesture recognition and the selection of a menu element were triggered manually by the supervisor. To keep any possible experimenter bias of the Wizard of Oz technique constant, the supervisor (i.e. the Wizard of Oz) was the same for all participants. For the initiation participants were required to wave their dominant hand shortly. For a selection, they needed to perform a grab gesture (i.e. to form and release a fist) as suggested by [7]. As soon as the accordant gesture was performed, the supervisor triggered the initiation or the selection via button press.

The operation area of the gestures was set between head and stomach. Prior to data collection, an introduction to menu type and practice time with each menu type were provided until participants have had understood the approach. A task consisted of three parts: initiation, main menu selection (menu elements were A-D or A-H) and submenu selection (menu elements were 1-4 or 1-8). After selecting a menu element on the main menu, the submenu with different menu labels (i.e. numbers instead of letters) appeared and the required menu element was selected. The

[1] http://kinectforwindows.org/

[2] http://www.microsoft.com/expression/

Table 1: Tested menu types in two versions controlled by various kinds of gestures

Menu type	Version with 4 menu elements	Version with 8 menu elements
(i) **H**and movement tracking (referred to as *H4* and *H8*), inspired by [6]: The movement of the user's hand is tracked and controls a hand symbol. The cursor-like hand symbol is manipulated directly by the hand movements of the user.	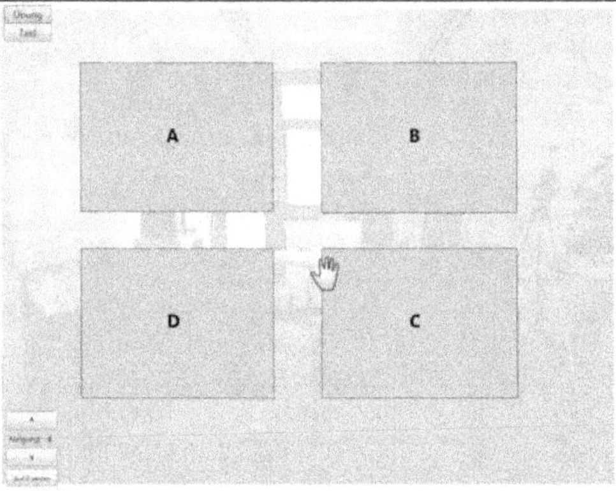	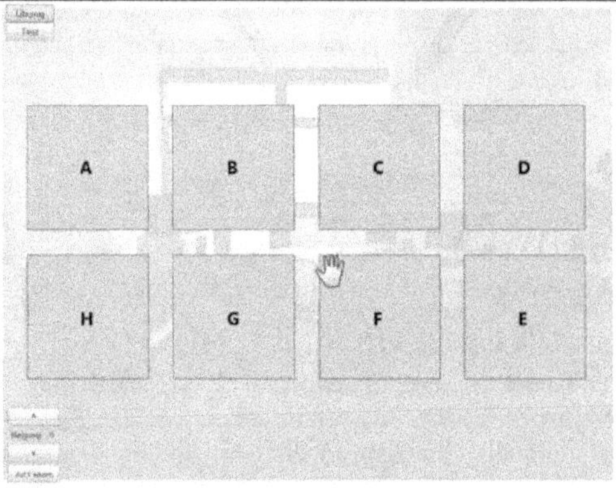
(ii) Static hand positions to control a **C**ursor (referred to as *C4* and *C8*), inspired by [24]: The static position of the user's hand in relation to the neutral center of the screen moves the white cursor in the accordant direction. As long as the user does not move his/her hand back to the center the cursor remains moving. The black arrow in the center indictates the direction of the current movement.	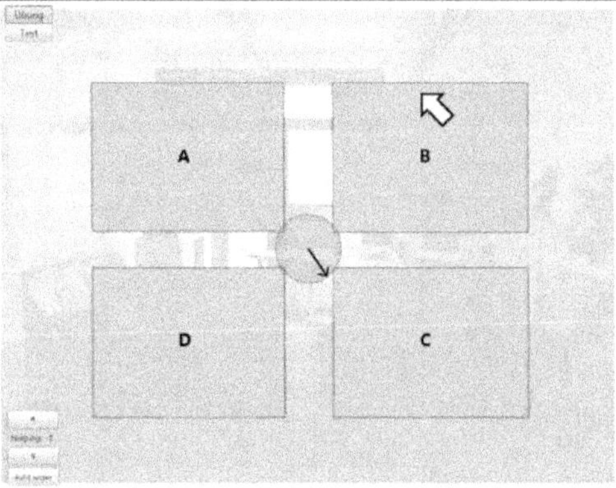	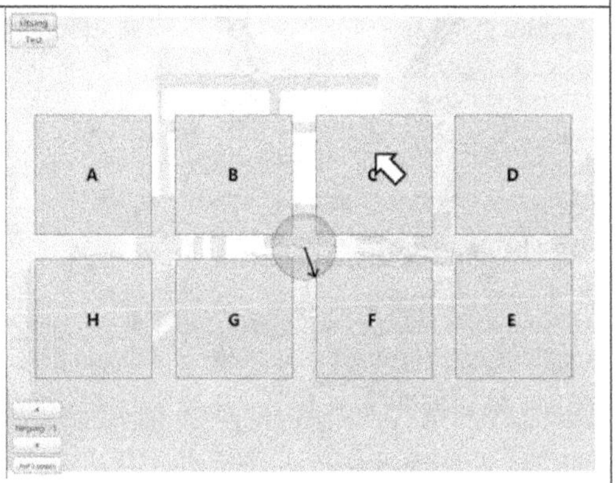
(iii) Hand strokes for **M**arking menu (referred to as *M4 and M8*), inspired by [14]: Starting from the neutral position in the center, the user just has to perform a stroke along one of the tracks to select the accordant menu element. As visual feedback of the movement a hand symbol shows the current position at the corresponding track.	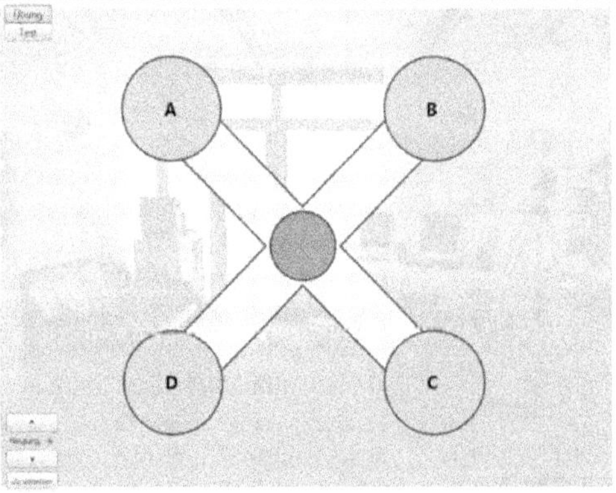	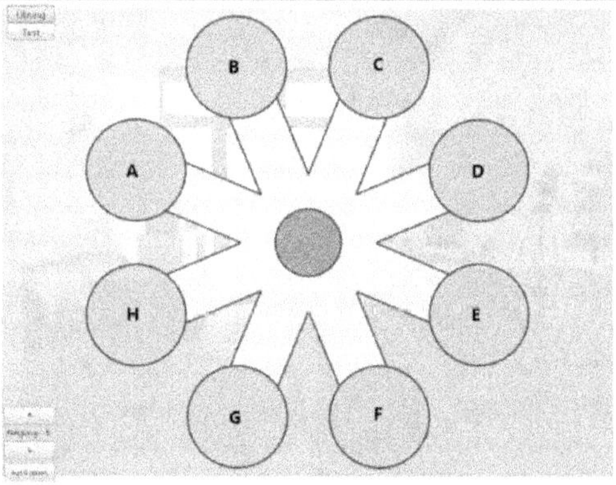
(iv) Dial plate for **R**adial menu (referred to as *R4* and *R8*), inspired by [4]: Circular hand movements parallel to the TV move the selection basket along the fixed ring, highlighting the current menu element. As the ring cannot be left one of the menu elements is highlighted at any time.	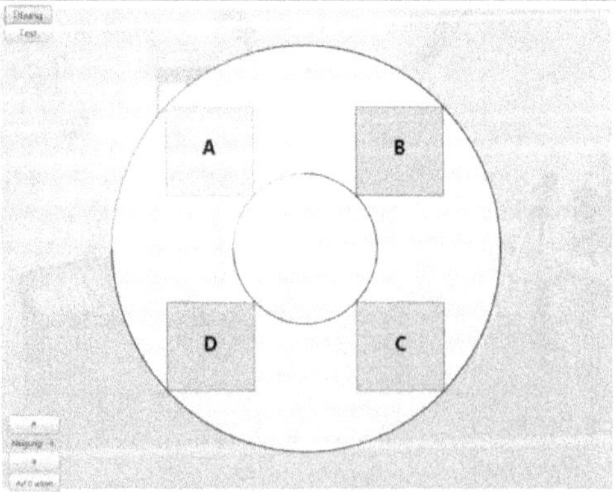	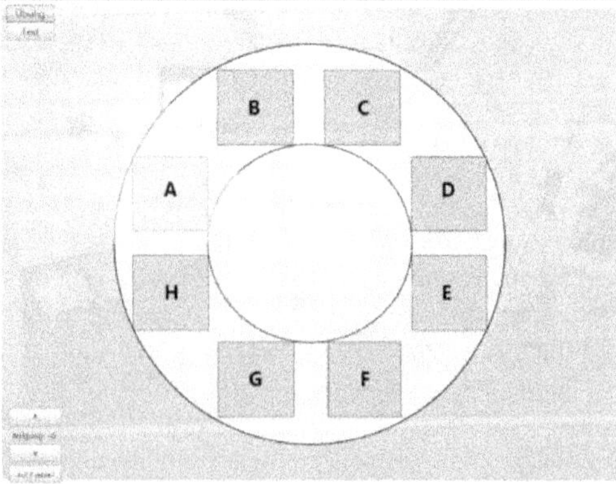

instruction before each task was e.g. "Please navigate to and select menu elements B and 3." All participants had to perform the same tasks for each menu type. Tasks were presented in random order to avoid any sequence or learning effects. They were constructed in a way that every possible distance between the two menu elements of main menu and submenu was covered once. This resulted in 60 tasks per participant which we considered as reasonable amount for older adults. The order of the menu types was counterbalanced by assigning every possible order once, which led to the amount of 24 participants (4! = 24). In case of a wrong selection the miss-hit was counted as an error and the participant had to repeat the task. Only for the successful selection the task completion time was measured. After each task participants had about 15 seconds to relax their arms until the supervisor provided the next task.

Performance was measured by logging task completion time and the amount of selection errors. After completing the tasks for one version of each menu type, participants answered selected items of the standardized technology acceptance questionnaire TAM3 [31]. This resulted in eight questionnaires per participant who had to rate the relevant items on a 5-point Likert-scale. The TAM3 questionnaire is based on a theory that models how users come to accept and use a certain technology [5]. The selection of TAM3 items was made to reduce the amount of items asked repetitively and because of testing a prototype where many items do not apply. The following seven items of the TAM3 were utilized to gain self-assessed feedback on the acceptance of the gesture-based menu interactions in terms of enjoyment, usability and behavioral intention (see [22][31]): Enjoyment (ENJ3), Perceptions of External Control (PEC1), Perceived Output Quality (OUT1 and OUT2), Perceived Ease of Use (PEOU4) Behavioral Intention (BI1 and BI2).. Furthermore participants ranked the four menu types according to their personal preferences, one ranking for the menu types with four menu elements and one for the menu types with eight menu elements.

3.3 Procedure

To realize the within subject study design we recruited 24 right-handed participants (12 men, 12 women) between 65 and 73 years (mean=68.3, sd=2.4) who did not use gesture-based interactions before. Participation was on a voluntarily basis and was compensated with 25€. Before we turned to the actual study, participants were asked to perform a simple motor test. Therefore, we modified the standardised Box and Block Test [18] which is a motoric performance test to measure the functionality of the upper limbs especially of older adults. Within our study participants had to put as many pralines as possible with the right hand (i.e. their dominant hand) out of a box to the corresponding place of an adjacent box, crossing a 15cm obstacle within 60 seconds (see Figure 1a). If they finished to move all 18 pieces before time ended they were asked to put them back again to the other side and keep going until 60 seconds had passed. The motor test was performed to better reflect the performance results of the evaluation of the gesture-based menu types regarding possible motor skill related differences between participants. In addition, participants were asked to assess their motor abilities subjectively on the basis of relevant items of the SMFA (Short Musculoskeletal Function Assessment) questionnaire [27]. It measures the functional status of a range of musculoskeletal injuries and disorders. The items most relevant to our study were related to activities of the upper limbs. Our intention to use two different methods for assessing the participants' motor abilities was to explore which kind and degree of reduced motor ability might be interfering with conducting free hand gesture-based interactions. By these means, we wanted to explore potential differences in performance values and the stated acceptance factors of the participants.

During the evaluation session participants were sitting in front of the TV while performing various selection tasks (see Figure 1b-c). We chose a sitting scenario for two reasons: sitting is the usual way of watching TV, and fewer effects of loss of balance [21]. The participants were seated on a staple chair and were asked to take a comfortable upright sitting position. The right shoulder was located in the middle of the TV (the Kinect sensor was placed on top), with a constant shoulder-TV distance of 2m. This standardized setup was designed to keep interfering positioning effects constant. A schematic view of the setup can be found in Figure 2.

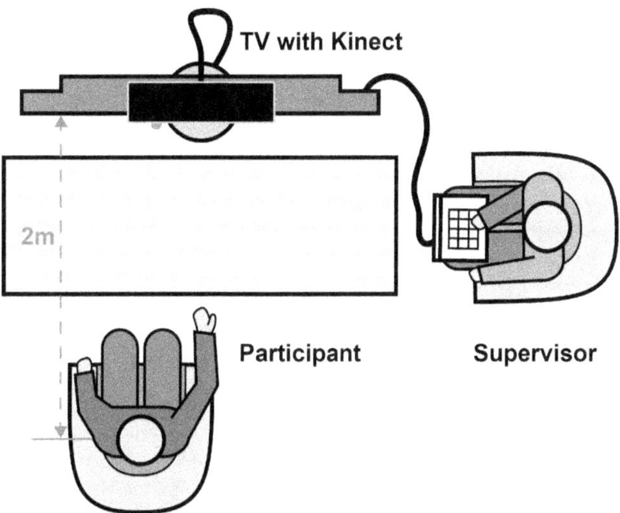

Figure 2: Schematic view of the study setup

As mentioned in section 3.2 participants first had training for each menu type and then conducted the tasks. During the conduction time and number of errors were recorded. After each menu type participants completed the TAM3 questionnaire After having completed all tasks using one menu type participants were asked to rank the menu type (once within the four menu elements version and once within the eight menu elements versions).

To sum up, our independent variables are the four menu types, as well as the number of menu elements (i.e. four or eight). Our dependent variables are therefore performance (task completion time and error rate), acceptance factors (i.e. enjoyment, perception of external control, perceived output quality, perceived ease of use, behavioural intention) and the preference ranking. To control effects of physical decline we assessed the motor abilities of the upper limb (modified Box and Block test, selected items of SMFA questionnaire).

4. RESULTS

In the following section the results of the objective measures (task completion time, error rate) and the ratings of the acceptance questionnaires are reported. We use the following abbreviations for the gesture menu types as introduced in **Table 1**: *H4* and *H8* stand for the two menu versions of Hand movement tracking, *C4* and *C8* stand for Cursor position control, *M4* and *M8* for Hand strokes for marking menu, *R4* and *R8* stand for Dial plate circle for radial menu, each with four or eight menu elements.

The 24 elderly participants (mean age=68.3, sd=2.4) of this study were rather experienced concerning the use of computer or laptop and TV (one participant skipped the questions on technology usage). Only two participants were completely inexperienced with computers or laptops, 20 use it on a daily basis. Watching TV was common to 23 participants as they claimed to use it every day.

We assessed the participants' motor abilities of hands and arms with the above mentioned modified version of the Box and Block Test [18], as well as with the SMFA questionnaire [27]. The selected arm-movement related items of SMFA questionnaire revealed no severe impairments of musculoskeletal functions in the respective body-parts. All participants rated themselves as physically fit. Ratings mainly range between *the activity is not at all difficult* and *moderately difficult*. Only three answers in total were set to *rather difficult*. The modified Box and Block Test resulted in an amount of moved pralines. This amount ranged from 9 to 44 (mean= 27.33, sd= 6.55). In contrast to the self-assessment the objective measures suggest certain variability related to the motor abilities of the participants upper limbs. No correlations were found between SMFA questionnaire and the results of the modified Box and Block Test.

4.1 Performance

Task completion time. A look at Figure 3 suggests that task completion times can be divided into three classes: *rather fast*, *medium* and *rather slow*. Tasks with menu type *H4* (mean=5.8s, sd=2.6s), *H8* (mean=7.3s; sd=1.8s) and *M4* (mean=6.4s; sd=2.4s) were completed *rather fast*. Tasks completed with *R4* (mean=9.9s; sd=3.8s) can be considered as medium, while tasks with *C4* (mean=13.0s; sd=9.0s), *C8* (mean=12.5s; sd=3.5s), *M8* (mean=13.0s; sd=5.4s) and *R8* (mean=12.6s; sd=3.6s) were performed *rather slow*. So, task completion times of *C4* and *C8* were about the same, while using *M8* took more than twice the time of *M4*. For an overview see Figure 3.

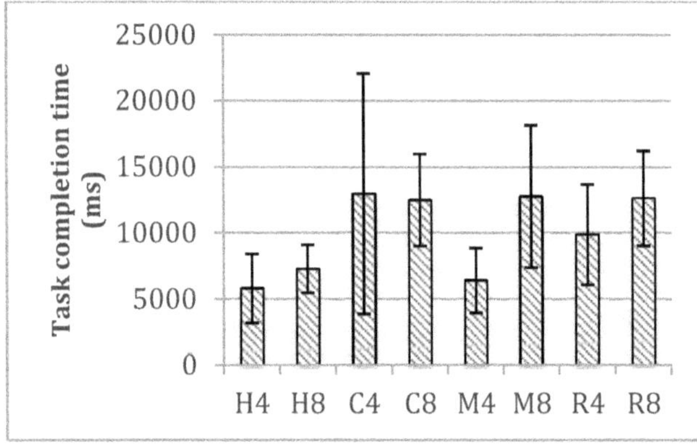

Figure 3: Completion time for all menu types.

Error rate. Most error rates show rather low values for gesture-based interaction. *C4* yielded the lowest error rate of 0.0%. Error rates of *H4*, *H8* and *C8* also remained under the aimed 5.0%. Even the 5.8% error rate of *M4* is still acceptable. Error rates of *M8*, *R4* and *R8* showed higher values wherewith the error rate of *M8* was almost three times higher as the error rate of its counterpart with four menu elements *M4* (see Figure 4).

Pearson correlations revealed that the results of the modified Box and Block Test did not have any relation to the error rate of the eight menu types, except of *M4* (r=-0.448; p=0.028). Concerning task completion time, only *M8* (r=-0.448; p=0.036) was slightly influenced by the results of the Box and Block Test. Pearson correlations of the SMFA score with task completion time showed a significant influence on the task completion time of *R4* (r=0.489, p=0.015), suggesting that the better the condition of the upper limbs of the participant, the faster he/she was able to complete the tasks of *R4*. Concerning the error rate, the SMFA score had an influence on the error rate of *R8* (r=0.509, p=0.013). The better the score, the more errors were made.

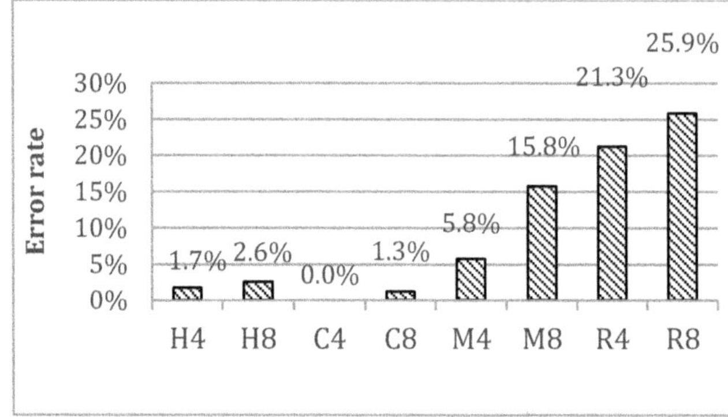

Figure 4: Error rate for all menu types

Q1: *Which kind of gesture control is the fastest for selection tasks and produces a low error rate?*

The answer of the first research question is easy to find as the results suggest that direct pointing with hand movement tracking (*H4* and *H8*) objectively perform best for our older participants.

4.2 User acceptance

Acceptance factors. The measured acceptance of the various gesture based menu types was rather high for every tested menu type. On the utilized 5-point Likert scale, ranging from *strongly disagree* (1) to *strongly agree* (5), the lowest average values of the whole sample were for *M8*, while the highest values were for *H4* and *C4*. Nevertheless, differences between the eight menu types are rather small (see Table 2).

Focusing on acceptance in terms of usability the values of the selected TAM3 items OUT1, OUT2, PEOU4 and PEC1 are relevant. However, there were only small differences, the highest

Table 2: Mean and standard deviation of acceptance values of the applied TAM3 items for the tested menu types

		H4	H8	C4	C8	M4	M8	R4	R8
OUT 1	mean	3.96	3.75	4.04	4.00	3.87	3.04	3.83	3.46
	sd	0.95	0.99	0.91	0.72	1.01	1.22	1.09	0.98
OUT 2	mean	3.88	3.71	4.04	3.92	3.74	3.00	3.67	3.46
	sd	1.08	1.12	0.91	0.78	0.96	1.17	1.09	1.10
PEO U4	mean	3.96	3.71	4.00	3.96	3.91	3.04	3.63	3.42
	sd	1.20	1.27	0.93	0.69	0.85	1.07	1.06	1.10
PEC1	mean	4.21	4.04	4.17	4.04	3.87	3.22	3.88	3.63
	sd	0.78	0.81	0.76	0.75	0.87	1.17	0.80	1.01
ENJ3	mean	4.21	4.04	4.17	4.17	4.04	3.52	4.13	3.96
	sd	0.88	0.99	0.57	0.57	0.83	1.04	0.85	0.96
BI1	mean	3.96	3.79	3.92	3.79	3.65	3.13	3.63	3.5
	sd	1.04	1.18	0.97	0.88	1.03	1.29	1.25	1.29
BI2	mean	3.88	3.79	3.88	3.75	3.43	3.04	3.58	3.63
	sd	1.19	1.29	0.99	0.94	0.99	1.33	1.28	1.28

scores received *H4*, *C4* and *C8*; the lowest receives *M8*. The values on TAM3 usability items in general range from 4.21 to 3.00. Details are illustrated in Figure 5 and Table 2.

We found high ratings on enjoyment (ENJ3) for all menu types. Except *M8* (mean=3.52, sd=1.04) all tested menu types received at least a value of 4.0. Therefore, enjoyment received the highest values of all tested items of TAM3 (see Figure 5 and Table 2).

Concerning the acceptance factor behavioral intention, all values for all menu types ranged between 3.04 and 3.96, which indicates a moderate intention to use of such a gesture-controlled system at the older adult.

According to the respective items of TAM3, the gesture controls seem to be acceptable for older adults. In this respect *H4* and *C4* score best. Although overall ratings were above mean, the worst ratings were given for *M8*.

The TAM3 items were neither influenced by the SMFA scores nor by the results of the modified version of the Box and Block Test.

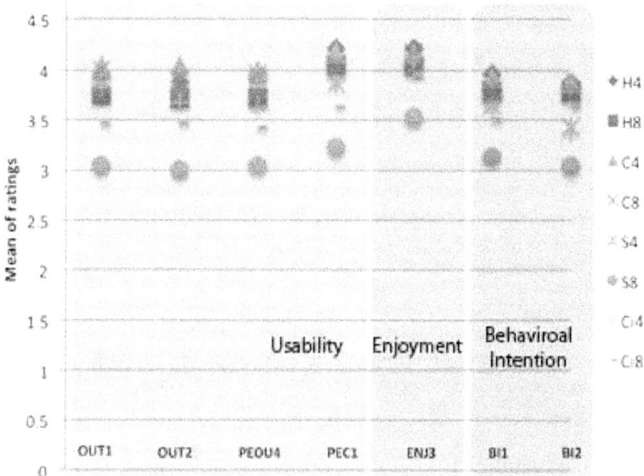

Figure 5: Respective TAM3 items clustered according to usability, enjoyment and behavioral intention

Preferences. The results of the personal preference ranking of the menu types by the participants (see Table 3) underline the measured findings in some respects. Hand movement tracking (*H4 and H8*) was ranked on top as it performed well in both, objective and subjective aspects. Dial plate circle for radial menu (*R4* and *R8*) was ranked worst with both versions although *M8* received the worst ratings in the acceptance questionnaire. Cursor position control (*C4 and C8*) and hand strokes for marking menu (*M4* and *M8*) lied in between.

Table 3: Median of the subjective ranking of the prototypes.

	H	*C*	*M*	*R*
Median of 4 menu elements	1.5	2.0	2.0	3.0
Median of 8 menu elements	1.0	3.0	3.0	3.0

Q2: *Do older adults accept freehand gesture-based interactions in terms of usability, joyfulness and behavioral intention and which kind of gesture control do older users prefer?*

According to the respective TAM3 items, freehand gesture-based interactions are generally accepted by older users. Participants enjoyed interacting this way with a TV-based control menu. The self-assessed preference ratings suggest that hand movement tracking interactions are perceived best.

5. DISCUSSION

The observed results are partly surprising and are discussed in this section based on the issues of the formulated research questions.

5.1 Performance

The observed results indicate that hand movement tracking (*H4* and *H8*) clearly performed best in this study. Influence of motor issues and fatigue could hardly be observed. However, we focused in this study on short interactions which allowed frequent relaxation of the arm. Follow-up work will be oriented to longer interactions and include the valuable comparison with younger users.

Task completion time. Both versions of hand movement tracking (*H4* and *H8*) performed *rather fast* and thus reached acceptable task completion times. This might be explained by the fact that most participants were experienced in using computers and therewith were familiar with the handling and the concept of a mouse-like cursor.

As expected, cursor position control (*C4* and *C8)* had *rather long* task completion times: For this menu technique only the direction of the movement is tracked. Therefore, a direct manipulation of movement speed was not possible. Instead, a constant, rather slow velocity of the cursor applies and participants had to wait until the cursor reaches the desired position. However, this applies especially for *C8* as there were long distances between the left and right outer menu elements. It remains unclear why participants needed similar amount of time for performing with *C4*. As the high standard deviation of *C4* indicates, some participants needed more time for some tasks which might be caused by the lower amount of tasks conducted with *C4* than with *C8*.

The rather long task completion times of the marking (especially *M8*) and the ring menu (*R4* and *R8*) were not expected. In contrast to cursor-based menu types, the concepts of stroke and circular movements are rather new to older adults which might explain the weaker task completion time. Research has shown that appealing to recognition works much better, especially for older adults, than completely new approaches [26]. Frequent usage of freehand gestures to control a TV menu might accordingly lead to a relative performance improvement of the not-cursor-based approaches of marking and ring menu. Since we used prototypes, some technical shortcomings might be a reason for the longer task completion times. While the cursor-based menu types relied on standard functions of the Kinect SDK the two other menu types (*M* and *R*) required the **implementation** of more advanced algorithms.

A common problem with the marking menus (*M4* and *M8*) was that after the initiation the hand symbol was not located in the center but already at one of the tracks. Thus, participants needed some time to position their hands in the center area. Besides, three participants commented for the version with eight menu elements (*M8*) that "it was difficult to find the entrance of the track" to the given menu element. To avoid a miss-hit some participants tried several times to start again by moving back to the center. A correlation between measured **motor abilities** (modified Box and Block Test) and task completion time for *M8* supports this observation. In other words, motor issues related to the Box and Block Test affect the performance with this kind of gesture technique. Considering by trend motor issues increase with ageing [21], more problems should be expected for older people than our participants.

The rather long task completion times with the ring menus (*R4* and *R8*) were partly caused by limitations of the prototype. It was not possible to transfer the circular hand movements synchronously at the controlled selection basket. The smallest detectable movement was a semi-circle. Hence, the direct mapping of hand and ring segment was lost and users had to crank along the ring to reach the given menu element. For example, to reach the menu element *E* starting from *A* requires the conduction of two full circular movements (see Table 1 iv). This results in longer task completion time.

Error rate. The error rates of both versions of hand movement tracking (*H4* and *H8*) and cursor position control (*C4* and *C8*) remained under the assumed 5%. Due to familiarity with cursor-based interaction and the absence of motor issues the participants had no problems with these gesture techniques. Especially the indirect movement control of *C4* and *C8* seemed to allow the participants to better concentrate on the selection itself resulting in the lowest overall error rates.

Concerning the hand strokes for marking menus, the error rate of *M4* could still be regarded as acceptable while the error rate of *M8* was almost three times higher. This difference might be explained by the increased amount of menu elements and the accompanying decrease of operation space for each menu element (see Table 1 iii). Thus, much more precision is required. The only correlation between motor abilities (modified Box and Block Test) and error rate was found for *M4*. We suppose that participants with slight motor issues tended to be more careful with the version with eight menu elements leading to longer task completion times with *M8* and higher error rates with *M4*. Hence, this gesture technique seems to be physically more demanding than the other ones.

High error rate of dial plate circle for a ring menu (*R4* and *R8*) could be caused by short performance delays of the prototype. In these cases participants often continued their circular movement until the selection basket moved further or shook their hands. The detected movements led to quick movements of the selection basket and the performed grab gesture applied to the wrong menu element. In contrast to the cursor-based techniques every selection gesture applies including those performed hastily.

The SMFA scores showed correlations with performance of the dial plate circle for a ring menu (*R4 and R8*) suggesting that the menu is controlled more accurate by people with little self-uncertainty concerning their motor abilities. Nevertheless, no correlation was found to the results of the modified Box and Block Test. The results of the SMFA questionnaire suggest that upper limbs of our participants were in a relatively good physical condition, at least not falling into a category of musculoskeletal injuries or disorders.

Lessons Learned. Overall we found out that older adults are able to control various TV menus with freehand gestures. Previous experiences with computers probably support older adults in using gestures controlling a cursor. However, it remains unclear which amplifying effects of motor issues on the performance occur with longer lasting gesture tasks, especially in comparison to younger persons.

5.2 Acceptance

Acceptance rates were overall very high. Additionally, the very high rating for **enjoyment** reflects the fun the participants had with gesturing, which goes along with the findings of [19]. The other investigated acceptance items for measuring **usability** and behavioral **intention** also received above-average assessments. These good ratings indicate that older adults accept gesture-based interactions in TV scenarios and they seem to be willing to invest the necessary learning efforts. One precondition for this success might be that no severe motor impairments hindered them in conducting the gestures. None of the tests for motor abilities had any influence on acceptance factors. Furthermore, the tasks were short enough to avoid the occurrence of fatigue.

When looking into more detail we see that cursor-based menu techniques (*H4* and *C4*) received the best results. Due to the best performance the positive ratings for *H4* and also for *H8* were expectable. In spite of requiring the longest performance time cursor position control (*C4* and *C8*) was rated very favorable. The low error rate might evoke a positive attitude, due to a relatively low frustration level, especially in comparison to the radial menus (*M* and *R*). Interestingly, *M8* received the worst (however still positive) grades for every respective TAM3 item. Although task completion time of *R8* was similar, its error rate was worse. *M4* performed better in both aspects compared to *R4* but did receive similar rates. A reason for this might be that this technique is more polarizing. Some participants were frustrated due to the performance problems and gave worse grades. In generally positive answers these grades are more conspicuous.

In the **preference** ranking created by the participants at the end of the study both versions of hand movement tracking stand at the top position. For explaining these clear preferences we rely to the already reported two main aspects: the overall best performance and the existing experience with cursor-based approaches. The low error rate and the good usability ratings support Cursor Position Control (*C4 and C8*) on rank 2 to 3, although performance time is poor. The highest error rate of all menu types is probably the reason why dial plate circle for radial menus (*R4* and *R8)* were ranked worse than the two versions of marking menu approaches (*M4* and *M8)* although *M8* received the worst values in the acceptance questionnaire.

It would be interesting to see if the general positive attitude reported in this study could be preserved when older adults have to choose between gesture-based interactions and the current remote control device of TVs. However, previous research showed that older adults are quite positive towards touch interactions [8]. Our study suggests that they are also keen to freehand gesturing. Novelty sensation seeking and the accommodation of their needs might be responsible that older adults are interested in these new forms of interaction. Hence, conducting an additional long-term study would be desirable to see if freehand gesturing remains an alternative control mechanism after the novelty bonus has disappeared.

Lessons learned. Older adults seem to have a very positive attitude toward freehand gestures for controlling TV menus. All measured acceptance factors received above-average ratings. It remains unclear if older adults would reduce the usage of standard TV remote controllers in favor for gesturing.

5.3 Further Issues

The diverging results of subjective and objective motor ability measures reflect a possible limitation regarding the appropriateness of the modified version of the Box and Block Test for answering our research questions. It is also questionable whether the self-assessment with the SMFA is helpful in this context. Since the SMFA was originally developed for rheumatic patients and our participants do not have severe bodily problems yet, the high variability of the granular spectrum of motor abilities of older adults may be assessed more reliable with objective instruments. Despite these issues our participants still were physically fitter than expected, which might led to the little amount of differences between the four menu types, especially in terms of acceptance factors.

In theory, the kind of gesture-based interaction used in this study can be transferred to other application areas than TVs. In similar contexts also menus of other distant displays like those of computers or game consoles can be controlled. Context in this case is a home scenario where the user can sit and is alone. When using more robust technology other familiar people can be around e.g. friends and family or other inhabitants of a residential home like in [19]. Application in public e.g. in front of a shop window is possible, however, depends on a broad range of additional factors e.g. standing vs. sitting, acting in public vs. at home, uncontrolled weather effects.

6. CONCLUSIONS

In this study, we could show that freehand gestures are an appropriate way for older adults to control a TV menu. With direct pointing using hand movement tracking the participants performed best. All four menu approaches utilized in this study were accepted in terms of enjoyment, usability and behavioral intention. However, older adults seem to prefer cursor-based interaction techniques. In this study, we just assessed short interactions wherewith we could not observe any influence of fatigue. Future research should investigate the influence of longer interactions and of more severe age-related impairments on this kind of gesturing. To better understand the performance results of older adults further research including studies with younger persons is required. Along with this, the limitation of the prototypes should be fixed.

7. ACKNOWLEDGMENTS

This research has partially been funded by the AAL JP project FoSIBLE (AAL-2009-2-135) and the Austrian COMET K-project AIR (Nr. 825345). Many thanks also to the developers of the prototype Michael Klein and Georg Regal.

8. REFERENCES

[1] Bailly, G., Walter, R., Müller, J., Ning, T., & Lecolinet, E. (2011). Comparing free hand menu techniques for distant displays using linear, marking and finger-count menus. *INTERACT'11 Proceedings of the 13th IFIP international conference on Human-computer interaction - Volume Part II* (pp. 248-262).

[2] Chaparro, A., Rogers, M., Fernandez, J., Bohan, M., Choi, S. D., & Stumpfhauser, L. (2000). Range of motion of the wrist: implications for designing computer input devices for the elderly. *Disability and rehabilitation, 22*(13-14), 633-637.

[3] Chen, M.-yu, Mummert, L., Pillai, P., Hauptmann, A., & Sukthankar, R. (2010). Controlling your TV with gestures. *Proceedings of the international conference on Multimedia information retrieval* (pp. 405–408)

[4] Chertoff, D. B., Byers, R. W., & LaViola Jr, J. J. (2009). An exploration of menu techniques using a 3D game input device. *Proceedings of the 4th International Conference on Foundations of Digital Games* (pp. 256–262)

[5] Davis, F.D., Bagozzi, R.P., and Warshaw, P.R. (1989). User Acceptance of Computer Technology: A Comparison of Two Theoretical Models. Management Science, 35 (pp 982-1003).

[6] Freeman, W. T., & Weissman, C. D. (1995). Television Control by Hand Gestures. *IEEE Intl. Wkshp. on Automatic Face and Gesture Recognition.*

[7] Hattori, T., Mine, Y., & Cohen, M. (2008). Gesture Interpretation for Domestic Appliance Control. *ICAT 18th International Conference on Artificial Reality and Telexistence* (pp. 343-346).

[8] Holzinger, A. (2003). Finger Instead of Mouse: Touch Screens as a means of enhancing Universal Access. *In: Carbonell, N., Stephanidis, C. (eds.) Universal Access. Theoretical Perspectives, Practice, and Experience.* LNCS, vol. 2615 (pp. 387–397). Springer.

[9] Hummels, C. & Stapers, P. J. (1998). Meaningful gestures for human computer interaction. *Proc. of the 3rd International Conference on Automatic Face and Gesture Recognition.*

[10] Jetter, H.-Christian, Gerken, J., & Reiterer, H. (2010). Natural User Interfaces□: Why We Need Better Model-Worlds, Not Better Gestures. *Natural user interfaces: the prospect and challenge of touch and gestural computing (Workshop CHI 2010)* (pp. 1-4).

[11] Karam, M., & Schraefel, M. C. (2005). A Taxonomy of Gestures in Human Computer Interaction. *ACM Transactions on Computer-Human Interactions* (pp. 1-45).

[12] Kim, S. H., Ok, J., Kang, H. J., Kim, M. C., & Kim, M. (2004). An interaction and product design of gesture based TV remote control. *CHI'04 extended abstracts on Human factors in computing systems* (pp. 1548–1548).

[13] Kelley, J.F. (1984). An iterative design methodology for user-friendly natural language office information applications. *ACM Transactions on Office Information Systems, March 1984, 2:1* (pp. 26–41).

[14] Kurtenbach, G. & Buxton, W. (1994). User learning and performance with marking menus. *Proceedings of CHI '94,* (pp. 258-264).

[15] Lee, T., Kim, H., & Park, K. (2010). Gesture-Based Interface Using Baby Signs for the Elderly and People with Mobility Impairment in a Smart House Environment. *Proceedings of ICOST 2010* (pp. 234-237).

[16] Liang, L., & Green, M. (1994). Geometric Modeling Using Six Degrees of Freedom Input Devices. *Computers and Graphics, 18*(4).

[17] Marras, W.S. (2006). Basic Biomechanics and Workstation Design. *In: Salvendy, G. (Edt.). Handbook of human factors and ergonomics.* Hoboken, N.J: John Wiley (pp. 340-370).

[18] Mathiowetz, V., Volland, G., Kashman, N., Weber, K. (1985) Adult norms for the Box and Block-test of manual dexterity. *American Journal of Occupational Therapy, 1985, 39* (pp. 386-391).

[19] Neufeldt, C. (2009). Wii play with elderly people. *International Reports in Socio-Informatics, 2009, 6*(3) *(pp.* 50-59).

[20] Ni, T., Bowman, D. a., North, C., & McMahan, R. P. (2011). Design and evaluation of freehand menu selection interfaces using tilt and pinch gestures. *International Journal of Human-Computer Studies, 69*(9), 551-562.

[21] Nichols, T. A., Rogers, W. A., Fisk, A. D. (2006). Design for Ageing. *In: Salvendy, G. (Edt.). Handbook of human factors and ergonomics.* Hoboken, N.J: John Wiley (pp. 1418-1458).

[22] Norman, D. A. & Nielsen, J. (2010). Gestural interfaces: a step backward in usability. *Interactions 17, No. 5* (pp. 46-49).

[23] Premaratne, P., & Nguyen, Q. (2007). Consumer electronics control system based on hand gesture moment invariants. *IET Computer Vision 1*(1) (pp. 35-41).

[24] Saleiro, M., & Rodrigues, J. (2009). Automatic Hand or Head Gesture Interface for Individuals with Motor Impairments, Senior Citizens and Young Children. *International Conference on Software Development for Enhancing Accessibility and Fighting Info-exclusion.*

[25] Saposnik, G., Mamdani, M., Bayley, M., Thorpe, K. E., Hall, J., Cohen, L. G., & Teasell, R. (2010). Clinical trial protocols Effectiveness of Virtual Reality Exercises in STroke Rehabilitation (EVREST): Rationale, Design, and Protocol of a Pilot Randomized Clinical Trial Assessing the Wii Gaming System. *International Journal Of Stroke, 5*(2) (pp. 47-51).

[26] Schieber, F. (2003). Human Factors and Aging: Identifying and Compensating for Age-related Deficits in Sensory and Cognitive Function. *In: Charness, N., Schaie, K. W. (Eds.). Impact of technology on successful aging.* Springer Publishing Company (pp. 42-84).

[27] Swiontkowski, M.F., Engelberg, R., Martin, D.P., Angel, J. (1999). Short musculoskeletal function assessment questionnaire: reliability, validity and responsiveness. *J Bone Joint Surg 81 A* (pp. 1245-1260).

[28] Stenger, B., Woodley, T., Kim, T. K., & Cipolla, R. (2009). A vision-based system for display interaction. *Proceedings of the 23rd British HCI Group Annual Conference on People and Computers: Celebrating People and Technology* (pp. 163–168).

[29] Stößel, C., Wandke, H., & Blessing, L. (2010). Gestural Interfaces for Elderly Users: Help or Hindrance? *Gesture in Embodied Communication and Human-Computer Interaction* (pp. 269–280).

[30] Tsukada, K., & Yasumura, M. (2002). Ubi-finger: Gesture input device for mobile use. *Proceedings of APCHI* (pp. 388–400).

[31] Venkatesh, V. and Bala, H. (2008), Technology Acceptance Model 3 and a Research Agenda on Interventions. *Decision Sciences, 39* (pp. 273–315)

[32] Yamamoto, G., Hyry, J., Pouke, M., Metso, A., Hickey, S., & Pulli, P. (2010). Senior Citizens' Interaction with Smart Ambient Environment. *16th International ICE-Conference on Engineering, Technology and Innovation.*

User-Defined Gestures for Free-Hand TV Control

Radu-Daniel Vatavu
University Stefan cel Mare of Suceava
13 Universitatii
720229 Suceava, Romania
vatavu@eed.usv.ro

ABSTRACT

As researchers and industry alike are proposing TV interfaces that use gestures in their designs, understanding users' preferences for gesture commands becomes an important problem. However, no rules or guidelines currently exist to assist designers and practitioners of such interfaces. The paper presents the results of the first study investigating users' preferences for free-hand gestures when controlling the TV set. By conducting an agreement analysis on user-elicited gestures, a set of gesture commands is proposed for basic TV control tasks. Also, guidelines and recommendations issued from observed user behavior are provided to assist practitioners interested in prototyping free-hand gestural designs for the interactive TV.

Categories and Subject Descriptors

H.5.2 [**Information interfaces and presentation**]: User Interfaces. Evaluation/methodology, user-centered design.

General Terms

Design, Experimentation, Human Factors.

Keywords

Gestures, gesture recognition, free-hand, Kinect, TV, living room, experiment, study, guessability, user-defined, interactive TV.

1. INTRODUCTION

Following the success of motion-sensitive controllers for video games (Wii/Kinect), gestural interfaces are slowly but steadily invading the rest of the controllable living room. Researchers and industry alike have been experimenting interface designs that allow users to control the functions of their TV sets by means of gestures only [2,4,7,12,13]. Such designs either augment the TV remote control with motion sensing capabilities [2,15]; replace the remote with smart mobile phones [7]; reuse video game controllers [13]; appropriate pieces of furniture as supporting equipments [12]; or employ free-hand gestures [4,5].

There are many good reasons for adopting gestures for TV control. Among the most often mentioned ones [2,12], gestures come to replace mis-designed remote controls that affect negatively the user experience. For example, ethnographic studies [3] have showed numerous times that many household members find remote controls complex and difficult to use with the main reasons being small buttons and high button congestions. Also, despite the large available palette of functionalities, people only use "*selected buttons of [their] remote controls ... [because] some are really useless*" [3]. Other weak points are the lack of backlighting on most remotes which reduces their usability in the dark; the fact that remotes can be lost; and their periodical need for fixing and battery replacement. On the other side, gestures feel familiar and natural to their users when properly designed while they also bring a new dimension of *fun* into the interaction (heavily exploited by today's gesture-sensitive video game controllers). However, probably the most important advantage of using gestures lies with the possibility of customization: users can provide their own commands without being constrained by the rigid design of the remote control.

Despite such advantages, we must also note that today's gestural interfaces are far from being ideal [9]. Although marketed as natural user interfaces, gestures have side effects such as misrecognition and poor designs of the gesture-to-function mapping [9]. Free-hand motions also induce fatigue with prolonged usage. However, as practitioners will learn more about their users in terms of execution capabilities and mental models for mapping gestures to tasks, gestural interfaces are likely to conquer the future living-room environment (either on their own [4] or as part of mixed designs [2,13,15]).

This paper contributes on the little researched area of designing intuitive mappings between gestures and TV functions. We report results from a study addressing users' preferences for free-hand gestures when controlling the TV set. We compile a set of gestures for basic TV commands and provide guidelines for practitioners interested in TV gestural designs. In this context, this work represents the first exploration of users' preferences for free-hand gestures for the interactive TV.

2. RELATED WORK

Researchers have always shown a strong interest in designing new interactions for the living room. An early prototype of Freeman and Weissman [4] employed a video camera which detected the location and posture of the viewer's hand for performing click-like interactions on the TV. The ARGUS system [5] extended the concept to multiple cameras employed to detect the direction of pointing in order to allows users to control multiple equipments with the same gestures. Vatavu and Pentiuc [12] showed how TV gestural interfaces can be developed robustly and without privacy concerns with the interactive coffee table prototype. WIMP-style interactions (Windows, Icons, Menu, and Pointing) were also explored for multi-screen home entertainment systems [13]. Such systems exploit the experience people had already acquired from working with windows-based operating systems in order to provide a smooth transition to other interactive spaces.

In the measure that gesture acquisition devices are becoming affordable (such as low-cost Wii/Kinect sensors), the main design problems are shifting towards finding the optimum mapping from gesture to function [11,14]. However, existing toolkits for gesture design only advise practitioners on how to obtain a high

EuroITV'12, July 4-6, 2012, Berlin, Germany.

recognition rate or help them organizing the gesture set [1]. As a consequence, the only options for finding *good* gesture mappings remain to rely on the designer's own expertise or to organize user studies. Norman [9] showed how the first option has often led to mis-designs and frustrating user experiences.

Involving users into the design process represents a viable alternative for collecting important data to inform design. In this direction, Lessiter et al. [8] employed users to suggest labels for the buttons of the remote and to rank their intuitiveness. Wobbrock et al. [14] introduced a methodology for eliciting gesture commands from users in order to compile sets of high-agreement gestures. Follow-up works verified the methodology for mobile phones [7,11], public displays, and tabletops [6]. However, no study yet exists for investigating user preferences for free-hand gestures despite many gestural interfaces being proposed in the TV community. This work tries to fill this gap by collecting and reporting user-elicited free-hand gestures to inform practitioners of the next generation TV gestural interfaces.

3. EXPERIMENT

An experiment was conducted in order to elicit user preferences for free-hand gestures for frequent TV control tasks. The experiment was designed and ran in accordance with domain practices for such guessability studies [11,14].

Participants

12 participants volunteered for the study (mean age 21 years, all right-handed, 6 females). Although volunteers were CS students, none of them had previous experience in interaction design nor had they used gestural interfaces before (such as Kinect).

Apparatus

Gestures were acquired using the Microsoft Kinect sensor[1] which was connected to a 3.0GHz computer running a custom software application which directed the experiment. The application logged video recordings and body tracking data of participants performing gestures. The Kinect sensor allows for 20 body points to be tracked in real time at about 30 frames per second. The PC was connected to a video-projected display (with a size of 2×1.5 meters and a resolution of 1024×768 pixels) which was emulating a large TV equipment. A sufficient amount of free space was secured for the testing area in order for participants to perform gestures in a confident and safe manner.

Referents

12 commands commonly used for controlling the TV set were selected for the experiment (see Table 1). By following the terminology of [14], commands are denoted as *referents*.

The set of referents contains frequently-used commands for controlling the TV set which cover channel navigation, volume control, accessing extra options through menus, performing general enquiries, and answering system questions. Although other commands could have been easily included, we opted for this specific and limited set for several reasons. First, ethnographic studies showed that participants focus and use few buttons only [3] and, when asked, redesign their own versions of the remotes with solely the functions they actually use or need. Second, the number of gesture commands people can remember for effective use should be limited in order not to increase cognitive load. More individual commands would translate into complex designs with a similar puzzling effect exhibited by today's remote controls [3]. This very observation has led the industry in proposing short versions of the remote such as the Tek Pal Simple Remote[2] or the Flipper[3] featuring 6 frequently-used buttons only (power, channel +/-, volume +/-, mute), all of which are part of our set. Also, menus represent a viable option to group other, less frequent, commands [2]. We need to note that the set can be easily enlarged to include air-drawn digits 0 to 9 (for quick channel change commands or similar short-cuts). For obvious reasons there was no point including digits in this study.

For each referent, a video demonstration depicting its effect was prepared in advance to be displayed during the experiment.

Table 1. Referents used for the elicitation experiment

REFERENT		NOTES
1.	SELECT/OPEN	Open TV or indicate a specific TV screen in a multi-screen environment
2.	CLOSE	Close the TV screen
3.	NEXT	Go to next channel
4.	PREVIOUS	Go to previous channel
5.	VOLUME +	Volume control
6.	VOLUME -	
7.	MUTE	
9.	OPEN MENU	Pop up contextual menu
9.	HIDE MENU	Hide currently opened menu
10.	HELP	Ask system for help
11.	YES	Answer to system question / Accept
12.	NO	Answer to system question / Reject

Procedure

Participants were asked to propose free-hand gestures using one or both hands for each referent in the set. Each referent was presented using a short text description (e.g. *volume up*) and by running a video demonstration of its effect. After participants confirmed they understood the effect, they were asked to suggest a suitable gesture command that would trigger the effect they had witnessed. Participants were encouraged to think aloud while searching for the best gesture to match the task. No visual feedback was provided during the gesture elicitation phase. The order of referents was randomized across participants.

4. RESULTS

We report results from 12 (participants) x 12 (referents) = 144 proposals for gesture commands. An agreement analysis was conducted in order to understand participants' level of consensus for each specific task/referent. The agreement rate measure of Wobbrock et al. [14] was used for this purpose:

$$A_r = \sum_{P_i \subseteq P_r} \left(\frac{|P_i|}{|P_r|} \right)^2$$

where P_r represents the set of all gestures proposed for referent r and P_i represent groups of similar commands. The agreement rate A_r ranges from $|P_r|^{-1}$ (no agreement at all) to 1 (perfect agreement).

The mean agreement for our set was $.42$ ($SD = .28$), comparable to values obtained by [14] ($.32/.28$) and [11] using the same methodology for surfaces and mobile phones. Individual rates for each task are shown in Figure 1.

[1] Kinect for Windows, http://kinectforwindows.com

[2] TekPal Remote, http://www.bigbuttonremotes.com/remotes-tekpal.htm

[3] Flipper Remote, http://www.flipperremote.com/

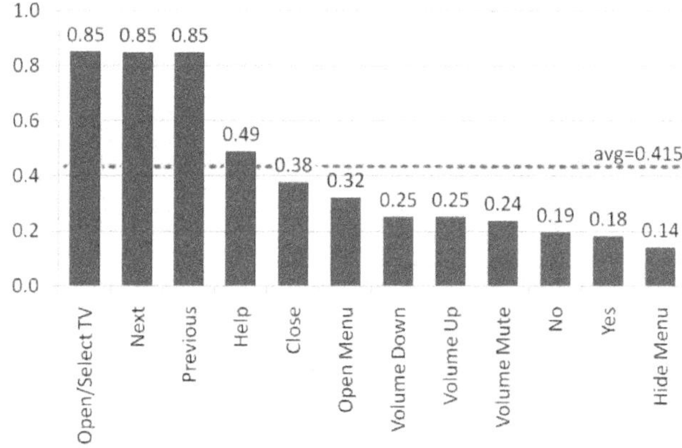

Figure 1. Agreement rates for user-defined free-hand gestures

Participants' gestures consisted in both motion and hand posture data. For some tasks (e.g. *Next*), the motion component was the most relevant whilst hand posture was just an artifact of the motion (i.e. non-intended). Other tasks clearly relied on hand posture (e.g. *Volume mute)* whilst hand location and motion was irrelevant. We consistently applied these rules when calculating the agreement rates. The highest agreement ($.85$) was obtained for *Open*, *Next*, and *Previous* (consensus among 11 out of 12 participants). The smallest levels of agreement ($< .20$) occurred for *No*, *Yes*, and *Hide menu*. In order to better understand what these values actually represent and extract meaningful information, we illustrate a few examples of how they could be obtained. For example, an $.50$ agreement level can be obtained when two groups of six participants propose the same command or when two commands are supported by two groups of 8 and 4 (suggesting a robust agreement):

$$A_r = \left(\frac{6}{12}\right)^2 + \left(\frac{6}{12}\right)^2 = .50;\ A_r = \left(\frac{8}{12}\right)^2 + \left(\frac{4}{12}\right)^2 = .55$$

An agreement rate of approximately $.25$ can be attained with four groups of participants each supporting a different command or with a group of at least 6 in consensus:

$$A_r = 4 \times \left(\frac{3}{12}\right)^2 = .25;\ A_r = \left(\frac{6}{12}\right)^2 + 6 \times \left(\frac{1}{12}\right)^2 = .29$$

Therefore, agreement rates above $.50$ are indicators of robust proposals; agreements above $.25$ suggest useful commands; while values lower than $.20$ indicate the need of expert design. In total, 4 referents had agreements over $.50$ (33%), 9 ($= 4 + 5$) over $.25$ (66%), and 3 were under $.20$ (25%).

4.1 A gesture set for free-hand TV control

The agreement analysis justifies an attempt to compile a gesture set for TV control. When performing the final gesture-function associations, the gesture occurring most frequently for a referent won the command. Figure 2 illustrates the final proposal.

Open/Select TV was performed by pointing towards the screen and confirming the command with either a hand posture or a quick push of a virtual air button (a technique we denote as *air-push*) by 11 out of 12 participants. In order to perform *Close*, participants drew letter *X* in mid air (mimicking the close icon of windows on PCs). Two distinct gestures were included in the set for *Open Menu*: letter *M* (4/12) and a double *air-push* (5/12). Low agreements were found for *Hide Menu* (0.14) for which participants suggested different options (*X* for closing; another *M*; *C* for close; move menu away with the hand; shake hand rapidly to ignore, etc.) Therefore, an artificial choice was made for *Hide*: the same gesture as for *Open Menu* inspired by the design of existing remote controls that only have a single menu button. *Next* and *Previous* were performed by moving the dominant hand to left and right (11/12).

Controlling the volume revealed interesting findings. *Volume Up* and *Down* exploited the use of both hands as well as the distance between hands as a control parameter. While the non-dominant (left) hand was held fixed, the right hand moved along one axis to control volume level (8/12). A considerable high (and unexpected) agreement was found for *Mute* despite its abstract nature. Almost half (5/12) participants performed a hand gesture by closing fingers simulating a closing mouth (shut up). In order to invoke system help, the majority of participants (8/12) drew a question mark in mid-air. *Yes* and *No* received culturally-dependent gestures such as thumbs-up (4/12), thumbs-down (4/12), and vertical/horizontal movements of the hand (2/12).

4.2 Guidelines for TV gesture set designs

Observations collected during the experiment and the follow-up analysis were compiled into a set of guidelines for practitioners:

(1) We found that one-hand gestures were heavily preferred to two hands (10 out of 12 commands use one hand). Two hands served for parameterized tasks (e.g. volume level). The same reasoning could therefore be reused for other similar situations (such as brightness or contrast adjustment);

(2) Hand posture was found to be important. The index finger pointed occurred most frequently but other postures such as thumbs-up, thumbs-down, and hand closed were equally employed. One participant performed *Close* by closing the fingers of her hand. Another participant used 3 stretched fingers in order to pop up a contextual menu (*Open Menu*). This shows the need of sensing technology with high enough resolution to capture such details (an important note for ambient video cameras);

(3) A clear preference was observed for drawing letters in mid-air (*X*, *M*, and question mark are present in the set; *Y* and *O* were suggested for yes/ok; *N* for no; *C* for close, *H* for help, etc.). This suggests possible extensions to other letter-like commands with the 0..9 digits falling into this category. Participants witnessed letters were easy to use and suspected they would also be easy to remember;

(4) Pointing was frequently used and WIMP-style interactions could be observed in many cases. For example, *air-push* simulates clicking a button while volume control gestures remind the use of track bars. An analogy with a long mouse click was used by a participant who executed *Open* with a long pointing (~2 sec) towards the screen. One participant imagined popping up a volume control (similar to the ones found in PC media players) by drawing letter *V*. Some preferences were observed for tangible controls. For example, one participant imagined a turning button in mid-air to be used for controlling the volume (wrist movements to right/left would change the volume level up/down);

(5) Cultural gestures were proposed due to their similarity with existing situations in the real-world (*Yes/No*). Although their generality is limited from culture to culture, their use should be exploited due to familiarity to their users [10];

(6) Some TV functions may be too abstract for participants to suggest meaningful gestures or to remember special designed ones. For such cases, on-screen widgets and menus should be used. This observation could also raise questions on the appropriateness of a gestural interface for some TV control tasks for which a mixed design (remote + gestures) might prove more appropriate;

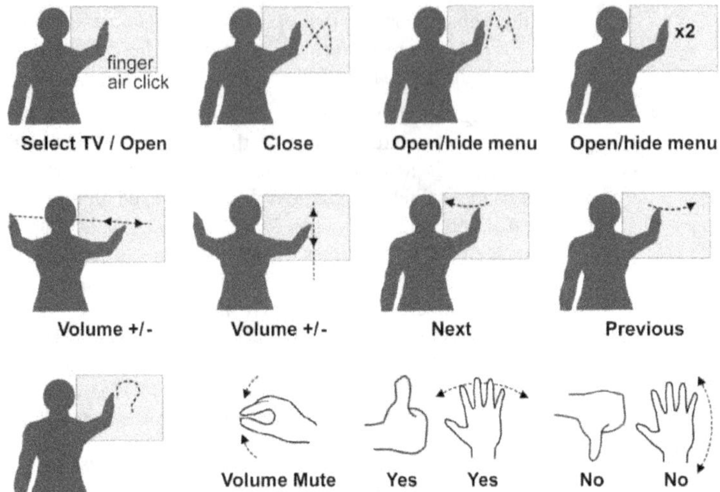

REFERENT	GESTURE
SELECT/OPEN	Point + air-push/air-click
CLOSE	Draw letter X
NEXT	Move dominant hand to the left
PREVIOUS	Move dominant hand to the right
VOLUME +	Non-dominant (left) hand serves as the reference the while right hand moves left/right or up/down
VOLUME -	
MUTE	Hand closes the fingers (shut-up)
OPEN MENU	Draw letter M or double air-push
HIDE MENU	Draw letter M or double air-push [gesture artificially created by copying Open Menu]
HELP	Draw question mark
YES	Thumbs-up / shake horizontally
NO	Thumbs-down / shake vertically

Figure 2. Gesture set proposed for frequent TV commands as compiled from the participants' agreement rate analysis.

(7) Although this study only investigated free-hand gestures, body-referenced gestures could be further explored. They occurred for *Volume Mute* for which one participant moved both hands to the ears covering them while another brought the hand close to her mouth. Also, one participant lifted his shoulders in order to invoke *Help*.

Cause of limited space we provide the complete set of gesture suggestions as a download from http://www.eed.usv.ro/~vatavu

5. CONCLUSION

The paper presented the results of the first study addressing users' free-hand gesture preferences for TV control. A set of candidate gestures was proposed for 12 common TV control tasks. We hope the results will benefit practitioners interested in designing gesture-based interfaces for the next generation of home entertainment systems and smart living room environments. We equally hope that the observations of this study will also raise questions on the usability of gestural interfaces for TV control, at least for some abstract tasks. Future work will investigate users' preferences for remotes vs. free-hand gestures.

6. ACKNOWLEDGMENTS

This paper was supported by the project "Progress and development through post-doctoral research and innovation in engineering and applied sciences- PRiDE - Contract no. POSDRU/89/1.5/S/57083", project co-funded from European Social Fund through Sectorial Operational Program Human Resources 2007-2013.

7. REFERENCES

[1] Ashbrook, D., Starner, T. 2010. MAGIC: a motion gesture design tool. In Proc. of CHI '10. ACM, New York, NY, USA, 2159-2168

[2] Bailly, G., Vo, D.B., Lecolinet, E., Guiard, Y. 2011. Gesture-aware remote controls: guidelines and interaction technique. In Proc. of ICMI '11. ACM, New York, NY, USA, 263-270

[3] Bernhaupt, R., Obrist, M., Weiss, A., Beck, E., Tscheligi, M. 2008. Trends in the living room and beyond: results from ethnographic studies using creative and playful probing. Computers in Entertainment. 6 (1), Art 5 (May 2008)

[4] Freeman, W.T., Weissman, C.D. 1995. Television Control by Hand Gestures. In: Proc. of IEEE Int. Workshop on Automatic Face and Gesture Recognition, Zurich

[5] Kohler, M. 1998. Special topics of gesture recognition applied in intelligent home environments. In: GW' 1997. LNCS, vol. 1471, 285-296. Springer, Heidelberg

[6] Kray, C., Nesbitt, D., Dawson, J., Rohs, M. 2010. User-defined gestures for connecting mobile phones, public displays, and tabletops. In Proc. of MobileHCI '10. ACM, New York, NY, USA, 239-248

[7] Kühnel, C., Westermann, T., Hemmert, F., Kratz, S., Müller, A., Möller, S. 2011. I'm home: Defining and evaluating a gesture set for smart-home control. International Journal of Human-Computer Studies, 69 (11), 693-704

[8] Lessiter, J., Freeman, J., Davis, R., Dumbreck, A. 2003. Helping Viewers Press the Right Buttons: Generating Intuitive Labels for Digital Terrestrial TV remote controls. Psychnology, 1(3), 355-377

[9] Norman, D.A. 2010 Natural user interfaces are not natural. Interactions 17, 3 (May 2010), 6-10

[10] Rehm, M., Bee, N., André, E. 2008. Wave like an Egyptian: accelerometer based gesture recognition for culture specific interactions. BCS-HCI'08, British Computer Society, 13-22

[11] Ruiz, J., Li, Y., Lank, E. 2011. User-defined motion gestures for mobile interaction. CHI '11. ACM, 197-206

[12] Vatavu, R.D., Pentiuc, S.G. 2008. Interactive Coffee Tables: Interfacing TV within an Intuitive, Fun and Shared Experience. In Proc. of EUROITV'08, Springer-Verlag, Berlin, Heidelberg, 183-187

[13] Vatavu, R.D. 2011. Point & Click Mediated Interactions for Large Home Entertainment Displays, Multimedia Tools and Applications, Springer, doi:10.1007/s11042-010-0698-5

[14] Wobbrock, J.O., Morris, M.R., Wilson, A.D. 2009. User-defined gestures for surface computing. In Proc. of CHI '09. ACM, New York, NY, USA, 1083-1092

[15] Smart TV by LG, http://www.lg.com/us/tv-audio-video/discoverlgtvs/smarttv/index.jsp

Comparison of Two Text Entry Methods on Interactive TV

Adam J. Sporka Ondřej Poláček Pavel Slavík

Faculty of Electrical Engineering, Czech Technical University in Prague,

Karlovo nám. 13, 12135 Praha 2, Czech Republic

{sporkaa, polacond, slavik}@fel.cvut.cz

ABSTRACT

This paper describes a study with 18 participants on two text input methods for use with interactive television, The Numpad Typer (TNT) and TwiceTap. Both methods were designed for use with a common infra-red remote control. Each character is entered using two keystrokes. After one hour and forty minutes of practice, split into 5 sessions, the participants were able to type faster than 9 words per minute. While the performance of both methods was similar, the TwiceTap required a smaller number of keystrokes per character, was less prone to errors, and was found to be more comfortable by the participants. Over time, the use of frequent *n*-grams in TwiceTap was reinforced while the use of infrequent *n*-grams was suppressed.

Categories and Subject Descriptors

H.5.2 Information Interfaces and Presentation: User Interfaces—Input devices and strategies

General Terms

Design, Experimentation, Human Factors, Measurement, Performance.

Keywords

Text input, Interactive Digital TV, performance, remote control, user study.

1. INTRODUCTION

Interactive Digital Television (IDTV) is a growing technology in terms of the number of users. According to the Leichtmann Research Group, 30% of all households in the US in 2011 have at least one TV set connected to the Internet. The IDTV enhances the television with interactive content, including web browsing and searching, social media, e-mail, etc. One of the vital parts of these applications is the text input.

There has been an extensive research in this context on various devices and methods of interaction, such as use of gestures, tablets, or mobile telephones. However, commercially available products are still significantly more expensive than the infra-red remote controls used commonly today. In this paper a user study of two text input methods with 18 users is presented. The methods can be operated using a common infra-red TV remote.

EuroITV'12, July 4–6, 2012, Berlin, Germany.

2. RELATED WORK

Probably the most popular text entry method on keyboards with a limited number of keys is Multi-tap, commonly available on mobile telephones. Each key is assigned three or four characters. To enter a character the user has to repeatedly press the same key until the desired character appears. The cursor advances upon a predefined timeout (user's inactivity). According to MacKenzie et al. [9] the KSPC measure (keystrokes per character) is 2.2. There were several modifications reducing the KSPC: Less-Tap (=1.6) [12], where the sequence of letters on the keyboard was no longer alphabetical or LetterWise (=1.15) [10] where the layout of keys dynamically shifted according to the previously entered text, which was on the expense of the clarity of the layout.

The T9 by Tegic Communications [4] is another method intended for use on mobile telephones that can be implemented on a TV remote control. The alphabet is subdivided in the same way as in the Multi-tap. The user selects the desired characters by pressing the corresponding keys and after a sequence of keys is entered, the word is disambiguated using a dictionary. Even though T9 is almost optimal in terms of the KSPC (close to 1), many users find it too difficult to use [5].

One of the first works on a text input method for the IDTV was *The Numpad Typer* (TNT) by Immargson [7] (see Figure 1). All characters can be entered by two keystrokes on a 9-button keypad on the remote control. The characters are laid out in two levels of 3×3 grids. The first keystroke selects a group. The second keystroke selects a character in that group. The speed of the keyboard varied from 9.3 up to 17.7 WPM (words per minute). A similar entry method, in which characters are entered by two keystrokes, was patented by Kandogan et al. [8]. This method is designed for a 12-button keypad commonly used on mobile phones. There is no evaluation of this method. Twist&Tap [1] is designed for text input on a TV using a remote control with accelerometers. Vega-Oliveros et al. [13] explored a multimodal text input on IDTV combining speech input, Multi-tap, and a virtual keyboard.

Iatrino et al. [6] compared Multi-tap and a virtual QWERTY keyboard for text input on IDTV. The virtual QWERTY keyboard was a grid reminiscent of a standard PC keyboard. Arrow keys were used to select a character. The "OK" button confirmed the selection. In a study with 36 participants, Multi-tap outperformed the virtual QWERTY in terms of speed and user satisfaction. However, a similar study by Geleijnse et al. [3] indicated that the virtual QWERTY keyboard is preferred by the users. The type rate of the virtual QWERTY, Multi-tap, and T9 are similar.

3. Introducing TwiceTap

We developed a novel method of text input called TwiceTap. The method is similar to the work by Kandogan [8]. It has the same layout of characters as the Multi-tap. Each character is entered by a sequence of two keystrokes. See Figure 2 for an example: To enter the letter `t`, first the key `t-u-v` is pressed to select this group. The individual letters of this group are then

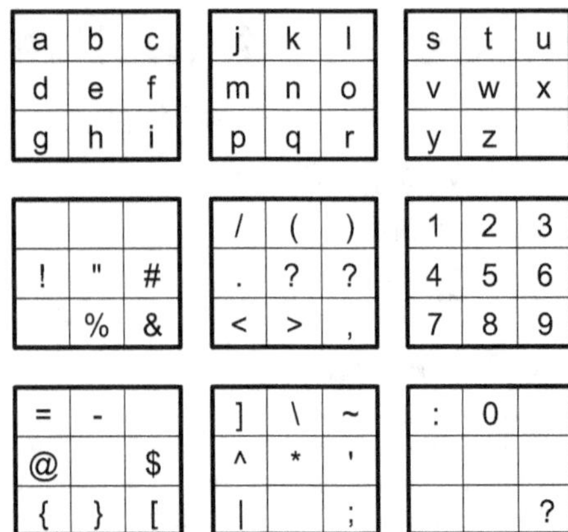

Figure 1: Layout of TNT

.,?!	abc	def
ghi	jkl	mno
pqrs	tuv	wxyz
147<	?	+-*?

a.

th	t	the
ut	u	us
ve	v	ver

b.

Figure 2: Layout of TwiceTap – a) as shown before the first keystroke, b) as shown after the user hit key tuv

displayed on separate keys in the same column (Figure 2b). The letter is entered upon pressing the corresponding key. Unlike the Kandogan's method, the blank spaces were filled with the two most frequent *n*-grams for each letter. The term *n*-gram further refers to a sequence of *n* characters. The *n*-grams with the length equal to one, two and three character are being called unigrams, bigrams and trigrams respectively. There is a fixed set of *n*-grams which were selected using a corpus containing 50,000 most common English words. The space, as the most common character in English, can be entered using one keystroke only.

4. Experiment

In this paper we perform a comparative study of the TwiceTap method and the TNT method [7]. Both methods can be implemented using low-cost off-the-shelf hardware.

The Multi-tap method would seem like a logical choice of the baseline, however we decided against it. We indeed intended to compare our method with a baseline that is established in the HCI literature but at the same time we were seeking for an input method that was unknown to the users so that the skills to use each method would be balanced (the TNT met these requirements) while the Multi-tap is a method that is known and used by a majority of the mobile telephone users.

18 participants (10 men, 8 female, mean age = 22.7, SD = 2.49) took part in a controlled experiment. They were not familiar with text input on IDTV, however they were all experienced mobile phone users. (3 of them used T9 on their phone; 2 people used a QWERTY keyboard. The rest of the group used Multi-tap.)

We expected KSPC=2 for the TNT, while for the TwiceTap the KSPC should be less than 2 because of the single-keystroke space and the availability of *n*-grams. A 9-button keypad is required for the TNT and a 12-button keypad for the TwiceTap. Both methods use a reference chart on the TV screen. The TNT occupies about 4 times more space on the screen than the TwiceTap.

The experiment was organized in 10 sessions per participant. Each session lasted 20 minutes. The participants were allowed to complete up to two sessions per day and used each method for 5 consecutive sessions. The order of the methods was counterbalanced in order to minimize any learning effects.

A 40" Samsung LCD TV was used for both methods. A remote control shipped with the Motorola VIP1003 set-top box was used. The participants were seated on a sofa about 2 meters in front of the screen. We implemented an audio feedback after pressing a key for both methods. Their task was to copy given phrases from Mackenzie's set for evaluating text entry methods [11] as fast and accurate as possible. The use of *n*-grams in TwiceTap was suggested but not enforced. A high-pitched click sounds upon the first keystroke, a low-pitched click upon the second, and a buzzer sound upon an error. The participants had to correct any typing errors before the application let them continue. At the end of the experiment the participants were asked to complete a post-test questionnaire to evaluate both methods. The participants were given a reasonable financial compensation for their time at the end of the experiment.

Our group of 18 users entered total of 118,811 characters of text. 57,048 characters (48%) were typed using TNT, 61,763 characters (52%) using the TwiceTap. The participans' type rate, measured in WPM, improved with each session for both methods, eventually reaching 9.1 WPM (TNT) and 9.6 WPM (TwiceTap). The type rate did not reach a plateau by Session 5, which indicates that the type rate reachable by the experts would be even higher. (See Fig. 3)

KSPC for TwiceTap was lower than for the TNT. In Session 5 it was about 2.25 for TNT (the users had to press at least two keys per one character on average) and 1.75 for TwiceTap. A paired *t*-test of the KSPC values measured for individual participants on the Session 5 confirmed that the difference was significant: $t(28.58) = 16.3$; $p < 0.001$. The TwiceTap method therefore requires less amount of physical effort than the TNT. The values somewhat decreased over the course of the entire data collection, by 5% (TNT) and 8% (TwiceTap) due to the decreasing number of errors. The error rate has been calculated as the number of backspaces pressed by the participants per amount of the correctly entered characters. Its development over the sessions is shown in Fig. 4. The mean error rate over all participants of the TNT and TwiceTap was about 5.1% and 3.8% in the last session. A paired *t*-test indicates that the TwiceTap was significantly less prone to errors than the TNT ($t(26.55) = 2.31$; $p < 0.05$).

A number of words could be written in different ways that were mutually exclusive. E.g. the word `"version"` could be entered using any of these sequences of elements: `(ve)(r)(s)(i)(on)`, `(v)(er)(s)(i)(on)`, or even `(ver)(s)(i)(on)`. We defined a usage of an element (an *n*-gram available at the keyboard or an individual character) as the ratio [number of occurrences in text] / [number of actual instances of use]. A KSPC of less than 2 in case of the TwiceTap implies that the participants made a systematic use of the *n*-grams. The Fig. 5 shows the combined usage of the most and the least frequent *n*-grams, compared against the usage of all *n*-grams. The overall strategy of the *n*-gram use has apparently shifted over the sessions: While the use of the most frequent *n*-grams was reinforced (60% in Session 1; 70% in Session 5), the usage of the least frequent *n*-grams dropped by 12% (for bottom 10 *n*-grams) resp. 23% (bottom 5).

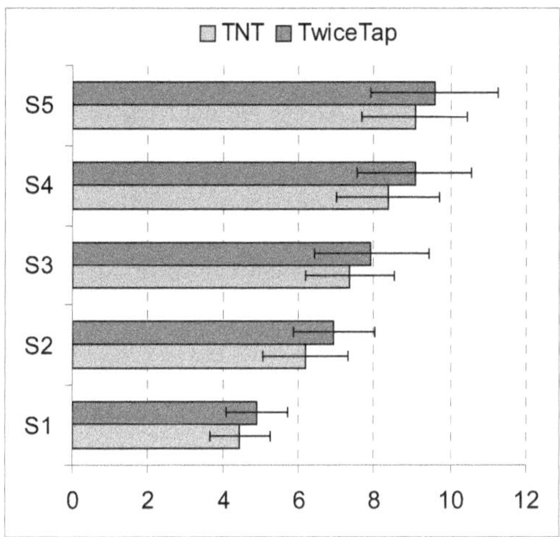

Figure 3: WPM by method and session. Mean values over all participants with SD in error bars for sessions S1 through S5

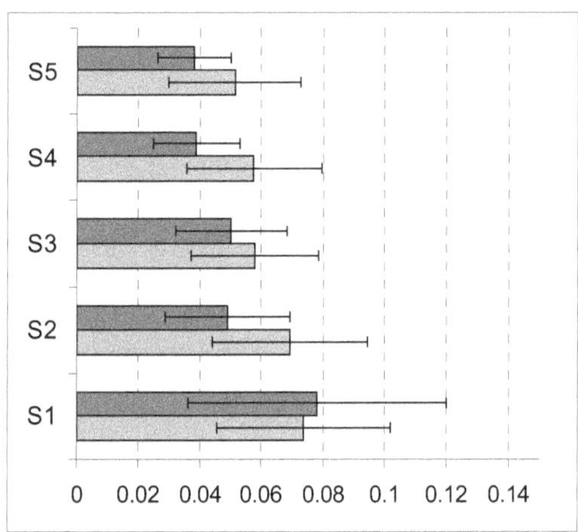

Figure 4: Error rate by method and session. Mean values over all participants with SD in error bars

This suggests that people recognized that the utility of the *n*-grams varied with their frequency, and learned to use those that were most frequent while giving up on those that did not notably contribute to the overall performance. (In the last session, there were total of 1322 opportunities to use one of the top 5 *n*-grams while only 193 opportunities to use one of the bottom 5 *n*-grams.)

The average time per character (the time needed to type a single letter of the English alphabet) was 1325 ms using TNT and 1633 ms using TwiceTap in the last session. A paired *t*-test of the times per character for TNT and TwiceTap shows that the TwiceTap was significantly slower in terms of typing individual letters ($t(49.44) = -4.396$; $p < 0.001$). This may be explained by the fact that the users did not see the whole TwiceTap layout at once. The final position of the letter was revealed only after the pressing of the first button, thus forcing the users to perform the visual search twice. The letter distribution in the test phrases roughly observed the common letter distribution in the English language, which in decreasing frequency was: `e`, `o`, `a`, `t`, `s`, ..., `v`, `j`, `x`, `q`, `z`. It could be expected that the more frequent a letter, the shorter time per character. The actual time per character, however, did not observe this expectation, as shown in Figure 6. Detailed

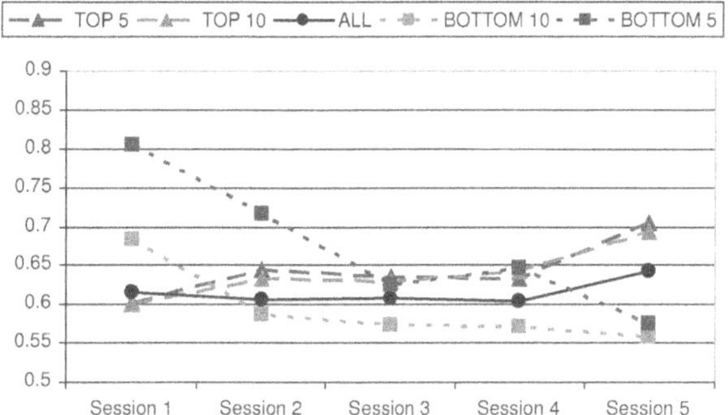

Figure 5: Usage of the most and least used *n*-grams by all users per session.

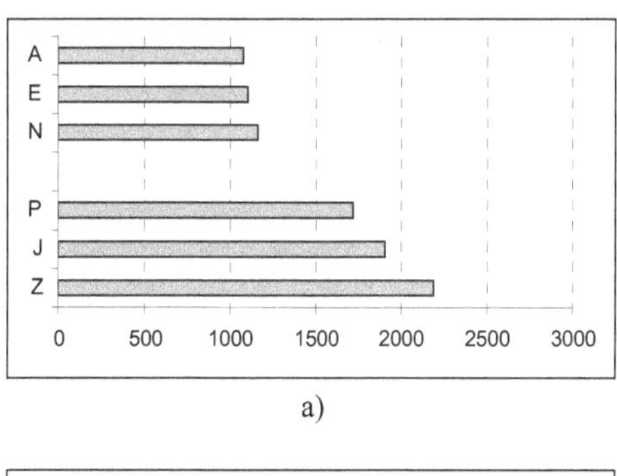

a)

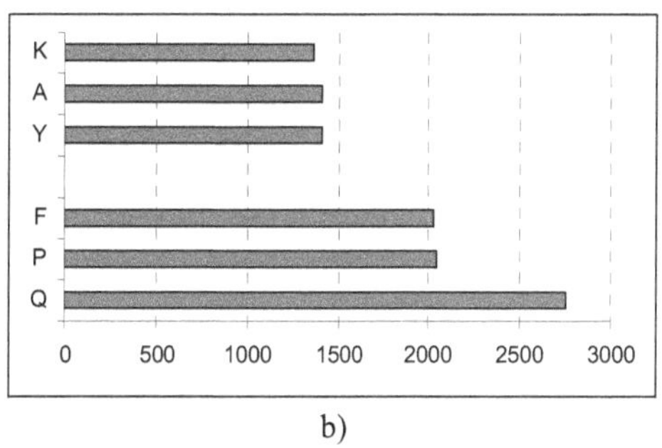

b)

Figure 6: Average time in milliseconds (horiz. axis) to enter individual characters (vert. axis). Three "fastest" and three "slowest letters" reported. a) TNT, b) TwiceTap

analysis suggested that the further apart the keys needed to enter a particular letter, the longer time per character.

For subjective evaluation we asked participants to complete a post-test and System Usability Scale (SUS; [2]) questionnaires for each method. They were also asked to make comments on both methods. The SUS was designed to quantify subjective usability of a product to allow comparisons. The item no. 5 ("I found the various functions in this system were well integrated") was not used in our case. A paired *t*-test was conducted to compare the SUS scores. There was a significant difference in the SUS scores for TNT (Mean=56.0, SD=20.8) and TwiceTap (Mean=70.7, SD=11.8); $t(17) = -2{:}58$; $p < 0.05$: Usability of TwiceTap method was therefore perceived significantly better than TNT. In the post-test questionnaire, five questions for each method were used to quantify other aspects such as fatigue and comparison with mobile phone text input methods. Five-scale Likert items were used (1="certainly no" ... 5="certainly yes") for the following questions as listed in Table 1. Median scores are displayed in Table 2. A paired Wilcox test showed that scores for the TwiceTap in Q1 and Q3 were significantly better than for the

TNT. We also asked the participants which method is better to use. 11 participants preferred TwiceTap, 4 preferred TNT, 3 expressed no preference.

Participants commented mostly on the keyboard layout and visual presentation of both methods. The two keys in the TNT were too far apart for some frequent letters (4 participants gave such a feedback), which caused pain in the thumb (1 participant) and a need to check position of fingers on remote control often (1). The TwiceTap layout is similar to Multi-tap, which was found positive (7) or negative (1). The *n*-grams in the TwiceTap were found useful (8). The TNT displayed too many letters on the screen (2), however visibility of all letters was appreciated (4); "I can search for the next letter while entering current letter" (2). The special characters such as apostrophe or exclamation mark were difficult to find on the TNT (2), but easy on the TwiceTap (1).

Table 1: Likert items for the post-test **questionnaire**

Q1	This method was comfortable to use.
Q2	This method was physically demanding.
Q3	This method is better than Multi-tap.
Q4	This method is better than T9.
Q5	I would like to use this method on my TV.

Table 2: Median scores for post-test **questionnaire and p-value for each item. Lines set in bold report a significant difference.**

Question	TNT	TwiceTap	p
Q1	**3.5**	**4**	**0.0113**
Q2	2.5	2	0.0617
Q3	**2**	**3.5**	**0.0077**
Q4	3	3	0.2885
Q5	3	4	0.1324

5. Conclusion

This paper presented a comparative study of two text input methods for Interactive Digital Television—the TNT and the TwiceTap. While the TNT supports only letter-by-letter typing, the TwiceTap also allows typing of the most frequent *n*-grams. The letters in both methods are entered by two keystrokes on a common TV remote control. Users preferred the TwiceTap, mostly because of its similarity to Multi-tap and the availability of *n*-grams. Even though the type rate was similar for both methods (TNT: 9.1 WPM; TwiceTap: 9.6 WPM), the keystrokes-per-character rate was significantly lower for the TwiceTap, indicating that this method required less physical effort. The TwiceTap was less prone to errors than the TNT.

Over the course of the experiment the participants adapted their own *n*-gram use strategy. By the end of the experiment they increased the use of the *n*-grams that were most frequent in the English language while ceasing the use of the less frequent ones, preferring to enter individual characters instead.

The TwiceTap keyboard can be further optimized by reordering the characters on each key according to the layout of Less-Tap [12]. Other interesting extension would be a dynamic *n*-gram suggestion based on the already written text.

Acknowledgements. This research has been supported by the MSMT research program MSM6840770014 and VERITAS, an Integrated Project (IP) within the 7th Framework Programme, Theme FP7-ICT-2009.7.2, Accessible and Assistive ICT.

6. REFERENCES

[1] Aoki, R., Maeda, A., Watanabe, T., Kobayashi, M., and Abe, M. Twist&tap: text entry for TV remotes using easy-to-learn wrist motion and key operation. Consumer Electronics, IEEE Transactions on 56(1) (February 2010), 161–168.

[2] Brooke, J. SUS: A Quick and Dirty Usability Scale. In Usability Evaluation in Industry, P. Jordan, B. Thomas, I. McClelland, and B. Weerdmeester, Eds. Taylor & Francis, London, 1996, 189–194.

[3] Geleijnse, G., Aliakseyeu, D., and Sarroukh, E. Comparing text entry methods for interactive television applications. In Proc. of EuroITV '09, ACM (New York, NY, USA, 2009), 145–148.

[4] Grover, D. L., King, M. T., and Kushler, C. A. Reduced keyboard disambiguating computer. Tech. rep., US Patent Publication, 1998.

[5] Gutowitz, H. Barriers to adoption of dictionary-based text-entry methods: a field study. In Proc. of the 2003 EACL Workshop on Language Modeling for Text Entry Methods, TextEntry '03, Association for Comp. Linguistics (Stroudsburg, PA, USA, 2003), 33–41.

[6] Iatrino, A., and Modeo, S. Text editing in digital terrestrial television: a comparison of three interfaces. In Proceedings of EuroITV'06 (Athens, Greece, 2006).

[7] Ingmarsson, M., Dinka, D., and Zhai, S. Tnt: a numeric keypad based text input method. In Proc. of the SIGCHI conference on Human factors in comp. sys., CHI '04, ACM (New York, NY, USA, 2004), 639–646.

[8] Kandogan, E., and Zhai, S. Two-key input per character text entry apparatus and method. Tech. rep., US Patent, 2004.

[9] MacKenzie, I. KSPC (Keystrokes per Character) as a Characteristic of Text Entry Techniques. In Human Computer Interaction with Mobile Devices, F. Paterno, Ed., vol. 2411 of Lecture Notes in Computer Science. Springer Berlin / Heidelberg, 2002, 405–416.

[10] MacKenzie, I. S., Kober, H., Smith, D., Jones, T., and Skepner, E. Letterwise: prefix-based disambiguation for mobile text input. In Proceedings of the 14th annual ACM symposium on User interface software and technology, UIST '01, ACM (New York, NY, USA, 2001), 111–120.

[11] MacKenzie, I. S., and Soukoreff, R. W. Phrase sets for evaluating text entry techniques. In CHI '03 ext. abstr. on Human factors in computing systems, CHI EA '03, ACM (New York, NY, USA, 2003), 754–755.

[12] Pavlovych, A., and Stürzlinger, W. Less-tap: A fast and easy-to-learn text input technique for phones. In Graphics Interface (2003), 97–104.

[13] Vega-Oliveros, D. A., Pedrosa, D. d. C., Pimentel, M. d. G. C., and de Mattos Fortes, R. P. An approach based on multiple text input modes for interactive digital tv applications. In Proceedings of the 28th ACM International Conference on Design of Communication, SIGDOC '10, ACM, New York, NY, USA, 2010, 191–198.

A Gesture Recognition Algorithm for Vision-based Unicursal Gesture Interfaces

Ryosuke Aoki, Masayuki Ihara, Toru Kobayashi, Minoru Kobayashi
NTT Cyber Solutions Laboratories
NTT Corporation
1-1 Hikarinooka Yokosuka-shi Kanagawa
Japan
{lastname.firstname}@lab.ntt.co.jp

Bessie Chan
University of British Columbia
2329 West Mall
Vancouver, B.C., Canada V6T 1Z4
besschan@interchange.ubc.ca

Shingo Kagami
Graduate School of Information Sciences, Tohoku University
6-6-01 Aramaki Aza Aoba,
Aoba-ku, Sendai 980-8579
Japan
swk@ic.is.tohoku.ac.jp

ABSTRACT

Network communication services such as Skype® or gaming applications using interactive TVs with cameras and IR-sensors have begun to appear. Vision-based recognition systems using hand gestures to control applications such as TV menus are gaining popularity in the market. It is crucial that the Vision-based Gesture Interface (VGI) is simple, easily used and allows users to comfortably command TVs. For simple and easy to use VGIs, we focus on vision-based unicursal gesture interfaces (VUGI) which recognizes both the shape of a unicursal figure drawn by a user and orientation indicated by the start position of the unicursal figure. In this paper, we propose Support Vector Machines (SVM) using Distance to Border (DtB) features to increase the number of recognized unicursal gestures. We evaluated the performance of the proposed algorithm in an experiment and the mean recognition rate of eight unicursal figures was 94.6% and the maximum recognition processing time was 9.56ms.

Categories and Subject Descriptors

H5.2 [**Information interfaces and presentation**]: User Interfaces – Input Devices and Strategies, Interaction Styles.

Keywords

VUGI, SVM, DtB, Gesture, Menu Selection.

1. INTRODUCTION

In the advent of interactive TVs with cameras and IR-sensors in the market, vision-based gesture interfaces (VGIs) are rapidly increasing in place of remote controllers with operating keys that allow users to control TVs. User-friendly VGIs where ordinary daily-life gestures are used to command external devices have been proposed [1-2]. As television content, service and functions increase, the number of gestures should also increase. However, gesture algorithms are complex and it is physically and mentally burdening for users to remember and perform the gestures to control a TV when there is a large number of gestures. We focus on vision-based unicursal gesture interface (VUGI) [3], which recognizes both the shape of a unicursal figure drawn by a user and orientation based on the start position of the unicursal figure. Unicursal figures include ones shown in Fig. 1, which users are familiar with in daily life. The combination of the shape and orientation decreases the total number of unicursal figures users have to remember for this interface. In [3], only two unicursal figures, the circle and the unicursal line were recognized. Therefore, an algorithm to recognize more gestures is desired. Furthermore, this algorithm needs to be able to recognize the gestures in real-time with high accuracy to control a TV.

To meet these requirements, we propose Support Vector Machines (SVM) using Distance to Border (DtB) features to classify the shape of unicursal figures as a recognition algorithm suitable for VUGI. We evaluate the performance and confirm the feasibility of this algorithm with eight kinds of unicursal figures. We assume that unicursal figures are drawn by user's forefinger. But subjects in this experiment draw unicursal figures with a laser light pointer with a white LED to evaluate the proposed algorithm easily and accurately. The results showed a mean recognition rate of 94.6% and a maximum recognition processing time of 9.56ms.

2. APPLICATION

Users can select items on TV menus by a menu selection method using VUGI shown in Fig. 2(A). VUGI-tags are assigned to each item when the user points his/her forefinger at a TV with a camera. Each VUGI-tag shows a different unicursal figure and the start position of the figure. In the VUGI-tags displayed in Fig. 2(B), the starting position is the point where the width of the line outlining the unicursal figure is thickest. Users can select an item of interest by drawing the unicursal figure on the tag assigned to the item. Users can navigate to another menu or scroll in a menu by drawing a unicursal line. This menu selection is applicable to menus such as Electronic Program Guide (EPG), On Demand TV and E-commerce. With the recognition system introduced, the increase of the number of unicursal gestures that can be recognized increases the number of selectable items on a menu or switchable menus. In a demonstration of Fig. 2, we used a laser light pointer with a white LED to recognize the position of hand. In the future, we will plan to use user's forefinger instead of this pointer.

3. RELATED WORK

The large number of proposed recognition algorithms is classified broadly into two popular gesture recognition algorithms: Hidden Markov Models (HMM) and Support Vector Machines (SVM). We clarify the requirements of a gesture recognition algorithm that can conveniently control TV menus with these methods.

EuroITV'12, July 4–6, 2012, Berlin, Germany.

HMMs can be used as a recognition algorithm for hand gestures [1] in which commands are based on the shape or a path trajectory by a hand or finger. HMMs can be especially useful for recognizing time-varying patterns such as those found in speech [4-5] and hand gestures [6]. For example, Elmezain et al. [7] uses HMMs to recognize Arabic numbers. Lee and Kim [8] use HMMs to recognize dynamic gestures for browsing PowerPoint® presentation slides and handles undefined patterns. However, HMMs are not suitable for real-time applications such as TV menu selection due to delayed response to user operation caused by the complexity of HMMs.

Meanwhile, SVMs are also used as a recognition algorithm for hand gestures [9]. Various ways of representing the gestures are simplified to feature vectors for SVM recognition. For example, the feature vectors of [9] are extracted from three images of a hand shape taken by three different cameras from different angles. However, we assume that TVs with one camera will soon become common in the future for communication services such as Skype® or for gaming with Kinect®. Willems et al. [10] tested various feature sets such as length, angle of bounding box, and distance between first and last point on multi-stroke gestures. However, a large number of features will require more computational power during recognition.

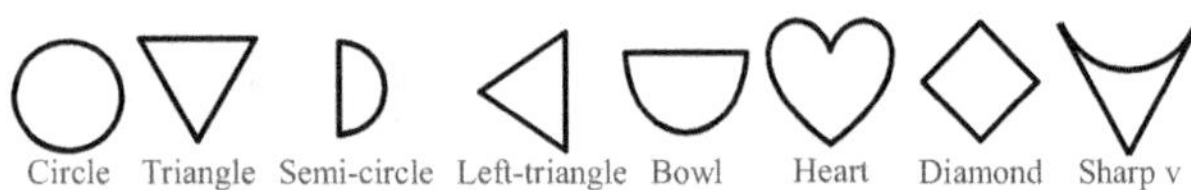

Figure. 1: Eight kinds of unicursal figures

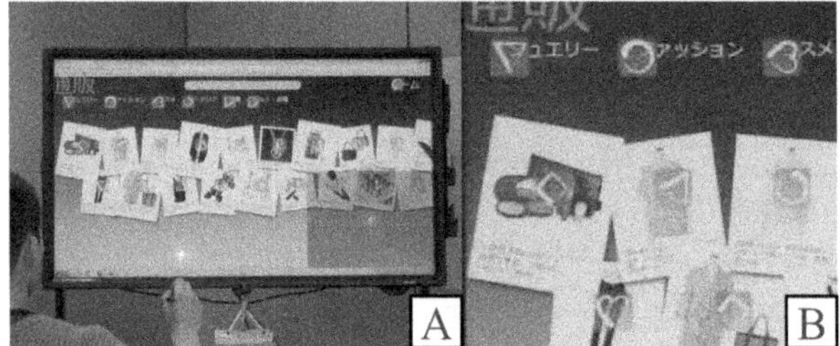

Figure 2: Menu selection using VUGI during a Demo

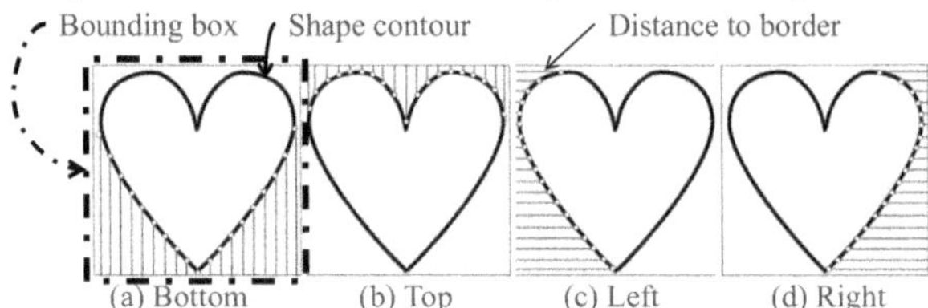

Figure 3: Menu selection using VUGI

4. SVM using DtB for VUGI

As mentioned in the applications and related works sections, it is preferable to increase the number of gestures for TV menu item selection and to have fast response times for user operations in real time applications such as TV menu navigation. To meet these conditions, we propose SVMs using the Distance to Border (DtB) feature as a unicursal gesture recognition algorithm for VUGI.

Lafuente-Arroyo et al. [11] introduces the concept of DtB as feature vectors for SVM classification of traffic signs. Their implementation of SVM is trained with DtB feature vectors extracted from binarized images. Concretely, DtBs are the distances from the edge of the shape to the shape's bounding-box, which is the minimum rectangle area including the shape. For example, Fig. 3(a) shows the vertical distance starting from the bottom border of the bounding box and ending at the edge of the heart. For each shape, there are four borders: the top, bottom, left and right borders. An SVM model can be constructed or trained for each border and used to classify the shapes. Thus, SVMs using DtBs is useful when recognizing external contours of unicursal figures.

There are four points worth noting for applying SVMs using DtB to VUGIs. Firstly, to create a command in VUGI, users draw simple unicursal figures whose shapes have different external contours such as figures shown in Fig. 1. Therefore, SVM using DtB is useful to recognize unicursal figures. To measure DtB in VUGI, the image of a unicursal figure drawn by users needs to be obtained. The VUGI extracts finger position data at each time frame from when a gesture starts and to when the gesture ends. A single image for calculating the DtB vectors for recognition is obtained by gathering position data. In comparison, [11] use precompiled photos of traffic signs and has not been tested in real time.

[11] employs a system in which calculations for all four DtB vectors are required for classification in their voting system. That is, to classify for example a circle, the top, bottom, left and right border vectors need to be calculated and compared with another shape. In comparison, our VUGI with SVM using DtB implements a multi-tiered system in which the gesture is classified using one SVM model at a time. As a result, the recognition system may not need to calculate all of the DtB vectors for classification.

Finally, VUGI can adapt to and recognize user varied unicursal gestures. Lafuente-Arroyo et al.'s [11] classification system was able to effectively classify three traffic sign shapes: circles, triangles and squares. However, traffic signs have mainly fixed, uniform shapes. In comparision, unicursal figures drawn by users do not have the same contour even if each user draws the same unicursal figure. The difference in each drawn figure is large especially if it is drawn in the air. Therefore, we need to design a system with a good combination of unicursal figures such that the users can learn and draw them easily. Furthermore, the recognition system should be able to recognize each figure accurately.

5. SYSTEM DESIGN

The system need to detect the position of hand or finger by which unicursal figures are drawn or of a tool such as a laser pen light instead of hand or finger. To get hand position via simple and easy image processing, either a forefinger attached to a white LED [3] or a laser light pointer with white LED is used.

Gesture segmentation of VUGI is detected by a circle zone shown in Fig. 4. We call the circle zone detection zone [3]. A gesture starts when the forefinger leaves the detection zone and ends when the forefinger returns to the detection zone. After the gesture ends, gesture recognition begins.

To make an image of a unicursal figure with hand position data in real-time, position data from the current point and the next position data point are connected continuously with a straight line. However, there is often a small gap between the start and end points of the gesture caused by using detection zones. It is possible for this gap to produce vectors that can confuse and decrease the accuracy of the SVM model due to insignificant vectors. Therefore, start and end points with a straight line are connected to make closed polygon such as unicursal figures. The contours of the gesture are found and the contour with the largest area is used to crop the image via region of interest (ROI). By selecting the contour with the greatest area, we can allow for variation in how the gestures are drawn. Gestures are sometimes drawn with extra smaller loops that are also detected by the contour finding method. The image is then resized into a 100x100 pixel image for feature extraction.

To distinguish each gesture shown in Fig. 1, which the users were able to learn and draw in a prior test, two SVM models trained with DtBs is used. The first SVM model classifies gestures given the Distance to Border vectors from the top. Gestures with similar top DtB vectors such as the upside-down triangle and the bowl in which both have flat tops are grouped together into the same class. Of the eight proposed unicursal gestures, all top DtB vectors are distinct with the exception of the upside-down triangle and bowl. Thus in total, we have 7 different classes for the top DtB SVM model. The second SVM model classifies gestures given the DtB border vectors from the bottom of the gestures. As with the first SVM model, similar bottom DtB vectors are grouped together. In total, there are 4 classes for the bottom SVM model (Fig. 5). Both SVM models were trained with a radial basis function (RBF) kernel. The top and bottom SVMs were trained with approximately 2000 preprocessed images of the eight gestures drawn by the researcher. After training the two SVMs with their respective training data, both are combined to classify the gestures.

6. USER STUDY

6.1 Experimental design

We conducted an experiment to evaluate the performance and feasibility of the proposed algorithm in two aspects which were accuracy of gesture recognition and real-time process. A within-subject experiment was conducted. The independent variable was the type of gesture such as circle, upside down triangle, right semicircle, left triangle, bowl, heart, sharp v, diamond in Fig. 1. The dependent variable was the recognition rate and recognition time. Ten subjects were recruited with an age range from 24 to 33. The subjects consisted of 3 females and 7 males. All subjects were right handed and held the LED pen with their right hands.

6.2 Apparatus

The experiment was conducted on a 2.66GHz Core 2 duo processor PC with Windows 7. User input was displayed on 640x480 pixel screen in a 20.1 inch LCD monitor. The gesture input devices include the Mitsubishi LED light and Grasshopper Point Grey camera (GRAS-03K2M-C). The frame rate of the camera was 60fps. Illuminance from an overhead lighting in the experimental environment was 940lux.

6.3 Procedure

Subjects got to view gestures on the screen in a 640 x 480 pixel box on the LCD screen. The display was a saturated grey camera image. The program detected and traced bright light sources, so we used a LED light for our experiment. A black line from the previously detected point to the currently detect point was drawn whenever the LED light was in the camera's field of view. Camera and position of the 640x480 screen displaying the gesture input were placed next to each other. That is, the camera was placed next to the LCD monitor, and the screen displaying the

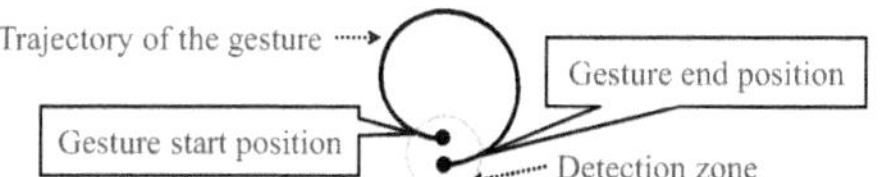

Figure 4: Unicursal gesture detection by detection zone

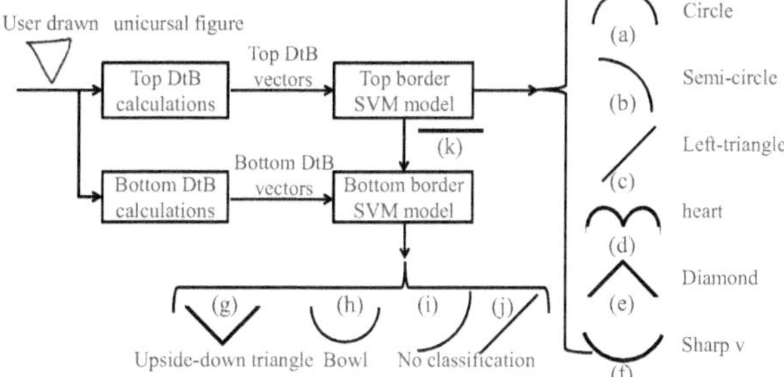

Figure 5: Recognition flow chart

gesture trace was placed directly to the left of the camera. A reference of each gesture was provided.

Prior to the actual test set, subjects were to perform a practice test set to get familiar with the equipment and gestures. The goal of each practice session was to correctly input each gesture 10 times or input each gesture a minimum of 20 times. The program indicated to the subject whether or not they drew the gesture correctly. During the actual test, each subject performed seven test sets where one test set consisted of inputting each gesture, 10 times each. The order in which the gestures were drawn was random. Users input each gesture continuously, starting from the initial position in the middle of the screen. Gestures were complete when the user returned to the start position. All of the gestures were recognized during real time and recognition rate was calculated after completion of all 7 test sets. Recognition time it takes to draw each gesture was also recorded.

6.4 Result

Table 1 shows the average accuracy rate and the average error rate of gesture recognition per gesture across all subjects. NULL means that the recognition system could not classify the gesture as any of the eight gestures shown in Fig. 1. The average recognition rate for all eight unicursal gestures was 94.6%. Meanwhile, the average of the recognition time was 8.33 ms for all gestures. The maximum recognition time amongst all gestures was 9.56ms. Thus, we have confirmed that the proposed algorithm is feasible.

Fig. 6(a) shows user ratings on how easy it was to draw each unicursal figure. Fig. 6(a) shows that it was difficult for subjects to draw semi-circle, bowl and sharp v. All of these figures in common consist of curved and straight edges. In comparison, the circle and triangle gestures which only contain either curves or straight edges require less effort and time to draw. Fig. 6(b) shows how easy it was to remember each figure. Evaluation of the bowl and sharp v was average and the evaluation for other figures was easy.

Subjects were also asked when they started to feel physically tired. The answers differed from subject to subject, but no subjects answered that they started to feel tired before the trial 3. Since one trial asked for 100 gesture inputs, all the subjects were able to input gestures as many as 200 times before they feel physical burden. Correlation between subject's fatigue and recognition rate was not observed.

7. DISCUSSION

The unicursal gesture with the lowest recognition rate was the bowl which was 84.3%. Table 1 shows that most of the recognition errors were due to classifying the bowl as a triangle instead. In the case of drawing figures in the air, the combination of a curve (Fig. 5 (h)) and sharp edge (Fig. 5(g)) is not preferred since the DtB vectors are similar and overlap each other. Thus, as with the semi-circle and right triangle, the bowl and triangle combinations should be avoided. During the experiments, many subjects commented on how difficult it was to draw the bowl's curve and ended up drawing the bowl similar to the triangle.

The unicursal gesture with the second lowest recognition rate among the eight unicursal gestures was the semi-circle which was 88.3%. In Table 1, recognition error for the semi-circle was due to gesture being classified as NULL. This error can be traced in Table 1 due to misclassification of the curve indicated in Fig. 5(b). The top border SVM first misclassifies the curve indicated in Fig. 5(b) as the straight indicated in Fig. 5(k), then the bottom border SVM detects the class in Fig. 5(i) which is NULL in Table 1. Thus, not only the combination of a curve in Fig. 5(h) and a sharp edge in Fig. 5(g) but also the combination of a curve in Fig. 5(b) and a straight edge in Fig. 5(k) should be avoided.

Due to the lowest recognition rate and poorest user rating, it is recommended that bowl shaped unicursal gestures are avoided. It would be possible to improve the proposed algorithm, but it is also important to take into account the choice of gestures when the system is designed. Since the recognition rate of the semi-circle was low but the recognition rate of the left-triangle was high, the right triangle should be used instead of the semi-circle. Although user ratings for the sharp v were poor in Fig. 6, the recognition rate of the figure was high. In the case of menu selection described in the applications section, we suggest that this figure is assigned to an item in which users select less frequently.

8. CONCLUSION

To control menus on interactive TVs with cameras conveniently, we focus on VUGI which recognize unicursal figures drawn in the air. We proposed SVMs using DtBs, which classifies a unicursal figure based on its external contour, as a unicursal recognition algorithm for VUGI. We conducted an experiment to evaluate the performance of the proposed algorithm and confirmed that the algorithm is feasible. In the future, we plan to evaluate the orientation recognition rate of unicursal gestures and a menu selection method using VUGI. Also, we will study how to recognize the position of user's forefinger. More detailed evaluation in various experimental conditions should also be carried out.

Table 1: Average recognition rate per gesture

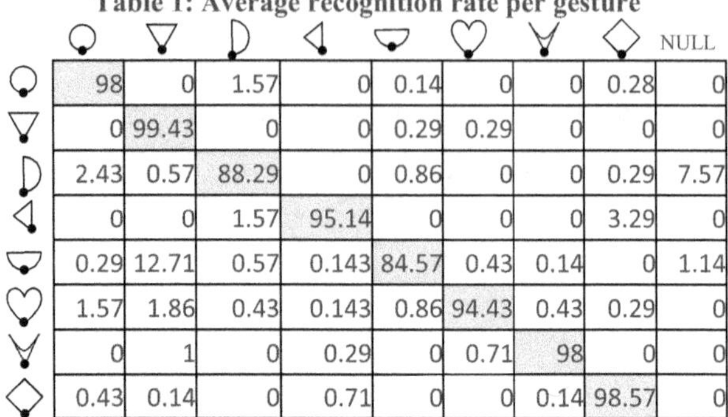

									NULL
	98	0	1.57	0	0.14	0	0	0.28	0
	0	99.43	0	0	0.29	0.29	0	0	0
	2.43	0.57	88.29	0	0.86	0	0	0.29	7.57
	0	0	1.57	95.14	0	0	0	3.29	0
	0.29	12.71	0.57	0.143	84.57	0.43	0.14	0	1.14
	1.57	1.86	0.43	0.143	0.86	94.43	0.43	0.29	0
	0	1	0	0.29	0	0.71	98	0	0
	0.43	0.14	0	0.71	0	0	0.14	98.57	0

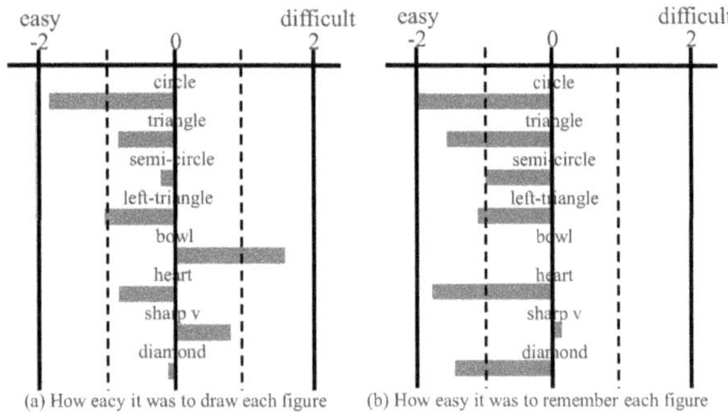

(a) How eacy it was to draw each figure (b) How easy it was to remember each figure

Figure 6: Questionnaires

9. REFERENCES

[1] Wu, Y., and Huang, T.S. 1999. Vision based gesture recognition: a review. In Proceedings of GW'99. London, UK, 103-115.

[2] Baudel, T., and Beaudouin-Lafon, M. 1993. Charade: remote control of objects using free-hand gestures. Communications of the ACM – Special issue on computer augmented environment: back to the real world. 36, 7, New York, USA, 28-35.

[3] Aoki, R., Karatsu, Y., Ihara, M., Maeda, A., Kobayashi, M. and Kagami, S. 2011. Gesture Identification Based on Zone Entry and Axis Crossing. In Proceeding of HCII'11. Florida, USA, 6762, 194-203.

[4] Ganapathiraju, A., Hamaker, J. and Picone, J. 2000. Hybrid SVM/HMM architectures for speech recognition. In Proceeding of International Conference on Spoken Language Processing, Beijing, China, 4, 504-507.

[5] Rabinera, L.R. 1989. Tutorial on Hidden Markov Models and Selected Applications in Speech Recognition. In Proceeding of the IEEE, 77, 2.

[6] Yang, J. and Xu, Y. 1994. Hidden markov model for gesture recognition. In Tech. Rep. CMU-RI-TR-94-10, Robotics Institute, Carnegie Mellon University, May.

[7] Elmezain, M., Al-Hamadi, A., Appenrodt, J. and Michaelis, B. 2008. A Hidden Markov Model-based continuous gesture recognition system for hand motion trajectory. In Proceeding of ICPR'08. 1-4.

[8] Lee H. and Kim, J.H. 1999. An HMM-based threshold model approach for gesture recognition. IEEETrans. Pattern Analysis and Machine Intelligence. 21, 10, 961-973.

[9] Chen, Y. and Tseng, K. 2007. Multiple-angle Hand Gesture Recognition by Fusing SVM Classifiers. In Proceeding of IEEE International Conference on Automation Science and Engineering. CASE'07. 527-530, 22-25 Sept.

[10] Willems, D., Niels, R., Gerven, M., and Vuurpijl. L. 2009. Iconic and multi-stroke gesture recognition. ACM Journal Pattern Recognition. 42, 12 (December 2009), 3303-3312.

[11] Lafuente-Arroyo, S., Gil-Jimenez, P., Maldonado-Bascon, R., Lopez-Ferreras, F. and Maldonado-Bascon, S. 2005. Traffic sign shape classification evaluation I: SVM using distance to borders. In Proceeding of IEEE Conference on Intelligent Vehicles Symposium, 557- 562, 6-8 June.

The Double Platform Structure of the Audiovisual Media Industry in Flanders

Valérie-Anne Bleyen
IBBT-Vrije Universiteit Brussel
Pleinlaan 9
1050 Brussels, Belgium
+32 2 629 16 65
vbleyen@vub.ac.be

Pieter Ballon
IBBT-Vrije Universiteit Brussel
Pleinlaan 9
1050 Brussels, Belgium
+32 2 629 16 65
pballon@vub.ac.be

ABSTRACT
In this article, the principles of multi-sided platform theory and value network analysis are used in order to give a detailed picture of the financing and revenue sharing models present in the audiovisual media industry in Flanders. By means of expert interviews, we verify whether the counter-logics of platform ecosystems and the double marginalisation effect of double platform markets pertain to the Flemish audiovisual media industry.

Categories and Subject Descriptors
H.5.0 [**Information Systems**]: Information Interface and Presentation – *Multimedia Information Systems.*

General Terms
Management, Economics, Performance, Design.

Keywords
Digital television, multi-sided platform theory, value network analysis, revenue sharing models, double marginalisation.

1. INTRODUCTION
The Flemish audiovisual media market is in flux. Both the market structure and the associated revenue models in the TV industry have been rather straightforward during the lengthy monopoly era of public broadcasters up to the 1970s and the initial 'comfortable' public-private duopolies in many European markets in the 1980s and 1990s [5]. Public broadcasters were financed through subsidies (be it a licence fee or direct government grant) and, occasionally, advertising income. Private broadcasters, for their part, mostly relied on advertising and sponsoring revenues. Since the beginning of the 21st century, however, a number of trends associated with digitisation have fundamentally changed the media industry, affecting both its structure and the associated revenue flows.

Firstly, in the analogue world, there was a direct relationship between broadcasters and consumers, and distributors were merely transporters of the electronic signals. The 'industry structure' was routinely characterised as a typical two-sided market, in which broadcasters operate as platforms that intermediate between advertisers and consumers, and that control the revenue flows between the different stakeholders [6]. In the digital era, telecommunication companies enter broadcasting markets, Internet companies enter telecommunication markets, cable companies enter both broadcasting and telecommunication markets, and so on. While these companies need to work together in order to create and capture value, and are thus part of the same 'value network', they at the same time (threaten to) disconnect broadcasters from consumers and advertisers. This leads to the inter-firm dynamic of 'co-opetition', i.e. the collaboration between firms with incomplete congruence of interests, and often in the presence of (market) power asymmetries [4]. While the outcome of this reconfiguration of the value network is not yet clear, it is evident that established audiovisual media provision models are under strong pressure, which leads to great uncertainty and causes clashes and conflicts between all sorts of companies that are repositioning themselves and are trying to reshape the value network according to their interests.

Secondly, the 21st century reveals a dramatic shift in consumer habits: user generated content, social media, interactivity, asynchronous service provision and mobile technologies are phenomena that force broadcasters to look beyond linear activities to connect with the audience in non-linear ways. At the same time, they offer opportunities for always-on service provisioning, a range of interactive and on-demand services, social TV offerings and so on. The question thus arises which actors in the value network are able to strengthen their customer relationship and take advantage of the new revenue streams.

A third trend affecting the broadcasting industry is that the TV advertising market is in relative decline. The digitisation of TV, which makes it possible for consumers to watch content in more flexible ways, e.g. in terms of recording TV content very easily, consuming 'micro-snacks' of content and/or skipping advertisements, has a negative impact on broadcasters' revenues from traditional ads. Accordingly, linear TV advertising suffered slow growth in the last decade. As a result, revenues from consumers[1] have started to outgrow advertising as the main form of funding for TV in several developed markets [13]. Whereas the yearly average growth rate of consumers' TV spend in the EU between 2005 and 2009 was 6.8%, the yearly average growth rate of TV ad spend amounted to -2.1% [14]. In Belgium, consumers' TV expenditure grew from € 614.5 million in 2005 to € 948.1 million in 2009 (i.e. a 54% rise, unadjusted for inflation), while TV advertising (in terms of gross value, and not taking into account any discounts) grew from € 980 million to around € 1,240 over the same period (i.e. a 26% rise, unadjusted for inflation). Finally, besides TV, online advertising is also rapidly gaining

[1] These include expenses by consumers for any kind of subscription to TV (basic, premium), as well as on-demand services provided by the distribution platform (cable, satellite, IPTV, DTT, telephone). Expenses related to the purchase or renting of the Set-Top-Box (STB) are excluded in these figures [Lange, personal e-mail request].

ground vis-à-vis TV advertising, especially in the most advanced media markets [15].

To explore the new configuration of the traditional two-sided audiovisual media industry that results from these trends – i.e. new patterns of co-opetition, changes in the customer relationship and the search for new revenues, this article focuses on the region of Flanders, Belgium. The Flemish media landscape faces a range of uncertainties as well as conflicts, brought about by the increasing complexity of the industry's structure, and its corresponding financing model. A prior research report [5, p.11] confirms this: *"At present, it is not clear at all where certain money flows go to or which revenue sharing models are applied. This creates suspicion [...] Moreover, for consumers, it seems not more than fair that they know what they are paying distributors and broadcasters for".*

Hence, the authors conclude that one of the most crucial challenges for the audiovisual industry is to achieve more transparency about the market structure and the breakdown and allocation of different revenue streams in the value network. This article aims to respond precisely to that challenge.

In the next section, we first frame the developments in the Flemish media industry within a theoretical overview of two-sided markets, and characterise digital media as a double multi-sided platform market. We then proceed by a detailed exploration of the value network of the audiovisual media industry in Flanders in Section 3.[2] At the end of Section 3, we devote specific attention to conflicts and bottlenecks that arise as a result of the counter-logics of platform ecosystems and the double marginalisation effect in the audiovisual value network. Section 4 concludes.

In order to validate all the revenue flows between actors in the double multi-sided platform market, we conducted expert interviews with the relevant stakeholders in the Flemish audiovisual media industry. The interviews took place with general and business directors and managers from 16 Flemish broadcasters, distributors, production houses and collective rights agencies, from October to December 2011.[3] They were semi-structured and open-ended, to allow for in-depth exploration and prioritisation of topics and issues by the experts. First, a list of topics was defined, which we further adapted and refined in line with the field of expertise of the interviewee.

2. THE AUDIOVISUAL MEDIA INDUSTRY: FROM A SINGLE TWO-SIDED TO A DOUBLE MULTI-SIDED PLATFORM MARKET

In this section, we address the theoretical concepts of two- and multi-sided platform markets. These will provide the framework for our value network analysis of the Flemish audiovisual media industry.

Two-sided network literature refers to platforms as mediating entities between agents that operate on different sides of the market, and whose utility is affected by participation and usage on the opposite side(s) (see e.g. [1,11,18]). Much of this literature offers a rather 'static' analysis in the sense that it concentrates on price equilibrium and allocative efficiency for a single platform or in relation to competition between two platforms. Recently, more 'dynamic' analyses have been conducted, that focus on two-sided platform strategies and business models, the evolution of platform boundaries, and cross-layer inter-platform interactions (see e.g. [3,8,9]).

As pointed out by [20], two-sided platforms arise in situations in which there are externalities and in which transaction costs prevent the two sides from solving this externality directly. In fact, the platform thus serves as a way of solving the externality in a way that minimises transaction costs. Well-known characteristics of two-sided markets include in first place the indirect network effects between the two sides of the platform, which in turn affect pricing and other strategies. Indeed, many two-sided platforms charge prices at one side below marginal cost (in some cases even negative) to enhance profit maximisation. This leads to the following formal definition of two-sided markets [19]: *"A market is two-sided if the platform can affect the volume of transactions by charging more to one side of the market and reducing the price paid by the other side by an equal amount; in other words, the price structure matters, and platforms must design it so as to bring both sides on board".*

Both in traditional media industries (e.g. advertising-supported media) and new media industries (e.g. software platforms and web portals), two-sided platforms prevail. The audiovisual media, especially private media, typically operate as a two-sided market, in which broadcasters function as platforms intermediating between advertisers on the one hand, and consumers of content on the other hand. The specificity in this market lies in the fact that advertisers derive a positive utility from the participation of as many consumers as possible to the broadcaster's platform, while for consumers mostly negative effects are associated with being exposed to advertising messages. This is one of the reasons why broadcasters usually let one side of the market (i.e. advertisers) cross-subsidise the participation of the other side of the market (i.e. consumers). This persistent cross-subsidisation, combined with the cross-platform (indirect) network effects described above, lead to the fact that broadcasters cannot maximise profits in each single market, but need to carefully consider the effect of pricing decisions at one side of the platform on the other side. It may explain why slower growth in advertising revenues leads to pressures to increase income from consumers. Also, it implies that broadcasters need to treat complementary businesses (such as advertisers) as clients rather than as traditional supply chain partners, and are thus incentivised to ensure healthy margins and sustainable ecosystems for these businesses.

Because of the trends mentioned in the introduction to this article, this basic structural and financial model of operation of the audiovisual media industry is now changing and becoming increasingly complex. First of all, the introduction of digital TV exploded the number of TV channels, provided the digital TV distributors with a direct consumer interface in the form of the Electronic Programme Guide (EPG), and made a range of interactive and on-demand services and new revenue streams possible. This has enabled TV distributors, whose business models up to that point had resembled that of utility providers, to start playing a two-sided platform role themselves, i.e. between 3rd party service providers (broadcasters) and consumers. As a result, there are now two platforms that interact with each other and serve as customer/supplier for each other, namely distributors and broadcasters. The actors who manage these two platforms can be named 'first' and 'second' layer platform providers, indicating how close they are to the end-users, or at which side they serve end-users. In case of the digital TV industry, the first layer platform provider is the distributor. Second layer platform

[2] It has to be noted that we excluded over-the-top players from our analysis, as this lies outside the scope of the study. Over-the-top players such as Netflix and Hulu are engaged in online delivery of video and audio without the Internet Service Provider being involved in the control of the content itself.

[3] A detailed list of the interviewees is available from the authors upon request.

providers, i.e. broadcasters, deal with first layer counterparts on one side and sell ads to advertisers on the other side. In some sense, they utilise first layer platform providers as a kind of distribution channel. They also monetise attention and information of end-users by selling ad space [10].

It is clear that such 'double platformisation' or 'layered platformisation' unavoidably leads to strong tensions between both types of platform 'wannabes', i.e. the distributors and the broadcasters, even if they are at the same time collaborators within the media value chain. This leads to a new set of strategic incentives, which are directly at odds with the platform logic explained above [25]. First of all, in this constellation, the distributor – and not the TV channels – sets viewer prices. This may be problematic since the distributor does not take into account the fact that high end-user prices have a negative impact on advertising revenue for the TV channels through reducing the size of the audiences. In other words, price coordination in this double two-sided market is difficult, as control over end-user prices for consumers is with the distributor [12].

To be more precise, in case of double 'layered' platforms, the 'double marginalisation' effect is prominent, which refers to the fact that any price increase by one platform constitutes a tax on the other platform, leads to price increases by the adjoining platform and thus to less consumption, and diminishes total welfare. It is well-known from economic literature that under these circumstances, the individual platforms will have strong incentives to vertically control prices of the adjoining platform, i.e. by vertically integrating activities (and thereby entering the other platform's territory), by commoditising or even destroying the adjoining platform's business, or by other means of influencing and coordinating prices. This article argues that many of the conflicts about roles and revenue streams between distributors and broadcasters in the audiovisual industry in Flanders today can be explained by the counter-logics of platform ecosystems versus double marginalisation, and will analyse whether such an interpretation of current developments is in line with the empirical evidence.

Furthermore, the audiovisual media industry is evolving from a two-sided towards a multi-sided market, with amongst others the introduction of independent production houses that produce content for various broadcasters' and distributors' platforms. These, then, in a sense may become a third side of the (double) platform market, and need to be included in new roles in the value network. The reconfiguration of revenue streams, and the associated conflicts, will thus also extend to the independent producers and rights holders. The end result is a set of highly complex and dynamic interdependencies that are very hard, if not impossible, to model formally. Figure 1 gives a high-level image of the double multi-sided platforms structure in the Flemish audiovisual media industry. Concerning the stakeholders in Figure 1, VRT, VMMa and group VT4/VIJFtv are the three major broadcasters (BCs) in Flanders, who together account for more than 80% of the viewers market. Telenet (DVB-C) and Belgacom (DVB-IPTV), for their part, are the two major distributors in Flanders, with a market share of 80%, resp. 15%. The remainder of the distributors' market is split between Mobistar, TV Vlaanderen (both DVB-S) and Norkring (DVB-T).

What this article will aspire to, is to provide a first empirical exploration of such new structures and interdependencies as depicted in Figure 1. In this exploration, the level of control executed by the platform beyond its own borders will thus be of crucial importance.

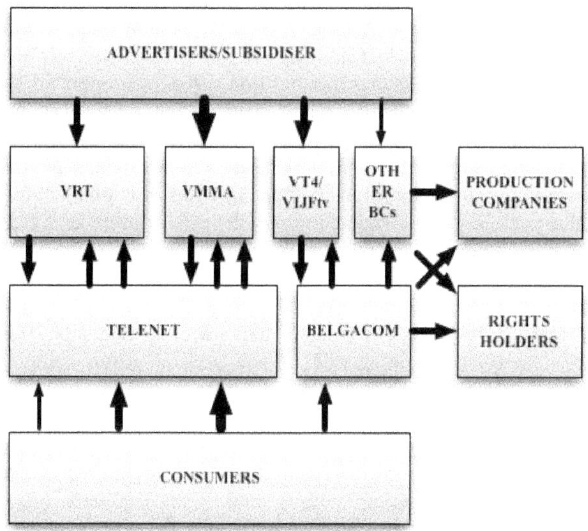

Figure 1. The audiovisual media industry in Flanders: a double multi-sided platform market

While an in-depth treatment of such models and their consequences for the Flemish audiovisual industry requires much more analysis, the following section will gather and present some first evidence on the structure and revenue flows that arise in this double multi-sided platform set-up. As the firms operating in audiovisual markets usually treat such information as strictly confidential, and since these markets have a long and complex history in which public and private stakeholders, regulation and private contracts, and various contextual factors are intertwined, this is not a straightforward exercise. This is to our knowledge the first academic article that has attempted to provide a full overview of the roles and revenue flows in such an audiovisual double platform market in Europe, and to analyse the current conflicts and bottlenecks in such a market in the light of the double marginalisation effect.

We will use the method of value network analysis to visualise and analyse the data on the Flemish audiovisual media industry's structure and finances. Value network analysis is a generally accepted technique from organisation science, of which the roots go back to [17]'s value chains, in combination with other schools of Industrial Organisation and Resource Based Management (e.g. [16, 22]). Essentially, a value network illustrates how companies, within the boundaries of their industrial activities, mobilise their resources in relation to surrounding actors. Typically, three building blocks can be discerned in a value network, namely business actors, business roles and business relationships.

1. Business actors are physical persons or corporations that create economic value through the mobilisation of (in)tangible resources (being financial, intellectual or social capital) within a business value network.
2. Business roles are logical groups of business activities that are fulfilled by one or more actors. Concretely, business actors provide value to and/or derive value from the business roles they play.[4]

[4] In case two roles are performed by the same actor, the money streams will flow internally between these two roles within this company, and these will be only visible to internal accounting. Conversely, when two roles are performed by different actors, the money streams will flow externally between two actors [21].

3. Business relationships can be the contractually defined exchange of products or services, financial payments or other resources [2].

The level of industrial concentration in a value network is determined by the extent to which certain actors perform more or less roles. Vertical integration implies the ownership by one actor of different vertical roles within the same industrial field. Horizontal integration, for its part, implies the ownership of multiple roles that are situated in parallel industrial environments. A high degree of vertical integration of one actor will have a direct impact on the feasible cooperation for all other actors involved in the value network. As integration becomes stronger, the interactions with other actors will lower in intensity. When very few roles are integrated in one and the same actor (i.e. modularisation of the ecosystem), more cooperation will be required between different actors [21].

Summing up, this section hypothesised that many of the current conflicts on roles and revenue streams between distributors, broadcasters, production houses and rights holders in the audiovisual industry in Flanders today can be explained by the counter-logics of multi-sided platform ecosystems versus double marginalisation. The following section will provide a first empirical exploration of such new structures and the associated revenue flows that currently shape the Flemish market.

3. VALUE NETWORK ANALYSIS: RELATIONS AND FINANCING MODELS

Over the past decade, there has been a dramatic shift in the production, distribution and consumption of media content. The model in which content is linked to a single platform and a specific revenue stream no longer stands. As a result, boundaries between sectors are increasingly becoming blurred. In subsection 3.1, we investigate the intertwining of business relations in the sector by presenting and explaining our value network.[5] In subsection 3.2, we give a qualitative discussion of the bottlenecks in the sector that transpired from the interviews with the stakeholders and are a result of the 'double marginalisation' effect that the shifting media ecosystem brings about. In doing so, this section focuses on the region of Flanders, Belgium.

3.1 The Value Network: A Double Multi-sided Platform Market

As was already mentioned in Section 2, there are now actually two platforms that interact with each other and serve as customer/supplier for each other in the audiovisual market, namely distributors and broadcasters; see Figure 2.

Starting with broadcasters, they aggregate the content that they produce internally and acquire externally. Subsequently, they transfer the content to the distributor, and receive a retransmission fee for this. Conversely, many broadcasters have to pay a carriage fee to the distributor for transportation and distribution of their signal. Broadcasters also receive income from the distributor for Video-On-Demand (VOD) transactions[6] and for 'red button' interactive applications, games, SMS votes and so-called astro services (i.e. 'late night' services related to astrology and so on). Another revenue stream related to the broadcaster comes from ad brokers that pay for advertising space and/or teleshopping. On the topic of rights clearing, broadcasters pay collective rights agencies for the authors represented by them (primary rights)[7] and for advertising.

Turning to our second platform operator in Figure 2, the distributor delivers the TV bundle to the end-user on a subscription base. In this subscription, possibly, a provision for author rights is included.[8] This author rights fee is paid partly to collective rights agencies for cable/satellite rights (CISAC[9]-members). The remainder of the author rights fee that the distributor passes on to the end-user – goes to the broadcasters ('retransmission fee') and AGICOA[10] (Non-CISAC).

An important remark should be made concerning the cable rights the distributor pays to the collective rights agencies. In 2006, Telenet filed a lawsuit against all Belgian collective rights agencies at the court of first instance of Mechelen. Basically, Telenet claims that, unlike for public broadcasters, it is not obliged to pay an author rights fee to the collective rights agencies for the retransmission of channels via direct injection (e.g. for VTM or RTL, channels that cannot be watched via the ether or satellite). However, the collective rights agencies oppose and say that, in case of direct injection, besides the primary rights collected from the broadcasters, distributors have to pay secondary rights. On April 12, 2011, Telenet won the lawsuit. The collective rights agencies entered an appeal but there has not yet been a decision. However, should the court decide in favour of the collective rights agencies, then Telenet will be obliged to pay cable rights to the collective rights agencies for private broadcasters, possibly also with retroactive effect.

Revisiting Figure 2, the distributor also pays a sum to the collective rights agency for VOD and for home copy.[11] Additional income for the distributor comes from the carriage fee it charges the broadcaster for transportation and distribution of their signal.

On the end-users' side, the distributor generates income from VOD transactions (on a pay-per-view or subscription base), from the rental/sale of the Set-Top-Box (STB) and from red button, games, SMS votes and astro services.

---

[5] Note that the government is also an actor, as its business roles include regulation and subsidies. However, studying government policy is outside the scope of this study, which is why we excluded this stakeholder from our value network analysis.

[6] The supply of Video-On-Demand (VOD) encompasses movies and series for which the operators have entered into agreements both with local and international producers and distributors. On top of this, an interactive library of catch-up TV and archival programmes has been developed in cooperation with almost each Flemish broadcaster. In this article, VOD is defined as all on-demand transactions related to TV series and movies, via subscription or pay-per-view.

[7] Alternatively, broadcasters may also pay the rights owners directly.

[8] In Flanders, only Telenet charges this author rights fee. The amount varies per postal code but comes down to on average of € 2.6 (excl. VAT) per month per subscriber.

[9] The International Confederation of Authors and Composers Societies' (CISAC) main activities include – amongst others – the strengthening and development of the international network of copyright societies. As of June 2011, CISAC numbers 232 authors' societies from 121 countries. For more information, please consult <www.cisac.org>.

[10] The Association of International Collective Management of Audiovisual Works (AGICOA) is a collective rights agency that represents Belgian and international producers for the collection of author and related rights.

[11] Depending on the STB's storage capacity, Auvibel collects home copyrights from the distributor amounting to € 3.30 and € 10.75 per STB.

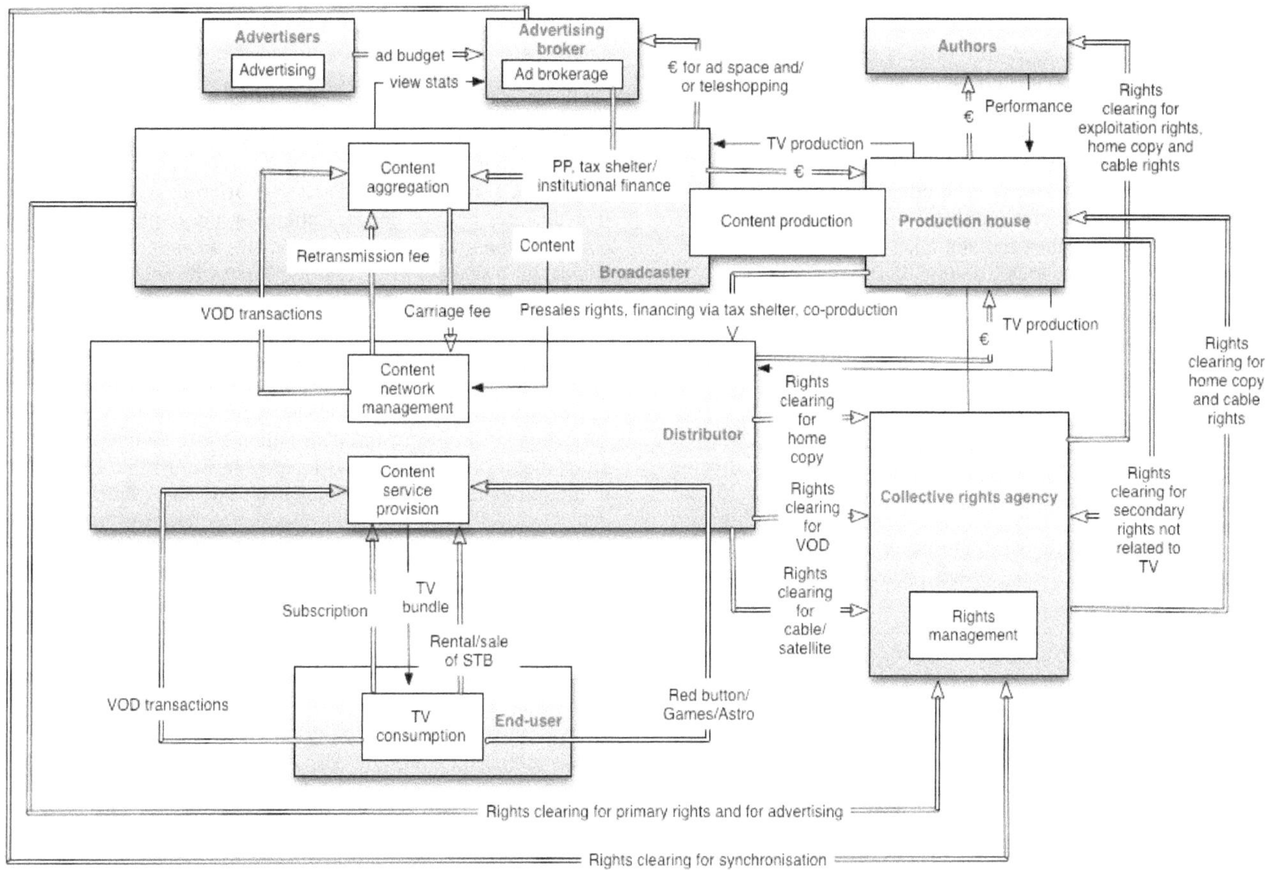

Figure 2. The value network for production and distribution of TV in Flanders

As was already mentioned in the previous section, independent production houses, as well as rights holders and collective rights agencies, constitute in a way the third side of the (double) platform market, and are being included in new roles in the value network.

Starting with the creation of content at the top right corner of Figure 2, an author always enters into contract with a producer, with the usual reservation for collective rights. This means that, in general, we are talking about an 'All Rights Included' contract with a provision for collective rights. Authors receive money for their performances from the production house and they receive money from the collective rights agency for the reproduction and for the public performance of their works, for home copy and for cable rights.[12]

The producer then proceeds along the value network with the contract and the content produced. Albeit not visible in Figure 2, broadcasters as well as distributors can have content that is produced internally. For instance, the VRT produces a lot of local programmes internally. Note furthermore that, on many occasions, broadcasters or distributors finance a production via a presales right, via tax shelter or via co-production. Besides, ad brokers can also finance a production via product placement, via tax shelter or via institutional finance. Depending on the individual contracts with respect to financing, the production house will deliver the content to the broadcaster (only for broadcasting purposes) or distributor (e.g. VOD). Concerning VOD, it is the distributor who refunds the broadcaster (for broadcast related programs produced by the broadcaster) or the production house for income received from VOD. On the topic of rights clearing, production houses have to pay collective rights agencies for secondary rights not related to TV. To illustrate, say newspaper X sells a collection of DVDs of the TV serial Y at discounted rate. In that case, the production company has to pay the collective rights agency for synchronisation and duplication. On the other hand, production companies receive a copyright fee for home copy and cable rights from the collective rights agency (that has been collected upfront from the importers/manufacturers of private copy devices and the cable operator respectively).

Our final two actors in Figure 2 are the advertisers and the ad broker. Advertisers pay an advertising budget to the ad broker. The ad broker subsequently develops a campaign and buys ad space with the broadcaster. On the topic of rights clearing, note that the ad broker pays the collective rights agency for rights clearing for synchronisation.

Summing up, Figure 2 provides a full overview of the actors, roles and revenue flows in the audiovisual market in Flanders. Its additional complexity compared to the 'simple' two-sided model in the analogue world reveals that the transition from a single two-sided to a double multi-sided market platform brings about

[12] Note that the collective rights agency does not always intervene for the collection of exploitation rights. This depends on the stipulations in the contract; it is possible that primary rights are settled directly between the rights holder and the licensee.

structural shifts in the media ecosystem. This relates to some extent to the roles the stakeholders play, and to a large extent to the revenue streams in-between each other. Naturally, such a shift to a double multi-sided platform market brings about various conflicts between the stakeholders involved.

The following subsection provides a discussion of the main bottlenecks in the sector that transpired from the interviews with the stakeholders, which all point directly to the tension between the need to cooperate and foster each other's growth (referring to the platform ecosystem logic) and the attempt to gain control over the major revenue streams and diminish competing platforms' revenues (referring to the double marginalisation effect).

3.2 Structural Conflicts Between Stakeholders

In this section we discuss the sharing of revenues between stakeholders, as well as the associated conflicts and tensions, per revenue stream, starting with retransmission and carriage fees (3.2.1), Video-On-Demand (3.2.2), advertising (3.2.3), delayed viewing and its impact on the two previous revenue streams (3.2.4), revenue streams related to the production sector (3.2.5) and author and related rights (3.2.6), respectively. Subsection 3.2.7 concludes and highlights where the double layered platform model that we observed earlier may cause a double marginalisation effect.

3.2.1 Retransmission and Carriage Fees

One of the main disputes between broadcasters and distributors relates to the payment of retransmission fees from distributors to broadcasters for the distribution of their content on the one hand, and the payment of transport and distribution costs by broadcasters to distributors in exchange for carriage on their networks on the other hand. These two transactions can take many forms, depending on the broadcaster and distributor involved in the commercial agreement. Indeed, as pointed out by [24], the contractual agreements between the different broadcasters and distributors are complex to such an extent that no univocal logic can be distilled from it. For instance, the public broadcaster VRT, which enjoys a must-carry status, does not pay a carriage fee while receiving (albeit not *strictu sensu*) a retransmission fee.[13] The latter is subject of an agreement to exploit the rights of the VRT through retransmission.

Next to the VRT, there are a number of foreign channels (including the Dutch public broadcasting channels, which also enjoy must-carry status) that receive compensation from distributors in exchange for the distribution of their content and do not have to pay a carriage fee either. This also applies to the Flemish regional channels (must-carry status) and to a number of foreign private broadcasters. The latter have no interest in being retransmitted by distributors in Belgium and, hence, they do not see the point of paying transport and distribution costs. Private broadcasters targeting the Flemish market pay a carriage fee and receive a retransmission fee. For broadcasters operating niche channels, there are two options; (i) they pay transport and distribution costs without receiving a retransmission fee; or (ii) they receive a fee per subscriber. These categories apply to the retransmission through cable. For xDSL, other arrangements have been made by the respective distributor that does not charge transport and distribution costs; neither does it charge consumers for author rights [5]. Note furthermore that, in some contractual agreements, commitments are included to spend high advertising budgets on certain channels [24].

Many broadcasters increasingly object the current agreements concerning retransmission and carriage fees – especially with the cable operator. First of all, the level of retransmission fees paid is disputed. Concretely, the broadcasters offering generalist channels feel that the current compensation for the exploitation of their content is too low given the traffic their content generates. Related to this, they also complain that the current compensations paid by the cable operator are in fact paid by the consumer who is directly charged for author rights contributions by Telenet. Consecutively, these are redistributed to broadcasters. Allegedly, the cable operator is thus not paying any compensation for transmission itself. A second point of discussion relates to the imbalance in collection of transport and distribution costs. Some broadcasters argue that it is unfair that they are paying while other broadcasters in the same market are not compelled to do so. A third problem is that it is unclear on the basis of which criteria the transport and distribution costs and retransmission fee are determined. This creates the perception among broadcasters that criteria are discriminatory in nature. The distributors counter by arguing broadcasters' compensation is already well above the European average. In any case, the balance between the transport and distribution costs and retransmission fee for most broadcasters in Flanders being carried by the cable operator is positive.

In order to resolve tensions, Telenet has proposed a new matrix model in which retransmission fees would be calculated on the basis of the CIM audience market shares (age 4+/all day) of all the channels of a given broadcaster. Some broadcasters argue that, although they might have preferred a different model, it is at least based on objective criteria that are applied in a non-discriminatory fashion (i.e. the same model for all players in the market). However, most broadcasters are highly sceptical about the matrix model, stating it is still not adequately compensating them for the distribution of their content. Another point of criticism is that it makes no sense to base retransmission fees on one criterion only, being the CIM audience market shares (age 4+/all day). Other criteria such as the reach of target groups (i.e. audience market shares in a given age or demographic group), local employment, investments in domestic content, etc. could be taken into account in order to come to a more balanced assessment of what a broadcaster's channels are worth. The biggest broadcasters were not particularly in favour of the model, arguing that they negotiate under which conditions their signal is retransmitted referring – among others – to Article 1, §1 of the Belgian Auteurswet. Telenet, for its part, has stressed the first point being the implementation of a matrix model that is objective and non-discriminatory. In addition, the cable operator also asserted that under the matrix model all local broadcasters would receive more money than they did in previous contracts. The starting idea of the cable operator is to rebalance current payments (generated on the basis of their consumers' author rights provisions) from foreign to local broadcasters in favour of the latter [5]. However, several broadcasters are convinced that the foreign broadcasters will take their current retransmission fee as the starting point of new negotiations with the cable operator. In this respect, it remains to be seen whether this rebalancing of retransmission fees will work out in practice.

Niche channel Acht's general manager foresees another risk related the matrix model:

[13] In contrast with the commercial channels in Flanders, the VRT does not engage in commercial exploitation contracts. Its contracts with Telenet and other distributors are based on IPR law and aim at compensating VRT for the use of its author rights. This said, throughout the article, for reasons of analytical straightforwardness, we use the term 'retransmission fee' for all broadcasters.

"If retransmission fees will be based on market share in the future, all channels will broaden their product offer in order to attract a wide audience as to increase their market share. This in turn will lead to boring uniformity, and hampers the cultural diversity of the media ecosystem" (Interview Acht).

Finally, in spite of the matrix model, several Flemish broadcasters have still not agreed on the terms of a new contract with the cable operator. This does not imply that their signal is not carried by the cable operator. Indeed, broadcasters need to reach audiences to generate advertising revenues. For that reason, asking to remove your signal from the cable is not an option – especially in a cable-dominated market with few alternative distributors [5].

3.2.2. Video-On-Demand

Over the years, platform operators have invested in the development of several non-linear services including the supply of VOD. As already mentioned, the supply encompasses movies and series for which Telenet and Belgacom have entered into agreements both with local and international producers and distributors, as well as an interactive library of catch-up TV and archival programmes in cooperation with Flemish broadcasters. Subscribers can then pay to (pre)view this content during forty-eight hours. A first type of conflict concerning VOD relates to distributors' offer of on-demand films. To be precise, broadcasters argue it is interesting for them to offer films of which they have acquired the linear rights in a non-linear way as well, but are bound by the exclusive offerings of the operators.[14]

A second conflict arises concerning VOD's revenue split. After deduction of VAT and the provision for author rights, the remainder of VOD income is split between the distributor and the broadcaster. The ratio is usually 60 for the distributor and 40% for the broadcaster, or 50-50%, and varies per broadcaster. According to one Flemish broadcaster, compared to other countries, broadcasters' revenue share from VOD is extremely low.

The interview with the Flemish public broadcaster revealed another conflict related to VOD:

"The Electronic Programme Guide (EPG) function that enables to record a complete serial at once, is a real killer for VOD on a pay-per-view base. Which is why broadcasters now focus on real-time TV, the 'live format experience' including red button voting applications" (Interview VRT).

In Section 3.2.4 we further elaborate on the impact of the EPG on VOD.

3.2.3 Advertising

Starting with the advertisers' perspective, a first concern for advertisers in Flanders relates to the audience they can reach. Due to the success of the public broadcaster, a lot of advertisers feel it is hard to reach a large part of the population. Furthermore, advertisements on the public broadcaster's channels may only last 5 seconds, and therefore a separate commercial has to be produced (next to the regular 30 second commercial). This obviously entails additional costs. Secondly, due to distributors' flexview services, a lot of consumers skip advertisements during a programme. The CIM (Centre for Information on Media) estimates that approximately 5 to 7% of consumers in Belgium watch programmes delayed. Apparently, especially young people avoid advertisements. In a recent study by Dear Media and Ehsal, 1,500 respondents between 18 and 25 years were questioned about their media behaviour. Strikingly, no less than 90% said they systematically avoid advertising on TV. More in detail, 70% of the respondents watch digital TV and hereof, one quarter skips advertisements every day [7]. Obviously, ad skipping has a baleful influence on advertisers' Return On Communication Investment (ROCI).

The issues mentioned above compel advertisers to find other ways to reach the audience, for instance through product placement.[15] However, it is difficult to measure the ROCI for product placement. Another alternative, namely advertising within the content, raises issues for advertisers as well. Specifically, it may cause friction with the programme producers since commercial aspects are hard to integrate into a programme's content. Another possibility, namely advertising via iDTV (the red button) has not taken off either and expired in the experimental stage. The Union of Belgian Advertisers (UBA) sees a number of reasons for this. Firstly, the pricing was too expensive. Also, in terms of campaign management, interactive advertising is rather difficult because it is only suitable for the final advertisement in a commercial break. If the consumer then clicks the red button, he obviously misses the beginning of the programme he is watching. Thirdly, the expected results were not met in terms of ROCI and, by consequence, advertisers ceased their efforts.

As a final remark, the UBA sees much potential in the EPG as a medium to exploit advertisements. Unfortunately, advertising with the distributor is still in its infancy. As pointed out by the UBA's CEO during the interview:

"For now, the 30-second spot still remains advertisers' main form of communication because it is measurable and efficient in the short-term. Besides, the advertising business is evolving more and more to an 'and-and' story, instead of an 'or-or' one. To be more specific, advertisers look for various channels to promote their products, for instance both online and on TV" (Interview UBA).

Continuing with private broadcasters' perspective, they claim that approximately 80% of their income still comes from advertising. However, this percentage is decreasing year-on-year, and income from consumers is becoming increasingly important. To counterfeit the flexview problem, many broadcasters resort to live programmes, possibly with the integration of second screen/social media applications (cf. supra).

3.2.4. Delayed Viewing and its Impact on VOD and Advertising

Until ten years ago, operators solely engaged in distribution. Nowadays, they also exploit broadcasters' content in another way offering so-called 'comfort services'. These allow consumers to, for example, store content and to watch it delayed. Given

---

[14] A linear TV service can be defined as a broadcasting service offered by the broadcaster to watch audiovisual programmes simultaneously, based on a programme scheme ('classical' TV watching). A non-linear TV service (or audiovisual broadcasting service on demand) can be defined as a broadcasting service offered by the broadcaster that enables the consumer to watch audiovisual programmes on individual request whenever he wants, based on the broadcasters' selected programme catalogue. Examples of non-linear TV services are VOD, pausing and rewinding live programmes (via Telenet's flexview and Belgacom's Comfortview), and interactivity services such as photos, games and digitext [24].

[15] Articles 78-101 of the Media Decree stipulate how advertising, teleshopping and product placement may be integrated in programmes.

technological evolutions, it is possible for consumers to record programmes while watching another programme, to record a programme while not watching anything, to resume a programme after a break – and if desired – skip advertisements, etc. Some operators also enable customers to record programmes from their computer or smartphone while being at work. These new services pose a threat to broadcasters' current business models that mainly rely on advertisement revenues. After all, if advertisers feel that they can no longer reach the audience they are paying for, it seems inevitable for advertising revenues to drop. Calculations of broadcasters indeed indicate that they miss out on considerable advertising revenues due to delayed viewing by consumers. Moreover, broadcasters argue that the offer of comfort services deviates from the simultaneous, unaltered and unabridged transmission of their signal. In their opinion, retransmission fees only compensate for the exploitation of their content in so far as it is retransmitted simultaneously, unaltered and unabridged. Comfort services go *beyond* such a retransmission and, hence, a remuneration for the exploitation of broadcasters' content is in place. Distributors largely disagree with this view. As a first argument, they say that broadcasters want to slow down technological evolutions. Comfort services merely meet consumer demands as they are a logical extension of VHS and other home taping technologies (allowing for a private copy). Secondly, it was also claimed that the more flexible product placement rules of the Audiovisual Media Services Directive enable broadcasters to recuperate a part of the alleged losses of advertising revenues. For now, the dispute on comfort services seems to be the most problematic and complicated one (see also [5]).

One broadcaster pointed out that paid-for reviews of programmes are declining strongly, whereas the number of STBs keeps growing. For free reviews and previews, the figures are more optimistic. Besides VOD, income from advertising also suffers from flexview. Importantly, these viewers cannot be measured, and hence, cannot be charged to the advertiser. For these reasons, broadcasters are dissatisfied with the current remuneration they receive from the distributors. They see a number of possible solutions for the future, such as (i) the retransmission fee remains equal and there will be an additional remuneration from the distributors' income received from the rental prices of the STBs, (ii) the distributor makes sure that – if a consumer fast forwards an advertising block – he/she is obliged to watch at least one commercial, (iii) the distributor pays the broadcaster a compensation for the loss of advertising due to delayed viewing, or (iv) the distributor makes it impossible for consumers to record premium content (e.g. fiction series that are very expensive), in such a way that the viewer *has* to see the advertisements and *has* to buy the episode in VOD in case he missed it.

Niche channel Acht's general manager further stated during the interview:

"The distributor should not adopt the same 'everything for free' mentality the consumer has. If he does, broadcasters will be forced to invest less in local content. And, if so, local affinity with the consumer disappears, as more and more foreign content will be available. Obviously, competition from alternative players such as Apple TV and Google TV will only increase by this" (Interview Acht).

Hence, broadcasters and distributors should preserve each other. If not, all other stakeholders will suffer from it, starting with the production sector.

Regarding income from the rental of STBs, one distributor noticed that STBs are in fact prefinanced, and that profit margins are small. He also mentioned that the STBs' rental model carries a risk, since there is a guarantee in case of product failure. Another distributor asserted that the maintenance of STBs is a very expensive undertaking. According to this distributor, it takes approximately 5 to 6 years to recover the costs on a STB and run break-even. He further noticed that the back-office procedures related to developments, applications, programming and updates of the STB are not only time-consuming, but also very expensive. Practically all distributors that were interviewed further argued they would be in favour of outsourcing the production, distribution, programming and maintenance of their STBs to an external organisation.

3.2.5 Revenue Streams Related to the Production Sector

There appears to be a trend away from shared revenue models between broadcasters and production houses. Nowadays, broadcasters increasingly claim all the rights on a production, while the production companies say they (continue to) bear most of the risk. Hence, a point of conflict that often arises with broadcasters, concerns the income that production houses receive (on average a 15% margin on year basis). Several production houses appear to be in favour of regulation, such as in France, where broadcasters are obliged to invest a percentage quotum in production companies, based on their turnover.

3.2.6. Author and Related Rights

As pointed out by [5], the current practices of dealing with author rights seem ill adapted to the new media environment and are highly untransparent. First, the current system of clearing rights is not up to date. Concretely, many legislative instruments date back from the 1990s and were in fact developed in response to evolutions of the 1970s and 1980s. As a result, the current ill-adapted legislation causes fairly high transaction costs. Despite the collective rights management, there is no 'one-stop-shop' for rights clearance. This fragmentation in turn hampers efficient dealings with author rights. A second problem is the lack of transparency with regard to author rights. Consumers pay distributors for author rights, distributors pay broadcasters and collecting societies for exploitation, broadcasters pay production houses for exploitation, etc. All these financial flows (or the 'author rights value chain') are – to the least – complicated.

More in detail, the current author rights mechanisms installed by the cable operator might be questioned. First, why is there a separate charge for author rights on consumers (with Telenet and VOO – the latter active in the Southern part of Belgium), while other operators do not have such a separate charge in place? Second, it is unclear whether author rights contributions are identical for all consumers and how increases are justified. Third, how the VAT-level on author rights contributions from consumers is dealt with, is uncertain. Without doubt, solving these questions is a prerequisite in order to make the system more transparent in the future.

It became clear from the interviews with the stakeholders, that they are dissatisfied with collective rights agencies' current practices. One production company complained that the way in which AGICOA collects and divides cable rights is highly untransparent:

"Considerable sums of money are involved, and more clarity concerning the breakdown of these collections is necessary" (Interview Eyeworks).

Concerning the collection of author rights for satellite transmission, one distributor at this stage has no agreement with the collective rights agencies. The company currently does pay a provision of 3.6% of the subscription price. However, collective rights agencies claim 10 to 15% of the distributor's content revenues, whereas in other countries, this provision is maximum 6%. The distributor argues that the price should be equal for all distributors and aligned with Europe.

Thirdly, all broadcasters agreed they would prefer a standardised system with one payment to all collective rights agencies. Nowadays, broadcasters often feel they are paying double, as everyone claims copyrights for the same repertoire. Moreover, collective rights agencies are not exactly 'communicating vessels'; there is a lot of tension, especially between SABAM[16] and SACD[17]. One specific concern for private broadcasters relates to the lawsuit Telenet filed against the collective rights agencies claiming it is not obliged to pay cable rights for the private broadcasters (cf. supra). In case Telenet looses the case, it will most certainly recoup the damage from the private broadcasters, as this was stipulated in the contracts. Specifically, according to these contracts, broadcasters should indemnify Telenet for claims from collective rights agencies.

This said, from the collective rights agencies' perspective, three types of possible conflicts may arise in the sector. For one, there is the opposition in interests between collective rights agencies and the rights licensees: collective rights agencies want to collect as many contributions as possible, whereas the licensees want to minimise their costs as much as possible. A second problem relates to the fact that the different categories of right owners feel that additional rights will in turn lead to a bigger pie, whereas distributors, broadcasters and producers take the view that the pie should remain unchanged and divided amongst all right owners. All licensees alike have a budget they reserve to pay right claimants. The question then remains who should get the most out of it, the artist, the producer or the authors. Related to this, there is the question of how much should be paid for the different types of repertoire. Finally, internationally, there is a lot of competition between collective rights agencies, which on occasions creates a field of tension.

3.2.7 Conclusion: Stakeholders at Cross-purposes?

Our value network analysis and the interviews with the stakeholders revealed that the audiovisual media industry in Flanders indeed is a typical example of a double 'layered' platform market. Furthermore, it became clear that the 'double marginalisation' effect is prominent; price setting in one platform market directly affects (the) adjoining platform market(s), and the major stakeholders are engaged in fierce conflicts to control and minimise 'taxes' levied by other platform players.

To start with, there is the interplay between broadcasters and distributors concerning the payment of carriage and retransmission fees. As a second example of double marginalisation, distributors' exclusive offer of on-demand films hampers broadcasters to offer films of which they have acquired the linear rights in a non-linear way. Thirdly, the EPG is a real killer for broadcasters' income from VOD and advertising. Distributors' offer of flexview services has repercussions in other vains of the value chain as well. For one, due to less advertising income, income from consumers is becoming increasingly important for broadcasters. Furthermore, in case distributors do not adequately compensate broadcasters for their loss in advertising income due to flexview, broadcasters threaten to invest less in local content, which in turn would harm the production sector. At the same time, competition from new entrants such as Apple TV and Google TV would increase. As this is harmful for distributors, this would in effect close the vicious 'double marginalisation' circle.

As already mentioned in Section 2, it is well-known from economic literature that individual platforms have strong incentives to vertically control prices of the adjoining platform, for example by entering the other platform's territory. Indeed, distributors do not only take care of network management and content transmission, they also engage in service provision and content aggregation offering company-owned broadcast channels or specific premium packages. In that sense, they play a triple role; they operate their network, distribute content and offer their own channels. As also pointed out by [5], premium content is a unique selling proposition that makes it possible for operators to differentiate themselves from competing platforms. Indeed, the bundling of electronic communication services (Internet, fixed/mobile telephone and digital TV) makes it difficult to discriminate on price, as there is no transparency regarding the cost of digital TV in the market. Also on the topic of premium content, both Telenet and Belgacom have started to launch thematic channels that focus on specific target groups. Telenet, for example, launched Studio 100 TV (kids) and, from June 2010 onwards, supports Disney (kids) [23]. This may cause friction since both channels directly compete for market share with the other kids channels (namely, VRT's Ketnet and vtmKzoom). The distributor with the weakest position on the Flemish market, Belgacom, owns only one niche channel (ANNE), which steers clear of competition with a particular established TV channel.

Another possible conflict may arise due to distributors' combined role of gatekeeper and content aggregator. As the operators select and package the channels, it is possible that platform operators are reluctant to offer good distribution conditions to stations that are a direct competitor of their own channels. This in turn may lead to conflicts of interest and an abuse of market power. To exemplify, say a new sports channel wants to enter the market. It obviously needs a distribution agreement with distributors to get its programmes to the viewers. But the possibility exists that the new channel will cannibalise the distributor's own channel, persuading the distributor not to take up the rivalling sports channel. As a consequence, media diversity and consumer choice may be harmed.

Summing up, this section revealed that many of the conflicts about roles and revenue streams between distributors and broadcasters in the audiovisual industry in Flanders today can be explained, and are even typical cases in point, by the counter-logics of platform ecosystems versus double marginalisation.

4. CONCLUSION

This article attempted to partly lift the veil of secrecy that covers the business arrangements and set-ups in the Flemish audiovisual industry. It offered a detailed picture of its structure and provided a number of heretofore unreported insights concerning the allocation of different revenue streams among relevant stakeholders in the sector.

---

[16] SABAM represents music authors, composers and publishers but also film directors, scriptwriters, poets, choreographers, painters, sculptors, photographers, architects, etc.

[17] SACD represents authors within the categories television and radio fiction, motion picture, theatre, dance, scene music and multimedia fiction.

While doing so, it became clear that the ecosystem of the TV industry in Flanders is tightly knit, though fragile, in the sense that shifts in the relationships between the players may cause the ecosystem to malfunction or even to collapse. It became clear that the relationships between broadcasters and distributors are fraught with tensions that relate directly to the new double platform structure of the industry. In the light of a range of potential over-the-top entrants, Flemish broadcasters and distributors nevertheless have a strategic incentive to preserve each others' economic sustainability.

As a suggestion for further research, studying the media value chain and revenue sharing mechanisms in other countries would be very interesting. In the Netherlands, Germany, the United Kingdom, France, etc. challenges concerning broadcasting and distribution arise as well. A comparison of cases and analysis of 'best practices' across Europe would further enhance our understanding of the Flemish situation.

5. ACKNOWLEDGEMENTS

The authors wish to thank Dr. Karen Donders for her research support and perceptive comments. Our gratitude also goes to all stakeholders for their fruitful cooperation and openness towards this study's research activities and findings. The study was made possible through a grant of the VRT Medialab.

6. REFERENCES

[1] Armstrong, M. 2004. *Competition in Two-Sided Markets.* Mimeo, University College, London.

[2] Ballon, P. 2005. Best *Practice in Business Modelling for ICT Services.* TNO-ICT Report. TNO-ICT: Delft.

[3] Ballon, P. 2009. "The Platformisation of the European Mobile Industry", *Communications & Strategies*, Dossier: Changeover in the mobile ecosystem, 75, 3rd Quarter 2009, 15-33.

[4] Dagnino, G. & G. Padula. 2002. "Coopetition Strategy: a New Kind of Interfirm Dynamics for Value Creation", Paper presented at *EURAM – The European Academy of Management Second Annual Conference - "Innovative Research in Management"*, Stockholm, Sweden, 9-11 May.

[5] Donders, K. and Evens, T. 2010. *Broadcasting and its Distribution in Flanders, Denmark and the United States: An Explorative and Future-Oriented Analysis.* Research Report for SBS Belgium. VUB-SMIT: Brussels.

[6] Doyle, G. 2002. *Understanding Media Economics.* Sage Publications Ltd., London.

[7] Droeven, V. and Deckmyn, D. 2012. *Jeugd lust geen reclame – enquête over kijkgedrag jongeren.* Online News Article, Destandaard.be, January 11, 2012, consulted on January 19, 2012, available at <http://destandaard.be/artikel/detail.aspx?artikelid=AO3KN4QL>.

[8] Eisenmann, T., Parker, G. and Van Alstyne, M., 2009. Opening Platforms: How, When and Why? In: Gawer, A. (ed.) Platforms, Markets, and Innovation. Edward Elgar, 131-164.

[9] Hagiu, A., 2009."Multi-Sided Platforms: From Microfoundations to Design and Expansion Strategies." Harvard Business School Working Paper, No. 09-115, April 2009.

[10] Hanbo, Z. 2008. *Emerging Business Models of the Mobile Internet Market.* Master's Thesis. Helsinki University of Technology: Espoo.

[11] Jullien, B. 2004. *Two-Sided Markets and Electronic Intermediation.* IDEI Working Papers 295, Institut d'Économie Industrielle (IDEI), Toulouse, France.

[12] Kind, H.J., Nilssen, T. and Sorgard, L. 2010. *Price Coordination in Two-Sided Markets: Competition in the TV Industry.* CESifo Working Paper Series 3004. CESifo Group: Munich.

[13] Knapp, D. 2011. Diversification. New impulses for TV advertising beyond the 30 second spot. *Presentation at '20 Years of Private Television' Conference* (Brussels, Belgium, April 29, 2011). Available at <http://www.privatetelevision.eu/cmimg/client44//File/Diversification_TV_Advertising_Brussels_29042011_DKabridged.pdf>.

[14] Lange, A. 2011. Challenges for the European TV industry. *Presentation at '20 Years of Private Television' Conference* (Brussels, Belgium, April 29, 2011). Available at <http://www.privatetelevision.eu/cmimg/client44//File/Lange.pdf>.

[15] Létang, V. 2011. Social Telly: Television & Social Media. *Presentation at 'Social Media Week' Conference* (London, UK, February 8, 2011). Available at <http://www.slideshare.net/Chinwag/social-telly-television-social-media-by-vincent-letang>

[16] Normann, R. and Ramírez, R. 1993. From value chain to value constellation: Designing interactive strategy. *Harvard Bus. Rev.* 71, 4, 65-77.

[17] Porter, M. E. 1980. *Competitive Strategy: Techniques for Analysing Industries and Competitors.* The Free Press, New York.

[18] Rochet, J.C. & J. Tirole. 2003. "Platform Competition in Two-Sided Markets", *Journal of the European Economic Association*, 1 (June 2003), 990-1029.

[19] Rochet, J.-C. and Tirole, J. 2006. *Two-Sided Markets: A Progress Report.* Working Paper. University of Toulouse: France.

[20] Schmalensee, R. and Evans, D.S. 2007. Industrial organization of markets with two-sided platforms. *Compet. Policy Int.* 3,1. Available at <http://ssrn.com/abstract=987341>.

[21] SMIT. 2010. *Techno-Economische Aspecten van Kabeltelevisiedistributie in Vlaanderen.* Research Report for SACD-Scam Belgium, AGICOA BELGIUM and SOFAM. VUB-SMIT: Brussels.

[22] Stabell, C. B. and Fjeldstad, Ø. 1998. Configuring value for competitive advantage: On chains, shops, and networks. *Strategic Manage. J.* 19, 5, 413-437.

[23] Telenet. 2011. Jaarrapport 2010. [*Annual report 2010*]

[24] VRM. 2010. Mediaconcentratie in Vlaanderen. *Rapport 2010.* VRM: Brussels.

[25] Weyl, E. Glen, 2008. Double Marginalization in Two-Sided Markets (July 2, 2008). Available at SSRN: http://ssrn.com/abstract=1324412 or doi:10.2139/ssrn.1324412

Loading Time Optimization in Broadcast TV Applications

Jean-Claude Dufourd
Telecom ParisTech; CNRS LTCI
37-39 rue Dareau
75014 Paris, France
+33145817733
dufourd@telecom-paristech.fr

Jean Le Feuvre
Telecom ParisTech; CNRS LTCI
37-39 rue Dareau
75014 Paris, France
+33145817169
lefeuvre@telecom-paristech.fr

Jean-Claude Moissinac
Telecom ParisTech; CNRS LTCI
37-39 rue Dareau
75014 Paris, France
+33145818088
moissina@telecom-paristech.fr

ABSTRACT

HbbTV, an emerging standard for interactive television, is being deployed in various European countries, creating bandwidth demand for interactive services in existing saturated broadcast networks. The problem of managing often-reused resources, such as script libraries, in broadcast interactive applications, becomes acute when trying to find a good compromise between bandwidth and waiting time. This paper explores the issues that TV channels have with on-air interactive applications and their optimized delivery. More specifically, this paper addresses the issue of data caching between broadcast carousel sessions as a way to optimize the bandwidth consumption of interactive applications. Proposed extensions to the current HbbTV specification to help solve the problem are given, and typical results include significant reduced waiting time, up to a factor of 3. The implementation complexity and other potential applications of the proposal are also discussed.

Categories and Subject Descriptors

H.3.5 [**Information Storage and Retrieval**]: Online Information Services – *Commercial services, Web-based services;* H.5.1 [**Information Interfaces and Presentation**]: Multimedia Information Systems; H.5.4 [**Information Interfaces and Presentation**]: Hypertext / Hypermedia – *User issues*

General Terms

Algorithms, Experimentation, Standardization.

Keywords

HbbTV, interactive TV applications, resource management in broadcast.

1. INTRODUCTION

HbbTV (Hybrid Broadband Broadcast TV), a standard targeting interactive TV, is getting more and more traction since its inception in 2009 and standardization by ETSI in June 2010 [1]. HbbTV is actually a conformance, certification and promotional effort as well as an industry standard adding interactive functionalities to TV by aggregating and profiling existing standards such as CEA for CE-HTML, MPEG for video, audio and transport, DVB for signaling, OIPF (Open IPTV Forum) for APIs to manage the link between the interactive HTML and the various subsystems, etc. It builds on well-known and proven technologies such as HTML, CSS and JavaScript to create interactive applications.

This standard differs from past standardization efforts in that its scope includes both broadcast (i.e. unidirectional link) and broadband (i.e. bi-directional link) delivery mechanisms. Applications can be delivered either in broadcast within a DSM-CC carousel [2], or in broadband by HTTP over the Internet. A carousel is a one-to-many distribution technique for the repeated transmission of a set of resources, usually a hierarchy of files, so that a client can start receiving data at any time and get access to any resource after a maximum waiting time; this time is usually referred to as the carousel period. Note that when a single carousel carries several resources, a different carousel period can be applied to each resource. Well-known examples of data carousel protocols are DSM-CC and FLUTE [3].

In the process of helping with the French roll out of HbbTV for TNT 2.0, the name of the future version of DVB-T in France, (promoted by the HD Forum), we have designed TV applications, tested applications designed by third parties, developed application validators, generators and other tools in the application production tool chain for HbbTV. During these developments, we faced a recurring problem with HbbTV applications in the management of resources. In a broadband environment, the browser, as mandated by the HTTP specification naturally caches reused resources; in other words, resource retrieval optimization happens automatically in broadband. In broadcast however, there is no mechanism available to enable caching of carousel objects between sessions. As a result, when broadcast of interactive applications is an important use case, like in France for TNT2.0, all resources need to be resent every time they are used, and no optimization is currently possible.

In this paper, we intend to optimize the waiting time of viewers when tuning into an HbbTV program with an interactive application by proposing a carousel organization and a caching scheme for script libraries. The rest of this paper is organized as follows: Section 2 provides an analysis of carousel mechanisms and explains the problem of data scheduling through the analysis of a real-world HbbTV application. A proposed solution to this problem is given in Section 3. Section 4 gives some result achieved with the given proposal, along with further considerations. Section 5 concludes this paper.

2. OF CAROUSELS AND CACHES

2.1 Carousel Basics

When carouseling data over a broadcast link, the main problem to solve is how to optimize the time taken for the data to be received at a given bandwidth, hereafter called *waiting time*. As shown in [7], usage of a carousel with multiple speeds often helps with the compromise between waiting times and the amount of bandwidth

EuroITV'12, July 4–6, 2012, Berlin, Germany.

allocated for interactive applications. For example, the set of resources to be transmitted in the carousel is split into three subsets: resources that need to be present before the application can start, resources that are important for the application, and resources that are nice to have (see [6] and [7] for a more detailed discussion of classes of resources to take into account for interactive services). The first set would be repeated at a certain period, the second set would be interleaved with the first set but with a slower repetition period, and the third set would be interleaved with the other two when bandwidth is available, with an even slower repetition period.

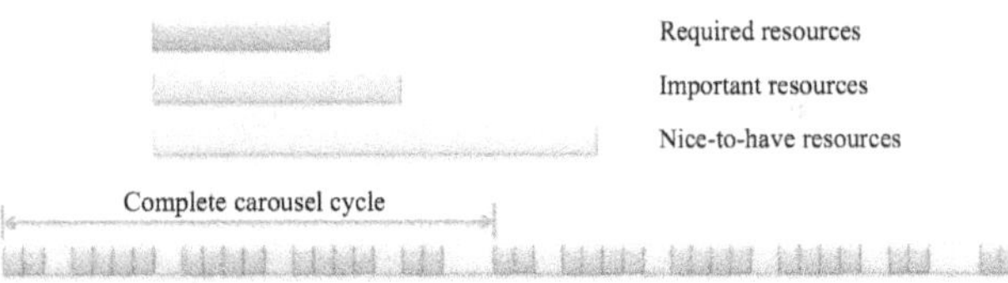

Figure 1: Multi-period carousel

The above figure describes a simplified situation where resources are sent in one piece, required resources are sent 4 times more often than important resources, which are sent 4 times more often than nice-to-have resources. In practice, resources of all types are cut into smaller sections and some interleaving reduces the impact of the variance on resource length.

For an HTML/CSS/JS-based application, as is the case in HbbTV or MHP (DVB-HTML), JS libraries required to construct the page would have to be allocated to the faster cycle to reduce the waiting time, so their impact on the required bandwidth is maximal.

2.2 Overheads in HbbTV Applications

In our experience, among the applications used within a certain TV channel, most of them come from a small number of application providers, in general specialized design studios. The applications coming from the same studios are usually designed the same way and share many JS libraries: jQuery, mootools, yui, dojo are such often used libraries, on the Internet as well as on mobiles and now on TVs. Using those libraries helps with blurring the difference of browsing quality of experience between TVs and PCs, which is an important need for TV channels. However, these libraries are sent with each application, thereby wasting precious bandwidth and potentially increasing the waiting time of the carousel.

Another source of duplication among the applications of a particular channel is the graphics charter of the TV channel: logo, background, buttons, styles, etc. However, since the application look and feel is often tuned to that of each broadcasted show, this may in practice be a smaller source of optimizations.

There are easy strategies to alleviate the impact of waiting for images; for example, using two images in the HTML document, a reduced quality version sent at a higher frequency in the carousel, which can therefore be displayed quite fast, and a full quality version sent at a lower frequency, whose availability is monitored through *onLoad* events in HTML <*img*> element.

There is no simple equivalent strategy for the JS libraries or most programmatic elements (e.g., Java Classes). Indeed, application authors tend to rely on existing libraries, well optimized for Web infrastructure but usually conceived as a monolithic piece of code: these libraries cannot be easily divided into a small initialization part for document preload, then a more advanced sub-library for document structuring and finally the rest of the library for visual effects, and are therefore not suitable for multi-period carousels.

Providing a caching mechanism for those resources, allowing them to be sent once in a while rather than within each carousel at high frequency, will greatly help in reducing the average waiting time and the management of bandwidth allocated to interactive applications.

2.3 A Real-Life Use Case

We base our analysis on a real-life HbbTV application from France Télévisions, available at the time of writing on all their channels. It includes text and images for general news, sports news, weather forecast and ads for various future broadcasts. This application intends to replace the older teletext system, and as such targets all receivers, whether connected (broadband) or not; this implies that all the application data is carried inside the broadcast link.

Figure 2 - Live France2 HbbTV application

The total size of this application is 550kb, of which 430kb are images and 113kb are scripts. Transmitted in a uniform carousel with 100kbit/s, where all resources are sent once per cycle, and counting 10 bits sent per byte to send to account for overhead, the maximum waiting time for any resource is 57s. In a carousel with images transmitted at a 10^{-1} priority, i.e. all other resources are repeated 10 times more often than images, the maximum waiting time would be 17s for other resources and 3mn for images. With scripts transmitted at a 10^{-1} priority than required resources, the maximum waiting time for required resources goes down to 5s.

This means that the very first time a TV uses a particular resource, it has to wait a maximum of 50s. For following accesses to the resources (i.e. after a tune out from the channel), the maximum waiting time would drop from 17s to 5s if scripts were cached. In terms of bandwidth, to achieve a similar gain of 3.4, we need to dedicate 340kbits/s instead of 100kbits/s to the carousel. Note that this simple caching would not change the waiting time of the first tune-in of the clients, as they still have to fetch the required resources with long carousel periods.

2.4 Caching in Broadcast

Caching is often mentioned in relation with DSM-CC carousels, e.g. in [5] as well as in [1] for the minimum DSM-CC cache size, but with a different focus. The caching starts when the carousel is accessed, and stops when the carousel is closed. Such caching improves the waiting time by anticipating requests for a particular resource: as soon as a carousel is open, received resources are stored in cache even if the application did not request them yet. When the request comes, if the resource is already in cache, the response is immediate. We refer to this mechanism as *intra-carousel caching*. This looks very good in theory, but does not solve our problem in practice. As shown previously, we need a persistent cache, such that JS libraries could be stored locally after closing the carousel and fetched back from the cache when re-opening the application carousel. We refer to this persistent cache as *inter-carousel caching*.

The DSM-CC object carousel mechanism, much like many tools used for file delivery over unidirectional links, does not provide for caching across sessions: when a session is no longer running, the transmitted files are no longer required and may be deleted. More importantly, identifiers used during the session are usually not meaningful outside of this session. Flute, used for unidirectional delivery of files over the Internet, provides similar carousel tools, as shown in [4]. It has however the interesting property of using URIs as file identifiers, and a useful possibility is to actually use a located URI as identifier, usually an HTTP URL. This design implies that:

- resource identifiers are independent from the carousel session, and can be interpreted once the session is killed,
- a connected device has always the choice of waiting for the resource to arrive over Flute, or to bypass waiting and get it from the Internet.

The first feature will be at the heart of our proposal; the second feature is a direct consequence of using, as an URI, an URL (e.g. HTTP URL) that resolves to a valid resource on the Internet network.

3. Inter-Carousel Caching

3.1 Design Principle

Inter-carousel caching is our answer to the aforementioned limitations: it allows sending data once for several applications, thereby avoiding duplication, and allows for sending application data before the application is loaded, thereby reducing loading times. Such a carousel can be sent whenever available bandwidth allows for it, preferably before the start of the application carousel if reducing the load time is the desired effect.

We want our solution to be as transparent as possible for the content creator (minimal or no changes in content), while providing an efficient cache for applications relying on broadcast and broadband networks. As said previously, we need a way to identify carousel resources even when the carousel is no longer received; our proposal uses URLs as resource identifiers, which gives us the possibility to identify network resources as well.

Finally, we would like our solution to provide a generic HTTP cache push system for any application, HbbTV or not. We have in mind usage of Push-VOD services relying on HTTP as transport mechanisms, such as HTTP Streaming solutions (e.g. MPEG-DASH).

3.2 Simple HbbTV Cache Proposal

Our first design is a very simple extension to the HbbTV framework, achieved by using a new attribute on elements using external resources, such as *<script>*, *<link>*, *<img>*, *<video>*. Let us take an example of a resource:

```
<script src="js/jquery.js" type="text/javascript" …/>
```

In our proposal, the resource would be marked as cachable as follows:

```
<script src="js/jquery.js" h:cacheName="jQuery142" .../>
```

The implementation would process the extended *h:cacheName* first, look for a matching resource in the cache, and if there is no such resource in the cache, request *js/jquery.js* from the carousel, then store the returned resource in the cache before handing it back to the browser. The above example assumes the definition of the attribute *h:cacheName* in another namespace, following strict XML extension rules. The value of *h:cacheName* is the global identifier for the resource, valid across sessions, channels and multiplexes. It may correspond to the official download URL of the resource if appropriate.

This proposal is quite simple and efficient, but it has some limitations:

- It requires some changes in the content.
- It cannot be used for sharing resources across applications from different providers for obvious security reasons: libraries could be overwritten with non-compatible or malicious versions, without any possibility to prevent it apart from keeping the caches separated between applications, or at least service providers.
- It cannot be used to cache data not referenced in the HTML page.

3.3 Generic HTTP Cache Proposal

To overcome these limitations, we designed a second proposal, which consists in sending the cache instructions together with the objects to be cached, in a regular object carousel. The carousel root directory contains a file labeled *cache.xml*, which provides an XML description of each item that needs to be cached in this carousel:

- name of the resource in the current carousel e.g. *jQuery142* in our previous example,
- for each carousel referring to this resource:
  - the name of the referred resource e.g. *js/jQuery.js* in our previous example,
  - optionally the DVB triplet identifying the referring service; this solves naming conflicts, when different resources, cached or not, are used with the same name in different channels.
- optionally, some HTTP header fields for cache directives, as a server would have replied if the resource were queried with an HTTP GET method.

The *cache.xml* file can be directly included in the application carousel, in which case caching is restricted to the current service provider. If caching needs to be shared across applications from different providers, a dedicated DSM-CC carousel is declared in one PMT, with a specific AIT type (currently a reserved one) and the AIT *autostart* flag set. Similar to DVB System Software Update, we force the device to process such a carousel as soon as it has the possibility. The proposal is naturally backward compatible with existing implementations, since the *cache.xml* file can safely be ignored; moreover, the proposal is very light, the cache file being quite small (potentially gzipped by DSM-CC) compared to other files in the carousel.

This second proposal allows the description of caching instructions of files in a carousel, possibly not tied to any particular TV channel. While more complex, this approach has the benefit of not touching the HTML part of the application, only requiring modification of the HTTP stack in a standard way, using the HTTP cache header fields given in the XML file. It can also be used to cache files not referenced by the current HTML application and with non-HTML applications.

4. Results and Analysis

4.1 Gains

Table 1 describes some more results of applying our proposals to 4 applications. The results are valid for any of our proposals, since we made sure not to break existing implementations by always including a long-period carousel for the required resources in each application. The first application is the one described in Section 2. The others are applications designed by different agencies for different customers. All are already on air in France at the time of writing. Although we studied more than 20 sequences using external JS libraries, we only show the most relevant applications.

Name	Nb res	Total Size	Scripts	Images	Max wait A	Max wait B	Max wait C
FTv	147	576k	113k	451k	57s	17s	5s
MS	30	391k	46k	334k	39s	9s	6.8s
CE	14	169k	40k	126k	17s	5.6s	2s
Go	30	395k	43k	346k	40s	8s	4.4s

Table 1: Waiting times for a bandwidth of 100kbits/s

The measurements were made using our HbbTV tools for bandwidth management developed in the openHbb project (www.openhbb.eu). All resources except images have been gzipped, which is a feature of DSM-CC modules. The **Max wait** columns describe the maximum time for the application to appear, even if it is incomplete. **Max wait A** is the waiting time when all resources are repeated once per cycle, regardless of their type: for the first application, the maximum waiting time is around one minute, but then the application is complete after 1mn. **Max wait B** is the waiting time when images are repeated ten times less often than other resources: it implies that the first application appears on the screen with no images in a maximum of 17s, and images appear gradually for the next 3mn. **Max wait C** is the waiting time when images and scripts are repeated ten times less often than other resources: if the scripts are in cache, the first application arrives after a maximum wait of 5s, then the images appear within the next 50s; if the scripts are not in cache (first time) then the maximum wait is for 50s. The improvement from using our proposal ranges from 25% to 70%, while maintaining reasonable maximum waiting times for cache misses. Our experiment showed that using a longer period (priority lower than 10^{-1}) for scripts does not help the overall waiting time much: an improvement of the waiting time of less than 10% is observed when scripts are in the cache, with the drawback of a first time wait increasing from 50s to 9mn for application FTv.

4.2 Discussion

The implementation requirement of our first simple HbbTV proposal is very small, affecting the resource loader of the HTML browser to hand over the value of the new attribute *h:cacheName* to the carousel manager of the device, which handles the caching. This caching can be done independently of the HTTP cache of the device, as the resource will always be accessed through the carousel transporting the application.

Our second proposal is just slightly more complex to implement, but it requires automatic mounting of the cache carousel and some processing for filling up the device cache. However, in order to be able to share the resources among applications, the cache has to be global to all carousels and therefore fits best with the HTTP cache of the device/browser. It should be noticed that better results in terms of bandwidth occupancy will be achieved by gathering small resources (e.g. JS files) into a single one when possible (e.g. a single library): although the cache description is gzipped, it still grows linearly with the number of files to cache.

One major advantage of our second proposal is its ability to push HTTP resources over a broadcast link, while keeping the possibility to access the HTTP resources online if any. We see several use cases benefiting from this feature.

Leveraging server usage: our solution can reduce the risk of overwhelming web servers distributing JS libraries or other resources at the beginning of a popular broadcast with an interactive application which uses for the first time a new version of the resource: such a situation could generate millions of quasi synchronous requests for the same resource. We avoid this by pushing the requested resource in the device HTTP cache.

Enabling Content Push: our solution allows pushing complete movies or trailers to the device, without change to the HTML content. It can also be used for more advanced HTTP streaming, by pushing the first part of the session to the device, enabling the playback to start without buffering, and then be switched to a regular HTTP streaming session if the device is connected.

5. CONCLUSION

In this article, we have reviewed the basic functionalities of data carousel, including multi-period ones; we have shown how HbbTV, the upcoming interactive TV standard, is used together with this mechanism and have identified some overhead in bandwidth management, leading to longer load time and bad user experience. We have proposed a new caching paradigm for DSM-CC, the inter-carousel cache, based on HTTP caching rules, which allows a better usage of the available bandwidth and a better user experience. We have shown how this mechanism could potentially be used for data caching at the service level (data shared among different providers) and explained the potential gains. Our future works include standardization related to this topic, on-air experiments with national broadcaster and upgrade of our HbbTV toolchain.

6. ACKNOWLEDGMENTS

This work was partly done within the French-funded openHbb project, www.openhbb.eu.

7. REFERENCES

[1] HBBTV, ETSI Technical Specification 102 796, "Hybrid Broadcast Broadband TV"

[2] R. J. Crinon, "The DSM-CC object carousel for broadcast data services," 1997, pp. 246-247.

[3] Flute - File Delivery over Unidirectional Transport, IETF RFC 3629, http://www.rfc-archive.org/getrfc.php?rfc=3926

[4] C. Neumann, V. Roca, R. Walsh, Large scale content distribution protocols, ACM SIGCOMM Computer Communication Review 2005 35 (5) (2005) 85–92.

[5] Steven Morris & Anthony Smith-Chaigneau, Interactive TV Standards: A Guide to MHP, OCAP, and JavaTV, Focal Press, 2005

[6] J.-C. Moissinac and C. Concolato, "A model for the delivery of interactive applications over broadcast channels," in *Proceedings of the 3rd workshop on Mobile video delivery - MoViD '10*, 2010, p. 15.

[7] C. Herrero and P. Vuorimaa, "Optimisation Techniques for Digital Television Applications Broadcasting," Proceedings of the 7th IASTED International Conference on Internet and Multimedia Systems and Applications, IMSA 2003, Honolulu, USA, pp. 689-694, August 2003.

Digital TV: The Effect of Delay when Watching Football

Rufael Mekuria
CWI
Sciencepark 123
1098 XG Amsterdam
+31(0)20 592 4020
Rufael.mekuria@cwi.nl

Pablo Cesar
CWI
Sciencepark 123
1098 XG Amsterdam
+31 (0)20 592 4332
P.S.Cesar@cwi.nl

Dick Bulterman
CWI
Sciencepark 123
1098 XG Amsterdam
+31 (0)20 593 4300
d.c.a.bulterman@cwi.nl

ABSTRACT

Hearing a neighbor cheer for a goal seconds before you see it can be very annoying. Currently, many people that upgrade their TV service from analog to digital TV are experiencing this. We briefly describe causes of these (relative) delays. To support this with practical evidence, we report field measurements of relative delays from 19 different receivers that show that up to 5 seconds occurs between technologies like IPTV, analogue cable, digital cable (both SD and HD), digital satellite, terrestrial and web TV. We present a controlled experiment that simulates the football watching experience with 18 participants watching clips in different rooms cheering over an audio connection. The results show that delays measured in practice disturb the experience significantly. Moreover it often took participants little time to find out if they were ahead or behind. Also many participants felt inclined to change their service to a provider with less delay. The results emphasize that delay is a quality factor that needs to be taken into account and minimized in digital TV. This is crucial for digital TV providers to entice consumers that want to be the ones to first cheer for a goal.

Categories and Subject Descriptors

H.5.1 [**Multimedia Information Systems**]: Video, Broadcasting,

General Terms

Measurement, Experimentation, Human Factors.

Keywords

Digital Video Broadcasting, Football, Quality of Experience, Delay

1. INTRODUCTION

The national team is playing a play-off match for the FIFA world championship football. John recently subscribed to his high definition TV package, and invited friends to watch the game at home. The streets are empty as John is not the only one watching the game. The striker has the ball and heads towards the goal. As he gets closer, John suddenly hears his neighbors shouting and cheering. Some seconds later John and his friends indeed see the goal scored. The striker passed back and a second line shot flew in. After the excitement, John and his friends realize that they are not watching the match live as others are ahead of them. Some other tense moments in the match occur and a second goal is scored. Every time the neighbors are cheering and shouting before John and his friend. John gets the question, how much money he is paying for his subscription. At half time John and his friends decide to watch in a local bar so that they can cheer all together when a goal is scored.

This experience has happened to many digital TV subscribers. Posts in popular media and Dutch national TV indicate that people are frustrated by this[1]. With increased urbanization, people tend to live closer to each other, and sounds from neighbors are often present. Especially for the continents where live football is popular such as Latin America and Europe this is true. As live football matches are very popular, these delays give many people a reason *not* to switch to digital TV despite its better visual quality. As this drawback is becoming well known to customers, digital TV service providers cannot keep ignoring this effect, as it may damage their current and future revenues. Football watching is a serious business for TV broadcasters. To give an indication, the owner of the rights to the English premier league is reported to have paid over £1 billion for them.

Digital TV broadcasting consists of multiple digital processing steps, the delay that each processing step introduces accumulates and can be large compared to analogue transmission. While much literature and standardization work on digital TV is available, the delays introduced in each step and the effect when watching football have not been studied systematically. This leads to our first research question:

1. What are the causes of delay in digital TV and how much difference between closely located receivers are common in real situations?

We will provide a table with delay causes in digital TV and a measurement study comparing different receivers in an urban area in the Netherlands. The second research question will be related to the Quality of Experience, the subjective experience of the user by answering the following questions:

2. How much (relative) delay makes people notice or get annoyed when watching football and does this discourages people from using digital TV?

This, we will investigate by simulating the football watching experience with audio feedback in a controlled trial with eighteen participants and artificially introduced relative delays.

The rest of the paper is structured as follows: in section 2 we present related work. In section 3 we identify the causes of delay in digital TV. In section 4 we present and analyze the results of a measurement study of relative delays between channels and technologies in a single urban area. In section 5 we present the

EuroITV'12, July 4–6, 2012, Berlin, Germany.

[1] http://wk2010.eenvandaag.nl/home/36140/irritatie_door_vertraging_digitale_tv (in Dutch)

setup of the controlled experiment for the user experience and its results. The paper concludes in section 6.

2. RELATED WORK

In most countries, analog TV broadcasts are phased out and are replaced by digital TV broadcast. An overview of digital TV standards worldwide is given in [1]. The compression and digital techniques employed in these standards introduce some delay that is taken into account in these standards. However minimizing these delays was not a primary design goal in digital TV. For example the DVB project described in [2] aims for constant delay in a given configuration. This resulted in different digital TV users experiencing different delays affecting the user experience when talking over an audio connection or when watching football. For example, a prototype to synchronize online video playback was presented in [3] for the talking/chatting scenario online where users watch content and communicate simultaneously. It showed initial evidence that elimination of relative delay is desirable in such scenarios. The authors investigated the effects in a controlled study in [4]. We found that when friends are watching a sociable genre, a quiz in this case, they may notice a relative delay of 1s or more when talking over a voice connection and when using text chat, the more active chatters noticed 2s or more. The study in [9] presented the idea that synchronization benefits the football watching experience. However, the result from the controlled study in [4] does not apply to football as large differences in viewing experience between different genres have been reported in [5]. Another use case where TV broadcasting delays can be annoying that received attention is the case when it causes channel zapping delay as in IPTV. Causes and possible ways to reduce channel zapping delays are described in [6] and the QoE of channel zapping delay was studied in [7]. The ITU Quality of Experience standard for IPTV [8] adapted these values and gives values for channel zapping and broadcasting delays. A paper [9] provides a use case for synchronizing receivers of IPTV, as it should benefit watching football.

These studies do not cover the QoE of the popular and commercially relevant case of watching football using digital TV. This paper aims to fill this gap by presenting a controlled studies of this effect. Moreover we will focus on digital TV in general which is currently widely deployed and used. As cheering neighbors can use different types of digital TV, such local differences between technology types will be measured here.

3. Delay in Digital TV

Some of the sources that cause delay in digital TV are presented in Table 1. Encoding and Capturing introduce delays at the studio/ broadcast source. This can introduce a relative delay between different TV stations when the broadcast the same live content. A conversion of the digital image format (for example to adapt to the screen size in DVB-H) can also introduce extra delay. Modulation, coding and propagation as used in digital TV can also introduce delays.

Table 1 Delay Sources in Digital TV

Delay Source	Location
Generation	Broadcast source/studio
Transcoding/image conversion	Operator
Modulation/ error coding	Operator
Propagation	Between operator and Source
Buffering, decoding, rendering	Receiver

For example when a satellite signal is used already a two way propagation delay of 120 ms occurs. In the case of IPTV, the access network may introduce some delays around 100 ms. Moreover decoding, buffering and rendering steps also introduce a delay based on the digital TV and set-top box hardware.

4. DELAY MEASUREMENT STUDY

A mobile TV receiver was deployed in homes with different TV services. A camera connected to a laptop recorded both the home TV image and the laptop image. The mobile TV receiver is shown in top of figure 1 and consists of a laptop connected to the portable DVB-T Anysee device. By comparing the scene changes happening on the TV with the ones at the mobile receiver, differences between the two were measured. An example front recording is shown in Fig. 1. By measuring at many different homes, we indirectly compared many TV services, resulting in a broad measurement study (17 locations, over 30 different setups). The results were collected in a spreadsheet and plotted in Fig 2 as error bars around the mean difference with the DVB-T laptop.

Fig. 1 Anysee DVB-T receiver (left) and the front recording of home TV and mobile receiver (right)

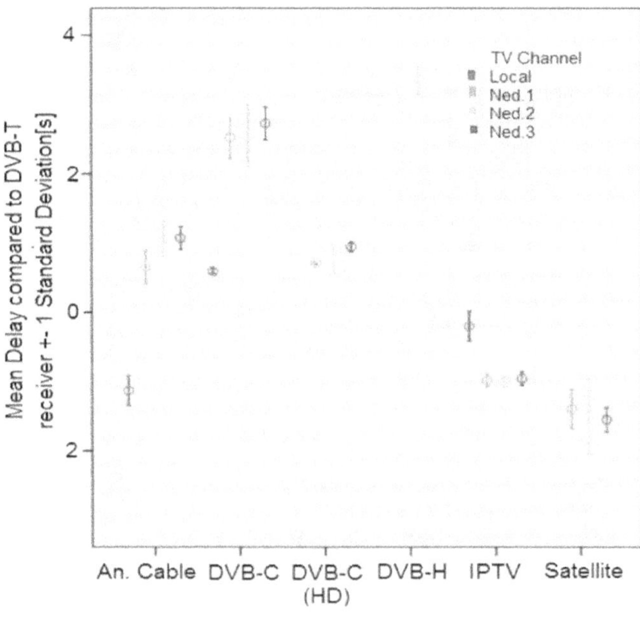

Fig. 2 Comparison study of synchronization between TV-based technologies

Fig. 2 shows the mean difference with the mobile DVB-T receiver and the standard deviation. The national broadcasting stations are represented by green, gray and purple and the local TV broadcast, recorded if available, in blue. Fig. 2 also shows that the means and standard deviations are clustered around the service type (technology) and channel. Analysis of Variance confirms this: $(8,249) = 37{,}38$ $p<0.001$. The DVB-C/HD difference showed that a large difference between quality level can exist, and that, in this case, the HD version was (somewhat surprisingly) faster. The digital satellite signal DVB-S was the fastest, maybe because other operators used DVB-S as source (we could not verify this). The DVB-H receiver, a broadcast technology optimized for mobiles, showed the highest delay caused either because of buffering or screen size conversion or other factors causing overhead.

5. FOOTBALL WATCHING EXPERIMENT

In this section we study the impact of the impact of such (relative) delay when watching football matches on the user experience.

5.1 Technical setup

The experimental setup involves two laptops that display football clips. The laptops run Ubuntu 11.10. The laptops are synchronized in time by setting the same local time server in the ntp.conf file and calling the system command ntpd to synchronize the stations. Then, to artificially introduce relative delays, we developed a small media player using gstreamer[2], an open source framework for developing media streaming applications. The media player asseses the Linux system time to start g-streamer playback at the two machines at (almost) exactly fixed or synchronized starting times of 0, 500, 1000, 2000 and 4000 ms. The program was written in C and uses the time.h library and the sys/timeb.h that provide millisecond accuracy. The system was validated by listening to the audio synchronization of the two laptops displaying the same video, a difference that was close to inaudible (a very small difference audible to the sensitive ear). To enable speech communication we used cisco IP telephones on speaker mode. The speech audio and voice audio were tuned in such a way that feedback from the football video through the speech interface was inaudible. A schematic of the experimental setup displaying the laptops, the NTP server and the phones is shown in Figure 3. Figure 4 displays a screenshot of the banshee media player initialized by gstreamer for playback of the football clip. The initialization and setting of the timing of each clip was handled by a bash script. After each clip the users are given time to fill the questionnaires and when they finish and when they press to continue, and the bash script starts the media player.

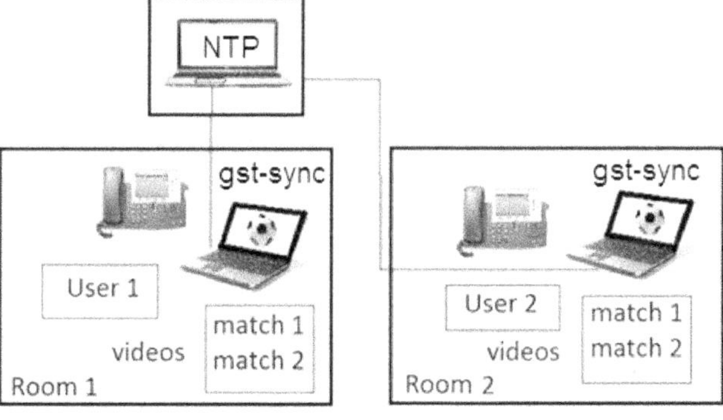

Fig. 3 Experimental setup

[2] http://gstreamer.freedesktop.org/

Figure 4 Banshee synchronized video player

5.2 Video Content

During the 90 minutes of a match, parts with more activity and parts with less activity occur. Intuitively, relative difference tends to be more disturbing in active parts than in quiet parts. To avoid this possible bias, we use 10 minute summaries that emphasize on the active parts and display goals and chances. Each clips show an approximately equal amount of possibilities to cheer or shout. The summaries presented contain the matches of one season of champions league in 1995 of Ajax, the team that eventually won and present very entertaining football to keep the participants interested. Another reason for choosing an old match is that participants will not have recently seen it recently, avoiding this type of user anticipation.

5.3 Experimental procedure

We utilize methodology and approach as in our earlier work presented in [4] where we measured the effect of such differences in Social TV .We are aware that a controlled setup takes away some realism from real world situations, but allows to test the specific different conditions in isolation and find the threshold values. We situated two participants behind their laptop in different rooms and asked them to cheer for the winning team in each of the ten minute videos. In order to avoid habituation effects, conditions are presented in randomized order. The values of the relative delays are selected as 0, 500, 1000, 2000 and 4000 ms, corresponding to real world measurements shown in section 4. After each ten minute clip participants are demanded to fill in the questionnaire. In fact the questionnaire is an adapted version of the degradation category MOS scale [10] shown in table 2. This scale is commonly used in QoE experiments. The participant is also asked in if this difference would encourage him to change service provider and if paying more would be an option. Recruitment was performed in friends, work, acquaintances and family circles. The participants were both men and woman of ages in the range of 20-40 years old. Most were at the time pursuing Masters or PhD degrees.

Table 2 Assessment scores on DCR scale

Score	Impairment
5	the play-back difference is not perceptible
4	the difference is perceptible but not annoying
3	the difference is perceptible and slightly annoying
2	The difference is perceptible and annoying
1	the difference is perceptible and very annoying

We asked participants to cheer as much for the goals as possible. In this way the effect of audible/noticeable difference was tested, instead of the more social/cultural aspects of this situation.

5.4 RESULTS

The majority of participants also watched football matches in their private time, mostly the European leagues or the leagues in Brazil or Turkey. Figure 5 shows the percentage of persons that noticed/and or got annoyed by the relative delay. At 1 second more than half the participants notice the differences, while at 4s most participants notice it and are annoyed.

Table 3 Participant willingness to change service

Difference[ms]	NO	MAYBE	YES
0 ms	78%	22%	0%
500 ms	72%	22%	6%
1000 ms	72%	22%	6%
2000 ms	39%	55%	6%
4000 ms	11%	28%	61%

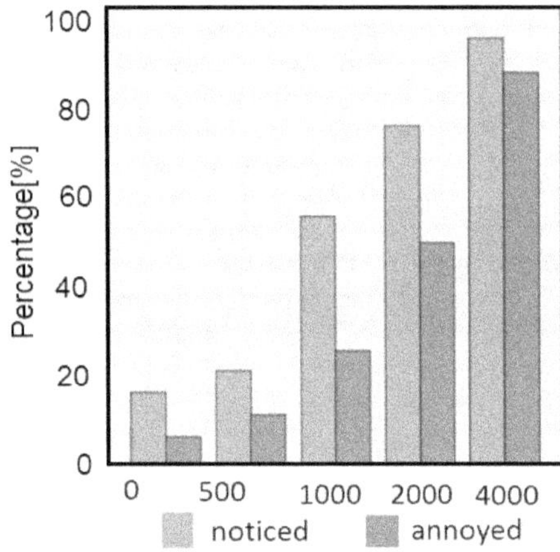

Figure 5 Experimental results

We also posed the question if such difference would make participants consider changing their service provider. The aim was to measure the intention of people. The responses are shown in Table 3. The results show a clear trend: at 2s people start to doubt and at 4s more than half indicates willing to change their service. Also, in that case 28% considers changing their service as an option. From the collected data, especially, the people that watch football often indicate the possibility to change provider.

6. CONCLUSIONS

In this paper we presented empirical evidence that relative delays encountered in digital TV degrade the football watching experience. Especially large differences are noticed quickly by participants and are a plausible reason to change provider. As the experiment had 18 participants, we refrained from statistical analysis. However from the results, 1 second is noticeable in over 50% of the cases and 4 seconds is annoying in more than 50% of the cases. These values can be used a motivation to develop solutions to palliate this problem and motivate business decisions to upgrade current digital TV infrastructures.

ACKNOWLEDGEMENTS

We thank all the participants for their time watching the matches. Moreover we thank Dr.Oskar van Deventer and Hans Stokking for their contributions. The research leading to these results has received funding from the European Community's Seventh Framework Programme (FP7/2007-2013) under grant agreement no. ICT-2011-7-287723 (Reverie project).

REFERENCES

[1] Wu, Y. Hirakawa,S .Reimers, U. Withaker, J. 2006. Overview of Digital Television Development. *Proceedings of the IEEE*, Volume 94 Issue 1 8-21. DOI=10.1109/JPROC.2005.861000

[2] Reimers, U. 2005. DVB *The Family of international standards for digital video broadcasting*. Springer , signals and communication technology, Braunschweig.

[3] Shamma, D.A. Bastea-Forte, M. Joubert, N. Liu Y. 2008. Enhancing online personal connections through synchronized sharing of online video. In *Proceedings of the SIGCHI Conference on Human Factors in Computing Systems* (Florence, Italy), April 05 - 10, 2008). CHI '08. ACM, New York, NY, 2931-2936. DOI= 10.1145/1358628.1358786.

[4] Geerts, D. Vaishnavi, I. Mekuria, R. Van Deventer, M.O. Cesar, P. 2011. Are We in sync? Synchronization requirements for watching online video together. In *Proceedings of the SIGCHI Conference on Human Factors in Computing Systems* (Vancouver, Canada), May 07 - 12, 2011. CHI '11. ACM, New York, NY, 311-314. DOI=10.1145/1978942.1978986

[5] Geerts, D. Cesar, P. Bulterman, D.C.A.. 2008. The implications of program genres for the design of social television systems. *Proceedings of the first international Conference on Designing Interactive Experiences for TV.* (Vancouver, Canada, October 22 - 24, 2008). UXTV '08. ACM, New York, NY, 71-80. DOI=10.1145/1453805.1453822

[6] Ramosa, F. Crowcroft, A. Gibbensa, R. Rodriguez, P. White, A. 2011. Reducing channel change delay in IPTV by predictive pre-joining of TV channels. *Elsevier Signal Processing: Image Communication* Vol. 26 Issue 7. pp. 400-412. DOI= 10.1016/j.image.2011.03.005

[7] Kooij, Ahmed, K. Brunstrom. K. 2006 . Perceived Quality of Channel Zapping. *Fifth IASTED Conference on Communications Systems and Networks,* Citeseer 2006 155-158.

[8] ITU-T. G.1080 Quality of experience requirements for IPTV services. (2008), ITU.

[9] Van Deventer, M. Stokking H., Niamut O., Walraven F., Klos V. 2006. Advanced interactive television services require content synchronization. *Proceedings of the 15th international conference on Signals Systems and Image Processing.* (Bratislava, Slovakia June 22-25 2008). IWSSIP'08 109- 112. DOI= 10.1109/IWSSIP.2008.4604379

[10] ITU-T. *ITU P.800 Mehods for objective and subjective quality assesment.* 1993-1996.

In-situ Everywhere: A Qualitative Feedback Infrastructure for Cross Platform Home-IT

Jan Hess, Lin Wan, Benedikt Ley, Volker Wulf
University of Siegen
Hoelderlinstr. 3
57076 Siegen, Germany
+49 271 740-4036
{jan.hess, lin.wan, benedikt.ley, volker.wulf}@uni-siegen.de

ABSTRACT

The domestic appliance landscape is becoming increasingly interconnected with different options to consume rich media, e.g. on TV, PC or Mobile with manifold options for additional services. From a participatory design oriented perspective, involving users into the design of new applications related to video and TV is a topic with growing importance. However, current options to provide feedback at use-time are limited to a standardized form, e.g. in traditional usability tests. In order to open the design space for long-term and more creative in-situ feedback, we will address this topic by a concept of a cross platform infrastructure that enables users to provide feedback on different devices in the context of the usage. This concept enables users to co-develop and improve a system over time in a continuous manner. Crossing the boundaries of various platforms, feedback can be enriched in a very comfortable way, e.g. by annotating a screenshot of the television screen with the smartphone.

Categories and Subject Descriptors

H5.1. **[Multimedia Information Systems]**: Evaluation/ Methodology

General Terms

Evaluation, Methodology, Human Factors

Keywords

Remote evaluation, in-situ feedback, cross platform infrastructure, community help

1. Introduction

Since many years, research has been putting a strong focus on involving users in the design process of new applications. Including employees in the design of computer systems as they are being developed [3], has its origins in Scandinavia, and participatory design (PD) also became important in domestic contexts. Previous work has put strong focus on real life contexts, with PD variations used for evaluation and exploration. 'Cultural probes' have been used to explore this approach in order to gain new ideas for improvement. Bernhaupt [2] for example created and tested the 'playful probes' – a collection of games and playful material aimed at encouraging user involvement. Other works focus on the question of how to evaluate new prototypes and how to improve usability along design guidelines [1, 5].

In our previous work we gave insight into how users could be involved over longer period of time, in order to collect new ideas and be able to improve functionalities continuously. Our previous experience with community driven development [9] has shown that feedback channels should be integrated directly in the artifact. Instead of only discussing new functionalities in an online forum, additional channels should enable users to provide feedback directly in the context of the usage. Such functionality should go beyond a simple error reporting system and give options to explain desired improvements through visual descriptions, e.g. by annotating a snapshot of the TV interface on the mobile device.

In a running research project we are developing a cross platform framework for the home entertainment domain to support the exchange of audio/visual content between different devices and to enrich this with community functionalities. From an empirical point of view, we have observed different kinds of usage jumps [8] on a single device (e.g. switching between TV and Internet module at the media center system) and between different devices as well (e.g. searching for additional content on the smartphone while watching TV). In order to support such behavior, services need to be adapted for the specific context, e.g. on a public screen or on personal devices. PD oriented work and concepts for remote evaluation may support the design process with adequate services for remote user participation.

Providing feedback on public devices, such as the television set, can be tricky. Normally controlled via remote control, the TV provides only limited options to enter text or highlight certain screen area. While designing for a cross platform infrastructure, we also scaled the feedback-issue on that level. It means that the users should be able to generate in-situ feedbacks on any device and annotate it easily with another one, e.g. capture a screenshot on the mobile device and edit it on the tablet. Options should provide the users with possibilities to enrich screenshots and photos with text, audio or other descriptive elements. The feedbacks then can be made available for the developers and other users as well, e.g. in an online forum. This opportunity would empower users to articulate their needs much easier and much clearer, which in turn makes it possible for the designers to understand the context much better.

2. Context & Motivation

The digitization of the media scene entails far-reaching changes in domestic appliances and information technology. More and more devices such as the television are being equipped with computer technology thus offer diverse additional functions because of their network capability. Full-video content is available on demand and in a nonlinear fashion in different contexts. In our research project SocialMedia we will take these developments into account by exploring new integrated techniques and concepts for cross-platform communication and exchange between users. Therefore, we focus on a dynamic home-IT infrastructure, in which the TV or the media center PC is an important component. We are particularly interested in concepts that support social exchange with regard to full-video content.

User participation in the design and evaluation process has an increasingly important impact on innovative application development [3]. The SocialMedia project has been following the participatory design principle right from the start. A Living-Lab consisting of 27 participants from 16 households has been established in the early stages of the project [10] and design and development has taken advantage of the long-term test studies from the Living-Lab. From the methodological point of view, long-term cooperation with testers requires a specific methodology toolkit that should include standard approaches (e.g. controlled lab studies or media diaries) and customized feedback tools as well. While we used both former methods in certain stages of the project (e.g. creative workshops with groups of participants, usability studies in controlled lab environments), we were also confronted with the need to involve participants in a more continuous way, in-situ at home. This was requested by both the developers and the users. Developers wanted to have feedback channels that were built into the prototypes they developed, in order to receive feedback directly from the actual context of use, so that they could understand the problems better and come up with solutions faster. Users wanted to have easier options to exchange their user experience with other users from the test group in order to help each other in the process of appropriation. Unlike any full automatic bug tracking system, our feedback infrastructure presented in this paper suits the best in a long-term qualitative research methodology. The motivation is to use feedback as a trigger for later discussion between developers and users. The developer will always contact the user and refer to the feedbacks together to help both parties understand the problem better, in this sense the users are able to "co-develop" with the developers.

Within the current development status of the project, we have built an alpha version of a social TV application running on the media center PC which is connected to the television screen, a mobile application running on Android powered gadgets, and a social platform on the web. The motivation of the feedback architecture described in this paper is to provide feedback channels for the interconnected application components during the design phase, so that the developers are able to gather first-hand user needs with preserved context in order to re-design the current (basic) version, as well as gather new ideas for further releases. On the other hand, such tools are important for the users as well to be able to support the appropriation of new applications by providing integrated help channels.

3. PREVIOUS WORK

From the literature there are different methodological approaches to empower the user to report usability and user experience aspects from the real usage context. When studying user interaction with a system imbedded into their real life usage context, in-situ studies are appreciated for its directness of feedback and preservation of the exact context [16]. As shown in the work of Obrist et al. [13], an in-situ field study is best suited for real usage context and actively engaging test sessions. However, it requires the developers to be synchronously and physically beside or next to the users, as direct communication between stakeholders is seen as key in this approach. The session is relatively action-intensive; this makes it difficult to apply this approach to a long-term evaluation.

While users and developers are involved in different Communities of Practice (CoP), there is a gap in the sense of time, space, and culture between both stakeholders [15]. In order to support the appropriation of new functionalities, tools for remote evaluation can also be used for remote participation between participants as well. Members of the community can be empowered to "help themselves" with issues and problems. Another quite important focus of using online technologies in participatory design projects is the definition of new product requirements through members of the community [9]. Online forums, wikis and options to provide feedback in-situ (here implemented as a voting function via TV) enable members of an online community to discuss and decide on their own, which functionalities are important.

Remote evaluation is a well-accepted method to overcome the limitation of distributed locations of users and developers. Different mechanisms can be used to support exchange between users and developers via audio and video. Such remote evaluation (e.g. semi-instrumented remote evaluation which features asynchronous information exchange) is quite interesting for us, although a brief training for the users is necessary to be able to identify and report the critical incidents [6].

Also relevant are previous workings on Technology Probes [12], Mobile Probes [11] and Infrastructure Probes (IPs) [p]. While mobile probes help to explore the mobile context in question for studying people's actions, technology probes are technical artifacts with the aim to evaluate a technology additionally. The aim of the IPs is close to our work and is theoretically informed by research on E-Infrastructures [14]. The IPs specifically aim at documenting 'infrastructure breakdowns' and 'use innovations'.

While services are becoming more and more interconnected with each other, with adequate interfaces on each device, this should be considered for concepts for distributed user participation. Optimally, meta-tools can be used in an open and more creative phase of design exploration and in a more structured feedback phase for evaluation as well. Compared to previous works [9, 11, 12] we have addressed a feedback concept that overcomes limitations of separated solutions. Ideas, improvements and breakdowns should easily be captured in context of use, accessible and annotatable from any other device with the easy options to share.

4. CROSS PLATFORM FEEDBACK INFRASTRUCTURE

One major problem when testing early stage prototypes in real world contexts is to identify and report critical incidents during usage. Current approaches only concern themselves with specific use contexts and devices. However, lots of applications are developed for multiple devices and in addition to the mobility of devices such as smartphones, tablets or laptops, users are able to switch their spatial usage context. In our concept, we will focus on a cross platform solution, which enables users to capture their current usage setting on any used device and in any usage context, regardless of e.g. whether they are at home watching TV, on the move at the train station or at work, while surfing the internet.

For an optimal specification of critical incidents, and to avoid forcing users to interrupt their workflow, feedback should be created directly from the main application without the need of leaving the usage context. The effort necessary to create a new report should be as low as possible. To simplify this process, we want to benefit from the devices' multimedia interfaces that allow the user to enrich feedbacks by various multimedia contents. Besides simple text messages it shall be possible to attach different types of images; like screenshots or pictures taken with the internal camera of a smartphone, or sketches. Furthermore, videos and audio recordings are helpful in enriching the feedback with meaningful information. This flexibility of being able to choose between multiple input options also has an advantage in regards to the limitations of input options on some devices. Text input, for instance, can be tedious on the smartphone thus voice recording might be a more comfortable option.

In addition, it would be helpful to be able to create and edit feedback on multiple devices. For instance, when using an application on the television, a screenshot of a critical incident can be captured, but making further text annotations or sketches is not possible on this device due to interface restrictions. Hence, the user should be able to switch to another, more suitable device and complete the report there. To make this possible, reports have to be stored temporarily on a central storage unit, where they can be accessed from any device. Besides, depending on the users' context, creating detailed feedback is not always desired or possible, e.g. due to lack of time. In that case, it is helpful to save a report and then complete it later. When a feedback report has been completed, it will be sent to the feedback pool. A forum manager filters the feedback in the first round, picking out those feedback that could advocate discussion within the test group and posts them in the forum of the community portal. Descriptions of problems, issues and improvements can be forwarded to the developers. The developer, or other representatives from the project team, can also contact the user and discuss the feedback with them together, referring to the feedback as a memory cue. In this sense we motivate the users to "co-develop" with us through the design process.

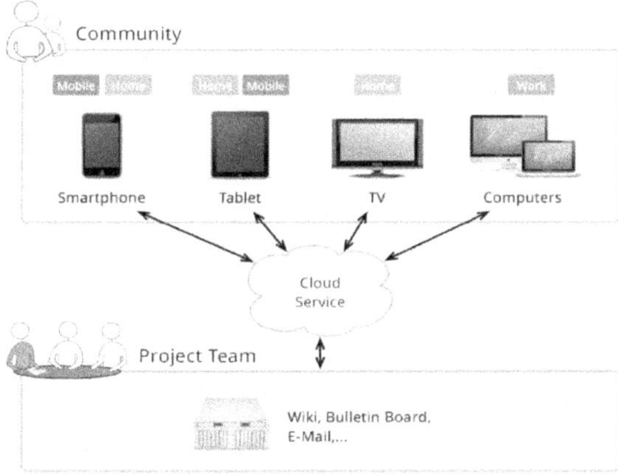

Figure 1. Cross Platform Feedback Infrastructure

Another relevant kind of feedback we are dealing with is the feature request. Due to the strong involvement of users in our design processes, suggestions for additional features will and should be made continuously. These requests can be created in a similar way as a bug report and then submitted to a community portal. This way, the members of the testing community have the opportunity to discuss the submitted feature requests, rate them and even enhance them to participate in the further development.

The overall concept of our cross platform feedback approach is shown in figure 1. Users from a testing community can create bug reports or feature requests on any device they use. To enable a cross platform editing or a subsequent editing, feedbacks are temporarily stored in a central cloud service, where they are accessible from any device at any time. When a report is finished, it will be sent either to a developer platform or a community platform for further discussion. A back channel allows for continuously status request both for the developers or the users.

5. Feedback App

The implementation of the feedback system is highly modular and extensible. The feedback component on each platform can be developed independently and then easily integrated into the whole infrastructure. Starting out, we discussed several options and decided that a feedback tool on a mobile platform should be the first step to the whole system. A feedback tool on a mobile platform can be used in a very flexible way to cover the other platforms when their native feedback counterparts are still in their early design phases. Using the built-in camera of the mobile phone, the user can easily take pictures of the interfaces of the project prototypes on other platforms, e.g. from the sofa and capturing the TV interface. In this way, cross-platform feedback composing can be achieved in a temporarily compromised way. The second reason is due to the different progress of the prototypes development in the SocialMedia project. The mobile application in the project has been the lead in the development compared with the TV client and web client, a feedback tool on the mobile platform to keep pace with the prototype development was then part of our consideration.

In the stage we are currently in, we have developed a feedback tool for the Android platform, which will be delivered together with the project mobile app for user evaluation. Figure 2 shows the user interface and an example feedback report. There are 3 ways to launch the feedback application. It can be started just like any other Android applications and this is meant for casual feedback composing, editing, or browsing. The user is also able to take a screenshot directly in the project mobile app by pressing a key combination of "Menu" and "Search". The feedback app will then automatically open and generates a new feedback report using the screenshot. This method is mostly used to capture use context directly from inside the mobile app. The 3rd method starts with a normal camera capture, the user can then send the photo to a list of applications that is shown to him when he opens the picture from the device's photo gallery. When the user selects the feedback app to receive the photo, the app will be launched and a new feedback report will be generated using the photo. This method is mainly designed for capturing photos of the other platforms.

The example feedback report in Figure 2 consists of a screenshot directly taken from within the project mobile app (in its remote control module) and a photo of the TV client. It was a complaint where, when the user pressed the info button on the mobile app, nothing happened on the TV client. The user was expecting the additional information panel to automatically pop up, so he manually opened the information panel and took a photo of it with the mobile phone to show the effect he would like to have. Each feedback is a combination of text comments, photos, or audio recordings. The 4 icons on the top right corner provide the user with the ability to attach this content to the feedback report. By choosing the send button, the current report is saved on the server's side. The designer can access the feedback and react, e.g. with adaptations of the software or by discussing the feedback in the online forum.

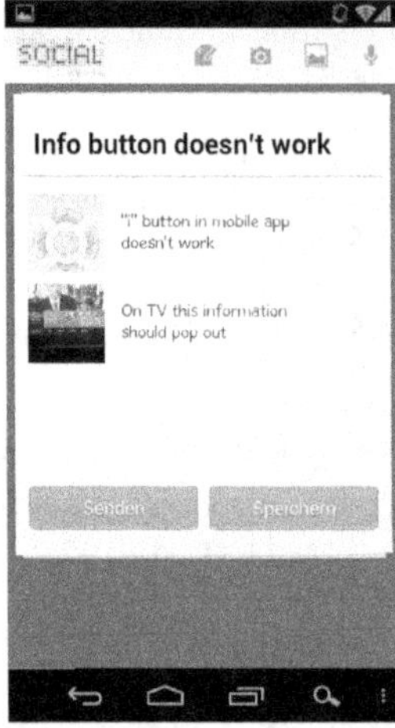

Figure 2. UI of the feedback tool on the mobile platform

6. TOWARDS META-DESIGN VARIATIONS

While infrastructure breakdowns and user innovations become especially visible during usage [14], our work is motivated by the need to involve users more in the design of their usage contexts and within development process. In order to support meta-design as proposed by Fischer [4], with tools that empowers users to continuously 'design' during use, we present the concept of a cross platform feedback infrastructure. It is designed to empower users to provide feedback directly from within the context of use, regardless of specific platform's limitations. The feedback can be sent to the developers for professional support, as well as to other users from the community, to take advantage of the collective wisdom.

For our further work we are planning to use the mobile feedback tool in combination with the project application bundle (the social TV application, the mobile application and the social network). We are aware of the current limitations, but we are able to support the feedback process at the current state. The concept of the cross platform feedback infrastructure can be used in various domains. Even though our current implementation is focused on functionalities that support the design process (e.g. reporting bugs or providing improvement suggestions), the concept can be further utilized for empirical studies, to explore the context in general (e.g. digitalized media diary). In our future work we are also thinking about adding more playful traits to the concept to better motivate users to participate, e.g. by earning badges or providing a 'tamagotchi' like interface.

7. ACKNOWLEDGMENTS

The project *SocialMedia* is funded by the Ministry for Innovation, Science, Research and Technology of the country of North Rhine-Westphalia, Germany with resources from the European Union and European funds for regional developments (Ziel 2) (280411902). Additionally we thank Martin Radvak and Benjamin Sprengart for their assistance in the coding.

8. REFERENCES

[1] Bernhaupt, R., Obrist, M., and Tscheligi, M. (2007). Usability and usage of iTV services: lessons learned in an Austrian field trial. ACM Computer Entertainment *5*, 6.

[2] Bernhaupt, R., Weiss, A., Obrist, M., and Tscheligi, M. (2007). Playful Probing: Making Probing More Fun. Proceedings of the 11th IFIP TC 13 international conference on Human computer interaction *4662*, 606-619.

[3] Bødker, K., Kensing, F., and Simonsen, J. (2004): *Participatory it Design. Designing for Business and Workplace Realities*, MIT press, Cambridge, Massachusetts.

[4] Fischer, G., and Scharff, E. (2000): Meta-Design – Design for Designers. Boyarski, D., and Kellogg, W. Proc. of the third International Conference on Designing Interactive Systems (New York City, August 2000), ACM, 396-405.

[5] Geerts, D., and Leuven, I. K. U. (2009). Supporting the Social Uses of Television : Sociability Heuristics for Social TV. Information Systems Journal, 595-604.

[6] Hartson, H.R., Castillo, J.C., Kelso, J., and Neale, W.C. *Remote evaluation*. ACM Press, New York, New York, USA, 1996.

[7] Hess, J., Dörner, C.; Pipek, V.; Wiedenhöfer, T. (2011): Expressing use: infrastructure probes in professional environments. IS-EUD'11: Proc. of the Third international conference on End-user development, Springer-Verlag.

[8] Hess, J., Ley, B., Ogonowski, C., Wan, L., and Wulf, V. Jumping between devices and services. *Proc. of the 9th international interactive conference on Interactive television 2011*, ACM Press (2011), 11-20.

[9] Hess, J., Offenberg, S., and Pipek, V. (2008): Community-Driven Development as participation? - Involving User Communities in a Software Design Process. In: Participatory Design Conference 2008, (Bloomington, IN, USA, 2008).

[10] Hess, J. and Ogonowski, C. Steps toward a living lab for socialmedia concept evaluation and continuous user-involvement. *Proc. of the 8th international interactive conf. on Interactive TV & Video 2010*, ACM Press (2010), 171.

[11] Hulkko., S., Mattelmäki, T., Virtanen, K. and Keinonen, T., Mobile Probes. Proceedings of NORDICHI 04, (Tampere, Finland, 2004).

[12] Hutchinson, H., Mackay, W., Westerlund, B., Bederson, B. B., Druin, A., Plaisant, C., Beaudouin-Lafon, M., Conversy, S., Evans, H., Hansen, H., Roussel, N., and Eiderbäck, B. Technology probes: inspiring design for and with families. in Proceedings of CHI '03 (2003), ACM Press, 17-24.

[13] Obrist, M., Moser, C., Alliez, D., Holocher, T., and Tscheligi, M. Connecting TV & PC: an in-situ field evaluation of an unified electronic program guide concept. *European Conf. on Interactive Television*, (2009), 91-100.

[14] Pipek V., and Wulf, V. (2009): Infrastructuring: Towards an Integrated Perspective on the Design and Use of Information Technology, Journal of the Association of Information System (JAIS), Volume 10, Issue 5, May 2009, 306-332.

[15] Stevens, G. and Wiedenhöfer, T. *CHIC - a pluggable solution for community help in context*. ACM Press, New York, New York, USA, 2006.

[16] Taylor, P. and Wong, W. Editorial : In Use, In Situ : Extending Field Research Methods. Science, 912280237 (2007).

Who is on Your Sofa? TV Audience Communities and Second Screening Social Networks

Mark Doughty
School of Computer Science,
University of Lincoln,
Lincoln, UK.
mdoughty@lincoln.ac.uk

Duncan Rowland
School of Computer Science,
University of Lincoln,
Lincoln, UK.
drowland@lincoln.ac.uk

Shaun Lawson
School of Computer Science,
University of Lincoln,
Lincoln, UK.
slawson@lincoln.ac.uk

ABSTRACT

Television viewing coupled with audience interaction through a second screen has gained popularity as second screen capable devices have become more pervasive and affordable. In this paper, we investigate the nature of television audiences which engage in second screen interactions. Two different television show audiences are explored though their message activity while using the Twitter social blogging service. Connections are made between users when retweeting messages or mentioning other users in a message. The networks of viewers which are formed when viewers connect through these means reveal different characteristics within the audience networks and imply that different motivations for second screening while watching television shows are in play.

Categories and Subject Descriptors

K.4.m Computers and Society: Miscellaneous

General Terms

Measurement, Human Factors

Keywords

Social computing, second screen, TV viewing, social viewing, co-viewing

1. INTRODUCTION

Watching television in conjunction with the use of a second screen, such as a tablet or laptop computer is a viewing model which has grown rapidly in popularity in recent times. This 'second screening' interaction constitutes a subset of the broader concept of social TV, [4] [9] [19], and facilitates rich levels of computer-mediated interaction between 'connected' viewers.

While social TV incorporates a full spectrum of sociability with respect to television viewing (including mobile device interaction, web streaming, recommender services and 'check-in' apps such as GetGlue[1]), the focus of this paper is on the loosely coupled interactions and subsequent transient ad hoc social networks facilitated by the use of second screens in a television viewing setting.

Specifically, our research investigates the social networks which are manifested within large groups of television show viewers who are using second screens to communicate and comment on the television show being watched. The use of a microblogging service such as Twitter facilitates this second screening process, and in turn allows the collection and archiving of the communication data as it is passed between users in the network. By applying well known social network analysis (SNA) techniques to this data and the associated metadata which reveals user id's and their followers, the structure and characteristics of the network of interacting viewers can be investigated. In particular, the community structures evident in the social network could help to further an understanding of viewers' engagement in second screen interactions. For example, by identifying community characteristics within a TV viewing social network, opportunities for enhancing the viewing experience may arise, viewing patterns and preferences may be assimilated and a deeper understanding of the social characteristics of TV viewing may be reached.

The structure of this paper is as follows. Firstly we present a background to the concepts of social network communities and second screen social networking modes of engagement in Section 2. Section 3 discusses related and supporting work, which is discussed and positioned with respect to this study. The methodology adopted for gathering our data and results of a subsequent analysis are presented in Section 4. The implications of our findings are then discussed in Section 5.

2. BACKGROUND

The use of SNA to understand micro-blogging communities within television audiences implies that the participating audience members have some level of connection with other audience members, and that these connections are traceable. The possible presence of communities of friends or other relational factors within the collected message data is an interesting concept for researchers and could lead to a greater understanding of audience engagement with TV shows. This section therefore begins with an overview of communities and their structures and significance within social networks. The discussion then focuses upon the

EuroITV 2012, July 4-6, 2012, Berlin, Germany.

[1] www.getglue.com

social networks formed by second screening TV viewers and what characterizes those particular networks. The contextual aspect of TV viewing as a driver for these social networks is discussed, and we conclude with a justification for why social networks formed by second screening TV viewers are worthy of research and investigation.

2.1 Social Network Communities and SNA

The tendency for like-minded people to group together is a natural part of society. The online domain has facilitated the formation of communities which transcend natural barriers. Whether these communities are online game players, blog posters and readers, or simply networks of 'real world' friends, these collections of compatible individuals are grouped by homophily: similar beliefs, common goals or similar interests. However, the categorization of a social network 'community' is not straight forward. Different types of sub-groupings within a network are categorized by differing descriptive parameters. As summarized by Fortunato and Castellano [10], community definitions can be categorized according to three main categories: 'Local', which focuses upon the nodes within the sub-group itself, 'global', which places the sub-groups within the context of the whole network, and 'node similarity' which groups nodes by similarity – the criteria for which may be either global or local.

Within a large network of connected nodes, the distribution of these sub-networks of nodes in terms of their 'connectedness' to the other nodes in the network can vary greatly from network to network. The measurement of such distributions can be by a number of different parameters, each of which measures a particular characteristic of the whole network. *Density*, being the measure of the level of connections between nodes, *betweenness*, which measures the extent to which a node lies between other nodes in the network, *centrality*, which broadly indicates the number of connections a node has to others in its locale, *reciprocity*, which measures the incidence of mutual connections between two nodes and *inclusiveness*, which shows the proportion of connected nodes to isolated, or unconnected nodes, in the network, are all measureable parameters which allow us to compute certain characteristics of a social network, and in turn determine the nature of any communities or sub-groups within the network. A full discussion of these parameters is provided by Scott [22], and a mapping of the concepts to networks of second screening audiences is made in the following section.

In practical terms, network communities or sub-groups are generally characterized by groupings of higher density node – node connections, but between which the connections are less dense [12]. For some networks these sub-groupings may be self organizing, as network members select their sub-groups consciously (for example, society memberships of University students, or football team supporting fans will be self selecting sub-groups of a broader network). For others, sub-groupings, or clustering, may arise through more indirect or emergent means.

2.2 Second Screen Social Networks

The shared or co-viewing experience afforded by the use of a second screen during television viewing sessions has rapidly grown in popularity [8]. The growth in significance of a connected and networked television audience which communicates through digital backchannels is becomming more commonly recognized by broadcasters, with many displaying Twitter 'hashtags' on screen to allow the second screening audience to 'tune' their data streams to one focused upon the particular broadcast being viewed.

The networks which are formed by viewers engaging in second screen activity can be interpreted in different ways. Network connections ('edges') between two different viewers ('nodes') can be generated by looking for when a 'retweet' or 'mention' has been generated in the hashtag stream for a particular show, indicating that a user has consciously re-broadcast another users Twitter message (a 'retweet') or who has directed a Twitter message at, about or including another user as a component in the message (a 'mention'). A connection between users in the context of retweets and mentions contributes to what could be called a 'conversational ecology' [3] and shows that a conversational connection exists between the users. Another form of determining network connections and structure is to look for 'follower' connections between users. Twitter users can opt to 'follow' another user. This constitutes a unilateral decision to form the connection (users do not have to formally 'accept' a follower request as is the convention with other social networks such as facebook). Users are, however, free to 'block' another user from messaging them directly. A follower will receive tweet messages from their followed accounts whenever they are generated.

In our research, we are focused upon the networks formed by retweets and mentions between users. The nature of a retweeted message or a mention indicates a strong affinity for the content of the tweet message or the identity of the mentioned user [6].

2.2.1 Second Screening

Second screening, or more informally, 'sofalising', is a term used to describe the act of coupling a TV viewing activity with second screen interaction. This additional screen may be that of a mobile device such as a smartphone or tablet, it may also be a laptop or personal computer screen [4], [5]. These devices may be more tightly coupled in an interactive TV environment for instance (ref:), or they may be utilized to enhance a more passive viewing experience by exposing rich, related data streams from social media platforms.

The use of a second screen while watching TV can be employed in different modes of interaction. Whether it is a social sharing mode where the screen connects the viewer to the wider co-viewing audience [8], an interactive, tightly coupled display which feeds additional content or recommendations to the viewer [4], or a control device for enhancing or tailoring the viewing content [1], the additional screen is a key portal to the new viewer experiences in each of these modes of interaction. The ready availability, affordability and ubiquity of second screen devices means that these types of interaction are accessible to a large proportion of the TV viewing audience.

2.2.2 TV as a Context Driver

The focal point and contextual driver for second screen co-viewing activity is the TV broadcast content. Predominantly 'live' or 'as scheduled' shows, the actors, participants and narratives are discussed, commented on or spoken to, by social networks of connected viewers using a range of social network platforms or technologies. While TV provides a *context*, then the social networking activity of the viewing audience is a *catalyst* to a new, more engaged viewing audience. Audience members may see themselves as more deeply integrated into the media 'ecosystem' rather than being passive consumers of media messages [24]. Audience members may also contribute to the content and currency of the broadcast. Hermida [14] discusses the role that

Twitter has in contributing to TV news for example. He describes 'microbursts' of journalistic information, which, with careful filtering and interpretation contribute to an emerging 'ambient journalism' culture.

The connections between audience members afforded by the retweet (RT) and mention structures within twitter allows us to view the information flows and links within a distributed TV audience. Opinions, observations and personal status updates related to the TV show are shared and connections made. Questions are raised however when we look at what the structure of a second screening TV audience might look like, and indeed what might be the range of experiences for individual viewers by becoming part of such a network during a TV show broadcast?

2.3 Why Study Second Screening Social Networks?

The rise in popularity of second screen activities amongst TV viewing audiences presents us with a new problem domain. The network of viewers which becomes active when a TV show is broadcast is made up of a sub-set of the total viewing public. This is a self-selecting cross-section of social network using television viewers, i.e. people who have made the conscious decision to use microblogging – sych as Twitter – whilst watching television and who, for the most part, want to post short messages about their watching experience. Marwick and Boyd [18] examine a user's motivation for posting Twitter messages in a general setting. They conclude that users could be 'mentioning' friends (using the @username notation), 'retweeting' or rebroadcasting a message to their own friend network, simply 'blogging' their thoughts with no particular audience in mind, or directing their message to an unspecified audience, but one which is interested in the topic of the message by using the #, or 'hashtag', topic classifier notation.

A TV audience within the context of the social network needs to be interpreted differently in the light of these networked activities. Individual audience members could metaphorically 'invite' other viewers of the show into their viewing circle. By mentioning another user or retweeting another comment, a conversation about the TV show is initiated which could possibly be analogous to a co-located TV viewing event on a communal sofa. As Marwick and Boyd conclude, the audience is no longer a stable group congregated around a media product, rather a network of groups of highly engaged people who produce as well as consume. A social networking technology such as Twitter allows the focusing of this production and consumption within a network of real, active co-contributors. The information flows and connections made in the viewing network are interesting as they could potentially reveal audience characteristics and community features which are normally hidden under the surface of a TV audience. Understanding these characteristics further may provide opportunities for addressing sub-groups within an audience directly, or possibly filtering or mining data produced in the information exchanges to better understand the nature of a networked TV audience.

3. RELATED WORK

As Twitter themselves acknowledge, television and Twitter have a 'special connection' [25]. Twitter's own analysis of this focuses upon the marketing potential of the Twitter stream as TV shows publicize hashtags, encourage 'trending topics' (a 'trending topic' is a word, phrase or hashtag which become popular very quickly as many users mention it in their messages within a short timeframe), or read tweets live on air. The benefit to the television show is increased exposure of their presence and content to the wider Twitter user base, and it also gives Twitter users a channel through which they can build a relationship with the show. The marketing activity of television shows through Twitter is a conscious strategic activity by television networks to exploit the dissemination potential of a dynamic social network [17], in particular, the role of influence and popularity of key users in the network in this sense, is drawing particular research attention, for example, Bakshy et al. [2], Cha et al. [6] and Wu et al. [30].

The communal aspects of television viewing within a 'social TV' infrastructure is a phenomenon which has gathered interest in recent years, for example Oehlberg et al. [20], Evangelia et al. [9] and Mitchell et al. [19] explore the social awareness issues related to audience interactivity within television show broadcasts. Projects which exploit the developing synergy between media broadcast activity and social media are emerging. Many projects focus upon the recommendation power of the social graph and the presentation of television content based upon user social media behavior, for example [19], [23] while Sofanatics[2], which launched during the 2010 FIFA World Cup, brings football supporters together in a social network context during live game broadcasts to discuss the action and comment on the games through a common interface. iOS apps such as Miso[3] and Peel[4] offer a hybrid TV check-in and recommender service within a social media context.

The actual structures and variability of viewer virtual communities formed when watching a common TV broadcast are not yet fully understood and many questions remain open. For instance, do viewers consciously invite other viewers or friends into their 'viewing circle' to discuss the show and exchange views or are the audiences more a homogeneous group of like-minded individuals all watching together?

4. ANALYSIS OF SECOND SCREEN SOCIAL NETWORKS

To explore the nature of viewer communities and audience structures which are formed while consuming TV broadcast events and interacting through second screen channels, we gathered Twitter data which was generated during two live television broadcasts in the UK: (i) BBC Question Time and (ii) Strictly Come Dancing.

BBC Question Time is a weekly political panel debate show during which contemporary political and other prominent individuals are questioned by a live studio audience. The show is a late night broadcast, usually airing shortly after 10.30pm. While there is no formal interaction between the programme and the TV viewers, the presenter does, however, promote the use of a hashtag *(#bbcqt)* to focus the discussion of viewers through Twitter. The message data was gathered during the BBC2 broadcast on Thursday October 27th between 10.35pm and 11.35pm UK time (GMT).

Strictly Come Dancing is a live TV show which features celebrities dancing with professional dance partners in ballroom dance styles. The viewing public vote for their favorite dancers

[2] www.sofanatics.com

[3] www.gomiso.com

[4] www.peel.com

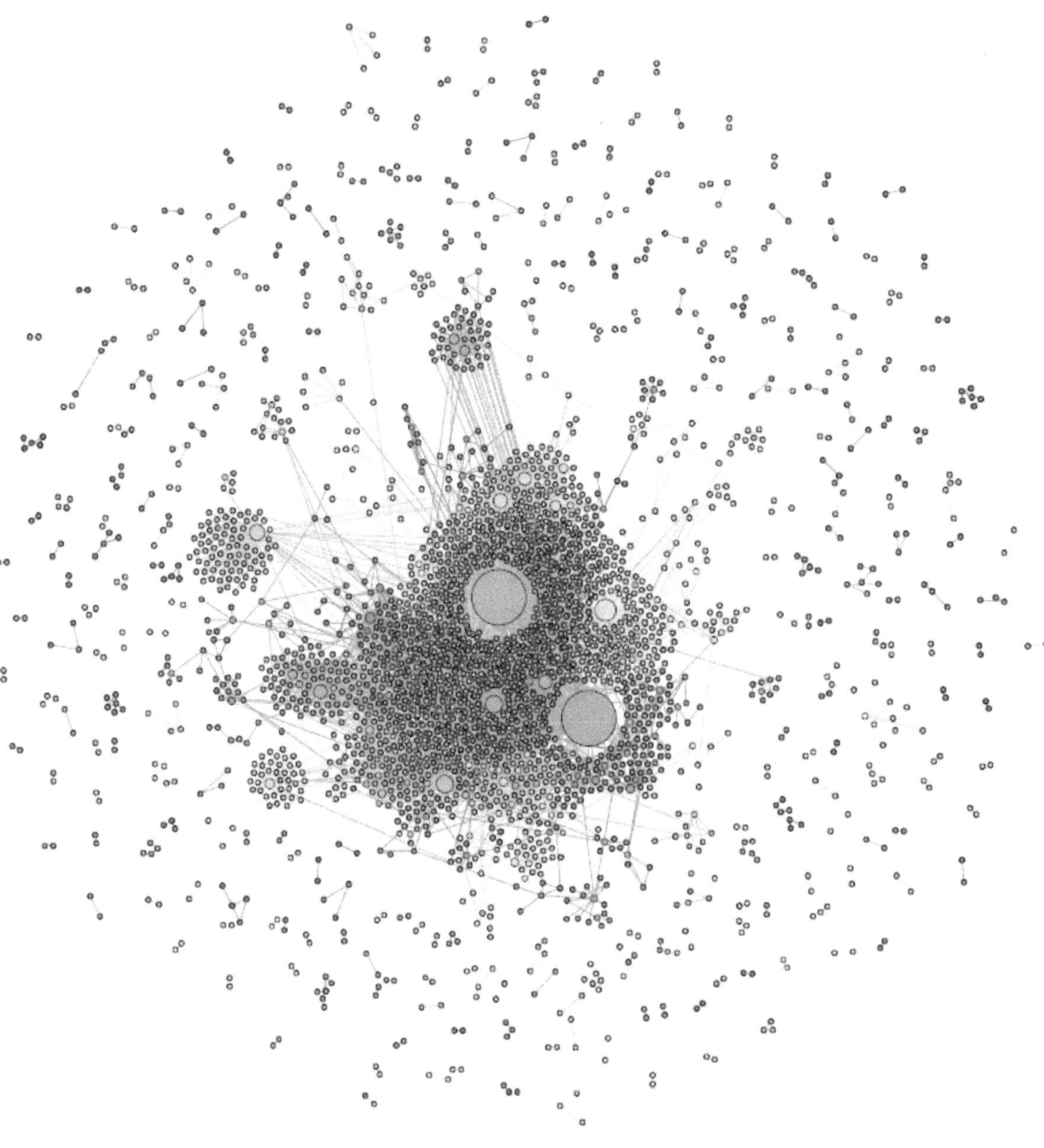

Figure 1: #scd mentions and retweets network

and a panel of judges pass critical comment, with these results being combined to determine which dance couples leave the show and who stays each week. The 2011 series ran between 10th September 2011 to 17th December 2011. Twitter message data (using the *#scd* hashtag) relating to the show was gathered during the BBC1 broadcast of the live semi-final on 10th December 2011 between 6.35pm and 7.45pm UK time (GMT).

4.1 Data Gathering

Tweet data was gathered in real time as the programmes were broadcast by accessing the Twitter Stream API. The Stream API allows the sampling of all public Twitter statuses in either a sample mode, where up to 10% of all Twitter status updates are gathered, or in a filter mode, where 'track' keywords or geo-location parameters can be used filter the stream for targeted tweets. By using the TV show hashtags as track keywords, we filtered relevant tweets from the Twitter Firehose (the entire stream of Twitter data). As we used only single track parameters, rather than a collection, we could rely on all occurrences of relevant tweets being returned [27].

The limitation of this method is that we only gathered tweets which contained the relevant hashtag. While this ensured that the collected tweets contained contextual information for the TV shows, users are not forced to use hashtags in their tweets.

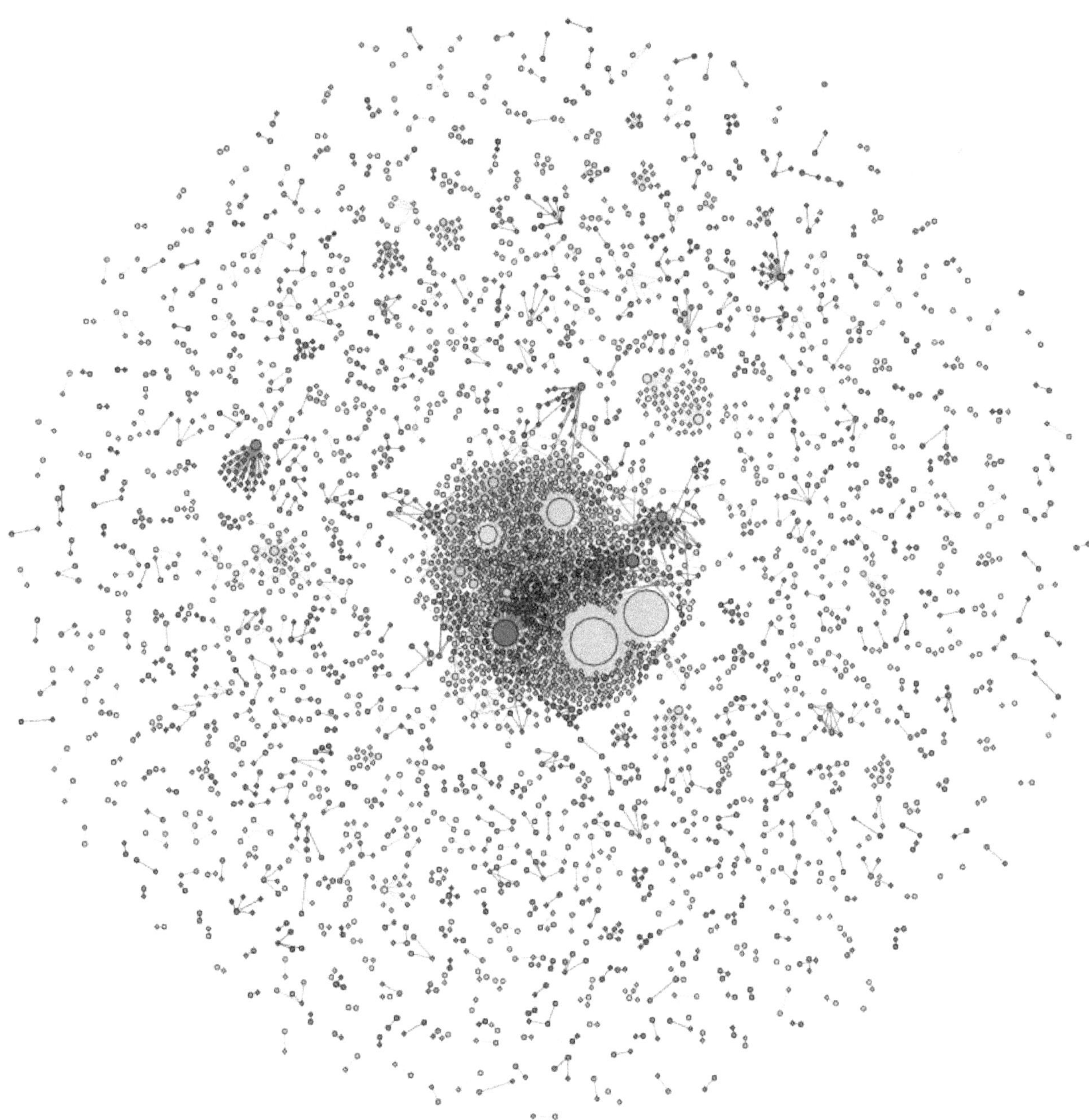

Figure 2: #bbcqt retweets and mentions network

Therefore it is reasonable to assume that tweets were posted about the TV shows which didn't contain the target hashtags. As discussed by Laniado and Mika [16], hashtags which are similar to common words and are simply differentiated with a preceding '#' are less specific as more Twitter specific tags which do not correspond to words in common usage. As our tags are *#bbcqt* and *#scd*, neither of which being commonly used words, we can be confident that their use was within our expected context, i.e about the TV shows in question. In addition, both TV shows advertised their 'preferred' hashtag corresponding to our search terms which reinforces their choice as tracking terms.

A total of 7011 tweet messages from 5367 users were collected during the Question Time broadcast, while 11840 tweet messages from 4891 users were collected relating to the Strictly Come Dancing broadcast.

4.2 Analyzing the Audience Network

As our intention is to explore the nature of the community structures within these socially interacting TV audiences, the message collections need to be processed to discover links and conversational threads between users, which could reveal potential community groupings and structures. To reveal the links between users, three indicators of influence within the network were considered as discussed by [6]: a) the identity of the followers of a user who were also watching the TV broadcast, b) the retweet patterns between users and c) the presence of user mentions in messages. While the followers measure indicates a connection between the follower and the followed user, its significance in conversations and community connections is lower than that of the presence of retweets and mentions in messages. We therefore took all of the collected messages and constructed a list of user connections. A directed connection was made between users when a message from a user contained a retweet signification or a user mention in the text. Messages which contained retweet indication and multiple mentions resulted in multiple connections from one user to a number of other users. There were some instances in both networks of users mentioning themselves in their messages, resulting in a self directed loop. These connections were compiled into a single list of connections, or 'edges' which indicated a directed connection between users, or 'nodes'.

The network for each TV show was constructed from these edge/node lists by importing them into the Gephi[5] network analysis tool. In order to view the networks, each data set was processed with the OpenOrd[6] network visualization algorithm plugin which emphasizes clustering and community structures within a network. The 'edge cut' parameter was set to 0.0 to ensure that all nodes were visible in the network representation. To better visualize status within the network, the 'in-degree' of each node which relates to the number of mentions or retweets that user has received, is represented by the relative sizes of the nodes. The larger nodes represent users which have received more mentions ands retweets.

A visible feature of both networks is the bimodal distribution of connected nodes. Communities or groupings of nodes are either in a disconnected, isolate form, or in a more connected major grouping within which are found the nodes with the greater in-degree. The more disconnected communities within the networks are distinguished by their isolation from the main grouping of nodes and also their separation from the main influencers or foci of attention within the network. These communities consist of dyads, which represent a conversation or relationship between two people only, and groupings with higher membership, but with varying structures and degrees of connection between the members.

The *#scd* network (Figure 1) consists of 3903 edges between 2895 nodes, of which 443 edges and 695 nodes are located in the isolated groupings. The *#bbcqt* network (Figure 2) consists of 3769 edges between 3955 nodes, of which 2640 nodes and 1913 edges are located in the isolated groupings.

The overall level of reciprocity, r, between users in each audience network, indicating the level of reciprocated mentions or retweets is at a similar level but very low. In the *#bbcqt* network, r = 2.17%, while in the *#scd* network, r = 3.07%. When compared to typical reciprocity measures for followers on Twitter (the proportion of user relationships which show a reciprocation in following) which is reported by Kwak et al. to be 22.7% [15] these figures are low. There is an observed difference however, when we compare the reciprocity of the connections between the users in the disconnected, isolated groupings and the more tightly connected and networked 'core' of each of the networks. For *#scd* those users in the disconnected groupings show reciprocity of r = 5.6% against 2.74% for those in the core connected group, while for *#bbcqt*, the disconnected users show r = 2.97%, against 1.34% for those in the core group.

[5] http://gephi.org

[6] https://gephi.org/plugins/openord-layout/

4.3 Community Clustering and Degree

The two audience networks display a difference in the types of viewer communities which are formed when audience members engage in messaging and discussing the shows through Twitter. The clustering coefficient, which is a measure of the ratio of the number of edges between a node and its immediate neighbourhood and the maximum number of edges which could exist, is an indication of the degree to which the network conforms to a 'small-world' principle [11] where users are connected to many others through their immediate connections. For *#scd*, the overall network clustering coefficient is 0.055, which compares with that of *#bbcqt* which is 0.066. Again these values are small when compared to social networks such as the Facebook social graph (0.167) [28]. For the central core of the networks where edges are more prominent, *#scd* clustering is a slightly higher 0.066, while *#bbcqt* is 0.116.

If we look at the clustering measurement within the context of the average degree of the nodes, then an interesting comparison is seen. The area of higher clustering in each graph corresponds to greater average degree for the nodes involved compared to the overall graph (*#scd:* average degree overall: 1.34, average degree core: 1.57, *#bbcqt*: average degree overall: 0.95, average degree core: 1.411).

5. DISCUSSION

The two audience networks described here are representative of two different genres of television show. Strictly Come Dancing is a prime time, dancing entertainment, celebrity oriented reality TV show, while BBC Question Time is a late night current affairs debate and panel discussion show. The interactions between the audience members through the social network medium of Twitter show some similarities however, as well as some differences. It is interesting to see a similar separation of the audiences into a tightly clustered and connected 'core', containing nodes of higher degree, and a less connected, collection of small membership communities which tend to display more reciprocity in network connections between users. In both networks, the core contains the nodes of highest degree, which in most cases represent the individuals featuring in the TV shows, other 'celebrities' and well known people or organizations. These individuals exhibit much higher 'in-degree' than the rest of the network but lower reciprocity, possibly reflecting their popularity or status within the audience network, but that the connection is mainly a one way dialogue. The presence of organizations such a media companies, bloggers and charities in the networks is an interesting one. They have no direct connection to the television show, yet through connecting with other users in the network, a level of exposure and self promotion is achieved.

The meaning of reciprocity within these networks is of reciprocated mentions in Twitter messages. In other words reciprocity is evidence of a two way conversation between the users with the TV show as the focus. The low overall levels of reciprocity in both networks indicate that edges which do not display reciprocated mentions could signify viewers who message friends who are not viewing the show to invite or remind them to view also, or to initiate a conversation about the show which is not followed up by the other user.

There is no temporal element to reciprocity of user links in this network. Unlike in a friendship network, where friendships can be made and withdrawn, once a mention or retweet has been made it is fixed. One solution to this could be to introduce a link 'decay' parameter to such connections whereby links could be removed if no reciprocal mentions are made within a particular time frame.

The difference in reciprocity levels through the networks and its apparent inverse relationship to areas of high clustering and average degree is a possible indication of the celebrity culture which drives many of Twitter users' 'following' activity. The evidence that the areas containing the users with the highest degree (i.e. the most mentioned or retweeted users) and clustering coefficient displays a lower level of reciprocity is an interesting example of the development of status hierarchies [13] (cited in [21]), whereby an unresponsive receiver of a mention in a tweet could effectively be asserting a position of superior status to the originator of the message in the network.

The less clustered areas of the network imply that different interaction mechanisms are at play between users. These connections are more likely between groups of friends and possibly represent more of a conversational interaction. The metaphor of inviting someone to 'share your sofa' through tweet mentions and retweets is a compelling one, with mini communities of users forming and discussing the television show through second screen interfaces. The development of companion applications to support and provide a more formal interaction space for these activities is a possibility which we are exploring in our ongoing investigations in this area.

6. CONCLUSIONS

Our investigation looks at the characteristics of a networked television audience which communicates in real time through a second screen interface. We explore two differing genres of television show and the characteristics of the audience groups show some similarity as well as differences. The prime time, celebrity oriented Strictly Come Dancing show has a greater proportion of its networked audience connecting with the celebrities and stars of the show, while the current affairs show, BBC Question Time, has a greater proportion of networked viewers engaging in conversation with friends. This is reflective of the content and tone of the shows.

Connections with celebrities and stars of the shows were made through mentions and retweeted messages. These tightly clustered connections were rarely reciprocated and represent recognition of the status of the higher degree users in the network. Higher rates of reciprocation of links were observed between the more disconnected, smaller communities within both networks. These communities appear to represent co-viewing, friendship relationships and are analogous to virtual gatherings on virtual sofas to watch and discuss the television show in question.

In conclusion we argue that users in these networks are displaying different behaviours. The common aspect of the behaviour is that it is directed through a second screen interface, but that viewers are either looking for a more communal viewing experience with friends or like minded viewers, or they are exploiting the closeness to celebrity which these networks facilitate, to possibly increase their own status or exposure within the network by taking advantage of the higher visibility and popularity of the central users in the network.

7. REFERENCES

[1] Alfaro, S., Bove, M., Surround Vision – A Hand-Held Screen for Accessing Peripheral Content around a Main Screen and Transfer Television Content, *LNCS*, 2011. 7069:324-345.

[2] Bakshy, E., Hofman, J., Mason, W., Watts, D., Identifying 'Influencers' on Twitter, *WSDM* 2011, ACM Press.

[3] Boyd, D., Golder, S., Lotan, G., Tweet, Tweet, Retweet: Conversational Aspects of Retweeting on Twitter, *HICSS*2010, Jan 5-8, 2010.

[4] Cesar, P., Bulterman, D., Jansen, A., Usages of the Secondary Screen in an Interactive Television Environment: Control, Enrich, Share, and Transfer Television Content, *LNCS*, 2008, 5066:168-177.

[5] Cesar, P., Knoche, H., Bulterman, D., From One to Many Boxes: Mobile Devices as Primary and Secondary Screens, *Human–Computer Interaction Series* 2010, 6:327-348.

[6] Cha, M., Haddadi, H., Benvenuto, F., Gummadi, K., Measuring User Influence in Twitter: The million follower fallacy, *In Proc. Fourth Int. AAAI Conf. on Weblogs and Social Media,* AAAI.org, 2010.

[7] Chou, B., Suzuki, E., Discovering Community-Oriented Roles of Nodes in a Social Network, *In Proc. DaWaK2010*, Bilbao, Spain, 2010.

[8] Doughty, M., Lawson, S., Rowland, D., Co-Viewing Live TV with Digital Backchannel Streams, *in proc EuroITV2011*, ACM Press, 2011.

[9] Evangelia, M., Lekakos, G., Vrechopoulos, A., Social TV: Introducing Virtual Socialization in the TV Experience, *uxTV'08*, ACM Press.

[10] Fortunato, S., Castellano, C., Community Structure in Graphs, *Encyclopedia of Complexity and System Science*, B. Meyers, ed., Springer Verlag, Heidelberg, Germany, 2008 (arXiv:0712.2716).

[11] Fraginiaud, P., Giakkoupis, G., On the Searchability of Small-World Networks with Arbitrary Underlying Structure, *STOC'10*, ACM Press, 2010.

[12] Girvan, M., Newman, M., Community Structure in Social and Biological Networks, *PNAS* 99:12 7821-7826, 2002.

[13] Gould, R., The Origins of Status Hierarchies: a Formal Theory and Empirical Test, *.Am. J. Sociol.* 107:1143–78, 2002.

[14] Hermida, A., From TV to Twitter: How Ambient News became Ambient Journalism, *Media/Culture* 13:2, 2010.

[15] Kwak, H., Lee, C., Park, H., Moon, S., What is Twitter, a Social Network or News Media? *In Proc. WWW'10*, ACM Press, 2010.

[16] Laniado, D., Mika, P., Making Sense of Twitter, *ISWC 2010*, in LNCS 2010, 6496:470-485, Springer.

[17] Lin, J., Pena, J., Are you Following Me? A Content Analysis Of TV Networks' Brand Communication On Twitter, *Journal of Interactive Advertising*, 12:1, 2011.

[18] Marwick, A., Boyd, D., I Tweet Honestly, I Tweet Passionately: Twitter Users, Context Collapse and the Imagined Audience, *New Media & Society* 13:1 114-133, Sage Journals.

[19] Mitchell, K., Jones, A., Ishmael, J., Race, N., Social TV: Toward Content Navigation Using Social Awareness, *in proc. EuroITV2010* ACM Press, 2010.

[20] Oehlberg, L., Ducheneaut, N., Thornton, J., Moore, R., Nickell, E., Social TV: Designing for Distributed, Sociable Television Viewing, *in proc. EuroITV2006*, ACM Press, 2006.

[21] Rivera, M., Soderstrom, S., Uzzi, B., Dynamics of Dyads in Social Networks: Assortative, Relational and Proximity Mechanisms, *Annu. Rev. Sociol.* 2010. 36:91 – 115

[22] Scott, J., Social Network Analysis, 2nd ed. Sage Publications, London, 2000.

[23] Sena, H., Dias, R., de Melo, J., Burlamaqui, A., Trend TV: An Architecture for Automatic Change of TV Channels Based on Social Networks with Multiple Device Support, *IEEE VECIMS 2011*, Ottawa, Canada.

[24] Stefanone, M., Lackaff, D., Rosen, D., The Relationship between Traditional Mass Media and "Social Media": Reality Television as a Model for Social Network Site Behavior, *Journal of Broadcasting and Electronic Media*, 54:3 508-525, Taylor Francis, 2010.

[25] Twitter blog: Watching Together: Twitter and TV, http://blog.twitter.com/2011/05/watching-together-twitter-and-tv.html

[26] Twitter API Documentation, https://dev.twitter.com/docs/streaming-api/concepts

[27] Valente, T., Fujimoto, K., Bridging: Locating Critical Connectors in a Network, *Soc. Networks* 32:3 212-220, 2010.

[28] Wilson, C., Boe, B., Sala, A., Puttaswamy, K., Zhao, B., User Interactions in Social Networks and their Implications, *in proc EuroSys'09*, ACM Press, 2009.

[29] Wohn, Y., Na, E., Tweeting About TV: Sharing Television Viewing Experiences via Social Media Message Streams, *First Monday*, 16:3, March 2011.

[30] Wu, S., Hofman, J., Mason, W., Watts, D., Who Says What to Whom on Twitter, *in proc. WWW'11*, ACM press, 2011.

FANFEEDS: Evaluation of Socially Generated Information Feed on Second Screen as a TV Show Companion

Santosh Basapur
Interactive Media User Research
Applied Research Center
Motorola Mobility Inc.
USA
+1 630 254 0490
sbasapur@motorola.com

Hiren Mandalia
Interactive Media User Research
Applied Research Center
Motorola Mobility Inc.
USA
+1 630 254 0490
hirenm@motorola.com

Shirley Chaysinh
Interactive Media User Research
Applied Research Center
Motorola Mobility Inc.
USA
+1 630 254 0490
Shirley.Chaysinh@motorola.com

Young Lee
Interactive Media User Research
Applied Research Center
Motorola Mobility Inc.
USA
+1 630 254 0490
younglee@motorola.com

Narayanan Venkitaraman
Interactive Media User Research
Applied Research Center
Motorola Mobility Inc.
USA
+1 630 254 0490
cnv002@motorola.com

Crysta Metcalf
Interactive Media User Research
Applied Research Center
Motorola Mobility Inc.
USA
+1 630 254 0490
crysta.metcalf@motorola.com

ABSTRACT

In this paper, we describe the development and field trial of a second screen iTV experience called FanFeeds. FanFeeds is a second screen application that allows authoring and consumption of time synchronized secondary content around TV shows. FanFeeds are created by one's social circle as a companion experience to TV shows. For the purpose of concept evaluation, we ran a four-week field trial in 12 households consisting of 4 social groups of 3 friends. A total of 23 unique episodes of 12 different shows were watched while using our prototype. Overall feedback to our concept was mixed. Participants found some good motivations to use the system but they also found a number of concerns related to the nature of the shows they watched and the social dynamics with their friends. Participants revealed that our prototype allowed them to better connect with their TV shows and have an enriched social life around live as well as time-shifted TV content. Participants also described some concerns like distraction from TV show. We explore this contradiction in the paper, along with other valuable lessons we learned. We also report on the motivations that made participants create posts for one another and the different ways in which they used the information from the second screen.

Categories and Subject Descriptors

H5.1 [Information Interfaces and presentation]: Multimedia information systems – audio, video; H5.m [Information Interfaces and presentation (e.g., HCI)]: Miscellaneous

Keywords

Interactive Television, Experimentation, HCI, User Experience, Second Screen iTV Application, Fan Generated Information Feed

1. INTRODUCTION

By 2015, the tablet PCs alone will have a projected U.S. market share of 23%. If all personal devices like the netbooks and laptops are considered, the percentage grows to 82% [12]. A recent report released by Nielsen in association with Yahoo Inc. in October 2011 revealed that 42% of tablet owners and 40% of SmartPhone owners use their devices while watching TV [26]. According to the report, approximately 40% visit social networking sites during the show or the commercial breaks, approximately 30% look up show related information on their personal device and 20% look up information related to products featured in the advertisements. These results indicate that the advent of powerful second screens is now an integral part of regular life in TV rooms during the content consumption experience.

While such proliferation of devices and usage trends create great opportunities for iTV experiences, new challenges come with it. Especially, the main challenge in the context of the second screens is to keep viewers engaged with the primary contents of TV rather than distracting their attention from it. Also, it is a challenge to figure out what shows work well with multi-device iTV experiences and in what different situations. Projects like CollaboraTV [25], RendezVous [28] and Motorola Inc.'s dual device iTV user experience [3] have attempted to provide asynchronous social commentary related to TV show on the TV, auto-generated and expert generated contextual information (related to TV show) on second screen respectively. But they all left out crucial element of "socially generated information bundles" in addition to just commentary on the second screen. For this reason, we aimed to investigate if socially generated media feeds on a second screen companion device enhance (or hinder) the TV viewing experience. Also, we wanted to understand the types of information feeds that people create and consume with each other. Investigation of social engagement among people around content and the second screen experience was important for us as well.

Our specific Research Questions were:

RQ1. What is the overall experience of TV viewing when FanFeeds prototype is being used?

RQ2. What are the different motivations (like social or gamification) for people to create supplemental content for their social circles?

RQ3. How do people consume the informational feeds and other social commentary from their social circles?

2. RELATED WORK

Recently, there has been an increase in commercial interest in two-screen iTV services that allow fans to interact with TV shows in different ways and to socialize around content. IntoNow is an application available on iPad that Yahoo Inc. released late last year. IntoNow allows users to tell their friends what television shows and movies you're watching in real time [20]. But unlike other media "check-in" services like Miso or GetGlue [17, 24], IntoNow listens and infers what you're watching using audio tracing technology. Boxee [6] and TVLoop [7] rely on the crowd to curate what is available online for consumption and to help people decide what to watch. The Buddy TV application [15], available on Android and IOS platforms, allows fans to connect with other fans of TV shows and share thoughts on new and past episodes. But this interaction is on a public forum and do not capture comments relative to the show timeline. Lastly, ScreenTribe is an application that allows people to share their TV watching activity with friends and earn points [31].

Second screen experiences have been around in iTV research since late 1990s. In 1996, Robertson et al. put browsing of floor plans of homes on second screen (PDAs) while users watched primary video on TV [29]. Other previous research in second screen based iTV experiences includes HyperTV [30] which provided internet content on second screen, Fallakhair's work in T-learning [14, 15] where language lessons and video content were presented on dual device user interfaces, and lately work in interactive EPGs like that of Cruickshank [11] and Obrist [27] has have also used mobile devices to support TV viewing experiences.

Two projects are quite close to this project of FanFeeds. In RendezVous project [28], users receive contextual information, related to the primary TV content, on their second screen. But the feed of information supplied, came from an automated system, which worked off of pre-established editorial rules. Even though interesting, this system runs the risk of automated recommendations being false positives or negatives when predicting "related" contextual content. The second was our paper from Motorola Inc. describing a field trial of a dual device user experience for iTV [3]. We described a field trial of a prototype experience wherein participants received TV show related contextual information on the secondary screen – a laptop. Unlike RendezVous, in our previous research the contextual information was manually generated by the researchers and fed in to the prototype, which was then consumed by the study participants. So in a sense "human experts" had generated the contextual information feed for the second screen. We found participants responded very positively to contextual information about their TV shows. The rich information allowed our users to better understand their shows and connect better with their friends and family using show related information as a conversation starter. But we did not have social commentary from friends as part of that prototype and subsequently found needs for it. Also, during the previous research, we found that the "experts" had to spend a lot of time to watch a TV show and create the additional information bundle. So we wanted to see if "friends" who watch similar TV shows could replace "experts". This would allow for a self-sustaining eco-system for contextual information that is well related to the TV show and highly relevant to the viewer. There seems to be not much research wherein social circles suffice the need for show related information while watching a TV show.

3. FANFEEDS CONCEPT

FanFeeds is a TV-related experience on a companion device that provides in-sync content-related supplemental media and information bits. Compared to RendezVous [28] and our previous research - Dual Device iTV User Experience [3], FanFeeds is a significantly different concept. FanFeeds relies on one's social circles to create contextual information for TV shows and not on automated systems or experts. This makes the information feeds more personal and potentially more targeted and relevant to the primary content. While many of the iTV experiences and applications discussed in related work above are designed for live TV, the FanFeeds concept attempts to address TV watching (synchronous and asynchronous) with socially generated commentary and additional information. FanFeeds also brings the element of time-coded delivery of secondary content on second screen, which makes the delivery time and context sensitive.

FanFeeds enables creation of supplemental media and information using built in search capability for attaching videos and web articles. In addition, FanFeeds allows users to earn points, by being active post creators and consumers. When a certain number of points are earned the person can become a "Guru" of the show within their social circle. We added this feature to encourage users' adoption of new concept, following the gamification principle. We wanted more people to engage in contextual information creation activity. The consumption side of the FanFeeds concept attempts to enhance the viewing experience of TV by providing in-sync access to socially generated relevant information. This allows people to watch their show and consume supplemental information feed about that show on a second screen. Our assumption, in keeping all the interactivity on the companion device, was that collocated groups could watch TV without too many distractions due to user interaction with FanFeeds.

3.1 The FanFeeds Prototype

Our concept prototype was designed as a second screen application to allow for authoring and consumption of the time synchronized secondary content around TV. A user can browse or search or select an episode from a list of live/recent TV show episodes. The episode page allowed a user to check-in to that episode, view comments, like or reply to existing comments and author new comments. It also featured a timeline with a time ticker that represents the timeline of the show and (an adjustable) marker to show how far the show has progressed.

The secondary content authoring interface is designed primarily to allow users to insert a comment and optionally attach an external piece of content (link or video) at any given time within the show. The authoring interface featured a built-in Google and YouTube search console to find relevant content on the web. In addition, a user could copy-paste a URL and automatically import an image (if available) and brief description from the webpage for preview.

A user can also reply to a comment. When a user posts a comment, the application captured relative (within show timeline) and absolute timestamp with the comment. For privacy, users were given an option of sharing comments with only friends or with everyone (public). To promote gamification among fans and motivate them to post relevant secondary content, the researchers decided to award points to users every time they posted a new comment. Users also earned more points each time their comment was liked or replied to by their social circle. This allowed participants in becoming Gurus of their shows.

By default, the comments from others were sorted in reverse order of relative timestamps. However, users had the option to sort comments based on absolute time or popularity (based on number of likes). Users could also choose to filter comments either from friends or from everyone. In addition, users were allowed to bookmark a comment for future quicker access. Our application also provided users with "All Feeds" page that presented an activity (commenting/replying/likes/check-ins) stream from all users on all shows. The intent was for the user to get a feel for what shows are currently "trending" high in the fan community and what fans are saying about them. Our application also provided users with a profile page that included the user's buddy list, recent activity history, check-ins, bookmarks and points.

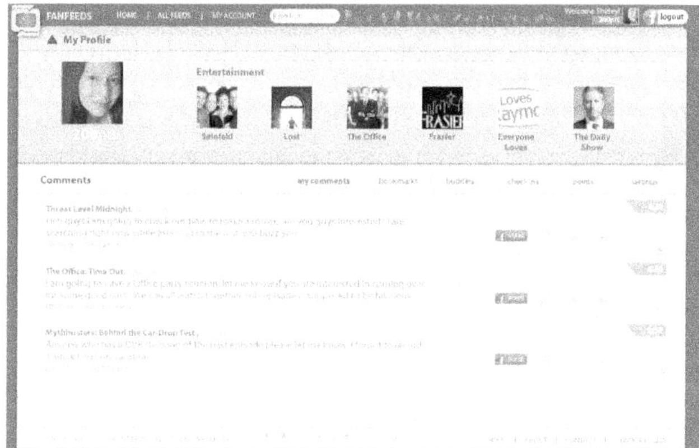

Figure 1. Screenshot of User Profile Page on FanFeeds.

Our prototype was developed as a website compatible with a Firefox browser, usable on a PC or Mac. For reasons of rapid development and technology familiarity, the researchers decided on a website option rather than an application on SmartPhone or a Tablet PC. Our prototype was developed using HTML, JQuery and CSS on the client side with a combination of PHP and MySQL on the server-side on top of Apache HTTP web server [2] The prototype was integrated with the Facebook API [13] to allow users to login using their Facebook credentials and thus automatically discover friends who have signed up with our application. Our web server was integrated with Google and Youtube API to allow users to perform web and video search from within the client website when looking for related content to post. TV program metadata and thumbnail images were received from a professional metadata hosting server. Time synchronization between our application and user's TV was manual whenever a user was watching recorded content from DVR. Users were highly encouraged to manually synchronize the time between the DVR playback and our application using the timeline on the episode page. For live shows synchronization happened naturally as everything was with respect to real time.

Our website relied heavily on AJAX [1] and JSON [21] to update secondary content in the background. The website used simple polling every few seconds to check for updates (new comments, replies, likes, score updates, check-ins etc.). Our prototype used PHP scripts that would periodically connect with the metadata server and ingest all the required metadata into MySQL. For the purpose of this user trial, our prototype imported the metadata for specific set of TV shows - chosen by the study participants.

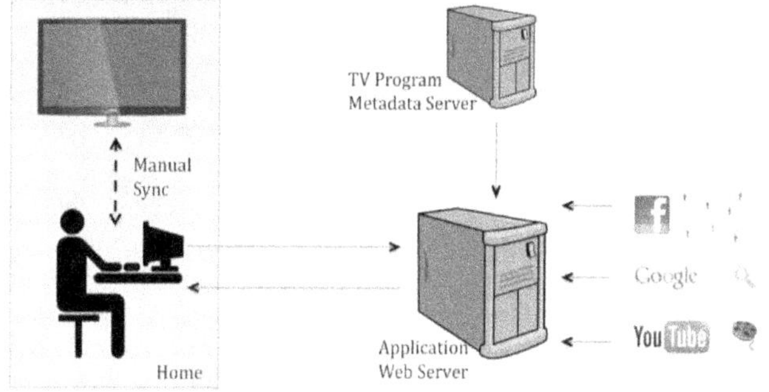

Figure 2. FanFeeds System Diagram.

4. THE FIELD TRIAL

We ran a four-week field trial of our prototype in 12 households. The study took place in the fall of 2011, mid-September to mid-October. Fall television season was a good time because usually in the US, almost all popular TV shows air new episodes. This allowed participants to choose their favorite shows and participate in our study. Shows chosen by users included a variety of genres, e.g., a talk show with video clips (aired every weekday), sports (American Football), reality shows (talent competition), a cooking show, a sitcom and an action drama. Participants were given complete freedom in terms of how to watch their TV shows – live or recorded. Participants also had full freedom as to when to watch the show, with whom to watch the show or the number of times to watch. Also, we were interested in knowing how many people would continue to use our prototype of their own volition. So, we instructed our participants that it was only mandatory to use the prototype for the first two weeks. The last two weeks of the trial were completely optional and they could choose to use or not use the website depending on if they found some value in it. Some basic tasks were given to the participants in the first two weeks to familiarize them with the FanFeeds website.

Figure 3. Participant 2's set-up for using FanFeeds.

4.1 Recruitment

Participants were recruited using a recruiting agency. They had no affiliation with the researchers and were compensated $200 for their four-week participation in our study, which included 2 visits to their home. Requirements for recruiting included watching at least 2 TV shows regularly and being active on social networking sites like Google+, Facebook and/or Twitter. Participants were recruited in groups such that we had 4 groups of 3 friends. The friends all had to watch similar TV shows in order to qualify for the study. The users varied from single person households to multi-person households and/or families. All participants lived in the Chicago city and suburb area. They all had a cable subscription along with digital video recorders, Wi-Fi broadband Internet and a Wi-Fi capable laptop. They all had experience watching both live as well as time shifted TV. Most of the participants had smart phones but that was not a requirement. Over all, we recruited 12 households – 7 male and 5 female participants whose ages ranged from 18 to 55years. Note that one participant, P7, dropped out of the study making our final count of participants 11. In the results section we will be discussing comments from participants using the codes P1-P12. They all had two shows in common and were asked to watch those shows for the duration of this field trial. Table 1 shows their information.

Table 1. Participants' Information

Social Groups	Gender	Age	Shows Watched
P1, P2, P3	1F, 2M	25-30 years	Tosh.0 and Football
P4, P5, P6	3F	40-55 years	Dancing with the Stars and The Biggest Loser
P7, P8, P9	3M	18-24 years	Dexter and Football
P10, P11, P12	1F, 2M	30-35 years	Big Bang Theory and Kitchen Nightmares

4.2 Data Collection

The field trial was four weeks long and consisted of an initial interview, a mid-trial phone interview and a final interview. Also, system usage logs were captured and the participants were requested to leave a voicemail every time they used FanFeeds with or without a TV show, thus creating a voicemail diary of their usage. The initial interviews were at the participants' home and were used to understand their TV viewing habits and to introduce the prototype. For the duration of the trial, logs were maintained of participants' activities on our prototype website. Participants left voicemails for us on a toll free number and explained each use and their overall experience. They were also encouraged to try FanFeeds for other TV shows that were available on the website. Also, they could see other people on the site depending on which show they were watching (not all shows had "strangers" on them). Strangers were other people in the study who weren't part of the participants' social circle. There was a brief mid-trial phone interview after the second week to clarify their voicemail descriptions of how they used the prototype and their experiences. At the end of four weeks a final interview was conducted at the participants' home. The final interview was our opportunity to prove the participants' usage patterns, issues they faced and their reactions to our prototype in general. All interviews were semi-structured to allow for exploration of uses, the various contexts and their overall experiences. All interviews were audio and/or video taped.

4.3 Data Analysis

Even though we had a prototype that we introduced in to people's homes, we did not have set hypotheses that we wanted to prove or disprove. What we did have is a set of well-defined research questions that we wanted to answer by understanding the use of our prototype in real life situations. We wanted to answer the research questions using the interview data and the voicemail diaries generated by the users. Hence we used the grounded theory based affinity analysis approach [4, 5, 23], which allowed us to draw conclusions regarding why, how, and when FanFeeds impacted participants' TV viewing and also the context.

We extracted approximately 1600 direct quotes from participants' data regarding their experiences with our system, from the initial, mid and final interviews along with the voicemails. We then analyzed the data as a team. Researchers, designers, developers who built the prototype as well as team management participated in the analysis of the data. All the direct quotes were printed on to sticky notes and then stuck on the walls of a big room and analyzed for patterns [5, pp. 154-163]. The notes were grouped and researchers identified certain patterns of behavior or user reactions in them. The patterns were then discussed, as a group, and finalized. Using the patterns "themes" were generated [23, pp. 67, pp. 95-112]. Themes, again, were discussed by the group and confirmed. Then, "theories" that answer our research questions were formulated using the themes [4, pp. 492 – 497]. The analysis was team based and extremely iterative in nature. Overall, three weeks of time was spent on the analysis of this data.

5. RESULTS

In this section we discuss our research findings regarding the general reaction of users to the FanFeeds concept. The overall experience of using secondary devices to create and consume socially sourced information related to the TV show is also discussed in detail. To have a manageable scope we restrict ourselves, in this paper, to mostly qualitative data findings.

5.1 Basic Descriptive Statistics

In our four-week long field trial of FanFeeds there were 12 households consisting of 4 social groups with 3 friends each. A total of 23 unique episodes of 12 TV shows were watched with our prototype that is FanFeeds. 6 out of the 11 final participants continued to watch their TV shows in the optional two weeks when it was not compulsory to do so thus showing their positive response to the concept. All the participants showed some positive and some negative response to the overall concept of FanFeeds. The following section of qualitative findings will demonstrate the value we found in user feedback.

Overall activity on the FanFeeds website over the field trial period is shown in Figure 4. One can see that there were a lot of comments but few videos, uploaded by peers, were watched. Some people were very active creators and got the "Guru" status within their social circles while most were just consumers of the "feeds."

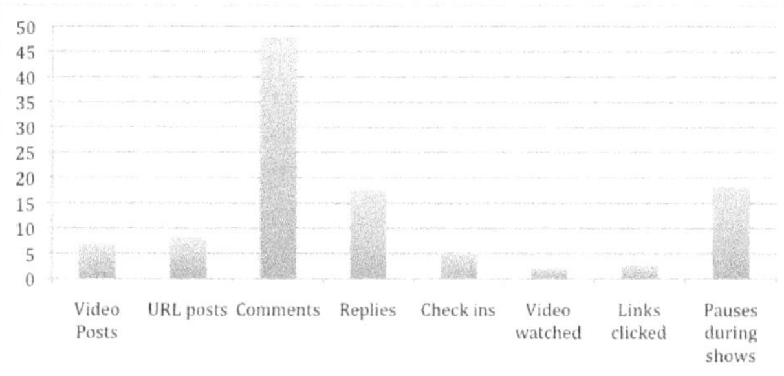

Figure 4. Participant activities during trial.

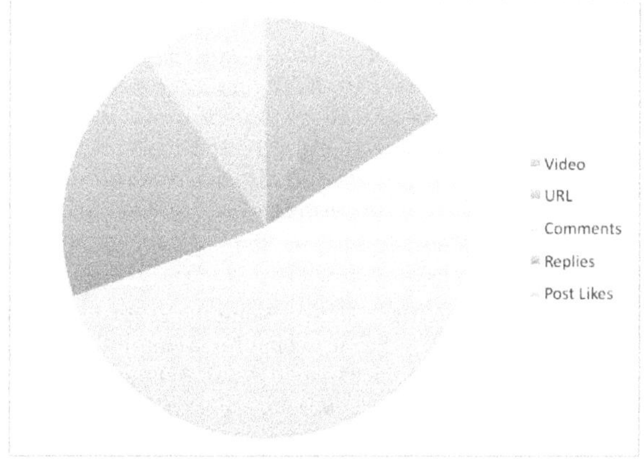

Figure 5. Participant consumption of different information.

Figures 4 and 5 show activities done by participants in our study (relative to each other). Figure 4 shows creation of different posts and Figure 5 shows consumption activity. Of all the videos posted, 24% of videos were consumed and similarly 29% of links uploaded by friends for them were clicked on by the participants.

5.2 Overall User Experience of FanFeeds

FanFeeds' different uses yielded different experiences, some good and some bad. Experiences varied between engaging and distracting depending on the show and supplemental feed created. We discuss only the major themes that addressed our first research question.

5.2.1 FanFeeds enabled Pseudo-Sociality around DVRed TV shows

One of the goals of our research was to see if the supplemental information feeds from friends better the time shifted TV watching experience. We found that FanFeeds made time-shifted TV experience "pseudo-social" for some of our participants and they liked the experience. This was a unique experience that FanFeeds enabled for participants by providing reactions from friends who had watched the TV show earlier and left behind comments and posts. P12 described experience as *"As for watching alone, it's technically really not watching alone, so like feeding along P11's comments, is kind of like he was right there, even though he watched it the day before."* P5 having used FanFeeds for a couple of weeks summarized her experience till that time saying *"It was interesting because obviously coming to those postings after [time shifted], I realized we [friends and her] had similar conclusions/perspectives that we could share even if they weren't [there with me]..."*

This is an important finding because, having done Social TV research previously [18, 19], we had consciously tried to avoid repeating that work and investigate creation and consumption of supplemental information with TV shows on second screens. But despite not designing for Social TV use cases, people still used our prototype in a manner very similar to social TV.

The feature of time-coded posts did garner good feedback. The timely cascade of posts onto the screen as the show progressed made feed appear as if it were happening in real time even if the feed was created in the past. P9 summarized this feeling saying *"...when I was not watching something live, I think that it was really cool to see that the ticker feed essentially recreating an experience for me even if I didn't watch it live. So it still felt like I was participating with everybody as they watched it even if I was doing it 3 or 4 days later."*

Participants made it clear though that some of the live conversations that happened were time-sensitive, hence ephemeral in nature and lost value as time moved on. We found that, informational posts, content-specific comments and video posts do retain their value better than just social commentary. Also the fact that FanFeeds enabled off-website asynchronous communication between people made the time-shifted TV watching more social.

But, asynchronous communication was not an attraction for all participants. P3 loved the live conversations with friends about the shows they watched as a group in real time and so he said *"But I don't think that even though that feature [time coded delivery of comments as show progresses] is cool, it [comments] popup where ever they did [in the episode] I still don't think that would be enough for me to do that, if I wasn't doing it at the same time as them."* P2 agreed with P3 about FanFeeds being good when live but not that valuable when used with time-shifted content. P2 said *"... you know its pretty cool when I watched something later on [off of DVR] to kind of see other people's comments pop up but it didn't add that much value when it [conversation] wasn't live."*

5.2.2 FanFeeds provided fodder for conversations with friends

FanFeeds provides fodder for conversation with friends, which in turn enhanced social-connectedness. P12 said FanFeeds led to SMS conversations offline *"After the whole fact was done. I would text him and say 'are you serious?' He thinks that Big Bang Theory is incredible and I find it a bit dry sometimes. I think its techie and geeky but I like Chuck and Modern Family..."* P12 continued saying *"Me and P11, were interacting and feeding off of each other. I don't know if he watched shows live or taped."* *P10 said that she used posts from FanFeeds to post to Facebook as her status and had conversations with others on that platform, "on Facebook, its just about current events and stuff. [I posted] Soft kitty [a song on a sitcom she watched while using FanFeeds]...just talked about it on Facebook because I saw it on here. P11 posted it and all three of us commented on it."* P10 also talked about how FanFeeds created conversation with her family members when they all watched TV together.

5.2.3 One location for both show-relevant information and people's reaction to the show

FanFeeds provide interesting show-related information in-sync (time-wise) with the show. FanFeeds also provided friends' reaction in the same place, which made it a good 'one-stop-shop' for information and social banter. More interestingly, this idea of one-stop-shop held true for both synchronous as well as asynchronous TV watching (live or time shifted TV watching). P11 said *"I personally like shows like Kitchen Nightmares a lot because when I travel I like to try new restaurants & stuff, so, sort of to have a forum to put that kind of information and reaction out there, I think it gives me a little more value to it (TV watching)."* P11 and his friends P10 and P12 did a lot of asynchronous communication due to FanFeeds posts. P2 described it as *"all of that stuff is stuff that I already do, it was kinda contained in one platform, so it makes sense with the way I think, with the way that I watch TV...we were always referencing other things and thinking of things that it (show) reminds us of ... its great to be able to pull that stuff in it [on FanFeeds]."*

5.2.4 FanFeeds is a place where personal memories can be shared with friends and relived

TV shows often-triggered memories of childhood years for our participants. Hence they became obvious things to post about and discuss. Users were quick to recall information from the past (childhood) and post related information that would invoke a laughter or nostalgia. For instance, during a football game, an advertisement made P1, P2 and P3 discuss an old Pepsi commercial from yesteryears. Similarly, a character in a sitcom made P11 and P12 discuss the old movie 'A Christmas Story' at length. All three users of the group greatly enjoyed that discussion.

5.2.5 FanFeeds is a distraction to engrossing shows

We knew from our website logs that only 6 out of 11 people had used the website of their own volition in the last two weeks, when it was optional to do so. So we knew that not all of our participants were thrilled with the current iteration of the concept. Hence, in our final interviews, we asked participants for the issues they encountered when they used the website. We also asked for feedback on how to improve the features and functionality of such a fan/friend created of information feed.

The mental and physical effort needed to engage properly with FanFeeds was cited, most often, as an issue to adopting FanFeeds with regular TV watching especially with engrossing shows. FanFeeds did not fit all the shows participants watched because it needed effort from users in terms of looking up extra media to post as an informational feed for peers. Social banter comes naturally to people so simple commenting is easier. Whereas, the effort needed to think of what to post, to look up (using the search tools provided), and then to make the post, took time and attention away from the TV show. This was not a surprise finding because we expected this to happen with shows of genre that demand complete attention from viewers. We ended up confirming that FanFeeds, with dramatic shows like Dexter, is a distraction. P8 said *"I don't want to be looking at anything other than the show [Dexter]."* P5 agreed with P8 but said she somewhat overcame the issue over time, *"I found that when I was watching something that I was more intent on, that in the beginning trying to post online simultaneously was a bit of a distraction."* Later in the user trial P5 said that FanFeeds became *"less burdensome"* once she knew the user interface better and knew how to use FanFeeds in a way that minimized her chance of missing action on the TV show.

6.6.2 FanFeeds, one more new social network

FanFeeds needs integration with existing social networks and should not be its own social network. That will minimize the burden of adoption as there will not be any effort needed in terms of creating and maintaining a new network. P2 said *"...the idea of using another application [is an issue], I use a lot of social media tools already and for there to be another one, I just don't know if I would actively go to it."*

5.2.3 Need offline notifications to spur social activity

One of the major issues that troubled participants was that FanFeeds didn't provide them any notification of activity around their posts on FanFeeds when they were off the website. We observed that the offline conversations would have been much more if there had been a notification mechanism in place. P1 was clear when he said *"the biggest improvement that could be possibly made would be notifications when someone comments on or likes [your posts]."*

5.2.4 Spoilers about TV shows are an potential issue

Lastly some posts by friends and strangers can be show spoilers. Posts can, accidently, give away the suspense and spoil the show for a viewer. P8 on seeing a comment from his friend P9 said, *"Before even watching he is already telling me 'that is really bad show' and it kind of ruined my expectations."* P9 too, got a spoiler in the form of final score of a football game, he said *"It happened to me on a Football show. I clicked on homepage or something and I learned the final score. It didn't ruin it for me but if it was for something bigger like a TV show that could have been a bigger deal."* P3 was wary of spoilers and took precaution to avoid spoilers. He said *"I didn't go through & scroll through a feed to see what people were saying before I got to that point in the program, I thought that would be spoiling it for me so I didn't want to do that."*

However, seeing a post right after viewing the event in the show created a cool experience. P9 on seeing his friend P8's comment said *"Deb [a character in Dexter] made lieutenant and that comment would have been a spoiler but seeing it after it happened on screen was cool to see. It was P8 asking if it was good or bad for Dexter and I was wondering the same question myself."*

5.3 Motivations to use FanFeeds

We discovered multiple motivations for participants to engage with FanFeeds prototype, thus answering our second research question. Motivations ranged from FanFeeds being an information source to a place where one can speak her mind. Each subsection is a "motivation" and quotes from users have been used to depict how they felt during these experiences.

5.3.1 The innate need for social validation

Participants who made comments or created informational posts to FanFeeds and seemed to seek validation from their peers – a validation that they thought alike and more importantly a validation that they belonged together as friends and as a social circle. P10 said *"Yes. For ones that I created on my own, I would think about how are they going to react to what I am saying. Are they going to think if what I am saying is true or funny or whatever. How can I stun them?"* P1 also described this very well when he said *"If you are sharing links and videos, it sounds like you are trying to one up each other. Oh you found that, I bet I can kind find something even more inane and ridiculous on top of that."* In this group there was an ongoing game of one-upmanship and a quest to get the others to acknowledge one user as a *guru* of *"silly things."* P2, on belonging to her group, mentioned this *"that was always kind of funny because they were posting and thinking the same things that I was when I was watching it."* P5 concurred even though she was from a very different age group and was watching quite different show genres *"...when I got comments for the my post, I felt it was interesting, to me, that everybody was thinking the same thing at the same time as I was."*

5.3.2 FanFeeds is a place to share ephemeral reactions

FanFeeds became a place for participants to post their ephemeral reactions that were directly and/or indirectly related to TV shows. They used it in a way very similar to that of Twitter or Facebook but they said that the show-centricity" of FanFeeds was different and better. Whatever came to their mind, as they were watching the TV show, was posted onto FanFeeds. So much so that after reviewing her own posts P5 described her feed as a *journal* of her experience. Despite being similar to Twitter and Facebook, FanFeeds had its own advantages. P9 described the advantage FanFeeds over Twitter as *"I use forums a lot to express my opinion. I felt FanFeeds is more of a public forum in real time. I like that I can reach out to people that aren't in my twitter circle or my Facebook circle, that are completely separate from me and nothing else in common but that we have this one show in common and that kind of creates an interesting conversation as well."* P12 described the benefit of FanFeeds over a Facebook as *"This site here, unlike FB, is only one little facet of who I am, that I like this TV show. On FB, people see everything about you...if people see everything [on FanFeeds] may be I will encourage someone to watch a TV show I like."*

5.3.3 FanFeeds is a place where one can show off their knowledge about TV shows

We observed that participants started using FanFeeds to show off their general knowledge. Participants were proud about knowing something unique about the show or the actors and were keen on sharing that knowledge with their group (especially participants P1, P2, P9, P10, P11 and P12). Many times if users didn't know or couldn't recall something then they would engage in elaborate search efforts. They would hunt for the piece of information they thought was interesting to the group and then post it. P11: *"[Emmy's video post] Just because I knew he [actor] had a new Emmy in a row for his role in the show as Sheldon, so I figured I would post a video of his speech."* P11 knew his group would love to see more of Sheldon's funny one-liners. So he found a video from YouTube that was a collage of one-liners from different episodes of The Big Bang Theory. Similarly, P9 knew his mates in the group would love to see behind the scenes video of the show they all liked. So he dug up a video and posted it for his group. In fact his friend, P8, thinking pretty much the same thing, posted the exact same video.

5.3.4 FanFeeds is a place to speak my mind and seek opinions/commentary from others

Users actively sought other people's reaction and feedback to their posts. They were constantly assessing their peers' posts and opinions about the show. P1 and P9 talked about how they felt like "stirring the pot" as in initiating discussions about the TV show that was being watched. Also, FanFeeds being a show-centric site acted as a good place to speak their mind about the show. P4 talked about how she posted on the show Biggest Loser to get her friends to react. P4's comment was not even about the The Biggest Loser, she posted about another show's controversy on The Biggest Loser show just to get her friends' opinion on what she thought. P9 said that during football games he spoke his mind on referee decisions and sought to create discussions: *"If there was a flag or if there was overturn that should have happened, something like that, I would like to put something out there and see if other people thought the same as me. Me being the first one I can generate that conversation."*

5.3.5 Points were noticed but full gamification is needed for engagement

We had tried to partially "gamify" the FanFeeds site with "Guru" status. This status could be achieved by being active on FanFeeds site. We wanted to incentivize creation and consumption activity. We observed that even though the points were described as "showing 'who' is the leader" they were not much of an incentive towards activity because they did not have a fully worked out rewards for them. P11: *"The points I think are interesting, I just want to know what would be the application for them if there is an application...my thought about this is how are they going to be utilized? Is it something similar to FourSquare? Yelp? Where if I have 25pts I get some sort of a word [password] for watching a certain show?..."* P9 had similar questions for us *"I like the idea that I have more points than some other people but it didn't add up to anything. So it didn't influence me all that much. There was no real value."* We found that the points system that we had introduced on the website was definitely noticed and reflected upon by the users. Participants showed us the points gained by their friends and the "Guru" status achieved by some participants in the final interview. But, it didn't lead to any significant activity on website or trigger conversations among participants. So our learning was that points could be exploited when deploying such a system because the users noticed them and separated out the lead users from the rest of the pack. But to trigger further activity more gamification is needed than just "Guru" status.

5.4 Different ways in which FanFeeds was used (RQ2)

We discovered multiple different ways in which participants chose to use FanFeeds, thus answering our third research question. We highlight three prominent uses in this section.

5.4.1 FanFeeds, a private forum

FanFeeds is definitely more interesting as a TV show-related group activity within one's social circle. In live group activity, even though people may be remote, the feedback is immediate and leads to more dynamic conversations while the TV show is being watched together. This finding confirms the traditional Social TV findings so we will not delve too much in detail. P3 summarized, *"This is a nice private forum to be able to do that [discuss/comment] without offending anyone...unlike a message board, where I would be a little bit more discerning w/ my comments, if its me & two of my friends we can say whatever."*

5.4.2 FanFeeds, a public forum too, as long as TV show is the tie-in

What was surprising was that for some participants, we found FanFeeds acted as a good public forum as well. This was a surprise because Social TV usually works well within one's own social circles and not with strangers. We observed several reasons why some participants liked FanFeeds as a public forum. First, for social chatter to happen with strangers the show has to be the tie-in meaning the forum should be made of fans of the show irrespective of whether they are close friends or strangers. Second, the posts produced by strangers may sometimes be better than the ones produced by friends, as the strangers may be experts on the subject producing more interesting posts than friends. P9 commented on this *"...it was really cool, kind of, to see these strangers trying to chime in on this stuff [TV show]. It really felt like a generation of a conversation between complete strangers about common interests, which was pretty cool."* P1 liked the idea of discussing show with strangers as well and said *"liked the idea, like, it is a live blog of a program, that you know, there are other people out there watching it whether its the same time as you or a little bit later on...it helps us to really have a camaraderie around that specific topic, whether its a specific show or program."*

5.4.3 FanFeeds, a source for extra media content

Participants used FanFeeds as a source for show related information and extra media content like pictures, songs and videos. P11 found interesting information about a celebrity chef through a post made by his friend P12: *"The post I found interesting is P12's link to IMDB entry for Gordon Ramsay. [I] Was able to find out stuff on Gordon and how he became a reality chef and star."* P10 found it useful to browse the site on its *own "I think it was couple of times [she went to site for some information]. Biggest Loser was one and I think it was Dancing with the Stars, I wanted to see who got voted off. I don't watch it but I wanted to see who was voted off. I couldn't find it online and I was at work...I found that information (on FanFeeds)."* P9 chose to watch only some videos out of the extra content using comments as his screening criteria *"I watched some of their (P8) posts (means videos) depending on what it was about and what their comment was on it."*

5.5 Different ways in which FanFeeds was accommodated into regular TV routine (RQ3)

We observed that people are very used to using secondary devices like laptop, tablets and smart phones while watching TV. So another "website" being used did not change their basic TV watching routines. They did say that the "creation" of posts was distracting (we cover that later in experiences section) but when we saw their usage over the four weeks we found a couple of different ways in which participants accommodated use of FanFeeds in their TV watching routine, thus answering our research question number 4.

5.5.1 Shows' narrative patterns were exploited to engage with FanFeeds

Participants to engage with FanFeeds exploited TV shows' narrative peaks and valleys. The timing and amount of interaction with FanFeeds was directly proportional to the narrative flow. Participants knew their TV shows very well and so knew instinctively when to take eyes off of TV and engage with the second screen. For example, American Football has brief breaks after each play and reality shows like Dancing with the Stars have judges discussing participants. Shows like Biggest Loser have participants of the show making personal comments after spurts of weight-loss exercises in the show, which allowed fans to disengage momentarily. P4, P5 and P6's opinion was that Biggest Loser was less visual and had breaks to be able to engage with FanFeeds than the dance show, Dancing with the Stars. P5 commented in voicemail *"it was different [with Biggest Loser than with Dancing with the Stars] because if you look away its not too terrible. Its not constant live action."* P9 compared use of FanFeeds for his multiple shows *"With Dexter not going to use it, needs all my attention. More so on Football where there is time when I can look away, and then Tosh.0, While I cant look away there are more commercials and so feed can be generated for that..."* P3 talked about how FanFeeds worked well for him with Football *"the thing about doing it with sports especially with football is that there is always 20 or 30sec between plays."*

Geerts et al. [16] discuss very similar results in their study of effect of genre on social TV activities like clip sharing or chat. They found that people do not talk while engaged in plot-structure of a show and they do talk during genres that have less of a plot-structure such as sports, quiz or reality shows. What our results add to that corpus of knowledge is that users are fans of shows and they pretty much know the patterns of the shows they watch regularly. So even if something is engaging they will know when to take off their eyes from primary content and when not to. So for instance, Dexter had no commercial breaks and an intense plot so activity was real low on FanFeeds. On Big Bang Theory there was activity whenever the show was in lull between jokes and during commercials.

5.5.2 Video clips were consumed during commercial breaks or right after TV show is over

Participants chose to watch videos during the commercial breaks or right after the show is over. P2 watched bookmarked video right after the show was over, she said she would have forgotten about them if she didn't do it right after the show. Similarly, P11 said *"We [his younger brother and him] watched Gordon Ramsay's interview on Top Gear a few times. It was right after the show though."*

6. DISCUSSION

6.1 Pseudo-Sociality: Social life around time-shifted content

This research addresses some important issues in terms of potential Social TV experiences for time-shifted content. We discovered how various aspects of information availability, time-coded delivery and offline discussion led to "pseudo-sociality" around time-shifted content. This experience refreshed offline conversations about a TV show and led to more social connectedness among people. We have not seen much discussion about this in Social TV literature [8, 10, 18]. There has been lot of research and discussion of live conversations with TV shows, the genre effect [16] and also social video annotation [23] but not about time-shifted content and social behavior around it. Also if someone is watching the show completely time shifted, now they can benefit from the social chatter and informational media feed left behind by their friends. They now get their friends' point of views about occurrences in the TV show as if they were with them. Nathan et al. [25] had found during their CollaboraTV project that their prototype, by preserving comments made by users who are asynchronous or virtually present, made TV viewing social. Their users had described the experience as "preservation of water cooler talk." But Nathan et al. in their study method had "asked users to do the task" of watching TV asynchronously with their friends and then give a survey response. Where as we had asked people to use the prototype of their own volition and as part of their regular TV watching. So participants did the asynchronous TV watching completely voluntarily and as part of their regular TV routine and enjoyed the asynchronous TV experience (as reported over voicemails and in interviews). Participants also enjoyed the time-coded delivery of social comments along with additional videos and informational links left behind by their friends who watched the show before them. So our results comprehensively confirm the results found by Nathan et al. and extend them. As for understanding the specific effects of show plots, genre and the amount of time-shift between consumptions on the social experiences, more longitudinal field trials are necessary.

6.2 Semi-live content consumption

Additionally this research brought to fore how content could be live, semi-live and/or completely time-shifted. Most discussions of social TV projects discuss live and non-live experiences but we found some interesting incidences of semi-live experiences in our trial. By semi-live we mean that one or more people, in a group are behind by a few minutes with respect to others. For the most part, we saw that when someone is semi-live with their group they still had a good experience if they had someone else semi-live with them. In this way they could discuss things that others had left behind and consume content live with someone else. P3 and P9 watched a football game together but they were semi-live with their groups. P9 summed it up well when he described the experience *"What I do like is that I can still maintain the conversation even if I watch the game delayed because of the Feed Timer keeping us at the same place. I thought it was pretty funny to see that Mike was watching the Bears game on delay as was I."* P9 pinged P1 during this even though they are not from same group and he also commented to P3. But more research is needed to flush out the details of such situations and the experiences. Nathan et al. [30] discuss briefly the concept of mixed-viewing situations but they do not delve into the semi-live situation. They found that mixing collocated and virtual audience and synchronous and asynchronous audience as being social and enjoyable.

Also, we found that whenever there was a case of semi-live session, there is a good possibility of a conversation of some sorts among people who are ahead in the timeline and those behind. And that complicates social exchanges and may even make it a negative experience because now the group is exposed to potential spoiler comments and may also be forced to re-do jokes/conversations that may have been temporal (so not very relevant anymore).

6.3 Social TV with strangers

Social TV [8, 9, 18, 19] literature has always discussed how people feel more connected to each other via shared TV watching and/or watching and discussing shows/sports that both parties like, be it a collocated situation or a geographically distributed experience among a group of friends. What this research newly indicated, when FanFeeds was used freely as a public forum, was that some people were OK with having a social TV experience with complete strangers who did not belong to their social circle. We did find people requesting the usual social TV features of communication with friends but additionally we also had people appreciating a community feeling around their TV shows with strangers as part of the community. There was no hesitation in interacting with strangers as long as the strangers were perceived as "other fans" of the show. We feel the use of social media has now ingrained itself in our society much more intrinsically than ever before because the caveat seemed to be that the community should be show centric and the strangers should be equally interested in the show as the participants. We further think that the anxiety about talking to strangers is reduced when there is a common topic to talk about. We saw that some users browsed other people's profiles and posts, people they did not know socially. Some TV shows were discovered from profile browsing as well. One participant, P9, added a new show to his NetFlix queue upon discovering it through a stranger's post. Further research in this seemingly new Social TV behavior is needed.

7. Implications

Keeping our research questions and results in mind, we have listed some practical suggestions and implications:

1. In designing FanFeeds features and the user interface, we had attempted to reduce the barrier for creation of supplemental information. We had created the prototype with the expectation that this would be a way for people to create a supplemental content feed for their friends, we did not create it to be a pure social experience (in terms of having conversations using the tool) – yet users chose to use the tool as a social TV enabler. Users preferred to consume more information rather than creating information for their friends. Participants most enjoyed the sessions where they were using the prototype live with their friends and were exchanging social banter along with contextual show relevant information. Most interactions were through comments and replies rather than through additional information. Our lesson is that the basic Social TV features are a must no matter what else is added new. First, there needs to be a way to seek and get "presence" information of friends. Participants need to know who else is on FanFeeds with them. Secondly, there needs to be offline activity notifications system, whereby users can know when their friends have liked or commented on their post. Including these features would benefit FanFeeds' user experience.
2. Asynchronous availability of time synched comments and additional media is a good experience as demonstrated by our results. When the users got the additional media in the relevant places as they watched the time shifted primary media, it was a compelling experience. But despite that, there were no revisits to DVRed primary content or the secondary content on the FanFeeds. This demonstrated that different posts had different temporal life and relevancy. We observed that informational posts were more beneficial to the experience than the ephemeral "this is great!" kind of comments. Conversational comments were in-between. If there's an expectation of someone seeing certain comment and being able to continue the conversation then only those comments remain relevant. Hence, offline activity notifications could increase the asynchronous commentary between people thus further improving the pseudo-social experience.
3. Creation of posts is still viewed as a distraction no matter what show it is done with. Creation therefore seems to be the forte of the "superfans" rather than average TV viewers. Hence we make an additional implication (or hypothesis) that superfans who want their friends to admire their special knowledge or creativity may be inclined to watch the show as soon as it airs and create feeds for others who watch time-shifted. This might imply that regular fan consumers could then concentrate on their conversations with their friends while consuming the feed created by superfans. We feel that this new experience should be further investigated as well. Furthermore, the passivity of people around creation could also be overcome by meaningful "gamification" of the creation experience. Even though we had very basic points system, it did get noticed. This phenomenon could be exploited by giving more tangible incentives like exclusive first-look of content or free bonus content.
4. Lastly, auto-synchronization is needed between the second screen and the primary screen. FanFeeds website timeline needs to be in auto-sync with the TV timeline to deliver best user experience. With technologies like IntoNow [27] this problem can be easily addressed. Also, for expediency reasons, we used laptop as our second screen and instead of an "application" on a tablet PC like Motorola Mobility's XYBoard or an Apple iPad. This too requires further research to see if tablets make better companions than laptops for FanFeeds-like experiences.

8. ACKNOWLEDGMENTS

We sincerely thank our Motorola Mobility's Applied Research Center members for helping with discussions and critiques.

9. REFERENCES

[1] AJAX. http://en.wikipedia.org/wiki/Ajax_%28programming%29

[2] Apache Web Server. http://httpd.apache.org/

[3] Basapur, S., Harboe, G., Mandalia, H., Novak, A., Vuong, V., and Metcalf, C. 2011. Field trial of a dual device user experience for iTV. In Proceedings of the 9th International European conference on Interactive Television (EuroiTV '11). ACM, New York, NY, USA, 127-136

[4] Bernard, H. R. 1998. Handbook of Methods in Cultural Anthropology. Altamira Press

[5] Beyer, H., and Holtzblatt, K. 1998. Contextual Design: Defining Customer-Centered Systems. Morgan Kaufmann Pu3blishers.

[6] Boxee Box. http://www.boxee.tv/

[7] BuddyTV Application. http://www.buddytv.com/

[8] Cesar, P., Chorianopoulos, K., and Jensen, J. 2008. Social television and user interaction. Comput. Entertain. 6, 1, Article 4 (May 2008), 10 pages.

[9] Cesar, P., Bulterman, D. C., and Jansen J. Leveraging user impact: an architecture for secondary screens usage in interactive television. Multimedia Systems Journal, 15(3):127--142, 2009

[10] Cesar, P., Bulterman, D. C. A., Jansen, J., Geerts, D., Knoche, H., and Seager, W. 2009. Fragment, tag, enrich, and send: Enhancing social sharing of video. ACM Trans. Multimedia Comput. Commun. Appl. 5, 3, Article 19 (August 2009), 27 pages.

[11] Cruickshank, L., Tsekleves, E., Whitham, R., Hill, A., Kondo, K.: Making interactive TV easier to use: Interface design for a second screen approach. The Design Journal 10(3) (2007).

[12] Epps, S. R., Gownder, J. P., and Wiramihardja, L. 2010. The US Consumer PC Market In 2015. Forrester Research Report accessed on 3rd Jan 2011 at: http://forrester.com/rb/Research/us_consumer_pc_market_in_2015/q/id/57210/t/2

[13] Facebook's PHP SDK Overview. http://developers.facebook.com/docs/reference/php/

[14] Fallahkhair, S., Pemberton, L., and Masthoff, J. 2004. A Dual Device Scenario for Informal Language Learning: Interactive Television Meets the Mobile Phone. In Proceedings of the IEEE International Conference on Advanced Learning Technologies (ICALT '04). IEEE Computer Society, Washington, DC, USA, 16-20.

[15] Fallahkhair, S., Pemberton, L., and Griffiths, R. 2005. Dual Device User Interface Design for Ubiquitous Language Learning: Mobile Phone and Interactive Television (iTV). In Proceedings of the IEEE International Workshop on Wireless and Mobile Technologies in Education (WMTE '05). IEEE Computer Society, Washington, DC, USA, 85-92.

[16] Geerts, D., Cesar, P., and Bulterman, D. 2008. The implications of program genres for the design of social television systems. In Proceeding of the international Conference on Designing interactive User Experiences For TV and Video, pp. 71-80

[17] GetGlue Application. www.getglue.com

[18] Harboe, G., Massey, N., Metcalf, C., Wheatley, D., and Romano, G. 2008. The uses of social television. Comput. Entertain. 6, 1, Article 8 (May 2008), 15 pages.

[19] Huang, E., Harboe, G., Tullio, T., Novak, A., Massey, N., Metcalf, C., and Romano, G. 2009. Of social television comes home: a field study of communication choices and practices in tv-based text and voice chat. *In* Proc. of the 27th international conference on Human factors in computing systems (CHI '09). ACM, New York, NY, USA, 585-594.

[20] IntoNow website: http://www.intonow.com/ci

[21] JSON. http://www.json.org/

[22] Krause, J. 2003. Enhanced TV: A Bridge Between Broadcast and Interactivity. Indiana Univ., Dept. of Telecomm. (http://www.indiana.edu/~telecom/people/faculty/krause/etv/etv_article16.pdf)

[23] LeCompte, M., and Schensul, J. (1999) Analyzing and Interpreting Ethnographic Data. Ethnographer's Toolkit, V.5, AltaMira Press, CA, US

[24] Miso Application. www.gomiso.com

[25] Nathan, M., Harrison, C., Yarosh, S., Terveen, L., Stead, L., and Amento, B. 2008. CollaboraTV: making television viewing social again. In Proceeding of the international Conference on Designing interactive User Experiences For TV and Video, pp. 85-94

[26] Nielsen Consumer Reports. 2011. State of Media: Consumer Usage Report at website: http://blog.nielsen.com/nielsenwire/mediauniverse/

[27] Obrist, M., Moser, C., Tscheligi, M., and Alliez, D. 2010. Field evaluation of a cross platform 6 key navigation model and a unified user interface design. In Proceedings of the 8th International European Conference on Interactive TV (EuroITV '10). ACM, New York, NY, USA, 141-144.

[28] Poivre, Sebastien. 2011. RendezVous Project, Orange Labs. Presentation at "iTV in Industry" session at EuroiTV 2011

[29] Robertson, S., Wharton, C., Ashworth, C., Franzke, M. 1996. Dual device user interface design: PDAs and interactive television, Proceedings of the SIGCHI conference on Human factors in computing systems: common ground, p.79-86, April 13-18, 1996, Vancouver, British Columbia, Canada

[30] Samuels, W.C. 1996. EarthWeb and ACTV unveil HyperTV™ breakthrough. Business Wire.

[31] ScreenTribe. http://www.screentribe.com/

[32] TVLoop Application. http://www.tvloop.com/

The Composition and Role of Convergent Technology Repertoires in Audiovisual Media Consumption

Cédric Courtois
IBBT-MICT-Ghent University
Korte Meer 7-9-11
BE-9000 Gent
+32 9 264 91 54
cedric.courtois@ugent.be

ABSTRACT

This paper departs from the observation that the amount and the nature of technologies affording audiovisual media consumption have increased exponentially in the past years. Therefore, we inquire what patterns of technologies, or technology repertoires, can be statistically derived from a large sample, consisting of three age cohorts. Moreover, drawing upon a socio-cognitive interpretation of uses and gratifications, we question whether different technology repertoires exercise a moderating effect on the extent to which consumption is explained by deliberate outcome expectancies on the one hand and habit on the other. The results indicate three technology repertoires: (a) predominant television viewers, (b) versatile viewers, mixing all kinds of devices and (c) predominant laptop viewers. Further analysis shows that the versatile viewers' consumption is only explained by habit, indicating this behavior to be strongly rooted in their daily routines. In contrast, both other repertoires are explained by expected outcomes as well, indicating a specific deliberation. Finally, drawing upon domestication theory and Norman's notion of perceived affordances, a qualitative follow-up study was set up, aiming to understand the effects found in the quantitative study. The results suggest remarkably strong distinctions in how technologies are socially constructed and how they are implemented in everyday audiovisual media consumption.

Categories and Subject Descriptors

J.4 [**Social And Behavioral Sciences**]: Sociology

General Terms

Management, Human Factors, Theory.

Keywords

Technological convergence, audiovisual technology repertoires, habit-goal interface

1. INTRODUCTION

In recent years, the means to consume audiovisual content have increased steadily [1]. Today, a large variety of devices allow consuming digital content through various, mainly digitized channels (e.g. digital television, the world wide web). Although for many people television retains its place as primary device, computers and mobile devices of all sorts and shapes have entered the field too, however convincing only few [2]. Still, consumers are able to develop complex patterns of affording technologies, bringing about an unprecedented ubiquity of audiovisual content consumption. In this paper, we look into these patterns and relate them to the most important factors known to explain media consumption. More specifically, by drawing upon a relatively recent socio-cognitive interpretation of uses-and-gratifications [3], we question to what extent these consumption patterns are differentially explained by intentional incentive motivators as well as by non-intentional habits. The underlying presumption is that people who employ different technologies are characterized by differently interfacing motivations and habits because each technology has its own type of application. Hence, this research offers a general overview of differentiation in consumption modes.

However, we extend this research by addressing the fundamental question of how we can understand these different modes. We subscribe to two theoretical, social-constructivist perspectives, aptly discussed in the literature. The first regards insights concerning the perceived affordances of technologies [4], whereas the second frames technology meanings within the larger framework of everyday life (i.e. Domestication Theory [5]). As such, we aim to develop a thorough insight in why certain technologies are embraced for audiovisual consumption and how they are able to attain a place in people's day-to-day consumption.

1.1 Changing media environment

A look with hindsight to the audiovisual media landscape, some ten to twenty years ago, immediately shows that a lot has changed in this time span. Whereas then, linearly connected television was basically the one and only affording technology, nowadays choices are much more diverse [6]. Due to digitization, content has become compatible with and hence distributable through various channels. Moreover, technological convergence brought about a tremendous increase in the number of devices suitable for audiovisual play back. This links in with what Jenkins refers to as the black box fallacy [7]. That is the observation that, in contrast to an earlier belief, technology is not mold into a single device. Instead, we witness a tremendous diversity of devices that adopt each other's functions. This ranges from televisions in all kinds of shapes and sizes to a multitude of computers (desktop, laptop, netbook, tablet) and mobile devices (smartphones, portable media players). For example, newscasts are repurposed for online viewing, paired with written articles and even made available through mobile applications. Likewise, various services, such as for example Netflix, furnish online viewing of movies and series. Hence, the once so rigid separations between broadcasting,

EuroITV'12, July 4–6, 2012, Berlin, Germany.

telecommunication, publishing and information technology industries have been consistently evaporating [8]. This trend, which is directly linked to corporate concentration, tore down the silo structures in which traditional media corporations used to function. This brings about a disappearance of the prior definite relationship between a medium and its content. Still, although most devices are quite widespread, not all of them are used to the same extent to consume audiovisual media; that is to say if they are used. Therefore we propose the following, first research question:

- *RQ1: What technology repertoires are used to consume audiovisual media?*

1.2 Explanatory factors of media consumption

As mentioned, different technologies enable audiovisual consumption, thus for now we presume that distinct repertoires exist. A second question then regards the kind of consumption these repertoires furnish and what explains this consumption. Usually in media studies, the emphasis is put on intentions by adopting the Uses & Gratifications (U&G) framework [9, 10]. This approach assumes an active audience, intentionally seeking to satisfy its needs, while among others, media function as possible gratifying means [11]. The U&G approach has generated a tremendous amount of informative empirical studies, directed towards compiling gratification typologies and uncovering their psychological and sociological origins.

Still, this approach has been firmly criticized for a number of reasons, including its confusing conceptual framework, lack of sound theoretical framework, and its rational account of media consumption, which is deemed 'too mentalistic' [12]. However, recent theoretical developments counter part of these criticisms by drawing upon theoretical insights originating from social cognition. More specifically, in their Theory of Media Attendance, LaRose and Eastin have successfully demonstrated how gratifications can be framed as incentive motivators [3, 13], which make up an essential part of Bandura's Social Cognitive Theory [14, 15]. In short, this theory of human behavior posits that people learn from different sources. Next to direct experience, they follow both social and symbolic models. Still, new behaviors are first evaluated for the likelihood that they could be successfully performed and the conviction that they will lead to favorable outcomes in six domains, which are easily mapped onto existing gratification typologies: (a) *novel incentives:* learning new experiences, seeking cognitive stimulation, hence information seeking; (b) *social incentives:* seek social acceptance and avoid disapproval, like social interaction; (c) *monetary incentives:* obtain tokens to obtain other incentives; (d) *activity incentives:* enjoyment of exercising a preferred activity, or entertainment; (e) *status incentives:* ability to exercise control and obtain social and material benefits; and (f) *self-reactive incentives:* which refers to the intrinsic motivating character of activities, which is often linked to escapism. In operational measures (cf. The Model of Media Attendance), these incentives are framed as expected outcomes, which hold the midst between the long-held distinction between *gratification sought* and *gratifications obtained* [16], which divides prior desires towards future media consumption and the post hoc evaluation of its instrumentality. More specifically, expected outcomes occupy a middle ground, as they are conceived as expectations that are informed by prior attained outcomes.

Yet, the most substantial innovation is the theoretically sound incorporation of the psychological habit construct [17]. In fact, most of our everyday behavior, including media consumption, is habitual. That is the automatic process that involves a lack of awareness, diminished control and cognitive parsimony. A habit is formed by consistently repeated, rewarding behavior, exercised in a stable context. This holds vast consequences for the U&G approach that only considers intentional motives, and neglects the fact that over time, these motivations crystallize into a habit [17]. Hence, a strong habit indicates that a behavior has a prominent, yet routine place in people's everyday lives. Likewise, strong expected outcomes point to intentional deliberation of consumption. However, media consumption is to be explained as an interface of both intentional and non-intentional factors. Hence, we question what the role of technology is in affording day-to-day consumption. This leads to the following research question:

- *RQ2: How do habit and expected outcomes interface in explaining audiovisual media consumption by means of different technology repertoires?*

1.3 The social construction of technology

Yet, the question remains how and why specific technology repertoires are compiled and implemented within the everyday. In that respect, two major lines of theory are apparent [18]. On the one hand there is the diffusion of innovations approach, while on the other hand the social shaping perspective has gained ground. Whereas the former draws upon a technological determinist point of view, the latter views technologies as social phenomena that derive their meaning from the social environment in which they are devised, adopted and used.

An enticing theory in the field of the construction of technology is the domestication perspective [5, 19, 20]. This theory, grounded in media sociology, was formulated as a response to the steep increase in consumer electronics, entering the majority of homes since the late 1980's and early 1990's. Until then, the focus was merely oriented toward media texts, mainly overlooking the affording technologies and the context they are rooted in. In fact, the physical dimension of media consumption lies at the core of domestication. This is exemplified by the key concept of a double articulation, referring to the significance of technological artifacts (first articulation) as meaningful, psychical prerequisites to consume media texts (second articulation), which, of course, carry meaning too. Hence, texts cannot be articulated without the object being articulated. One of the major merits of domestication is to view this process within its proper context, which in recent theoretical and empirical accounts has been proposed as a distinct articulation within media consumption. This context of the home is usually referred to as the moral economy of the home. That is viewing the home as a micro-economic entity in a larger macro-economic system in which cognitions [20], values and aesthetics are transferred and negotiated. More specifically, this means that media consumption meanings, both on the level of technology and content, are ideally constructed within the social environment of the home, while there is a constant communication with the public world.

As mentioned in the previous sections, technologies have become content-independent due to technological convergence and the ongoing digitization of audiovisual materials. This leads to an increased number of possibilities to furnish the consumption of similar texts. As such, it becomes increasingly interesting to get a clear view on what and why technologies are used for a specific practice. In theory, many devices afford the same practices, but it is very unlikely that this is effectively the case. In fact, it is not because a technology has the capability of allowing a certain behavior that this capability is identified and used as such. This links with the concept of perceived affordances [4], which refers to *'the perceived and actual properties of the thing, primarily those fundamental properties that determine just how the thing could possibly be used'* (p. 9). That is what people see, not what the object is inherently capable off. Meaning can only exist when users identify an affordance as useful. More specifically, people devise a mental model of objects, sketching the flow of how and for what to use objects, including various physical, semantic, cultural and logical constraints. These can all be linked to people's social environments and how these are constructed as spaces packed with routines and goal-directed behavior. Hence, to get a clearer view on this, we propose a third research question?

- *RQ3: How can we understand audiovisual technology repertoires in terms of their affordances in people's everyday social environments, interpreted as an interface between routines and goal-directed?*

2. METHODOLOGY

2.1 An research funnel

In order to answer these two research questions, we implemented an integrated funnel approach. In a first phase, we devised a large-scale paper & pencil survey with operational measures drawn from the Theory of Media attendance. Moreover, as will be discussed in the measures section, we included a set of items inquiring what technologies are used to consume audiovisual content, in order to compile technology repertoires, using latent class analysis [21], First of all, these patterns allowed a multi-sample analysis of the Model of Media Attendance. Secondly, the classes were used to sensibly recruit participants for a follow-up phase, consisting of domestic interviews. Chosen on the basis of very high to even absolute membership probabilities, the interviewees are treated as representatives for their respective classes. In the interview, we tapped into how media technologies are made meaningful and how it allows the exercise of everyday media consumption routines.

Still, we first need to explicit our operationalization of audiovisual media consumption in today's increasingly converging media landscape. As put in the introduction, multiple devices furnish the consumption of audiovisual texts through various channels, while situated in a diversity of environments. Hence, we subscribe to an earlier empirically grounded recommendation for an agnostic approach towards media consumption [22], inciting to tap into the experience, independent of a specific type of device, content or socio-spatial context. However, this poses another problem concerning the differences in experience of for example quickly watching a short news clip on a laptop computer at a desk versus taking time and making yourself comfortable to watch a film or series on the very same device. We strongly believe it is a mistake to treat both viewing modes as chips from the same block. Therefore, based on literature on human-computer interaction [23, 24], we heuristically distinguish between a haphazard lean forward viewing style and a much more dedicated lean back viewing style. In the survey questionnaire, both viewing styles were aptly introduced and familiarized by a situational sketch.

2.2 Quantitative survey

The paper and pencil questionnaire was administered on a large quota sample, targeting three age cohorts: young adulthood (18-30y), middle adulthood (31-50y) and late adulthood (50y+), equally dispersed over gender. The data were gathered in the context of a research methodology seminar at a large Belgian university. This led to a total number of 1,559 valid responses (51% male, 49% female; M_{age} = 40.61, SD_{age} = 16.79). The following paragraphs enumerate the applied measures.

Technology usage consists of six relatively common devices to consume audiovisual media: (a) television, (b) desktop computer, (c) laptop computer, (d) mobile media player, (e) mobile phone and (f) portable DVD player. The respondents were asked to indicate how often they used these technologies to view audiovisual content of whatever kind. The ordinal response categories were (a) never, (b) less than weekly, (c) weekly, (d) every 2-3 days and (e) at least once a day.

Content consumption comprised of ten items measuring the frequency in which popular content genres are consumed, regardless of what device: (a) news casts, (b) current affairs, (c) documentaries, (d) soaps/series, (e) human interest, (f) films, (g) sports, (h) reality shows, (i) shows/game shows, (j) online clips. All categories were aptly illustrated by popular examples. The response categories were (a) never, (b) less than weekly, (c) weekly, (d) every 2-3 days, (e) once a day and (f) more than once a day.

The measures below, which make up the Model of Media Attendance, were gathered for lean back viewing as well as lean forward viewing. The constructs' means, standard deviations and measures of internal consistency are summarized in Table 1.

Habit strength was assessed by Verplanken and Orbell's Self-Report Index of Habit Strength [25]. In line with current applications, items concerning past behavioral frequency were omitted [26]. The ten remaining items were rated on a seven-point Likert scale ranging from 'totally disagree' to 'totally agree'.

Expected outcomes were measured by twelve items drawn from previous research [3, 27]. The original items were slightly adapted to fit audiovisual consumption. The four most recurrent expected outcomes that match U&G research on television were retained [13]. Hence, novel, social, activity and self-reactive outcomes were assessed with seven-point Likert scales, ranging from 'very unlikely' to 'very likely'.

Consumption frequency was measured by inquiring the hours and minutes spent on viewing moving images one and two days before the survey administration. This measure's metric was eventually converted to minutes.

Table 1: Questionnaire measures

Construct	Lean back viewing style			Lean forward viewing style		
	M	*SD*	α	*M*	*SD*	α
Expected outcomes						
Social	3.16	1.24	.79	2.93	1.34	.80
Novel	4.67	1.20	.79	4.89	1.35	.84
Self-Reactive	4.39	1.12	.70	3.30	1.15	.76
Activity	5.07	1.05	.82	3.77	1.33	.88
Habit strength	4.74	1.34	.88	3.43	1.31	.91
Consumption frequency	108.77	77.62	(r = .43)	24.95	34.10	(r = .70)

2.3 Qualitative follow-up

After the initial quantitative phase, a small-scale qualitative research was set up, recruiting typical cases from the derived latent classes. The participants were then interviewed in their domestic contexts. The aim is to generate a better understanding of the effects found in the quantitative study. Several topics were addressed: (a) the devices adopted and how they are used, (b) the perceived affordances and how these fit in to daily consumption practices and (c) the role of audiovisual consumption in the everyday. A total of ten participants agreed to participate: five males and five females, ranging from 20 to 57 years old. Hence, this is a rather small sample that will be extended in supplementary research. Still, the results generate a rather clear view on how to interpret the first study's results. Nonetheless, these views will be refined as supplementary interviews are included in the analysis. The analysis itself was performed using the NVivo 8 software package. More specifically, all topics were coded and crossed with latent class membership, allowing the analysis of cross-patterns.

3. RESULTS

3.1 Technology repertoires

In order to identify patterns in technology usage, a latent class analysis was performed on the six inquired technologies. This renders a well-fitting three-class model ($L^2(1481) = 1552.24$, $p = .10$). The response probabilities per class, depicted in Figure 1, indicate that the first class predominantly exists of *television viewers*, whereas there are rather small chances of frequently using a computer to view content. A different situation is noticed within the second class, which is made up by *versatile viewers* who combine various technologies. Although television remains dominant, they also frequently employ computers and mobile phones. Finally, the third class is made up by *laptop viewers,* displaying the relatively highest chances of using a laptop on a daily basis for audiovisual consumption.

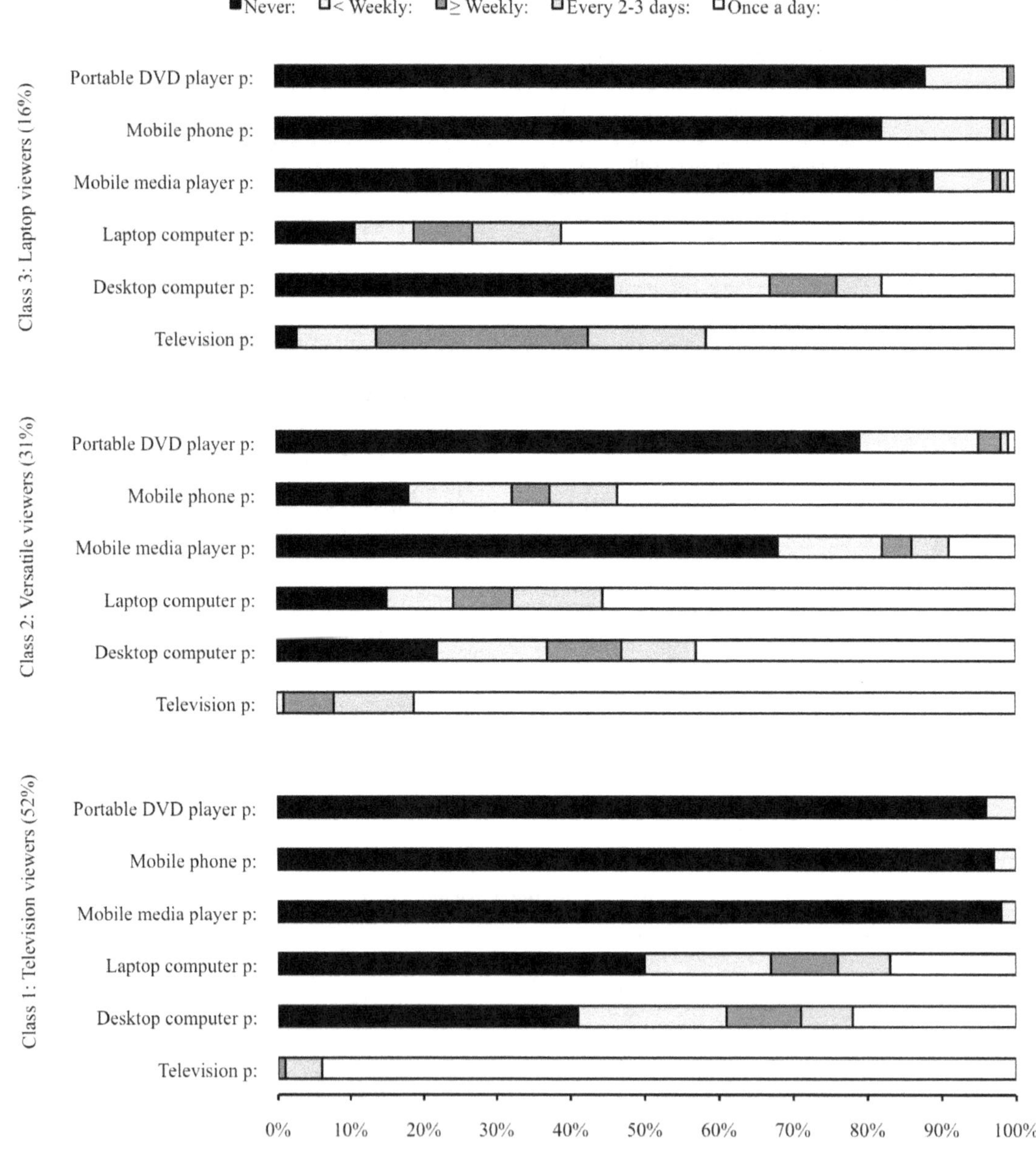

Figure 1: Latent class analysis of technology repertoires

Table 2: Descriptive table of content consumption, age and gender per technology repertoire

	Mdn Television viewers *(Mean Rank)*	Mdn Versatile viewers *(Mean Rank)*	Mdn Class 3 Laptop Viewers *(Mean Rank)*	χ^2	
News casts	Once per day *(820)*	Once per day *(758)*	Every 2-3 days *(464)*	121.26	***
Current affairs	Once per week *(793)*	Once per week *(771)*	Less than weekly *(549)*	49.86	***
Documentaries	Once per week *(787)*	Once per week *(762)*	Less than weekly *(580)*	37.71	***
Soaps/Series	Every 2-3 days *(754)*	Every 2-3 days *(823)*	Once per week *(574)*	42.89	***
Human Interest	Every 2-3 days *(823)*	Once per week *(756)*	Less than weekly *(473)*	100.64	***
Films	Once per week *(717)*	Every 2-3 days *(892)*	Once per week *(644)*	66.67	***
Sports	Once per week *(762)*	Once per week *(811)*	Less than weekly *(597)*	32.62	***
Reality shows	Less than weekly *(737)*	Less than weekly *(836)*	Less than weekly *(634)*	33.53	***
Shows	Less than weekly *(787)*	Less than weekly *(797)*	Less than weekly *(507)*	73.56	***
Online clips	Less than weekly *(609)*	Once per week *(970)*	Once per week *(971)*	267.27	***
Age cohort (%)				294.76	***
Young adulthood (18-30y)	19	58	68		
Middle adulthood (31-50y)	42	26	22		
Late adulthood (50y+)	39	17	11		
Gender	53% F, 47% M	43% F, 57% M	49% F, 51% M	10.71	**

The descriptive table above (Table 2) indicates that the older cohorts make up *television viewers*, who often consume news content, soaps and series and human interest. The *versatile viewers*, who have a similar consumption pattern, albeit extended by regular consumption of films are however much younger. The same goes for *laptop viewers*. Furthermore, they are characterized by limited consumption frequencies.

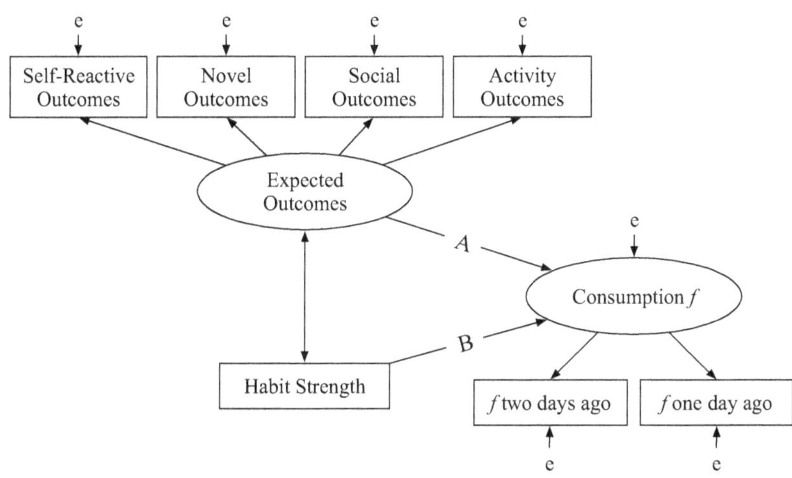

Figure 2: Specified structural equation model

3.2 Explanatory factors

To answer the second research question, concerning the factor that explain audiovisual media consumption accomplished by distinct technology repertoires, two separate structural equation models - one per viewing mode - were ran simultaneously on three subsamples, each consisting of a technology repertoire class. These models attain an acceptable model fit for both lean back ($\chi^2(36) = 157.32$, CFI = .95, TLI = .92, RMSEA = .05, CI_{90} = .04, .06) and lean forward viewing ($\chi^2(36) = 109.85$, CFI = .98, TLI = .94, RMSEA = .04, CI_{90} = .03, .05). Next, additional models were computed, constraining the paths from expected outcomes and habit strength to equality. As such, we can assess the extent to which the consumption by means of a specific constellation of technologies is explained by both intentional and non-intentional factors. The results in Table 3 reveal that *versatile viewers'* lean back and forward consumption is uniquely explained by habit strength. *Television viewers* however demonstrate a lean back viewing equally explained by expected outcomes and habit, whereas their lean forward viewing behavior is strongly explained by habit. Finally, *laptop*

Table 3: Multi-sample parameter estimates

Path specifications	Parameter estimates†					
	Class 1: (53%) *Television viewers*		Class 2: (31%) *Versatile viewers*		Class 3: (16%) *Laptop viewers*	
	B	*SE*	B	*SE*	B	*SE*
Lean back viewing:						
Path A: Expected outcomes → Attendance	16.40***	*3.29*	4.69	*3.89*	18.32***	*5.28*
Path B: Habit strength → Attendance	19.67***	*1.99*	19.27***	*2.03*	11.46***	*2.13*
Models with both paths constrained to equality:††	$\Delta\chi^2$ = .60		$\Delta\chi^2$ = 9.07**		$\Delta\chi^2$ = 1.35	
Lean forward viewing:						
Path A: Expected outcomes → Attendance	.51	*1.15*	-2.10	*2.38*	5.37*	*2.60*
Path B: Habit strength → Attendance	10.63***	*.82*	15.06***	*1.22*	7.71***	*1.01*
Models with both paths constrained to equality:††	$\Delta\chi^2$ = 44.81***		$\Delta\chi^2$ = 35.55***		$\Delta\chi^2$ = .60	

viewers also demonstrate equal explanations of expected outcomes and habit strength for both viewing types. In sum, these results indicate that technologies furnish different orientations towards audiovisual media consumption. However, to further clarify the role of these supporting technologies as physical objects, allowing the playback of audiovisual content, there is an apparent need for further deepening research.

3.3 Understanding technological repertoires

In order to address the third and final research question, we draw upon the results of the qualitative follow-up study. A first finding is a rather sharp division between participants who embrace and welcome convergent technologies and those who maintain a more traditional stance, or what we like to refer to as *pre-convergent schemata*. In the latter case, the traditional television set still plays a dominant role, allowing a habitual consumption in a specific space. These people, not surprisingly part of the class of *television viewers*, still value the television set as a primary device and fully acknowledge its supposedly superior screen quality, ease of use, not requiring any specific technical skills and ability to consume in a social setting. This is especially important given the life phase in which this age cohort is often situated (middle and late adulthood), having a partner and children. Moreover, these people tend to discard other technologies to consume audiovisual content. A telephone is for calling and text messages; a computer is for office applications and browsing the Internet, albeit coinciding with the encounter and haphazard viewing of online video clips. This is reflected in the modest probabilities of using a desktop of laptop computer for audiovisual content consumption. Other mobile devices, such as portable DVD players or mobile media players are considered nice, yet unnecessary and sometimes even clumsy gadgets that add little to no value. In sum, the pre-convergent scheme of media technology usage boils down to the acknowledgement of a very limited set of affordances per device, whereas very little overlap exists. As such, in everyday life, technologies are narrowly constructed within narrowly defined compartments.

Hence, when people with pre-convergent meaning structures engage in watching television, it is usually the dominant activity at that specific time; especially when they take the time to sit down comfortably, in a lean back fashion. Although this is a part of a daily routine - especially at night - it also prevents people from fully engaging in all kinds of alternative activities. Hence, it is dedicated time that is not spent on other things. This helps to understand the effects found within the quantitative study for *television viewers*: their behavior is equally explained by a habit and expected outcomes. Still, lean forward viewing is dominantly explained by habits, pointing to an overall coincidental, haphazard behavior. It is in other words an unplanned activity, fitting in with other simultaneous activities or even part of a larger activity, such as browsing the Web. Rita (54, F) exemplifies this sense of compartmentalization:

> Rita: *In the morning, when I wake up I make coffee; turn on my laptop for reading mails and the newspaper. When I'm at home, it stays on for the rest of the day, just to check up every once and a while. Moving images, those for in the evening, on my television. In the daytime I would watch a short clip, sent by someone, or a video clip that is part of a news article. But I won't watch series during the day on my laptop. In the wintertime, I would tend to watch a series during the day, but that's on my television.*

Still, most interesting are the technology repertoires of people who have constructed strong *convergent schemata* on media technologies. That is the acknowledgement of media technologies as affording multiple activities, valuing them as elements in a larger constellation of linked or networked devices and actually using them in diverse patterns. This is most apparent for the *versatile viewers*, who combine the traditional television screen with computers and even mobile phones. For both viewing types, these viewers exemplify strong effects for lean back and lean forward consumption. These imply that these people strongly embedded this type of media into their daily habits and apparently draw upon the technological ubiquity to furnish this habit. In our experience, these are young professionals, starting a family. In fact, technologies are used in a complementary fashion: a television at night for comfortable viewing, a computer for obscure or short content and a mobile device, such as a smartphone containing a favorite series to watch on the train, during commuting. For example, Christopher (25, M), explains that because it is the same trajectory each time, his time is much better spent watching a video. Likewise, Maria Alicia (34, F) says:

> *I think it is handy* [mobile device] *but then again, I don't use it that often, so I don't mind the screen being smaller.*
>
> Interviewer: *Did this technology affect your viewing behavior?*
>
> Maria: Yes it did, I watch more. Before, I used to watch a lot of television, now I also watch when I'm on the train.

Yet, the acknowledgement of the benefits of technological convergence can also lead to a substitution of devices with similar affordances. This is found with the laptop viewers who demonstrate higher chances of frequently using a laptop for audiovisual consumption than a television set. As such, they divert from the traditional scheme. Moreover, in general, the behavior seems to be rather strongly motivated for both viewing types. During the interviews, mostly with younger people, it surfaced how a laptop is constructed as an overall affording device that should be seen as the absolute center of their networked, digital media consumption:

> Caroline (24, F): *I think compatibility is very important. I can connect my laptop to every device: I connect it to my television; I can connect my iPod, my mobile phone... So these three devices that I use quite often, I can all connect them to my laptop, making it my most important device. I transfer photo's from my mobile, and, something I do quite often, is connecting my laptop to the television, using a HDMI cable to watch a film in the living room...*

The latter situation shows us how using the device as an audiovisual playback device is paired with specific arrangements that need to be done. These range from relocating the device, hooking it up to other devices or networks to getting yourself into a position that diverts from the usual. Still, we learned to understand this substitution by framing it into the participants' everyday life circumstances. As the *laptop viewers* are usually situated in late adolescence and early adulthood, they still live at home, or only recently left the parental home. As such, they are limited in financial, spatial and material means, hence, using a similar device for a range of activities is especially interesting for them. Moreover, they regularly engage in individualized viewing, which conforms the perceived affordances of the device. Also, this is further reinforced by the ability to use an Internet-connected laptop to download and stream various types of content, free of cost.

4. DISCUSSION

The results of this study have showed that in a broad sample, consisting of various age groups, three distinct profiles are to be identified. Each one represents a distinct orientation towards media technologies suitable for audiovisual consumption. In specific, we have noticed trends of status quo (*television viewers*), of expansion (*versatile viewers*) and substitution, in which one technology serves as an alternative for another (*laptop viewers*). Moreover, these profiles are linked with equally distinct patterns for concerning the factors commonly considered as the substrate for media consumption. Both expected outcomes, pointing to a deliberate use and habit strength, which is indicative of a non-intentional routine-driven media use, seem to play vital, albeit different roles. In the expansion scenario, the consumption itself is strongly driven by routines. This was confirmed by the interviews with exemplifying participants. They mentioned to consume more often, in various situations on various devices. In that respect, technology offers the opportunity to broaden media use to almost any possible situation, furnishing a strong habitual situation. On the contrary, the other scenarios, status quo and substitution, are relatively more driven by conscious deliberation. In such a case, audiovisual consumption is much more of choice that puts constraints on the liberty of exercising alternative behaviors. For the television viewers it means to go and stay in a specific context, whereas the laptop viewers are confronted with the apparent need of rearranging their physical environments.

Interestingly, the employed technological repertoires are to be understood by the everyday social environments in which people live. The television viewers, who are of older age and are mainly situated in distinct life phases identify their television set as most prominent and suitable because the device serves their needs best. That is comfortable, social viewing in a specific space. Otherwise, the versatile viewers claim to embrace the ubiquity of devices by implementing them into various situations. These people, mostly young professionals, demonstrate a technological savvy and an open orientation towards innovative technology. Last, the laptop viewers, mostly students and very young adults, experience several constraints in terms of means. Hence, they have embraced their laptops as all-affording devices that meet their most basic media consumption needs.

5. CONCLUSION

In conclusion, the results from this study offer insight in the on-going diversification of technologies for audiovisual consumption. Rather than just focusing on adoption figures, it goes beyond this by inquiring actual usage and devoting attention to diversity in this respect. Although we are limited to a quota sample that is not representative for a given population, it does suggest that the majority of users is bound to a conservative consumption pattern. This experience little to no incentive to embrace alternative devices. Nonetheless, this is true for a smaller proportion of users, either because of the strong routine of consuming content or because of various constraints that make them more prone to use other devices. Hence, technology use seems to be coupled with age cohorts and life circumstances. An important question however is whether these trends will increase for future younger generations and whether today's diversifying and substituting consumer will persist in their behaviors. In the latter case we believe this is very unlikely, as we hypothesize that the shift to a next life phase will induce different circumstances that might lead them to a more 'traditional' technology consumption pattern. On the other hand, they might as well slide into a more versatile pattern. For that reason, we encourage future research that aims at monitoring these potential trends.

6. REFERENCES

[1] Tsekleves, E., et al., *Converged Digital TV Services: The Role of Middleware and Future Directions of Interactive Television.* International Journal of Digital Multimedia Broadcasting, 2009.

[2] Courtois, C., P. Verdegem, and L. De Marez, *The Triple Articulation of Media Technologies in Audiovisual Media Consumption.* Television & New Media, In Press.

[3] LaRose, R. and M. Eastin, *A Social Cognitive Theory of Internet Uses and Gratifications: Toward a New Model of Media Attendance.* Journal of Broadcasting & Electronic Media, 2004. **48**(3): p. 358-377.

[4] Norman, D.A., *The design of everyday things.* 2002, New York: Basic Books.

[5] Silverstone, R. and L. Haddon, *Design and the domestication of information and communication technologies: technical change and everyday life*, in *Communication by Design*, R. Mansell and R. Silverstone, Editors. 1996, Oxford University Press: Oxford.

[6] Doyle, G., *From Television to Multi-Platform : Less from More or More for Less?* Convergence, 2010. **16**(4): p. 431-449.

[7] Jenkins, H., *Convergence Culture: Where old an new media collide.* 2006, New York University Press: New York.

[8] Dwyer, T., *Media Convergence.* 2010, Maidenhead: Open University Press.

[9] Rubin, A.M., *The Uses-and-Gratifications Perspective of Media Effect*, in *Media Effects: Advances in Theory and Research*, J. Bryant and D. Zillman, Editors. 2002, Lawrence Erlbaum Associates: Mahwah.

[10] Ruggiero, T., *Uses and Gratifications Theory in the 21st Century.* Mass Communication & Society, 2000. **3**(1): p. 3-37.

[11] Katz, E., J.G. Blumler, and M. Gurevitch, *Utilization of Mass Communication by the Individual*, in *The Uses of Mass Communication*, J.G. Blumler and E. Katz, Editors. 1974, Sage Publications: London.

[12] Swanson, D.L., *The Uses and Misuses of Uses and Gratifications.* Human Communication Research, 1977. **3**(3): p. 214-221.

[13] LaRose, R., D. Mastro, and M. Eastin, *Understanding Internet Usage: A Social-Cognitive Approach to Uses and Gratifications.* Social Science Computer Review, 2001. **19**(4): p. 395-413.

[14] Bandura, A., *A social cognitive theory.* 1986, Englewood Cliffs: Prentice-Hall.

[15] Bandura, A., *Self-Efficacy: The Exercise of Control.* 1994, New York: Freeman.

[16] Palmgreen, P., L.A. Wenner, and J.D. Rayburn, *Relations Between Gratifications Sought and Obtained A Study of*

Television News. Communication Research, 1980. **7**(2): p. 161-192.

[17] LaRose, R., *The Problem of Media Habits.* Communication Theory, 2010. **20**(2): p. 194-222.

[18] Lievrouw, L., *New Media Design and Development: Diffusion of Innovations vs. Social Shaping of Technology*, in *Handbook of New Media*, L. Lievrouw and S. Livingstone, Editors. 2006, Sage: London. p. 246-265.

[19] Silverstone, R., *Television and Everyday Life.* 1994, London: Routledge.

[20] Silverstone, R., E. Hirsch, and D. Morley, *Information and Communication Technologies and the Moral Economy of the Household*, in *Consuming Technologies*, R. Silverstone and E. Hirsch, Editors. 1992, Routledge: New York. p. 15-31.

[21] Vermunt, J.K. and J. Magidson. *Latent Class Analysis.* 2006; Available from: http://www.statisticalinnovations.com/articles/Latclass.pdf.

[22] Courtois, C., P. Verdegem, and L. De Marez. *Audiovisual consumption as the interplay of objects, texts and contexts.* in *EuroITV 2011.* 2011. Lisbon, Portugal: ACM.

[23] Ruy, H. and A. Wong, *Perceived usefulness and performance of human-to-human communcations on television.* Computers in Human Behavior, 2007. **24**(4): p. 1364-1384.

[24] Tsekleves, E., et al., Entertainment Computing, 2011. **2**(3): p. 151-161.

[25] Verplanken, B. and S. Orbell, *Reflections on Past Behavior: A Self-Report Index of Habit Strength.* Journal of Applied Social Psychology, 2006. **33**(6): p. 1313-1330.

[26] Verplanken, B., *Beyond Frequency: Habit as a Mental Construct.* British Journal of Social Psychology, 2006. **45**(3): p. 639-656.

[27] Peters, O., et al., *Explaining and analyzing audiences: A social cognitive approach to selectivity and media use.* Communications, 2006. **31**(3): p. 279-308.

Large-Area Moderator Tracking and Demonstrational Configuration of Position Based Interactions for Virtual Studios

Dionysios Marinos   Chris Geiger   Jens Herder

University of Applied Sciences Düsseldorf
Josef-Gockeln-Straße 9
40474 Düsseldof
+49-211-4351-830
{dionysios.marinos, geiger, jens.herder}@fh-duesseldorf.de

ABSTRACT

In this paper we introduce a system for tracking persons walking or standing on a large planar surface and for using the acquired data to easily configure position based interactions for virtual studio productions. The tracking component of the system, radarTRACK, is based on a laser scanner device capable of delivering interaction points on a large configurable plane. By using the device on the floor it is possible to use the delivered data to detect feet positions and derive the position and orientation of one or more users in real time. The second component of the system, named OscCalibrator, allows for the easy creation of multidimensional linear mappings between input and output parameters and the routing of OSC messages within a single modular design environment. We demonstrate the use of our system to flexibly create position-based interactions in a virtual studio environment.

Categories and Subject Descriptors

D.2.12 [**Interoperability**]: Data mapping. I.3.6 [**Methodology and Techniques**]: Interaction techniques. I.4.8 [**Scene Analysis**]: Tracking.

General Terms

Measurement, Performance, Design, Reliability, Experimentation, Human Factors.

Keywords

Body Tracking, Virtual Studio Interaction, OSC Mapping.

1. INTRODUCTION

In live virtual studio productions (Figure 1), interactive art installations, theatrical performances or other occasions, where people interact with real or virtual objects, there is often the need to track the position of the participants in order to support the ongoing interactions. The current position of the user can be used to control, for example, the light and sound elements of an interactive set or to trigger certain events once the user reaches a certain position. A tracking system has to allow for easy configuration, especially if people with little technical experience use it. Looking at today's live productions in virtual studios there are few approaches that allow for user-specific triggering of interactions. Instead, most interactive elements in a virtual set are controlled from outside the set, e.g., an operator controls the set elements during the production by keyboard/mouse or dedicated hardware controls. We have addressed these issues and have extended a commercial large-area tracking system consisting of a laser scanner device with an additional software tracker allowing to track position and orientation of one or more users on a large planar surface without the need for special markers often used by optical tracking systems in virtual reality applications. The developed software offers an easy configuration of the tracking

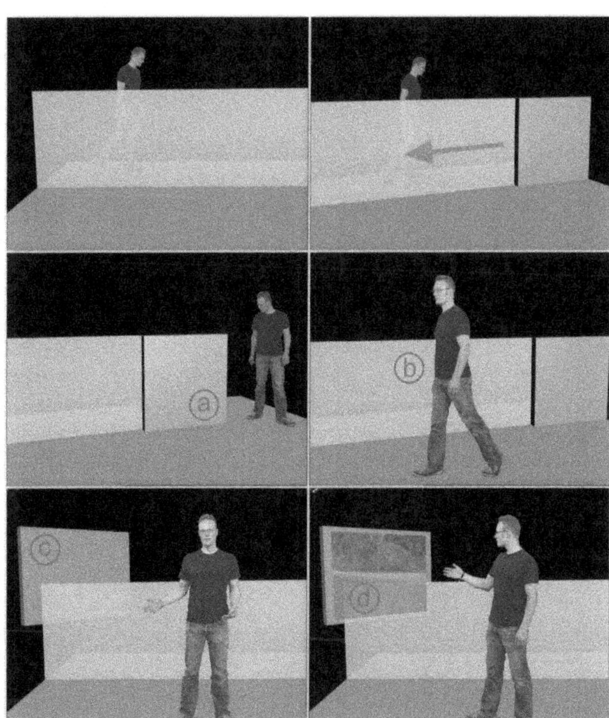

Figure 1. A moderator inside a virtual studio set interacting with some objects based on his position and orientation. Available interactions: (a) the red door opens up, (b) the wall gets occluded by the moderator image, (c) a virtual display appears, (d) a video is played back

EuroITV'12, July 4–6, 2012, Berlin, Germany.

area and additional areas, where certain interactions may take place. In order to create position based interactions, there is some effort involved concerning the need to process the acquired tracking data and to pass it on to particular interactive components e.g. a suitable software framework like 3D graphics engines, virtual studio software or media frameworks like *MAX/MSP* or *vvvv*. For such interactive systems consisting of a large number of components, this may be a laborious and time-consuming task, often requiring programming skills and know-how about the exact interfacing behavior of the components. In this work we wanted to solve part of this problem and created a tool that acts as a connecting link between tracking systems and interactive components. The idea was to get the user tracking data from our tracking system and to be able to comfortably map this data into new value spaces that make sense for the available interactive components. Having flexibility and compatibility with existing systems in mind, the tool was designed to receive and send Open Sound Control (OSC) [13] messages from and to any number of hosts, allowing for the flexible routing of control data. The mapping of incoming control or tracking data into useful value spaces for the specific interactive components is based on examples provided by the user. In this way interactions can be *"calibrated"* on-site by the user, who is just manipulating the outgoing values, while watching the effect of his actions in real-time, in order to create useful mappings between incoming control data and outgoing interaction values without traditional programming. This method resembles a programming-by-demonstration paradigm, like seen in [7].

2. RELATED WORK

In [5] Jung S. and Woo W. introduced an infrared-based tracking system for indoor environments, which was able to robustly track users even in noisy environments. The environments had to be equipped with a grid of IR transmitters and the users with an IR receiver. Orr and Abowd in [8] created a floor system that was able to identify and track people based on their footstep force profiles. User tracking using multiple uncalibrated cameras has been researched in [6]. Organic Motion [15] created tracking systems based on multiple camera setups that enable the tracking of one or more users in a certain volume without the use of any markers. Microsoft's Kinect [12] used with the right software also provides a marker free tracking system for multiple users, it offers however a pretty small tracking volume. In comparison to our system, the above systems consist of multiple devices and their setup can be proved to be complicated for someone who wants to quickly create a large indoor or outdoor tracking area for multiple users with the possibility to effectively provide tracking data in real time to most modern audio or graphics authoring systems. Frieder Weiss, a German software developer, has worked on many artistic projects including audio-visual dance performances, museum exhibits and music videos. He is the developer of the eyecon software framework that allows triggering events based on previously defined areas in the camera image [10]. Instead we use the object/actor space for tracking and triggering events.

In the area of routing and mapping control data for artistic and other forms of interactive performances, an interesting work by Bergstrom [2] was presented at ACE'09. The proposed piece of software, called Mediator, was able to gradually re-route OSC messages, expanding the artistic potential of musical or other technologically mediated performances. Another piece of software allowing the user to create flexible routings for OSC and other control data like MIDI is Osculator [16]. Although such kinds of tools provide a good example of the possibilities that open up by flexible routing in the field of artistic performances and music creation, they don't address complex mappings and flexible OSC message conversions. The flexible and easy design of interactions is also goal of many frameworks, that focus on multi-touch gestures for finger/hand interaction. A good overview of selected systems is presented in [9] where the authors also describe the declarative MIDAS framework that allows to declaratively specify gestures using a rule-based inference engine. This allows defining new complex gestures with little programming overhead. We follow the same goal but as we focus on complete body movement we do not consider the life cycle of "touch-points" that form a gesture but only the current position. Looking at the related work we identified the following requirements and differences for our purposes:

- Large area tracking beyond the range of otherwise suitable devices like the Kinect or similar time-of-flight depth cameras. Also we need to track in the object space and not in the image space like the eyecon project.
- Marker-less, non-tethered tracking that allows actors to move freely within the tracking area in a virtual studio. Thus we cannot use traditional VR tracking approaches with IR sensitive marker bodies.
- Position based tracking of actors that recognizes only the position and orientation of the whole body and not fine-grained gestures that require the detection of arm or finger postures.
- Multiple actor support. While the primary goal is to track one person for a "One-Man-Show", support for multiple actors should be available.
- Easy configuration of tracking setups for non-programmers, using state-of-the-art protocols like OSC for interfacing commercial frameworks for virtual studio production.

3. RADARTRACK

In order to track people on a large planar surface (up to 20x20m), we extended a compact laser scanner system with an additional piece of software (Figure 2). This laser scanner system, known as radarTOUCH (Figure 3), deploys a safe laser IR beam and a precisely timed rotating mirror to create an invisible plane, on which intersecting objects can be detected and tracked with the use of special software. The size and the position of the interaction plane can be easily configured and the detected intersection points are transmitted as touch events according to the TUIO protocol specification. The touch events are independent from one another and do not contain any further information regarding the position of the user who generates them. Our software extends the system and analyzes the user tracking data so that it can be easily configured to enable position based interactions. In order for the system to work properly, the interaction plane of the radarTOUCH device has to be set parallel and close to the floor, which the people move or stand on. This way the tracked points provided correspond ideally to the feet of the users.

In order to analyze the tracked interaction points and provide user tracking data, like the two-dimensional position and the body rotation of the user, the following steps are considered:

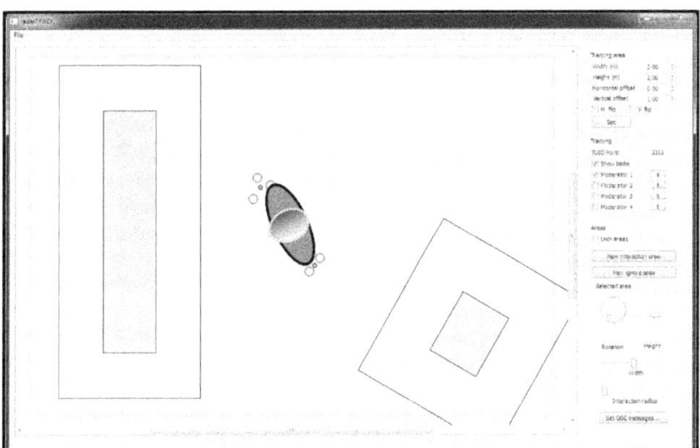

Figure 2. The radarTRACK software interface. On the right side, there is the configuration control panel. On the left side, a top view visualization is provided showing the tracking space, the interaction areas with their surrounding proximity space and the user representation with the detected interaction points and derived foot positions (small circles).

- Interaction points that appear close to each other are clustered together based on a certain threshold, so that they form a single robust foot position. The position of the foot is calculated as the weighted center of the clustered points, based on the life cycle of the points inside the cluster.
- When two detected feet are close enough to each other they are assumed to be the feet of a user. The position of the user is then defined as the midpoint of his/her feet. The rotation of the user body is derived from the axis that goes through his feet. At the beginning it is assumed that that user is facing the radarTOUCH device, but as soon as the user walks a certain distance, the user orientation is defined by the walking direction under the assumption that people walk forward in most situations.
- If only one foot is detected, it is at first assumed the user feet are so close to each other, that they are detected as a single point. The position of the user corresponds to this single foot position. If the speed of the moving user remains under a certain threshold, the last calculated rotation is considered. Exceeding this threshold leads to a change in the orientation, assuming the tracked user faces the direction he/she is moving in.
- The user position and body rotation are then exponentially smoothed to avoid big leaps in the tracking data.

The resulting tracking data per user are then sent at a specified host as OSC messages with three float values: the 2D position values X and Y and the rotation value of the user body. Our tracker also provides the possibility to define areas, in which the detected points are ignored. These "ignore" areas are quite useful for real world situations, on which statically positioned objects are not supposed to be detected as actors, like a moderation desk in a virtual studio. In addition to that, it is possible to define square formed interaction areas for the triggering of various events. When the user enters such an area, a custom defined OSC message is sent to a specified address. An additional area around the interaction area can also be defined, so that an OSC message with a proximity parameter varying between 0 and 1 is sent, when the user approaches the interaction area.

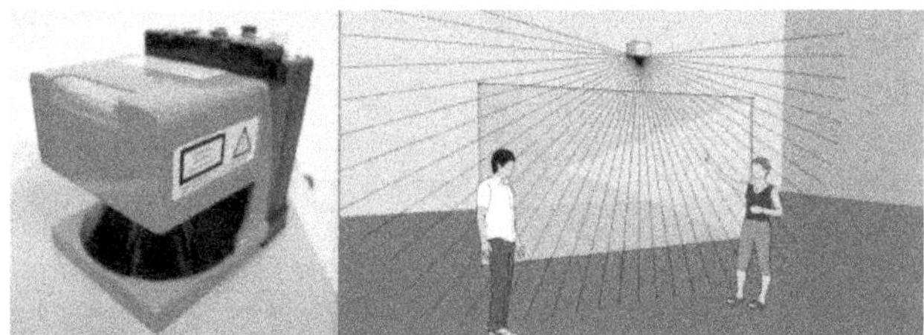

Figure 3. The radarTOUCH device (left). Illustration of its use as an input device for a vertical interactive surface (right).

radarTRACK has been successfully used to track a moderator and to automatically trigger certain events for an educational production about the virtual studio technologies available in our facilities (Figure 4).

Figure 4. Captured frame from a virtual studio production utilizing radarTRACK (left), screenshot of the radarTRACK software depicting the defined interaction areas for the specific virtual scene (right). When the moderator steps over an interaction area, the corresponding explanatory panel shows up.

4. OSC CALIBRATOR

In this work, we also address the routing of control or tracking data and their multidimensional mapping to new value spaces to support the creation of interactions. Interactive systems often consist of many different tracking devices and modules that communicate with each other to exchange tracking values or to signalize different events. A protocol often used for this purpose is the Open Sound Control protocol [16]. OSC messages can be easily created and send over a network in form of UDP packets. The protocol's flexibility and ease of use led to its rising popularity, so that nowadays almost every authoring software for real time interactive graphics or audio applications supports it. The protocol keeps evolving [3] and it gradually finds its place to new application areas, like e.g. in our case the virtual studio. Although the OSC protocol is pretty straight-forward in its use, it always requires some effort in order to add new components or to change the message flow across an interactive system. Apart from that, there is often the case, in which different components are developed outside the scope that they should work together. Making such components work together requires transforming the data sent from one form into another, so that the receiving component is able to interpret it correctly: often a time consuming task that requires the modification of the components in question. Our software, called *OscCalibrator*[1], offers a delicate way to

[1] OscCalibrator is available as free GNU GPL v3 software at http://code.google.com/p/osccalibrator/

solve this kind of problems, allowing for flexible routing and easy multidimensional mapping of OSC control data and supporting the implementation of interactive systems. This tool offers the possibility to accept OSC messages from different hosts, individually extract the corresponding control values, pass these values through mapping processors, create new OSC control messages out of the available raw or processed values and send them to specified hosts. The interface of the software resembles a typical modular design environment, where processing nodes can be added and connected with each other. There are only three available nodes:

- The *OSC Input Node* for receiving an OSC message.
- The *OSC Output Node* for composing and sending an OSC message.
- The *Calibrator Node* for configuring a mapping between input and output values by demonstration.

Before we go into detail in describing how the Calibrator Node works, the OSC routing capabilities of the software are first demonstrated. The user can add a new OSC Input or Output Node by right clicking on the tools working area and selecting the corresponding option from the pop up menu, which shows up. A double click on the node brings up a configuration dialog, which allows setting up the OSC message parameters. For the OSC Input Node these are the OSC message address, the listening port number and the number of expected control values. In addition to that, the configuration dialog for the OSC Output Node asks for the address of the host to receive the composed OSC message. The configured nodes appearing in the application working area have a title and labels for the available input and output connectors that can be edited by the user at any time. The user can connect an input to an output by simply dragging one connector over another. This schema allows for a fast, clear and flexible OSC routing configuration.

To create a mapping between input and output values the user can use a Calibrator Node, which is one of the main particularities of our software in comparison to other mapping tools. Such a node can be added in the same style like the other nodes. Through a dialog window the user specifies the number of inputs and outputs that the node should work with. After that, the Calibrator Node can be connected to the OSC Input and Output Nodes to accept

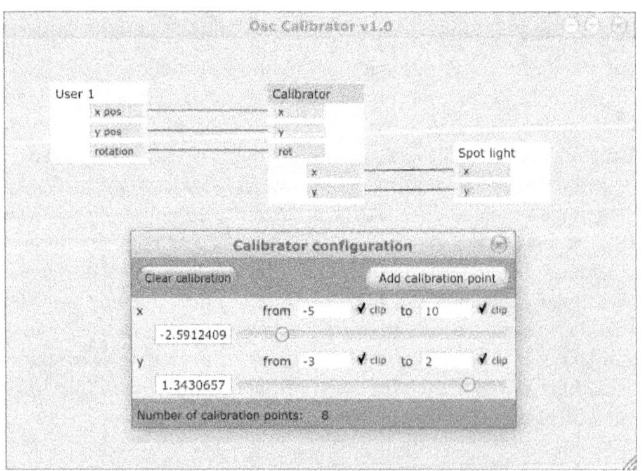

Figure 5. The configuration dialog of a Calibrator Node accepting three input and delivering two output parameters.

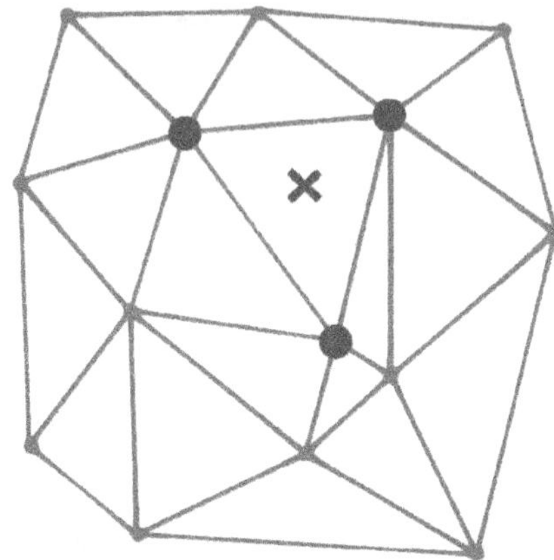

Figure 6. A Delaunay triangulation in two dimensions. The graph nodes represent the calibration points. The input point is denoted with an 'x'. The three surrounding vertices form a triangle containing the input point and are used to perform the necessary data interpolation.

the desired input values and to deliver the resulting mapped values respectively. In order to create a mapping, the user has to provide output examples for the current input value vector. This is possible by calling the configuration dialog of the Calibrator Node. In this dialog there is a list of faders that correspond to the desired output values. The user can operate these faders to define output values for the current input vector and press a button to add this association to the current configuration, which we will from now on call a *calibration point*. When moving the faders, the Calibrator Node outputs the corresponding values in real-time, so that the user can directly watch the influence of his action on the system, which he/she wants to control. After adding enough calibration points the user can close the configuration dialog (Figure 5), in order for the Calibration Node to start producing output values based on the defined calibration points.

The output values are produced by interpolating or extrapolating the output values of a subset of the available calibration points, based on the input value vector. Assuming that the input vector consists of n values representing a point in an n-dimensional space, the available calibration points are considered to be scattered points inside this space. In order to produce an output, the following steps have to be followed:

- A delaunay triangulation (Figure 6) of the calibration points in n-dimensions takes place using the CGAL framework [11].
- Based on the input value vector, which represents a point in the n-dimensional space, the best simplex produced by the delaunay triangulation is selected. That implies the simplex that contains the input point or the simplex with the closest centroid to the input point.
- The barycentric coordinates of the input point inside the selected simplex are calculated. The vertices of the simplex correspond to certain calibration points.
- A barycentric interpolation/extrapolation takes place to produce the output value vector.

The following algorithm describes the procedure above:

Output Parameters Computation

Input: A vector of calibration points *CP*. Each calibration point contains a position *Pos*□□^{n} and a vector of parameters *Par*□□^{m} with *m*□□. A position in space *InputPos*□□^{n}.
Output: The output parameter vector *OutputPar*□□^{m}.

```
for each calibration_point in CP
    push calibration_point.Pos to Vertices;
end
Simplices = Delaunay_Triangulation(Vertices);
bestsimplex = Simplices[0];
mindistance = distance(Simplices[0], InputPos);
for each Simplex in Simplices
    tempdistance = distance(centroid of Simplex, InputPos);
    if (tempdistance<mindistance)
        bestsimplex = Simplex;
    end
end
for each Vertex in bestsimplex
    push CP element with (Pos == Vertex) to CPoints;
end
Matrix T; //n×n Matrix
for i = 0 to n-1
    push column CPoints[i].Pos-CPoints[n].Pos to T;
end
bar_coordinates=T^-1·(InputPos-CPoints[n].Pos);
push 1- \sum_{i=0}^{n-1} bar_coordinates[i] to bar_coordinates;
Matrix P; //m×(n+1) Matrix
for i = 0 to n
    push column CPoints[i].Par to P;
end
OutputPar=P·bar_coordinates;
```

The above method expects to have enough calibration points (at least $n+1$ for an n-dimensional space) in order to form a simplex in the given dimension. If less calibration points are available simpler strategies are followed:

- If only one calibration point is available, the output of the Calibrator Node corresponds to the given output of this single calibration point.
- If two calibration points are available, the input point is projected on the line formed by these points. The interpolated values for the projected point are used.
- If the space has three dimensions but only three calibration points are available, the input point is projected on the plane formed by the calibration points. The projected point is then used to produce the interpolated output.
- In any other case the Calibrator Node delivers the current values defined in its configuration dialog.

The user is able to define limit values for every output parameter of a Calibrator Node in its configuration dialog. By activating clipping for those parameters, output values stay inside the desired interval even in extrapolation cases. This is a useful feature for controlling interactive elements that require values in a certain range in order to work properly.

Another important feature of the Calibration Node configuration dialog is the possibility to remotely control the sliders and the other GUI elements over OSC. The user can simple drag and drop a GUI element over the desired output connector of an OSC Input Node to allow the remote controlling of this GUI element. This way, by using a portable device like a smartphone or a tablet, it is possible to configure the calibration points while interacting inside the tracking area, without needing another person to set the proper calibration points. Another possibility is to directly use control or tracking values that are already available in the OSC infrastructure of the respective virtual studio application as example values for a calibration. The use of this feature will be presented in the test cases that follow.

5. TEST CASES

In this section two simple and arbitrary test cases are presented, in which user position based interactions were implemented using radarTRACK in combination with OscCalibrator and Ventuz [18], a 3D authoring program for the creation of interactive graphics content. Ventuz supports the OSC protocol, which makes it an ideal candidate for experimentation with our system. Moreover, Ventuz offers a broadcast edition for synchronous video output, allowing its use with other video equipment found in a virtual studio. Other popular virtual studio authoring environments, like e.g. VizArtist [19] or Orad 3Designer [14], can also work with our system by using an OSC receiver plugin.

5.1 Creating an Interactive Virtual Set

In this test case we created a simple virtual television studio set with the goal to demonstrate the effectiveness of our system to configure user position based interactions. Related interactions were implemented and explored in [1]. Although our test case only focuses on interactions in a virtual studio environment [4] with a moderator moving around a virtual set triggering events and controlling virtual objects, it provides a good example of the design process that our system supports for configuring and fine-tuning such interactions. The virtual set consists of a flat area, on which a studio moderator stands and walks (Figure 7). This area is divided in two regions separated by a thin semi-transparent wall. On the one side of the wall there is a sliding door. In one of the two regions there is a virtual display for video content playback.

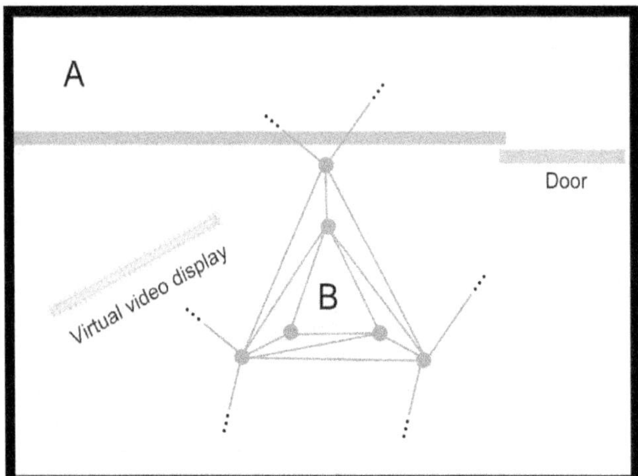

Figure 7. A top view illustration of our virtual set. The start position of the moderator is designated with an "A" and the end position with a "B". The calibration points required for the apperance of the video display with the corresponding triangulation are shown.

The described hypothetical production scenario involves the moderator starting at a certain position and walking along the semi-transparent wall towards the door. When he/she reaches the door, the door opens and the moderator enters the second region. The moderator moves toward the center of the second region, while the door closes behind him. Once the moderator reaches his/her end position the virtual display, which until then was invisible, appears showing a paused video clip. The moderator turns his body toward the display to simulate the effect of wanting to watch the video clip. Then the playback of the video clip starts (Figure 1).

In a traditional virtual studio production a person would sit in the control room, watching over the production and controlling the virtual set by operating some sort of software or hardware faders and buttons that are connected to the virtual studio authoring environment. The obvious controls needed for carrying out the production described above are for the opening and closing of the door, the appearing of the display and the starting of the video playback. Another important issue here is the necessary resolving of occlusions. Only the virtual objects of the set that reside between the studio camera and the moderator should occlude the moderator. In a studio without the possibility to track the moderator position, someone in the control room will have to make the virtual objects appear in front or behind the moderator by pressing the right buttons. These interactions have to be extensively trained by the production crew, before the show would go live on air. If there is a moderator tracking system in the studio, there is the possibility to use the logic functions provided by virtual studio authoring software, in order to automate the interactions described above. This is a time consuming process and involves an expert with programming skills as well as knowledge about the progression of the show events. All these factors make a live virtual television production, trying to give the impression of a highly interactive virtual set, rather difficult and have led to today's productions, which are based on some rather static and safe-to-use interaction templates that can be used by non-experts. Our system allows for defining and fine-tuning interactions like the ones described above in a delicate way, making it possible even for non-experts to express their creativity.

Let us assume we start with the necessary task of designing the virtual set for the hypothetical virtual studio production above and offer the following real-time control parameters:

- *Door-Openness*: a parameter that takes a value between 0 and 1 and controls the openness of the door (on 0 the door is closed).
- *Display-Appearance:* a parameter between 0 and 1 that controls the transparency of the video display (on 0 the display is invisible).
- *Video-Playback*: a parameter for starting the video playback, if it is other than 0. A value of null stops the video playback.
- *Occlusion-Activation*: a parameter for making the wall and the door occlude the moderator, if it is on 1.

The next step in our design process is to place the radarTOUCH device on the virtual studio floor and configure it, so that the interaction plane is aligned to the virtual set floor. Then we start the radarTRACK software and input the interaction plane parameters. After that, the tracker is able to robustly track a person moving around the blue box. Sequentially we start the OscCalibrator tool. We add an OSC Input Node, in order to receive the tracking data. Four OSC Output Nodes are added to send the necessary control data to Ventuz, for the direct controlling of the parameters listed above. As next, a Calibrator Node per control parameter is added. The whole configuration of the interaction now only consists of defining the necessary calibration points for each parameter. For that purpose an operator sitting in the control room instructs someone to move around the set and sets the calibration points accordingly. An alternative would be to use the OSC control feature of the Calibrator Node dialog to set the output parameters through the use of a portable control device, like a tablet or smartphone running an OSC control application (e.g. [17]). This way it is possible for a single person to configure the desired interactions, assuming that he/she is able to get feedback for his/her actions while remotely operating the dialog of the Calibrator Node.

The calibration process for each parameter follows:

- *Door-Openness*: The door resides on the right side of the set. This means that a single coordinate describing the position of the moderator on the left-right axis would be enough to make the necessary interaction work. The operator has to feed the Calibrator Node with the x-coordinate of the moderator position. The moderator is instructed to move from left to right and the operator sets to calibration points. While the moderator is far away from the door side the output value should be 0. When he reaches the door area the output value is set to 1.
- *Occlusion-Activation*: Similar to the Door-Openness parameter, this parameter only depends on a single coordinate: the y-coordinate of the moderator's position. The moderator takes his start position behind the wall and a calibration point is set with the output value of 1. The moderator moves then in front of the virtual wall and another calibration point is added with the value of 0.
- *Display-Appearance*: The display is supposed to appear when the moderator reaches a certain position. The necessary information for this interaction is the 2-D coordinates of the moderator position. The Calibrator Node is therefore fed with

these two tracking values. The moderator moves to the desired position and the operator sets a calibration point with the output value of 1. Some additional calibration points around this point are needed to precisely define the area that activates the display and additional transition areas around it (a minimum of 6 calibration points like in Figure 7).

- *Video-Playback*: The video playback occurs when the display is visible and the moderator turns his body towards it. In order to configure this interaction the Display-Appearance parameter and the body rotation of the moderator are fed into a Calibration Node. The moderator takes the display activation position and supposedly looks at the virtual display. The output of the corresponding calibration point is set to 1. He turns away from the display and some other points are calibrated with the value of 0. He then goes away from the display activation area, so that the operator sets a last calibration point with the output value of 0, for the case that the moderator display is not visible. This way the video playback cannot get started, if the moderator turns towards the display before it appears.

The above configuration (Figure 8) can be simplified if we use the available feature of radarTRACK to send OSC messages when the user approaches and enters specified areas. The reason we configure the whole interaction only through the definition of calibration points is to demonstrate the flexibility of the Calibrator Node. Apart from that, the definition of the calibration points at the phase of rehearsal is something that does not require additional effort for the production crew, because during this phase all interactions have to be tested with real people anyway: a phase in which the calibration points can be set at the first place. Another advantage of our system is that calibration points can be added at any time. So if the crew decides to make a certain interaction more complex, it just has to add some additional calibration points.

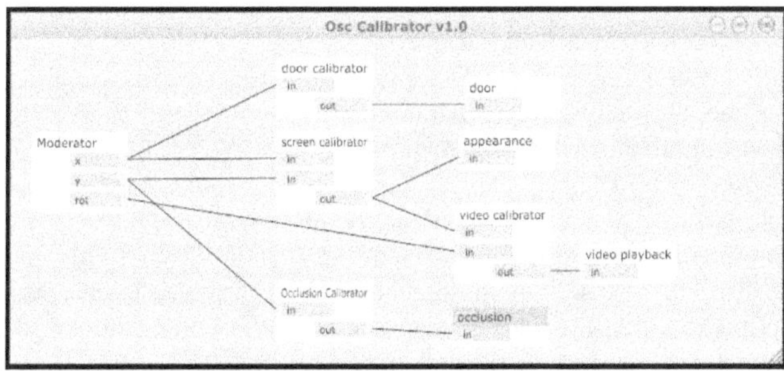

Figure 8. The OscCalibrator configuration for the deployed interactions in the virtual studio set.

5.2 Coupling Two Tracking Systems Together

If a tracking system fails to track an object or a person, then the tracking data from another system can be used to drive the interaction, increasing the robustness of the system. Another motivation for this test case is to increase the tracking space by coupling more than one tracking systems with partially overlapping tracking areas. Through the use of the OscCalibrator, a developer or interaction designer can effectively deploy the above ideas. In order to demonstrate this, we describe a case in which the desired interaction is impaired from the tracker limitations and how an additional tracker can be used to resolve the problem. Let us assume we have an interactive display in the middle of a virtual studio that provides e.g. visual feedback to the moderator. The table, on which the interactive display resides, has a rectangular form and is attached to the floor. Depending on the position of the moderator around it, the table should display different pieces of information in different formats. The challenge here is to robustly track the user around the table and provide the necessary data to its software.

Suppose we use radarTRACK to track the user location. We place the radarTOUCH device on the floor and configure the tracking area dimensions to match the ones of the room. The interactive table is attached to the floor and therefor there is no way with radarTRACK to follow a user, when his/her feet are occluded by the table. In this case, we have to integrate an additional sensor to cover the untrackable area. This integration has to be transparent to the table software, in order for it to keep working without needing to reprogram the available interaction model. Figure 9 illustrates the problem and the use of an additional Kinect sensor as part of the solution. By using the Kinect sensor with suitable open source software it is possible to get the user position from Kinect in form of OSC messages. The position is delivered in Kinect's coordinate system. The first step is to transform the coordinates into the desired coordinate system, in our case, into the radarTRACK coordinate system. For this purpose, we feed the three dimensional position data from Kinect into a 3-to-2 Calibrator Node. A person stands at different positions inside the areas that are trackable from both tracking systems. For each of these positions we set a calibration point with the output value vector equal to the position delivered by the radarTRACK. This can be easily done using the OSC control feature of the Calibrator Node dialog, by controlling the corresponding sliders with the values received from radarTRACK. The use of the OSC control feature allows for the addition of new calibration points by the person who is standing inside the tracking area, making the calibration process more comfortable. After setting enough calibration points the output of the Calibrator Node corresponds to the output of radarTRACK, making the Kinect data suitable for use with the table software.

The next step is to select on the fly which tracking data should be used. This can be done through a weighting factor w that signifies which system is currently tracking. So if w is 1, this means that

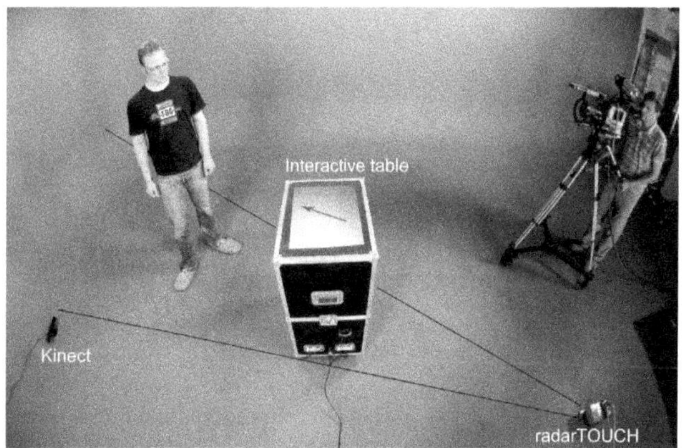

Figure 9. The moderator resides in an area that cannot be tracked using radarTRACK. Through the use of an additional Kinect sensor and its transparent integration, the interactive table in the middle receives the right moderator position and works without any modifications.

only the values delivered by radarTRACK are valid, while a weighting factor of 0 signifies the validity of the Kinect data. Let *rt* denote a two-dimensional vector representing the tracking position delivered by radarTRACK and *kt* the corresponding position vector delivered from Kinect through the Calibrator Node mentioned above. The desired position to be used for the interaction is: $Pos = w \cdot rt + (w-1) \cdot kt$. The last step involves configuring an additional Calibrator Node to deliver the right weighting value *w*. A 2-to-1 Calibrator Node is sufficient this task. As input vector we use the *kt* vector. We let the user stand at the edges between the areas that are only covered from Kinect and the ones where the tracking areas from Kinect and radarTRACK overlap and we set a couple of calibration points with an output value of 0. Then the user stands at the edges between the overlapping areas and the purely radarTRACK tracked area and we set a couple of calibration points with 1 as the output. The resulting output, when we put the Calibrator Node in use, is a value floating between 0 and 1 signifying how reliable the data from radarTRACK is. This value corresponds to the weighting factor *w* and can be used directly. To complete the solution, we just have to perform the calculation described by the equation above. This can be easily done in almost any program that allows the manipulation of control data, like Ventuz. In conclusion we were able to effectively use a cheap sensor like the Kinect, to cover an area of an interaction space that could not be completely tracked with radarTOUCH. The resulting data, composed by the weighted combination of the tracking data delivered by both systems, is in the right format and can be used transparently with the available interactive table.

6. DISCUSSION AND FUTURE WORK

Our tracking system proved itself to provide a sufficient way to track one or more moderators inside the blue box of a virtual studio or on other large surfaces. The main disadvantage was associated with the orientation of the user. If the user was walking backwards and spinning around, the system could faulty interpret this, delivering a rotation value as if the user has been looking at the opposite direction. However, the tracked position of the user is not impaired by this kind of problem, allowing most interactions to continue working properly. Nevertheless, in order to overcome the problems associated with the user orientation, the possibility to change the user orientation on-demand was considered by adding the necessary button next to each moderator label on the radarTRACK software interface. This way, an operator watching over a live production can detect a problem in the tracked orientation and directly correct it. Another issue with our tracking system is occlusion. Tracking more than one person may become unreliable, considering the fact that one person's feet can occlude the other person's feet from the laser scanner's point of view. For the future, we are examining the combination of more than one radarTOUCH devices to increase the reliability.

The OscCalibrator provides a flexible yet simple tool to support the creation of position-based interactions. Its combination with radarTRACK and other tracking sensors allows for the creative transformation of tracking data into useful interaction values, making it possible to easily create and expand interactions while exploring and testing the available tracking space. In our test cases, a person operated the OscCalibrator while another person was moving inside the tracking area. If needed, this kind of configuration process can be replaced with a single-person-configuration process. This is possible through the OSC controlling of the calibration nodes and the use of a portable OSC controller.

At the moment of writing, OscCalibrator does not provide a visualization of the calibration points or the possibility to edit them. Such functionality would allow for the authoring of the available interactions, providing a way to adapt them to new virtual sets without the need to repeat the calibration process.

In order to expand the spectrum of useful possible interactions, the idea of value snapping has also to be explored. Certain interactions are driven by discrete values, like the selection of an item on a list, where the important parameter would be the index of the item. In such cases the interpolated values output by the Calibrator Nodes would not be very useful. With a mechanism for snapping the current tracking values on the nearest calibration point, the output would take the calibrated discrete values needed. A combination of interpolated and snapped output values would also make sense, assuming that an interface for defining the snapping thresholds for the available calibration points was provided. In order to further improve the usability of the OscCalibrator in real life scenarios, delay nodes could be added allowing to model time constraints or delaying data in order to synchronize them with other events.

CONTRIBUTION: Real interaction in live virtual studio productions is currently not widely applied and most interactive behavior is prescripted or controlled by an external operator. Virtual studio frameworks had to be programmed similarly to VR systems to allow interactive behavior during a live production. With our radarTRACK system we provide an efficient, yet easy-to-use approach to track a person's position and orientation on a large area and to trigger different events when he/she steps over or approaches different configurable areas. To our knowledge, currently no such system for virtual studios exists. The mapping of different tracking and control data is well known in research areas like virtual and augmented reality (e.g. [12]), but most often the general approach of these powerful systems requires substantial technical (programming) know-how. With our OscCalibrator software we focused on a narrow application area (position-based interactions for virtual studios) and we successfully managed to create a tool that interfaces with commercial virtual studio frameworks and allows for rapid creation of interactivity through exploring the interaction space and demonstrating control parameter relationships without the need for programming. Such a method opens up the way to the creation of complex interactions for live productions even by non-programmers, contributing to the evolution of virtual studios into a more expressive, interactive medium.

7. ACKNOWLEDGMENTS

This work was partially supported by the research grant "IVO [at] hiTV" funded by German Federal Ministry of Education and Research (BMBF) under the program "FHprofUnt 2010", contract no. FKS 17010X10.

8. REFERENCES

[1] Ballendat, T. et al. 2010. Proxemic interaction: designing for a proximity and orientation-aware environment. *ACM International Conference on Interactive Tabletops and Surfaces*. (2010), 121–130.

[2] Bergstrom, I. et al. 2009. Mutable mapping: gradual re-routing of OSC control data as a form of artistic performance. *Proceedings of the International Conference on Advances in Computer Enterntainment Technology*. (2009), 290–293.

[3] Computational Geometry Algorithms Library: *http://www.cgal.org/*. Accessed: 2012-01-16.

[4] Features and Future of Open Sound Control version 1.1 for NIME: 2009. *http://cnmat.berkeley.edu/node/7002*. Accessed: 2012-01-19.

[5] Gibbs, S. et al. 1998. Virtual Studios: An Overview. *IEEE Multimedia*.

[6] Jung, S. and Woo, W. 2004. UbiTrack: Infrared-based user Tracking System for indoor environment. *ICAT'04*. 1, (2004), 181–184.

[7] Khan, S. et al. Human tracking in multiple cameras. *Proceedings Eighth IEEE International Conference on Computer Vision. ICCV 2001* (Vancouver, BC, Canada), 331-336.

[8] Kinect: *http://www.xbox.com/kinect*. Accessed: 2011-10-20.

[9] Li, Y. and Landay, J.A. 2005. Informal prototyping of continuous graphical interactions by demonstration. *Proceedings of the 18th annual ACM symposium on User interface software and technology* (New York, NY, USA, 2005), 221–230.

[10] Open Sound Control: *http://opensoundcontrol.org/*. Accessed: 2011-10-20.

[11] Orad 3Designer: *http://www.orad.tv/3designer*. Accessed: 2012-01-17.

[12] Organic Motion: *http://www.organicmotion.com/*. Accessed: 2011-10-20.

[13] Orr, R.J. and Abowd, G.D. 2000. The smart floor: a mechanism for natural user identification and tracking. *CHI 00 extended abstracts on Human factors in computing systems*. (2000), 275–276.

[14] Osculator: *http://www.osculator.net/*. Accessed: 2011-10-20.

[15] Performance projects and eyecon framework: *http://www.frieder-weiss.de/*. Accessed: 2011-10-20.

[16] Scholliers, C. et al. 2011. Midas: a declarative multi-touch interaction framework. *TEI '11 Proceedings of the fifth international conference on Tangible, embedded, and embodied interaction* (2011), 49.

[17] TouchOSC: *http://hexler.net/software/touchosc*. Accessed: 2012-01-17.

[18] Ventuz: *http://www.ventuz.com/*. Accessed: 2011-10-20.

[19] VizArtist: *http://www.vizrt.com/products/viz_artist/*. Accessed: 2011-10-20.

Seeing the Bigger Picture: A User Perspective on 360° TV

Lizzy Bleumers, Wendy Van den Broeck, Bram Lievens & Jo Pierson
IBBT-SMIT, Vrije Universiteit Brussel
Pleinlaan 2
1050 Brussels, Belgium
+32 2 629 16 47

Lizzy.Bleumers@vub.ac.be

ABSTRACT
Omnidirectional video (ODV) is a type of video in which viewers can look around in 360° as if turning the camera themselves. This type of video presents opportunities for new interactive television formats. The development of such new formats, however, is accompanied by challenges in terms of user experience and technical and creative development. In this paper, we discuss which issues and opportunities users anticipate. These findings are the result of a human-centered design study in which we first introduced potential users to ODV, gathering their feedback, and then encouraged them to envision suitable ODV-based enhancements of television genres.

Categories and Subject Descriptors
H.5.2 [User Interfaces]: User-centered design.

General Terms
Human Factors, Design.

Keywords
Omnidirectional Video, Television, Participatory Design, User Research.

1. INTRODUCTION
Omnidirectional video (ODV) refers to moving images that have been captured so that the viewer can look around in the image in 360°. There are several terms in use to refer to ODV. Synonyms include panoramic, 360°, spherical, and surround video. In essence, people can freely choose the viewing angle while the omnidirectional video plays, as if they are turning the camera. As such, ODV provides viewers with a new form of interactivity. For an example, see [17].

Although combinations of the two are possible, ODV has to be distinguished from multi-angle video. In the case of multi-angle video, users have the opportunity to choose between alternate video streams, often showing a single event from different viewpoints (recorded by cameras standing at different positions). With regular ODV, the viewer can choose their viewing direction from a given viewpoint, not the viewpoint. This extended field of view is the result of either using a single-camera solution with curved lenses/mirrors or a multi-camera system in which each camera films part of the surrounding space and images are stitched together afterwards [4].

ODV can be displayed in various ways (as shown in Figure 1). Within a spherical or cylindrical set-up, users look at an area of interest through eye and head movement. On a head-mounted display, the viewing area is confined to the glasses and users look around by moving their head. In case of more common displays (such as television, computer and tablet displays), the viewing area is confined and developers have to either capitalize on the existing interface or provide new interaction devices/modes.

While ODV provides an opportunity to create, develop and distribute new television formats, ODV on 2D displays has only been offered online. This is due to the difficulties of televising ODV. The challenges that accompany this process, with respect to concept creation, technical development and user experience are currently being tackled in the xTV (explorative television) research project [29].

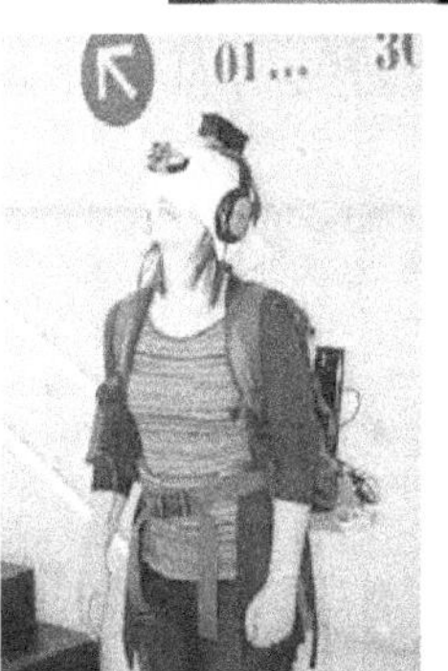

Figure 1. ODV displays. Top: Multi-projection home cave. Bottom left: Head-mounted display. Bottom right: 2D display on website.

The main motivation for an interdisciplinary approach in xTV is the realization that whether new interactive services fulfill their promise, does not merely depend on tackling technical challenges. The switch from analog to digital television and the introduction of cross-media interactive platforms has clearly taught us that there are other obstacles. Producers wish to retain authoring control, while many TV viewers at the same time appear satisfied with the current types of 'lazy interaction' (e.g. pausing and voting) that do not really call for high involvement [25].

For example, experiments with interactive services such as access to additional content (e.g. accessing diary of a TV-presenter and contestants, watching behind the scenes movie clips) showed that these features were only appealing for those viewers that already liked the specific program [26]. With regard to interactive narrativity, a Dutch study showed that that viewers had little interest in choosing between alternative endings for a particular program [28]. TV is still considered as a storytelling medium [7] and viewers tend to want to leave this storytelling to the professionals.

The concern to look beyond technical challenges is echoed in the work of Steen [22] who warns for the risk inherent to purely technology-driven innovations. When user needs and wishes are neglected, innovations may well lead to a product that is quickly abandoned, or not even adopted at all. He argues for human-centered design as an alternative to technology push, in which an active attempt is made to bridge the worlds of users on the one hand, and researchers, developers and engineers on the other.

The xTV study that will be described in this paper was conducted in the fall of 2011. It presents an attempt to inscribe potential users of televised ODV in the development process. Treating users as equal, knowledgeable partners, we engaged in a dialogue with them on what characteristics, if any, would make television programs suitable for use in conjunction with ODV.

In what follows, we will first describe the methodology of this human-centered design study and then discuss users' perspective on televised ODV (for convenience dubbed ODTV or 360° TV). This will encompass both users' concerns as well as perceived opportunities.

2. METHODOLOGY

2.1 Human-centered design approach

Before elaborating on the particular set-up of our study, we want to position our general approach. Specifically, we aimed to implement a human-centered design approach: an approach that in 2010 was formalized as a standard for user experience (referred to as ISO 9241-210).

In his doctoral thesis, Steen [22] describes how human-centered design can be situated across two dimensions. The first dimension describes the tension between designing with users and designing for users. In certain approaches, the user is positioned as a knowledgeable partner in the design/research process, while in others, researchers and designers seek to enhance their knowledge of users to feed into this process. The second dimension describes the tension between the concerns for what is and for what ought to be. Certain approaches focus on studying the current situation of the user, while others focus on imagining a future situation.

Given the study's aim, it becomes apparent that our main concern is envisioning a future situation. Television formats using ODV do not exist yet and as such, the users are not yet defined. This does not mean that the current situation is not important. When thinking up completely new formats, the generated ideas will be shaped by people's actual context and TV experiences.

Secondly, we want to involve users and other stakeholders as knowledgeable partners in the development process. The rationale for this choice is not simply the belief that this will benefit the development process, as other human-centered design approaches can accomplish the same. It is the belief that users and other stakeholders should be given a voice, should be empowered within the design process. We note, however, this is not the same as positioning them in the role of designers and researchers. What is key to us is treating their expertise as equally important.

2.2 Set-up and data collection

2.2.1 Overview

Table 1 describes the research set-up of the individual sessions with users that we conducted to answer our main research question: *What characteristics make a TV-program suited for enhancement with ODV according to adult digital TV viewers?*

As exploratory research at the start of our project hinted at gamers and non-gamers having different expectations about ODV. Indeed, gamers' extensive experience with games as interactive media, with navigation through virtual environments, and with game concepts and mechanics may trigger different needs and perceived opportunities. Hence, we decided to investigate the following research question as well (as a subtopic): *Do gamers and non-gamers have different ideas and preferences with regard to enhancing television through ODV?*

Table 1. Session overview

Phase	Description	Timing
Introduction & intake	Going over informed consent; getting acquainted with participant's media use (focus on television and gaming)	10 min
ODV demo & inquiry	Demo: Participants explore a ODV demo (Eva de Roovere fragment) Inquiry: Participants complete a survey concerning the fragment and are asked to recount their experience.	20 min
Vision	Extracting program attributes: Establishing which characteristics make a particular program genre interesting for ODV. Grouping: Establishing which characteristics are seen as identical or related. Prioritization: Establishing which of the attributes matter most. Moving up the ladder: Settling on why these attributes are important.	1h

In total, 20 people participated in this study[1]. Participants were recruited via two channels: (1) an existing representative user panel in Flanders maintained by our project partner and research facilitator, iLab.o, and (2) a call for participation spread out via colleagues. All participants were selected so that they had access to and watched digital television at home. Furthermore, the group was composed so that half of the participants played games on average about 3 hours or more a week and half played less than 3 hours a week. We will refer to the first group as the gamer group and the second as the non-gamer group.

The gamer group consisted of 5 females and 5 males. The average age in this group was 32.6 (range: 22 – 54, STD = 10.93). The non-gamer group consisted of 4 females and 6 males. The average age in this group was 32.3 (age range: 22 – 48, STD = 8.96).

Most participants were professionally active with the exception of three persons: a university student, one person recently graduated and one disabled participant. Although we did not inquire into this, it was apparent from participants' job positions that the majority held a college or university degree. While most participants used several platforms to consume digital content, all but one participant had never heard about omnidirectional video.

As can be seen in Table 1, the 1.5h sessions consisted of three phases, which we will describe in more detail below.

2.2.2 Introduction & intake phase

In the introduction and intake phase, we situated the session by going over an informed consent form. After they signed the form, we briefly interviewed participants to be able to contextualize our findings. Questions addressed current television viewing behavior (e.g. viewing times, program preferences, use of interactive digital television services, social viewing) and for the gamer group also their gaming practices (e.g. amount of game play, game preferences, platforms played).

2.2.3 Demo & inquiry phase

In the ODV demo & inquiry phase, we first familiarized participants with omnidirectional viewing by letting them look around in an ODV fragment, featuring a concert by a Belgian music artist [17]. The demo was viewed on a laptop. Participants were explained how they could change their viewing angle and zoom in and out, as the main aim of this phase in the research was to give them experience with the technology rather than to investigate usability issues.

After the demonstration, participants were asked to complete a short survey. This was followed by a brief discussion of their responses, to get a better idea of how participants had experienced the demo and how they conceived of possible television use of ODV based on this experience.

The survey used to inquire into the experience of the ODV demonstration contained ten statements. Participants had to indicate to what extent they agreed with the given statements (on a 5-point scale ranging from 1 = "don't agree at all" to 5 = "completely agree"). The statements, originally in Dutch, were:

1. **Fun**: I enjoyed looking around in the image.
2. **Ease of use**: Looking around in the image went smoothly.
3. **Interactivity (Control)**: While the movie was playing, I was able to decide what to look at.
4. **Presence**: I had the feeling that I was in the same place as the artists and the audience.
5. **Interactivity (Exchange)**: There is an exchange between the viewer and the form and/or content of the image.
6. **Quality**: The visual quality of the movie was good.
7. **Interactivity (Synchronicity)**: While watching the movie, the image adapted without any delay.
8. **Directing**: While watching the movie, I felt like I was directing it.
9. **Story**: I missed a story line while watching the movie.
10. **Identification**: I identified with people from the audience.

Items pertaining to interactivity (item 3, 5 and 7) were based on items from the Interactivity Scale developed by Liu [12], which consists of three subscales: Active control, Two-way communication and Synchronicity. The item pertaining to presence (item 4) refers to physical presence and was based on an ITC-SOPI questionnaire item [11]. Finally, the identification item was derived from a player identification scale [27].

2.2.4 Vision phase

In the final phase, the vision phase, we prompted users to envision possible opportunities for future usage of the new technology, letting them think about enhancements of existing types of television programs with ODV. The previous phases can be seen as a warm up for this phase, making participants aware of their own TV viewing and gaming experience and practices and familiarizing them with the new technology.

In this phase, we used 'laddering' as a research method. Laddering was first introduced in consumer research to capture consumers' perception of a product so that marketing could be matched to this perception ([19] and [20]). It is based on Means-End Theory [8], which states that consumers choose certain products because they believe that the products' attributes result in consequences that support their personal values. The goal of laddering is to reveal these perceived attribute-consequence-value chains or 'ladders' through interviewing and content analysis.

Laddering, as explained by Reynolds and Gutman [19], starts with establishing which product attributes are important for the person that is being interviewed. Often these attributes are elicited by letting participants compare existing products, express their preference and explain what it is about the preferred product that makes it better. When a substantial list of attributes is extracted, it is suggested to let participants prioritize attributes [19]. The researcher then proceeds to prompt the participant to explain why he or she believed each particular attribute to be important (making sure the most important ones are covered).

Given our human-centered design approach detailed earlier, it may seem a bit unconventional to use a method that was developed in a marketing context. However, we believed that provided some adaptations as explained below, we could retain the method's merit – extracting perceived links between product

---

[1] Sixteen of the 20 sessions involved face-to-face contacts. We also conducted 4 remote sessions following essentially the same procedure but via Skype (for interviewing) and Google Docs (for facilitating the post-survey and the vision exercise).

attributes, product experiences and personal values – while putting it to use in a human-centered design approach[2]. In what follows, we describe this in more detail. We note that we tested our approach in two pilot sessions with one gaming and one non-gaming respondent to assess whether it was viable.

To help participants express what program characteristics they thought could be important, we first let participants compare television genres (one pair at a time!). Instead of asking them their preferred genre, which is typically done, we asked them:

- For which of these two types of programs do you think ODV would be more suitable?
- What is it about this type that makes it more suitable? (and/or) What is it about the other type that makes it less suitable?

The TV genres we asked participants to compare were drawn from the list of genres used by Geerts, Cesar and Bulterman [6]. They deployed it to investigate the impact of program genre on social interaction during and after TV viewing. They compiled this list by selecting popular genres from the content classification scheme issued by the European Broadcasting Union [5].

We omitted animation and movies from the list as out of scope for the current study, but added consumer magazine, human interest and touristic program, which we felt were missing. This yielded a list of 20 genres (such as news, documentary and comedy series), which we illustrated on cards with well-known Flemish TV programs. The list and program examples are available on request.

Each elicited attribute was written down on a post-it by the facilitating researcher. Once all card pairs had been compared, we asked participants to group post-its describing essentially the same attributes. We added this step to avoid redundancy. We then had participants prioritize attributes.

After prioritization, the researcher proceeded by moving the participant gradually up the ladder from attributes to consequences and finally to values by asking the following:

- Why do you find this program characteristic is important? What consequences do you think it has for your viewing experience?
- Why is this consequence important? Which personal values does it support?

Similar to the attributes, elicited consequences and values were noted down on post-its. The session was ended with the question whether the participant felt a genre that would be particularly suitable for ODV was not mentioned.

2.3 Analysis

Both the findings from the demo & inquiry phase and the vision phase were subjected to qualitative and quantitative analysis.

2.3.1 Analysis of the demo feedback

We tested for significant differences between the ratings of the non-gamer and gamer group by applying two-tailed t-tests for unpaired samples per survey item. Significance level for these tests, α, was set at .05. The discussions following the survey were categorized according to survey items and then summarized.

[2] In fact, we are not the first to use laddering in a design and development context. Laddering was previously also adapted for product likeability evaluation (see [24] and [30]).

2.3.2 Analysis of the vision results

The direct results of a laddering interview (Figure 2) are analyzed in two consecutive phases: a qualitative and quantitative phase [19]. The user session that we organized yielded a set of unstandardized chains of attributes, consequences and values. These unstandardized ladders formed the main input for a first qualitative analysis phase:

1. All unstandardized ladders were listed in EXCEL, including corresponding interview notes
2. Summary codes (i.e. standardized labels per ladder level) were created and numbered. Interview notes and recordings helped determine which raw labels referred to the same concept
3. The ladders were re-coded, using the summary codes, yielding standardized ladders

Figure 2. Example of output of a laddering interview.

The standardized ladders (63 ladders, average ladder length of 3.14 elements) were then entered in the LadderUX tool (ladderux.org) ([10] & [24]) developed to automate the quantitative analysis of laddering data. Specifically, the software automates the following steps:

1. Construction of summary score matrix: This contains all participants' ladders
2. Construction of implication matrix: This specifies the strength of all the code links registered
3. Construction of the hierarchical value map: This is a graphical map of dominant links between attributes, consequences and values

Dominant links are determined by the cut-off level. This is the number of links needed to call a link dominant. We set this level at 3 in LadderUX. This resulted in 79% of perceived links being above cut-off level and hence being represented in the hierarchical value map.

3. FINDINGS

3.1 Feedback to ODV demo

In this first results section, we describe participants' feedback to the ODV demo. Table 2 shows the average ratings per item in the survey following the demo. Recall that the highest rating (5) refers to strong agreement with a given statement. For example, a high mean rating for fun means that on average participants found use of the ODV a fun experience.

The descriptive statistics have been collapsed across gaming groups as statistical analyses showed no significant differences between the average ratings given by the gamer and non-gamer group. Nevertheless, we did find a marginally significant effect for synchronicity ($p = .054$). This item was on average rated lower in the non-gamer group.

Table 2. Mean rating and standard deviation per survey item

Item	Mean	Standard deviation
Fun	4.0	0.89
Ease of use	4.3	0.73
Control	4.5	0.61
Exchange	2.9	1.04
Synchronicity	4.2	0.59
Directing	2.4	1.19
Presence	2.6	1.00
Quality	2.9	1.14
Story	2.9	1.50
Identification	2.1	1.19

3.1.1 Fun

While overall participants enjoyed the ODV demo, there was disagreement on whether such content would continue to be entertaining and on whether one would like to have television programs with the opportunity to look around. In this regard, some respondents expressed skeptic arguments, which we can summarize as follows:

- **Information load**: Television may threaten viewing experience as a relaxing experience.
- **Social viewing**: ODV may compromise watching television together on a single screen.
- **Privacy**: As a member of the audience in an event (e.g. performance or show) that is broadcast, one can be observed continuously by viewers. This could negatively affect the live experience of the event.
- **Narrative processing**: Specifically in programs with an elaborate narrative (e.g. fiction), looking around could cause viewers to lose focus and miss the essence of the program.
- **Absence of triggers**: A participant in the gaming group noted that when there is no clear purpose in looking around (unlike games), one may easily get bored with this viewing activity.

3.1.2 Ease of use

The demo was considered easy to use. For television, however, following considerations should be taken into account in order to improve ease of use:

- **Pre-set viewpoints**: Participants felt ease of use could be improved by enabling viewers to jump between points of interest, instead of having to continuously drag the image. This could include jumping back and forth between the personally selected and the directed view.
- **Zooming and moving**: One of the gamers noted that it was impossible to zoom in or out and look around simultaneously. This could be enabled to improve viewing efficiency.
- **Gestural input & precise control**: The ODV demo was controlled by handling a computer mouse. When asked what type of control would be considered easy to use on television, several respondents suggested control by hand gesturing would be most intuitive (cf. Microsoft Kinect). They are concerned that the current remote control would be imprecise, and they disliked the idea of having to hold a device all the time. They were least interested in purchasing and using a separate device specifically for controlling ODV on television.
- **Asynchronous use of second screen**: While participants watched the demo on a single screen, we also asked about the possibility of watching a directed view on one screen and ODV on another, either simultaneously or successively. Participants expect synchronous viewing of a primary and secondary view to be complex. They also worry that co-located viewers will perceive using a second screen as asocial behavior. Successively viewing television-related ODV content on a secondary platform (e.g. computer, handheld) appeared to raise more interest.

3.1.3 Interactivity

On average, perceived interactivity of the demo can be described as follows:

- **High degree of control**: Participants felt in control over what they could look at by being able to choose the viewing angle. They did note the potential relevance of being able to control viewpoint as well, for instance, during a sports game.
- **High degree of synchronicity**: Participants experienced high correspondence between their actions and the image update.
- **Moderate level of exchange**: Viewers felt there was essentially a unidirectional influence originating from themselves and exerted on the image. For the content that was shown, they did not really feel that the image directed their behavior (cf. Absence of triggers).

3.1.4 Directing

Most participants **did not feel as if they were directing the video**, given that they only had control over the viewing angle and not over other factors (i.e. viewpoint and scene content). Those who gave a low rating for this item (i.e. the majority) noted that they felt more like a cameraman/woman or a voyeur, rather than a director. The few people that did give a higher rating for this item, referred to feeling part of the performance (i.e. presence) or to the possibility of customizing the video fragment.

3.1.5 Presence and identification

Ratings of presence and identification varied strongly across individuals, but people tended to recount both experiences in the same way. Factors that were believed to influence these experiences were:

- **Display size/type**: Participants believed a larger display or a surround display (and surround sound) would enhance their sense of presence.
- **Personal focus**: Some participants noted that they tended to focus on the technical aspect of the demo. They believed that one's attitude towards the demo, sometimes referred to as willingness to suspend disbelief [13], affected their sense of being there.
- **Camera position**: Participants noted the camera was not at eye-level position. Because of this, it seemed as if one was hovering somewhat above the audience instead of being part of the crowd.
- **Audience & content appreciation**: Being able to see other people enjoying the music was noted to enhance the sense of being there as well (cf. social presence). However, this seemed

dependent on another factor; certain participants did not like the music(ian) and claimed that because of this they could not identify with and feel part of the crowd. This stresses the importance of content in relation to presence and identification.

3.1.6 *Quality*

Overall, image quality was perceived as neither exceptionally poor nor great. The following quality issues were reported:

- **Stitching artefacts**: At certain moments, participants perceived slight stitching errors.
- **Blind spot**: Participants noted the absence of an image at the position of the actual camera.
- **Zooming**: Zooming in/out had a detrimental effect on perceived image quality. The resulting resolution drop and image distortion were considered to be a major issue. Quality should be maintained across the zooming range, if need be the range should be limited.

While the specific quality of the image can influence the overall quality of experience, it must be noted that some participants found the quality issues more troubling than others. Furthermore, not all reported issues were considered equally problematic. It was mainly the impact of zooming on image quality that was perceived as disturbing.

3.1.7 *Story and content*

With regard to the particular demo, most participants did not really miss a story line, noting that for a concert the story line is per definition limited. It was acknowledged, however, that narrative elements could contextualize the viewing experience and stimulate presence (e.g. through character identification).

In addition, several participants argued that the presented content could not fully illustrate the added value of ODV as viewers tend to focus on musicians and the directed versions thus show what the viewer wants to see. Discussing what might constitute more appropriate types of content, participants referred to content where the viewer and director are likely to have different opinions on what constitutes an interesting view (e.g. broadcast of live events). They also emphasized that the risk of missing essential content when looking around should be minimized.

3.2 Envisioned opportunities

The vision phase yields a set of ladders, i.e. attribute-consequence-value chains that illustrate how people believe that existing formats can be enhanced using ODV and why they find such enhancements meaningful.

In what follows, we will describe each ladder structure separately (visualized per section). Specifically, we will point out per ladder what characteristic is considered to make a television program suitable for omnidirectional viewing (i.e. attribute component), which desirable impact ODV is believed to have on the viewing experience (i.e. consequence component) and why this is considered meaningful on a personal level (i.e. value component).

As will become evident from the discussion, some of the preferred program characteristics can be linked to particular genres, while others appear to be more generic and can be applicable in various programs.

3.2.1 *From the uncharted to exploration*

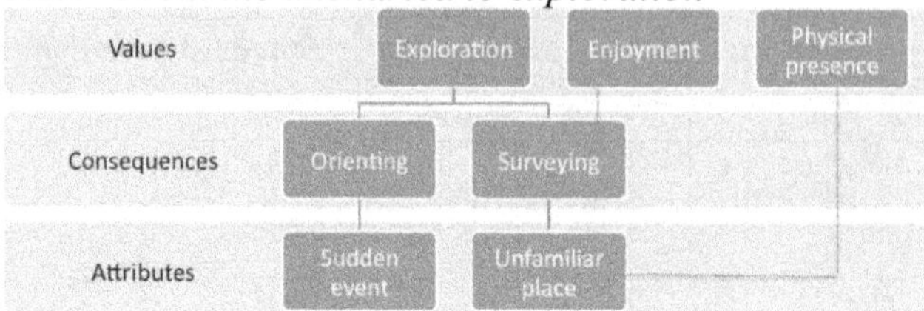

Programs featuring an environment previously not (well) known by the viewer are considered suitable for omnidirectional viewing. ODV is believed to give viewers an opportunity to survey the displayed space, getting a bigger picture of what is going on. This fulfills the desire to satisfy one's curiosity and be informed. ODV was also seen as something that allowed participants to feel present in the mediated space.

Exploration can be self-initiated or triggered. On the one hand, viewer may seek to enjoy the beauty of a space or pursue other goals such as planning a trip. On the other hand, they may be triggered to attend to a sudden event featured in the program (e.g. a sound originating from outside the given view).

In essence, when showing places is key to the program itself, ODV enables viewing behaviors that support exploring the environment from within. In this respect, program genres such as documentaries, touristic programs, but also programs featuring houses and interior design are considered to be particularly suitable for ODV-based enhancements.

3.2.2 *From procedures to skill*

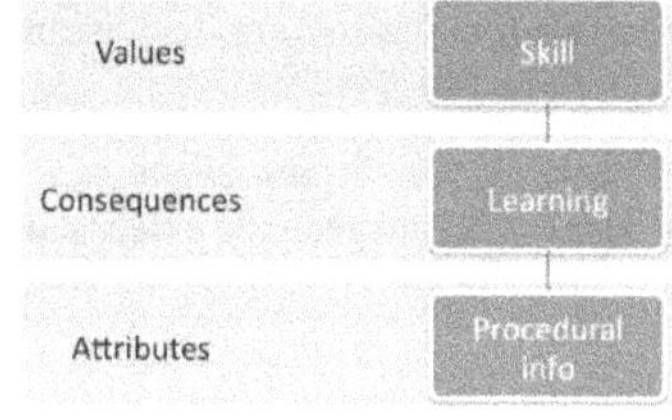

In programs that show how certain procedures are performed, viewers expect that omnidirectional viewing will allow them to observe components of the procedure more closely and thus will facilitate learning about it. This supports the interest they might have in mastering a certain skill or to at least have knowledge about how something is done.

Genres that tend to feature this procedural information, according to participants, are hobby programs (e.g. cooking programs). Some participants, however, also expressed interest in gaining knowledge about the procedure of making a program ("making of").

To watch the making-of, the ODV camera would be placed alongside the commonly used camera-setup. There was not a specific program type for which the respondents want to see this creation process. Instead, people's preference was linked to what they already enjoy watching. Participants also considered this to be a feature that they would use only once. Once they have seen the process, they know it.

3.2.3 *From human interaction to social presence*

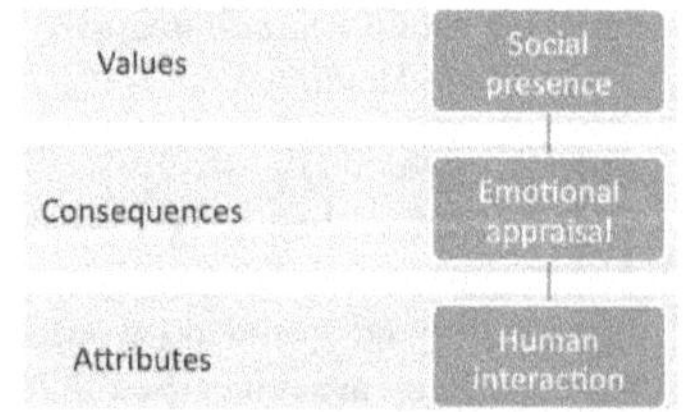

When human interaction plays a central role in a program, omnidirectional viewing is also potentially relevant.

Commonly, when human interaction takes place, the

focus is on the human actor that is speaking. ODV is thought to provide the possibility to look around at will and assess the emotional, non-verbal response of others that are part of the interaction, yet (momentarily) in a more passive role: the audience, quiz candidates, participants in a debate that are listening, and so on. This emotional appraisal supports the need to capture and interpret human emotion, to understand people's intentions and the social situation as a whole, and in some cases even feel part of it.

As apparent from the previous paragraph, programs that were often linked up to this preference structure are debate programs and quiz formats. Also mentioned were consumer magazines in which there is a test audience, stand-up in which the comedian heavily interacts with the audience, and music contests with several jury members.

3.2.4 From portrayal of facts to veracity

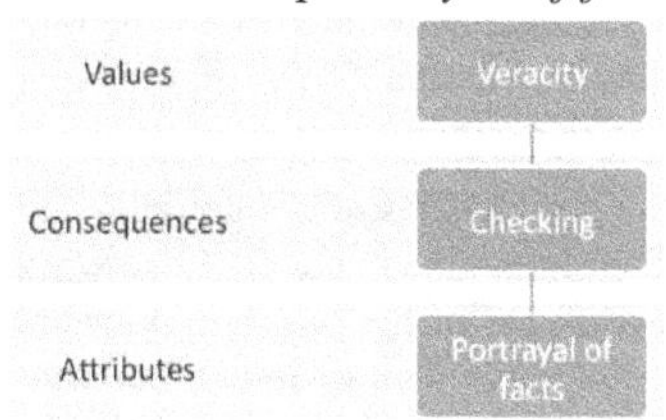

In the case of programs featuring events that are portrayed as facts, yet leaving the viewer uncertain that the events are actually staged, participants were also interested in having an omnidirectional view. They believed that this would allow them to verify what is going on. Such viewing behavior would be in line with the desire for truth and authenticity.

Programs that are seen as operating on the border of fact and fiction are reality shows, docu-soaps and human-interest programs. Aside from these typical examples, there was also mention of blurring of fact and fiction in other genres such as in news reports.

Interestingly, while participants considered this particular opportunity of ODV, some of them started to reflect on the impact ODV might have on the production of the aforementioned programs. While some believed that ODV might lead to a more authentic ways of televising content, others felt that producers would likely find a work-around to "manipulate" viewers.

3.2.5 From little progress to excitement

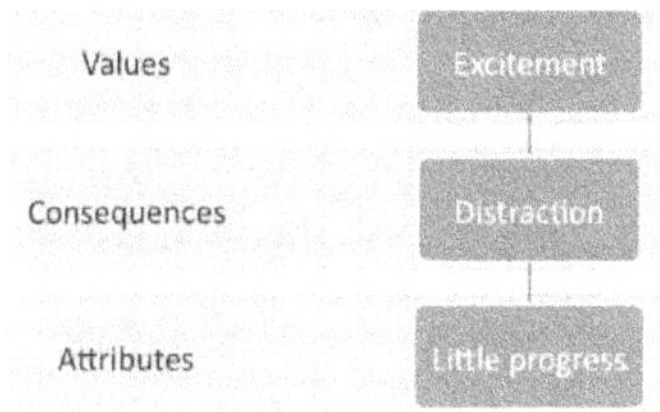

Omnidirectional viewing was considered to provide some distraction in programs that are slow paced in nature or momentarily exhibiting little progress. As such it would be a way to keep one's mind occupied and to avoid boredom. Looking around could be an alternative to zapping away, with the added advantage that the viewer can still hear what is going on and return to a more focused, linear view when the pace picks up again.

This ladder cannot be linked to a particular program genre. Dull moments can occur in any program. Long conversations during soaps, debates and talk shows, slow pace in documentaries, sports and music programs were mentioned to trigger looking for distraction. Even participants that were highly skeptical about ODV on television felt that slow content provided an opportunity. This does require that there is something visually interesting available. Otherwise, people will turn to other activities (e.g. doing dishes) while using the television as a radio.

3.2.6 From persons of interest to connectedness

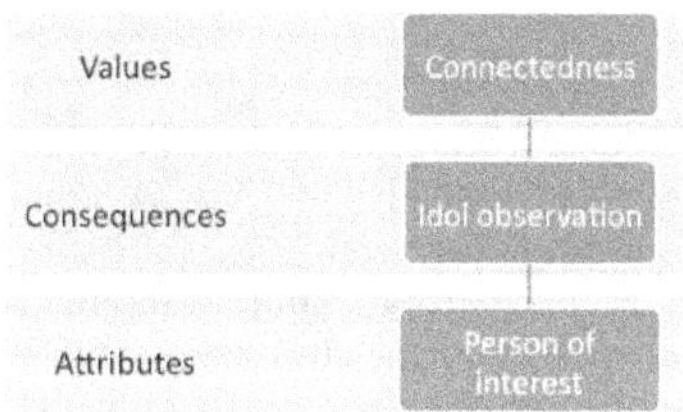

Programs that feature a person that is of interest or becomes of interest to the viewer are seen as potentially suitable for omnidirectional viewing. In this case, ODV could afford observing this person and his/her context from a first-person or even from the idol's view. Such viewing behavior would meet people's need to understand (the context of) the people they relate to better, to feel more connected to them.

Genres that are likely candidates in this regard include sports programs (featuring a sportsman of interest), music programs (with one's favorite musician playing in a band), programs in the style of MTV "Cribs" (featuring an idol who showcases his or her house) and fiction series (featuring one or more characters that one relates to). In this respect, it must be noted that most participants considered fiction series to be problematic genres for ODV-based enhancements. However, in the case of fan fiction, it was noted that one could make use of ODV when watching an episode again.

3.2.7 From simultaneous events to self-determination

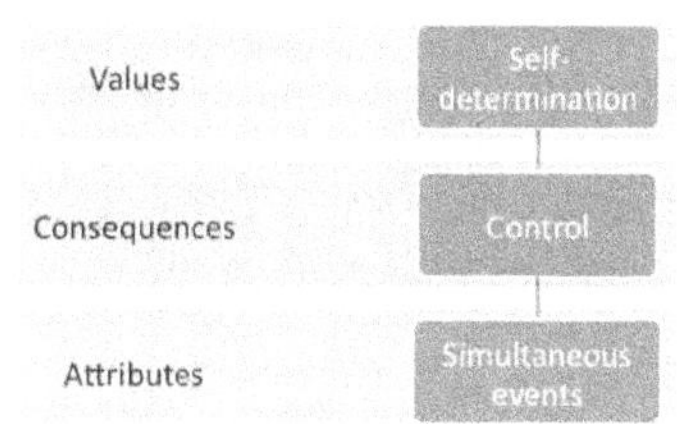

When a program features several events at the same time, omnidirectional viewing allows the viewer to choose for him- or herself which event is of more relevance. This supports the viewer's interest in having freedom of choice.

This preference structure emerged explicitly in the context of sports programs such as omnisports (e.g. Memorial Van Damme) or cycling (e.g. different events going on among pack vs. front runners). It is apparent, however, that the value of self-determination is also implicitly present in the other preference structures as well.

3.2.8 From familiar places to recognition

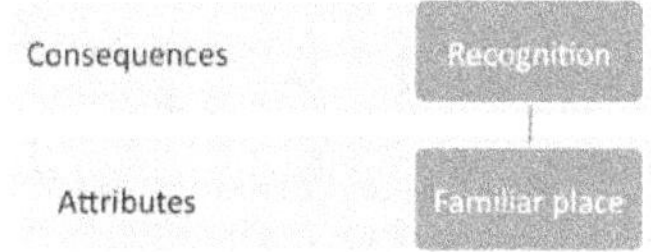

Unlike the ladder structures discussed so far, the analysis yielded also two partial ladder structures (i.e. attribute and consequence only) that will be described in the current and the following section (3.2.9). The lack of a value element in these ladders seems to be due to the fact that these ladders were mentioned less and the fact that they were associated with divergent values.

The partial ladder in this section represents the following. A small number of participants pointed out that when they would see a familiar place featured on television, they would appreciate looking around for landmarks, elements in the landscape or cityscape familiar to them. In the case of the place where they live, it would be a way to feel more connected to it or look at it in a different way. In the case of a place they once visited or lived in, it would be a way of finding out how much the place had changed over time. This is in line with the current success of the Google Street View service that enables users to look around on a map.

3.2.9 *From challenge to engagement*

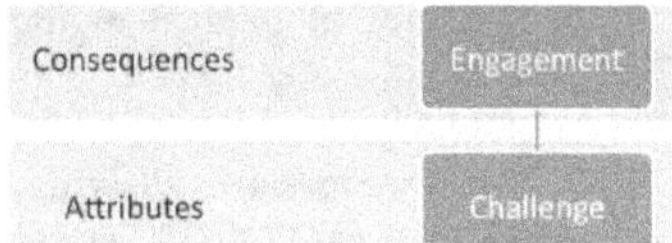

A few participants pointed out that when the program features a particular challenge (e.g. solving a murder mystery), ODV would allow participants to be more actively, cognitively engaged, as if rising to the challenge themselves. For some, this would support the desire for creative thinking, finding the way clues are given in current crime series often far too obvious. Others saw an opportunity for joint fun, competing with or playing together with others.

3.2.10 *Final note*

We also compared the preferences of non-gamers versus gamers. In both groups, there is a ladder structure leading up to the need for exploration. Orienting to sudden events, however, was only mentioned by the gamer group. A possible interpretation for this result may be that, due to their gaming experience, this group may be more inclined to think of triggers as a relevant way of encouraging exploration.

The remaining ladders that reach value level are different for the two groups. In the non-gamer group, the ladder structures leading up to social presence and connectedness described earlier resurface. In the gamer group, the ladders leading up to skill, excitement and veracity reappear. This suggests that non-gamers we interviewed were more drawn to the social affordances of ODV, while the gamers were more occupied with its individual affordances.

We do want to emphasize the above comparison should be treated with caution. Given the small number of participants per group (i.e. 10), generalizing the outcome of this comparison would be inappropriate.

4. DISCUSSION

In this paper, we describe the results of a participatory design study in which we encouraged potential users, gamers and non-gamers, to envision suitable enhancements of television genres based on omnidirectional video (ODV). Specifically, the study was driven by the following, respectively, primary and secondary research questions:

- What characteristics make a TV-program suited for enhancement with ODV according to adult digital TV viewers?
- Do gamers and non-gamers have different ideas and preferences with regard to enhancing television through ODV?

To address these questions, we first familiarized participants with ODV and then applied a method called laddering tailored to a human-centered design *approach.* During laddering, we asked participants to choose between program genres and discuss which one they preferred for ODV and why. The underlying rationale for a preference is elicited by prompting participants to make explicit expected positive consequences and the values these are thought to support. We believe that any television study that aims to provoke an in-depth discussion with viewers on which characteristics make a TV program suitable for a particular interactive service (if any) can benefit from this approach.

One could argue that by opening up genre conventions for personal interpretation through dialogue, we also subscribed ourselves to a cultural approach to understanding genre [14]. The attribute-consequence-value chains that we elicited in fact acknowledge that a genre cannot be defined on the basis of program characteristics alone, but are coupled to personal, social and cultural values. In this respect, we believe that laddering may also be a fruitful approach to studying people's interpretation of genre.

What did our findings tell us? With regard to our *main research question*, we found that certain genre-specific content elements can make a program suitable for ODV from a user perspective. For example, the confrontation with an unfamiliar space typically found in touristic programs trigger the desire to explore. Hobby programs trigger interest in mastering the skills that are displayed. Debate programs elicit the wish to understand the social situation. In each of these cases, it is anticipated that ODV may enable viewing behaviors and experiences that satisfy these needs.

Aside from these genre-specific characteristics, more generic, and circumstantial elements could potentially also make ODV viewing worthwhile. When there is little progress in the program, viewers can seek temporary distraction. When a person of interest or well know region happens to feature in a program, viewers can actively act upon the connection they feel with this person or place.

With regard to our *secondary question*, the answer is nuanced and tentative. In giving feedback to the ODV demo, gamers would refer to their specific experiences including their gaming knowledge to explain why they did or did not like something about the demo. However, they did not rate the demo significantly different from the non-gaming group. The analysis of the vision results suggests that gamers were mere prone to pick up on the individual benefits of ODV on television, while the social benefits were more apparent to the non-gamers. However, further research with larger group sizes is warranted to validate this.

That participants see potential in 360° TV may be surprising given the evidence on viewers' limited enthusiasm with regard to interactive television services (see intro). We note that we did see skeptic arguments from older studies on interactivity resurface. Participants, some more than others, feared that interactivity might compromise watching television as a social, relaxing and compelling experience. Nevertheless, by comparing various genres participants picked up on opportunities where ODV could contribute to their viewing experience, instead of detract from it. They may not always want to look around, but do foresee occasions where their own interest in terms of what to look at may differ from what the director believes people want or should see.

The reader may ask to what extent participants' overall viewer preference played a role. Given that we asked about participants' current viewing preferences at the start of the session, we are able to establish that participants indeed also took their general viewing preference into account when deciding in which program they would prefer to look around and zoom in. A genre they strongly disliked was not a likely candidate for ODV viewing. This is in line with earlier findings on the link between viewer preference and interest in interactivity (see supra). However, it does appear that mild disinterest could be turned around.

Seeking to relate our findings to previous work, we were surprised by the dearth of user research concerning ODV. Since its conception, panoramic video has been applied to various domains. Takács discusses examples in surveillance and security, spatial mapping, teleconferencing, entertainment, healthcare, education and his own work on mobile delivery of cultural content [23]. With regard to television, several broadcasters have experimented with providing supplementary ODV material online ([1], [3] and [16]). Research seems to have focused primarily on the technological challenges particular to the different application domains.

Work that goes beyond anecdotal user data is that by Rizzo et al. [21] and Chen [2]. Rizzo and colleagues [21] outlined a series of diverse scenarios, which they subjected to production experiments and user evaluation, ranging from therapeutic to information and entertainment applications. This body of work has mainly focused on viewing panoramic video by means of HMD.

Chen [2] conducted user research, i.e. requirement elicitation and prototype evaluation, to inform his work on capturing and online delivery of enhanced ODV content on a virtual zoo website. His investigation was highly specific to the given application domain and the envisioned system that also supports annotation and navigation between viewpoints.

Given that the limited user research available on ODV has considered its use in other domains and as part of different interfaces, it is difficult to relate our findings to previous work We do see a correspondence between the needs that emerged from our inquiry and the requirements outlined by Neng and Chambel for online video players showing hyperlinked[3] ODV [15]. Some of our participants noted they would rather look around in retrospect, when they knew what to expect. This reflects the authors' requirement of giving the user a view of the complete image. The concern that one would lose interest in looking around when not triggered corresponds with the requirement to hint people about where interesting information (in their case: links) might be. Finally, the desire to have pre-set reference points to jump to, in our view does not only reflect a desire for efficiency but also the need to combat disorientation as identified by Neng and Chambel. The need was also pointed out and addressed by Chen [2].

Overall, our results show that viewers foresee both problems and opportunities for 360° TV. Some of the anticipated issues were particular to the given ODV player and content used during the demo and can be tackled by technical improvements, adjusted content selection and platform adaptations. In fact, at the time of writing, some of these issues have already been addressed by technical improvements. Other matters, however, represent current attitudes about what it means to watch television alone or together and of which it is unclear how they will interact with future solutions once introduced. This brings us to the final part of this discussion: the next steps we plan to undertake in this project.

Indeed, while our approach was successful in capturing user attitudes towards and expectations of 360° TV, follow-up work is needed in three respects. First, the attitudinal data do not yield actual solutions. We plan to organize a workshop in which the expertise of viewers and the skill of professional stakeholders are joined to generate new formats based on ODV. These professional stakeholders could include both stakeholders in television production as well as external professionals with relevant expertise such as interaction and game designers. A facilitating technique for this workshop we are thinking of using is letting participants map out a user journey [18].

Secondly, the given methodology cannot tell us how widespread these attitudes are. Hence, we are interested in conducting a large-scaled survey to assess interest in ODV at the level of the general population. Finally, once the first prototypes are available for testing, we plan to undertake a longitudinal study of actual appropriation of a prototype introduced at people's home in order to investigate actual user practices for a longer period of time (after the 'novelty effect' has faded).

With this study, we hope to have made a first step towards describing the promises and challenges related to 360° TV from a users' perspective. We will continue our joint efforts with content creators and technical developers so that together we can come closer to seeing the bigger picture.

[3] ODV content with links embedded that lead to other content.

5. ACKNOWLEDGMENTS

This study was part of the xTV project. This project is co-funded by IBBT (Interdisciplinary institute for BroadBand Technology), a research institute founded by the Flemish Government, and project support of IWT for the companies participating in it (see [29] for a complete list our partners). We thank our project partners, in particular, Philippe Bekaert (IBBT-EDM) who captured the ODV content used in this study and made the viewer for showing ODV content [9] available to us. In addition, he and Jan Van Looy (IBBT-MICT) provided us with material to illustrate this paper (PB: Top & bottom right pictures, JVL: Bottom left picture. The latter picture was taken during a performance of xTV project partner CREW. Finally, we acknowledge Vero Vanden Abeele for granting us access to the LadderUX software and David Geerts for sending us the list of genres deployed in the Geerts, Cesar, & Bulterman study [6].

6. REFERENCES

[1] BBC Oceans 360 degree experience. http://www.bbc.co.uk/oceans/360/lemonsharks.

[2] Chen, W.-H. 2010. *An investigation into Web-based panoramic video virtual reality with reference to the virtual zoo.* Doctoral Thesis. De Montfort University at Leicester, UK.

[3] CNN special coverage: 360° video on Haiti earthquake. http://edition.cnn.com/interactive/2010/01/world/haiti.360/index.html.

[4] Decock, J., Van Looy, J., Bleumers, L. and Bekaert, P. 2011. The Pleasure of Being (There?). An Explorative Study into the Effects of Presence and Identification on the Enjoyment of an Interactive Theatrical Performance using Omni-Directional Video. In *Proceedings of the International Society for Presence Research Annual Conference* (Edinburgh, Scotland, October 26-28, 2011). ISPR 2011. Edinburgh Napier University, Edinburgh, Scotland, UK, 12p.

[5] European Broadcasting Union 2007. *Escort: EBU System of Classification of RTV Programmes.* Technical report.

[6] Geerts, D., Cesar, P., and Bulterman, D. 2008. The implications of program genres for the design of social television systems. In *Proceedings of the International Conference on Designing Interactive User Experiences for TV and Video* (Silicon Valley, CA, USA, October 22 – 24, 2008). uxtv'08. ACM, New York, NY, USA, 71-80.

[7] Gerbner, G. 1997 *The electronic storyteller*. Media Education Foundation, Northampton, MA.

[8] Gutman, J. 1982. A means-end chain model based on consumer categorization processes. *J. Marketing. Res.* 46(2), 60-72.

[9] Iv-viewer. Software tool for displaying ODV content (developed by Philippe Bekaert, IBBT-EDM).

[10] LadderUX. Laddering the user experience, software tool, access request is required. http://www.ladderux.org.

[11] Lessiter, J., Freeman, J., Keogh, E., and Davidoff, J. 2001. A Cross-Media Presence Questionnaire: The ITC-Sense of Presence Inventory. *Presence-Teleop. Virt.* 10(3), 282-297.

[12] Liu, Y. 2003. Developing a scale to measure the interactivity of websites. *J. Advertising Res.* 43 (2), 207-216.

[13] Lombard, M. and Ditton, T. 1997. At the heart of it all: The concept of presence. *J. Comput-Mediat. Comm.* 3(2), Retrieved from: http://jcmc.indiana.edu/vol3/issue2/lombard.html.

[14] Mittell, J. 2001. A Cultural Approach to Television Genre Theory. *Cinema J.* 40(3), 3-24.

[15] Neng, L. A. R. and Chambel, T. 2010. Get around 360° hypervideo. In *Proceedings of International Academic Mindtrek Conference 2010* (Tampere, Finland, EU, October 6 – 8, 2010). ACM, New York, NY, USA, 119-122.

[16] Net5 Reality Show with 360° streaming. http://www.secretstory.nl.

[17] ODV example by project partner IBBT-EDM. http://www.360video.org/eva/keizern.html.

[18] Parker, S. and Heapy, J. 2006. *The journey to the interface: How public service design can connect users to reform.* Demos, London, EU.

[19] Reynolds, T. J. and Gutman, J. 1988. Laddering theory, method, analysis, and interpretation. *J. Advertising Res.* 28(1), 11-31.

[20] Reynolds, T. J. and Olson, J. C. 2001. *Understanding consumer decision making: The means-end approach to marketing and advertising strategy.* Lawrence Erlbaum Associates, New Jersey, NJ, USA.

[21] Rizzo, A. A., Ghahremani, K., Pryor, L., and Gardner, S. 2003. Immersive 360-degree panoramic video environments: research on creating useful and usable applications. In *Human–computer interaction: theory and practice, vol 1*, J. Jacko and C. Stephanidis, Eds. Lawrence Erlbaum Associates, Mahwah, NJ, USA, 1233–1237.

[22] Steen, M. 2008. *The Fragility of User-Centered Design.* Doctoral thesis. TUDelft.

[23] Takács, B. 2011. Immersive interactive reality: Internet-based on-demand VR for cultural presentation. *VR*, 15, 267-278.

[24] Vanden Abeele, V. and Zaman, B. *Laddering the User Experience!* Paper presented at User Experience Evaluation Methods in Product Development Workshop at Interact2009 (Uppsala, Sweden, EU, August 25). UXEM'09.

[25] Van den Broeck, W. 2005. *New Media, new audiences, new practices. Is iDTV indeed a paradigm shift?* Paper presented at International Association for Media and Communication Research Conference (Taipei, Taiwan, July 26-28 July). IAMCR 2005.

[26] Van den Broeck, W., & Pierson, J. 2008. The i in iDTV: How interactive is interactive digital television. In *Workshop Proceedings Cost Action 298 Participation in the Broadband Society – Digital television revisited: Lining users, markets and policies* (Budapest, Hungary, EU, May 15). COST 298 – OPOCE, Brussels, Belgium, EU, 41-49.

[27] Van Looy, J., Courtois, C., and De Vocht, M. 2010. Player identification in online games: validation of a scale for measuring identification in MMORPGs. In *Proceedings of the 3rd International Conference on Fun and Games* (Leuven, Belgium, EU, September 15 - 17). Fun and Games '10. ACM, New York, NY, USA, 126-134.

[28] Van Zoonen, L. and Aalberts, C. 2005. Televisiekijken in het digitale tijdperk. *Tijdschrift voor Communicatiewetenschap* 33(4), 347-365.

[29] xTV IBBT-project description and partners. http://www.ibbt.be/en/projects/overview-projects/p/detail/xtv-2.

[30] Zaman, B. 2008. Introducing contextual laddering to evaluate the likeability of games with children. *Cognit. Tech. Work* 10(2), 107-117.

Exploring Children's 3DTV Experience

Marianna Obrist[1,2], Daniela Wurhofer[1], Magdalena Gärtner[1], Florian Förster[3], Manfred Tscheligi[1]
[1]Christian Doppler Laboratory for "Contextual Interfaces",
HCI & Usability Unit, ICT&S Center, University of Salzburg, Salzburg, Austria
[2]Culture Lab, School of Computing Science, Newcastle University, Newcastle upon Tyne, UK
[3]Studio MicroLearning & Information Environments, Research Studios
Austria Forschungsgesellschaft, Salzburg, Austria
[1]{firstname.lastname}@sbg.ac.at, [2]marianna.obrist@ncl.ac.uk,
[3]florian.foerster@researchstudio.at

ABSTRACT
3D is expected to transition from cinema to personal consumer electronics. Given that children are heavy users of consumer electronics and represent a driving force when it comes to the adoption of new technologies, it is important to investigate and understand children's experiences with new technologies. Within this paper, we explore children's 3DTV experience with respect to attributed viewing qualities, willingness to view 3DTV at home and influences by age and gender. The study was conducted as part of a three-day science event organized within a shopping mall. Within these three days, feedback from more than 600 children was collected using a combination of quantitative and qualitative methods. Next to a one-page, pre-structured questionnaire, which was developed in particular to explore the quality of children's 3DTV viewing experience, we used open feedback cards on which the children could note their positive and negative experiences of watching 3DTV. The questionnaire results indicated that older children found watching 3DTV requires higher attention and is more exhausting, although – at the same time – they experienced it as more realistic than the younger children. Furthermore, three-fourths of the children indicated that they would like to watch 3DTV at home. The study results provide a first step towards a richer understanding of children's experience with 3DTV.

Categories and Subject Descriptors
H5.2. Information interfaces and presentation (e.g., HCI): User Interfaces, *Evaluation/methodology*.

General Terms
Measurement, Documentation, Experimentation, Human Factors.

Keywords
3DTV, children, user study, viewing experience, user experience, context, method.

1. INTRODUCTION & BACKGROUND
Within the last few years, mature technology and advanced special effects helped 3D especially in the cinema to reach the mainstream [35]. Furthermore, children are a target group of the movies industries, when it comes to 3D (e.g. see [4]). Children therefore also represent an interesting user group, concerning the adoption of 3D technology beyond movie theatres, e.g. 3DTV at home, especially considering that *"...the family home becomes a key site for the integration of telecommunications, broadcasting, computing and video, with satellite and cable television, computer games, Internet and other interactive media already transforming the everyday lives of children and young people..."* [25].

However, little is known about how children experience 3D technology, neither in cinema theatres nor in any other setting. Therefore the main goal of our research was to investigate children's experiences with 3DTV to shed light on this emerging technology whilst also bringing a user-centered perspective to this topic. By investigating the experiences collected in the public context, including assumptions for the future acceptance in the home context, we aim to contribute to the current discussion regarding 3D technology and 3DTV in particular.

There is only limited research published on the user's perspective and perception of 3DTV (e.g., [23][42]). The majority of evaluation studies on viewing experiences are conducted in controlled laboratory environments (e.g., [17][30][36][39]). Only a few exceptions can be found in mobile 3DTV research (e.g., [11][23]). In general, lab studies are perfectly suitable for evaluating perceptual qualities, however, when it comes to assessing the user experience (UX), the conclusions drawn from such studies have limited use. Field studies can bridge the gap and provide richer insights on how people experience a technology. As children are more and more becoming primary users of software and technology, a broad number of research methods on how to involve them in the development process have evolved (e.g., [19][10][24][15][33][14]). With respect to 3DTV, no studies on children's UX have – to our knowledge – been conducted to date.

Within this paper we try to contribute to this research gap by presenting initial study results on users' experiences with 3DTV. Thereby, the focus is put on children as a relevant user group, building on their role as "change agents" regarding the adoption of new technologies in the home [31]. Our main research question was: *How do children experience 3DTV?* In detail, we explored the following sub-questions:

- *Which attributes do children assign to their 3DTV viewing experience? I.e., which attributes characterize children's viewing experience?*
- *How does the viewing experience influence the children's willingness to watch 3DTV at home?*
- *What factors influence children's experience of 3DTV (e.g., age, gender)?*

In the following, we present the results of a study conducted to explore children's experiences with 3DTV in a public space,

EuroITV'12, July 4–6, 2012, Berlin, Germany.

namely within a shopping mall, as part of a three-day University science event. This setting provided us with the possibility to establish contact with a huge amount of participants. In addition, this event enabled us to reach the intended target group, because a large number of schools organize field trips to the University science event in order broaden children's interest in different project topics and science in general. This public set up, the methods used and the major findings, which combine quantitative and qualitative data are presented and discussed in the following sections. Furthermore the results of this study lay ground for a more in depth investigation of 3DTV and children, presented in the last section, future work.

2. RELATED WORK

Although 3D technology is no recent invention and has been around in different forms for almost 100 years, for most of its lifespan it has been seen as a gimmick more than something that truly enhances the watching experience [6]. Nevertheless, within the last few years mature technology and advanced special effects helped 3D especially in the cinema to reach the mainstream, as successful movies like James Cameron's "Avatar" and Disney's "Toy Story 3" illustrate. In particular, "Avatar" is considered an important trigger for ongoing public enthusiasm for and interest in 3D technology, as well as for first use of 3DTV at home [5]. Since 2009, when "Avatar" reawakened 3D technology, the number of movies published in 3D has constantly risen, with nearly three times as many 3D movies released in 2011 as in 2009, and even more 3D movies expected to be released in 2012. This increased enthusiasm for 3D movies has pioneered the way for the adoption of 3D technology beyond the public context to more private spaces like the home context [27].

2.1 Variables Affecting the Take Up of 3DTV

The diffusion of 3DTV beyond the cinema will mainly depend on the prize, improvements in technology, content availability and finally on the users' adoption and acceptance of such new technology in their home context. *"We were a long time in the chicken-and-egg situation for cinema. 'Do we need the content first or the theatres?' You can see the same happening in [3D]TV right now – and that reminds you that it is going to be a process, not an overnight thing"* ([5], p. 35). 3D technology for the living room is still in a stage of development and is not assured to be a success in the near future. Prognoses and assumptions about the take up and adoption of 3DTV by the consumers in the home are varying from a few years up to ten or twenty years (see [11][6][5]). However, people do not tend to replace technical equipment, which is still in working order. New media devices, such as 3DTV sets have to compete with older ones if people are to incorporate them into the household [31]. However, new devices are desirable, not only regarding enhanced functionality and usability but also the prestige value, which comes along with innovative and modern technology.

Major global market researchers (e.g., [6][33]) state that consumers want 3DTV, especially if they have already experienced the visual quality of 3D somewhere else, e.g., in cinema movies. In addition, almost every notable television manufacturer is offering 3D-capable TV screens for the living room at present or will have them in their product range soon [11]. Nevertheless, the final adoption will depend on the benefits identified by the consumers and the quality of experience and perception of 3DTV. Whether a new device finds its place in the home or not, is always the result of an interplay between the technology itself and the user context [31].

2.2 Relevant 3DTV Consumers: Children

Quandt and Pape [31] report that in households with children the children's bedrooms contain the second highest number of media in the home just after the living room, which is the definite monopole for technical devices. They also discovered a concentration of new technologies within the children's space, which concurs with results of other studies on children's media use, underlining their role as "change agents" regarding the adoption of new technologies.

There is another aspect regarding the physiology of children, which underlines the particular position they have in the evaluation of 3D technology. Children are more tolerant towards stereoscopic variances than elderly people, as with increasing age people more and more lose their ability to adapt to alterations affecting their visual perception. In other words, children are in a kind of learning phase concerning their visual senses, therefore their eyes can adapt more quickly to changes in digital 3D movies [38].

Animation movies, which are mainly made for families and especially children (e.g. see [5]), are particularly appropriate for the application of 3D technology given their digital, computer-based production process. Almost any animation movie shown in cinemas in the past two years was released in an additional 3D format and the mainly young audience, the target audience of these movies, appreciated that. Consequently children and teenagers can be assumed to be a target group of the movie industry when it comes to 3D [25].

2.3 Evaluating Children's Experiences

When it comes to evaluating the user/viewer experience with 3DTV a number of different methods and approaches exist. The most common way to evaluate the users' viewing experience are laboratory studies focusing on the perceptual and technical qualities of 3DTV (e.g., [17][30][36]). Perceptual quality evaluations are often used to assess the video quality perceived by the user and to limit discomfort. Viewing durations for judging the quality have short time spans, varying from 5 to 15 seconds [3]. Evaluations of this kind are conducted in lab environments to control for factors like background and room illumination, or viewing distance. A low perceptual quality does not only cause an unpleasant viewing experience, but can also cause physical side effects. Thus, the International Telecommunication Union (ITU) addresses recommendations for such evaluations, originally designed for 2DTV, but now also designated for 3DTV[1].

In contrast to mere perceptual studies, which often rely on objective quality metrics [1], wider approaches exist. These approaches either combine perceptual evaluations with qualitative methods like interviews and questionnaires [12], or solely rely on the latter [e.g., 15]. These qualitative approaches aim to identify underlying factors for the subjective viewing quality of 3DTV [21]. Jumisko-Pyykkö et al. [21] for instance, conducted 90 semi-structured interviews to reveal viewing experiences after a psychoperceptual quality evaluation. Their developed model on quality of experience integrates four components: 1) quality of visual modality in depth, spatial and motion domains, 2) viewing experience, 3) content, 4) audio and audiovisual quality.

Moreover, Häkkinen et al. [15] compared the perception of stereoscopic and non-stereoscopic content. Their results show that

---

[1] See International Telecommunication Union (ITU) website: http://www.itu.int/net/itunews/issues/2010/02/index.aspx

people experiencing 3DTV most often report on physical symptoms as well as five subjective attributes: depth impression, life-like versus artificial, presence in the scene, emotional experiences and more richness of detail [15]. Other approaches for assessing 3D content include the measurement of the users' feeling of presence [22][9], feeling of sickness [15] [23] and usability [20].

In recent years a number of studies on 3D are grounded on a user-centered design approach, especially within research on mobile 3DTV [11][23]. These studies coin the term user experience (UX), as they take user characteristics and goals, content and context of use into account. The closer 3DTV comes to usage in a home context, the more important these additional factors become. The scope of UX supersedes the concept of usability and other performance oriented measures by including for example users' emotions as well as motivations and a strong focus on the context of use. Following the ISO definition, UX contains various contributing factors such as *"users' emotions, beliefs, preferences, perceptions, physical and psychological responses, behaviors and accomplishments that occur before, during and after use* [of a product, system or service]" [ISO]. Overall, we need to keep in mind that we cannot design UX but only design for UX, because people appropriate technology individually, as McCarthy and Wright [28] point out.

As children are increasingly becoming primary users of software and technology, many efforts are undertaken to shape technology according to their abilities, interests and development needs [18]. Hence, a broad number of research methods on how to involve children in the design and development process have evolved [26][10]. Hereby, children act as users [24], testers [15], informants [33] as well as design partners [14]. Independent of the purpose of research and the methods used, attention has to be paid to adapt or design research methods considering children's abilities and needs differ from those of adolescents (see e.g. [4]). Regarding research that focuses on the evaluation of interactive systems numerous tools and methods have been designed [19]. Two such examples are a questionnaire for the evaluation of communication technologies with children [40] and a tool to improve self-reporting by children in user-centered evaluations [31].

With respect to interactions with 3DTV, the majority of studies on 3D viewing experiences are conducted in controlled laboratory environments. A few exceptions can be found in mobile 3DTV research. In general, lab studies are perfectly suitable for evaluating perceptual qualities, however, when it comes to assessing the UX, the conclusions drawn from such studies only have limited use. In addition, to our best knowledge these studies are mainly limited to adult participants with respect to 3DTV. Thus, by going out into the field and collecting feedback from people in the wild, additional insights can be gathered and will contribute to the interpretation of children's 3D viewing experiences.

3. STUDY AND METHOD

The study took place in a shopping mall as part of a bigger annual scientific university event in November 2010. The main research goal was to utilize the public setting to generate a substantial amount of data on children's experiences.

Children visiting our booth were accompanied either by their parents or teachers. The children as well as their chaperons were orally informed about the procedure and the aim of our study including information about the potential effects of watching 3DTV content (e.g., possibility of feeling sick). In addition to two chairs positioned in front of one of the 3DTV screens (see Figure 1), there were other seating possibilities available around the booth. Children could only take part in the study when their parents or teachers allowed them to participate. A minimum of four researchers were available at the booth at any time to take care of the participants: from the moment they were given the 3D glasses, while they were watching the 3D content, until they were asked to fill in the questionnaire and give feedback on the feedback cards.

3.1 Study Objects and Set Up

In cooperation with an industrial partner, four of their produced 3D movies, namely "skiing" (3 minutes), "base jumping" (3 minutes), "breakdance" (2.30 minutes), and "body painting" (3 minutes), were used in our study. The movies were displayed randomly on two 3D screens (JVC 3D LCD Monitor/GD-463D10E) over three days at our booth in the shopping mall. Each of the two screens was connected to a Sony PlayStation for a random playback of the movies.

Children visiting the shopping mall could get involved in our study by using one of the 40 polarization 3D glasses available at the booth. Participating children could either stand or sit in front of the TV screens (see Figure 1).

Figure 1. Evaluation set up in the public context, namely a shopping mall, enabling watching the 3DTV movies while standing or sitting in front of the TV screens.

The public study environment did not allow a controlled set up with exact time fixations. We estimate that the approximate viewing time for the 3D movies varied between 3 and 10 minutes.

3.2 Method Used

A quick evaluation approach was essential within the shopping mall context. Therefore, a one-page, pre-structured questionnaire consisting of four parts was developed as a main means of collecting the children's feedback. The questionnaire was based on existing research on viewing experiences with 3DTV (see [21]) and on positive experiences with this questionnaire method in a previous public study with children (focusing on interactive technology) [41]. The questionnaire (see Figure 2) was designed to especially suit children aged between 8 and 14 years, being the most frequent user group of such a science event (based on our previous years' experiences).

Question one focussed on the children's overall viewing experience. The second question aimed at further understanding this viewing experience, asking children to choose one or more of ten attributes to describe their physical and emotional state after watching 3DTV. The ten items were derived from the five subcomponents of the quality of users' viewing experience identified by Jumisko-Pyykkö et al. [21]. Each subcomponent consists of a pair of items representing the positive and the negative aspect of the component: *(1) ease of viewing* (items: easy to watch / strong need to focus), (2) *pleasantness of viewing* (items: pleasant / unpleasant), *(3) enhanced immersion* (items: realistic / unrealistic), *(4) comparison to existing technology* (items: better than regular TV / like regular TV), and *(5) visual discomfort* (items: relaxing / exhausting).

We decided not to use the pairs on separate scales but arranged the ten items freely on the questionnaire, as we wanted the questionnaire to be suitable for all children – especially for the youngest – and to reduce the bias of answers when narrowing down the attributes to bipolar pairs [1]. Furthermore, this open approach allowed us to investigate, which attributes children select for describing their experience, without pre-categorizing them in a positive or negative way.

The third question addressed the children's willingness to watch 3DTV at home in order to acquire first impressions of their potential future interest on 3D technology beyond the cinema and public viewing context. Finally, we asked for some basic demographic data (gender and age). In addition to the questionnaire, open feedback cards were given to the children to collect further information on their positive and negative experiences. The cards prompted the children to freely write down their impressions after watching 3DTV.

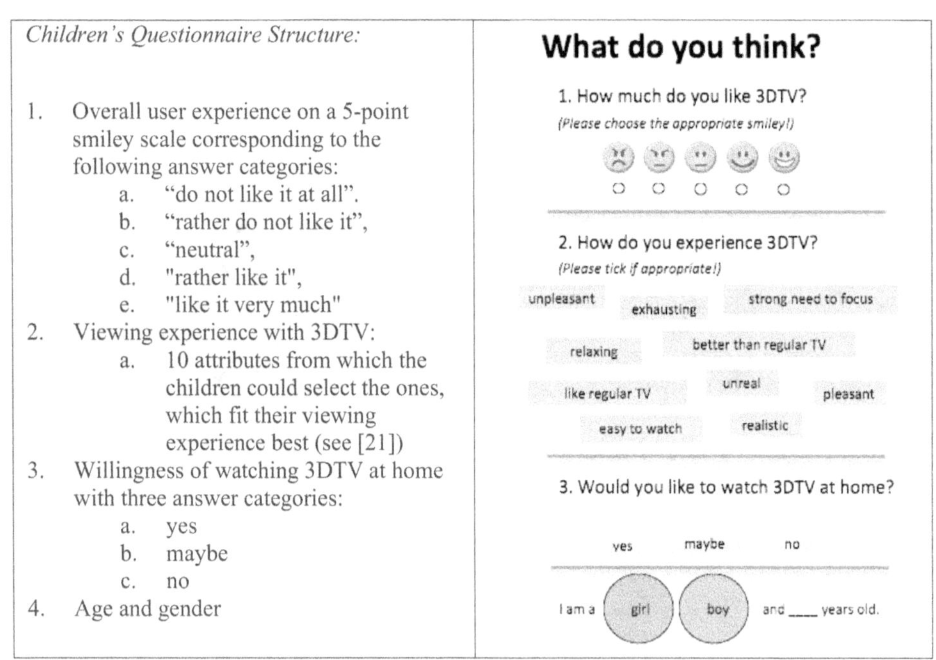

Figure 2. Questionnaire consisting of Four Main Parts.

Table 1. Distribution of Age Groups

		6 to 10 years	**11 to 14 years**	**15 to 18 years**	**Total**
Female	N (% within age groups)	62 (43%)	157 (40%)	43 (55%)	262 (42%)
Male	N (% within age groups)	84 (57%)	238 (60%)	35 (45%)	357 (58%)
Total		146 (100%)	395 (100%)	78 (100%)	619 (100%)

4. STUDY RESULTS

Overall, 639 participants aged between 6 and 18 years filled in the questionnaire[2]. The mean age of the participants was 11.83 years (SD=2.48), with 58% male and 42% female participants. In order to look for differences between different stages of life, three age groups were defined ("6 to 10 years", "11 to 14 years", and "15 to 18 years"). See Table 1 for details.

4.1 Overall Experience

The questionnaire revealed that the majority of participants (95%, N=625) liked 3DTV, while only 2% of the participants disliked it. We found a significant difference in the ratings of the youngest age group (6-10 years) and the oldest age group (15-18 years), with the youngest group having more positive ratings of the overall experience (M=4.70, SD=0.64) than the oldest group (M=4.49, SD=0.77); $t(131)=2.03$ $p=0.045$. With a mean of 4.64 (SD=0.67), the average rating of age group 2 (11 to 14 years) lies in between.

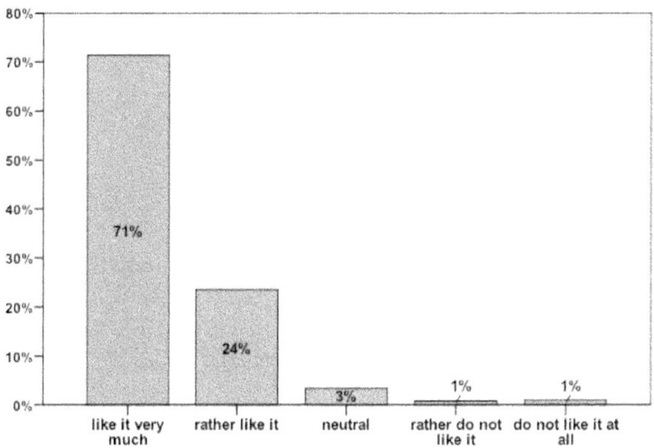

Figure 3. Ratings on the Question "How much do you like 3DTV?" (N=625).

Concerning the willingness to watch 3DTV at home, the majority of children were positive (73%, N=621). The highest percentage of those who did not want 3DTV at home were aged between 15 and 18 years (15 to 18 years: 9%, 6 to 10 years: 4%, 11 to 14 years: 5%). A one-way analysis of variances to compare the age groups and the willingness to watch at home showed a significant effect for age, with younger participants exhibiting a higher willingness to have 3DTV at home. We found significant differences in the willingness to have 3DTV at home between age group 1 (6 to 10 years) and age group 3 (15 to 18 years) as well as between age group 1 (6 to 10 years) and age group 2 (11 to 14 years); $F(2, 612)=8.68$, $p<0.001$.

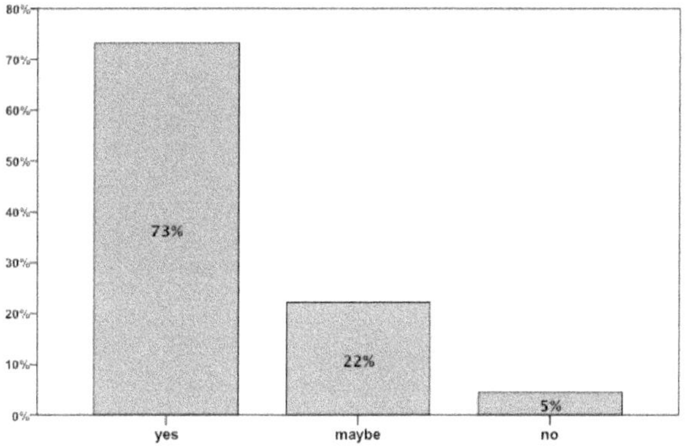

[2] Although participants older than 14 years are usually not considered as children, but rather as adolescents, we refer to them as children within this paper.

Figure 4. Ratings on the question "Would you like to watch 3DTV at home?" (N=621).

A one-way ANOVA showed that the willingness to watch 3DTV at home had a significant effect on the ratings of the overall user experience, with a lower rated overall user experience for the children who were indecisive or not willing to have 3DTV at home; $F(2, 604)=110.08$, $p<0.001$.

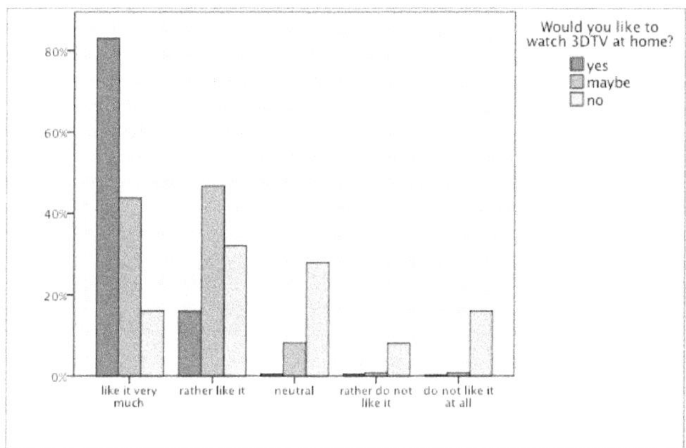

Figure 5. Ratings of Overall Experience according to Children's Willingness to watch 3DTV at Home (N=607).

4.2 Attributed Viewing Experience

The viewing experience of the participants was measured by letting them choose one or more of the 10 attributes regarding the perception of 3DTV.

Table 2 presents a ranking of the attributes according to their frequency of selection, showing that the positive statements were selected much more often (n=1062) than the negative ones (n=223). Two-thirds of the children (67%, N=639) considered 3DTV to be "better than regular TV". About half of the children (46%) selected the attribute "realistic", followed by one fifth (21%) who indicated they feel "pleasant" while watching 3DTV. "Relaxing" (17%) and "easy to watch" (17%) were other positive attributes children associated with 3DTV. The attributes "exhausting" and "strong need to focus" were chosen by 12% of the participants. In comparison the attributes "unpleasant", "unreal" and "like normal TV" were rarely chosen (all 4%).

Table 2 Ranking of Statements for the Question "How do you experience 3DTV?" according to Frequency of Selection

Ranking of Statements	Frequency (Percent of Cases)
Better than regular TV	423 (67%)
Realistic	289 (46%)
Pleasant	132 (21%)
Relaxing	110 (17%)
Easy to watch	108 (17%)
Exhausting	76 (12%)
Strong need to focus	74 (12%)
Like regular TV	26 (4%)
Unpleasant	25 (4%)
Unreal	22 (4%)
	N = 1285

Concerning age and ease of viewing, we found that the older the children were, the more frequent they indicated that 3DTV requires higher attention ("strong need to focus"). A Pearson's Product Moment Correlation showed a marginal correlation between age and attention; (r(624)=0.185, p<0.001). In addition, older children more often chose the attributes "realistic" and "exhausting" when being asked to indicate their viewing experience. However, we only found a slight positive correlation between age and "realistic" (Pearson's r(624)=0.175, p<0.001) and between age and the item "exhausting" (Pearson's r(624)=0.145, p<0.001). Thus, the frequency of choosing negative attributes does increase with age in terms of ease of viewing (strong need to focus) and visual discomfort ("exhausting") as well as for the positive attribute enhanced immersion ("realistic").

Pearson's Product moment correlations for overall experience and willingness to watch 3DTV at home with attributed viewing experience were computed. The attribute "unpleasant" showed a low negative correlation with overall experience (r(625)=-0.33, p<0.001), indicating that attributed unpleasantness results in a negative rating of the overall experience. Concerning the willingness to watch 3DTV at home, we also found that attributed unpleasantness is directly related to the unwillingness to watch 3DTV at home (r(621)=0.31, p<0.001). The same tendency was found for the attribute "exhausting", meaning that those participants, who considered 3DTV to be exhausting, showed a tendency towards a negative rating of the overall experience (r(625)=-0.22, p<0.001) and an unwillingness to watch 3DTV at home (r(621)=0.30, p<0.001). For the attribute "better than regular TV", the opposite was the case: choosing this attribute correlates with a positive overall experience (r(625)=0.21, p<0.001) and a willingness to watch 3DTV at home (r(621)=-0.27, p<0.001).

Table 3. Pearson's Product Moment Correlations for Overall Experience and Willingness to Watch 3DTV at Home with Attributed Viewing Experience.

	How much do you like 3DTV? [Overall Experience[a]]	Would you like to watch 3DTV at home? [Willingness to Watch[b]]
Unpleasant	-0.33***	0.31***
Exhausting	-0.22***	0.30***
Strong need to focus	-0.07	0.13**
Relaxing	0.09*	-0.14***
Better than regular TV	0.21***	-0.27***
Like regular TV	-0.06	0.60
Unreal	-0.14**	0.19***
Pleasant	0.10*	-0.10*
Easy to watch	0.08*	-0.07
Realistic	0.02	-0.05
	(N=625)	(N=621)

Note. *= p < .05, **= p < .01, ***= p < .001. [a]Overall Experience: 1=*do not like it at all* to 5=*like it very much*. [b]Willingness to Watch: 1=*yes*, 2=*maybe*, 3=*no*.

4.3 Open Questions: Positive and Negative Experiences

In total, 437 open feedback cards were collected during the three-day study. 246 cards contained positive statements (57%) and 189 cards negative statements (43%). For the qualitative data analysis, in which we followed an inductive categorization process, one researcher pre-structured the cards by classifying and grouping similar comments towards the overall positive and negative categories (i.e., *I like...; I don't like...).* Afterwards, the revealed sub-categories were presented and discussed with the other research group members, which led to an iteration and refinement of the categories, especially with respect to the labelling. Finally, nine sub-categories were formulated based on the qualitative data

Concerning positive feedback (see Table 2) about one third of the participants indicated to enjoy the visual quality of 3DTV, stating for example *"It's great, like real life"* or *„It's so realistic"*. Experiencing pleasant emotions was noted as another positive aspect of 3DTV by one fifth of the participants: *"You can feel what is happening on the screen much better, and it is adventurous"* or *"Cinema-feeling"*. One tenth experienced enjoyable physical effects, such as the feeling of presence: *"You feel like you're involved in what's going on, yourself."* Furthermore, participants were pleased about the design of the 3DTV devices and indicated to like the 3D content. Finally the children also provided positive feedback for the study approach, such as the booth set up for 3D viewing (summarized in the category "Misc").

Regarding negative feedback about one third of the participants perceived the technological aspects, especially the need to wear glasses as negative. Typical statements were for example: *"Who really wants to wear glasses while watching TV at home?"* or *"After a while it's simply annoying that you always have to wear these glasses"*. Another third indicated to have experienced unpleasant physical effects like eye strain, headache or nausea, noting for example: *"I don't like that my eyes start hurting after a while and it's so exhausting"* or *"The quick and constant panning of the camera causes stomach troubles."* About one tenth of the participants noted that they were annoyed about the high prices and sparse availability of 3DTV devices. Some participants were not satisfied with the visual quality of 3DTV, with blurring pictures and double vision mentioned as the main problems. Only a few noted dislike of the 3D content/movies shown.

Table 4. Ranking of the Positive and Negative Experience Sub-Categories revealed from the Open Feedback Cards according to Frequencies of Mentioning.

Ranking ***"I like..."***	**Frequency (Percent of Answers)**	**Ranking** ***"I don't like..."***	**Frequency (Percent of Answers)**
Visual Quality	91 (37%)	Technological Aspects	55 (29%)
Emotions	53 (21%)	Physical Effects	50 (27%)
Technological Aspects	29 (12%)	General Dissatisfaction	43 (23%)
General Satisfaction	26 (11%)	Availability	17 (9%)
Physical Effects	22 (9%)	Visual Quality	11 (6%)
Availability	10 (4%)	Misc	5 (2%)
Design	6 (2%)	Emotions	4 (2%)
Content	5 (2%)	Content	3 (2%)
Misc	4 (2%)	Design	1 (0%)
	N=246 (100%)		N=189 (100%)

5. DISCUSSION

As the results show, the children in general experienced 3DTV in a very positive way. Comparing our results for the ten used attributes with the five subcomponents of the users' viewing experience quality [21], children most often selected the "enhanced immersion" and "comparison to existing technology" components to describe a positive 3D viewing experience (addressing our first research question *"Which attributes do children assign to their 3DTV viewing experience?" I.e. which attributes characterize children's viewing experience?).* In terms of what led to a negative viewing experience the most frequently chosen negative attributes belonged to the subcomponents of "ease of viewing" and "visual discomfort". The experienced visual discomfort is further supported by the results from the open feedback cards, where unpleasant physical effects like eye strain, headache or nausea were stated by more than one-fourth of the participants.

The results from the questionnaire showed that the majority of the children (95%, N=621) reported liking 3DTV. The study revealed that younger age groups (6-10 and 11-14 years) rate the overall experience with 3DTV more positively than the oldest age group (15-18 years). And this difference in overall experience was statistically significant. These findings could be confirmed by the theory of Tauer [38], who reports that the younger children are, the better and faster their eyes adapt to visual variances. Our findings support his theory that older children experience watching 3DTV as more demanding in terms of the level of attention needed (more need to focus) and more exhausting than younger children.

Furthermore, we can assume that participants from the older age groups, who experienced negative effects more frequently, have a reduced willingness to adapt and watch 3DTV at home. Our findings in general revealed a high willingness to watch 3DTV at home (addressing our second research question *How does the viewing experience influence the children's willingness to watch 3DTV at home?)*, with 73% of the participants indicating their willingness to watch 3DTV at home, 22% being undecided, and only 5% disapproving the idea. But within the latter category, the highest percentage was again found in the oldest age group. Furthermore the willingness to watch 3DTV at home had a significant effect on the ratings of the overall user experience. Children rated the overall user experience lower if they were indecisive or not willing to have 3DTV at home. Children's positive attitude towards 3DTV is also reflected in the attributes selected to describe their overall experience. They mostly selected positive attributes to characterize their experience, such as 'superior to regular TV', 'realistic', 'pleasant', 'relaxing', and/or 'easy to watch'. The children reported far less frequently that their experience of watching 3DTV was 'exhausting' or 'difficult to focus on', as well as 'unpleasant', 'unreal', or 'just like normal TV'. Concerning gender, our data did not reveal any differences between girls and boys and their willingness to watch 3DTV at home.

In addition, having a closer look at the attributed viewing experience in relation to the participants' age revealed some interesting results for our third research question *What factors influence the children's experience (e.g., age, gender)?*. Two-thirds of the children evaluated 3DTV to be 'better than regular TV'. The older the children, the more they indicated that watching 3DTV requires higher attention (more need to focus) and is more exhausting. At the same time the older participants experienced it as more realistic than the younger ones. In addition, one-third of the collected positive feedback cards referred to a realistic and attractive visual quality of 3DTV. From a methodological perspective we know from previous research that older participants are more critical in their responses than younger participants. Previous research has already shown an effect of age on responses' variability and the tendency for higher ratings (e.g., [1]). This has to be taken into account in the interpretation of the findings and can be further explored in future studies.

Finally, almost one-third of the statements on the negative feedback cards were related to the 3D glasses and the children's dislike of wearing them while watching 3D content. This supports previous research results [8]. Meesters et al. [30] claim, that a usual technical distinction concerning 3D is made between stereoscopic and autostereoscopic displays. Regarding stereoscopic displays the viewer of 3DTV content wears an optical device (aided viewing) whereas the autostereoscopic techniques enables the viewer to experience 3D content without any additional device (free viewing). Further details with regard to these display techniques are given by Sexton and Surman [36].

"Panasonic's Suetsugi admits that in a perfect world, consumers should be able to have the immersive 3D experience without wearing glasses. But he said that it will be at least 10 years before the technology is advanced enough to provide a similarly robust 3D experience without glasses" [35]. This statement is traced back to 2006. Since then, 3DTV without glasses gained a lot of attention from manufacturers, as the need to wear 3D glasses is one of the major barriers to the mass acceptance of 3DTV as a truly popular entertainment medium.

6. CONCLUSIONS AND FUTURE WORK

Although emerging 3D technology changes the way people experience movies, scientific research on this issue from a user-centered perspective still lacks behind. The data presented in this paper is based on a three-day user study conducted as part of a broader science event organized in a shopping mall. Feedback was collected using a short pre-structured questionnaire and open (positive and negative) feedback cards.

With respect to the overall research question *How do children experience 3DTV?*, our study results represent a first step towards reaching a richer understanding of children's experiences with 3DTV. We are aware about the methodological restriction of our study, not having control over the duration of watching the 3D content or the influences of the different movies (content) on the experiences. However, first insights on the children's experiences were explored and build the basis for further examinations. In addition, we are conscious about the need for a better distinction between the different age groups and the selection of methods for future studies.

Thus, our study provides a starting point for exploring 3DTV with respect to the particular target group of children – considered highly relevant as early adopters of newly evolving technologies. The following research directions can be summarized:

- Exploring the differences in viewing experiences dependent on time of viewing and type of content (e.g., skiing versus break dance).
- Exploring the viewing experiences of 3DTV over a longer timeframe (several weeks) in order to study changes in the viewing experiences.
- Understanding the attributed characteristics for 3DTV with respect to contextual influences and different contextual settings for watching 3DTV (e.g., cinema, home, mobile).
- Investigating children's viewing experience with and without 3D glasses. Wearing glasses is perceived bothersome in a public setting, such as a shopping mall, and could be assumed to be much higher in a private setting, such as at home, in the living room.
- Studying new approaches on how the narrative structure for 3DTV should be. What is the storyline for a 3D environment and how does this compare to traditional and interactive TV? Insights on the narrative construction of 3DTV content will open up new design spaces and business opportunities (e.g., 3D content for educational purposes).

As a first future work piece, we have successfully conducted a follow-up study in November 2011. This time the study focused on differences regarding children's experiences when watching 3DTV with glasses (polarization glasses) and without glasses (autostereoscopy). In particular, we focused on the user experience factors presence, engagement, feelings, and sensorial impressions. We also constructed and deployed a more advanced questionnaire for children. During the field study over 250 questionnaires were collected, covering the answers of children aged between 6 and 13 years. The analysis of the questionnaires is currently in progress.

7. ACKNOWLEDGMENTS

The financial support by the Federal Ministry of Economy, Family and Youth and the National Foundation for Research, Technology and Development is gratefully acknowledged (Christian Doppler Laboratory for "Contextual Interfaces"). Finally, we want to acknowledge the great support of all members of the ICT&S Center.

8. References

1. Boev, A., Hollosi, D., Gotchev, A., and Egiazarian, K.: Classification and simulation of stereoscopic artifacts in mobile 3DTV content. In: Proceedings of SPIE-IS&T Electronic Imaging, Stereoscopic Displays and Applications XX, San Jose, CA, USA. (2009)
2. Bruck, M., Ceci, S. J., and Melnyk, L.: External and internal sources of variation in the creation of false reports in children. Learning and Individual Differences, 9(4):269{316, 1997.
3. Chen, W., Fournier, J., Barkowsky, M., and Le Callet, P.: New Requirements of Subjective Video Quality Assessment Methodologies for 3DTV. Author manuscript, published in Video Processing and Quality Metrics (VPQM), Scottsdale, United States. (2010)
4. Christensen, P. and James, A. Research with Children. Perspectives and Practices. 2nd edition. Routeledge,Abdingdon, UK. (2008)
5. Dempsey, P. Children of Pandora. In: Engineering & Technology, issue 16, pp. 32-35. IET, London (2010).
6. DisplaySearch: Quarterly TV Design and Features Report. Retrieved from: http://www.displaysearch.com/cps/rde/xchg/displaysearch/hs.xsl/quarterly_tv_design_features_report.asp (January 2010)
7. Dubravac, S. G.: Understanding where 3DTV fits in. In: Consumer Electronics Vision, Vol.14, No. 2, p. 6. CEA, Arlington,VA, USA (2010)
8. Fehn, C., Barré de la, R. and Pastoor, S.: Interactive 3-DTV – Concepts and Key Technologies. In: Proceedings of the IEEE, Vol. 94, No. 3, pp. 524-538. (2006)
9. Freeman, J., and Avons, S.: Focus group exploration of presence through advanced broadcast services. In: Proceedings of SPIE the International Society for Optical Engineering, pages 530–539. (2000)
10. Garzotto, F.: Broadening children's involvement as design partners: from technology to "experience". In: Proceedings of the 7th international conference on Interaction design and children (IDC'08), pages 186-193, NY, USA, ACM. (2008)
11. GfK-Gesellschaft für Konsumentenforschung: Innovative technology for the living room. In: GfK Consumer Electronic Conference 2010: growth trends. Retrieved from: http://www.gfk.com/ (January 2010)
12. Goldmann, L., and Ebrahimi, T.: 3D Quality is more than just the Sum of 2D and Depth.
13. Gotchev, A., Jumisko-Pyykkö, S., Boev, A., and Strohmeier, D.: Mobile 3DTV System: Quality and User Perspective. In: Proceeding of 4th International Mobile Multimedia Communications Conference, Mobimedia, Oulu, Finland. (2008)
14. Guha, M., Druin, A., Chipman, G., Fails, J., Simms, S., and Farber, A.: Working with young children as technology design partners. In: Communications of the ACM, 48(1):39-42. (2005)
15. Häkkinen, J., Pölönen, M., Takatalo, J., and Nyman, G.: Simulator sickness in virtual display gaming: a comparison of stereoscopic and non-stereoscopic situations. In: Proceedings of the 8th Conference on Human-Computer Interaction with Mobile Devices and Services, pages 227–230. (2006)
16. Hanna, L, Neapolitan, D., and Risden, K.: Evaluating computer game concepts with children. In Proc. IDC'04, pages 49-56. (2004)
17. Hoffman, D., Girshick, A., Akeley, K., and Banks, M.: Vergence–accommodation conflicts hinder visual performance and cause visual fatigue. In: Journal of Vision, volume 8(3). (2008)
18. Hourcade, J.P. Interaction Design and Children. In: Foundations and Trends in Human–Computer Interaction. Vol. 1, No. 4, 277–392. (2007)
19. Jensen, J. J. and Skov, M. B.: A review of research methods in children's technology design. In Proceedings of the 2005 conference on Interaction design and children (IDC '05), NY, USA, ACM, 80-87. (2005)
20. Jin, Z. X., Zhang, Y. J., Wang, X., and Plocher, T.: Evaluating the usability of an autostereoscopic display. In: Proceedings of the 12th international conference on Human-computer interaction: interaction platforms and techniques, HCI'07, Berlin, Heidelberg, pages 605–614. (2007)
21. Jumisko-Pyykkö, S., Strohmeier, D., Utriainen, T. and Kunze, K.: Descriptive quality of experience for mobile 3D video. In: Proceedings of the 6th Nordic Conference on Human-Computer Interaction: Extending Boundaries (NordiCHI '10). pp. 266-275. ACM, New York, NY, USA (2010)
22. IJsselsteijn, W., de Ridder, H., Hamberg, R., Bouwhuis, D., and Freeman, J.: Perceived depth and the feeling of presence. In: 3DTV Displays, 18, 207-214. (1998)
23. Jumisko-Pyykkö, S.,Weitzel, M. and Strohmeier, D.: Designing for user experience: what to expect from mobile 3DTV and video?. In: Proceeding of the 1st international conference on Designing interactive user experiences for TV and video (UXTV '08). ACM, New York, NY, USA, pages, 183–192. (2008)
24. Kaplan, N., Chisik, Y. and Levy, D.: Reading in the wild: sociable literacy in practice. In: Proceedings of the 2006 conference on Interaction design and children (IDC '06), pages 97-104, NY, USA, ACM. (2006)
25. Livingstone, S.: Young People and the New Media: On learning lessons from TV to apply to the PC. In: Réseaux, 1999, vol. 7,no. 1., pp. 59-81. (1999)
26. Markopoulos, P., Read, J., Hoÿsniemi, J. and MacFarlane, S. Child computer interaction: advances in methodological research. Introduction to the special issue of cognition technology and work. In: Cognition, Technology & Work Journal, Volume 10, Number 2, 79-81. (2008)
27. Marks, G. Digitale Leinwand. 3D-Filme. Retrieved from: http://www.digitaleleinwand.de/3d-filme/). (Jänner 2012)
28. McCarthy, J., and Wright, P.: Technology as experience. Cambridge, Massachusetts: MIT Press. (2004)
29. Media Awareness Network: How Marketers Target Kids. Retrieved from http://www.media-awareness.ca/english/parents/marketing/marketers_target_kids.cfm (January 2010)
30. Meesters, L. M. J., IJsselsteijn, W. A., and Seuntiens, P. J. H.: A Survey of Perceptual Evaluations and Requirements of Three-Dimensional TV. In: IEEE Transactions on circuits and systems for video technology, Vol. 14, No. 3. (2004)
31. Pasch, M. Improving children's self-report in user-centered evaluations. In Proceedings of the 9th International Conference on Interaction Design and Children (IDC '10). ACM, New York, NY, USA, 331-334. (2010)
32. Quandt, T., and Pape, T.: Living in the Mediatope: A Multimethod Study on the Evolution of Media Technologies in the Domestic Environment. In: The Information Society, 26, pp. 330-345. Taylor & Francis, LLC. (2010)
33. Quixel Research: Consumers Prefer 3D Content from Cable and Satellite Providers over Blu-ray and DVD Players. Recent 3D Study Finds Consumers Eager for 3D TV and

Content. Retrieved from: Quixel Research, http://www.quixelresearch.com/ (2010)

34. Read, J., Gregory, P., MacFarlane, S., McManus, B., Gray, P., and Patel, R.: An investigation of participatory design with children-informant, balanced and facilitated design. In: Interaction Design and Children, 53-64. (2002)
35. Reardon, M.: 3D is coming to a living room near you. Retrieved from: CNN.com/technology, http://edition.cnn.com/2009/TECH/01/15/3d.tv/index.html (December 2009)
36. Sexton, I. and Surman, P. Stereoscopic and autostereoscopic display systems. In IEEE Signal Processing Magazine, volume 16, pages 85-99. (1999)
37. Shao, H., Cao, X., and Er, G.: Objective Quality Assessment of Depth Image Based Rendering in 3DTV System. In: Proceedings of the 3DTV Conference: The True Vision - Capture, Transmission and Display of 3D Vide. (2009)
38. Tauer H. Stereo 3D. Grundlagen, Technik und Bildgestaltung. Schiele & Schön, Berlin (2010)
39. Yang, J., Hou, C., Zhou, Y., Zhang, Z., and Guo, J.: Objective quality assessment method of stereo images. In: Proceedings of the 3DTV Conference 2009: The True Vision - Capture, Transmission and Display of 3D Video. (2009).
40. Yarosh, S. and Markopoulos, P. Design of an instrument for the evaluation of communication technologies with children. In Proceedings of the 9th International Conference on Interaction Design and Children (IDC '10). ACM, New York, NY, USA, 266-269. (2010)
41. Obrist, M., Igelsböck, J., Beck, E., Moser, C., Riegler, S., and Tscheligi, M. "Now You Need to Laugh! " – Investigating Fun in Games with Children. In: Proceedings of the International Conference on Advances in Computer Entertainment Technology (ACE '09). (2009).
42. Obrist, M., Wurhofer, D., Förster, F., Meneweger, T., Grill, T., Wilfinger, D. & Tscheligi, M. Perceived 3DTV Viewing in the Public: Insights from a Three-Day Field Evaluation Study. EuroITV2011: Proceedings of the 9th European Interactive TV Conference. ACM, New York, NY, USA, 167-176 (2011).

Documatic: Participatory, Mobile Shooting Assistant, Pre-Editor, and Groundwork for Semi-Automatic Filmmaking

Andrew Quitmeyer
Georgia Tech – Digital Media
TSRB 85 Fifth St.
Atlanta, GA, USA
andrew.quitmeyer@gmail.com

Michael Nitsche
Georgia Tech – Digital Media
TSRB 85 Fifth St.
Atlanta, GA, USA
michael.nitsche@gatech.edu

ABSTRACT
While digital filmmaking has broadened the accessibility of documentary film and television creation, legacy production practices persist of first gathering information (shooting) and later structuring the audio-video narrative (editing). The open-source app Documatic combines shooting and editing processes via synchronized smartphone–camera annotation systems that automatically generate non-destructive video "rough-cuts" for *Adobe Premiere*. Harnessing the correct digital affordances can enable small documentary productions to enjoy some of the production efficiency traditionally belonging only to large scale filmmakers, while maintaining the artisanal quality control of a small team. The paper outlines the design, implementation, and example usage of this production and editing assistant, which is aimed at supporting small independent documentary filmmaking teams.

Categories and Subject Descriptors
H5.m. Information interfaces and presentation (e.g., HCI): Miscellaneous.

General Terms
Design, Experimentation, Human Factors.

Keywords
Television, filmmaking, documentary, editing assistant, pre-editor, smartphone, collaborative, categorical documentary, procedural model, automation, Android, open-source

1. INTRODUCTION
Digital filmmaking has significantly impacted documentary television and film by decreasing the costs of production, editing, and distribution. Few digital affordances, however, have been applied to improve the actual filmmaking process. Currently, most documentary productions continue to abide by the legacy practices that were formed by the conditions of traditional, celluloid film practices. First, documentarians gather massive amounts of subject information from archival footage, recorded interviews, and text. Next, the documentarians are forced to sort through the collected data and derive a structure for the eventual audio-video narrative [1]. While this structural synthesis period distinguishes documentary from other film formats, as a stand-alone process it can be quite arduous.

Some video logging systems attempt to address this problem of sorting through droves of audio and video. These systems, however, are typically only used in large commercial or theatrical filmmaking as they rely on pre-established concrete master structures (such as shot lists).

Following a different approach altogether, database film projects automate the structuring of video into procedurally arranged segments or present spatialized, interactive clips. With these systems, the construction of any sort of distinct narrative that could function in linear TV still requires the sorting and editing process of traditional filmmaking.

Documatic[1] is a free, open-source Android app created as a proof-of-concept for a dynamic and efficient digital video creation process. It simplifies the arduous structural synthesis process by combining it with the more exploratory, spontaneous information gathering period. Via a synchronized Android app and an arbitrary digital camcorder, annotations can be added in real-time to recorded footage. Users structure these tags and – guided by *Documatic*'s open design – generate a malleable structure for their film during production itself. Finally, as the amassed data is downloaded to a computer, *Documatic* utilizes this structure of tags with its custom-built Project Generator to create "pre-edited," rough-cut video sequences for *Adobe Premiere Pro* [2]. In that way, it utilizes digital affordances during production to allow for a new form of content assembly. Since annotations utilize universal timestamps, the system can be paired with any digital camcorder, and audio-visual fidelity need not be sacrificed or limited to the capabilities of current phone cameras.

Documatic's structural basis evolved from theories and research of analogue documentaries in order to preserve the cinematic grammars culturally developed over the past century. The end product is not meant to be an interactive movie but will be more or less indistinguishable from a traditional, linear documentary film. The audience's ability to "read" the final artifact will be preserved, while the new formative process exemplifies simpler, more efficient ways for digital documentary production.

2. PROBLEM SPACE
Even though both, small independent films and large studio productions can be shot, edited, and distributed completely digitally, a major production company is still able to create cinematic content more efficiently due to its ability to sort through

EuroITV'12, July 4–6, 2012, Berlin, Germany.
Copyright 2012 ACM 978-1-4503-1107-6/12/07...$10.00.

---
[1] http://www.semiautomaticfilmmaking.org

and organize massive amounts of collected content. Where a small documentary team may take years to plan, shoot, and edit a 120 minute film, the sheer manpower of a large studio can produce a similar amount of content in a matter of weeks.

Concerning his thesis on the "Evolving Documentary," Michael Murtaugh describes the "traditional" method of making a documentary film: "filmmakers collect a large amount of raw material -- original film footage, archive photographs, text articles. These raw materials are organized in progressively larger chunks: shots, scenes, and sequences. Finally, sequences are edited together to form the final "cut" of the film. [...] In this way the filmmaking process may be seen as a kind of funnel [where] a large collection of content [...] is gradually refined and reduced" [3]. This is a work- and time-intense approach.

Another hindrance arises in that documentaries, in particular, tend to be produced in a more dynamic fashion than large theatrical studio films. A fiction film can follow *a priori* storyboards and scripts as blueprints for shooting and editing. Documentaries, on the other hand, must allow for unforeseen events and interviews with outcomes far different than could have been planned.

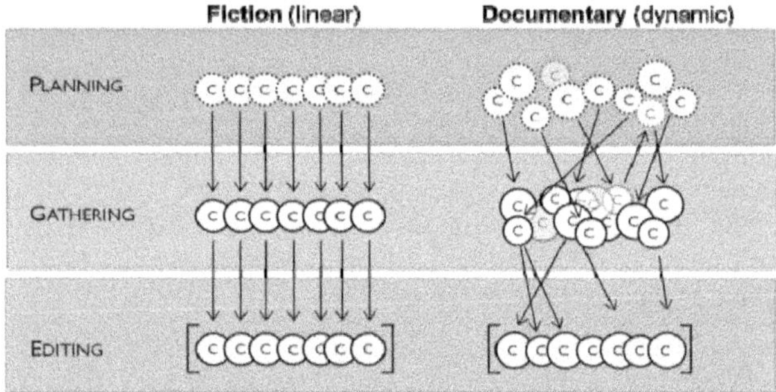

Figure 1. Differing content management in fiction and documentary video production

Whereas fiction film production has pre-assembled content (e.g. in the form of a screenplay and shot list), documentarians often face unforeseen changes in their content units (marked "c" in fig. 1). This applies even more to the practices of *YouTube* directed filmmakers catching unpredicted events on video.

Rigid filmmaking structures grant process efficiency to large, assembly-line-style teams but impede the work of small-team video creators. If we could however, digitally automate and/or parallelize some of the steps of the production process, the individual can begin to enjoy some of the filmmaking efficiency afforded to the big filmmakers, while maintaining the quality control and flexibility of a small team.

3. CURRENT FIELD

3.1 Video Tagging/Metadata Systems

Video logging systems, such as Adobe's *OnLocation* software [4], permit filmmakers to add supplementary information to movie files such as shot number, scene, description, camera information, timestamp, and ownership. Most of these logging systems are intended for large commercial or theatrical video productions, however, and they function as little more than a modern "clapboard." This linear style of metadata (shot, scene, and camera information) must be used with a previously established master structure since the tags themselves bear little semantic meaning. Thus, these current systems do little to aid documentary filmmakers whose movies' structures are dynamic and malleable.

3.2 Database Filmmaking

Meanwhile, other systems, like Michael Murtaugh's "evolving documentary", *ConTour*, Manovich's *Soft Cinema*, or the work of Murray's Experimental TV Lab, were developed to automatically generate cinematic experiences from information databases that reference collections of video clips [5]. These systems permit dynamic exploration of large content bases but creating these complex databases can be just as hard as editing the footage directly. Furthermore, the output of these database systems is usually a dynamic and interactive explorative moving image piece. It more resembles a web-based browsing approach and does not fit into the traditional format of linear TV and film.

While both approaches offer unique affordances, they also highlight the lack of an assistive, dynamic system for small-scale productions that could benefit from a combination of the two.

4. DESIGN

Analysis of the historical and structural difficulties in television, cinema, and documentary filmmaking, form the here-proposed design goals for a "semi-automatic filmmaking" activity. Overall, *Documatic* strives to enhance filmmaking; it does not replace the established techniques. It focuses on five core design goals: A) *Efficiency*: data needs to be intelligently collected with the automated structuring. B) *Agency*: creators should have full agency to direct the outcome of the project, and the digital component should be entirely non-destructive; that is, even if the system breaks, or performs oddly, the documentarian is still left with all the footage, as if they have shot a traditional documentary. C) *Readability*: The system's output should be indistinguishable from a traditional documentary and follow conventional film grammar. D) *Independence*: a filmmaker should not have to rely on external data networks, e.g. cell signals to capture the shots needed. This is necessary as many documentary productions operate in difficult territory such as nature reserves or foreign places where instant connectivity is not given. E) *Adaptability*: Finally, as Bernard notes [6], a system should react to the dynamics of the documentary creation process. A balance is needed to allow pre-planning of certain situations, while also allowing fast reactions to unforeseen developments.

Technically, the functionality of this product is derived from the pairing of a pool of raw, unorganized data (folders of unlabeled video content) with a collection of semantic data (xml annotations of specific time-periods) via global timestamps in order to automatically generate an editable sequence in an editor like *Adobe Premiere*. Building on the design goal of technological independence, the raw data can be collected from one-to-many digital video recording devices, while separately annotation data is captured by the *Documatic* app running on an Android device. By synchronizing the internal clocks of the desired camcorder(s) and the Android device with the current internet time (such as nist.time.gov), no further communication is necessary to allow the devices to work together.

4.1 Procedural Model: The Categorical Documentary

The first step in any automation process is the creation of rule sets. These rules are necessary to transform any continuous real-world process, into a discrete series of manageable steps that can be completed programmatically [7].

In their book, *Film Art*, Bordwell and Thompson identify a primary rule-set governing many documentary films, the "categorical documentary" [8]. This format follows a simple, consistent pattern regardless of the topic. First, the subject is introduced, and the viewer is then presented with series of interviews or narrations grouped into topics associated with the overall subject. The order in which these sections are arranged forms the overarching narrative experienced by the viewer. The narrative flow and continuity of these films is provided by characters and themes recurring throughout the distinct categories.

Because this approach is clearly defined, yet broad enough to allow for a high level of flexibility, the categorical model provides a firm basis for organizing footage. This is why *Documatic*'s tagging system uses a basic categorical documentary approach to structure the referenced video segments. It automatically provides "Introduction" and "Ending" segments and allows users to create their own sections, which they tag while filming to group semantically similar pieces of footage across different interviews.

To aid filmmakers in editing the footage once it has been organized into categories, a supplementary, syntactical rule-set is included. This secondary rule-set is based on a study of categorical style documentaries such as Errol Morris's *Fast Cheap and Out of Control* [9]. It breaks down individual sections of a documentary into three fundamental footage elements: *Interview*, *Exhibit*, and *Narration*. *Documatic* uses these three sub-elements to automatically intelligently layer footage in the editing stages.

Interview footage serves as the bulk of the content for most categorical documentary films. It consists of video from a camera pointed at a person (typically a close-up head shot), who is making a statement or answering questions. A single interview is often cut into smaller clips and takes from different interviewees can be grouped according to topics regarding what was being said in each clip. These groupings by topic form the individual sections of the overall categorical documentary.

Exhibit footage consists of superimposed shots that illustrate what is being discussed by an interviewee or narrator.

Narration adds the filmmaker's voice as a transition between categories or explanation a particular piece of exhibit footage.

By using these simple rules to guide the production process many steps of the film material assembly process can be automated. They can support the filmmaker in terms of organization and structuring without limiting the artistic approach or content. Using a logical, yet semantic, system has the additional benefit in that individual projects can be handed off to a third-party with a clear and pre-implanted structure.

4.2 System Overview and Walkthrough

What follows is a sample walkthrough to illustrate the functionality of the *Documatic* system, based upon a set of actual use cases/user tests. "Mary", one of the first users of *Documatic*, is interested in creating a documentary about people and their dogs in the park. Mary asks her friend "Adam" for help filming the documentary, but wants main directorial control of the project.

4.2.1 Pre-Production

As a very first step, Mary launches the *Documatic* app from her Android-powered smartphone (Google's Nexus One [2.3.6]). She creates a new project called, "Long Dogs." A new project is automatically generated for her with initial "Introduction" and "Ending" sections. The team discusses possible topics and interview questions. For each topic they add another section to the overall project via the "New Section" button. Eventually, they compile a list of topics which represent both the questions they want to ask, and the sections that will comprise the final film (see fig. 2 left). This dynamic list can be re-arranged at any time, but provides an initial structure to the evolving documentary.

Figure 2. Example screen shots for setting up the initial structure (left); tagging during shooting (right)

4.2.2 Production: Recorder and Annotator

When the duo arrives at the park, they synchronize the clocks on Mary's phone, and Adam's camera. After they find an interviewee, Mary, acting as the "annotator," inputs the subject's preliminary information into the Android app. From now on, the new subject's information – e.g. "Henry and Spot" – can be automatically applied to shots. Adam acts as the "recorder," sets up the shot, and starts recording as Mary begins the interview.

At this point, the recorder's role is exactly the same as in a larger film production. He is responsible for the quality of the shot itself, keeping the person in the frame, in focus, and monitoring audio levels. He does not have to engage with the responses and is thus able to get the highest quality footage possible.

Similarly, Mary's job of conducting the interview is made easier through this division of labor. The initial layout of topics serves as a supportive list of talking points for her to cover, and it also provides the necessary real-time tagging annotation of the footage recorded by Adam's camera. Mary taps the sectional tag in the interface's list corresponding to the topic being discussed by the interviewee and creates additional tags as the interview evolves. If the subject, for instance, begins by discussing the breed of the pet, but then immediately starts talking about what factors affect its cuteness, Mary simply taps the "Cuteness" menu item, and any video being recording during this time is automatically categorized into the "Cuteness" section and linked to the subjects, "Henry and Spot." While footage is being annotated, the theme of the user interface flashes bright red to indicate that virtual clips are being recorded. New sections can be added on the fly, even in the middle of an interview.

After the interview, one can use the system to collect *Exhibit* footage that illustrates what the interviewee was discussing, and these clips will be automatically linked to that specific person. The documentarians can also optionally record audio snippets of *Narration* to introduce specific sections of the film for later use.

4.2.3 Post-Production: Pre-Editing / Refinement

Whether the team is prepared to produce finalized, distributable video, or just wants to get a quick feel for how the video is coming together, the post-production process is made simpler with the *Documatic* system. One first copies the project's folder from the Android device to the editing machine. Next, they copy the "raw" video files from the camera's card to this folder. Then, they can use a Project Generator program. *Documatic* automatically synthesizes a new, "pre-edited" XML sequence based on the information from the tags and the corresponding time code on the raw footage. Dragging the new sequence file into a Non-Linear editor like *Adobe Premiere CS5*, reveals this labeled, annotated, and pre-structured video sequence (fig. 3).

Technically, all the arranged clips are tagged subclips of the full video files. If anything important was cut off a particular clip by the automatic generator, the human editor can adjust the in- and out-points of any subclip at any time.

Figure 3. Outcome: automatically, intelligently segmented video, with pre-generated name-tags for interviewees

Unlike rigidly structured video systems, the documentarians can go back and forth throughout these Pre-Production, Production, and Post-Production phases at will. At any time they can generate a full sequence, plan new topics, or collect more interviews and add them to the editing project.

4.2.4 Collaboration

The *Documatic* system is not a unidirectional process. Instead, it harnesses Murtaugh's "Evolving Documentary" idea to let documentarians iteratively augment and share their works. Multiple project folders from distinct film crews can be copied together, and the Project Generator synthesizes them together intelligently. Since the Documatic production process is based on structuring the collected footage in a meaningful way (as opposed to the pure syntax of shot/scene numbers), it can be much easier to share or pass along a documentary project to other filmmakers without prior knowledge of an overall theme or outline.

5. DESIGN EVALUATION / EVOLUTION

One of the most important discoveries made during the design process and the testing phase of *Documatic* was the value in exploiting the unique timestamps. In the initial phases of the design, there was much focus on determining the optimal way to directly communicate and pair the semantic data of the annotations with the raw data of the video files in real-time. Several different systems were designed to use either Bluetooth or network communication to share these two sets of data between phones, but none of these methods met the design criteria for agency and independence.

To better situate the annotator's attention more on the interview than the device, the UI's design went through several iterations. Haptic feedback and categorical clustering led to a less obtrusive interface.

6. Extensions

Since *Documatic*'s underlying framework is based on universal timestamps it can be adapted to a wider context. The interactor's tags can be used not only as annotations of a specific video, but rather of a unique *time* and *place* in history. This opens up several ways to extend the system to encompass a wide variety of additional features and uses.

For large events, like a political protest, one could have an indiscriminate amount of people, filming and annotating throughout the day. Then they could separately upload these video files, and time-stamped XML annotations to a central server. Based on combinations of this data interesting views of the day could be automatically generated representing individual or merged experiences from the group as a whole. Films like *Burma VJ* [10] or the Beastie Boys' documentary [11] would be ripe for this approach to digital participation.

A documentary is just one possibility of this fully digital video production process. By modeling other cinematic genres, one could begin producing digital, semi-automated sitcoms, thrillers, or dramas. In fact, one could create a procedural model creation system, where users generate their own rule-sets of custom complexity to replace the current categorical model – leading to an auto-generation of custom-build content tailored to their own preferences. A single audience member might query a large database with her list of interests, which are checked against the existing tags, and a pre-cut movie could be generated for the viewer. This supports the database approaches mentioned above.

7. CONCLUSIONS

The most important aspect of *Documatic* is that it provides a complete workflow for producing and assembling video data procedurally. By pairing annotation with video, and forming intelligent rule sets, it simplifies the labor intensive video-editing process. However, it remains an assistive system that supports but not replaces a filmmaker's creativity. It thus avoids any limitation to the filmmaker's ideas while easing the workload.

8. ACKNOWLEDGMENTS

Thanks to the participants, like Mariam Asad, for their help in evaluating and improving the system.

9. REFERENCES

[1] Murtaugh, M. 1996. *The Automatist Storytelling System: Master's Thesis*. Cambridge: MIT.

[2] Adobe. *Premiere Pro CS5*. http://www.adobe.com/products/premiere.html

[3] Murtaugh, M. 1996. *The Automatist Storytelling System: Master's Thesis*. Cambridge: MIT.

[4] Adobe. *On Location* http://www.adobe.com/products/onlocation.html

[5] Manovich, L. (n.d.). *Form*. Retrieved Sept. 2010, from Lev Manovich: Soft Cinema: http://softcinema.net/form.htm

[6] Bernard, S. C. (2004). *Documentary Storytelling for Film and Videomakers*. Oxford: Focal Press.

[7] Manovich, L. (2000). *Language of New Media*. 27

[8] Bordwell, D., & Thompson, K. (2004). *Film Art*. 132

[9] Morris, E. *Fast Cheap and Out of Control*. 1997.

[10] Ostergaard, Anders. *Burma VJ*. 2010.

[11] Yauch, Adam. *Awesome I Fuckin' Shot That!*. 2006

A Comparative Study on Distant Free-Hand Pointing

Ondřej Poláček, Martin Klíma, Adam J. Sporka
Faculty of Electrical Engineering, Czech Technical University in Prague,
Karlovo nám. 13, 12135 Praha 2, Czech Republic
{polacond, xklima, sporkaa}@fel.cvut.cz

Pavel Žák, Michal Hradiš, Pavel Zemčík, Václav Procházka
Graph@FIT, Brno University of Technology
Božetechova 1/2, 612 66 Brno, Czech Republic
{izakpa, ihradis, zemcik}@fit.vutbr.cz
xproch12@stud.fit.vutbr.cz

ABSTRACT
In this paper we present a comparative study of free-hand pointing, an absolute remote pointing device. Unimanual and bimanual interaction were tested as well as the static reference system (spatial coordinates are fixed in the space in front of the TV) and novel body-aligned reference system (coordinates are bound to the current position of the user). We conducted a point-and-click experiment with 12 participants. We have identified the preferred interaction areas for left- and right-handed users in terms of hand preference and preferred spatial areas of the interaction. In bimanual interaction, the users relied more on dominant hand, switching hands only when necessary. Even though the remote pointing device was faster than the free-hand pointing, it was less accepted probably due to its low precision.

Categories and Subject Descriptors
H.5.2 [**Information interfaces and presentation**]: User Interfaces – *Input devices and strategies*

General Terms
Experimentation, Measurement, Performance.

Keywords
Free-Hand Pointing, Remote Pointing Device, Mouse, Bimanual Interaction, Fitt's Law, Kinect, Wii

1. INTRODUCTION
Since Bolt's famous Put-That-There system [1], the distant pointing techniques and devices have made a large progress. Today we witness a great commercial success of computer games that are controlled by body motion and limb gestures, which is a very intuitive and responsive way of input. Playing such games requires a system that is capable of tracking the current position and motion of the user. In our work, we investigated performance of two existing commercial systems, *Kinect* and *Wii,* in terms of speed and pointing precision.

In our study we target two scenarios where the user can navigate the user interface distantly and no direct touch is required. The first scenario is an Interactive TV. Both *Kinect* and *Wii* are intended to be used with a TV as a special remote control device. Besides playing games, they both can be used to control a user interface of an Interactive TV. The other scenario is a large public display presenting information such as indoor navigation, planned events, booking of rooms and seats, etc. in a public building like a library. Let us further imagine that the display is large enough to let several users work at the same time. In this case, we can introduce a dedicated user interface for each detected user. As the user moves along the large display, the UI controls are following her or him.

EuroITV'12, July 4–6, 2012, Berlin, Germany.

Figure 1. A silhouette of the user interacting bimanually

2. RELATED WORK
Several works exist that have focused on the remote large display navigation, gesture recognition, and remote pointing. The Fitt's law [2] is a well described model and it has been proven, that it works for touch as well as for remote pointing with Wii [3]. Test of two remote input devices for Interactive TV [4] resulted in conclusion that the mouse is strongly preferred technique. According to Riek et al. [5], the Fitt's law is surprisingly not violated in bimanual aiming task.

The distant display pointing techniques have been elaborated for menu selection problem [6] or button pressing [7]. Clark et al. [8] explored multimodal interfaces for distant and close interaction.

Several different techniques have been introduced for pointing. Some of them (e.g. [9,10]) are based on computer vision using regular cameras and are able to handle both pointing and touching while not requiring any additional devices held by the user. *Samsung ES8000* is an example of a commercial product operated by gestures. Others (e.g. [11, 12]) require additional hardware which can be an obstacle for use in our proposed scenarios. Vogel et al. [13] used a commercial motion tracking system that allowed emulating click by precise finger gestures.

3. OUR SOLUTION

Our free-hand pointing solution utilizes motion sensing device *Microsoft Kinect* originally developed for *Xbox 360* game console. The device is placed below a screen and it monitors area in front of the screen. *OpenNI* library (http://www.openni.org/) was used to track the user. Compared to professional motion tracking systems, this solution is much cheaper but less precise.

A silhouette of the user is displayed on the screen and two cursors are shown on the user's palms (see Figure 1). As the palm moves the cursor moves accordingly on the screen. Click operation is performed by moving palm forward or backward the screen by 3 inches (approx. 7.5 cm). These movements resemble pushing and pulling a button.

Besides a user interface, in which elements do not change the position (fixed reference system, further referred to as *static*), we also implemented a user interface, in which the reference system follows the center of the user's body (body-aligned reference system, further referred to as *dynamic*). In other words, whole user interface moves on the screen along with the user's motion. The difference between these two user interfaces is depicted in the Figure 2.

Figure 2. a. Static interface – the UI element, depicted as green circle, do not change the position as the user moves. b. Dynamic interface – the UI element moves along with the user.

4. EXPERIMENT

The aim of the experiment was to compare four versions of the free-hand pointing interface with a remote pointing device and a PC mouse. The PC mouse was the only indirect pointing device and it was used only as a baseline method. We expected the mouse to outperform the other mentioned methods. The following interaction methods were prepared for the comparison test:

- *Free-hand dynamic bimanual.* The user interface was following the position of the participant who could use both hands for pointing.
- *Free-hand dynamic unimanual.* The user interface was following the position of the participant, who used only dominant hand for pointing.
- *Free-hand static bimanual.* The participant could use both hands for pointing.
- *Free-hand static unimanual.* The participant used only dominant hand for pointing.
- *Remote pointing device. Nintendo Wii* remote control was used. The remote control has the ability to determine its position using a built-in infrared camera that monitors infrared LED diodes mounted on top of the TV, called sensor bar. The mouse cursor was directly manipulated by the device. Mouse click was actuated by pressing the trigger on the bottom of the device.
- *Mouse.* A common computer optical mouse was used. *Enhanced pointer precision* option in *MS Windows* was turned off.

The performance of each method was measured using a sequence of 100 point-and-click target acquisition tasks. Each participant was requested to aim and click on circles that appeared one-by-one on the screen. There were three levels of size (32, 64, and 128 px in diameter) and three levels of distance between the successive circles (128, 256, and 512 px). Both levels were being randomly selected during the task. The objective data collected in the task were processed into three indicators as follows:

- *Point time*, which is the duration needed to move the pointer to a circle.
- *Click time*, which is the duration needed to perform a click operation on a circle.
- *Selections per turn*, which is a number of how many times the pointer crossed the border of the target in one turn (the point-and-click task). This measure is a quantification of precision of the interaction method.

The point-and-click experiment ran on a personal computer connected to a 40" Samsung LCD TV with resolution 1280x720 pixels. All participants were told to stand 6 feet (approx. 1.8m) far from the TV.

12 participants took part in the experiment. They were recruited from the university staff (4 women, 8 men, mean age=34, SD=8.6) and were all experienced computer users, however they had no previous experience with *Kinect* or *Wii* systems Ten participants were right-handed. Within-subject experimental design was used, the factor was the choice of the interaction method.

Participants were asked to complete the sequence of 100 tasks for each input method. The order of presentation was counterbalanced using a Latin square to compensate for a learning effect. The entire session (all six series) lasted for approximately 30 minutes. After completing all tasks, the participants were asked to complete a questionnaire.

5. RESULTS

5.1 Speeds

The measured values in the experiment are summarized in the Table 1. The ANOVA test and pairwise t-test with Bonferroni correction were used to find statistically significant differences in mean quantities among the methods. The task times suggest that pointing device is slightly faster than free-hand pointing. However, the only significant difference in the task times ($F(5,66) = 11.9$, $p<<.001$) is between the mouse and all other methods as expected. Using dynamic interface is a bit slower than static as a distant circle gets even farther while the user trying to reach it. The static unimanual interface is significantly faster than the dynamic unimanual interface for both pointing ($F(5, 7032) = 207.0$, $p<<.001$) and clicking (($F(5, 7032) = 61.7$, $p<<.001$). Bimanual interaction is faster than unimanual and it is significantly faster in dynamic interfaces in the point and click times. Remote pointing device was faster than all the free-hand pointing methods in point time but it is less precise as selection per turn suggests. Compared to the static interfaces, the pointing device is even significantly less precise ($F(5, 7032) = 48.9$, $p<<.001$).

Table 1. Mean times and standard deviations (SD) for each measured value and modality.

	dynamic bimanual		dynamic unimanual		static bimanual		static unimanual		remote pointing device		mouse	
	mean	SD	mean	SD	mean	SD	mean	SD	mean	SD	mean	SD
Task time [s]	215.3	26.0	263.4	85.6	201.8	40.6	213.2	50.6	186.4	52.5	110.7	13.3
Point time [ms]	1073	428	1173	552	1054	432	1102	438	889	419	685	226
Click time [ms]	1022	1184	1188	1269	961	1054	962	1033	953	914	432	225
Selections per turn	1.64	1.3	1.7	1.3	1.5	1.1	1.5	1.1	1.7	1.2	1.1	0.3

5.2 Hands usage

In case of bimanual interaction, participants relied more on their dominant hand. The Figure 3 shows ratio between left and right hand for the right-handed participants on the screen divided into 9x5 grid. The number in each cell indicates the percentage of use of the right hand in that region. Note that in front of the body, the participants used mostly right hand (70-77%). For the left-handed participants the situation is mirrored. Figure 4 shows mean point times for each region when using right hand in static unimanual interaction. Mean times on the right of the screen are generally shorter than those on the left.

Figure 3. Ratio of right hand usage in different positions on the screen. Red and blue colors (light and dark grey on B/W print) correspond to left and right hands respectively

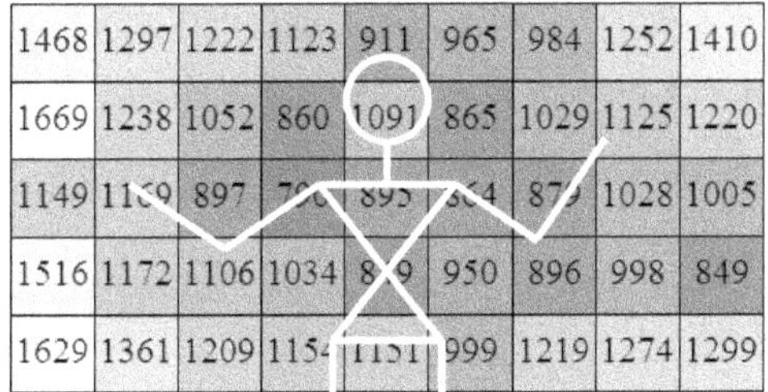

Figure 4. Mean point times in different positions on the screen when using right hand in static unimanual interaction.

5.3 Fitt's law

Fitt's law [2] provides model of human movement in simple pointing task. It predicts the time required to point (movement time, MT) at a target. The model can be mathematically formulated as follows:

$$MT = a + bID \tag{1}$$

$$ID = \log_2(2A/W) \tag{2}$$

where a and b are device-dependent parameters, ID is index of difficulty of a combination of target distance (or amplitude, A), and width W. In our experiment, there were three different amplitudes (distances between successive circles) as well as target widths (circle diameter), which yielded 5 different indices of difficulty.

In order to find models for each method, a linear regression was performed. The results are shown in the Figure 5. The Table 2 shows a and b values as well as correlation of a model for each method. Note, that correlations are high even for bimanual interaction methods. We believe that this is caused by participant's strategy of changing hands – they tend to use one hand until a circle was too difficult to reach. Then they switched hands and continued in the same manner. The bimanual interaction actually consisted of series of unimanual interaction.

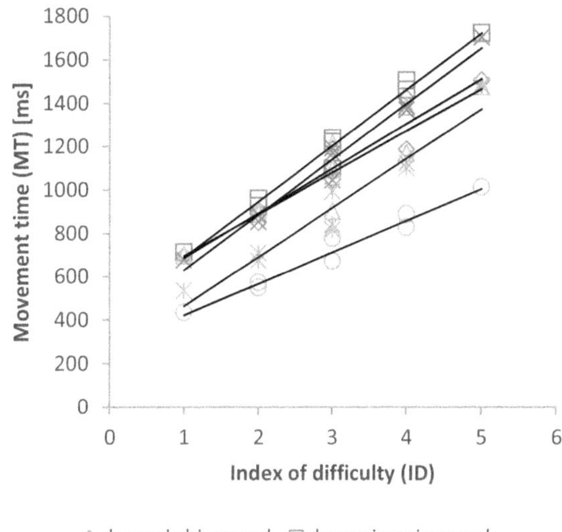

Figure 5. Linear regression between the pointing time (MT) and index of difficulty (ID)

Table 2. Parameters of Fitt's law model for each method.

	A	B	correlation (r)
dynamic bimanual	481.7	205.9	.962
dynamic unimanual	430.5	258.2	.990
static bimanual	504.2	192.3	.926
static unimanual	373.9	255.8	.988
pointing device	235.4	227.5	.968
mouse	275.5	145.6	.981

5.4 Subjective results

The participants were asked to rate all the methods in terms of perceived speed, comfort and accuracy on a five-item Likert scale (1 – certainly yes, 5 – certainly no). The median values of collected data are depicted in the Figure 6. Static interfaces were rated better than dynamic ones and they were also rated better than the pointing device. However, the mouse received the best scores among all the methods.

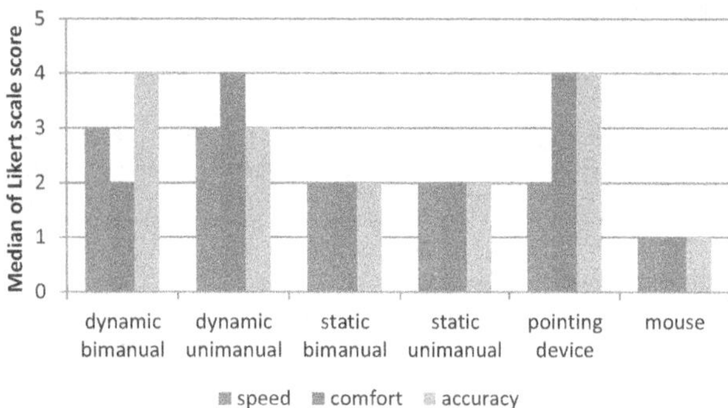

Figure 6. Subjective scores

Free-hand pointing was quite intuitive for all participants but the click operation was found cumbersome. As already mentioned, click was triggered by moving palm forward or backward the screen by 3 inches. This was found difficult to perform. We observed that the instruction "*move your palm forward*" was interpreted by the participants as palm movement in a straight line defined by shoulder and current position of palm (see Figure 7a). When the arm is stretched, the meaning of the command is to rotate the arm forward (or backward) in the shoulder.

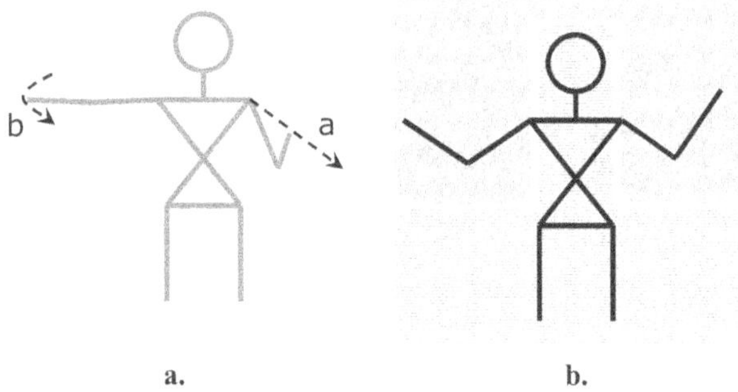

a. b.

Figure 7. a. Meaning of command "move the hand forward" for bent (a) and stretched (b) arm positions. b. Regions suitable (blue vertical lines) and unsuitable (red horizontal lines) for interaction.

We also asked the participants to comment comfortable and uncomfortable hand positions when using free-hand pointing. The regions suitable for interaction are depicted in Figure 7b by blue horizontal lines. The less comfortable positions are shown in red vertical lines. Almost all participants complained about interaction in front of their head as they did not see the screen properly. Six participants did not like to interact in front of their body, four of them complained about lower positions of the hand. On the other hand, they mostly appreciated positions besides their body and higher positions. In unimanual interaction they complained about interaction on the other side of their body.

6. CONCLUSION

The comparative study has shown that free-hand interaction with dynamic interfaces is slower and less accepted by the users than static interfaces. Even though remote pointing device was faster than free-hand pointing, it was less accepted probably due to its low precision. The study has also shown that in bimanual interaction, the users rely more on dominant hand and they switch hands only when necessary. We have also identified suitable regions for free-hand interaction.

We believe that these results can be applied for future designs of user interfaces for both Interactive TV and public large displays. In the future work we would like to aim at finding actual usability of a dynamic interface, not only its performance.

7. ACKNOWLEDGMENTS

This work has been supported by the EU FP7 project TA2: Together Anywhere, Together Anytime ICT-2007-214793, grant no 214793, and the grant OHK3-048/10 Automatically generated user interfaces in nomadic applications.

8. REFERENCES

[1] Bolt, R. 1980. "Put-that-there": Voice and gesture at the graphics interface. Proc. of SIGGRAPH '80, ACM Press, 262-270.

[2] MacKenzie, I.S. 1995. Movement Time Prediction in Human-Computer Interfaces. Readings in human-computer interaction (2nd ed.), Morgan Kaufmann, 483-493.

[3] McArthur, V., Castellucci, S. J., MacKenzie, I. S. 2009. An empirical comparison of "wiimote" gun attachments for pointing tasks. Proc. of EICS'09, ACM Press, 203-208.

[4] MacKenzie I.S., Juosh, S. 2001 An Evaluation of Two Input Devices for Remote Pointing. In Engineering for Human-Computer Interaction, Springer-Verlag, 235-250.

[5] Riek, S., Tresilian, J.R., Mon-Williams, M., Coppard, V.L., Carson, R.G. 2003. Bimanual aiming and overt attention: one law for two hands. Experimental Brain Research, vol. 153, Springer-Verlag, 59-75.

[6] Bailly, G., Walter, R., Müller, J., Ning, T., Lecolinet, E. 2011. Comparing Free Hand Menu Techniques for Distant Displays Using Linear, Marking and Finger-Count Menus. Proc. of INTERACT'11, Springer-Verlag, 248-262.

[7] Cesar, P., Chorianopoulos, K. 2009. The Evolution of TV Systems, Content, and Users Toward Interactivity. Foundations and Trends in Human–Computer Interaction, vol. 2, Now Publishers, 373-395.

[8] Clark, A., Dunser, A., Billinghurst, M., Piumsomboon, T., Altimira, D. 2011. Seamless Interaction in Space. Proc. of OzCHI '11, ACM Press, 88-97.

[9] Freeman, W. T., Weissman, C. 1995. Television control by hand gestures. International Workshop on Automatic Face- and Gesture- Recognition, IEEE Computer Society,179-183.

[10] Schick, A., Camp, F., Ijsselmuiden, J., Stiefelhagen, R. 2009. Extending touch: towards interaction with large-scale surfaces. Proc. of ITS '09, ACM Press, 117-124.

[11] Parker, K., Mandryk, R. L., Inkpen, K. M. 2006. Integrating Point and Touch for Interaction with Digital Tabletop Displays. IEEE Computer Graphics and Applications, vol.26, IEEE Computer Society, 28–35.

[12] Bi, X., Shi, Y., Chen, X. 2006. uPen: A Smart Pen-like Device for Facilitating Interaction on Large Displays, Proc. of Conference on Horiz. Interactive Human-Computer Systems, IEEE Computer Society, 160-168.

[13] Vogel, D., Balakrishnan, R. 2005. Distant freehand pointing and clicking on very large, high resolution displays. Proc. of UIST'05, ACM Press, 33-42.

A Set of Recommendations for the Control of IPTV-Systems via Smart Phones based on the Understanding of Users Practices and Needs

Regina Bernhaupt, Mael Boutonnnet, Bastien Gatellier, Yannick Gimenez, Christian Pouchepanadin, Latifa Souiba
IRIT, Université Paul Sabatier
118, Route de Narbonne
31062 Toulouse, France
+33 561 55 8209
{regina.bernhaupt, mael.boutonnet, bastien.gatellier}@irit.fr
{gimenez.yannick, c.pouchepanadin, latifa.souiba}@gmail.com

ABSTRACT
This paper describes recommendations for the design of a smart phone application enabling users to control IPTV-systems including all connected devices. Recommendations are based on findings from a media study focusing on how people currently use their IPTV systems and associated devices in their homes. The media study applied an ethnographic oriented method called playful probing. From the user's perspective the ideal smart phone application provides them on a general level with a simplified set of (touch-enabled) buttons to control and navigate. The application should support them in their most frequent tasks (e.g. watching TV, listening to music) and overall shall enhance the experience by providing additional information to the TV channel currently selected, by supporting their need for privacy and by allowing them to achieve a certain level of security. In terms of interaction techniques, users prefer flexible touch interaction and (a limited set of) speech commands over gesture, with the exception of being able to directly point at a device to identify it for direct control.

Categories and Subject Descriptors
H. 5.2. [User Interfaces] I.5.2 [Design Methodology] Mobile Phone application design.

General Terms
Design, Human Factors.

Keywords
mobile phone applications, remote control, control, entertainment environment, cultural probing.

1. INTRODUCTION
The IPTV landscape is continuously changing. While watching TV is still a rather passive activity, there is a variety of activities related to the consumption of moving images including video, movies, short clips or standard TV formats, that has become rather active, involving handling and controlling a variety of devices and controls.

As simply watching TV, selecting media content, or setting up any form of entertainment devices has become more complicated than ever before, there is a need for new forms of control in the entertainment environment. One possibility is to use smart phone applications to enable the user to control a variety of devices and to perform additional tasks that enhance the overall entertainment experience. Smart phones additionally enable the user to use new forms of interaction techniques to control their entertainment environment, like speech, gesture or touch. Instead of navigating with a set of different (infra red based) remote controls through a set of menus, users might simply talk to the mobile phone, perform a gesture or select quickly interact via touch with the smart phone application.

Goal of this paper is to provide a set of design recommendations for the next generation of smart phone applications that enable the control of all IPTV systems and connected devices in users homes. The set of recommendations is based on a media study that investigates how people currently use their smart phone as part of their entertainment environment, what ideas users have for future usage of smart phone applications, to understand what type of problems related to IPTV can be successfully solved with smart phone applications and how to enhance the overall user experience of today's IPTV offers with such a type of application.

2. STATE OF THE ART
2.1 IPTV and Media Usage
Gauntlett and Hill [11] have studied TV usage in the home in one of the largest media studies, including 500 participants. Their key findings were that the TV is still a focus of attention and watching TV is influenced by social interaction. Viewing habits differ immensely between age groups, gender and personal interests. Bernhaupt et al. [5], have investigated media consumption in a

series of ethnographic studies, reporting that (1) the living room is still a social and an individual place, and that technology is only becoming part of that personal space if it supports the feelings of being at home, respecting people's privacy, (2) TV is strongly related to other activities in the home, (3) interaction techniques, especially the growing number of remote controls, are perceived as difficult to use, and that (4) watching TV is still a social activity allowing people "to be together".

TV is principally seen as a leisure activity, and most often TV is a rather passive activity [14]. Several studies have shown that the interactivity of interactive TV systems is not always welcomed, but a series of studies demonstrated that additional services and supports can enhance the overall user experience: Ethnographic studies and ethnographically-oriented field studies investigated the application of new services and systems in the home, including the application of new recommender systems [5], personalization approaches and the enhancement of the social experience [8]. Other studies on media consumption typically focused on a particular media technology, for example the introduction of a set-top box in people's home [24]. Seager et al. [28] investigated the use of triple-play services, focusing on the different devices employed in the households.

To summarize, media consumption is steadily changing. While five to seven years ago, the TV was the main source for entertainment-related content like movies, series or news, today Internet access and a multitude of new (specialized) devices have changed who is consuming what kind of media. Especially in the area of interactive TV, these changes in media consumption are important, as the future generation of iTV systems shall support new forms of media consumption without having iTV and IPTV completely replaced by a simple combination of a PC/Laptop and a large screen. To support the development of future interactive TV systems and services there is a need to understand user practices and behaviors.

2.2 Interaction Techniques related to Mobile Phones

Smart phones do support the following three basic ways to enhance the interaction: (1) touch-based interaction (2) gesture and (3) voice/speech. Other possible ways of interaction (e.g. using the camera) were not focus of this study.

2.2.1 Voice/ Speech

The study of using voice as means of interacting with a computing system has its root in the area of natural language processing [11]. Elder was one of the first ones to consider speech as an interaction technique [10]. Applying speech as interaction technique for iTV systems seems advantageous: Speech interaction can be hands free, thus enabling the user to naturally interact with the system without the need to take any device in his hands. For the interaction with an iTV system two possibilities exist: the user can either use natural speech or the speech entry is restricted to a certain set of commands. Natural speech as been investigated by Goto et al. [16] conducting a Wizard-of-Oz experiment to investigate natural language for interacting with TV. Based on their goal to design a "television operation interface easy enough for anybody to use" results were promising. Participants in the study stated that program selection was easy, that they could directly access any information necessary without the need to go through hierarchical structured menus or program information. Balchadran [3] presented in 2007 a standard remote control that allowed natural language input for the dialog management.

In 2009, Turunen et al., [31] presented a multimodal media center interface, combining voice, gesture and physical touch. Users were given full control over the media center via its speech user interface. It's grammar was containing about 110 words, which reached a high recognition accuracy of more than 93%. In their user experience evaluation they found that users preferred physical touch and gesture interfaces. Speech input was less preferred by the users: speech input was considered not robust by the users, which was probably due to the "small" number of words. Turunen et al. explained the low preference rating with the fact that the multi-modal interaction with gesture and vocal might have disturbed the results of the vocal interaction (e.g. the microphone was in a "more challenging" angle).

The second approach for speech is the usage of voice as a triggering sound. Igarashi et al. [17] present in their study three different types of a what they call "Voice as Sound" (VaS) technique. The first one is to control functions induced by continuous voice, meaning the user has to keep making a sound (e.g. "Volume up, ahhhhhhh") for the command to continue. The second one is an extension of the first one, where the pitch of the voice is used as a one-dimensional joystick. For instance, if the user is using "Volume up, ahhh" and is raising the pitch of his "ahhh", the volume will increase faster. It is combined with a speed-dependent automatic zooming interface. The last one is a slightly different one, considering it is a discrete control by tonguing. The objective was to offer an alternative for non-continuous variables, such as channel, for instance. For the tonguing the user has to simply clap their hands or snap their fingers instead of the use of short voice-noises. The advantage of these techniques is that the users can stop its command as soon as they are satisfied, because of the immediate feedback.

While such a type of interface can be helpful for users that cannot use their hands due to physical disabilities, the participants in the evaluation study were less positive. This type of interaction has been perceived as unnatural.

Voice/speech interaction is in general well perceived by users, but it poses a set of difficulties when applied in the context of iTV: with the main goal of enjoying media, including sound/speech recognition in this environment is difficult. It implies the necessity that the user actively activates the speech recognition, to avoid any misleading interpretation of the sound in the living room. It additionally needs enhanced technical solutions (e.g. special microphones in the TV or remote control) to enable the user to perform speech input.

2.2.2 Gesture

Gesture has been become accepted widely as a possible means of controlling devices due to its success in video games. It offers the advantages that it does not require visual attention from the user on the remote control, but supports a completely blind usage, enabling the user to solely focus on the TV screen. Gesture interaction has been reported to be well accepted by users [19], [26]. What is important to note is weather mobile phones can be reasonably well used as pointing devices. Evidence here is contradicting showing that pointing is not possible [32], while others have shown the ability to use them for pointing [25].

Gesture interaction based on a Wii-mote has been recently investigated in the context of TV [2] replacing traditional remote controls. Findings indicate that users perform naturally pitch and yaw gestures when interacting with a gesture instead of the remote control. Gestures seem appropriate to enable eyes-free interaction, and to avoid the continuous problem of selecting buttons on a standard remote control. In a second study the same authors studies free hand gesture. It was shown that the optimal mapping between mid-air gestures and directional actions strongly depends on context [1]. Using linear, marking and finger-count menus the authors achieved an accuracy rate in their user tests above 93%. In their conclusion they state that typing on a physical remote control will remain faster than using gesture to control the iTV with free-hand gesture. However, users mentioned that they would appreciate to be able to use freehand gesture as a "complementary tool" for specific actions.

Hybrid techniques combining mid-air gestures and buttons were especially efficient, with the further advantage of compatibility with pure button-based techniques. As designers will want to look for eyes-free interactions, techniques using a directional pad or pitch and yaw for transposing 2D marking menus to the mid-air space are recommended. Though, purely gestural techniques tend to be slightly lower, in terms of performance. It is necessary to focus on keeping it simple, and to keep in mind that designing for the entertainment in the home, especially for the living room, poses a unique context.

2.2.3 Touch

To enhance or replace remote controls with touch-based input has been suggested by Mackenzie and Enns [22]. They presented a remote control including touch and gesture. In general, touch interaction has been getting more and more important with the rise of smart-phones. Nowadays, almost everyone is able to touch a screen, almost naturally. While touch interaction was well researched within the last 20 years [15], it still seems to have difficulties to enter in today's living rooms [26]. The drawbacks of classical remote controls are said to be their lack of scalability and their difficulty in supporting new technologies. Touch-based interaction for remote controls could help to simplify the interaction, supporting flexibility in terms of task-oriented support, simply changing the number of buttons shown on the screen.

Mobile phones including touch may not only be used to directly control iTV devices. Tsekleves et al. [30] investigated the usage of mobile phones as second screens. Users preferred the PDA prototype over the standard remote control.

Touch interaction can pose a set of usability problems, including the limitation that touch interfaces cannot be used blindly (compared to a standard remote control were users can feel the buttons), that touch interaction needs new forms of communication with the TV and iTV system (standard devices still operate with infra red as input) like connectivity in a wireless LAN. On the other hand, touch has been proven to provide a better overall user experience when interaction with an iTV system [26].

2.3 Mobile Phone Applications and Devices for ITV systems

Using mobile phones to control an ambient media player has been proposed by Lorenz et al [21] proposing an set of gestures to control the ambient media player. A complete survey of the smart phone as input devices for ubiquitous environments is available in [4].

From the user perspective, there is a variety of smart phone applications currently available for controlling iTV and IPTV systems. All producers of set top boxes and the majority of I(P)TV providers in Europe, North and South America and Asia offer this type of applications. Provider from over the top services also offer such applications, for examples Apples *Remote* developed for iPhones, iPod and iPad. To a limited extend such applications are also available for mobile phones with the Android operating system. The limitation of all these applications is that they typically can only control the set-top box. Once the user wants to control any other device in the living room, it is necessary to use an additional remote control. The smart phone thus only becomes another remote control, but has the advantage that it can be operated independent of its position. (Remote controls are still based on infra-red, so users have to point to the device they want to control, on the contrary smart phone applications operate via other technical infrastructure like WLAN.)

To overcome the limitations of WLAN based control of only the set top box, there is a set of devices allowing to control any type of IR-based device in the living room. Examples are L5 or myTVRemote for iPhones. These products are simple add-ons that are fixed on the phone via power consumption or USB, and that are able to emit infrared. A set of single standing solutions like Peel or Gear4 (Unity Remote) offers the user the possibility to put the device in their home, without the need to plug it on the smart phone. Other products additionally allow to control the whole home infrastructure including heating or lights for example BeoLink from Bang & Olufsen.

Devices enabling the control of all different types of technical protocols used for entertainment devices are (to the best of our knowledge) currently not available on the market, neither have they been investigated from a scientific media study perspective.

3. STUDY MOTIVATION AND OBJECTIVES

This study was motivated by findings within an industrial project called "Living Room 2020" financed by ruwido Austria. The goal of the project is to investigate current media consumption patterns in the living room and beyond to inform the next generation of IPTV user interfaces and interaction concepts. What we learned in this project is that a number of IPTV providers in Europe and Canada complained that their hotlines have a steady increasing number of calls related to the connection of devices and access to various sources of media content that they are not able to solve any more. One of the proposed solutions currently is to use smart phone applications to allow users to perform their TV- and entertainment oriented tasks in an easier and more enjoyable way. The success of these applications is limited, most likely due to the fact that they only allow to control one device.

Goal of the study was to understand how people currently use media systems and to identify problems and users experiences in IPTV households. Based on these findings, a set of design recommendations to inform the development of a next generation of smart phone applications is developed. The study was guided by the following research questions: (a) how people use their smart phone as part of their entertainment environment, (b) what type of problems related to IPTV can be successfully solved with smart phone applications and (c) how to enhance the overall user experience of today's IPTV offers based on such applications.

4. METHOD

To investigate what problems people currently face when using mobile phones, entertainment oriented devices, IPTV systems and other devices for entertainment in the home, and what requirements people would have for a future generation of smart phone applications, we chose an ethnographic oriented method. The method is a variation of the cultural probing approach [13] called playful probing. The methodological approach has proven to be helpful in understanding users habits, needs and requirements in a series of previous studies **Error! Reference source not found.**.

4.1 Playful Probing

An ethnographically-oriented study can be a fruitful method to investigate media usages. To investigate the above research goals and questions the study used a methodological variation of cultural probes called playful probing [6] that includes creative and playful aspects.

Playful probing uses playful elements in the probing material including participatory design tasks that are based on modeling clay. To enhance the commitment of the participants in the study a game is designed that addressed the thematic topic of the study.

In order to gain a holistic understanding of people's practices and needs and the potential for new interaction techniques, we triangulated qualitative probes material (e.g. photos, videos, interview data, some of the creativity cards, sketches) and quantitative probes material (e.g. questionnaire data, some of the creativity cards). This does not go in line with the traditional cultural probing approach proposed by Gaver et al. [13], who only used qualitative probes materials as source of inspiration for design concepts. However, the triangulation of various kinds of materials allowed us to be more confident of the collected data (consistency check) and it stimulated a richer understanding of household's technology usage patterns by addressing different aspects [18].

4.2 Households and Participants

The study was conducted in November 2011, recruiting 15 households in Toulouse, France, by local announcements, mailing lists and recruiting via Facebook. Households did not know each other. In total 30 participants older than 8 years participated in the study. As one of the goals of the study was to identify different usage practices and needs related to the usability and the overall user experience of a smart phone application, three different groups of households were recruited: (a) households with (technological-oriented) singles, (b) households with (technological-oriented) young couples or families that finished their education and (c) households with families including at least one child older than eight years. Each group had 5 households.

All households had as primary TV with one of the available IPTV offers in France (eight had Free, three had the offer called Neuf, one Bouygues, three missing).The IPTV offers all included triple play (TV, Internet and phone via IP). For thirteen of the IPTV offers there is already a smart phone application available that allows to directly control the IPTV set top box given that the mobile phone is in the same wireless LAN. The solutions do not support to control any other device in the living room.

All households had broadband internet access, ten had activated the local wireless network from the IPTV provider, seven had additionally a LAN. At least eight of the households had access to the internet via the set-top box available. Households had between one and six remote controls in their living room to control the (entertainment related) devices around the TV, only one household owned a universal remote control which was not in use.

The main TV was positioned in the living room, five households had a second TV positioned in the sleeping room, one household had three TVs. All TVs in the households received digital TV, as analog TV is no longer available in this region.

Adult participants in the household were between 19 and 51, n=22, with an average age of 33,27 (SD=9,8), 9 female, 13 male. People obtained a broad range of education levels typically for this region and professions included secretary, coiffeur, sales persons, technical engineer, household help, students and one un-employed person. The majority of participants (15) had French as their primary language, seven indicated to be bi-lingual (3 Arabic, 2 Tamil, 1 Creole, 1 Chinese). All participants indicated to speak at least one additional language (English/Spanish). Choosing multilingual participants should allow to gain insights in needs related to accessing international offers and content that is typically available in various languages.

4.3 Procedure and Material

Households were visited at the beginning of the study by the interviewer and received a household questionnaire to focus on devices and equipment that was currently installed in the household and the playful probe package (see Figure 1) including creativity probing cards, modeling clay, pens, post-it notes and a specially designed game called 1000 miles. The modeling clay was added to the probe package to encourage the participants to build some designs of simplified versions of the controls they would want to have.

The participants were asked to document important aspects of their daily life by recording videos and taking photos as well as solving tasks on the creativity cards.

At the end of the one week observation period households were visited again and a final interview was conducted. Final interviews were conducted (if possible) with all household members at the same time. In the final interview the probing material was discussed with the participants using additional questions to focus especially on the experience of the households regarding interaction techniques that could be supported by standard smart phones today (touch interaction, gesture, voice).

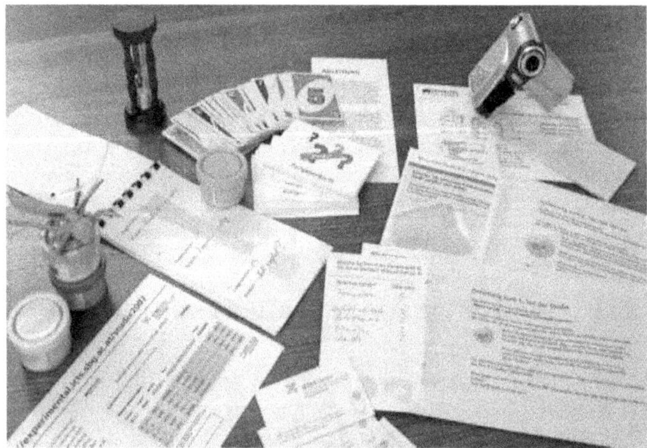

Figure 1: Example of playful probing material distributed to the households.

5. RESULTS

The results of the study were categorized using grounded theory [29] as methodological background. Results were categorized by three native speakers on an agreement basis. Based on the first open coding the axial coding focused on the research questions that guided this study. A variety of other dimensions including requests for enhanced media content, broader media offers etc were found, which are not reported in this article. Media usage is reported based on the quantitative probe material.

5.1 Media Usage

From the 22 adult participants, seventeen participants watched TV on a daily basis, 5 watched several times a week. Table 1 shows the indicated usages for various media types. The usage of media is rather high, which is in line with the three household types we recruited. Thirteen participants have been installing applications on their mobile phone, and ten have been searching application for their mobile phone in the internet. *None* of the participants *used the available application to control the set-top box* in their home.

Table 1: Media usage frequencies of the 22 adult participants: D= daily, STW=several times a week, STM= several times a month, R=rarely, N= never, AVG(SD)=avg. time spent per day in minutes with this activity (Standard deviation in min).

Media	D	STW	STM	R	N	AVG (SD)
TV	17	5				129 (74)
Radio	6	5	1	3	6	44 (38)
CD's	2	4	3	1	8	45 (28)
Reading	9	3	3	4	2	64 (35)
Notebook/PC	16	1	2		1	172 (155)
Video games/PC	1	4	2	4	8	251 (243)
Video games/Console	2	3	2	7	7	82 (83)
Internet (private)	19	1	2			-
Facebook	7	2	1	4	7	-
Mobile phone (calls private)	15	5	1	1		-
Internet via mobile phone	9	4	1	0	6	-
E-mail via mobile phone	11	3	1	0	6	-
SMS	11	7	2	1		-
Photo/Video mobile phone	2	8	2	9	1	-
Music mobile phone	4	3	1	1	7	-

Eight participants in the study were children between 8 and 17 years old, mean 12,5 (SD=3,5). They reported to watch TV at least several times a week on average 153 minutes per day (SD=98). Especially the usage of mobile phones, internet and facebook was high among the children with the majority on a daily basis.

Thirteen households reported on the probing cards, that the TV (including the set-top box) is still the most often used device in the living room, one household mentioned the PC as most used, one household the X-Box (in France, there are various offers to receive TV via the X-Box).

5.2 Direct Control and Navigation

Participants were asked on the probing cards to protocol what functions and buttons on the remote control were really important to them and what buttons they would keep for a simplified control. In terms of direct control all but one household agreed on the necessity of a simplified remote, either by reducing the number of buttons or regrouping buttons. The most important functions were changing the TV channel, Volume control, Navigations keys including ok. The households all mentioned the importance of changing volume for a specific devices (e.g. controlling the volume for the DVD player, the TV or the set-top box). Three households mentioned explicitly pause/record, one household mentioned the color keys (which are used to access important functions in the IPTV system the household used), and one household mentioned the need to access the Teletext service on the TV (to access language subtitles). These statements replicate findings from recent recordings of buttons used on IR-based remote controls in households [23].

We prompted participants to think about how a smart phone application can help to overcome the identified problems:

(1) Remote controls typically offer direct access to a range of services. Participants reported usability problems with labels that were difficult to understand and remember, or simply meaningless to them."I do not understand this abbreviation, the [smart phone] app should just have a longer label, that would make it clearer to me" [1] (household 2 (HH2), female adult). "I just don't know what happens when you press this button, there should be written something else" HH3. A smart phone application should thus provide direct control of IPTV and entertainment related devices including direct control of channels and volume, basic navigation, a limited number of usage-oriented scenarios (e.g. turn all devices on/off).

(2) To enhance the layout of the remote control to the individual needs and to support different tasks study participants would want to perform in a more efficient way, buttons should be grouped in new forms on the smart phone application.

(3) Minimal design: Study participants reported that they observed that they only need a minimal set of buttons to control their iTV experience: the application should simply offer a minimal set of buttons, and all other functions should be made available in the interface displayed on the TV.

(4) Simplification of long tasks: to support users that did not manage to solve complex tasks (e.g. accessing the latest recordings on the external hard drive), the application shall allow to simplify these tasks providing a one-button solution.

(5) Flexible display of (touch based) buttons: The application should just present buttons that are related to the currently performed task.

(6) Participants stated that the mobile phone itself would help to overcome some recurring usability problems, like the missing background light on some of the remote controls, that makes it

[1] all statements were translated from *French*

impossible for them to use them in the dark. They mentioned that the application should have the ability to restart/reinitialize devices (mobile phone app is informing about the need to update the device). Other needs were to enhance the switching between channels which is perceived as slow.

5.3 Enhancement of Interaction Technique

Touch was the preferred type of interaction with the mobile phone, but was also seen as a preferable means to enhance the current forms of remote controls. Touch was mentioned as being helpful for personalization of the controls: "I simply want to have a list of buttons and then I drag the important ones on one page" (HH5). When applying touch to any form of remote controls users requested to have a combination of buttons and a touchpad on the remote control for the most important tasks. In household 7 the participant suggested to have a touch pad to write down the three numbers with the finger, to be able to change to the channel: "I know that 637 is my favorite foreign language channel, and I could simply write that down".

Gestures were less welcomed by the users. Due to the limited functionality of the gesture based remote control that is currently in their households, users neglected to use gestures: (HH 8) "I tried to navigate the internet with these gestures, but I immediately gave up and went to my PC". Ideas on gesture usage were more related to enabling to point with the mobile phone towards a device or user interface element. "I just point on the DVD and the volume directly it [the DVD device]". HH2 wanted the same type of selection of a device by pointing but simply change the language of the program. One household member (HH12) suggested to enable interaction with the TV like in "minority report, you know, where everything is see-through and you can just move objects around".

To enhance direct access to frequently used services or functions users described speech input as a possible means. The speech input should consist only of a limited set of commands, which "you can speak directly into the mobile phone" (HH9). In household 2 one of the children (girl, 15) made a design including speech as one of the icons that can be selected in the main menu of the TV, enabling speech input.

To improve the interaction with the IPTV system participants requested to have the intelligence of all the device in the IPTV system and a simple haptic device in their hands. Household 7 said in the final interview "I just one to have one button, with a good tactile feedback, and the menu on the TV is simply showing me the things I want to get the latest movie".

5.4 Usage-Oriented Scenarios

To enhance the overall user experience households suggest to have various functions, tasks and activities grouped together. The needs and requirements stated were broad, what they had in common is that they were all around certain usages of the entertainment system or IPTV system. We refer to them as usage-oriented scenarios.

5.4.1 Supporting the user experience of watching TV

Participants reported to watch TV still on a daily basis or several times a week. A smart phone application would best support their TV experience enabling them to watch TV: simply changing channels and changing the volume is one of the basic requirements. While this sounds obvious as a request, changing volume has become a complicated task involving the volume control of the set top box and the volume control of the TV. Typically two remote controls have to be used to set the volume to an agreeable level. For watching TV it is necessary (a) to select the input source the signal is coming from (typically labeled on the remote control as "source"). This action allows to select between the various connected devices including the set-top box. (b) Once the set top box is selected, the TV offer has to be chosen in the user interface of the set-top box, for example the standard offer of the IPTV provider, or the premium content (using the remote control of the set- top box) and then (c) the user can switch between channels.

To enhance the user experience of TV watching, a smart phone application should simply allow to control the volume (hiding from the user any necessary adjustment of different volume regulations on different devices), and give the user a simple TV mode (without the need of selection in any menus or other activities). Households mentioned additionally that volume is depending on the time of the day ("you know, when I come home it is just running in the background, but when I watch a movie after dinner I want automatically a different volume value", HH11, male, 27).

5.4.2 Usage-oriented control

Beyond the need to enable the simple activity of watching TV, users stated that their most often used activities include watching DVD, to listen to music or to play. To enhance the control of such usage-oriented scenarios they suggested to have a set of buttons on one page of the application to be able to control them. The application should additionally allow to set-up, modify and delete such control settings that are related to usage-oriented scenario. The usage-oriented control (households called them control pages) should be easily accessible in one menu and should adapt to the current usage situation or personal preferences chosen.

5.4.3 Turning on and off

Enjoying any type of moving pictures in a living room means to turn on and off a multitude of devices. Depending on the usage-scenario (e.g. watching TV, watching a DVD or simply listening to music) this can involve various different devices. Users expressed their wish to have an intelligent function that automatically turns on and off the requested devices for the various usage scenarios. Other households suggesting to have just all devices turned on and off, independent of the usage scenario.

5.4.4 Selecting and handling content

Naturally, the first step to enjoy any type of content is to be able to choose and select it. Content selection has become a challenge: users reported that they have a multitude of devices or what they called "places" to look for content. This includes for example the hard disk of the set-top box for recorded programs, movies that were bought on different portals (in the IPTV systems the household owned there is a range on video-on-demand offers available, and access to (rented) movies requires to navigate to the appropriate portal), content on DVDs, content on external (additional) hard disks, content that is accessed via the local area network, content that is accessed via the games consoles (either reading a DVD, receiving premium content or accessing content via the Internet) and content that was downloaded on a PC and transferred to the TV via a USB stick.

The smart phone application should enable them to display all possible "places" where content can be accessed from a menu providing a general (device independent) overview. This would allow them to easily select the content, without the need to navigate through several interfaces and without the need to change devices.

Close to the support of such a unified views st the wish of users to display all connected devices, as a first step to select the content source, but also as a means to understand what devices are currently actively connected. "You know, I am really upset when I am already installed on the couch and then I realize that the kids unplugged the [DVD] player, to be able to connect their game [game console]". HH 3.

5.4.5 Service usages including the home context

Users presented a set of scenarios that can be supported by the smart phone application that included the control of the PC, telephone, lights, personal calendar or access to information on personal devices and services (e.g. reminders, ...). Especially for the control of web-pages on the TV screen they suggest to enhance the interaction with number and text input on the smart phone.

5.5 Design Ideas and Two-Screen Design

The probing package requested household members to provide some design ideas on how to display information on the mobile phone and on the TV screen. Users primarily kept the current form of interaction: the TV screen is the user interface, displaying the content, while the mobile phone screen is simply used to control the information displayed on the TV screen. Information on the TV screen should be shown at the borders of the screen (not like the majority of current IPTV user interfaces use the whole screen). More space of the screen should be used, the more important the information is becoming. This confirms industry attempts to design the next generation of user interfaces following the level of engagement of the users: if users are only limited engaged (e.g. they just choose the main menu) this should not hinder them from enjoying the (TV) content, but the more selections the user is making (e.g. the user chooses a sub-menu or additional information), the more space can be used.

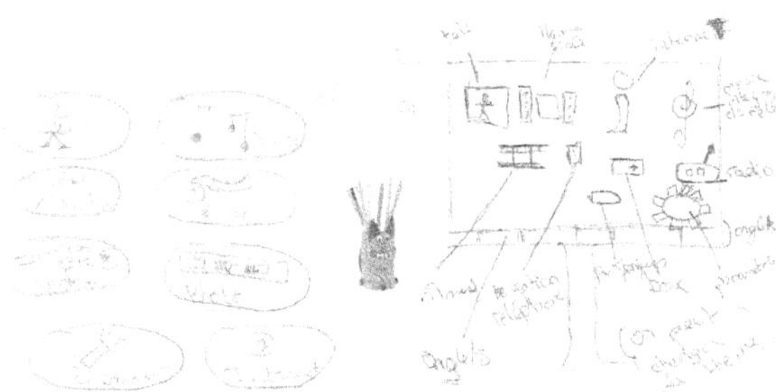

Figure 2: Depiction of two designs that were suggested by HH 2 (girl, 17, girl, 13,5). Noticeable is that both drawing suggest Internet as important category (left: button down to the right; right: depiction "i".

Designs from the users ranged from iconic views ("they simply should use the same icon view as I have on the iPhone", HH2, girl 17), to presenting the information as a pie chart or as a list (HH2, mother; HH2, girl 15,5). Figure 2 shows some of these designs. The majority of households referred to the standard design currently available (a bar, enabling the user to select items navigating left or right), or a mosaic view. Users that were speaking Arabic/Tamil preferred the user interface to be positioned at the right side of the screen.

Households today are comfortable with the idea that the user interface of the TV is structured similar to other devices like the PC, the mobile phone or Internet pages. HH 15 suggested to have a windows oriented graphical user interface, to enable to listen to the music at the same times as selecting information in the user interface displayed on the TV.

5.6 Differing Needs for Usability and UX

User practices, needs and requirements were different in the three household groups. Table 2 shows and overview on what needs households had in terms of enhanced usability and what households suggested to enhance the overall user experience.

Table 2: User needs mentioned in the study related to usability and user experience, split by household groups.

	HH with children	Technology oriented, single	Technology oriented, couple
Needs/Requirements related to the usage of the system (usability)			
Less functions; less usability problems with buttons	4	4	2
Less actions necessary, faster actions	4	5	3
Easier learning	3	4	3
Less memorizing (less cognitive load)	3	4	3
Universal remote control	1	1	2
Context awareness	2	5	1
Central control	1	1	2
Help to solve problems	1	2	1
Enhance feedback	1	0	2
Lights	0	0	1
Needs/Requirements to enhance the overall user experience			
Privacy	3	5	3
Profiles/Personalization	1	2	2
Easier recording of programs	4	2	4
Social networks	2	3	3
Additional/Enhanced information to current program	1	2	0

In terms of privacy the participants saw the mobile phone as an ideal mean to achieve privacy: private information should be displayed on the phone while information (for example photos) should be shared on the TV screen. The mobile phone was indicated to be helpful for personalization (HH6: "I can get a list of all the movies I like on the mobile phone, and I do not have to look that up on the Internet again [referring to using Internet on the PC]". The smart phone could support people in terms of recording: either by suggestions on what to record on the mobile phone or by helping to administer (one central) list of recordings for all entertainment devices. To enhance the overall user experience, participants suggested to enable access to social networks on the TV or in combination with the mobile phone, and to display additional information that accompanies the running program.

6. DESIGN RECOMMENDATIONS

Based on the user requirements identified in the field study using a playful probing approach the following design recommendations can be helpful for the development of a smart phone application.

(1) Enable the control of ALL devices related to the IPTV experience

Current smart phone applications limit the user to the control of one device (e.g. the set top box), to a set of devices that have one type of communication protocol (e.g. all infra-red controllable devices) or to the control of all devices that are in the same wireless LAN. From a user's perspective this means that the smart phone application is just another form of remote control, with the need to use additional remote controls for various tasks. To enable users to overcome current usability problems when accessing media from a set of entertainment devices the application must allow to control all the devices in the living room. This includes the support of controlling devices via infra-red (IR), various radio frequencies (RF, RF4CE) and wireless LAN. This might include the necessity to provide additional infrastructure that goes beyond standard solutions.

(2) Design for 'usage-oriented' Scenarios

When designing the application it is important to help the user perform the most important tasks, independent of the number of devices involved. This requires a detailed analysis of the tasks users typically perform with their IPTV system, including watching TV, buying and watching movies, watching DVD's, playing or listening to music. The mobile phone application should allow the user to select one of these activities and provide the most important controls related to that activity. If possible the control should be supported by some intelligent mechanisms (e.g. in the case of automatic turn on/off of the devices, or when information shall be accessed across devices.)

(3) Design for Personalization and Personal Usage

To support the user in their personal usages, the interface must enable the user to flexibly generate "quick access pages" for the most often used controls, devices, functions and services. Included should be the ability to perform a sequence of control events (for example as macros). Lessons learned from universal remote controls clearly indicate that macros are difficult for users to develop, maintain and program. We thus recommend to support the user with a set of pre-defined macros or usage scenarios that can be adapted to fit the personal needs and infrastructure in the households.

(4) Support the User to Control the Connected Home

Users need support to understand the ever increasing complexity in the living room. A smart phone application can help them to understand what devices are connected to the IPTV system, and how to perform tasks that involve the usage of different devices.

(5) Enhance the Overall User Experience

A smart phone application can be helpful to enhance the overall experience. Changing a channel today can need up to 3 seconds. People do enjoy the experience to "see what is on other channels", but with channel switching times of up to three seconds this becomes tedious. Smart phone applications can bring back this experience, allowing the user to flip through lists of channels and their content description, even allowing to give pre-views on the selected content. Thus the usability problem of slow channel switch can become a user experience in terms of enjoyment.

Other possibilities to enhance the user experience is to enable the support of privacy and security. While TV today is still used by several members of the household, the mobile phone typically is a personal device [5]. The smart phone app thus can be used to control access to special content (e.g. payment can be done via the mobile phone), to allow the user to control what is displayed on the large screen (e.g. what photos shall be shown on the TV screen, what should stay private) or by enabling context dependent display of services (e.g. the user can select on the smart phone if he wants to have the latest twitter messages displayed or not).

(6) Support Touch and Speech as Interaction Techniques

Users are open to new forms of control in their living room. Touch interaction with a smart phone has become widely accepted and was also suggested as an enhancement of current standard remote controls. Gesture was less welcome due to negative experiences with the currently available systems, but was seen as important to select devices or items by a pointing gesture. Using a limited set of speech commands is a promising approach, due to the ability of a smart phone processor to process language (maybe by simply processing speech recognition in the cloud).

7. SUMMARY AND DISCUSSION

This study presents the results from a field study using playful probing investigating user needs and requirements related to smart phone applications that enable the control of all entertainment devices. While the majority of insights seems to simply confirm our daily experiences with entertainment devices, insights in this study are unique as participating households owned the latest generation of IPTV systems including Internet access, remote controls that supported gesture, and the ability to use smart phone applications that allow the control of the set-top box.

To summarize, from user's point of view, a smart phone application that shall be successful in terms of usability and user experience shall support them with the following: (a) direct control of all devices in the living room (b) support of usage-oriented scenarios (c) enabling personalization (d) supporting control of the connected home (f) and enhancement of various user experience dimensions including enjoyment and personalization. Additionally any smart phone application can be helpful to support users in their daily usage and to overcome existing usability problems (see Table 2).

What seems to be clear is that the current generation of smart phone applications is likely to fail, as it does not support users in their initial wish to have only one central control for all their entertainment devices.

In terms of interaction technique the usage of smart phone applications is a promising step as flexible touch interaction, speech and a limited set of gestures can be used. This is partly in-line with recent findings in the literature that touch has become an acceptable means of interaction. It replicates and supports findings from [19] that gesture interaction has to be carefully designed in terms of number and type of gestures and that the simple button remote control might outperform gestures [1]. Using a smart phone for interaction via speech seems acceptable for the users. From a user perspective talking to a smart phone might feel just natural, compared to talking to a remote control.

The development of an application taking into account the above design recommendations will be a complicated endeavor. It involves the development of new types of hardware (to control IR, RF, WLAN), new forms of (bi-directional) connections (to detect all devices that are connected to a TV), and might require changes in current software on almost all devices in the living room. We are currently developing a set of new applications that will be based on the above design recommendations which should be available end of 2012.

ACKNOWLEDGEMENTS

We would like to thank all participants in the study. This research was funded in part by the project "Living room 2020".

8. REFERENCES

[1] Bailly, G., Vo, D.-B., Lecolinet, E. and Guiard, Y. 2011. Gesture-Aware Remote Controls□: Guidelines and Interaction *Techniques Proceedings of ICME 2001*, 263-270. DOI: 10.1145/2070481.2070530

[2] Bailly, G., R. Müller, W. J., Ning, T. and Lecolinet, E. 2011. Comparing Free Hand Menu Techniques for Distant Displays Using Linear , Marking and Finger-Count Menus. *Proc. of Interact 2011, LNCS 6947*, 248-262, DOI: 10.1007/978-3-642-23771-3_19

[3] Balchandran, R., Epstein, E. P., Potamianos, G. and Seredi, L. 2008. A multi-modal spoken dialog system for interactive TV, *Proceedings of the 10th international conference on Multimodal interfaces - IMCI '08*, 191-198.

[4] Ballagas, R., Rohs, M., Sheridan, J. and Borchers, J. 2006. The smart phone: A ubiquitous input device. *IEEE Pervasive Computing*, 5(1): 70 - 77.

[5] Bernhaupt, R., Pirker, M.M., Weiss, A., Wilfinger, D. and Tscheligi, M. 2011. Security, privacy, and personalization: Informing next-generation interaction concepts for interactive TV systems. *Comput. Entertain.* 9, 3, Article 17 (November 2011), 33p. DOI=10.1145/2027456.2027463

[6] Regina Bernhaupt, Marianna Obrist, Astrid Weiss, Elke Beck, and Manfred Tscheligi. 2008. Trends in the living room and beyond: results from ethnographic studies using creative and playful probing. *Comput. Entertain.* 6, 1, Article 5 (May 2008), 23 p. DOI=10.1145/1350843.1350848

[7] Bernhaupt, R., Weiss, A., Obrist, M., Tscheligi, M.(2007). Playful Probing: Making Probing more Fun, INTERACT 2007, 10 -14 Sep 2007, Springer LNCS, 606-619.

[8] Cesar, P., Chorianopoulos, K., and Jensen, J. F. 2008. Social television and user interaction. *Comput. Entertain.* 6, 1 (May. 2008), 1-10. DOI= http://doi.acm.org/10.1145/1350843.1350847

[9] Chorianopoulos, K. and Lekakos, G. 2007. Learn and play with interactive TV. *Comput. Entertain.* 5, 2 (Apr. 2007), 4-14. DOI= http://doi.acm.org/10.1145/1279540.1279544

[10] Elder, H. 1970. On the feasibility of voice input to an online computer processing system, *Communications of the ACM*, 13, 6, 339-346.

[11] Furnas, G. W., Landauer, T. K., Gomez, L. M. and Dumais, S. T. 1987. The vocabulary problem in human-system communication. *Communications of the ACM*, 30, 11, 964-971.

[12] Gauntlett, D. and Hill, A. 1999. *TV Living: Television, Culture and Everyday Life*. Routledge, London.

[13] Gaver, W. W., Boucher, A., Pennington, S., and Walker, B. 2004. Cultural probes and the value of uncertainty. *interactions* 11, 5 (Sep. 2004), 53-56. DOI= http://doi.acm.org/10.1145/1015530.1015555

[14] Gawlinski, M. (2003) *Interactive Television Production*, Oxford: Focal Press.

[15] David Goldberg and Cate Richardson. 1993. Touch-typing with a stylus. In *Proceedings of the INTERCHI '93 conference on Human factors in computing systems* (INTERCHI '93), S. Ashlund, A. Henderson, E. Hollnagel, K. Mullet, and T. White (Eds.). IOS Press, Amsterdam, The Netherlands, 80-87.

[16] Goto, J., Kim Y.-B., Miyazaki, M., Komine, K., Uratani, N., 2003. A spoken dialogue interface for TV operations based on data collected by using WOZ method. *Proc. of the 41st Annual Meeting on Association for Computational Linguistics 2003*, 101-104. doi>10.3115/1075178.1075191]

[17] Igarashi, T. and Hughes, J. F. 2001.Voice as Sound□: Using Non-verbal Voice Input for Interactive Control, *Proc of UIST 2001*, 155-156.

[18] Jick, L. 1979. Mixing quantitative and qualitative methods: Triangulation in Action. *Administrative Science Quarterly*, 24, 4, 602-624.

[19] Kela, J., Korpipo, P., Marvi, J., Kallio, S., Savino, G., Jozzo, L. and Di Marca, K. 2006. Accelerometer-based gesture control for a design environment. *Personal Ubiquitous Comput.* 10, 5 (July 2006), 285-299. DOI=10.1007/s00779-005-0033-8

[20] Krol, L. R., Aliakseyeu, D. and Subramanian, S. 2009. Haptic feedback in remote pointing. In *Proceedings of the 27th international conference extended abstracts on Human factors in computing systems* (CHI EA '09). ACM, New York, NY, USA, 3763-3768. DOI=10.1145/1520340.1520568

[21] Lorenz, A. and Jentsch, M. 2010. The Ambient Media Player - A Media Application Remotely Operated by the Use of Mobile Devices and Gestures, in *Conference Proceedings of MUM'10*, 372-380.

[22] Mackenzie, S., I. and N. Enns, "Touchpad Based Remote Control Devices," *Human Factors*, no. April, 2008, 229-230.

[23] Mirlacher, T. and Bernhaupt, R. 2011. Breaking myths: inferring interaction from infrared signals. In *Proceedings of the 9th international interactive conference on Interactive television* (EuroITV '11). ACM, New York, NY, USA, 137-140. DOI=10.1145/2000119.2000146

[24] O'Brien, J., Rodden, T., Roundefield, M. J. and Hughes, J. 1999. At home with the technology: An in-home computing and ethnographic study of a set-top-box trial. *ACM Trans. Computer-Human Interaction*, 3, 3, 282-303.

[25] Pelling, C., Sko, T. and Gardner. H. J. 2009. Be careful how you point that thing: Wiimote aiming for large displays. In

Proceedings of the 21st Annual Conference of the Australian Computer-Human Interaction Special Interest Group: Design: Open 24/7 (OZCHI '09). ACM, New York, NY, USA, 397-400. DOI=10.1145/1738826.1738908

[26] Pirker, M., Bernhaupt, R., and Mirlacher, T. 2010. Investigating usability and user experience as possible entry barriers for touch interaction in the living room. In *Proceedings of the 8th international interactive conference on Interactive TV&Video* (EuroITV '10). ACM, New York, NY, USA, 145-154. DOI=10.1145/1809777.1809808

[27] Rico, J. and Brewster, S. 2010. Usable gestures for mobile interfaces: evaluating social acceptability. In *Proceedings of the 28th international conference on Human factors in computing systems* (CHI '10). ACM, New York, NY, USA, 887-896. DOI=10.1145/1753326.1753458

[28] Seager, W., Knoche, H., Sasse, M. 2007. TV-centricity - requirements gathering for triple play services. EuroITV '07: Adjunct Proceedings of the European Conference on Interactive Television. 274-278.

[29] Strauss, A. and Corbin, J. 1990. *Basics of qualitative research: grounded theory procedures and techniques*. Newbury Park, Calif, Sage Publications.

[30] Tsekleves, E., Cruickshank, L., Hill, A., Kondo, K. and Whitham, R. 2007. Interacting with Digital Media at Home via a Second Screen," *Ninth IEEE International Symposium on Multimedia Workshops (ISMW 2007)*, 201-206.

[31] Turunen, M., Melto, A., Hella, J. et al. 2009. User expectations and user experience with different modalities in a mobile phone controlled home entertainment system. In *Proceedings of the 11th International Conference on Human-Computer Interaction with Mobile Devices and Services* (MobileHCI '09). ACM, New York, NY, USA, , Article 31 , 4 pages. DOI=10.1145/1613858.1613898

[32] Lin, J., Nishino, H., Kagawa, T. and Utsumiya, K.. 2010. Free hand interface for controlling applications based on Wii remote IR sensor. In *Proceedings of the 9th ACM SIGGRAPH Conference on Virtual-Reality Continuum and its Applications in Industry* (VRCAI '10). ACM, New York, NY, USA, 139-142. DOI=10.1145/1900179.1900207.

Second Screen Applications and Tablet Users: Constellation, Awareness, Experience, and Interest

Cédric Courtois
IBBT-MICT-Ghent University
Korte Meer 7-9-11
BE-9000 Gent
+32 9 264 91 54
cedric.courtois@ugent.be

Evelien D'heer
IBBT-MICT-Ghent University
Korte Meer 7-9-11
BE-9000 Gent
+32 9 264 84 77
evelien.dheer@ugent.be

ABSTRACT
This study investigates how tablet users incorporate multiple media in their television viewing experience. Three patterns are found: (a) only focusing on television, (b) confounding television viewing with other screen media (e.g. laptop, tablet) and (c) confounding television viewing with various media, including print and screen media. Furthermore, we question how the incorporation of screen media in this experience affects the practice of engaging in digital commentary on television content. Also, we inquire the uptake and interest in so-called 'second screen applications'. These applications allow extensions of the primary screen experience on secondary screens (e.g. tablet). The results, based on a sample of 260 tablet users, indicate that there is only a modest uptake and interest in using secondary screens to digitally share opinions. However, the use of second screen interaction with television content is not discarded: although there is still little awareness and experience, we notice a moderate interest in these apps.

Categories and Subject Descriptors
J.4 [**Social And Behavioral Sciences**]: Sociology

General Terms
Management, Human Factors

Keywords
Tablet, Second Screen, Interaction

1. INTRODUCTION
Whereas in earlier days, the living room was solely dominated by the television set, in recent years many other (screen) media have permeated into this shared family space; a laptop on the coffee table, a smartphone in each pocket and a tablet in the sofa. All of them connected to the Internet of course. As such, the overall media exposure proliferates and saturates [1], existing in complex interaction patterns. Although this proliferation is wildly acknowledged, very little research exists on their interconnected modes of consumption for a user perspective. In this paper, we present the results of an exploratory study on a relatively recent development in consumers' media repertoires, namely the adoption of tablet PCs. We question (a) whether these easily accessible, tangible and continually web-enabled devices are integrated in the television viewing behavior, taking into account other available (screen) media, and (b) if there is a potential to support the existing television viewing experience by providing a direct feedback channel and affording so-called second screen apps.

1.1 Changing media constellations
The notion of mediation has become prominent in the age of interaction and network-enabled 'new' media technologies [2]. We have entered a media-drenched, data-rich, channel surfing age, were according to for instance Deuze [3], we no longer live with, but *in* the media. People nowadays are more than ever participating in and engaging with media through various platforms and channels [4]. Convergence is not only about merging technological systems, but has become a genuine aspect of our everyday life [5]. Our first concern is (RQ1) how multiple media have entered the space of the television experience, especially focusing on tablet devices. Second, (RQ2), we are enticed to know how these tablet devices are used and whether there is a synergy with television viewing by using computer-mediated communication to share opinions about television content. In this respect, we acknowledge the importance of the paradigm 'mass self-communication'. This new type of communication is simultaneously mass communication but also multi-modal and self-generated, self-directed and self-selected [6]. Although much of this communication does serve self-expression and self-representation, it does provide the networked self a gateway to the public. As such, we want to know (RQ3) to what extent television viewers who own a tablet are interested to communicate about television content and whether they are interested to participate via second screen applications.

1.2 Second screen feedback mechanisms
Although in recent decades, quite some experiments have been performed on feedback mechanisms for television, it has been found that these do not really fit the relaxing nature of television viewing and require too much effort of the television consumer. Moreover, as it usually a social activity, interactive application on the primary, television screen tend to interrupt, rather than enhance [7]. Nonetheless, broadcasters have shown interest to embrace the potential of secondary screens to engage with television content (e.g. voting or participating in quizzes). These (commercial) 'top-down' initiatives in the form of applications run on a secondary screen device. They aim to extend the experience derived from the primary, television screen. It allows taking part in quiz shows (e.g. answering the questions on the primary screen by entering the answer through the second), obtain extra information, air an opinion, etc. A tablet device could be

most suitable for several reasons: it is easy, intuitive and comfortable to operate, small in dimensions, has good graphical capabilities, and is in the majority of cases connected to the Internet (where it can operate in symbiosis with the television as long as it is digitally connected as well, cf. ip-TV). Yet, we have no clear view on the degree to which tablet owners (RQ4a) already engage in such activities, and (b) whether they are drawn to these kinds of extensions.

2. METHODOLOGY

This paper draw upon data obtained from the VRT/Research Department-Medialab. VRT is the Flemish Public Service Broadcaster, focusing on the Northern (Flemish) region of Belgium. The data originate from a CAWI (Computer Aided Web Interviewing) questionnaire. This entails a web survey that automatically adapts to previous answers, tailoring the questions and their formats to specifically to the respondent at hand. The fieldwork was performed from June 30th until July 24th 2011. The respondents (N = 260) were sampled from a market research panel, on the basis of the criterion of having a tablet pc. On average, the survey took 28 minutes to complete. The survey consisted of several blocks, regarding technology adoption and use, social networking, interest in interactive services, second screen services and socio-demographics.

The majority of respondents were male (62%, versus 38% females). The youngest respondent was 18 years old, while the oldest was 65. This results in an average age of 39.15 years (SD = 12.07). The respondents live in families with an average size of 2.93 members (SD = 1.46). About 22% are married/living together without children, whereas 46% do have children. There were 3% single parents, 10% lived at home with family. 17% of the respondents live in a single-person household. The majority of the sample is highly educated (34% college degree, 24% university degree), whereas 22% has a higher secondary degree. The remainder obtained a primary degree or lower secondary degree.

3. RESULTS

3.1 Multi-media viewing patterns

In order to answer the first research question, a latent class analysis (LCA) is performed on a set of nine dichotomous variables, inquiring what devices are used, simultaneous with television viewing (at least once a week). LCA is a multivariate technique to reveal latent structures in categorical data. A common strategy is to iterate the analysis with an increasing number of clusters, until a fitting model is reached (with an non-significant L^2-value). In this specific case, this criterion is met as soon as with two clusters (Table 1). However, because a three-cluster model shows a lower Bayesian Information Criterion (BIC) - an index for model performance comparisons - we prefer to go with a three-cluster solution.

Clusters	*LL*	BIC(*LL*)	*N*par	L^2	df	*p*
1	-1163.65	2371.78	8	585.12	247	0.00
2	-1002.34	2099.22	17	262.51	238	0.13
3	-955.49	2055.55	26	168.81	229	1.00
4	-934.27	2063.17	35	126.37	220	1.00
5	-923.72	2092.12	44	105.28	211	1.00

Table 1. Iterative model testing

The graph in Figure 1 plots the response probabilities of each variable per cluster. The first cluster, named *'Television and screen media'* is characterized by relatively high probabilities of using laptop and especially tablet devices while watching television. The second cluster is characterized by an absolute probability of not combining any other media activity with watching television. Finally, the third cluster - *Television and multimedia* - consists of respondents that share high chances of pairing television viewing with various other (digital) media. In fact, there is a nearly absolute chance of using the tablet during television viewing at least once a week.

Further analysis shows there are no differences between clusters for what concerns age [F(2, 257) = 1.23, p > .05] nor gender [$\chi^2(2)$ = 1.14, p > .05]. Hence, we find rather distinct profiles, two of which tend to use multiple screens during television viewing, whereas a third, yet smaller profile solely concentrates on a single screen.

3.2 Tablets in the home

Now we have a view on the relation between tablet devices and television, we proceed by looking into how tablets are dispersed into their users' everyday environments and for what they are appropriated. As shown in Table 2, the majority of respondents claim they use the tablet present in their homes, although the *TV Only* viewers seem somewhat less likely to do that. Also, the tablet device is most commonly shared with other household members, especially partners, followed by their children. The most popular places to use a tablet are the living room (79%), the bedroom (42%) and the home office (31%). There is however no difference concerning places of use between the multi-screen viewing patterns as outlined above.

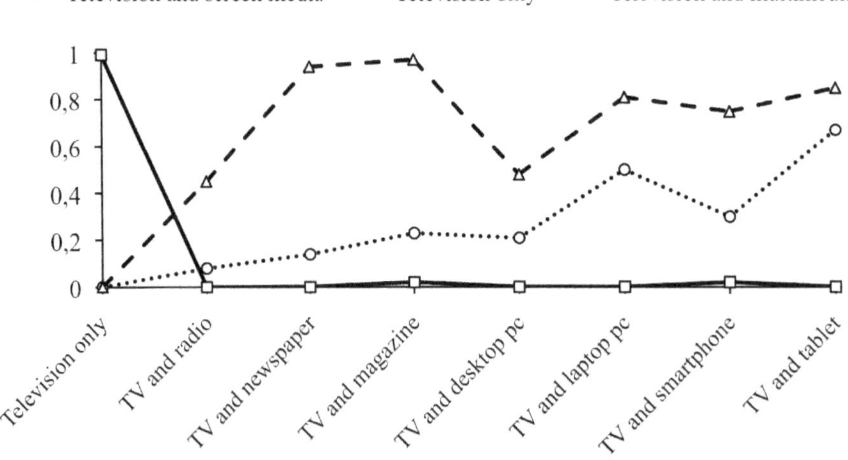

Figure 1: LCA results, repsonse probabilities of each variable plotted per cluster.

	TV and screen media (Mdn)	TV only (Mdn)	TV and multimedia (Mdn)	$\chi^2(2)$	*p*
Overall use	Several times per week	Several times per week	Several times per week	3.00	0.22
Specific use:					
E-mail	Several times per week	2-3 times a month	Several times per week	12.59	0.00
Agenda	Once a month	Less than every 2-3 months	Several times per week	7.09	0.03
Search info	Several times per week	About once a week	Several times per week	14.94	0.00
Surfing	Several times per week	About once a week	Several times per week	11.93	0.00
Online shopping	Less than every 2-3 months	Less than every 2-3 months	2-3 times a month	9.21	0.01
Social networking	About once a week	Less than every 2-3 months	Several times per week	10.97	0.00
View online video	About once a week	Every 2-3 months	Several times per week	12.70	0.00
Watch live tv	Less than every 2-3 months	Never	2-3 times a month	16.45	0.00
Use second screen apps	Never	Never	Once a month	15.03	0.00
Watch films	Less than every 2-3 months	Less than every 2-3 months	Once a month	4.65	0.10
Gaming	Once a month	Less than every 2-3 months	Several times per week	6.50	0.04

Table 3. Frequencies of tablet activities per cluster

	TV and screen media	TV only	TV and multi-media	$\chi^2(2)$
I use the household tablet	99	93	100	10.64**
I am the only user	59	67	56	1.20
In case of other users:				
Partner	71	88	73	2.12
Children	49	41	47	0.36
Other family members	16	12	7	0.96
Friends	10	12	13	0.15

Table 2. Social use of tablet devices

All of the distinguished patterns appear to make a similar, regular use of their tablet device. The median usage frequency is 'several times per week'. When we look into the exact activities that are performed (Table 3), we notice that the *Television and multimedia* pattern is more prone to perform various activities, such as searching online info, browsing online shopping, social networking, but also consume online video and even watch films and, most important: they use second screen applications. However, the median frequency is limited to once a month, which is nonetheless twice as much as the other two patterns.

3.3 Interaction and second screen apps

On the whole, the tablet users in the study are quite active on Social Network Sites. No less than 79% have an account on Facebook (despite a significant lower percentage of account for the *TV Only*, 64%, $\chi^2(2) = 10.69$, $p < .05$). Furthermore, 42% has a YouTube account, 27% owns a Twitter account and 26% has a Netlog account (no significant account differences among profiles).

First, we focus on the most prominent SNS, Facebook. There are no differences between multi-screen viewing patterns in the level of activity on the platform. On average, respondents indicated to spend 14 minutes on Facebook on weekday, and 12 minutes on a weekend day. At least multiple times per week, 24% posts at least on status update, 58% keeps track of others' status updates, 46% checks friends' profile pages, 17% posts photos/videos, 51% looks at others' photos/videos and 34% sends private messages. Moreover, 36% participates in a game or a quiz at least once per week, while 29% becomes a fan of a group or organization. Most interesting, 44% of the respondents with a Facebook account claims to be a fan of media-related Facebook group (e.g. Television program, broadcaster, celebrity).

Second, we zoom into Twitter. About 25% of the respondents with a Twitter account claim to tweet multiple times per week, 30% retweets a message with a similar frequency. Most relevant is that 33% of the Twitter users claims to follow celebrities or trends multiple times per week. Moreover, 14% comments on TV or radio programs with a similar regularity.

These findings raise questions on the extent to which these Social Network Sites are prone to instigating and/or facilitating audience participation. On a rating scale ranging from *'extremely uninteresting'* to *'extremely interesting'*, with a mid-category labeled *'interesting'*, the respondents' average score amounts to 2.68 ($SD = 1.10$). This means that the sample as a whole is not that interested in providing their thoughts on TV programs through SNS, albeit not substantially discarding it. Furthermore, there seem to be no significant differences in whether experience is present and how often those who already aired their opinions on programs engaged in that kind of endeavor. Nonetheless, among those who did not yet share their opinion, it shows that the members of those clusters characterized by multi-screen usage share higher intention scores, especially the respondents who belong to the *TV and multimedia* pattern. In terms of socio-demographics, it shows that there are significant, negative, yet small correlations between age and interest in airing an opinion ($r = -.24$, $p < .001$), experience with the activity ($r = -.28$, $p < .05$) and, - for those without experience - the intention to engage in this activity in the near future ($r = -.19$, $p < .001$). Still, there are no effects of gender on interest, experience, frequency or intentions.

	Interest in airing opinion	Experience	Frequency	Intention future (have not engaged so far)
TV+ screen media	2.71	18	At least once a month	2.38
TV only	2.42	18	At least once 2-3 months	2.00
TV + multimedia	2.94	29	At least once a month	2.58
Difference?	No	No	No	Yes
	$F(2.257) = 6.22, p > .05$	$\chi^2(2) = 2.62, p > .05$	$\chi^2(2) = 0.74, p > .05$	$F(2.207) = 6.71, p < .05$

Table 4. Digital interaction about TV content

One of the possible means to interact with television content is the use of the discussed second screen applications, which are in most cases especially suited for application-built devices such as smartphones and tablets. However, the tablet users in this study, especially those who do not combine watching television with other screens, share a rather low awareness of the existence of second screen apps. The overall small proportions of respondents who claim to have experience with these apps echo this finding. Also, it is noteworthy that there is no contingency between being the only one that uses a tablet and experience with second screen apps. Furthermore, there are significant differences in both the interest in these applications and the intention to use them in the near future (ranging from *'definitely not'* to *'definitely'*, employing *'perhaps'* a mid-point). In both instances, the patterns that combine television viewing with various media score the highest, closely followed by those who pair television and screen media. Still, second screen apps do not seem to persuade the respondents who are not (yet) relating their television use to other, simultaneous activities. Concerning socio-demographics, it seems that the younger respondents are not more often aware of second screens apps, although they are more experienced ($r = -.21$, $p < .001$) and are somewhat more interested ($r = -.20$, $p < .001$). Moreover, younger people who claim no prior experience are slightly more inclined to try it in the near future ($r = .14$, $p < .05$).

	Know about 2nd screen apps	Experience with 2nd screen	Interest in 2nd screen apps	Short term use intention
TV and screen media	46	15	2.71	2.68
TV only	26	10	2.25	2.18
TV and multimedia	53	21	3.09	2.88
Difference?	Yes	No	Yes	Yes
	$\chi^2(2) = 8.99$, $p < .05$	$\chi^2(2) = 1.93$, $p > .05$	$F(2,257) = 8.10$, $p < .001$	$F(2,257) = 6.13$, $p < .005$

Table 5. Digital interaction about TV content

4. DISCUSSION

Our analysis shows that tablet owners tend to appropriate their devices in multiple spaces, however the living room appears most popular. Although this setting used to be solely dominated by the television set, it is permeated by multiple other screen devices that are incorporated in the experience of watching television. We found three distinct patterns of how this cross-medial potential is put into practice. Although there is a small group that maintains an undivided attention for the television screen, we encountered two other patterns, in which multiple screens are used, in one instance also next to established print media. It was not so surprising that, most likely due to its tangible and accessible properties, tablet owners are likely to combine this particular device with their television viewing activities.

Furthermore, it is clear that tablets serve two important purposes: they afford a swift search for information, and enable social networking activities that are commonplace in today's Web use. This opens a window of opportunities in linking this with television viewing. In fact, we noticed that our respondents are relatively active on SNS at tend to join groups on television content and celebrities. They even, albeit to a lesser extent, post messages about what is happening on the primary television screen. Still, we must take into account that in general, there is only a weak inclination to engage in this kind of interactivity: the respondents in our sample are only slightly interested, and do not have that much experience. Apparently, they would rather make use of established channels (e.g. personal FB account) than to engage in specially designed 'second screen' applications.

On the other hand, the potential of second screen applications that extend beyond mere commenting and opinion sharing seems somewhat brighter. In general, although far from overwhelming, there is a modest interest. Still, we must acknowledge that almost half of the respondents did not know about the existence of these applications. Moreover, in case of those who have no experience mixing screens, there is a lower interest, which paired with a very limited awareness. In the other multi-screen patterns, the awareness is somewhat more pronounced, yet not reaching over 53%. As such, it seems that at the moment, the potential of second screen apps is heavily underutilized. Although people might be aware of their existence, they might need to be remembered by the primary screen in case the program they are watching is supported on secondary devices. In addition, benefits and added value might also be unclear. On the brighter side, respondents in the TV and multimedia pattern seem to somewhat prone to 'perhaps' try second screen apps in the near future. Still, it is clear that the adoption potential of these apps remains precarious, not even with people who own the appropriate, scarcely adopted hardware and are thus quite likely to fit an 'innovator' profile. Finally, we must stress that we found various, albeit small, correlations between younger participants in the interest in second screen apps. Therefore, on the basis of this study, we advise to concentrate more on younger viewers, as they appear to be more likely to embrace these initiatives. Finally, venues for future research are the search for integration with existing modes of interaction with television content and further research to discern in-depth why people are (not) interested.

5. ACKNOWLEDGMENTS

The authors would especially like to thank VRT-Studiedienst-Medialab for their help and sharing data.

6. REFERENCES

[1] Newell, J., J. Pilotta, and J. Thomas, Mass Media Displacement and Saturation. International Journal on Media Management, 2008. 10(4): p. 131-138.

[2] Silverstone, The sociology of mediation and communication, in The sage handbook of sociology, C. Calhoun, C. Rojek, and B. Turner, Editors. 2005, Sage: London. p. 188-207.

[3] Deuze, Media life. Media, Culture, and Society, 2011. 33(1): p. 137-148.

[4] Livingstone, The challenge of changing audiences: Or, what is the audience researcher to do in the age of the internet? European Journal of Communication, 2004. 19(7): p. 75-86.

[5] Jenkins, Convergence Culture: Where old and new media collide. 2006, New York: New York University Press.

[6] Castells, Communication Power. 2009, Oxford: Oxford University Press.

[7] Tsekleves, E., et al., Investigating media use and the television user experience in the home. Entertainment Computing, 2011. 2(3): p. 151-161

An Approach for T-Learning Content Generation Based on a Social Media Environment

Iván D. Claros
Universidad Autónoma de Madrid
Department of Computer Science
28049, Madrid, Spain
+34 914972419
ivan.claros@uam.es

Ruth Cobos
Universidad Autónoma de Madrid
Department of Computer Science
28049, Madrid, Spain
+34 914972243
ruth.cobos@uam.es

ABSTRACT

The T-Learning paradigm facilitates to the viewer/learner to take an active and leading role in his/her teaching-learning process through the digital interactive television. In this sense, quality educational contents and simple interactive mechanisms with them are required, but there aren't strategies that facilitate the composition of educational material and procure continuity of education across platforms. To solve this lack, a model for generating educational content for cross-platform is presented in this article. This article propose a social media environment where their users can search, share and argue video format resources available on the Web and then combine them with interactive mechanisms to generate interactive multimedia educational content. A real blended learning experience was made to evaluate this proposal.

Categories and Subject Descriptors

K.3.1 [**Computers and Education**]: Computer Uses in Education. I.7.2 [**Document and Text Processing**]: Multi/mixed media. H.5.1 [**Information Interfaces and Presentations**]: Multimedia Information Systems - Audio, Video.

General Terms

Documentation, Design, Experimentation, Human Factors.

Keywords

Social Media Education, Interactive Multimedia Content, Collaboration Learning, SMIL.

1. INTRODUCTION

The interactive digital television (iDTV) is a suitable alternative for accessing to information and a powerful platform for creating services that extend the coverage and quality of education [1], because it has some characteristics that favour the teaching-learning processes [2, 3], e.g. i) users are used to TV, so the cognitive overload is reduced; ii) pervasiveness, especially in remote rural areas [4]; iii) trustfulness, general population tend to trust in the TV-content, which enhances effectiveness in educational processes; but especially iv) *interactivity*, which allows at the viewer/learner to take an active role in his/her teaching-learning process. According to [4], interactive TV is a user experience that involves at least one user and one or more audio-visual and networked devices; so even traditional TV is potentially interactive. In this context, educational activities and training supported by iDTV technologies are called T-Learning [5, 6].

EuroITV'12, July 4–6, 2012, Berlin, Germany.

From a technological point of view, Web and iDTV have some commercial approximations, e.g. GoogleTV, Yahoo TV-Widgets; and some entities are trying to ensure that Web works well on TV, for instance W3C [7]. However, It is not convenient use iDTV as a Web-browser to support the educational tasks, because it difficult the affordance of this environment [8]. Additionally, there are not strategies for adaptation of the contents from the Web to iDTV and each other, into the educational field.

Meanwhile, the technological developments around the Social Media [9] phenomenon have demonstrated many capacities that can enhance education [10], too. Some of these capacities are: i) the identification of quality contents and their classification with high precision are possible thanks to appropriate strategies [11], ii) the effectiveness and fast diffusion of these media, iii) the high acceptation of this media in Internet, and iv) this phenomenon is not only supported by computers but also mobile and TV.

Therefore, we propose the development of a service that harnesses the capabilities of both Web and TV through a web-based social media system that is used to generate interactive multimedia educational content as a T-Learning content. Two environments are proposed: first, a social media tool as a collaborative learning environment that allows to their users to search, share and argue video format resources available on the Web, and then, to combine them with interactive mechanisms to generate interactive multimedia educational material like a learning object called Learning Script (LS); second, a Multimedia Player, an environment that allows deployment and management of LS like interactive content over Web, mobile or iDTV.

SMIL [12] seem to be an appropriate language for describing mix of multimedia content and already it was used for iDTV [13]. However, there are limited supports of interactive mechanisms, so an extension of SMIL was proposed and was used like documents model for LS objects.

We compare some related research works to our approach below. CAV project [14] (T-learning services to support a virtual academic community) proposes supporting of services like forums, chats, wikis, syndication, content and information in a Virtual Academic Community through the platform Web and iDTV [15]. In our approach, we have considered pertinent maintaining those tasks on a Web environment and the possibility to extend them towards the composition of educational content as LS objects, because we believe that it can be more suitable to the mental viewer's model. In similar way as *T-learning Authoring tool* [16] from ELU project, each LS object is a Learning Object [17] that describes interactive content and is interpreted at runtime by a Multimedia Player; however, *T-learning Authoring tool* doesn't consider the composition of material like a collaborative learning process as ours. Other important aspects have been reviewed of *T-Maestro* [18] like personalization, adaptation and e-Learning standards. Also, mechanisms for indexing and classification of metadata-based audiovisual content, collaborative tagging system, and semantic annotations [19, 20], and time-based annotations [21] was considered in the present work.

In the next section, structural and functional aspects of this proposal are shown. After, a brief description of prototype and experimentation developed, and finally conclusions and future work are exposed.

2. OUR PROPOSAL

The figure 1 presents the conceptual model of this proposal. Two kinds of environments are defined: first, a collaborative learning environment, that allows to search, share and argue video format resources available on the Web; and second, the Multimedia Players, a cross-platform solution that deploys and plays the LS objects.

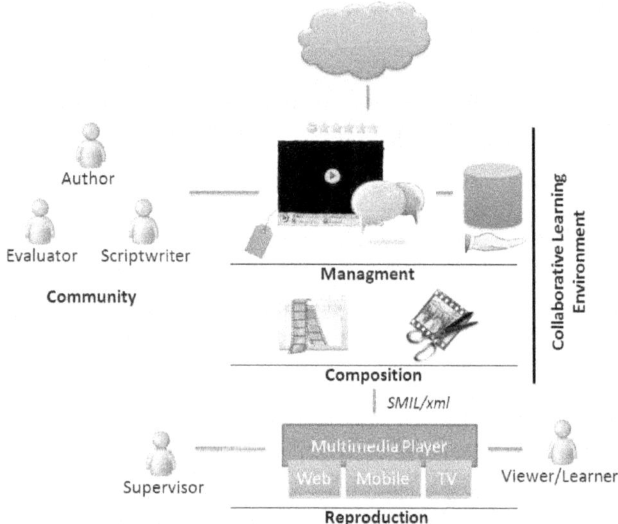

Figure 1. Conceptual model for system proposed

Users group of this environment is called *Community*, and they are responsible of generating educational content or LS, while they learn and work in a collaborative way. Then, a collaborative guideline is required. Several Roles of users are proposed in this collaborative process: *Author*, *Evaluator*, *Scriptwriters*, *Supervisor* and *Viewer/Learner*, their interactions are presented below. On summary, the mentioned guideline is divided in 4 steps [22]:

i. *Analysis*: community is created around a knowledge domain. Each *Author* searches and shares resources available on the Web. Each resource is described with metadata and tags, and then *Evaluators* qualify the resource with votes and comments, highlighting relevant information. This task is similar to a brainstorm, and helps community to explore and build a database of quality resources.

ii. *Synthesis*: usually, the knowledge domain is wide, so is divided into topics. Each topic is feeding with resources that form structures as lists. This classification task is a collaborative learning technical called *Affinity Grouping* that allows to users improving their abstraction skills [23].

iii. *Composition*: in this point, *Scriptwriters* use *Authoring Tool* to design and compose new educational material where resources and interactive mechanisms are mixed in a document descriptor called "*Learning Script*" (LS). Collaboration and feedback of Community is done for each LS object. The manipulation of objects and information is an effective way to improve motivation and learning and is part of new education trends.

iv. *Playing:* each LS object is deployed and played over Multimedia Players; while the Supervisor monitors the interaction between LS and *Viewer/Learner*. Each interactive LS mechanism triggers several events and information, e.g. time of play, answers, jumps, etc. those are keeping on an interactive database that the community could analyze.

The implementation of a tool that supports this proposal was dealt as a Social Media solution. We called to this solution **SMLearning System**; some services of this environment are presented below:

Collaborative indexing of resources: for this process, the system deals with a variety of information sources, such as: metadata (e.g. creation location, date, creator, duration, formats available and dimensions), content description provided by the Author (e.g. title, abstract and keywords), collaborative tagging, rates of content quality and content complexity level (i.e. if it is suitable for beginners or for experts). The indexing process can improve the navigation by the content and can allow identifying knowledge areas without enough contributions. Moreover, that information could be used in recommendation services.

Time-based Annotations: it provides to add annotations over specifics points in reproduction time of multimedia resources. This service can facilitate the understanding of a resource because granularity and identification of concepts is increased [21]. Also, identification of key points for the insertion of interactive components associated is possible.

Interactivity mechanisms: a simple interactivity model is proposed. Some examples of this kind of interactivity are the following: i) activities without technology support, e.g. to draw an object in a sheet of paper, talk to someone or to visit a place; ii) comments, images or text with summaries of key ideas; iii) questionnaires and polls and voting mechanisms; v) communication mechanisms, like chat or forums; and vi) games (e.g. puzzles or word searches).

Learning Script Composition: it allows composing a logical playback sequence with embedded interactive components based on debugged resources. This sequence can be guided by a list of keywords sorted by priority, timeline events in content, or just by a structure proposed by the *Scriptwriter*. Different LS objects could be designed over different criteria, such as, user skill levels or background, for example.

We have used SMIL 3.0 like a document model of LS, but some extensions were required: it was included the tags *parameter*, *action*, *embedded* and *question*. *Parameter* is a tag with name and value attributes, and helps to support e.g. over *video* tag, the *volume* and *mute* properties. The *action* tag was included to allow send special interactive command to the Multimedia Player e.g. *play, pause, resume, stop, mute and unmute*. *Embedded* is used to support *Adobe Flash Object*, *IFrames* or *Java Applet* like content in a LS. *Question* is used to make simple test or polls supported with *option* tag. In addition to this, some meta-tags was adopted of e-Learning standards like LOM [24] and Dublin Core [25] for describing LS like a Learning Object, e.g. Title, Summary, Targets, Target audience, Self-Assessment, and others. Resources like video or images are referenced by URL.

3. PROTOTYPE

The home page of SMLearning System is shown in figure 2. We have developed a prototype like a Web application with Facebook integration. API Facebook has allowed managing users and notifications, but especially, is a well-known Social Media often visited by the users. *Youtube* API was used as video repository because allows access to meta-information of videos and to manipulate events of reproduction within JavaScript code.

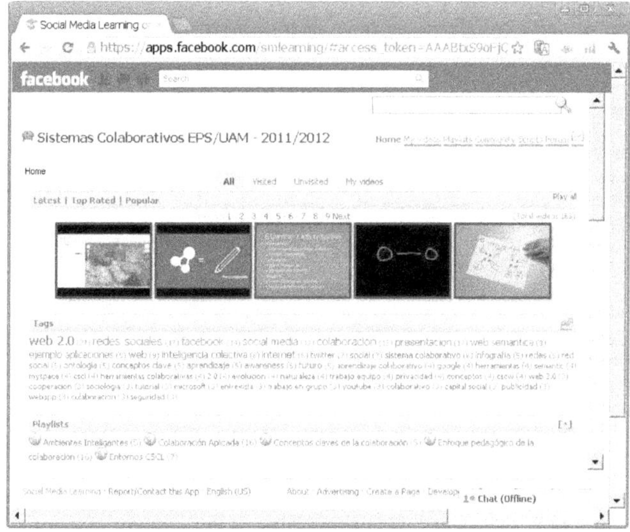

Figure 2. SMLearning System like a Facebook Application

According to these capabilities, we have developed a component that allows the addition of time-based annotation. These annotations are visualized using the *fisheye* technique, where we present annotations about current time in foreground while others are presented in background. Also, we have presented the annotations as a histogram, which shows in a timeline a count of comments. Additionally, some mechanisms of monitoring and evaluation, and *Awareness* were developed.

In this prototype, a web-based Multimedia Player was implemented like a *JQuery* plug-in that interprets LS and reproduces it on Web-Browser. Videos and images are prefetch before LS is played. The *Youtube* API was used to play, pause and seek the video resources. A new interpretation of *src* attribute in *<video>* tag was required to integrate *Youtube* sources. The player controls and a video with subtitles are shown in Figure 3 like a partial view of the Web Multimedia Player implemented.

Figure 3. Partial view of Multimedia Player

In this prototype, videos and images are linked from their original internet location. Then, prefetching and adaptation process are made on client-side. That has implications to Web browser performance when LS have a lot of resources. Therefore, a *prefetch* process on server-side could be required to adapt on mobile and TV.

4. EXPERIMENTATION

SMLearning System was evaluated in a blended learning experience with students enrolled in a Master course called *Sistemas Colaborativos* (Collaborative System) at Department of Computer Science of *Universidad Autónoma de Madrid* (Spain), from September-2011 to January-2012. The Community was integrated by 10 users between students and teachers. They accessed to SMLearning Facebook application (https://apps.facebook.com/smlearning/) and managing their membership across a Facebook Group called "*Sistemas Colaborativos EPS/UAM - 2011/2012*" (https://www.facebook.com/groups/291903894159359/).

Regular classes were interleaving with control sessions for the experience. In those sessions, functional and methodological aspects of SMLearning System were instructed. Four weeks was assigned for the first step of methodology, while second and third step, two weeks each one. The fourth step (Playing) was developed like three Face-to-Face sessions, where each LS author exposed their concepts and design decisions.

Logs of interaction and a satisfaction survey were used to analyse this experience. The course knowledge domino was divided on 18 topics. At the end, 163 resources were added, 268 annotations, 25 lists and 16 LS. Some pedagogical aspect were evaluated, such as motivation and learning (based on qualification). The users manifested a motivation average of 8.33 with a StDev of 2.3, and user qualification average was 8.96, and StDev 0.05 (scale 1, minimum, to 10, maximum). We find that lineal coefficient of determination (R^2) between motivation and qualification was 0.57; that is coherent with direct positive relation between motivation and learning. Finally, the Community considered useful the inclusion of interactive mechanism to multimedia content.

5. CONCLUSIONS AND FUTURE WORK

This article has presented a methodology guideline and technical approach for create interactive multimedia educational content, based on a collaborative process supported in a social media system, called SMLearning System. That system has two parts: a Web-based CSCL system that allows composition of new educational content like a mix among multimedia resources and interactive mechanisms, called Learning Script (LS); and a Multimedia Player, a cross-platform tool where LS objects are reproduced. SMIL/XML with some adaptations was used for the document model of LS.

This proposal was validated in a real blended learning experience. The experience evaluation was shown that users were motivated and they reached learning goals. According to users, functional and usability aspects of SMLearning system were satisfactory. An analysis of user interaction was made, where the linear coefficient of determination (R^2) between motivation and qualification was calculated like 0.57. This value is coherent with the pedagogical principles.

In future work, new experimentations will be made to improve the collaborative guideline and the SMLearning System. In this article, a Web-based Multimedia Player was presented, but the support by mobile and iDTV are being developed. These environments require adaptation of video-content and a technology in control level where there is a wide range of possibilities, e.g. Android, Apple TV, DVB / MHP, Boxee, UbuntuTV, HTML, among others, which hinders the approach of a unique solution. However, future prototypes are developing on Android as mobile technology and a Media Portal (http://www.team-mediaportal.com/) as a TV media center.

6. ACKNOWLEDGEMENTS

This research was partly funded by the Spanish National Plan of R+D, project number TIN2011-24139; by the CAM (Autonomous Community of Madrid), project number S2009/TIC-1650; and Universidad Autónoma de Madrid Teaching Plan, project number EPS-L2/4 (2011).

7. REFERENCES

[1] Sancin, C., Castello, V., Dell'Aiuto, V., Di Genova, D. 2009. T-learning for social inclusion, Genova DIDA, Italy, eLearning Papers, 12.

[2] Moeller, B. 1996. Learning from Television: A Research Review. CCT Reports, 11, 1-37.

[3] ORT France (eds.) Project ELU. 2007. Deliverable D 2.3. - State of the Art on Learning Using iDTV, [Online] http://www.elu-project.com

[4] Chorianopoulos, K., Lekakos, G. 2007. Learn and play with interactive TV. Comput. Entertain. 5 (2).

[5] Herweg Filho, G.H. and others. 2009. Interactive TV standards: a guide to MHP, OCAP, and JavaTV. Comunicação & Sociedade, 29 (48), 200-203.

[6] Aarreniemi-Jokipelto, P. 2005. T-learning model for learning via Digital TV. In Proceedings of the 16th annual conference on innovation in education for electrical and information engineering, Lappeenranta, Finland.

[7] W3C, 2011. Web and TV Interest Group. [Online] http://www.w3.org/2011/webtv/

[8] Collazos, C., Rusu, C., Arciniegas, J., Roncagliolo, S. 2009. Designing and Evaluating Interactive Television from a Usability Perspective, Advances in Computer-Human Interactions. ACHI '09. 381-385.

[9] Kaplan A., Haenlein M. 2010. Users of the world, unite! The challenges and opportunities of social media, Business Horizons, 53, 1, 59-68.

[10] De la Torre, A. 2006. Web Educativa 2.0. Revista Electrónica de Tecnología Educativa, 20. [Online] http://www.uib.es/depart/gte/gte/edutece/revelec20/anibal20.htm

[11] Agichtein, E., Castillo, C., Donato, D., Gionis A., and Mishne, G. 2008. Finding high-quality content in social media. In Proceedings of the international conference on Web search and web data mining (WSDM '08). ACM, New York, NY, USA, 183-194.

[12] W3C. 2008. SMIL 3.0. [Online] http://www.w3.org/AudioVideo/

[13] Cesar, P., Bulterman, D.C.A., Jansen, A.J. 2006. An architecture for end-user TV content enrichment. In Proceedings of the EuroITV 2006, 39-47.

[14] Campo, W., Chanchi, G., Arciniegas, J. 2010. Arquitectura para el Soporte de Comunidades Académicas Virtuales en Ambientes de TDi. Memorias del V Congreso Colombiano de Computación.

[15] Day, M., Crump, E., Rickly, R. 1996. Creating a virtual academic community, Computer networking and scholarship in the 21st-century university. 291-314.

[16] F. Bellotti, S. Vrochidis, E. Parissi, P. Lhoas, D. Mathevon, M. Pellegrino, G. Bo and I. Kompatsiaris Bellotti, F. 2008. T-learning Courses Development and Presentation Framework. IEEE Multidisciplinary Engineering Education Magazine, 3 (3), 69-76.

[17] Wiley, D. 2000. Connecting learning objects to instructional design theory: A definition, a metaphor, and a taxonomy. D. A. Wiley (Ed.). The Instructional Use of Learning Objects. [Online]. http://reusability.org/read/chapters/wiley.doc

[18] Rey-López, M., Díaz-Redondo, R., Fernández-Vilas, A., Pazos-Arias, J., López-Nores, M., García-Duque, J., Gil-Solla, A., Ramos-Cabrer, M.. 2008. T-MAESTRO and its authoring tool: using adaptation to integrate entertainment into personalized t-learning. Multimedia Tools and Applications, 40 (3), 409-451.

[19] Rey-López, M., Díaz, R. Fernández, A., Pazos, J. 2010. T-learning 2.0: a personalised hybrid approach based on ontologies and folksonomies. Computational Intelligence for Technology Enhanced Learning, Springer, 273, 125-142.

[20] Tsunoda, T., Hoshino, M. 2008. Automatic metadata expansion and indirect collaborative filtering for TV program recommendation system, Multimedia Tools and Applications, 36 (1-2), 37-54.

[21] Laiola, R., Cesar, P., Bulterman, D. 2010. Creating and sharing personalized time-based annotations of videos on the web. In Proceedings of the 10th ACM symposium on Document engineering (DocEng '10). ACM, New York, NY, USA, 27-36.

[22] Claros, I. Cobos, R. 2011. Un entorno Social Media para la Composición de Material Educativo Basado en Videos Interactivos, ISELEAR'11. 181-189

[23] Barkley, E., Cross, K., Howell, C. 2005. Collaborative learning techniques: a handbook for college faculty, John Wiley and Sons.

[24] IEEE Learning Technology Standards Committee, IEEE LOM working draft 6.1, [Online] http://ltsc.ieee.org/wg12/index.html

[25] Dublin Core Metadata Initiative, [Online] http://dublincore.org/

SentiTVchat: Sensing the Mood of Social-TV Viewers

Flávio Martins, Filipa Peleja, João Magalhães

Dep.Informática, Faculdade de Ciências e Tecnologia,
Universidade Nova de Lisboa, Portugal

flaviomartins@acm.org, filipapeleja@gmail.com, jm.magalhaes@fct.unl.pt

ABSTRACT

In this paper, we propose a novel Social-TV chat system integrating new methods of measuring TV viewers' feedback and new multi-screen interaction paradigms. Viewers' messages in chat services are a valuable asset for their peers in general, and for the cable TV operator in particular. The proposed system analyses chat-messages to detect the mood of viewers towards a given show (i.e., positive *vs* negative). This data is plotted on the screen to inform the viewer about the show popularity. Although the system provides a one-user / two-screens interaction approach, the chat privacy is assured by discriminating information sent to the shared screen or the personal screen. We evaluated the system on a first experiment with labeled data to assess the accuracy (78%) of the chat analysis algorithm and a second experiment with live chat data to validate the user interface.

Categories and Subject Descriptors

H.5.1 [**Multimedia Information Systems**]

General Terms

Design, Experimentation, Human Factors.

Keywords

SocialTV, chat, sentiment analysis, multi-screen interaction.

1. INTRODUCTION

TV-viewing is still a social experience but nowadays the audience is connected through the Internet and makes use of social networks like Twitter and Facebook to share thoughts in real-time while watching TV content. The living room TV entertainment environment has been enhanced by new interactive services that keep the user engaged and active. According to Haythornthwaite [6] media popularity is linked to social interactions in the new media. They concluded that social ties and social media are important to users' media viewing habits. More recently, Harboe et al [5], conducted an experiment examining the influence of Social-TV watching, i.e., users watch television alone but get instant notifications of what their friends and family are watching. Oehlberg et al. [8] went one step further and proposed a series of guidelines for designing distributed Social-TV viewing. In a related user study Weisz et al. [9], examined the activity of chatting while watching video online. Their technological solution was designed to observe human factors and not improve usability. In contrast, Cattelan et al. [3] implemented a system for chatting and drawing over video. Zaletelj et al. [10] adapted the live shows on-the-fly according to users' explicit votes/audiences collected from set-top-boxes. Several authors have proposed to analyse user messages in different domains. Bollen [2] and Dan et al. [4] addressed the domain of Twitter microposts and proposed to detect the sentiment expressed in user messages. Recently, Ariyasu et al. [1] proposed to detect the topics of twitter messages and to associate them to the correct show. In our system, the show is known and we proposed to infer the sentiment of the message towards the show. Thus, we set out to develop a Social-TV system prototype that allows users to chat with each other, in an integrated way. The paper's contribution is twofold:

- **Multi-screen interaction paradigm**: the system User Interface spans several screens and users interact with media through two screens. The first screen is intended for media visualization and it is assumed to be shared. The second screen is intended for personal use – it is where the user can watch previews, control the system and chat with peers.
- **Measuring TV chat feedback**: the chat component is powered by Google Channel API, thus a large base of users already exist. Sentiment analysis technology observes the sentiment expressed in opinions towards an item [7]. A novel viewer feedback metering method is proposed by integrating sentiment analysis technology into a Social-TV chat system.

With the proposed system, user messages are processed in real-time by a sentiment analysis algorithm, allowing the plot of the emotions felt by viewers, Figure 1. Another advantage of the proposed visualization method is that viewers can get a quick glimpse of the show's popularity in the last few minutes.

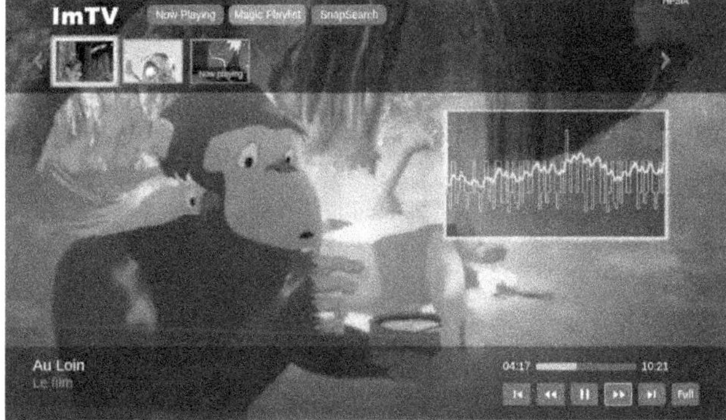

Figure 1. The SentiTVchat player with the sentiment graph.

In the following section, we shall describe the system architecture and components, and detail the chat analysis algorithm. An experimental evaluation and the corresponding discussion conclude this paper.

Figure 2. Media player with SentiTVchat graph.

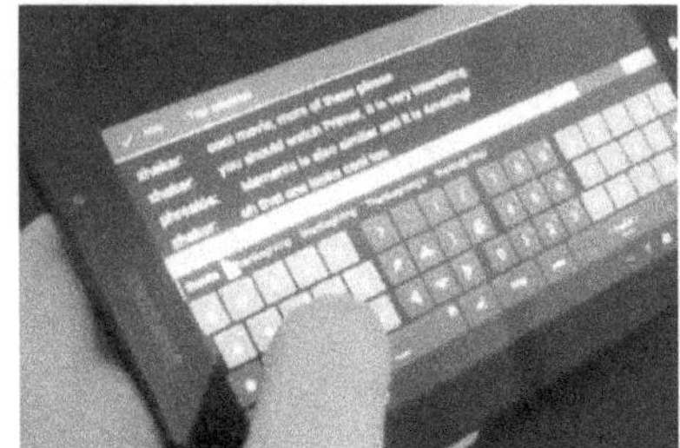

Figure 3. Tablet device in chat mode.

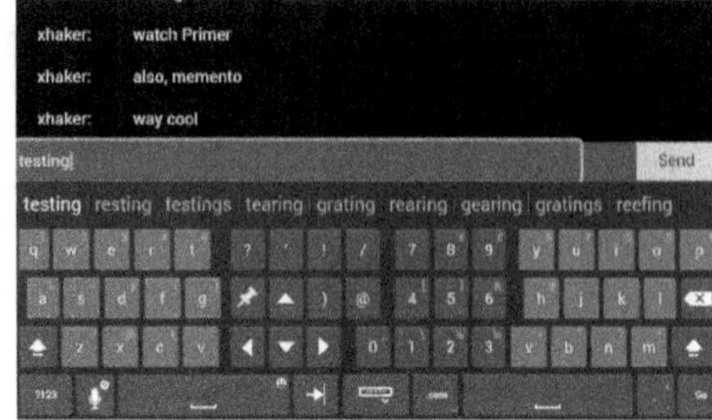

Figure 4. The personal control user interface.

2. A SYSTEM FOR SOCIAL-TV CHAT

The SentiTVChat system, allows "Social-TV-viewers" to communicate with each other during TV-viewing activities using a simple chat interface, shown in Figure 3 and Figure 4. The main goal was to develop a system for multi-screen TV-viewing activities and to enable the system to collect chat interactions with real-time analysis of the chat text to sense user moods.

2.1 System architecture

The system is divided in two parts: a Social-TV service and the SentiTVchat service, see Figure 5. The Social-TV service is responsible for the main media application and for binding user devices in the same session with a common communication channel. The chat system implements the chat service and messages analysis technology.

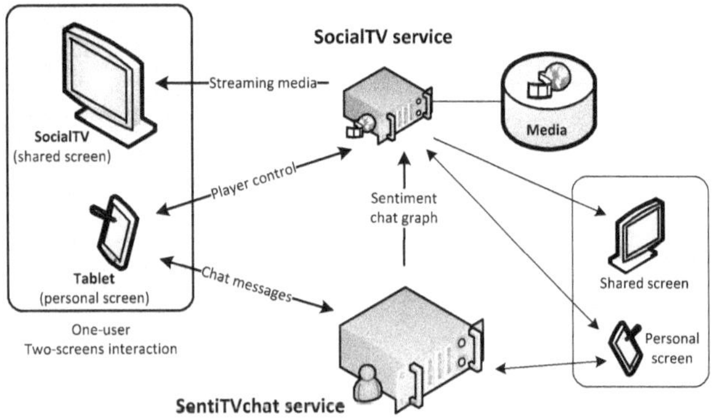

Figure 5. System architecture.

2.2 Social-TV service

Users can access the system by using any Web browser, capable of running JavaScript, which includes most modern browsers for desktops, laptops and the browsers included in mobile platforms such as iOS and Android. In Figure 2, we show the remote-control client interface running on an Android tablet, for example. The users can use mobile devices, such as tablets, to remote control the TV and participate in chat rooms with other people.

TV-Screen: The Media Player UI
To build the TV-screen interface, in Figure 2, we used the resources provided in the Google TV documentation for HTML5. In addition, popular browsers started shipping preliminary support for the Full screen API allowing the player to turn most modern browsers into a full-blown media consumption screen.

Tablet-screen: The Personal Control UI
The remote-control functionality includes standard controls such as Play/Pause and other control tasks, it also offers directional keys for navigating between user-interface buttons on the TV-screen. After authentication, a bidirectional channel is opened between the Tablet-screen and the TV-screen. This allows the TV-screen application to send updated media metadata information such as program title and progress to the secondary devices.

To authenticate the user, we use two factors: the user's Google account login information and a random alphanumeric 5-digit code that is available to the user in the TV-screen display corner. This provides better security and allows a single user account to be able to control a number of TV-screen devices.

Binding devices: a session based communication channel
To bind the user's devices and to implement communication channels between them we looked into Web Sockets. Current browser support for Web Sockets is limited and implementations differ substantially between browsers providing this API. Thus, we decided to make use of Google App Engine APIs to build our system so we could utilize the Channel API available on this platform. The Channel API is similar to Web Sockets, it allows Web applications to establish bidirectional communication channels. However, browser support is improved, since the API is provided to the client-side in a JavaScript library. This means that any JavaScript capable mobile browser should be able to communicate with a multitude of HTML5 ready devices running the player, such as a Web TV, a PC or a tablet.

2.3 SentiTVchat service

The implemented chat system supports the chat communications among users seamlessly. The Tablet-side UI gets the current TV-channel from the updates received from the TV-screen application. Thus, when users access the chat section in the Tablet-screen it will automatically enter the corresponding chat room for the TV-channel being watched on the TV-screen. We considered that each TV-channel has a chat room with an identical *name*, so, if the user is watching the *tv1* channel, for example, the Tablet-screen retrieves the URL: *chat-host.tld/?room=tv1*. The page obtained displays the latest 1000 messages from the chat room. Moreover, a subscription is registered on the server, so that the client can receive further messages instantly. A subscription is registered with the chat room, the user, and the communication channel. When a message is received, it is relayed to all the subscribers of the corresponding chat room through each of their channels. However, to send messages, the client makes a POST request to the */newMessage* endpoint instead of using the channel.

The system also allows read-only subscriptions to chat rooms, which do not require authentication. These were used to implement SentiTVMeter. This feature visualizes the chat room activity in a novel way: it draws a sliding line chart showing each message "sentiment analysis" value and a weighted moving average of the last 20 messages. This visualization was superimposed into the TV-screen display, so users can always monitor what is the general sentiment at each moment. The chart is drawn client-side using the Canvas element and JavaScript, making it lightweight, because the server just needs to annotate the messages with the sentiment analysis value, and pipe it through the communication channel.

2.4 Chat sentiment analysis

Sentiment analysis aims at detecting the preferences expressed within user-comments. To tackle this problem in an automated way, comments are represented as a vector of unigrams (words) which occur within each user-comment. In sentiment analysis not every word is useful for detecting the preferences of users [7], thus, in our approach only *adjectives*, *adverbs*, *verbs* and *nouns* are considered. In the following sections, the methodology to represent and classify user-comments will be detailed formally.

2.4.1 Problem formulation

Consider a set of N user-comments, $D = \{(c_1, p_1),...,(c_N, p_N)\}$, where a user-comment c_i is labeled as positive $p_j = 1$ or negative $p_j = 0$. Taking a machine learning approach and considering the training set D, sentiment chat analysis aims at learning a classifier function,

$$\Phi : c_i \rightarrow p_i \in [0,1], \tag{1}$$

such that for all new user-comment, $c_i \notin D$, the function Φ will infer a polarity value $p_i = 1$ for positive comments and $p_i = 0$ for negative comments. User-comments, are represented as a vector of *opinion words*, i.e., $c_i = (ow_{i,1},...,ow_{i,m})$ where each component $ow_{i,m}$ depicts the opinion word m of the user-comment i. An opinion word is a word that can express a preference, which can have different intensities and different orientations (positive or negative).

2.4.2 Orientation and intensity of an OW

The orientation of an OW indicates whether a word expresses a positive or negative preference. Turney [8] proposed the pointwise mutual information (PMI) to estimate the orientation of a phrase. This metric measures the degree of statistical dependence between two words by observing the probability of co-occurring together and individually. Hence, in this context the correlation will be measured by using a positive, and negative, reference. Thereby one can compute the semantic orientation (SO) of a word as

$$SO(ow_{i,j}) = \log_2\left(\frac{hits(ow_{i,j},"excellent")hits("poor")}{hits(ow_{i,j},"poor")hits("excellent")}\right), \tag{2}$$

where $hits(ow_{i,j})$, and for instance $hits(ow_{i,j},"excellent")$, are given by the number of hits a Web search engine returns using these keywords. In this paper, we tested the reference words listed on Table 1.

Table 1. Semantic orientation and word polarity references.

Technique	*Word polarity references*
T: Turney [8]	"excellent"/"poor"
G: Generic	"good"/"bad"
DS: Domain Specific	"best movie"/"worst movie"
DS+T	"excellent movie"/"poor movie"

Another factor to be considered is the intensity of an *opinion word.* OWs may express different intensity values, such as: "*contented*" versus "*ecstatic*" [7]. Thus, the lexical resource SentiWordNet [7], defining the intensity of opinion words, is crucial in this phase. In this lexical resource, each feature is associated with two numerical scores (positivity and negativity). In this context, given the SO of an OW, SentiWordNet will return its sentiment intensity. Therefore, the SentiWordNet (swn) for an OW will be given by,

$$swn(ow) = \begin{cases} posSWN(ow), & SO(ow) > 0, \\ negSWN(ow), & SO(ow) \leq 0 \end{cases} \tag{3}$$

where $posSWN(ow)$ corresponds to the positive score value given by SentiWordNet and $negSWN(ow)$ will correspond to the negative score. In Table 2 the *family* column refers to the words' family: N (noun), V (verb) and R (adverb). Regarding the sentiment intensity, the lexical resource SentiWordNet associates each word with a positive (*posSWN*) and negative (*negSWN*) value.

Table 2. SentiWordNet weights for the sentence "Love it or hate it, however someone tell me what on earth…".

word	*family*	*posSWN*	*negSWN*
love	N	1.375	0.0
hate	V	0.0	-0.75
however	R	0.5	0.5
someone	N	0.0	0.0
tell	V	0.875	-0.625
earth	N	0.0	-0.625

2.4.3 Classifier function

For classifying reviews, we used a linear classifier to assign a confidence value to that review. The classifier identifies the orientation and intensity of all opinion words of a comment $c_i = (ow_{i,1},...,ow_{i,m})$ and computes its rating based on the sigmoid function,

$$\Phi(c_i) = \frac{1}{1 + \exp\left(-\sum_j ow_{i,j} \cdot w_j\right)} + b. \tag{4}$$

The weights w_j are learned with a gradient descent algorithm to train the function to rate comments between positive and negative. The constant b is a bias factor for adjusting the sentiment curve.

2.4.4 Sentiment graph

Since the sentiment graph is plotted on the player screen (which might be shared), all chat posts are plotted on the graph anonymously. Figure 1 and Figure 2 shows the sentiment graph on the player screen: instant messages are plotted in grey and a smoothed curve is plotted in a bright green to offer a better sense of the show popularity.

3. EXPERIMENTS

The system's sentiment analysis module was evaluated on two settings: a first experiment assessed the accuracy of the sentiment analysis algorithm on labeled data; and a second experiment validated the system on live chat data captured from Justin.tv.

3.1 Accuracy assessment

The language analyzer Freeling (http://nlp.lsi.upc.edu/freeling) was applied to identify word families (nouns, verbs, etc). Later, user-comments were split into sentence level with the Natural Language Toolkit (http://www.nltk.org/home). A dataset from IMDB reviews was used to assess the accuracy of the sentiment analysis algorithm. The data is evenly split in two categories: positive and negative. We have used 1400 training and 600 test reviews along with a number of positive and negative reviews equally divided.

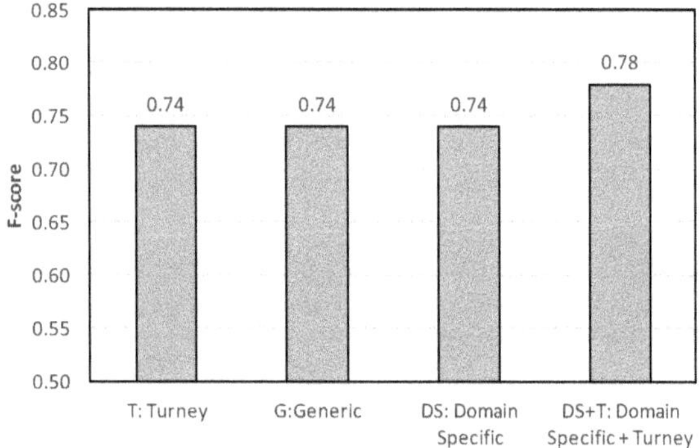

Figure 6: F1-score for IMDB.

Figure 6 shows the classifier performance in terms of F-score, i.e., $F\text{-score} = 2\ Precision \cdot Recall / (Precision + Recall)$, also known as the harmonic mean. This figure illustrates the sentiment analysis performance under different settings. We can observe here the importance of choosing adequate reference words for the Semantic Orientation (Equation 2): the best performance was achieved with "excellent-movie"/"poor-movie". This implies that a combination of a domain specific term ("*movie*") with general string positive and negative terms ("*excellent*"/"*poor*") is the best setting. These results illustrate the sentiment analysis ability to evaluate the sentiment within user comments.

3.2 Real-data experiment

To validate the system on real chat data, we collected chat data from two live Justin.tv channels: 4744 sentences for the *IGN Pro League* channel and 4553 sentences for the *this WEEK in TECH* channel. Figure 7 illustrates the real-time sentiment analysis graph of this data. These graphs present the results obtained with an analysis of the sentiment expressed in the last 100 sentences. There are several fluctuations on the instant messages (gray line) and the popularity trends of the show are clearly visible on the red curve. In this experiment, we observed that the algorithm was not capable of correctly analyzing some of the messages since viewers used slang expressions not recognized by the system.

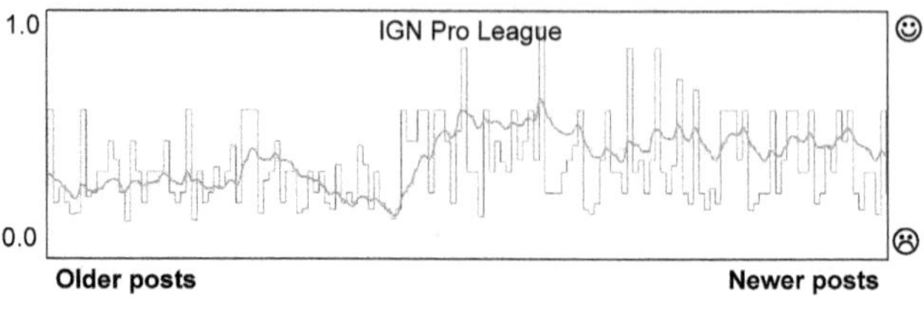

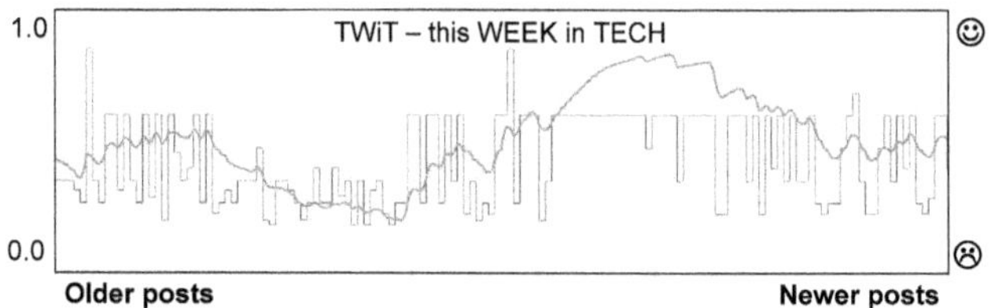

Figure 7. Real-time sentiment analysis graph.

4. DISCUSSION

This paper proposed a novel Social-TV chat system that measures in real time the viewers' mood / show popularity. By measuring and plotting viewers' mood, users that are zapping through channels will have instant access to the show popularity over the last minutes. Additionally, this measure will be closer to real viewers' preferences than by simply measuring audiences. Evaluation on the IMDB dataset demonstrated the ability of the sentiment classifier in identifying the preferences within user-comments. As future work, we will improve the sentiment analysis for other languages and for chat slang.

Acknowledgements. This work has been funded by the Foundation for Science and Technology by projects UTA-Est/MAI/0010/2009 and PEst-OE/EEI/UI0527/2011, Centro de Informática e Tecnologias da Informação (CITI/ FCT/ UNL) - 2011-2012.

5. REFERENCES

[1] Ariyasu, K. et al. 2011. Message analysis algorithms and their application to social tv. *EuroITV '11*, Lisbon, Portugal, Jun. 2011.

[2] Bollen, J. 2010. Determining the public mood state by analysis of microblogging posts. *Alife XII Conf. MIT Press*. (2010).

[3] Cattelan, R.G. et al. 2008. Watch-and-comment as a paradigm toward ubiquitous interactive video editing. *ACM Transactions on Multimedia Computing, Communications, and Applications*. (2008).

[4] Dan, O. et al. 2011. Filtering microblogging messages for social tv. *Proceedings of the 20th international conference companion on World wide web - WWW '11* (New York, USA, Mar. 2011), 197.

[5] Harboe, G. et al. 2008. Ambient social tv: Drawing people into a shared experience. *ACM SIGCHI Human Factors in Computing Systems*. ACM.

[6] Haythornthwaite, C. 2001. The Strength and the Impact of New Media. *Proceedings of the 34th Annual Hawaii International Conference on System Sciences (HICSS-34)*.

[7] Liu, B. 2010. Sentiment analysis and subjectivity. *Handbook of Natural Language Processing*. (2010), 978-1420085921.

[8] Oehlberg, L. et al. 2006. Social TV: Designing for distributed, sociable television viewing. *Proc. EuroITV* (2006), 25–26.

[9] Weisz, J.D. et al. 2007. Watching together: Integrating text chat with video. *ACM SIGCHI Human Factors in Computing Systems*..

[10] Zaletelj, J. et al. 2009. Real-time viewer feedback in the iTV production. *EuroITV 2009*.

Maps-TV: A Software Architecture to Support Development of Collaborative Maps in DTVi

Izequiel Norões
Laboratório de Engenharia do Conhecimento
Universidade de Fortaleza (UNIFOR)
Fortaleza – CE – Brasil
izequiel@gmail.com

Vasco Furtado
Laboratório de Engenharia do Conhecimento
Universidade de Fortaleza (UNIFOR)
Fortaleza – CE – Brasil
vasco@unifor.br

Elizabeth Furtado
Laboratório de Estudos do Usuário e Qualidade de Sistemas
Universidade de Fortaleza (UNIFOR)
Fortaleza – CE – Brasil
elizabet@unifor.br

ABSTRACT

This paper proposes a software architecture for the development of collaborative maps applied to the model of the Brazilian Digital Television System (SBTVD), called MAPS-TV. We describe the modules of MAPS-TV, how they interact, and how we extend the content representation model used by TV-Anytime to allow this interaction. For the purpose of validating our proposal, we also demonstrate how MAPS-TV facilitated the creation of collaborative maps – related to urban problems – to be used in the SBTVD, with no need for participation of software developers in the process.

Categories and Subject Descriptors

H.3.5 [**Online Information Services**]: Web-based services; D.3.3 [**Language Constructs and Features**]: Frameworks; H.5.1 [**Multimedia Information Systems**]: Hypertext navigation and maps; D.2.2 [**Design Tools and Techniques**]: User interfaces. J.7 [Computer Applications]: Computers in Other Systems.

General Terms

Experimentation, Human Factor.

Keywords

WikiMapps, Interactive Digital TV, Web Services, Urban Mobility.

1. INTRODUCTION

In Web 2.0, many applications support the ample production of information by Internet users. A specific type of application that is emerging, in this context, are mashups of different sources of information, particularly with the use of integration of services for digital maps, also called collaborative maps [16]. On these collaborative maps, the digital map functions as a blackboard to receive stories told by people about what they want to share in their social networks.

Parallel to the explosion of collaborative activities on the web, media convergence is occurring and has been opening space for the generation of digital content to be done in a ubiquitous manner. The Brazilian Digital TV System (SBTVD) [18] – using Ginga [8] as the basis for interactive features – is one of these spaces and can foster the collaborative process of the social web through the use of television.

Although this context is auspicious, in order for it to become a reality, the ecosystem of SBTVD application production must be developed and certain issues must be resolved. First, it should be understood that this ecosystem involves content producers that are not necessarily software developers. There must be tools that help them to produce content, integrate such content with applications, and make it available via SBDTV. Moreover, one cannot assume that this ecosystem will be isolated from applications that already exist on the web and the content produced there. It is necessary to provide tools that aid the integration of applications, with the provision of standards and methods to support the exchange of data and content between such applications.

Our research is part of the aforementioned issue. In particular, we define an architecture to support the development of collaborative maps in the SBTVD. This architecture, here called MAPS-TV, starts out from the principle that the process of generating an application for DTV (here called a DTVi application) takes place on the web, and the enhancement of this process takes place by the decoupling and modularization of activities for software development and content production. The decoupling of these activities required us to define a model to represent information that is communicated between the different modules of the architecture, which is what we did with the extension of the model used in the TV-Anytime standard (TVA) [23].

The MAPS-TV architecture includes services (provided through web services or directly through the website) for communication with the WikiMapps [3] platform of collaborative map generation on the web. The outputs of these services were represented in an extension of TVA, a model originally intended to represent interactive and multimedia content on DTVs, but requiring more details that would allow it to represent characteristics inherent to collaborative map content.

In this article we describe the modules of MAPS-TV, how they interact, and how we extend the content representation model used in TV-Anytime to allow the treatment of georeferenced content. For the purpose of showing the viability of our proposal, we will demonstrate how MAPS-TV facilitates the creation of a collaborative application of DTVi maps using a structure similar to a content management system, using templates in the application, and the WikiMapps tool as content provider.

EuroITV'12, July 4–6, 2012, Berlin, Germany.

2. COLLABORATIVE MAPS

As an example of an application for the use of collaborative maps, we can take the WikiMapps tool, which appeared in an earlier proposal aimed at obtaining information about crimes through maps called WikiCrimes (http://www.wikicrimes.org) (see Figure 1). The term WikiMapps comes from the combination of three words: Wiki (Wikipedia) + Map + Apps (applications). The purpose of WikiMapps (http://www.wikimapps.com) is to offer an environment for creating and maintaining collaborative maps. It is not simply to make a website to mark something on a map on the web. This is a site where the map and the markers (pins, routes, images, areas or icons) that will be placed on it are the instruments around which the processes of collaboration and interaction will occur. The collaborative maps generated by WikiMapps also rely on features typical of a social network, because people can comment, vote and indicate the recorded information, identify friends' markers, add a user as a friend, and therefore generate interaction among the members of the social network. The WikiMapps differential is the inclusion of the social networking concept (through functionalities) to collaborative maps.

A collaborative map offers different means whereby the user can interact with the map and with other users. The main feature of interaction is the marker. Through it, the user associates the information to a location on the map. In other words: to map, to mark or to record means to georeference information. The WikiMapps tool allows the creation of markers, classifying the information into different types: people, establishments, buildings, events, reports, routes, regions, and others.

Let's take the example of a map of reports of crimes in dangerous locations in the city. With the map already created in the WikiMapps application, we intend in this proposal to provide the registration of new reports of crime collaboratively via DTV. The problem that appears is that specific solutions, such as this one, already have information in the metadata of this map, such as the type of crime, the person who reported it, etc. But in order to record information in a collaborative way, for any type of map, there is the need to generate the interfaces dynamically to the map applied.

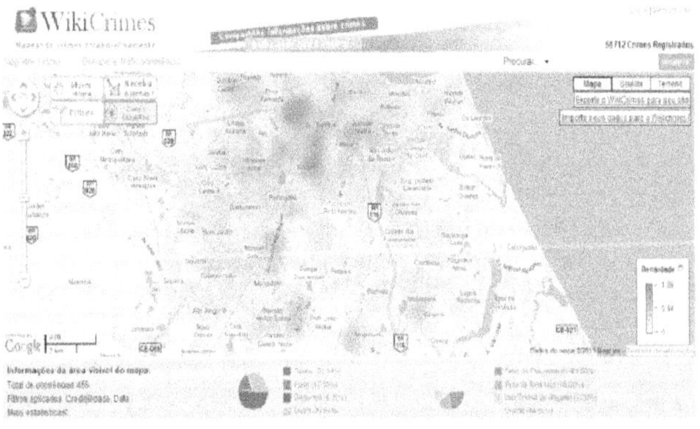

Figure 1. Application of a collaborative map on the web – WikiCrimes.

3. THE ECOSYSTEM OF SOFTWARE DEVELOPMENT FOR DIGITAL TV

When the SBTVD standard was defined in 2009, a window of opportunity was opened to developers, in light of the possibility to create applications based on Ginga to fully utilize the interactivity resource featured in this newly-adopted standard. DTVi applications have a tremendous chance for popular use because of the possibilities of the Brazilian model, which has a massive range, considering that nearly all Brazilian households have a TV set.

3.1. Development of DTVi Applications

Companies and universities have maintained their progress regarding the development of interactive applications, which has generated applications developed for specific purposes such as the T-Gov application, of the government-owned company Dataprev, with its project called "*TV Digital – Social*" [20]. There are also commercial interactivity platforms based on Ginga (AstroTV middleware [12]), such as the StickerCenter [12] project, opening the range of T-Commerce applications of the Totvs company, which – in addition to the applications disclosed by broadcast companies – allows for the download of applications and brings a degree of customization to DTVi applications, by merging with the use of IPTV and Ginga.

Even considering the advances that have occurred in the development of DTVi applications, there is still a demand for the generation of applications for the consumption of television content of information to be supplied, and improvements to be made in the development of tools designed for DTVi programming. In the current context, these tools follow two approaches:

- Textual, requiring code writing. These are programming environments [2] and development frameworks (AstroDev, cited above) that allow the automatic generation of applications for interactive environments. These tools still represent the majority, and allow greater flexibility in the development of applications for a wide range of needs. However, they are more geared toward experienced users with knowledge of programming. Users who are content producers – who will make better use of content production for interactive TV and are part of producer-companies, television channels or networks – usually have little or no programming knowledge to have satisfactory experience with these tools. To make interaction of non-programmer users possible, it is necessary to provide tools that facilitate the creation of DTVi tools that can access content already created in other media, as well as update such content, thereby contributing to improving the quality of content and even the dissemination of use of interactive applications via television.

- Editing of DTVi applications with visual resources. These are authoring tools that theoretically facilitate and increase speed in the process of developing software for interactive environments. But the tools available on the market [9] are proprietary and those that are available still have limitations. For example, they do not provide a preview of created content, which can be viewed before being transmitted and validated for TV programming. The preview is a requirement for these tools that would make it possible to create applications for DTV that are closer to the concept of "What You See Is What You Get" [1] and thus facilitate the interaction of novice users in content production.

Limitations of this type have implications for the design process for the interaction of DTVi applications and, consequently, to support the automatic construction of a user interface. They happen mainly because these tools work with an environment of emulation, hindering the process of content production. In other words, once content is generated, it will be shown via an application previously defined to present it, or by using virtualization to show the preview.

Finally, another analysis we performed is in regard to interoperability, i.e. the ability of environments to work on any DTV standard and the solution found to communicate content created across platforms, such as web and digital TV. In the first case, we evaluated how the tools make use of the middleware of the standards in order to facilitate the development of interactive applications. Ginga, in the Brazilian context, allows the development of interactive digital applications in both the declarative language NCL (Nested Context Language) – Ginga-NCL [21] – and in a non-declarative manner using the Java language – Ginga-J [6]. The equivalent in European DVB (Digital Video Broadcasting) is the MHP (Multimedia Home Platform), where we have the applications and development environments, GINGA-J and GEM (Globally Executable MHP).

We have surveyed the following tools for edition of DTVi applications such as CUICA[22], Jame Author[7], Icareus Suite[10], Composer[9], iTV Project[15], Contextual Ginga[4], T-Vilo Maker[17] and Stiker Center[12] (see Table 1), only the tools [4], [9], and [17] are specific to the Brazilian standard. The tools [22], [6], [10] and [15] are in the European standard (MHP/GEM), but only [15] is capable of interoperability among standards. Regarding interoperability to communicate the created content across platforms, we analyzed how they undertake the mapping among the interactive media to be transmitted along with the DTVi application. Most of them use XML files. In [17], for example, all of the relations between the media are represented in an XML file, such as order and runtime of the media, synchronization, and temporary attributes, among others.

	Offers generation of dynamic interfaces	Requires a specialist	Editing with visual resources	Supports interoperability
Cuica	NO	NO	NO	NO
Jame Author	YES	YES	NO	NO
Icareus Suite	YES	NO	NO	NO
Composer	NO	YES	YES	NO
iTV Project	NO	NO	YES	NO
Contextual Ginga	NO	NO	YES	NO
T-Vilo Maker	YES	YES	YES	NO
Sticker Center	YES	YES	YES	NO

Table 1. Comparison among development tools for DTVi applications.

One can see in Table 1 that none of the authoring tools included in the study meets all the needs presented, thus making it necessary to develop an architecture capable of covering this need and thereby promote the generation of applications with greater ease, especially for non-specialist users.

3.2. Representation of Multimedia Content for SBTVD

We have elaborated a comparative analysis (see Table 2) of the existing metadata. This table shows the gap related to the representation of information for collaborative mapping. A demand found in this study was in regard to a model for representing georeferenced content (metadata). The DVB makes use of MPEG-21 and TV-Anytime for description of multimedia content and thus represent/describe their data and make use thereof in the chain of information flow to which their architectures permit.

There are two types of metadata formats for DTV, hard and soft [20]. The main difference between these two formats is that the first one (such as XMLTV and Information & Service Tables) does not allow the extension of the pre-defined information descriptors in such a way that the existing systems that treat metadata are able to interpret the new descriptors. However with the second one (as is the case of the TV-Anytime, MPEG-7 and MPEG-21 metadata standards), it is possible to create new descriptors based on existing ones and allow the system to incorporate this new information.

We can see a brief comparison among a few different multimedia description metadata, as follows:

- XMLTV is an XML-based file format for describing Programming Grids, better known as Electronic Program Guide (EPG). The TV channels or distributors use it as a base template in their systems and extend its functionality according to their business needs. It has a static structure and cannot be extended. It does not have fields for comments or any other interaction of the users. Also, it does not contemplate any reference to geographic features, which are necessary for collaborative maps.

- MPEG-21 is a format standardized by the ISO/IEC, where the different elements form an infrastructure permitting the delivery and consumption of media content to work together. Moreover, it seeks to decrease the illegal distribution of files among users on the web. It is a flexible structure and defines a set of terms and concepts that are able to compose a model for the representation of a digital item, which is a generic content.

- TV-ANYTIME contemplates several services demanded by the industry and academia [21]. It supports the producers to capture, store, verify and distribute content. One of its main advantages comes from the fact that it uses metadata to describe audiovisual content as well as the flow of the content production and distribution. It is also extendable, allowing the description of new features, which is particularly relevant for our purposes of describing information for collaborative mapping.

	XMLTV	MPEG-21	TVA
Description of data (EPG)	Yes	Yes	Yes
Allows use of interactivity	Yes	Yes	Yes
Personalization	No	Yes	Yes
Collaboration / Sharing	No	Yes	Yes
Extension / Interoperability	No	Yes	Yes
Description of multimedia content	Yes	Yes	Yes
Use of geolocation data	No	No	No

Table 2. Comparison of the metadata studied.

All current open DTV systems adopt hard metadata models. Nonetheless, studies carried out mainly by European researchers [11] have examined the incorporation of flexible models. However in these works there are references to the SAVANT [5] project, which is a typical case of extension of TVA. But an extension was not found in these models [11] to represent georeferenced content. Furthermore, these models are not part of the set of metadata (SI tables) and available functionalities for the development of applications for SBTVD. But they can be used as a reference or basis for implementing a model that can be adapted and applied primarily in the communication of data between WEB and DTV applications.

4. CREATING CONTENT FOR COLLABORATIVE MAPS IN DTVi

The analysis presented in section 3 allowed us to identify the deficiencies that exist in the authoring tools for the generation of applications in the context of maps, and the lack of a model for the representation of information that flows among the participating elements in the process of content generation in DTV standards. In the case of this proposal, we present the MAPS-TV architecture based on the decoupling and modularization of activities of developing DTVi applications and content production for collaborative maps. We also propose a model for the representation of content, called MapsTVXML, used to allow automatic generation of DTVi applications for manipulating maps via DTV, as shown below.

4.1 Basic Architecture of the Application

The MAPS-TV architecture, for validation of this study, makes use of the information base and services of the WikiMapps tool, as an example of a content provider. The main element of this architecture is the Interactive Service Provider (ISP) [13], which is responsible for requesting a collaborative map for a DTVi application related to a given content to be aired in TV programming. This requisition is made through a query to web services related to this context. These services communicate with the WikiMapps tool through the use of metadata generated automatically with information from a map. A DTVi application makes use of metadata in the process of consumption and generation of information, making interactivity and collaboration possible with regard to the maps.

Consider the existence of a map of urban mobility, containing records of potholes (occurrences) on the streets of a big metropolis. This map is accessed via the web by the *WikiMappsPotholes* application and was generated by the WikiMapps tool. An occurrence is configured as a marker in WikiMapps and the data transmitted about the occurrence would be an event associated with that marker. One possible scenario for use of this map in DTV would be to reference it during a report on a local newscast, when the news anchor reports a traffic-related incident. The viewers watching the newscast would be invited to see further information about the reported fact and also to participate interactively. They would interact with the remote control using the DTVi application, which would present the occurrences from the *WikiMappsPotholes* map.

Figure 2 illustrates the architecture; the elements of this architecture that participate in the process of generating map applications for DTVi carry out the steps described below (numbering according to the architecture). The user of this process is the content producer, who could be the writer of the newscast described above.

FLOW 1: The user queries a list of available maps, previewing them in the respective DTVi applications. To do so, the ISP makes a request to the WikiMapps web service through the Maps-TV API to locate each map.

FLOW 2: After locating the map, it generates a set of metadata linked to the example we took for the *Potholes* Map. Once the metadata are compiled, the information is returned by means of an HTTP request that will initially occur in the collection of information in the WikiMapps base, which will generate an XML file formatted in the MapsTVXML standard. This file will provide information such as: the type of incident and the person/agent who reported it, pertaining to a specific map of the application initially defined by a marker. It is worth mentioning that the ISP can either consume the XML for use in an editing tool for DTVi applications, or download the file with the WikiMappsTV application through the automatic generation thereof, based on application templates available in the WikiMapps web tool.

FLOW 3: Given that the ISP chooses to consume the XML integration file, it is sent to the authoring tool, with the aim of creating an interface for a DTVi application. If the ISP chooses to download the WikiMappsTV application, it will also make use of the XML tool, but will be using a tool generated automatically from the WikiMapps web application that was compiled with a map generated specifically for this application and also with the MapsTVXML, with the data from *WikiMappsPotholes*.

FLOW 4: The broadcaster receives the application packets from the ISP, which was customized in an authoring tool, or the one that was generated with the WikiMappsTV template along with the application content, with the information passed through the metadata described in the MapsTVXML format. These will be transmitted along with the television program related to the map, which could be a newscast (as in the case of our example), an entertainment program, or even a documentary, which will be associated to a map according to its programming.

FLOW 5: In the last step, the reception of the DTVi application occurs by means of the receiver set. If there is the record of new information on the part of the viewer and there is a return-channel, the result of the viewer's interaction will be transmitted directly to a Web service in WikiMapps, which will receive the data via HTTP through a request from the application itself. These data received can either bring the information that will complement a marker on the map, or generate statistics with the interactions of viewers.

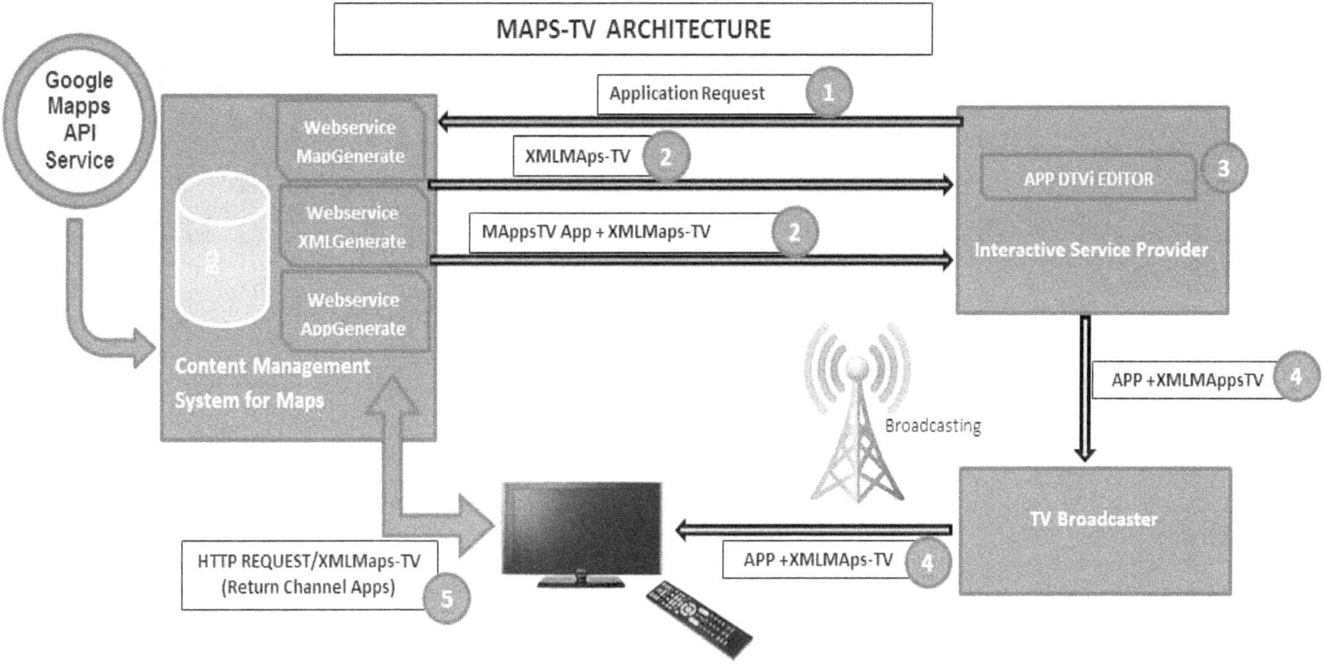

Figure 2 - Complete architecture with the flow required to create an application.

The flow above describes how the Maps-TV architecture works for the purpose of generating DTVi applications, which will serve as consumers and suppliers of content for the maps, clearly indicating the decoupling of the steps of content generation and application to TV. We perceived this based on flows 1 and 2 with the use of information from the Map Content Manager, where we will have services of generating maps, generating content linked to the maps, plus the possibility of generating a pre-formatted application (using pre-established templates), thus being of great value to the Interactive Service Providers who will make use of the XML or of the application of generated Maps.

The ISP that has the application can send it to the TV broadcaster or, if needed, customize an application based on the XML received. Thus the application can now be delivered to the TV broadcasters and we will therefore have the transmission of the application to the customers, i.e., the viewers' TV signal receiver set, as seen in Flow 4.

It is noteworthy that in the generation of the application (at the source of the content) and in the PSI, an expert software developer was not used for this purpose. This is the main contribution that we have in this proposal, as well as services, architecture modules and the XML model presented here.

4.2 Representation of Maps-TV Content

As previously stated, the metadata generated in the compilation of the elements by the WikiMapps application will be passed to an XML file, which contains the specifications of the Maps-TVXML model. This file represents the basic structure necessary for the assembly of the PSI interactive application. Maps-TVXML is based on the TV-Anytime (TVA) model, which among the existing models [19] has a greater extensibility and flexibility, serving and being adopted in the Brazilian standard as we saw in the analysis of the state of the art.

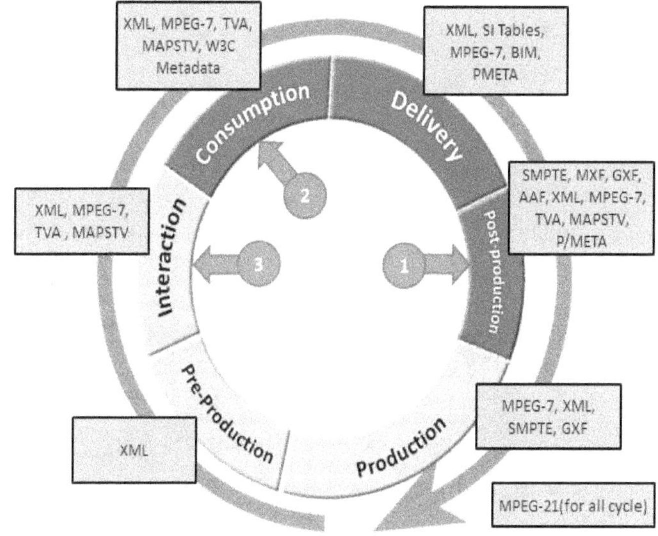

Figure 3. Life cycle of metadata to DTVi (adapted from [21]).

The flow of content to DTVi according to the lifecycle of metadata [11] can be seen in Figure 3. Here we indicate the three stages where Maps-TVXML is used: (1) when the content provider compiles the XML for the application; (2) consumption of the content, when the application is delivered via broadcast on TV and it makes use of data application; and finally (3) the interaction, when the viewer needs to use the return channel and thus send its data application response.

Observing the data presented in the comparison, we can see that a specialization for the use of maps would be necessary, as well as the data for the collaborative applications that may come to be used through this application. Hence, one can justify the proposal of an extension of TVA. The main elements of MapsTVXML are (see Figure 4):

- App – description of the application features such as the author of the app, the title, the URL, the creation date, and the type of map;

- Ads – advertisement information such as banners, texts and links;

- Wikiuser-Account – information about the author of the map;

- Map – the map used in the application;

- Marker – this is the main element of a collaborative map application because it represents the events that will be plotted on the map. The model represents the name of the marker, an icon, the creation date, the expiration date, and a classification to define the type of event (buildings, artistic production, report, event, people);

- Location – the place associated to the marker with longitude and latitude;

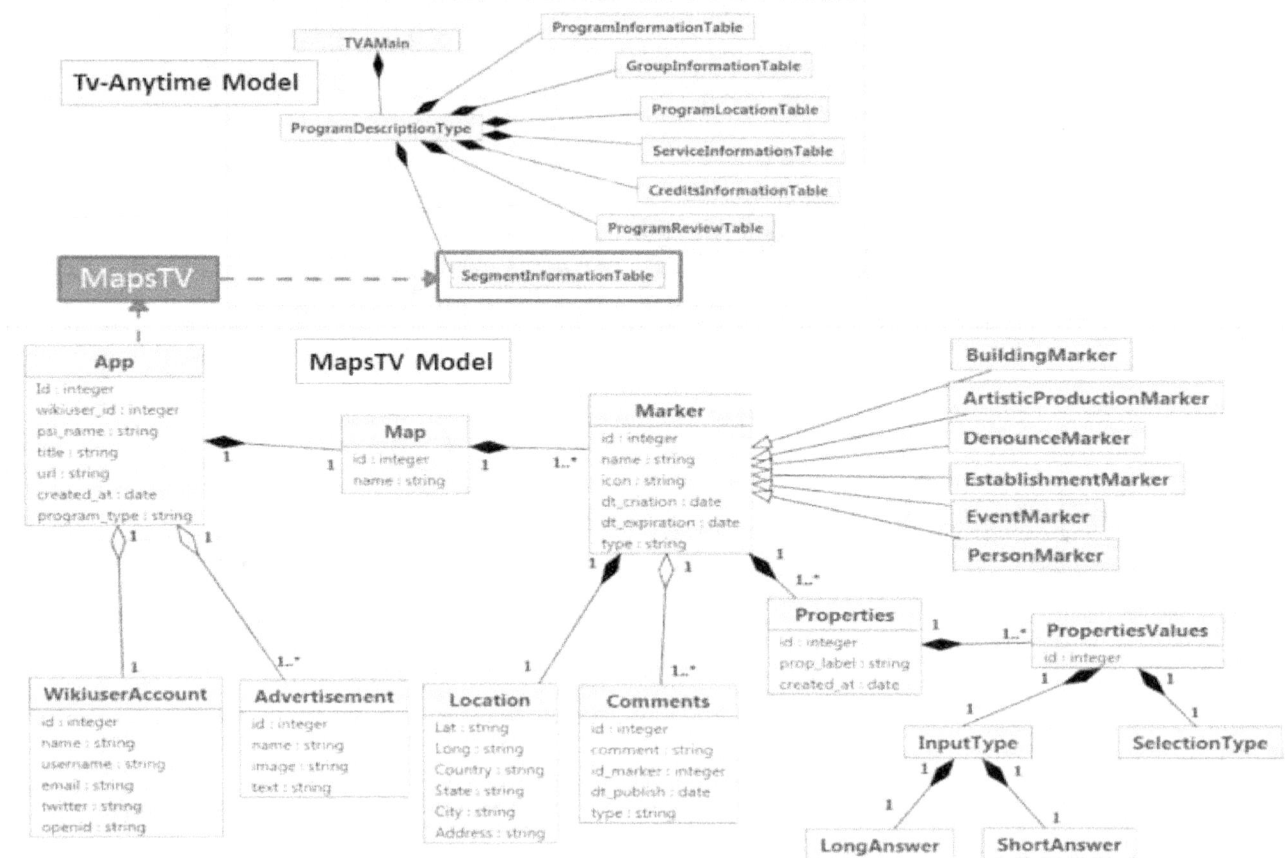

Figure 4 – The Maps-TVXML model integrated to the TVA model.

- Comments – comments about the marker;

- Properties – each marker has properties. These properties characterize the marker and require the specification of the type of interface to be used. That is why in the model we have defined two types of data input: free text input and selection (in which the values of the properties are predefined).

4.3 Using the Metadata with Tools for Generation of DTVi Applications

Applications made for the Digital TV environment use the languages NCL and Lua, and these are not very simple to use by a TV editor or developers of a TV programming grid. In the related works section, we have some examples of content editors who are actually editors of DTVi applications; one of them [17] uses an XML file to specify multimedia content but any metadata standard can be applied.

In order for these editors to be able to use the context of collaborative maps, they must have the capacity to interpret XML files to obtain data for an application according to the proposed Maps-TV API. Considering that the XML model used in the proposal of this study can be adopted, such applications make use of metadata so as to incorporate this functionality into their resources and can thus apply to the generation of their applications.

5. VALIDATION OF THE PROPOSAL: GENERATION OF A DTVI APPLICATION USING THE WIKIMAPPS TOOL

To validate the functionality of the architecture presented in this paper, we describe and illustrate below how a DTVi application was implemented for the SBTVD standard that manipulates maps generated by the Wikimapps tool.

5.1 Automatic Generation of the DTVi Application

A web application can provide the generation of a DTVi application with the use of templates. A DTVi application is made with a specific language, in this case NCL+Lua, according to the platform determined for the exportation of the service.

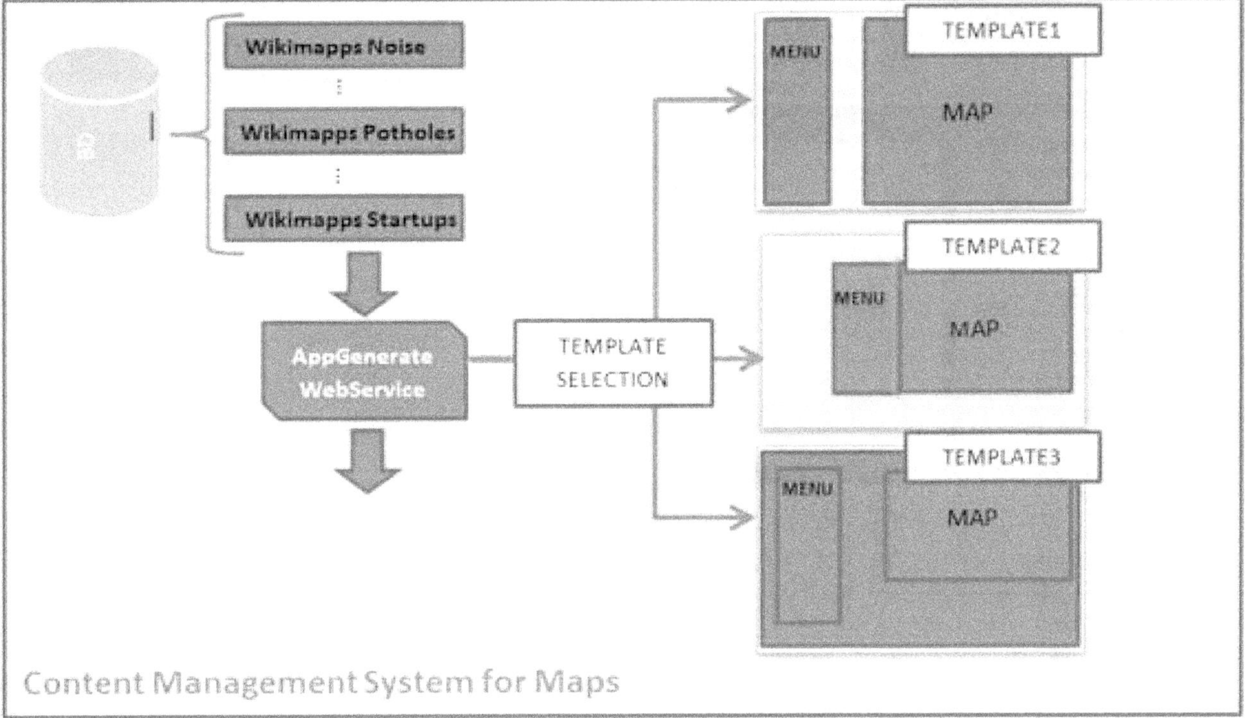

Figure 5. Generation of a DTVi application.

The ISP limits this application only to the context of the map applied/chosen at the time of its query to the content generator, in our case, WikiMapps.

To demonstrate this, we have a web service created in the WikiMapps tool that – upon generating the maps – offers the user the possibility to create applications related to such maps for DTV in an automatic fashion.

Figure 5 illustrates the chain of generation of a particular DTVi application, in which its interface can be defined according to a selected template.

5.2 Interaction with a collaborative map through the TV

Assume a hypothetical scenario in which a local news television program discusses urban problems such as the occurrence of potholes on certain streets. The problem could cause accidents, which could make the citizens angry and eager to report the occurrence of potholes. During the news, the map could be displayed to show where the potholes are, as well as asking the users to inform new occurrences they are aware of. Figure 6 shows an example of how the interface displays the events occurring in the places. Each event, coming from the Wikimapps website, could be selected for a detailed view via interaction with the map. Assuming also that the return channel is available, other kinds of interaction are available. The user can, for instance, plot new events on the map, such as potholes that could also reduce the speed of traffic.

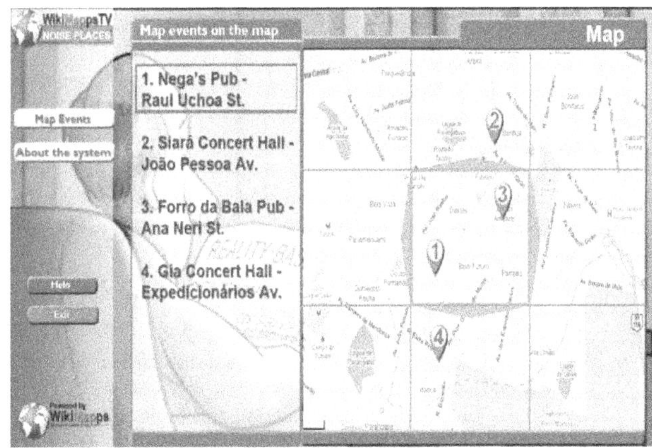

Figure 6. Interface of the WikimappsTV DTVi application.

After confirming the data, the application being run on the receiver device will send, via an HTTP request, the result of interaction with the viewer to the WikiMapps web service. This result will be stored and made available for informative return to the ISP or even the TV operator/broadcaster.

Note that our proposal in this paper is generic to any wikimapps. It is also possible to create other maps in different domains. Currently we are developing a specific solution to manage traffic problems. It will be possible to indicate slow traffic, accidents, nearby schools, etc. In this application, we are also using smartphones to guide the users during the route. Figure 7 exemplifies how this is displayed on the screen of the DTVi.

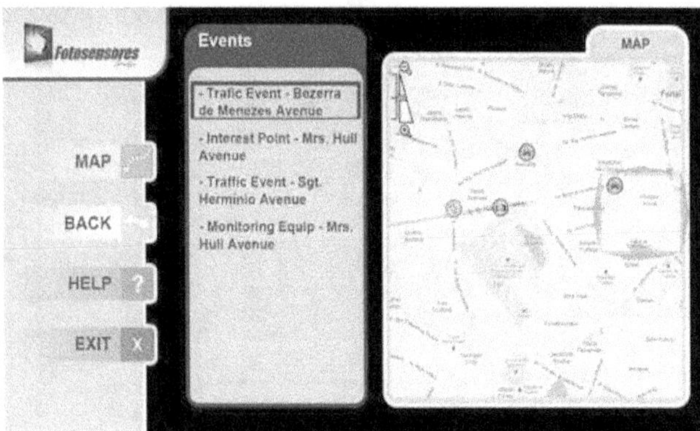

Figure 7. DTVi SICIT-Photosensors.

6. CONCLUSION AND FUTURE WORK

In this article we propose an architecture, called MAPS-TV, for the development of a collaborative maps application in DTVi that has, as a basic feature, the decoupling and modularization of development activities. MAPS-TV proposes a data model for transmission of information from the elements participating in the architecture. It allows the automatic generation of DTVi applications through the WikiMappsTV tool, which offers functionalities to enhance interaction for this purpose.

For this activity, we created an interactive application that makes use of a web service along with the WikiMapps database. The purpose of this application is to offer an environment to generate the necessary data and applications for DTVi that will populate collaborative maps with data on the registration of information related to the requested map. The main features of the WikiMapps tools were described, as well as the precautions and challenges for the use of maps in Digital TV to be successful. We concluded the article with an example of a DTVi application that populates collaborative maps created for use in TV programming as a public service, whereby incidents related to urban mobility are represented.

As future work, it would be necessary to define a mechanism to synchronize the information on the map with the content to be broadcast. In our case, when transmitting the application, the synchronization was left up to the TV operator, because the TVA standard calls for the use of a timeline related to the programming. But in this case we have an issue of how it would possible to obtain the maps automatically. It would be of great interest to define how to associate the map to the content of the TV program through the proposed use of metadata.

The automatic generation of maps presents some challenges because it depends on the following features: i) limiting the size of the area to be used in the collaborative map generated, ii) the way the map would be used by the user (with or without a return channel), and iii) using the Google API restricts the creation of map images to images sized 640x640 pixels at most. The creation of a library with functions to treat vector maps as well as a library for the interaction of objects for the manipulation of maps in the DTVi will comprise an important future development.

Even though in Brazil the use of the return channel is not yet widely disseminated, we have envisioned MAPS-TV and MAPSTVXML with features to use a return channel. The application of these features in real case scenario is also a subject for future work.

7. ACKNOWLEDGMENTS

The authors of the paper would like to thank the insightful comments of Teresa Chambel. The second author was partially funded by CNPq grant: 55977/2010 and 304347/2011. The third author was partially funded by CNPq and CAPES grant, respectively: 310247/2009-8 and 133/2008/CII/CGPE/DB-Capes.

8. REFERENCES

[1] Araújo, E. C. NCL Live: ambiente de autoria visual para prototipação de aplicações para TV Digital Interativa. Master's thesis. Universidade Federal do Maranhão. (2009).

[2] Barbosa, S. D. J. & Soares, L. F. G. TV digital no Brasil se faz com Ginga: Fundamentos, Padrões, Autoria Declarativa e Usabilidade. PUC RIO. Pg. 105–174. (2008).

[3] Caminha, C., Furtado, V., Vasconcelos, E.; Ayres, L. Uma ferramenta de autoria para criação de mapas colaborativos para aplicações em E-gov 2.0. In Proceedings of the XXX CSBC 2010 – WCGE, II Workshop de Computação Aplicada em Governo Eletrônico. Minas Gerais, Brazil, July, p. 20 – 23. (2010).

[4] Carvalho, A. P. B. A., Ferraz, C. A. G. 2010. Contextual Ginga: Uma ferramenta de autoria de Aplicações Interativas Sensíveis ao Contexto de TV digital para Ginga-NCL. In Proceedings of the WebMedia - Simpósio Brasileiro de Sistemas Multimídias e Web. Minas Gerais, Brazil, October, p. 5 – 8. (2010).

[5] Durand, G., Kazai, G., et al. A metadata model supporting scalable interactive TV services. Proceedings of the IEEE conference on Multi-Media Modeling. (2005).

[6] Filho, Guido Lemos S., Leite, Luiz Eduardo C., Batista, Carlos Eduardo C. F. Ginga-J: The Procedural Middleware for the Brazilian Digital TV System. J. Braz. Comp. Soc. pp. 47–56. (2007).

[7] Geuer, Olaf et al. JAME – System Concepts and New Technologies for iTV Services. Fraunhofer Institute for Media Communication IMK. (2009).

[8] Ginga Home Page. Retrieved April 11, 2012, from Official Site of Ginga Middleware: http://www.ginga.org.br.

[9] Guimarães, R. L., de Resende Costa, R. M., e Soares, L. F. G. Composer: Ambiente de autoria de aplicações declarativas para a tv digital interativa. WEBMEDIA: Brazilian Symposium on Multimedia and the Web. (2007).

[10] Icareus iTV Suite Author. Retrieved April 11, 2012, from Icareus Technology Home Page: http://www.icareus.com.

[11] LUGMAYR, Artur; NIIRANEN, Samuli; KALLI, Seppo. Digital Interactive TV and Metadata: Future Broadcast Multimedia. Springer. (2004).

[12] Middleware AstroTV. Retrieved April 11, 2012, from TQTVD Home Page: http://www.tqtvd.com.

[13] Neves, Rogério Baldini. Explorando o canal de retorno em sistema de televisão digital interativa: uma abordagem centrada no suporte à comunicação entre aplicações e provedores de serviços. Pontifícia Universidade Católica de Minas Gerais. Belo Horizonte. (2010).

[14] NoTube project. Retrieved April 11, 2012, from NoTube Project Home Page: http://www.notube.tv.

[15] Oliveira, M. R., Filho, C. B., and Fer, A. F. iTV project: An authoring tool for MHP and Ginga-J based on a web environment. In UXTV '08: Proceeding of the 1st international conference on designing interactive user experiences for TV and video, pages 179–182, New York, NY, USA. ACM. (2008).

[16] Rouse, L.J., Bergeron, S.J., Harris, T.M. "Participating in the geospatial web: collaborative mapping, social networks and participatory GIS," in Scharl, A., Tochtermann, K. (Eds.),The Geospatial Web: How Geobrowsers, Social Software and the Web 2.0 are Shaping the Network Society, Springer, New York, NY, pp.153–158. (2007).

[17] SANTOS, Ítalo Matos Cavalcante. T-VILO TOOL: ferramenta orientada a serviços para interação e produção de conteúdos educativos baseada no sistema brasileiro de televisão digital / Ítalo Matos Cavalcante Santos. Master's thesis. Universidade de Fortaleza. (2011).

[18] SBTVD Forum Home Page. Retrieved April 11, 2012, from STBVD Forum: http://www.forumsbtvd.org.br.

[19] Silva, F. S. et al. Análise Comparativa de Metadados em TV Digital. In: 24º Simpósio Brasileiro de Redes de Computadores, SBRC, Curitiba. (2006).

[20] Silva, Marco A. M.; Castilhos, Edson L.; Eichler, Flávio A. V.; Nogueira, Roger F. 2010. T-government: O Projeto "TV Digital – Social" um "case" de Oferta de Serviços Interativos para os Cidadãos. In Proceddings of the Simpósio Brasileiro de Sistemas Multimídia e Web (WebMedia). Minas Gerais, Brazil, October, p. 5 – 8. (2010).

[21] Soares, Luiz Fernando Gomes; RODRIGUES, Rogério Ferreira & Moreno, Márcio Ferreira. Ginga-NCL: The Declarative Environment of the Brazilian Digital TV System. Journal of the Brazilian Computer Society. Vol. v12, pp. 37–46. (2007).

[22] Soares, P. H. S. CUICA - Uma Ferramenta para Suportar a convergência da TV Digital com a WEB através da criação de conteúdo digital. Master's thesis. Universidade de Fortaleza. (2007).

[23] TVA. TV-Anytime Forum Home Page. Retrieved April 11, 2012, from: http://www.tv-anytime.org.

Engaging Viewers through Social TV Games

Pedro Almeida
CETAC.MEDIA
University of Aveiro
3810 – 193 Aveiro
Portugal
almeida@ua.pt

Jorge Abreu
CETAC.MEDIA
University of Aveiro
3810 – 193 Aveiro
Portugal
jfa@ua.pt

Ana Pinho
CETAC.MEDIA
University of Aveiro
3810 – 193 Aveiro
Portugal
pinho.ana@ua.pt

Diogo Costa
CETAC.MEDIA
University of Aveiro
3810 – 193 Aveiro
Portugal
diogo.perez@ua.pt

ABSTRACT

IPTV platforms have revealed a great potential for the viewers' involvement by allowing the development of services and applications related with the TV content. Taking advantage of both the potentialities of these platforms and game related dynamics new ways to promote interaction between viewers may be achieved. This research focuses on searching and validating innovative forms of entertainment through television. In this context we designed, developed and evaluated the Wize application that combines some social games characteristics with interactive television features. This paper presents the functional specification of this application, implemented in an IPTV platform and describes a Field Trial carried out with 22 users. To accomplish this evaluation those persons were provided at their homes with a sub-set of the Wize features integrated in an iTV application of a popular TV show. The results provide a better understanding of the expectations towards social TV related games and reveal that users have strong motivation to continue to use such an application and a strong interest in doing it with their friends. The results also showed the potential of this type of applications to engage in a deeper manner the viewers with the TV content.

Categories and Subject Descriptors

H5.2 [**Information Interfaces and Presentation**]: User Interfaces – *Prototyping, Screen design, interaction styles.*

Keywords

Interactive Television, Social Games, Bets, Quizzes, evaluation, Field Trial.

1. INTRODUCTION

In the current technological scenario the creation of interactive services related to television content may become even more interesting as they incorporate social components allowing the viewer to feel more connected to the TV show and close to those who share the same interests - a strong motivation for communicating and engaging with others [13].

EuroITV'12, July 4–6, 2012, Berlin, Germany.

Considering the success that social games have been gaining in the Web, we may expect that this type of games, when adapted and supported by IPTV platforms, may provide an interesting interaction model among the viewers, especially when coupled with dynamics that take advantage of the TV content.

The proposed application described in this paper was conceptualized and implemented using a regular IPTV infrastructure based on Microsoft Mediaroom. The application allows the user to answer to questions and make bets related with television programs, gaining points that can be exchanged for prizes. Taking advantage of the potential for social engagement offered by IPTV platforms, the game also allows the user to define his friends' list, which may lead to increase his sense of belonging and visibility on the (players) network. A sub-set of the developed features was later integrated in an iTV application of a popular TV show, Biggest Loser, and it was evaluated by means of a Field Trial carried out with 22 users for one month.

2. SOCIAL (TV) GAMES

For a better understanding of what could be the model to use for this application some examples of games already developed for iTV platforms were studied. From this analysis it was possible to identify two main types of games characterized by taking place, or not, around TV content.

Regarding the games that take place around TV content, they are typically related to Quiz shows, such as "Test the Nation"[1] or "Family Fortune", both developed by Two Way Media[2], in partnership with FremantleMedia[3]. In such cases viewers can have access to games through the Red Button mode and play it in real time, being faced with similar challenges to those presented to competitors who are in studio participating in the related TV show. In "Test the Nation" it is important to highlight a complementary application developed and tested in a lab environment: the Telebuddies system. As reflected in its name, this service explored the potential of social interaction and communication mechanisms [8] around the TV content. The viewer was able not only to enjoy a playful moment but also to share it with friends or relatives.

It is also appropriate to highlight the iTV games based on betting systems. One relevant example is the widget for Samsung's Connected TV, developed by Betfair[4]. This widget was available during the 2010 World Cup allowing viewers to place bets on

[1] http://www.bbc.co.uk/testthenation/howto.shtml#dsat

[2] http://www.twowaytv.com/

[3] http://www.fremantlemedia.com/

[4] http://corporate.betfair.com/

games they were watching or on future games contributing to a higher level of engagement with the soccer matches viewing experience. Another example comes from Sky who launched in 2004 Sky Vegas Live[5], in which viewers could participate, in an interactive way and through television, on a bingo game guided by a TV host in the studio, who acted as a promoter of the viewer's participation and engagement [12].

Aside these examples, most of the games released for iTV are based on a set of applications that use the brand of popular TV shows but are not prepared to take advantage of synchronized uses during the live broadcast of these shows. One can refer the Playjam[6] games that allow, among other features, the participation in a game inspired by the famous TV show "Who Wants to Be a Millionaire?". Just as in the television show, the viewers can answer to quizzes playing asynchronously with the content. Others like "Britain's Got Talent", which also follows the Quiz/Trivia model, are provided by Two Way Media. These also take advantage of the brand of popular TV shows.

In Portugal the offer is very similar to the examples referred. In the case of the main IPTV operator, a set of games is offered through its applications dock. Two of them, "Who Wants to Be a Millionaire?" and "Quiz Master", may also be categorized in the Quiz type. In this context, the Wize project showed up as the first prototype for Portuguese IPTV platforms to allow a synchronous gaming experience with the television content.

Other experiences provide valuable information on how to design social TV games. Goldenberg [6] developed the SyncGame, a proof-of-concept project that allowed viewers to play a game, collecting items related with what appears on TV while watching a cartoon show. The author proposes using layers to allow viewers to play without any interruption of the show, providing conditions for an high *semantic connection* between the game and the TV content.

Considering both analyses, the researchers conducted an exploratory Focus Group [7] in order to expose participants with the preliminary concepts developed for the social TV game. The results are presented in the next section.

3. FOCUS GROUP

Eleven potential users, mostly students, attended the session. The group was composed by 7 males and 4 females, ranging from 21 to 33 years old, with an average TV consumption between 2 and 4 hours a day and very active when it comes to social networks use. The group revealed a clear preference for television series, sport events and talent shows. The Focus Group session was divided into two distinct phases: in the first part, the researchers, who were moderating the Focus Group, presented the preliminary concepts for the Wize project and invited the participants to give their opinion on the proposals for the main features of the application; in the second part, the participants were challenged to create interface mock-ups, based on a prototyping paper technique. During the session, the data was collected through video recording and then analysed using observation grids. The main considerations gathered in each phase are presented in the following section.

[5] http://www.broadbandbananas.com/content/view/57/57/

[6] http://www.playjam.com/

3.1 Results

From the discussions on the game concept the possibility of developing a program around a Quiz show, like "Who Wants to Be a Millionaire?" was one of the first proposed hypotheses. Linking the game to a more complex genre of television, such as fiction, embedding it with a related narrative was considered valid, however, the participants noted that this format could require much more attention from viewers and, as such, could hamper the ability to follow the game during a live show. Concerning the impact that the game could have on viewing, it was consensual that playing it could not follow a dynamic that forced the viewer to divert his attention from the television content for a long time.

In order to displace the narrative from a strictly individual game, participants mentioned that it is very important to create systems that stimulate competition among players and different levels of experience/difficulty. According to participants, along with scoring systems, a key factor to attract players, is ensuring that they create a connection to the game and to the goal of achieving a better performance. Concerning specific features the participants referred that determination of a time limit to perform a set of tasks could make the game more appealing, like reported by Diakopoulos and Chiu [5]. Another referenced feature was the possibility of creating a friends list, which could be composed either by members of their already established community or even by strangers. Along with this option, participants suggested that it would be important to allow the creation of a user profile, which could support the establishment of teams, by similarity or complementarity between players.

Considering team play, and communication between team members, the participants recommended using a chat but also the possibility of exchanging messages asynchronously (through private messages or comments). Since recording features are usually available on IPTV platforms and therefore time shifted viewing habits become common, Focus Group participants found the proposal for an asynchronous component of the game important, allowing them to play anytime.

The possible connection to a social network was mentioned as another feature, emphasizing the idea, confirmed by the literature review, that when combined with interactive television these social networks may contribute to a more immediate and effective exchange of information between users [2] and to a potential increase of the exposure and visibility of the game results.

When asked about the importance of prizes the participants agreed that these rewards might help the player feel more attracted to the game and increase his involvement and commitment in achieving the defined goals.

In the second part of the Focus Group the participants were divided into two groups (A and B) and were invited to collaboratively build interface mock-ups based on paper prototyping techniques. The aim was to find how participants would arrange, on a TV screen, the different elements provided, corresponding to possible game areas (Figure 1). In the end, each group made a presentation of its proposal and the main suggestions were discussed. In order to adapt the interface to the player's preferences one of the groups proposed the existence of two viewing modes while running the game: i) an embedded mode with the video reduced to a small area; ii) and an overlay mode with the video in full screen. In both proposals, the permanent visible areas were directly linked with the player's basic information (like status or game score).

Figure 1. Group A - creating interface mock-ups.

Taking in consideration the game proposal, consolidated as a result of the Focus Group, the participants referred that the viewer might feel not only more involved with the related television content but also closer to those with whom he shares the experience. However, despite the game's importance, the interactive content should be designed in order to add value to what is already offered by television and not to override it [3]. This concern is even more evident in the synchronous gameplay mode. It should be assured that both play and viewing must operate on complementarity, so that users can take full advantage of both experiences.

Based on the analysis previously done, the preliminary concepts developed by the research team and the feedback from the Focus Group, the Wize application, a prototype for a social TV game, was designed and developed.

4. THE WIZE APPLICATION

The Wize application explores the potential of IPTV platforms, providing users with interaction models that may bring high levels of entertainment while watching their favourite programs. The proposed concept rests on a game that challenges players, testing them in different knowledge areas. Combining a Quiz dynamics with a betting system, the game seeks to innovate by merging two formats that have proven to be able to attract and keep the public. One example is the success of games like "Who Wants to Be a Millionaire?", "Trivial Pursuit" and "Buzz"[7] or betting systems as "Bwin"[8] (offering up to 30,000 possibilities of bets a day). Besides that, these Quiz shows typically have a great potential in fostering social interactions around television content, for example, gathering the family members around television [4]. Thus, based on a simple narrative, it was tried to adapt these models, combining them with the television consumption patterns and enriching them with social interaction dynamics. The main idea consisted in the development of a game that could be integrated with television programs or live broadcast shows, related to popular. Typically, these shows may be, among others: Talent Shows; Reality Shows; or Live Sport events, around which questions and bets could be made. These challenges could be placed into two distinct modules of the game: a synchronous mode, only available through Red Button while a TV show is broadcasted; and an asynchronous mode, always available through the IPTV operator applications dock system.

4.1 Main features

In the synchronous mode, when watching a show, the viewer may answer thematic questions, released for testing his knowledge. These questions allow the player to earn points (the faster he answer the more he wins), which could be exchanged by exclusive content about the show or, eventually, merchandising. At the same time, the correct answers, given by the player, are used to enrich his profile in terms of knowledge about the show or the corresponding thematic area. This property is illustrated by a set of badges that reveal the player's achievements.

If, on one hand, the knowledge test increases the visibility and enhances the player's credibility in the game's social network, on the other hand, the bets, available in the asynchronous mode, enable a greater engagement in the game and may strengthen the loyalty of viewers to it. In this mode, the player has the ability to make bets on unpredictable events of the shows, around which the game is built (information that normally only will be revealed in the future live broadcasts). The bets allow the player to increase (or lose), in a play of chance, the points earned during the synchronous mode.

In both modes, before playing for the first time, viewers should sign up to the application (Figure 2:B). This sign up is made directly on television, through an available registration form. He may choose to store data on the set-top box, helping him in future logins (Figure 2:A).

Figure 2. Entry screen – sign up/login.

During registration, the viewer can also decide to activate a connection to Facebook, which allows him to use his profile photo on Wize and automatically share game information on that network.

In the first screen, aside with the sign up and login, an help option (Figure 2: C) is provided. This could be a benefit for inexperienced viewers at early stages of usage.

The remaining application features will be presented in the next section, with reference to the corresponding modes.

---

[7] http://pt.playstation.com/ps2/games/detail/item45283/Buzz!-O-Mega-Quiz/

[8] https://www.bwin.com/pt/default.aspx

4.1.1 Synchronous Mode

In this mode, the application runs in overlay, with the information about the player's current score permanently available (Figure 3: A). The thematic questions, that need to be pre-prepared by the content managers in a back office, are shown time to time, based on a schedule previously defined or shown whenever the content managers decide accordingly to the TV content being broadcasted at the time. As seen in Figure 3: B these questions appear in overlay, occupying a small area of the screen, minimizing the disruption on the content that is being broadcasted. Each question has four possible answers. For example, in the Figure 3: B, the question is "Which team won the UEFA Cup in 2003?" and the viewer may select one of four available answers "1) FC Porto, 2) Sporting CP, 3) SL Benfica, or, 4) SC Braga". When a question is provided, the number of points granted by the correct answer is shown and a timer, signalling the remaining time to choose an option, appears on the screen. The intention is that viewer provides his answer as quickly as possible, since the number of points he can earn decrease with time.

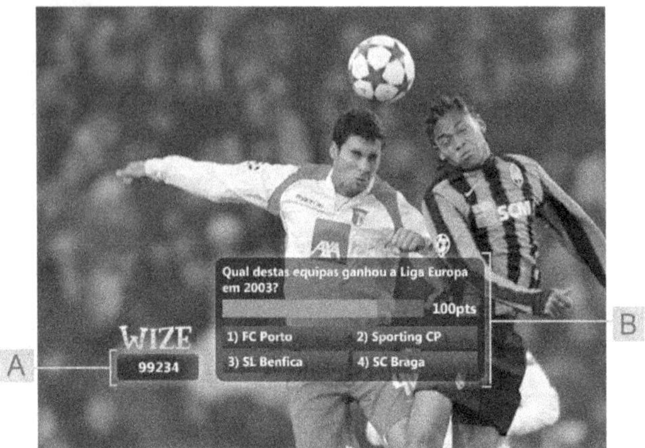

Figure 3. A new question is released (synchronous mode).

The points collected on this module can now be used to place bets (in asynchronous mode) or exchanged by prizes.

4.1.2 Asynchronous Mode

Players can, at any time, access this mode available through the IPTV operator applications dock. This module allows viewers to be in contact with the television show with which the game is associated, even when it's not being broadcasted.

As in the synchronous mode, the user starts with a login. From the moment he is logged in, the game menu becomes available providing access to the different playable areas: profile; bets; friends; ranking; history; notifications and; market (Figure 4).

Figure 4. Menu (asynchronous mode).

The profile area allows the viewer to define his identity as a player leveraging his visibility on the social network made up of his friends or all the Wize users. In this area, the player's personal information (Figure 5: A), including name, location and photo/avatar is shown. His game performance, earned points (Figure 5: C), bets won (Figure 5: D) and conquered badges (Figure 5: E) are also shown. In this area he can also edit his personal information (Figure 5: B) and manage his friends list.

Figure 5. The player's profile (synchronous mode).

When the user wants to make a bet, he may choose the show he wants to play with; access a list of open bets; and choose one of the available options. The possible gain of each guess is estimated according to the odds, assigned to each option. Along with the information of the possible options for each bet, a dynamic chart provides information, in real time, about the tendency of the guesses made by friends and by all the viewers who use the application. This information may be used by him to help with the decision.

In the friends area, the viewer has access to his list of friends (Figure 6: A) and the ability to search for new ones (Figure 6: B).

Figure 6. Friends list (asynchronous mode).

In the ranking area, players can find three of the top-rated Wize players, having the ability to filter the results by location or to restrict it to their friends' network.

In the market area (Figure 7) players are able to exchange their points to various prizes, as explained in the next section.

Figure 7. Market (asynchronous mode).

4.2 Score System and Business Model

After presenting the game features and areas, it is important to summarize how players can collect points. It can be by:

- Questions: each correct answer, launched through live shows, adds a certain number of points to the player's score;

- Bets: if a player wins a bet, he increases, in a single hit, the number of points earned until that moment. Likewise, he may lose those points if he makes a wrong guess;

- Badges: the player gets extra points on his score when he completes one of the thematic groups or the entire grid of badges;

Regardless of the possibility of earning points and exchanging it by real prizes, it is possible to foresee other benefits for the player, as a viewer, like the ability of taking a more active role as a TV consumer, contributing for closer liaisons with his favourite programs.

Moreover, by winning badges, which reflect his knowledge in a particular area, and earning points, which will give a prominent position in the ranking, the player will contribute to increase his visibility and credibility among his friends network.

5. ARQUITECTURE AND SYSTEM MODEL

The set-top box (STB) used for the development of the Wize application was a Scientific Atlanta – model KMM3210 – with the Microsoft Mediaroom™ 2.0 operating system installed, providing some new capabilities when comparing with the previous version, like its physics effects. The Wize application was developed using Presentation Framework. However, various restrictions were found, while developing this module, mostly related to the available STB memory.

The system is based on a client and server-side architecture complemented with a web management application. The client-side communicates with the server-side, which is running a .NET application, through Extensible Markup Language (XML) files that are interpreted by the STB's middleware. The Hypertext Transfer Protocol (HTTP) server also interacts with a Structured Query Language (SQL) database in order to provide the dynamic content to the application, which is responsible in the STB for the presentation on the TV screen. Additionally, a back-office (Figure 8) allows administrators to create, edit and publish the final application contents.

Figure 8. The Wize back-office.

This web management application is also based on a .NET system interaction with the main SQL database. The client-side is based on XHTML and Javascript.

6. FIELD EVALUATION

Considering that the Wize application was developed using Microsoft Mediaroom Presentation Framework, the research team worked to get conditions to perform a Field Trial at the home of some of the clients of the leading IPTV operator in Portugal. However, in order to get the advantage of having the social TV game related with a popular TV show, the Field Trial (FT) was prepared using only a part of the features of the prototype described in this document. To achieve this, these features were included on the iTV application that supported a Portuguese version of the Biggest Loser reality show (Figure 9). This solution, however, compelled the developing team to follow the design guidelines of that application.

For preparing this FT the research team benefited from the previous experiences, namely when evaluating the WeOnTV application [1] with the collaboration of the same operator and other documented Field Trials results ([9], [10], [11]). By this, the research team aimed to get qualitative insights about the Wize features and game dynamics.

Figure 9. The Biggest Loser iTV application with betting features.

Due to some legal limitations related with betting licenses, impossible to solve in the available short period of time, the iTV application powered with some Wize features was only available to a group of 22 users. These users had access to exactly the same Biggest Loser application of any other user enriched with the following Wize features that allow to:

- Make bets about future events in the TV show;
- Track the position of each user in the ranking (Figure 10);
- Get some information and help on the game rules;
- Win some exclusive prizes (merchandising from the operator and TV show).

Figure 10. The users started with an initial credit of 1000 units to bet.

Although the application only included a sub-set of the Wize features, with this Field Trial the research team aimed to:

- Identify, from the viewers' perspective, the application strengths and weaknesses;

- Evaluate the level of appropriateness of the features available to the user's expectation;

- Check the ability to incorporate the game in TV viewing habits;

- Understand, in the viewers' perspective, the application capabilities for engaging users with the television content.

The Field Trial was explained to the beta testers as a game, divided in 3 betting rounds during a period of 1 month, in July 2011. In the end of each round, the gaming results were confirmed and the 3 best players granted with prizes. Being a Field Trial, this game dynamics had the potential to have the participants involved more actively and simultaneously in a more familiar atmosphere [10].

As referred, the FT took place at the home of 22 beta testers (IPTV clients) and the application was available in their set-top boxes without the need for any local intervention or installation. All the users were notified and informed about the FT development process. During the FT they received some e-mails (in average one each week) to remind them of the betting application or providing information on the winners of each round as shown in Figure 11.

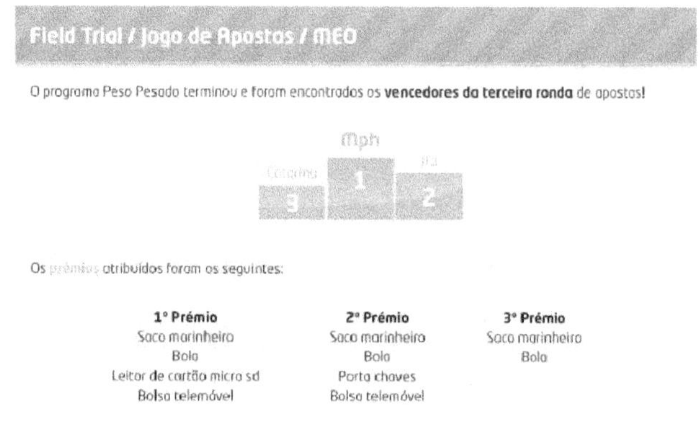

Figure 21. The information about the winners of each round was sent by email.

At the end all beta testers were invited to answer to an on-line questionnaire.

6.1 The results

From the total of 22 beta testers, 11 filled in the questionnaire. The results along with the data collected during the FT by means of logs of the application are organized in the next sections.

6.1.1 The users characterization

The users that answered the questionnaire were below 45 years old, with the majority (45%) having an age between 25 and 34. Most of the users (91%) watched TV in a regular basis (at least once a day). But when asked about the experience with interactive applications on TV (DVR, Pause TV, widgets, …) 36% referred that they used them once a day, but only 18% stated that they used it more than once a day.

Considering the preferred TV genres, we can see in Graphic 1 that the preference relies in news, movies and sports. In the opposite position we can find the variety shows and soap operas. The reality shows were not among the top preferred TV shows. The graphic highlights the results for all the genres ordering the preference from 1 (most seen) to 5 (less seen).

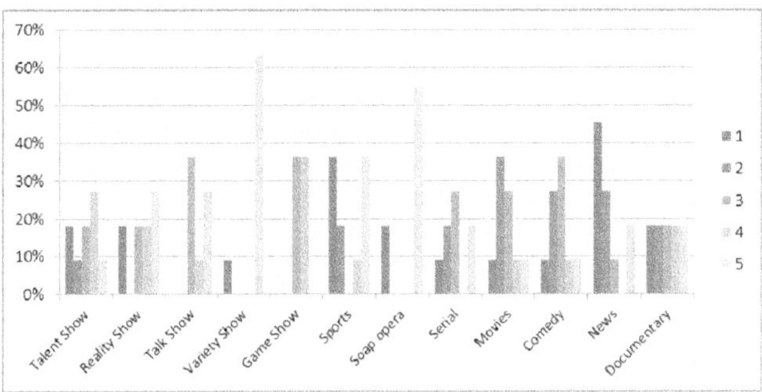

Graphic 1 – The TV genres preferences.

6.1.2 *The uses, concept and game dynamics*

Considering the uses of the betting features we can mention that 54% of the bets were made in the first round, 28% in the second and 18% in the third.

Most of the beta testers used the application at least once a week (55%). The use of the betting features was made mostly (64%) during the time slots where the Biggest Loser show was not being broadcasted. Even so, 27% of the users referred that at some time they turned on the TV set just to make or track a bet.

When asked about the ability to understand the concept of the betting features, 72% referred that the concept was clear while the remaining provided a neutral opinion. Most of the users mentioned that they would like to use, in the future (73% agree and 27% strongly agree), a betting application with similar characteristics even if applied to different TV genres. So, the next question tried to get the information about which could be the best TV genres to benefit from this application. As seen in Graphic 2, talent shows, reality shows, game shows and sport events were clearly highlighted by the users, although these genres were not the most watched by them (Graphic 1). With this context it is important to highlight that 73% admitted that their curiosity in the Biggest Loser show (a reality show) increased because of their participation in the Field Trial and the experience in using the application.

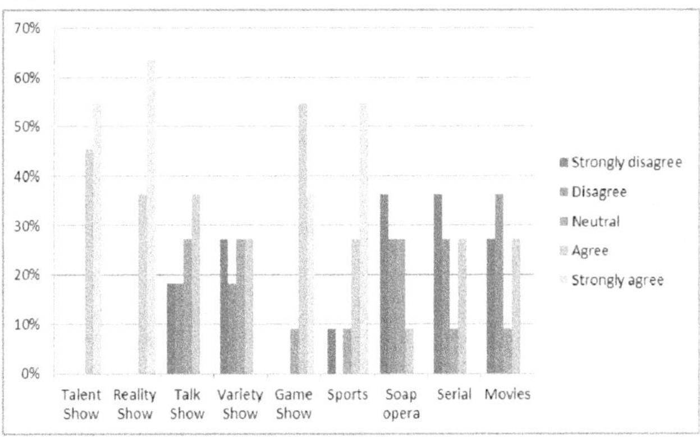

Graphic 2 – The compatibility of each TV genre with a betting application.

6.1.3 *The standard features*

The following questions on the questionnaire were targeted at getting the users opinion on the features available in the betting application and other possible future features (some of them already available at the Wize application).

The first question focused on the ability to provide a username to identify each player. 91% referred that they agree or strongly agree with the feature. 100% were favourable to having a ranking with the top players.

Concerning future features, all the beta testers expressed their willing to have the ability to define different users for a same set-top box. For login purposes the users were asked for their desire for a connection with Facebook. Although 45% referred to agree with this feature, 27% expressed their disagreement or strong disagreement.

About the possibility of creating a personal profile all agreed with the feature and 65% agreed with the ability of checking others profile. However, in what relates with providing personal information, only 45% were willing to do so, 36% expressed a neutral opinion and 19% revealed their disagreement with openly showing personal information in the profile. When the information is game related, all agreed with the public release of that, particularly the position in the ranking.

6.1.4 *The social features*

The Wize application relies in many social features and is targeted at promoting social interaction around a TV program. Through the results gathered we can refer that all the users were favourable to search in the application for new friends and almost all to create a friends list (Graphic 3).

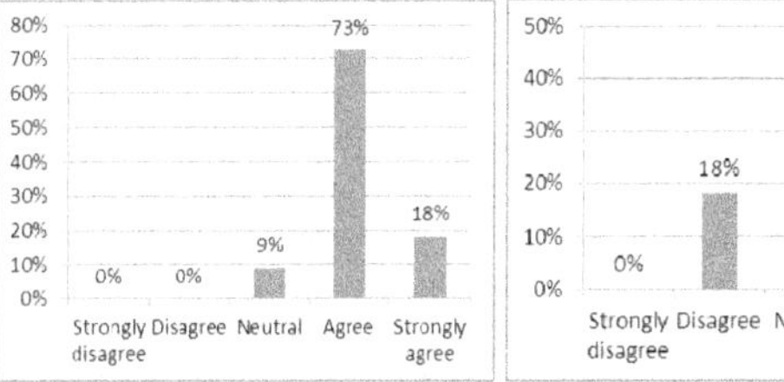

Graphic 3 – Interested in creating a friends list (left); Interested in (text) chatting with friends (right).

The users were also asked about the ability to text chat, through a virtual keyboard or triple tap, with their friends through the application. The results are positive but not in a total clear way (Graphic 3 - right).

Another Wize feature allows the users to get live information on the trend of answers in each bet. When presented with this feature 91% were interested in having the bet trends from friends (and 82% from all the community) before deciding on what option to bet on.

The Wize concept also introduced the possibility of creating teams to play the game. In this context, 91% of the users referred that they would be willing to be in a team that could work together to get better results and a better ranking.

Another important feature of Wize, not available at the Biggest Loser application, is the live game mode, to be played synchronously while the related TV show is on air, based on the deployment of time or manually triggered questions. The users were then asked to state their opinion on this feature. 91% were in favour of answering live questions, related to the TV content being shown at the moment. 81% were interested in knowing which of their friends was playing at the same time, although for these live moments, the users were not very motivated in having chatting features.

Finally, the game is based in getting the best results and earning points to exchange in a market of prizes. 72% revealed interested or most interested in having such a market and the remaining revealed a neutral position, eventually because they were not able to test the market in the prototype.

6.1.5 *The motivation for the future*

One goal of this research was related with trying to understand the players' motivations to use such an application related with a TV program.

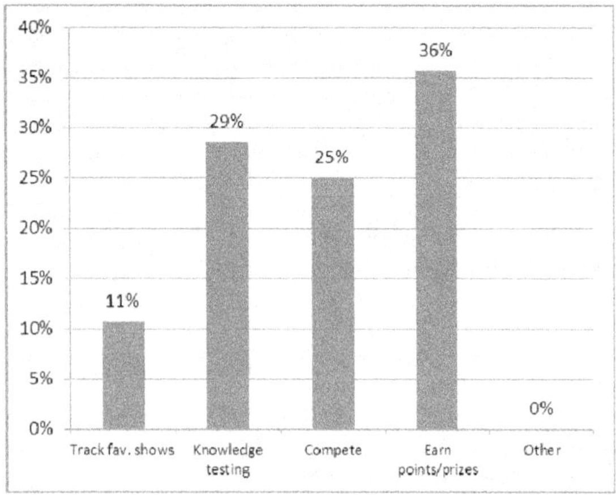

Graphic 4 - The reasons to use such an application.

For this, the users were asked about the reasons for using it. 36% referred that they will do it to earn points that allow them to exchange for prizes. The second most selected motivation was "testing my knowledge" and the third "competing". The second and third answers seem to reveal the motivation of users in competing and carrying challenges, which is supported by the referred interest in getting a ranking with the players' performance.

The least chosen motivation for using the application was "tracking my favourite shows" as the application was not seen as information oriented or a simple enhanced TV application.

7. DISCUSSION

The Field Trial was carried out with only a sub-set of the features proposed and implemented in the Wize application. Nevertheless, the users were able to try and experience the dynamics of a betting game with questions and bets related to a specific TV program. But, apart from this limitation, the users were able to get a better understanding of what a social TV game related to TV content may provide.

The results gathered from a small number of users were very positive towards the integration of social games related to TV programs and shows. Users showed strong motivation to continue to use such an application and a strong interest in doing it with their friends.

It is also important to highlight that, although the main reason to use such an application is not the TV show itself, but competitive related reasons, the use of this type of applications may engage in a deeper manner the viewers on the featured TV show.

The results did not allow the researchers to get a clear idea on the reasons that justified the decrease of bets in the second and third round of bets. But some possible reasons may be presented, namely the time period when the Field Trial was carried, the month of July. The second and third round took place in the last weeks of that month which is a traditional time for holidays. Some of the users could be away in that period. As the FT was carried at the home of users, and without interference of the evaluators it was not possible to confirm this fact.

But a possible decrease in the motivation to use the application could be softened with the introduction of team features granting an extra motivation for a regular use.

8. CONCLUSIONS

At a stage where social games are getting a major presence in social networks and starting to gain attention from iTV operators, it was appropriated to carry out an analysis of its key features and explore the social game possibilities for interactive television platforms.

Through literature review, (social) game analysis and a Focus Group, the researchers were also able to identify some of the viewers' preferences regarding the most popular TV shows, and television consumption habits. The researchers combined the results of these methodological steps in order to design a social TV game, correlated to TV content, able to take advantage of social network dynamics.

Throughout the development of this prototype, some technical constraints challenged the researchers to look for mechanisms that allow to overcome the limitations imposed by the platform of development, namely in terms of the available memory in the set-top box, so that it was possible to take greater advantage of its capabilities, creating a more appealing interface for viewers.

The results from a Field Trial support the research team with extra motivation to continue working on new mechanisms for social exchange and entertainment around TV content. Recent Deutsche Telekom Interactive Awards[9] reinforced the interest of iTV operators in betting and gaming applications for expanding the TV experience and engagement.

The researchers will continue to work on new models that may provide conditions to enrich the TV experience.

9. ACKNOWLEDGMENTS

The research leading to these results has received funding from PT Innovation. Our thanks to Eng.º Bernardo Cardoso and labs.sapo/UA team.

10. REFERENCES

[1] Abreu, J., Almeida, P., Figueiredo, C., Pinto, R., Teixeira, V., Designing a Social ITV Field Trial For Real Customers. Adjunct Proceedings of the 8th International Interactive TV&Video Conference (EuroITV 2010). Peng, C., Vuorimaa, P., Näränen, P., Quico, C., Harboe, G. & Lugmayr, A. (eds.). Tampere, Finland: Tampere University of Technology (TUT) p. 933-934, (2010).

[2] Baca M., Holtzman H. 2008. Television Meets Facebook: Social Networks Through Consumer Electronics. Conference Workshop. EuroITV 2008.

[9] http://www.interactive-tv-award.de/en

[3] Chorianopoulos K., Lekakos G. 2008. Introduction to Social TV: Enhancing the Shared Experience with Interactive TV. International Journal of Human-Computer Interaction, 24:2,113 — 120.

[4] Christensen, L. H. 2004. Out of Interactive TV. Conference Proceedings. Enhancing the Experience, 2nd. European conference on interactive television.

[5] Diakopoulos N., Chiu P. 2007. PhotoPlay: A collocated Collaborative Photo Tagging Game on a Horizontal Display. Proceedings addendum of User Interface Software Technology (UIST). Newport, Rhode Island, October 2007.

[6] Goldenberg, S. 2008. Creating augmented and immersive television experiences using a semantic framework. Proceedings of the 1st international conference on Designing interactive user experiences for TV and video (UXTV '08). ACM, New York, NY, USA, 45-48.

[7] Gondin, S. 2003. Grupos Focais como técnica de investigação qualitativa: desafios metodológicos. Paidéia, 2003, 12(24), 149-161.

[8] Luyten K., Thys K., Huypens S., Coninx K. 2006. Telebuddies: Social Stitching with Interactive Television. Paper presented at CHI'2006, Montreal, Canada.

[9] Obrist, M., Moser, C., Tschelig, M. and Alliez, D. 2010. Field evaluation of a cross platform 6 key navigation model and a unified user interface design. In Proceedings of the 8th international interactive conference on Interactive TV&Video (EuroITV '10). ACM, New York, NY, USA, 141-144.

[10] Obrist, M., Moser, C., Alliez, D., Holocher, T., and Tscheligi, M. 2009. Connecting TV & PC: an in-situ field evaluation of an unified electronic program guide concept. In Proc. of the Seventh European Conference on European interactive Television Conference (Leuven, Belgium, June 03 - 05, 2009). EuroITV '09. ACM, New York, NY, 91-100.

[11] Basapur, S., Harboe, G., Mandalia, H., Novak, A., Vuong, V., and Metcalf, C. 2011. Field trial of a dual device user experience for iTV. In Proceedings of the 9th international interactive conference on Interactive television (EuroITV '11). ACM, New York, NY, USA, 127-136.

[12] Tuomi P. 2009. i(TV) Brings People Together? How the Feeling of Togetherness Can Be Build. Conference proceedings. EuroITV2009, Leuven.

[13] Ursu F. M., Cesar P., Williams D. 2009, Enhancing Social Communication and Belonging by Integrating TV Narrativity and Game-Play. EuroITV2009, Leuven.

New Technology@Home: Impacts on Usage Behavior and Social Structures

Jan Hess, Benedikt Ley, Corinna Ogonowski, Tim Reichling, Lin Wan, Volker Wulf
University of Siegen
Hoelderlinstr. 3
57076 Siegen, Germany
+49 271 740-2098

{jan.hess; benedikt.ley; corinna.ogonowski; tim.reichling; lin.wan; volker.wulf}@uni-siegen.de

ABSTRACT

Studying domestic usage contexts has become an important field in research. Recent technological improvements have made media available on different devices, in different contexts and from different places. The adoption and appropriation of new devices and technologies has led to a more flexible usage behavior. However, even if we know about such a behavior, many questions, regarding how new technology changes the user's media usage and how these changes affect the social structure in a household, are still unanswered. We will address this topic in our work and want to provide an insight on how recent media consumption patterns have changed due to the appropriation of new technologies in the home. Based on a qualitative long-term Living Lab study we will present various patterns based on changes in media usage routines and their influences on households as social systems. The results provide a detailed understanding of how the new technology is embedded within domestic life by considering potentials and conflicts that also address further design oriented work.

Categories and Subject Descriptors

H.5.1 [**Information Interfaces and Presentation**]: Multimedia Information Systems – *Evaluation/methodology.*

General Terms

Design, Human Factors

Keywords

Living Lab, diary study, television, living room, media usage

1. INTRODUCTION

Television is the one mainstream mass media that can be found in every living room. It is not only a source of information, but also an established medium for relaxation and entertainment that is consumed alone, together with friends, or with other household members. While the reasons for TV consumption have remained the same, manifold technological developments have changed the way it is typically used [5,22]. From a technological point of view, television has been transformed into a medium that is uncoupled from the traditional television screen and is complemented by on-demand services on the Internet that can be consumed on a PC or mobile device [3,24]. Instead of watching television purely along the traditional TV schedule, users today can decide on their own, what they want to watch and when [2,18]. Beyond these changed consumption options, a variety of other web-enabled devices, e.g. smartphones, game consoles, Media Center systems or tablet PCs, are available at home and offer a large number of new possibilities to handle and consume media. Therefore, research on television, as a changing phenomenon, has become an increasing focus in Human-Computer Interaction (HCI) in the sense of developing new devices and interaction concepts for domestic environments.

Mobile technologies, such as smartphones and tablet computers, additionally enrich the TV experience [10]. The personal device as a secondary screen enables many options to access additional content, e.g. tagging and sharing content or complementary chat functionalities. But at the same time, these new options also correlate with the basic single use of devices versus the shared use of devices, which then brings up questions concerning ownership and privacy. Aspects of personalization, security and privacy in interactive television (iTV) environments are related to each other and need to be handled carefully [7].

Understanding how users appropriate new technologies and how they integrate them into their daily routine or how routines can change due to new technologies, are important aspects when developing new designs that are closer to the user's needs. Several user studies have provided insights into how new technologies are applied in practice. Earlier studies have explored patterns of technique usage [23] and the nature of communication among household members [11]. Other studies, e.g. [8], have focused on the users' practices of how new video-on-demand technologies have influenced the way media is consumed.

In our research we will focus on technologies and concepts which make value of current home infrastructures that include different devices, media and TV access from different sources and access to social services via the Internet. Together with partners from the industry and users, we co-develop new prototypes for the home. In order to understand the design context and to evaluate the concepts, we set up a Living Lab were households participate in a long-term manner. A phenomenon called 'cross media jumps' already was identified in previous work [16]. However, many questions regarding how new technology changes the user's media usage and how these changes affect the social structures within a household, were still unanswered. The empirical data presented in that paper summarizes results of the media usage behavior before and after equipping households with state of the art technologies. We provide insights on how users adapt new

EuroITV'12, July 4–6, 2012, Berlin, Germany.

functionalities and how these technologies influence media usage behavior within households.

We have conducted a two-stage qualitative empirical study with 16 households from our Living Lab. Under real world conditions, we explored each households media usage behavior before and after introducing new devices (a smartphone and a Media Center system). We compared the results from both studies with regards to changes in media usage and identified several phenomena related to the devices and media usage itself, as well as social influences in the households. We also received interesting insights into the users' individual perception of the changes that occurred to their media usage behavior. The relevant findings are discussed and presented in the form of usage patterns that may be of relevance to consider for further design.

2. TECHNOLOGY STUDIES AT HOME

Searching through the literature we found a large number of television related studies. One of the early studies about traditional television viewing was done by Lull [19] in the 1980s, in which he was already exploring established social practices of behavior in families when watching television in the living room. As shown in the study, television can nurture interpersonal relationships, e.g. by having a common topic to talk about. Nowadays, new technologies have changed the once simple act of watching broadcast television in several respects. Television is embedded in a process that Barkhuus & Brown [3] described as the video media lifecycle. Watching television today means much more than the simple consumption of planned programs; it facilitates a number of possible functionalities related to searching, obtaining, sharing, collecting, and discussing the content. New technologies such as personal hard-disk video recorders and download/streaming portals on the Internet support these processes and have changed the way in which users watch television [8]. Smith and Krugman [25] investigated these practices with regards to established consumption patterns and how users perceive changes in their media usage. They found that personal hard-disk video recorders lead to a more flexible and controllable TV consumption, which makes the user's viewing behavior more convenient. In this context, Irani et al. [18] dealt with the concept of rhythms and plasticity in order to analyze new temporalities of media consumption. Both rhythm and plasticity co-exist and effect watching experiences. The plasticity of time describes the way users interrupt or reduce the time they spend watching content by using, for instance, time-shifting or skipping functions, rhythm refers to the organization of when and with whom content should be watched, which is related to daily routines. Hence, they were able to analyze more flexible and open uses regarding TV consumption in the home [18]. In this regard, Wonneberger et al. [30] developed a process model of sequential-viewing patterns that allows investigating the dynamics of the entire viewing process, namely from the beginning, when users start watching TV, until they turn off the device. Therefore, a typology of influential factors has been deduced from the existing models of watching television. The factors that influence and change viewing habits fall into four categories: individual characteristics, program structure, social environment and context. Applying these factors when investigating existing phenomena would help clarify television watching behavior [30].

In recent years a lot of research on audience behavior and design-related issues has inspired new insights into the domestic space. In their work, Bernhaupt et al. [5] presented new trends in the living room. Based on two ethnographical studies, they analyzed 7 aspects that became important in the context of iTV. Apart from the importance of privacy, security, personalization and communication, watching television is still characterized as a communal activity that is relevant to the user's social life. Obrist et al. [22] also identified similar user requirements, based on their findings, they derived recommendations for an iTV concept that should offer, for instance, content related information, recommendations and communication services. In relation to this, Tsekleves et al. [28] have investigated the role of television in the living room. In their findings, they emphasized the importance of the television set as a shared device - not only for watching television together but also to make sharing information on the Internet possible or to share data stored on the computer via the TV screen. Bernhaupt et. al. [6] then specifically investigated the changes an interactive TV system will bring to the living room behaviors in terms of security and privacy. The results indicated that new forms of user interaction were required, which should enable personalized access to the content on the television and the new forms of connectivity for all devices used in the living room.

From a sociological point of view, Turkle [29] investigated how the phenomenon of mobile devices, as an additional source of media content, changes our social life with respect to our communication behavior. The fact that users get the feeling of being together but also being alone was one of the findings that was emphasized. Turkle deducted that users prefer text messages instead of physical appointments or if they meet, everyone is busy on their mobile device and face-to-face conversations will be reduced. In addition, Barkhuus [3] explored in her study the phenomenon of watching television on a computer and how the Internet influences user behavior. She showed that especially tech-savvy users combine original characteristics of the computer as a working instrument with leisure activities and entertainment aspects of television. The Internet as an additional channel for video content offers users the chance to break away from well elaborated program schedules of broadcasters and enables a more specific and time-independent access to content. Even if such new technologies and services enable a personalized and individual media consumption, the well elaborated program schedules still have a huge influence onto the users' viewing habits. Embedded in social practices, television series for instance are shared among friends or recorded content is watched the same day it is broadcasted live [2]. Knowing about this social importance, research often focused on concepts that allowed shared experiences on TV remotely via exchange and communication functionalities [14,17,20].

Besides computers, portable web-enabled devices such as smartphones or tablet PCs have also become increasingly important for accessing video content, and also content is normally customizable and can be shared on the go [10]. In their study O'Hara et al. [24] also focused on video consumption on mobile devices. They noted that mobile video consumption is more than just a personal pastime. Mobile video is seen as an important feature in bringing video content into social situations and places, which is not possible with a fixed TV set. Basapur et. al. [4] developed a secondary device concept that enhances watching TV by providing auxiliary information and media. The additional content is semantically related and synchronized to the ongoing TV content. A three-week field test with 11 households confirmed that the experience with a second device for additional information is quite positive. O'Hara et al. [24] also stated that people have an additional opportunity to effectively coordinate their various viewing interests without losing their proximity to the family. In the context of simultaneous use of mobile devices, those multi-media devices are often referred to as 'second devices' or as a 'second screen' [10,27,28] used to retrieve additional information or to use it for associated social activities. The work of Steimle et. al. [26] tried to identify the usage pattern of tabletop systems involving both physical and digital media, and concluded with design implications for hybrid tabletop systems.

In our present study, we want to contribute to the altered consumption process of audiovisual content by using new technologies and devices in the living room. Moreover, we will fill the gap of how media usage behavior is influenced by new technologies over a long period of time. While changing habits are mostly investigated in the use of single devices, as for instance the aspect of computer or mobile use to watch broadcast or video content, it is reasonable to look at the whole usage setting with all its influencing factors in order to understand the interplay of different multi-media devices in the living room. Therefore, our aim is to explore established media usage behavior and accumulated social interactions before technical interventions have happened and after they were appropriated as new functions. These two steps allow an immediate comparison of established media usage behavior and its changes regarding social experiences and individual TV and video consumption in households.

3. METHOD

Our study aims to explore the daily media usage behavior in domestic environments on a long-term basis, which will influence the design of new entertainment concepts. As an empirical frame for these investigations we used the Living Lab concept [1,12]. The concept offers a setting where several players, e.g. academia, industry, public facilities, and users, come together in an innovative and open development process that takes real usage contexts into account [21]. As users have become an important factor for research and development, they were involved actively, from the early research stages to the entire design cycle. The synergy of both, utilizing real world settings and conducting long-term inquiries, workshops and interviews, contributed to a co-creation process with a potential output in acceptable and usable applications and services. These characteristics lead up to the unique value of the concept. Our Living Lab [15,16] consists of players from academia, media companies and of participants of a local user sample. We applied this research setting to the strength of co-creation opportunities and long-term investigations in real usage contexts such as peoples' homes. Within the understandings of usage contexts, established media usage and appropriation of new media constitute one of the core aspects of our design paradigm. Thus, research and design cycles proceed strongly circumstanced and affects positively on bridging identified gaps and users' needs.

In the context of our two-stage empirical study, we at first wanted to gain an in-depth understanding of current media usage and device usage of households in relation to the consumption of audiovisual content and social aspects in their daily routines. After the first study we undertook a technical intervention while providing Living Lab households with current marketable technologies at this point. Each household was equipped with a Media Center system with Windows Media Center which was connected to the TV set and an Android OS smartphone. Households with a tube television were additionally equipped with a high definition television. We chose this system based on the fact that the Windows Media Center offers a stable performance software solution for TV consumption. In addition, it basically helps reach a common experience within households regarding the Media Center's technical functionalities. Again, Android OS was chosen because of its openness for application development, as well as because of its strong acceptance within the user market. Due to a limited budget, we were only able to equip each household with one smartphone, so that only one person at a time was able to use the device, unless they shared it with other household members, which was rarely the case. By implementing the marketable technologies in the peoples' home, we gave a brief introduction to the systems and their functionalities, but didn't demonstrate to do specific tasks or had them use the systems if they felt uncomfortable with it. In most households marketable technologies are replacing existing TV systems. One of the two households, who already had a Media Center system, even replaced the existing solution with the new one. The reason for that was the easier handling of the new system itself. The other household used their Media Center system until our framework was running, because their own system was perfectly integrated into their own network. The participants spent a couple of months using and learning the new functionalities on their own and integrating the technologies into their daily routines. Then, in the second stage we investigated how the new technologies were appropriated and how the media usage behavior had changed over time.

In an interval of 9 months, we conducted two self-documenting diary studies (February and December 2010) with our Living Lab households. The first study consisted of a three week documentation period, while the second study was designed for a two week period. Therefore, we designed a cultural probe [5,13] that helped participants with self-reflection and stimulated them in an open and creative manner, to give researchers an insight into their private space. Our probe contained one media diary for each participant in the household, a digital camera, a privacy policy, a stand-up display to remind participants of the documentation and some sweets for motivation. The diary study is also a common approach in exploring the context in question through the participants themselves [9]. Therefore, the method helped gain structured and in-situ feedback. The diary study is also a favorable way to establish a trusting relationship between participants and researchers, which is necessary for long-term investigations.

The diary represents the most important part of the study. It contains semi-structured pages, on which the participants are asked to document every single audiovisual media usage with the following information:

- Date and time of usage
- Number of persons involved
- Kind of media (TV, video, Internet, cinema, or other) and synchronous usage with other media
- Content of media
- Motivation for media usage
- Communication with others about the content

Apart from the camera, which was used to get more visual insights into the consumption settings, the diary of the first study also included special creative pages with different tasks, which helped us to understand the households better, in regards of their social structure, life style, experiences and individual opinions without invading the household's privacy. One task, for example, involved asking participants to sketch the layout of their homes and their technical equipment within each room. Beyond that, they were asked to mark their favorite spot, helping us gain some understanding of where household members feel most comfortable and relaxed, and to understand the relationship between their comfort and the organization of technical equipment in the household. These tasks were also used to make the documentation period less monotonous and to keep the participants motivated.

After each study, we collected the probes from the households and conducted additional semi-structured feedback interviews with each participant of the household to reflect on their own media usage behavior, the relevance of devices, changes in consumption behavior, and the diary study itself. In our study, we had 27 participants (14 m, 13 f) from 16 households (5 couples with children, 5 couples without children, 2 single households with children and 4 single households without children), which also made up the user group of our Living Lab (see table 1). They all resided in the urban region of Siegen-Wittgenstein, Germany, and were between 13 to 51 years old. The sample was divided into two groups to reproduce a heterogeneous sample with various types of users. Upon doing so, we did not aim at creating a representative profile, but with regards to our design focus, we wanted to address mainstream media users. One group (11 participants) consisted of users with existing experiences in using smartphones and/or Media Center systems. The other group (16 participants) only possessed minor technical experience within these fields and applications, but they all had a high daily TV and Internet usage in common. The participants were recruited via a call for participation in local newspapers and radio stations. The following selection process was based on semi-structured telephone interviews and predefined characteristics (e.g. sociodemographic factors, broadband connection, technical skills, communicative competence) and is also described in detail [15].

Table 1. Characteristics of Living Lab participants

Households	Characteristics of participants (sex, age, tech. experience [high +, low –])
Couples with children	F1_1 *(m 51 –)*, F1_2 *(f 41 –)*, F1_3 *(f 13 –)* F2_1 *(m 38 +)*, F2_2 *(f 34 +)* F3_1 *(m 43 –)*, F3_2 *(f 44 –)*, F3_3 *(f 18 –)* F4_1 *(m 38 +)* F5_1 *(m 37 +)*
Couples without children	C1_1 *(m 32 +)*, C1_2 *(f 36 –)* C2_1 *(m 29 –)*, C2_2 *(f 24 –)* C3_1 *(m 37 +)* C4_1 *(m 38 +)*, C4_2 *(f 34 +)* C5_1 *(m 34 +)*, C5_2 *(f 24 –)*
Single households with children	E1_1 *(f 43 –)*, E1_2 *(f 15 –)*, E1_3 *(m 16 –)* E2 *(f 38 –)*
Single households without children	S1 *(m 44 –)* S2 *(f 46 –)* S3 *(m 35 +)* S4 *(m 28 +)*

Out of the first diary study, we received an overall of 26 duly completed diaries (14 m, 12 f), with a number of 669 entries in total (average 25 entries per person). One female participant was absent during the study and was not able take part. From the second study, we received 20 diaries (11 m, 9 f) with a number of 296 entries in total (average 15 entries per person). Seven participants did not complete the diary due to their limited time during the stressful pre-Christmas period. Two participants explained in the additional interview that they did not see any sense in documenting their media usage again, because they believed it had remained the same.

The collected data, the entries in the media diaries and interviews, were digitalized and transcribed. By using inductively and deductively derived categories, the data was coded, analyzed and triangulated afterwards, with regard to media usage patterns, changes in media usage behavior due to the intervention of the described technologies, social phenomena, and individual perception of change.

4. RESULTS

Our results give an insight into how people use current multi-media devices in their domestic environment, how they appropriate recent technologies into their daily routines and how technologies affect and change those routines. We have looked at the changing role of devices within consumption processes and their flexible usage opportunities, the corresponding social phenomena and at the users individual perception of change through the intervention of new technologies.

4.1 Device and Media Usage Behaviors

From a technological perspective, current media usage behavior is permanently influenced by both new functions and possibilities on existing platforms and on new devices. Thereby, the usage of a single device changes individually and will be supplemented by the functionality of other devices or even substituted by others. One of the interesting phenomena identified in our long-term study, was the changing media usage behavior assigned to available devices and the special kind of expedient device usage.

4.1.1 Integration of new Devices

The Media Center system became an important role in daily routines and changed the role of PC/laptop usage. A good example is given by F2_2, who was using a laptop intensively for email, social networks and news before the introduction of the marketable technology happened. Her laptop had a fixed place in the kitchen, so that the usage of the television and the Internet happened spatially divided. As the results of our second study revealed, her usage behavior changed by using the Media Center system now, which offered additional opportunities for accessing online content. TV and Internet usage became flexible and more integrated in the living room as F2_2 explained in the interview: *"I turn the computer [Media Center system] on and then watch breakfast television to relax [...] switch to the Internet, check Facebook for new messages, check web.de, surf a bit on bild.de, switch to the TV program again, [...] it is much faster then using my laptop in the kitchen, until it is booted [...] that is much easier with the computer [Media Center system].* Due to the introduction of the Media Center system, additional opportunities for accessing online content emerged out of its functionalities. However, this device did not substitute the laptop usage at all, but offered a situational flexible media usage within the households.

Other participants, who already used the laptop simultaneously to the television in the living room, as we knew from our first study, also switched to the Media Center system instead: F5_1 described a simultaneous usage of the laptop in order to check e-mails, Facebook, Amazon or eBay. In the second study he reflected that the Media Center system partly substituted these functions previously done on the laptop. But F5_1 also explained that more active tasks, such as printing or writing mails, were still done on the PC. *"Actually, it [the laptop] is replaced [by the Media Center system]. We own a laptop, it is also here [under the coffee table], but it is being used very rarely. From this point of view things will be done mostly with the Media Center system. With the exception of checking email and printing, which is done on the stationary PC."* For a more spontaneous usage of the Internet, such as searching or retrieving situationally relevant information while sitting on the couch, one participant (C3_1) enhanced this usage directly via the TV. In the meantime, in such situations he did not use the smartphone or netbook anymore.

In addition to that, we could also identify another interesting usage behavior with regards to the Media Center system: it's full list of features makes it a perfect media hub for parties., C5_1 reflected on his party experience and pointed out that because of the all-round features, he really appreciated the Media Center system as a party media hub: *"When my friends were here, we used mainly the Media Center system to listen to music and watch YouTube videos. That's also what I valued especially. With the Media Center system, one is able to do everything: to surf the net, to watch a film, or listen to music."* (C5_1)

We could also identify shifts from PC/laptop towards the smartphone. Several participants used the smartphone instead of the laptop to regularly check email. In case of S1, this change became visible very well. Before technologies were introduced, he was not using any media in the morning (with the exception of the radio from time to time), because the morning was a busy time for him. In the second study he already used the smartphone in the morning to check his email. A similar behavior could be identified by S2. She described it with the reason of prioritizing follow-up activities based on her business email: *"After I get up in the morning I check my email. [...] Maybe that is just curiosity, is there something important, is it necessary to react immediately? Or will I have time to handle other things?"*

The introduction of the smartphone established practices of flexible media usage. S4 described this practice with a 'just-in-time' behavior. Through the permanent availability of the smartphone and the option to go online, media usage is flexibly distributed throughout the day and is not limited to the evening anymore. S4 explained this kind of improved flexibility as follows: *"Information and exchange have turned into a 'just-in-time' behavior. If you want to look up something, or because you're bored, you can directly check what's new, scroll down a bit and then exit again. I'd say that's rather flexible."*

4.1.2 Flexible Device Usage

Besides the above described integration of new devices in users' daily routines, an interesting behavior regarding the choice of devices for simple and short-term online activities, e.g. looking for brief information or checking email, could be identified when watching television. As almost all of the present devices (laptop, Media Center system or smartphone) were appropriate for these activities, participants described choosing a device based on a "least-effort" consideration. C4_1 for example stated: *"in case the laptop is not in my grasp, I'll use the iPad as it is ready immediately. And if the iPad is not in my grasp [...] I would use the smartphone. However, if the laptop is next to me, I will of course use the laptop".*

For more complex online activities that involve entering large amounts of text or complex graphical output, participants chose their device more carefully. For this purpose S1 described situations where TV content made him gather brief information using his smartphone. However, *"in case I wanted more in-depth information, I would boot up the laptop, as it has a larger screen".*

Moreover, the presence of other household members is taken into consideration when choosing a device: *"The PC must run parallel to watching TV together with other family members and then it's difficult to watch TV and check email simultaneously on the TV"* (F3_1). He also stated that it was no problem, if no other family member was sitting next to him in front of the TV. *"Then I use this function during commercials"* (F3_1). In addition to this, when watching TV alone, the simultaneous usage of a smartphone can be beneficial, as the watched content will not be interrupted or covered. For this purpose E1_2 explains, that *"when I sit in front of the PC or TV [watching video content in both cases], I normally use the smartphone for surfing and texting with other people or checking if someone emailed me. The advantage is that you don't need to interrupt the video to do something else".*

Besides those short-term role assignments, we also recognized long-term assignments, where devices were given fixed roles for significant periods of time. This was especially obvious by the fact that participants separated leisure activities from working activities in the living room, if they worked at home (for their business, studying for school or university).

Concerning this phenomenon S2 realized that after appropriating new technologies, she now uses the smartphone and the Media Center system to surf the Internet on weekends. She did not turn on her PC any more when she wasn't working, despite the fact that TV/Media Center system and computer were not spatially divided in the living room. In a similar way C5_1 said that for him the laptop *"has a well-defined scope. Of course I'm working on it. Furthermore I use it for surfing, occasionally for gambling, while the Media Center system is primarily used for movies and music".* Also a clear task specific and physical separation could be found in other households. C2_2 explained that after the introduction of the marketable technologies, her laptop *"now remains in the room where she studies or works. In the past, it was also used in the living room since it was the only device with internet-capability [...]. I have established a total separation between university [work] [...] and private affairs – for the fun of it".* Another participant (E1_3) used her computer to do homework in the afternoon. After she had finished her tasks, she went to the living room to chat online with friends and play online games on the Media Center system. Particularly, in both of the latter cases, the introduction of the Media Center system clarified the assignment of fixed roles for the devices and their physical configuration within the households.

4.2 Social Phenomena

The introduction of the Media Center system and the smartphone changed the landscape of electronic appliances in the households. As a result, a new usage pattern for each individual user has been observed, which was presented in the previous chapter. Nevertheless, social structures within the households also adapted to the change. We identified some subtle yet interesting changes that happened during our entire study.

4.2.1 Conflicts in Device Sharing

Sharing devices in households is sometimes tricky, as some household members may dominate and monopolize some devices for a certain period of time. Almost every household has an established hierarchy of access for each device, e.g. children occupy the TV during animation time. Device domination used to be a problem before the new hardware was introduced. After the hardware introduction - although this domination continues to exist - this problem has become less severe by the decoupling of content and device. There is now a wider range of possible devices from which to access the same content. Thus the device no longer plays a decisive role in this situation.

In one household the mother (F1_2) had very little chance to use the computer before our hardware introduction, because her husband and her daughter were always occupying it. *"I've noticed that I seldom use our computer. Looks like I don't need it and my husband spends quite a lot of time sitting in front of it, playing, my child also. To be honest, I think I have neither the time nor the chance to use it."* After we introduce the hardware, she started to use the Media Center system to surf the Internet when the computer was not available. Interestingly she claimed her Internet usage in the second study to be 'relatively high', given that she didn't even realize that she needed the Internet during the first study.

In another household, the situation was similar. C1_2 had very little access to the computer, regardless of the first or the second study. But through the introduction of the new devices she then had the possibility to fall back on to the smartphone or the Media Center system to surf the Internet: "*I could barely use it [PC] earlier (laugh). But now, I don't actually need it. Because now most of the time I use the smartphone to surf the Internet, or the TV [Media Center system]*". The PC is not always the first device for browsing the web. In another case the participant (F2_2) first tried to use the Media Center system to surf the Internet, if not possible, she then turned to the laptop: *"When the children don't let me use the TV, for example. They want to keep watching their program, but I want to check something on the Internet...They don't let me. Then I'll turn to the laptop, it's in standby mode all day long."*

4.2.2 Family Obligation

As a family, the members have an intrinsic tendency for physical proximity, even when this sometimes seems obligatory. From our study we realized that this phenomenon commonly exists in multi-person households. The representative pattern of "co-watching but with different interests" happened in the living room when some household members were bored by the TV program being watched. Instead of leaving the living room, they choose to stay but to use another device to do something else parallel to watching television.

For example, in one household, one participant (C2_2) is interested in a TV series but her boyfriend (C2_1) is not. C2_1 then used the smartphone to browse the Internet in the meantime. In another household the introduced smartphone also turned out to be used when co-watching. C1_2 described her usage as follows: *"I use the smartphone when C1_1 is watching something on TV but I'm not interested. I'll still sit beside him and just watch with 'one eye open', most of the time though I'll be playing or surfing the Internet on the smartphone."* We could identify the same phenomenon in households with children. In one case the child (F1_3) now has the opportunity to do more things while sitting next to its parents. *"When my parents are watching the television and I'm bored with what they're watching, I use the smartphone [to play and text with friends]"* (F1_3).

4.2.3 Plasticity of Time

8.15 p.m. used to be considered as 'prime time' for watching television. One has to align his social life to the planned TV program, if he doesn't want to miss it. But now, with the help of recording and time-shift, users are able to uncouple their personal timeline from the elaborated program schedule of broadcasters.

One household reported that with the function of recording and time-shift provided by the Media Center system, they felt quite relaxed at dinner. As they normally cooked around 8 p.m., they used to hurry so that they could catch up to the TV program by 8.30 p.m. But after the hardware introduction, they let the Media Center system record the program. In this way they could have dinner without being under pressure and enjoy the show later, and were then also able to manually skip the commercials: *"Now we often start watching TV at 8.30 or 8.45 p.m.. We let it record first, then we watch and then we can skip the commercials. We actually do this quite often."* (C2_2)

Another quite surprising way of use we identified, was that the electronic program guide was used for baby-sitting. One participant (E2) reflected that she was arranging the children's day according to the TV schedule. E2 stated that: *"EPG helps me a lot when I have to be away and leave the children alone. Then I'll say: 'now this program is broadcasted, then this, then this and I'll be back by this program'. In this sense I often structure the children's day according to the TV program."*

4.3 Perception of Change

As shown before, the implementation of technologies in households has led to changes in the daily routine of media consumption and social behaviors within a household. Even if the severity of these changes differs between various participants, they were always obvious. However, the participants' reflection and the degree of awareness of individual changes were distinguishable from the empirically ascertained behavior.

Some of the participants described their altered usage behavior in a detailed and well aware manner. C2_2 for example mentioned that the TV consumption remained constant or even decreased, because of the opportunity to surf the Internet on the television set as an alternative to watch low-quality TV content. Furthermore, the boot time of the Media Center system often led to the decision to leave the device off and thus to a more conscious television consumption. In contrast, the same participant described that the cell phone usage increased strongly and was kind of like an addiction. In the past she often left her phone at home but now she thinks to herself: *"Oh my god, you left your smartphone at home!"*. F2_2 said that there are no changes concerning her consumption behavior or time, but that the usage itself became more convenient due to the new integrated internet-capability of the television. *"You just remain seated on the couch and you have your keyboard. Otherwise, during commercials I would go to [the laptop in] the kitchen and log on to Facebook or elsewhere. [Now] I can just remain under my blanket and do it on the TV. That's great!"*. Another good example for a distinct awareness of individual changes in media usage behavior is found in a statement of C5_1. For him the opportunity to now be able to watch high definition content already poses a fundamental improvement.

In contrast to that conscious perception of individual changes in media usage behavior, other participants did not recognize any changes. Also, participants that before had described changes for several usage situations, did not discern existing changes in other situations. C2_2 for example, who described variances in her TV consumption and cell phone usage behavior, said that a simultaneous usage of various media did not take place in her household. Her boyfriend (C2_1) however said that when watching TV together, he sometimes used the smartphone to surf the Internet when he was bored of the TV content his girlfriend was watching. The missing awareness regarding the changes becomes even clearer in the following statement of E1_1:*"I always do the same. Because until now the Media Center system doesn't offer much new."* Although she is aware of the new devices, for her, there is no change happening when using same functions (e.g. browser games, Internet, instant messaging) on different devices (PC at the desk or TV screen). Her daughter (E1_2) even confirms that her mothers usage behavior has changed insofar that she now uses the Media Center system excessively: *"When I come home from school I use the Media Center system to watch animes on the Internet until 8 p.m, when my mother chucks me out.".*

Another good example is the following excerpt from the feedback interview after the second diary study with F3_2:

Interviewer (I): *"What changes did you recognize that are associated with the new devices?"*
F3_2: *"[...] regarding the box [Media Center system]?"*
I: *"Exactly!"*
F3_2: *"Ehm... No. Well, I record more now. I like recording, yes. But actually no changes."*
I: *"Did your daily routine change?"*
F3_2: *"No, not at all!"*
I: *"Everything remained the same?"*
F3_2: *"Yes!"*
I: *"Did the TV's role change?*
F3_2: *"No, no!"*
I: *"You use it the same way as before?"*
F3_2: *"Yes!"*
I: *"The same intensity, the same content?"*
F3_2: *"Yes, right. Nothing's changed."*
I: *"How do you organize your TV consumption? How do you plan watching TV? Has something changed?"*
F3_2: *"I don't plan watching TV. I always watch the same things, I don't have to plan."*
I: *"Regarding the Media Center system: Which functions do you use exactly?"*
F3_2: *"The recording function."*

This example illustrates clearly that the participant, despite the fact that she is using the new recording function of the Media Center system now, is not aware of any changes in her TV usage behavior. The statement also shows that when she says, she does not plan her TV consumption, this statement is contradicted by the fact that recording in principle requires planning (e.g. programming the timer). In the interview with F1_2 we had a similar experience. She also mentioned that the usage of the TV set did not change, but in her answer to the question about what functions she used on the Media Center system, she mentioned several services she could not use before (e.g. watching shared movies from the PC via Wi-Fi, recordings, Internet).

An additional interesting result concerns the fact that the participants' reflection upon changes in individual media usage was often induced by the applied diary study. Some participants assumed that they were aware of their usage behavior and the accompanied changes. Only by keeping the diary did they come to see significant differences between their assumed and real usage behavior. S1 describes this experience as follows: *"This is interesting. After the first diary I had no idea what could happen and I never thought that I would change. But this already started with the second diary, realizing that a lot has changed."*. S3 stated something similar and challenged his self-perception. *"I am appalled at how much media I consume and also by how standardized it actually is. Once I regarded myself as an individualist, but in actually I am a normal person. Through the project I became more aware of my media usage."*

5. DISCUSSION

The introduction of the new devices in our Living Lab households caused several expected changes within the participants media usage behavior. Many of our general findings about the meaning of television and the flexibility of TV consumption underline earlier research: Obrist et al. [22] investigated the TV usage and the television's role in daily life, Barkhuus [3] explored convergent media usage but only focused on the computer. Brown & Barkhuus [8] showed how the introduction of a PVR influenced the TV watching behavior. Moreover, we identified interesting phenomena in regards to how changes were induced by new devices and how they affected daily routines and social structures within the households.

Device-Shift: The trend of converging functions on various devices offers users the freedom of choice with regard to the used device. We identified that both the Media Center system and the smartphone take over various tasks of the PC or laptop regardless of whether if they are used in a single or multi-person household. However, this substitution occurs only in specific situations, an entire replacement could not be observed. In case of the Media Center system, the usage primarily takes place simultaneously to watching broadcast television (e.g. using the Internet during commercials or retrieving additional content) or as a new alternative to habitual TV consumption (e.g. watching on demand content from the Internet or hard disk). Here it is an interesting result that the new functions the Media Center system brings to the TV, are frequently used but did not result in an increasing usage of the TV set as a whole. The situation is different with the smartphone. Its permanent presence led to a more frequent usage and an altered usage behavior of the service itself. Email or social networks for instance were no longer used at specific times, but it was at hand all day long. This characteristic also led to changes in the synchronous device usage while watching TV. While the laptop was previously the device mainly used for this purpose, after the introduction of the new devices, it was in many cases substituted by the smartphone. This could be observed with participants with lower technical experience. Participants who already had experience with smartphones, had already shown this usage behavior before.

This raises an interesting question concerning the 'second devices' or 'second screens' and its integration into the situations, when media were consumed [4,10,27,28]. However, our study did not confirm an implicit order, where the television came first, and computer / laptop / smartphone / tablet PC were second, instead the order changed according to the users' attention and his main activity.

Expedient choice of devices: We found out that despite the fact that many services and functions (e.g. Internet, email) can now be accessed and used platform independently, the choice of the device is, however, not arbitrary. The users made unconscious decisions based on (a) *what effort* they would be willing to put into satisfying their information or communication needs and (b) *which device* to use. This obviously (a) depends on the urge and importance while (b) depends on a set of different influences. The following list of encountered factors from our study is derived from the classification of influencing factors for TV viewing of Wonneberger et al. [30]:

- **Individual influences:** tiredness, comfort, joy of use, individual role assignment of devices, etc.
- **Physical influences:** location of the device, mobility of the device, boot time, usability aspects, interdependency with synchronous activities, etc.

- **Social influences:** device is occupied, consideration for others, privacy concerns, ownership situations, etc.

Particularly in multi-person households, we could identify a stronger influence of social factors. In these cases, users sometimes had to choose an alternative device, because the preferred one was occupied by another family member. Otherwise, the more devices exist in households, the more opportunities emerge, which allow diverse access to media content. The phenomenon of expedient choice of devices hence confirmed the assumption that the convergence of media does not lead to a substitution of existing devices, but to a more flexible and complementary device usage. While this on the one hand enhanced the user experience, on the other hand, it also created a challenge for the right design. The same function is now used on different devices, which requires function sets to be defined to adapt to the characteristics and capabilities of each device. The user now has access to a wider range of devices, and "jumping" between devices becomes more frequent. Therefore, an awareness function is needed, to accurately locate the user so that corresponding services could be provided. The increased number of devices has also increased the difficulty of personal configurations. In this sense a cloud setting capability to centrally and dynamically arrange the configurations on all devices should be promising.

Role assignment: A surprising result is that after the introduction of the new devices, some of the participants assigned specific roles to their devices. The laptop or PC was previously the sole web-enabled device in most of the Living Lab households and used for any internet-based activities. Now, with the new devices, it was assigned the role of a work computer, while the Media Center system and the smartphone were used for leisure time activities. Another example is that the Media Center system was only used for multimedia (TV, YouTube, music, etc.) while communication applications were used on the laptop or smartphone. Both phenomena could be found in all household structures, as well as in both types of experienced users. This raises the questions of whether this behavior is based on traditional device roles (PC/laptop as a working tool), which are still embedded in the users' way of thinking, and what this means for the future design of new devices and interfaces. To answer these questions more investigation into this behavior is necessary.

Restricted device access: Because the devices were previously limited in numbers (mainly the PC), the members of many multi-person households had to share. This led to the situation that some household members gave others the advantage to use the devices more often, or that hierarchical structures were a handicap for household members when it came to device access. This was often the case in households with a mixed technical experience. Participants with less experience dedicated devices to other household members with more experience. However, the first diary study showed that the missing or restricted access to devices, respectively the Internet, did not effect the users needs being satisfied or unsatisfied. Instead they mentioned that there was no need for an intensified usage. The introduction of the Media Center system and the smartphone, made two new devices available, which solved the problem of restricted access. Interestingly though, this led to a heavily increased use by those participants with primarily less technical experience, who previously had to deal with restricted access to the then existing devices, even if they had mentioned before that they were satisfied with their amount of device usage. This phenomenon shows on the one hand that the need for device usage depends on the access possibilities, and that easier access causes more intensive usage. On the other hand we can see that a larger number of devices within a household does not dissolve hierarchies of device sharing. but leads to an easier device access for any household member.

The living rooms' social situation: Our study still confirms earlier findings e.g. from Bernhaupt et al. [5], that watching TV in multi-person households is an important social activity and an unspoken family obligation, where family members come together in the living room, to spend the evening together. However, it is not invariably the case that the program choice is to everyone's liking, so that compromises have to be found and that some are bored with the program. The smartphone as a new ultra-mobile device offers the possibility to follow individual interests without breaking up the physical coming-together, but also does not result in enhanced conversations. This behavior, which was critically discussed by Turkle [29], helps on the one hand to ease conflicts regarding the program choice, but on the other hand it breaks up the existing social cohesion within households. Family members are present in the room but no longer interested in common activities, so that they focus on other online activities on their mobile devices and were limited in following conversations. Therefore, the design of new concepts for tabletop systems should be seen as a challenge in order to recreate social cohesion in the living room.

Loose binding to elaborated program schedules: One of the frequently used functions of the Media Center system was the recording feature. The study showed that many households, regardless of their household structure and technical experience, used the EPG to plan recordings for the entire week and watched the content on the weekend. However, contrary to the findings from Brown & Barkhuus [8], the given program schedules are often established by daily routines and TV content is watched when broadcasted. As a consequence, other activities have to be shortened or aborted in order to not miss the beginning of a television show. In our study we identified an interesting behavior that deals with this circumstance and extends earlier findings from Irani et al. [18]. The participants were still guided by the given schedule but in order to finish previous activities (e.g. cooking and dining), they used the time shift feature to record the TV show and then watch after they had finished dinner. This allowed for a more relaxed evening schedule on behalf of social activities within the household.

Methodological challenges: The results of our study show that the participants' perception of their changed usage behavior strongly differs from each other. While some of the participants did not notice any changes, others reflected on their changed usage in a very detailed manner. One point we found, was that especially the smartphone was identified as a new device that fundamentally changed mobile usage, while changes based on the Media Center system were noticed less strongly. This brings up the question, if new devices or functionalities that are embedded in existing usage scenarios (TV set in the living room) are less perceived than devices that evolve new habits of usage (smartphone). In addition to that a more general question is how pronounced the changes have to be, so that users notice them as such. Hence, the participants' reflective faculties pose a major challenge for such a long-term field study. Because of this, the selected methods have to aim at continuously stimulating the users' reflection. A good example is the interview excerpt in chapter 4.3, where the interviewee helped the participant by asking specific and precise questions to reflect and describe her unconscious usage behavior.

Furthermore, we consciously used self-documenting methods in order to keep the living room a private space and to built trust for further interviews and long-term investigations within the field. Even if our data base is not completed, for our explorative procedure it was important to get an insight into the real life, understanding usage behavior and changes that occur over time. It could be seen as a limitation of the qualitative study that we did not use a tracking system which gathers more quantified data about the devices, used functionalities, timeframes and consumed content. Otherwise, it has to be considered carefully, if to use a tracking system without destroying natural TV consumption behavior as well as the trusted relationships. For further investigations it could be helpful to track timespans and used functionalities, but not the detailed content information.

Another study limitation is related to the limited budget, due to which we could fit each household with only one smartphone. For more extensive results especially within multi-person households it would be helpful to equip households with more than one device, because of their characteristic as personal device. Within our study only two households shared the smartphone with the other household members, most of them used it as a personal device. As a positive feedback from the field, we noticed that three of the households purchased another device, so that we could get a better understanding of the smartphones' integration into daily routines.

6. CONCLUSION

In this work we explored current practices of adopting and using new marketable devices in domestic environments. For this purpose we conducted a qualitative long-term study with 27 participants in 16 households of our Living Lab. In the first step of the two-stage empirical study, we wanted to gain an in-depth understanding of the current media and device usage. After the first stage we introduced the marketable devices – each household got an Android OS-equipped smartphone and a Microsoft Media Center system. In the second step, nine months later, we wanted to figure out how the new devices had changed the media usage behavior and how these changes impact on social structures within the households.

We identified several social and usage phenomena concerning device-shifting, expediency of devices, roles of devices, restricted access to devices within families, campfire effect in the living room, and the binding to program schedules. Furthermore we identified a strongly diverging reflective faculty regarding the individual perception of changes among the participants. Our results show that new devices and services are adapted rapidly within a household and result in a better, more flexible and more comfortable media usage. But our results also indicate that current concepts bring forth several issues that need to be investigated further in future research. On the one hand, even if proposed as 'convergence' of current solutions, it is not supported at an optimal level, e.g. when switching between television and Internet on the Media Center system. On the other hand, further solutions need to better address the expediency, e.g. using related services on a secondary device that is in a reachable distance or the separation of shared and personal use, e.g. by additional personalized content on mobile devices.

The results of our study provide insights that may affect design of new cross-platform concepts in current home IT infrastructures. Such environments are characterized by a diversification of devices, services and content offers. Content is accessible on different devices and can be enriched with functionalities that support personalization and social exchange as well. However, as an important issue we should address the social cohesion also within households. We observed different patterns including conflicts in device sharing, role assignment and expedient choice related to personal interests. But these observations also raise a more critical aspect, that everyone is consuming media only for himself, even if sitting together in the living room. Further work may address this issue by approaches that support activities also within households, e.g. by using an interactive secondary public display. Also privacy aspects need to be considered carefully. New and flexible options to access content and services also are related to management, e.g. roles and rights, and profile, e.g. household vs. personal profiles.

7. ACKNOWLEDGMENTS

The project *SocialMedia* is funded by the Ministry for Innovation, Science, Research and Technology of the country of North Rhine-Westphalia, Germany with resources from the European Union and European funds for regional developments (Ziel 2) (280411902).

8. REFERENCES

[1] Almirall, E. and Wareham, J. Living Labs and open innovation: roles and applicability. *The Electronic Journal for Virtual Organizations and Networks 10*, 3 (2008), 21-46.

[2] Barkhuus, L. and Brown, B. Unpacking the television: User practices around a changing technology. *ACM Transactions on Computer-Human Interaction (TOCHI) 16*, 3 (2009), 1-22.

[3] Barkhuus, L. Television on the internet. *Proceedings of the 27th international conference extended abstracts on Human factors in computing systems - CHI EA '09*, ACM Press (2009), 2479.

[4] Basapur, S., Harboe, G., Mandalia, H., Novak, A., Vuong, V., and Metcalf, C. Field trial of a dual device user experience for iTV. *Proceddings of the 9th international interactive conference on Interactive television - EuroITV '11*, ACM Press (2011), 127.

[5] Bernhaupt, R., Obrist, M., Weiss, A., Beck, E., and Tscheligi, M. Trends in the living room and beyond: results from ethnographic studies using creative and playful probing. *European Conference on Interactive Television*, ACM (2008), 1-23.

[6] Bernhaupt, R., Pirker, M.M., Weiss, A., Wilfinger, D., and Tscheligi, M. Security, privacy, and personalization. *Computers in Entertainment 9*, 3 (2011), 1-33.

[7] Bernhaupt, R., Weiss, A., Pirker, M., Wilfinger, D., and Tscheligi, M. Ethnographic insights on security, privacy, and personalization aspects of user interaction in interactive TV. *Proceedings of the 8th international interactive conference on Interactive TV&Video - EuroITV '10*, ACM Press (2010), 187.

[8] Brown, B. and Barkhuus, L. The television will be revolutionized: effects of PVRs and filesharing on television watching. *Conference on Human Factors in Computing Systems CHI'06*, (2006), 663.

[9] Carter, S. and Mankoff, J. When participants do the capturing. *Proceedings of the SIGCHI conference on Human factors in computing systems - CHI '05*, ACM Press (2005), 899.

[10] Cesar, P., Bulterman, D.C.A., Jansen, J., Geerts, D., Knoche, H., and Seager, W. Fragment, tag, enrich, and send:

Enhancing social sharing of video. *ACM Transactions on Multimedia Computing, Communications, and Applications (TOMCCAP) 5*, 3 (2009), 1-27.

[11] Crabtree, A. and Rodden, T. Domestic Routines and Design for the Home. *Computer Supported Cooperative Work (CSCW) 13*, 2 (2004), 191-220.

[12] Følstad, A. Living Labs for Innovation and Development of Communication Technology: A Literature Review. *The Electronic Journal for Virtual Organisations and Networks 10*, (2008), 99-131.

[13] Gaver, B., Dunne, T., and Pacenti, E. Design: cultural probes. *interactions 6*, 1 (1999), 21-29.

[14] Harboe, G., Metcalf, C.J., Bentley, F., Tullio, J., Massey, N., and Romano, G. Ambient social tv. *Proceeding of the twenty-sixth annual CHI conference on Human factors in computing systems - CHI '08*, ACM Press (2008), 1.

[15] Hess, J. and Ogonowski, C. Steps toward a living lab for socialmedia concept evaluation and continuous user-involvement. *European Conference on Interactive Television*, (2010), 171-174.

[16] Hess, J., Ley, B., Ogonowski, C., Wan, L., and Wulf, V. Jumping between Devices and Services: Towards an Integrated Concept for Social TV. *Proceedings of the European Conference on Interactive Television*, (2011).

[17] Huang, E.M., Harboe, G., Tullio, J., et al. Of social television comes home: a field study of communication choices and practices in tv-based text and voice chat. *Proceedings of the 27th international conference on Human factors in computing systems*, (2009), 585-594.

[18] Irani, L., Jeffries, R., and Knight, A. Rhythms and plasticity: television temporality at home. *Personal and Ubiquitous Computing 14*, 7 (2010), 621-632.

[19] Lull, J. *Inside Family Viewing: Ethnographic Research on Television's Audiences*. Routledge, 1991.

[20] Nathan, M., Harrison, C., Yarosh, S., Terveen, L., Stead, L., and Amento, B. CollaboraTV. *Proceeding of the 1st international conference on Designing interactive user experiences for TV and video - uxtv '08*, ACM Press (2008), 85.

[21] Niitamo, V.P., Kulkki, S., Eriksson, M., and Hribernik, K.A. State-of-the-art and good practice in the field of living labs. *Proceedings of the 12th International Conference on Concurrent Enterprising: Innovative Products and Services through Collaborative Networks. Italy: Milan*, (2006), 26-28.

[22] Obrist, M., Bernhaupt, R., and Tscheligi, M. Interactive TV for the Home: An Ethnographic Study on Users' Requirements and Experiences. *International Journal of Human-Computer Interaction 24*, 2 (2008), 174-196.

[23] O'Brien, J., Rodden, T., Rouncefield, M., and Hughes, J. At home with the technology: an ethnographic study of a set-top-box trial. *ACM Transactions on Computer-Human Interaction (TOCHI) 6*, 3 (1999), 282-308.

[24] O'Hara, K., Mitchell, A.S., and Vorbau, A. Consuming video on mobile devices. *Proceedings of the SIGCHI conference on Human factors in computing systems - CHI '07*, ACM Press (2007), 857.

[25] Smith, S.M. and Krugman, D.M. Exploring Perceptions and Usage Patterns of Digital Video Recorder Owners. *Journal of Broadcasting & Electronic Media 54*, 2 (2010), 248-264.

[26] Steimle, J., Khalilbeigi, M., Mühlhäuser, M., and Hollan, J.D. Physical and digital media usage patterns on interactive tabletop surfaces. *ACM International Conference on Interactive Tabletops and Surfaces - ITS '10*, ACM Press (2010), 167.

[27] Tsekleves, E., Cruickshank, L., Hill, A., Kondo, K., and Whitham, R. Interacting with Digital Media at Home via a Second Screen. (2007), 201-206.

[28] Tsekleves, E., Whitham, R., Kondo, K., and Hill, A. Bringing the television experience to other media in the home. *Proceedings of the seventh european conference on European interactive television conference - EuroITV '09*, ACM Press (2009), 201.

[29] Turkle, S. *Alone Together: Why We Expect More from Technology and Less from Each Other*. Basic Books, 2011.

[30] Wonneberger, A., Schoenbach, K., and Meurs, L. Van. Dynamics of Individual Television Viewing Behavior : Models , Empirical Evidence , and a Research Program. *Communication Studies 60*, 3 (2009), 235-252.

Everyday Life *in* (front of) the Screen: The Consumption of Multiple Screen Technologies in the Living Room Context

Evelien D'heer
IBBT-MICT-Ghent University
Korte Meer 7-9-11
BE-9000 Gent
+32 9 264 84 77
evelien.dheer@ugent.be

Cédric Courtois
IBBT-MICT-Ghent University
Korte Meer 7-9-11
BE-9000 Gent
+32 9 264 91 54
cedric.courtois@ugent.be

Steve Paulussen
IBBT-MICT-Ghent University
Korte Meer 7-9-11
BE-9000 Gent
+32 9 264 91 83
steve.paulussen@ugent.be

ABSTRACT

Today's (home) media environment is becoming increasingly saturated. Smartphones, tablets and laptops enter our living room and possibly alter our television viewing experience. In this paper, we want to grasp how 'screen technologies' are interrelated on a textual (content) and a material level (technological object), from a user perspective. By means of domestic in-depth interviews with owners of multiple screen technologies, we interpret the integration of multiple secondary screens in the everyday television viewing behavior. In most cases, the use of second screens is not related to television content. Nonetheless, we also found evidence of changing dynamics concerning public and private spaces, as people extend television text on their second screens into online social spaces or more generally, the Internet. These interactive structures provide individuals with opportunities as well as threats. In conclusion, we identify directions for future research on the consumption and reception of television.

Categories and Subject Descriptors

J.4 [**Social and behavioral sciences**] - *Sociology*

General Terms

Measurement, Human Factors

Keywords

Convergence, Audience, Individualization, Public

1. INTRODUCTION

In this media-drenched, channel-surfing age, Deuze, Blank & Speers [1] posit - on a somewhat provocative way - we no longer live *with*, but *in* media (cf. 'Media Life'). The intrusiveness and ubiquity of communication and informative technologies as well as the need to rethink audiences and media consumption is widely acknowledged [2]. The domestic media environment is indeed changing, with multiple media appliances entering our homes and occupying our living rooms (e.g. laptops, smartphones and tablets). In this respect, we aim to empirically understand convergence as a socio-cultural process by investigation everyday TV viewing behavior within a multi-screen media repertoire.

2. CONVERGED MEDIA, AUDIENCES, PRACTICES AND PLACES

The convergence or fluidity of post-industrial society, and media in particular, will be addressed at micro-level, i.e. the domestic context of the home. The latter no longer refers to the private, but interweaves multiple configurations of the public and the private [3]. The networked self extends the private sphere beyond the physical boundaries of the home, with the 'multiplication' of spaces as a result [4, 5], or as Castells [6] refers to it: the 'space of flows'. Whereas much work has been concerned with online communities and identity in cyberspace, very little is known on how online and offline spaces relate or converge [7].

Although television consumption is predominantly related to the domestic life, where meaning is ideally constructed, The Internet allows family members to interact via multiple 'meso-publics' (e.g. Twitter) [8, p. 65]. In this respect, the audience, a discursive construct related to broadcasting media, shifts to a more hybrid and fragmented constellation. People are more connected than ever, participating in and engaging with media through various platforms and channels [2]. It is up to the individual to select, mix and match the media technologies at hand to manage social contact, regulate time and space, self-representation and media consumption [3, 9].

The constant flux of audience roles, spaces and technologies allows control, autonomy and creativity. At the same time, uncertainty reigns in this liquid, reflexive times [10, 11]. Individuals are required to constitute themselves, as we are all 'artists of life' [12]. In this respect, Beck [10] posits that individualism, much criticized, is 'moral and political' in a new sense. He refers to 'individualization' as a structural concept, characteristic for late modernity. The emerging virtual context in combination with the multiplication of home media appliances indeed led to the popular thesis of increased privatization and individualization of media use within the home [e.g. The bedroom culture, 13].

3. TAMING THE MEDIATOPE

In order to grasp contemporary 'media culture', we preferably study media as an element of the everyday life [14]. In reference to Meyrowitz [15], we see media as *an environment*, emphasizing a holistic approach, by considering 'new media' in the light of older media and focus on their capacity to transform time, space and social relations. We do not focus our study on media effects (i.e. effects of specific mass media messages on audience's behavior and beliefs), but rather on meanings, uses in and impact on our everyday lives. Alasuutari [14], points to the need to incorporate the increased *reflexivity* on the part of the audience, as they reflect on media consumption, the media as an institute and the reality claims they make, both offline but potentially also through the World Wide Web.

Domestication, as a theory and a research concept, provides an understanding of the 'careers' of media technologies within the micro context of the home [16-18]. In our research, we emphasize the incorporation in time and space of *multiple* screen technologies, as well the relationship between the household and the outside world (conversion). Concerning media technologies, we distinguish both the physical (the object) and the symbolic (the message) ['Double articulation', 18] as well as the immediate social and spatial context ['Triple articulation', 19]. We will focus on the living room space and its socio-temporal dimensions, in which multi-screen consumption takes place.

In this paper, we want to grasp the interplay of screen technologies' material dimension and how they relate on a textual level. In doing so, we shed light on the changing dynamics between the private and the public and the articulation of the (reflexive) individual in the networked media ecology. This will enhance our understand convergence as a socio-cultural evolution.

4. METHODOLOGY

4.1 Respondent sampling and recruitment

In accordance with our theoretical framework discussed above, we recruited respondents of multi-screen households. Here, a multi-screen household denotes the ownership of at least one television, one portable computer/tablet and one smartphone.

Based on two large-scale surveys on media ownership and use, respondents were recruited for an in-depth interview. In total, 26 semi-structured interviews were conducted late 2011, early 2012, with respondents living in Flanders (Northern region of Belgium). Of the 26 participants, 15 are males and 11 are females, ranging from age 20 to 57. Next to age and sex, respondents vary in their family situation: alone (6); alone with children (1); living together/married without children (9); living together/married with children (8); living with parents (2). The diversity of respondent profiles yields a wide range of possible multi-screen consumption patrons in different contextual settings.

4.2 Interview procedure and analysis

During the interview, we elaborate on the interconnectedness of screen technologies, both as objects and as texts within the living room context (and its social and temporal specificities) from a user perspective.

The interviews started with the description of a typical evening routine with focus on the use of screen devices and the socio-temporal setting. In addition, respondents were asked to draw their living room and the physical location of the screen technologies when reflecting on their daily routines.

The interviews were conducted by the author and were audio-recorded. The interview transcripts were analyzed with use of CAQDAS. The literature outlined above serves as 'sensitizing concepts' for the analysis. The qualitative analysis consists of three stages [20], whereby we start from very concrete response categories of issues emerging from the data to evolve to more abstract (conceptual) levels of analysis.

5. RESULTS

First, we will focus on the role of screen technologies in our everyday routines. Secondly, we relate the consumption of multiple screens to the social dynamics within the living room context. Finally, we provide insight in the blurring lines between the private realm of the home and the online world.

5.1 Screens and everyday routines

The description of a typical evening confirms television's structural use [21]. The television set is turned more or less habitually and serves as a time regulator. The news preludes the start of the evening and is often combined with dinner-time, because '*just listening is enough*' (Paul, 34, M). When comparing the family situation and the habitual use of the television, we see that mostly in families with children, television is on for *or* put on by the children.

Although the television screen still dominates, to a lesser extent we see the integration of computers (fixed or laptops) and tablets in the evening routine. The respondents that turn on their computer when arriving at home, do not vary in age and gender. They are all less TV-oriented, meaning that they do not view a lot of broadcasting TV programs or do not need television as a 'companion'. In addition, in all cases, the (fixed) computer is located in 'social places' as the living and/or kitchen area. In four cases, the tablet is used *'in between cooking'* (Clara, 45), mostly by females or when the kitchen is separated from the living area where the television screen is located.

When taking place in the sofa 'to watch television', which still mostly happens between 7 and 8 pm, secondary screens are part of the daily television viewing routine. They are within reach and used regularly throughout the entire evening. Only two respondents deliberately refuse to confound television viewing with the use of second screens.

Tablets are perceived 'easier' than laptops to consume in the sofa and at the same time the bigger screen offers a better experience than the smartphone.

Joris (36, M): *The tablet is very easy…it is within hand reach and when you feel like playing a game, you take the tablet for 5 minutes. I don't need to be concentrated for 3 hours* […].

As stated above, not only the device itself, but also its text is easy to consume in front of the television. There is no continuity in the use these devices, as games, browsing and checking emails entail small tasks, allowing us to constantly switch easily between the computer screen and the TV screen.

Television's role as primary or secondary screen corresponds with the TV content that is consumed. Routine television content (e.g. daily soap series) is said not to require full attention. This routine TV viewing mode, or 'monitoring viewing style' [22], makes television both a first and a second screen, whereby viewers pay just enough attention to keep up with the program.

Most frequent activities on the small screen are checking Facebook, e-mails and purposely browsing the endless web. Hence, during television watching, there is an almost systematic connection with 'the outside world' (i.e. one's social network). Or as one of the respondents reflected upon it:

Freso (33, M): *Actually you want to stay up to date, not about the news, but about what happens around you…*

Rather strikingly however, in most cases, the use of second screens is related to television content *other* family members are watching. Apparently, respondents are not into compromising on television content and will privately consume their preferred texts on their personal screens (e.g. tablet, laptop) while other family members watch television. In what follows we will link second screen consumption with the social context of the living room and elaborate on (5.2) individualization as well as (5.3) socialization processes of this multi-screen environment.

5.2 Collective individualization

When sitting in the sofa, we see that most of the respondents (19) have their screens (preferably the tablet, if they possess one) within reach, regardless of whether they are alone or together with family members. As stated above, the 'small screens' are used to avoid watching television content one is not interested in.

Samuel (29, M): *He* [partner] *likes to watch those ridiculous reality programs on MTV. As I am not interested, I do something on the tablet. Mostly things that don't make any noise… for example just randomly browsing the web.*

This works in both ways, as Thomas points out:

Thomas (32, M): *If she watches 'All Saints'* [soap series] *I use the tablet, but I sometimes watch 'Top Gear'* [program on cars] *and then she uses the tablet.*

As Samuel points out, family members remain 'accessible' to one another despite their individual screen consumption. In this respect 'affiliation' [21] or interpersonal communication is still possible due to the proxemic nature of family members in front of the television set. Hence, it is achieved by the physical togetherness of family members rather than being induced by television viewing. In this respect, they report that multiple technologies have minimal impact on the amount of offline social interaction. The small screens' physical characteristics as well as its 'interruptible' activities comfortably enable offline interaction.

Although the above does not mean television is no longer a family activity, as not all TV programs are watched privately, we need to acknowledge the changing dynamics of the consumption of multiple screens in the living room context. Family members are physically close to one another, nonetheless, content is consumed separately (e.g. one family member watches television and the other reads the newspaper on his or her tablet), making the living room a place where media technologies are consumed 'alone together'. Hence, the increased privatization and individualization of media use within the home not only reflects the physical dislocation of family members, but also the mental dislocation of family members within the same physical location. The living room remains the social hub of the family, but at the same time it is a highly technological environment. The presence of these multiple screens of is rarely questioned or even perceived as such, which points to the 'invisibility' and accordingly the significance of the multi-media environment [23], as it silently changes the social practices surrounding TV consumption. It is indeed these the social practices of TV viewing (i.e. viewer talk and thought on television consumption), through which 'the audience' is constituted [21].

5.3 Converging (social) spaces

The online social environment, to which we are chronically connected, allows conversation and reflection on TV whilst watching, which we refer to as the *remediation* of TV consumption. Overall, this practice remains rather modest. Six respondents report about the remediation of television consumption, both those that live alone as well as the ones with partner (and children). Respondents report making comments on television content (news, current affairs & reality TV) via Twitter or Facebook. The respondents that do *not* share these reflections with family members, exclude the private (domestic) sphere, by taking domestic television consumption *into* the media without taking it back into the living room. Individuals both inside and outside the family then become the main 'reproduction unit' for the social in the life world [24, p. 128]. The Internet, and social media in particular, allows individual family members to reconnect through fluidly constructed audiences, united by broadcasting television, disconnected afterwards, with the predominant common feature being the act of viewing.

In a second instance, the Internet allows us to be reflexive concerning our TV consumption. People report looking for translations (e.g. when watching BBC), geographical locations, holiday destinations or ratings of specific series (e.g. IMDb) that allow us to control, manage and enrich television content.

Boris (27, M): *When watching 'Terzake'* [current affairs]*, I sometimes visit Wikipedia for some background information. In case of Maggie De Block* [secretary of state on asylum & migration], *I wanted to know what her background is. I mean, is that really an authority sitting over there?*

As Boris' quote shows, the Internet as an information gateway, provides avenues to reflect upon television content, the media as an institute and the reality claims they make.

In addition, the remediation of television consumption allows us to control and manage our identity. Online platforms such as Twitter and Facebook are not only sites of opinion and though but also places for self-creation and manifestation. This becomes salient when respondents talk about the aspects of their private consumption they do *not* want to 'share' publically:

Helga (52, F): *But I certainly do not want people to know I watch 'Komen Eten'* [reality TV]*, that's something I'd never share… or maybe under a different name.*

The above quote also signifies how costly privacy is in contemporary media life (social interaction versus privacy), or as Papacharissi [3] calls it 'a luxury'. The technologies at hand *collectively* provide us with possibilities concerning individual agency (empowerment), nonetheless we all need to define our privacy *individually*. Four respondents report to be very well aware of the potential risks of the Internet, hence, carefully manage their online identity, or as cited below, self-censorship occurs.

Tom (30, M): *I work in the IT sector and I know how fast everything goes and how traceable information is. Everything you say can be used against you. I work as a consultant* […] *I need to be neutral. Not that sharing my opinion would be that big of a deal, but you never know whether it could be used against you.*

Paradoxically, the Internet provides us control but at the same time can render our actions uncontrollable. We see respondents with an IT background, mostly man, reflect upon contemporary media life (both its potential and pitfalls) remarkably more than other respondents. In this respect, the need for awareness, skills and knowledge on the new media ecology's potential and drawbacks is significant.

6. DISCUSSION

It should be noted that the above results reflect a gradual trend in audience transformation, as the majority of the people do not own multiple devices and still make rather 'conventional' use of television. Nonetheless, the findings are emblematic of the fluidity of contemporary society and the networked self.

Although television still plays an important rol in structuring time and space, we see laptops, tablets or smartphones are integrated in our everyday routines and television viewing behavior. Paradoxically, this multi-screen environment simultaneously induces both privatization (individual domestic consumption) as well as socialization processes (online social interaction). In addition, broadcasting television content reaches all people on an identical way, nonetheless, it is up to the digitally equiped (multi-screen) individual to determine how he or she will control and manage this mass media content. In this respect, the importance of literacy to be able to benefit from this participatory digital culture, is salient.

Future research, both on micro, meso and macro niveau should occupy with new conceptualization of anachrostic dichotomies as offline and online. Consumption, reception and meaning making of television content can no longer be limited to the viewers and their television screen. As we are confronted with more hybrid forms of communication today, which reshape media behavior, also our research on media consumption needs reshaping, which will prove challenging in this flexible and fluid environment.

7. ACKNOWLEDGMENTS

The research takes part in the IWT-project Smarter Media in Flanders (SMIF). The SMIF project (Smarter Media in Flanders) is a project co-funded by IWT (Agency for Innovation by Science and Technology), a Flemish government agency. The authors would especially like to thank IBBT – iLab.o and the VRT Studiedienst – Innovation Centre for sharing their data to recruit respondents.

8. REFERENCES

[1] Deuze, M., P. Blank, and L. Speers, *A life lived in media.* digital humanities quarterly, 2012. **6**(1).

[2] Livingstone, S., *The challenge of changing audiences: Or, what is the audience researcher to do in the age of the internet?* European Journal of Communication, 2004. **19**(75): p. 75-86.

[3] Papacharissi, Z., *A private sphere. Democracy in a digital age. Digital media and society series*2010, Campridge: Polity Press.

[4] Moores, S., *The doubling of space: electronic media, time-space arrangements and social relationships*, in *Mediaspace: Place, scale and culture in a media age*, N. Couldry and A. McCarthy, Editors. 2004, Routledge: London. p. p. 21-36.

[5] Couldry, N. and A. McCarthy, eds. *Mediaspace: Place, Scale and Culture in Media Age*. 2004, Routledge: London.

[6] Castells, M., *The rise of the network society*1996, Oxford: Blackwell.

[7] Silverstone, R., *The sociology of mediation and communication*, in *The sage handbook of sociology*, C. Calhoun, C. Rojek, and B. Turner, Editors. 2005, Sage Publications: London. p. 188-207.

[8] Warner, M., *Publics and counterpublics*2005, New York: Zone Books.

[9] boyd, d., *Social network sites as networked publics. Affordances, dynamics and implications*, in *A networked self. Identity, community, and culture on Social Network Sites*, Z. Papacharissi, Editor 2011, Routledge New York. p. 39-58.

[10] Beck, U., *World Risk Society*1999, Cambridge: Polity Press.

[11] Bauman, Z., *Liquid modernity*2000, Cambridge: Polity Press.

[12] Bauman, Z., *The art of life*2008, Cambridge: Polity Press.

[13] Bovill, M. and S. Livingstone, *Bedroom culture and privatization of media use*, in *Children and their changing media environment: a European comparative study* 2001, Lawrence Erlbaum Associates: Mahwah, New Jersay. p. 179-200.

[14] Alasuutari, P., *Rethinking the media audience: the new agenda*1999, London: Sage Publications.

[15] Meyrowitz, J., *Images of media: Hidden ferment - and harmony - on the field.* Journal of Communication, 1993. **43**(3): p. 55-66.

[16] Morley, D. and R. Silverstone, *Domestic communication: Technologies and meanings.* Media, Culture and Society, 1990. **12**(1): p. 31-55.

[17] Silverstone, R., *Television and everyday life*1994, Oxon: Routledge.

[18] Silverstone, R., E. Hirsch, and D. Morley, *Information and communication technologies and the moral economy of the household*, in *Consuming technologies. Media and information in domestic spaces*, R. Silverstone and E. Hirsch, Editors. 1992, Routledge: London. p. 115-131.

[19] Courtois, C., P. Verdegem, and L. De Marez, *The triple articulation of media technologies in audiovisual media consumption.* Television and New Media, in press.

[20] Glaser, B. and A. Strauss, *The discovery of grounded theory*1967, Chicago: Aldine.

[21] Lull, J., *Inside family viewing: Ethnographic research on television's audiences*1990, London: Routledge.

[22] Lindlof, T.R., J.S. Milton, and D. Wilkinson, *Accommodation of Video and Television in the American Family*, in *World Families watch television*, J. Lull, Editor 1988, Sage Publications: Newbury Park, CA. p. 158-192.

[23] Bolter, J.D. and R. Grusin, *Remediation: Understanding new media*2000, Cambridge: MIT Press.

[24] Beck, U., *Risk society. Towards a New Modernity*1992, London: Sage Publications.

Sharing the Viewing Experience through Second Screens

Mark Lochrie
School of Computing and Communications
Infolab21, Lancaster University
Lancaster, LA1 4WA, UK
+44 (0) 1524 510537
m.lochrie@lancaster.ac.uk

Paul Coulton
School of Computing and Communications
Infolab21, Lancaster University
Lancaster, LA1 4WA, UK
+44 (0) 1524 510393
p.coulton@lancaster.ac.uk

ABSTRACT

Despite the ever expanding forms of digital entertainment and the emergence of consumer recording facilities, allowing viewers to time shift their TV viewing habits, there are still certain TV shows and events that create an audience desire to be part of a mass shared experience. In the past direct inter-audience interaction of such events has been restricted to either a shared location at the time of broadcast or later discussions amongst friends and colleagues often described as 'water cooler moments'. With the advent of online social networks that facilitate status updates these moments can be instantly shared in real-time using mobile phone creating a second screen for interaction with TV. In this paper we investigate the emerging role of mobile phones as the facilitator of second screen for TV. This is achieved through the analysis of *tweets* for a highly popular UK TV show the X Factor and comparing tweets from this show with other shows from a different format. The results highlight the rich source of information that can be extracted in real-time and how audiences are creating their own parallel narrative of the show through Twitter. This interaction has enormous potential for broadcasters and producers both in terms of reinvigorating live TV viewing and creating new forms of audience interaction.

Categories and Subject Descriptors

H.5.1 Multimedia Information Systems

Keywords

Mobile, second screen, interactive, television, Twitter, shared experience, narrative, performance

1. INTRODUCTION

In the last decade we have seen the introduction and rise of Digital Video Recorders (DVRs) changing the way viewers time-shift and consume their TV entertainment [3]. The initial increase in DVR ownership resulted in a decrease in watching live TV as there wasn't a real-time need to consume at the time of broadcast. As in the past if you wanted to discuss what you have just watched, you had to wait till the next day at work, typically around the refreshments, thus the term "water cooler moments". . The increase and popularity of Saturday night prime time competition and reality shows depend on facilitating some form of viewer engagement [3] bringing about the requirement a return channel between program and viewer. In terms of the device to utilise for such a purpose the obvious choice is the ubiquitous mobile phone, as an increasing amount of these devices have low barriers to entry in accessing data services. This access is facilitated by cheaper data plans on mobile networks and widespread connectivity using home Wi-Fi networks enabling new methods to engage users through web or rich application based content. These so-called 'second screen devices' are now becoming the first choice for multitasking whilst watching TV. Yahoo and Razorfish surveys report that 88% were mobile multitasking whilst watching TV (15% of which were on their mobile devices the entire duration of the show and 38% using their mobile device for consuming content relating to the show).

EuroITV'12, July 4–6, 2012, Berlin, Germany.

At the same time we have seen the dramatic rise of social media services, such as Facebook, and Twitter that link into existing social networks, being used to curate forums for debate around a range of topics including TV shows. Twitter in particular with its ability to share topics through '*hashtags*' and '*re-tweets*' are now being used by audiences to discuss TV programmes in almost real-time. Twitter recently introduced new ways to discover and engage with current social buzz content on the mobile device through its "Twitter Discovery" service. Twitter has also made it even easier to re-tweet, mention and to include hashtags with prepopulated tweet windows. This further bridges the gap between the viewer and the TV show, by providing a means of users to browse stories and read tweets around the story.

It is important here to differentiate the use of Twitter by TV programs to enable audiences to participate within the program (effectively making it an alternative to text messages) and the general discussion amongst the audience within the Twitter stream itself which will be the main thrust of the research in this paper.. Broadcasters increasingly embracing Twitter as a means of extending their audience relationship and to drive viewership by integrating: on screen *hashtags* as closed captions, TV personalities live tweeting during aired show, vote by tweet (DM), tweets used as part of the TV show, specific show related standalone applications and follow me as closed captions (usually depicted as flashy banners that are located either along the footer or in the corners of the screen).

Studies from Twitter[3] suggests that when broadcasters combine the real-time elements of Twitter, there is a direct and immediate increase of viewer engagement from anywhere from two to ten times more the amount of *mentions*, *follows* and *hashtags* used whilst the show airs. This is highlighted by the 2010 Grammy Awards, which saw a 35% increase on viewing figures from 2009, one of the suggested reasons for this increase is the integration of social media in the 2010 event. Confirmed by the Mobile World

Congress 2011 in Barcelona, during Dick Costello's keynote which outlined the future of Twitter in the TV entertainment business, adding value to live TV shows and deterring viewers from DVRs, as 'real-time' viewing is preferred so they could *tweet*.

2. RELATED WORK

Whilst previous research has focused on how such devices can best facilitate the provision of shared content, enabling recommendations from friends, or sharing an interactive link with friends, few have addressed real-time interaction between the whole viewing audience. Direct inter-audience interaction amongst large groups could provide a greater sense of shared experience for the audience, as it allows for the free and frank interactions such as those seen on fan forums and discussion boards [3, 4, 5].

Although the use of Twitter within the American Presidential Debates was studied [7], it was not performed in real time on individual *tweets* but rather through later the time synchronised rank analysis of terms used both tweets and transcript of what each speaker had to say. We have also seen similar studies analysing the effects that in vision closed captioning has on the Twitter stream i.e. how people were described [6] on TV and what impact this had on ranked terms that appeared in the Twitter stream [6, 7]. While both these studies are based on spoken dialogue the study presented in this paper considers TV shows that present a more visual spectacle and examines whether this changes the influence of the discussion within Twitter.

Therefore to gain a better understanding of this activity we developed a system to record and analyse in real-time all the *tweets* associated with the highly popular UK TV show 'The X Factor' during the 2010 series.. It was subsequently used to collect tweets on the 2011 shows of The X Factor and The X Factor USA. The X Factor USA which was the first show to directly integrate Twitter into its show, by utilising Twitter's Direct Messaging (DM) service for registering contestant votes and incorporating hashtags on screen for the show, the contestants and judges and to promote live tweets from the judges.

3. BACKGROUND TO STUDY

This paper provides a detailed analysis of The X Factor in particular the 2010 and 2011 series and its recently aired American counterpart. The X Factor is a reality TV show in which aspiring pop singers compete against each other for a recording contract. The shows format differs from other singing contests by characterising each contestant into groups mentored by one of the judges; each judge is assigned a category and then aids the contestant with song selection and styling. The contestants are competing for the public vote in the form of phone calls and text messages. Generally the judges make the final decision between the bottom two contestants after the public vote. In its opening weekend X Factor attracted 11.1 million viewers representing a 48% share of the national TV viewing audience and rose to 19.1 million viewers for the final, which is 61.9% of the national audience, making it the highest rated television episode of 2010 in the UK.

To enable us to perform this study Twitter's Streaming API was used to capture all tweets that contain the #xfactor hashtag in its raw form. The tweet data is then parsed into different tables (tweet data, mentions, tags, urls and users), this allows deeper analysis of the tweet content, its source, the tags used, any urls included and who tweeted it. To analyse the use of mobile for a 'second screen' it was also important determine the origin of each *tweet*. Based on the tweet data collected volume information can thus be calculated on a minute-by-minute basis.

4. TWEET DATA RESULTS

4.1 The X Factor 2010 analysis

Due to the sheer volume of data generated during this research project we limit data presented in this paper to the build-up and coverage of the finals weeks and live show. In terms of structure we see a definite narrative in relation to volume of *tweets* related to the contestants that correspond directly to the running order of the show.

Having evaluated the narrative of the show through Twitter it is interesting to compare this with other measures such as the phone votes received for each contestant during the wholes series (Total votes cast: 15,448,019)[1]. What is very clear is that Matt had the most support from beginning of the show and interestingly the final phones for Matt and Rebecca were 44% and 38% which is a greater difference than the weekly *tweet* results although confirms greater support for Matt.

4.2 The X Factor UK and USA 2011

The X Factor franchise finished airing on America's FOX network, running from 21/09/2011 to 22/12/2011, that averaged around 12 million viewers per episode. It was also the eighth year The X Factor appeared on British television, although the show didn't manage to retain the average UK viewing figures from its previous year (14.13 million) it still achieved an average of 12.03 million (higher than its American counterpart).

Similar to the UK series, the viewer engagement surged once the live shows started and they introduced vote by tweet, the vote by tweet are kept private as they are sent via DM. A similar trend was seen in The X Factor UK 2010 where the youngest contestants were the most popular amongst social network discussions. The US shows young contestant Astro, Rachel Crow and Melanie Amaro attracted the highest peaks of discussion on social networks. During the first week of vote-by-tweet the youngest contestant Astro (15 years old, an urban rap singer) was the most popular amongst Twitter users (this could be down to the demographics that use social network and watch these types of TV shows thus having more in common and can relate more with the song choices by the contestant).

4.3 Tweeting Platforms

4.3.1 The X Factor UK 2010 tweet data

In order to analyse the platforms used to create *tweets* source, a classification system of *MOBILE*, *NON-MOBILE* and *MIXED* was adopted from previous research [3] as limitations of Twitters metadata which details the agent used rather than the exact platform [3].

Figures 1.A (final week snapshot 05/12/2010 – 13/12/2010) illustrates the role of mobile for *tweeting* during the actual live TV shows and there is clearly a big difference between the performance show (Figure 1.B 11/12/2010 19:00 – 21:00) and the results show (Figure 1.C 12/12/2010 19:30 – 21:30). It seems likely this is due to the difference in show formats as one is performance led and the other a time slot filled with pieces to

---

[1] Twitter Blog
http://blog.twitter.com/2011/05/watching-together-twitter-and-tv.html

make a show before the phone in results are announced. This could suggests that there is perhaps less combined viewing on the main TV screen and thus an increased need for the second screen although this would need to be confirmed with more targeted research. Another interesting distinction is that viewers are more likely to watch the performance show and *tweet* during the commercials, whereas on the results show, viewers were more likely to engage with discussion and express their support on who they want to win during the show.

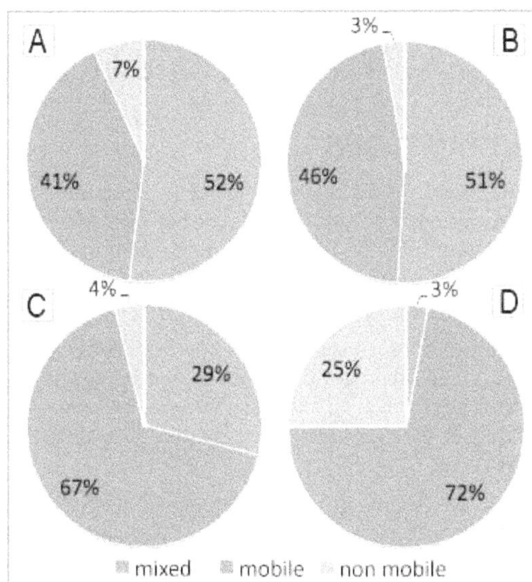

Figure 1. Tweet device data for mobile, non-mobile and mixed platforms

4.3.2 *The X Factor UK 2011 tweet data*

As previously mentioned, we captured and analysed a range of TV show formats, ones similar to The X Factor and some completely different in terms of show format. It was interesting to re-analyse the following year's (2011) mobile impact on the same show, as this time around social media has more of the spotlight, integrated more effectively into the shows programme. Unlike the US counterpart, the UK show hadn't moved over to vote-by-tweet, but by researching the impact it had in the US show, it would make a reasonable presumption similar features will appear in the UK show in the not too distant future. However the UK show definitely made more attempts at integrating the show on Twitter; by having tweet names and hashtags appear on screen as closed captions, a rise in judges and contestants joining and using Twitter, connecting with their audience not just through the TV screen impacting on audience voting influences.

Similarities were apparent when comparing the shows (both seasons of The X Factor 2010/2011). A snapshot of the final show was taken to identify which tweeting platforms were commonly used. Figure 1.D represents the percentages of platforms used to tweet during the live final results show (11/12/2011 19:00 – 22:00). The biggest difference is mixed platforms have decreased, this could be related to the fact Twitter has improved its tweet sourcing data. Also notably is the increase in mobile tweeting platforms. This increase can be associated with how the producers closely integrated Twitter more into its show with on screen captions, contestants and judges on Twitter themselves, the integration of Twitter into the OS (Operating System) in iOS devices and the increase could also be related to the growth in tablet sales last year [2].

5. SECOND SCREEN FOR TV: FUTURE

If we look more closely at the demographic for mobile Internet users that use their smartphone or tablet whilst watching TV (86%) 92% are 13-24 year olds. Since conducting this research a number of mobile applications have appeared attempting to bridge the gap between TV show and its audiences. For example, *X Factor* reintroduced their 'Tap to Clap' feature in the shows official application.

Pepsi recently sponsored The X Factor USA and developed "The Pepsi Sound Off" [//pepsisoundoff.com] adding a gamification element to boost viewer discussions. The platform allowed fans to chat about the show, contestants and judges, creating a narrative of the show amongst viewers, each viewer would earn points for every discussion they make and players are then ranked on leaderboards to compete with their friends.

Arguably the best example so far is 'Heineken Star Player' [//heineken.com/gb/ucl/star-player/] which encourages viewers to anticipate an outcome of in-game events e.g. where the ball will end up on a penalty. The viewers are awarded points if they successfully predict the outcome and are represented in leaderboards and badge system to reward their participation.

Recent announcements that Mark Burnett (producer of The Apprentice) and ACTV8 [//actv8.me] are developing ways of reinvigorating and innovating viewer engagement using the traditional smart phone and tablet. Mobile platform users will have the platform to interact, socialize, consume, share and participate in real time, all while watching their favourite TV shows. The application synchronizes a user's mobile device to any live or recorded video broadcast providing rich interactive content delivered straight to the users' mobile device relating to the programme they are watching. Not only does the application synchronised with the TV programme it also links into users' social networks, thus providing a platform for users to voice their opinions. ACTV8 have also realised the potential for broadcasters and advertisers by bringing the viewer directly into the TV programme providing programme enhancements, line extensions, quizzes, trivia, gaming and products seen in TV shows and also during commercials. Not only will this type of viewer engagement be rewarding for broadcaster and advertiser the application attempts to reward its users for their participation with content, including special offers and coupons from many of the leading TV advertisers.

Similarities can be seen with zeebox [//zeebox.com/] a combination of social networking, live programme information, TV remote control and real-time viewing figures application. The mobile and desktop application allows viewers to socialise immerse and interact whist watching TV. Both applications outlined show great potential for leading the way for utilising mobile devices as second screens.

6. CONCLUSION

In this research we presented a study into how the social networking service Twitter is increasingly being used as a channel for real-time inter-audience interaction for TV and implications for the role of mobile as the 'second screen'. To facilitate this

[2] The Guardian – UK tablet sales http://www.guardian.co.uk/technology/2011/dec/25/ipad-tablet-dominates-third-quarter-2011

research a system was created that allowed the storage and analysis in real-time of *tweets* on a minute-by-minute basis for the highly popular UK TV show the X Factor.

The data collected illustrates the high levels of interaction, already developing in the use of Twitter as an inter-audience forum, around TV and how the narrative of the show is played out through this interaction. Whilst the narrative is obviously driven in time by events in the show, many of the *tweets* also exhibit a great deal of humour, and irony which could be considered almost performative in nature, possibly demonstrating the notion of performing to the 'invisible audience' [1]. Compared with the previous study on the Presidential Debate which showed little correlation between what was in the tweets and what was said by the debaters in this format there was often a significant correlation between what was appearing on screen and the tweets suggesting a confirmation of the study involving closed captions that visual imagery has a more significant impact for this dual mode interaction.

In terms of using Twitter as a possible guide to predicting events it is clear that whist in this case the Twitter stream did replicate the phone voting in the majority of cases, anomalies do still occur suggesting that there are significant differences, in the demographic of the online community compared with those actually voting. Therefore producers and broadcaster wishing to use real-time Twitter analysis for audience interaction, should consider how best to weight the importance of such interaction in relation to their whole audience, as we have found out that different levels of audience interaction depends on the type of show in question.

As stated previously the *tweet* data captured provides an indication of who was being talked about and when, however it does not provide us a platform to analyse if this is positive or negative. To perform a deeper analysis the *tweet* language would have to be taken into consideration, this would be very problematic due to Twitter's status update constraints (140 characters) as in order to perform a deeper language analysis more words are required [8]. Twitter's API does provide a simple approach to this by using Emoticons (happy/sad faces depicted by punctuations i.e. ☺ ☹), however this method for detecting emotion in *tweets* is limited, as the majority of *tweets* captured in this study do not contain Emoticons to express emotion.

As this research did not consider the motivations of the individual involved it would seem appropriate that further research on this topic addressed these motivations more specifically.

Whilst this study included *tweets* from a variety of mediums the information obtained about the clients used to up-load the *tweets* indicates over 40% are from mobile, which is consistent with the figures reported by Twitter. Further, as reported widely in the media in February 2011 an IDC report showed that smartphone manufacturers shipped 100.9 million devices in the fourth quarter of 2010, while PC manufacturers shipped 92.1 million units worldwide in other words smartphones outsold PCs for the first time ever. As this trend is likely to continue then accessing internet services through mobile are likely to increase dramatically in the near future [2].

Overall this study highlights that mobile phones are already becoming the second screen for TV but not through broadcaster provision of personalised services, or service providers enabling them to act as a new form of remote, but rather by audiences themselves creating their own forums for inter-audience interaction. It is therefore important for broadcaster and producers to be able to better understand the nature of this interaction and how it may be utilised to create new forms of interactive TV and thus is a topic requiring further research.

7. ACKNOWLEDGMENTS

Many thanks to Lancaster University Network Services (LUNS) for providing a high bandwidth connection used to stream tweets from Twitter.

8. REFERENCES

1. Boyd, D., Why Youth (Heart) Social Network Sites: The Role of Networked Publics in Teenage Social Life, MacArthur Foundation Series on Digital Learning – Youth, Identity, and Digital Media Volume (ed. David Buckingham). Cambridge, MA: MIT Press, 2007.
2. Eronen, L. & Vuorimaa, P., User Interfaces for Digital Television: a Navigator Case Study. Proceedings of the working conference on advanced visual interfaces - AVI 2000. Palermo, Italy, 23-26 May 2000, pp.276–279. New York: ACM Press.
3. Lochrie, M. & Coulton, P., 'Tweeting with the telly on!: Mobile Phones as Second Screen for TV', Paper presented at Social Networks and Television: Toward Connected and Social Experiences at IEEE Consumer Communications & Networking Conference, Las Vegas, United States, 14/01/12 - 17/01/12, .
4. Park, J., Blythe, M., Monk, A., and Grayson, D. 2006. Sharable digital TV: relating ethnography to design through unuseless product suggestions. In extended abstracts on Human factors in computing systems, 119-1204. 2006.
5. Robertson, S. Wharton, C. Ashworth, C. and Franzke, M., 1996. Dual device user interface design: PDAs and interactive television. In Proceedings of the SIGCHI conference on Human factors in computing systems: common ground (CHI '96), Michael J. Tauber (Ed.). ACM, New York, NY, USA, 79-86.
6. Sayaka Akioka, Norikazu Kato, Yoichi Muraoka, and Hayato Yamana. 2010. Cross-media impact on twitter in japan. In Proceedings of the 2nd international workshop on Search and mining user-generated contents (SMUC '10). ACM, New York, NY, USA, 111-118.
7. Shamma, D.A. Kennedy, L. and Churchill, E.F., Tweet the debates: understanding community annotation of uncollected sources. In Proceedings of the first SIGMM workshop on Social media (WSM '09). ACM, New York, NY, USA, 3-10.
8. Simm, W.; Ferrario, M.-A.; Piao, S.; Whittle, J.; Rayson, P.; , "Classification of Short Text Comments by Sentiment and Actionability for VoiceYourView," Social Computing (SocialCom), 2010 IEEE Second International Conference on , vol., no., pp.552-557, 20-22 Aug. 2010.

Incremental Validation of Digital TV Applications in Nested Context Language

Rodrigo Costa Mesquita Santos[1], Jos Rios Cerqueira Neto[1], Carlos de Salles Soares Neto[1,2], Mario Meireles Teixeira[1,2]

Laboratory of Advanced Web Systems - LAWS

[1]Programa de Pós-Graduação em Ciência da Computação

[2]Departamento de Informática

Universidade Federal do Maranhão
Av. dos Portugueses, Campus do Bacanga
São Luís, MA – 65085-580 – Brasil

{rodrim.c,rios,csalles,mario}@laws.deinf.ufma.br

ABSTRACT

This paper presents an incremental validation process for multimedia documents describing interactive digital TV (iTV) applications. This work delves more specifically into documents defined in Nested Context Language (NCL), a declarative language standard adopted by ISDB-Tb and ITU-T for IPTV. The focus of incremental validation, the approach proposed in this work, relies on checking only the pieces of code that have been modified since the latest validation as well as those parts that have suffered any side effects, thus eliminating the need for a thorough checking of the document. The implications of performing this type of validation in a declarative language such as NCL are discussed and implementation details are given. Performance tests comparing the standard and incremental validation approaches have been carried out revealing a significant improvement concerning the latter.

Categories and Subject Descriptors

D.3.4 [**Programming Languages**]: Processors – *incremental compilers.*

General Terms

Performance, Experimentation, Languages, Verification.

Keywords

NCL, Nested Context Language, Incremental Validation, Source Code Validation, Ginga, Performance Tests.

1. INTRODUCTION

Digital interactive TV (iTV) applications are embedded in a context where the stages of application development and presentation have a clear physical separation: the development phase takes place in the broadcasters and content producers while the presentation occurs in TV viewers' households. In both phases there is a need to verify whether or not applications are in accordance with the current standard. In the development stage this need ensures that applications will be able to run on any device from any manufacturer that adheres to the standard rules. In the presentation stage, it will help saving computational resources by preventing the execution of applications that are corrupted or which are not in accordance with the standard.

Recent innovations in the multimedia arena, however, have made TV gradually migrate from its role of merely delivering content to viewers to take a central role in what is now known as home networking [30]. We have seen an increase in the development of applications known as Social TV, where viewers no longer just watch and interact with interactive applications, but also create and share content using the infrastructure of digital TV [16]. The advent of this class of applications gives rise to a form of authoring that pushes the boundaries of TV broadcasters and content producers to reach the house of the viewers, now happening within the set-top box.

The iTV application development is based on two main paradigms: imperative and declarative. Several digital TV middlewares adopt Java as imperative language. The authoring and validation of source code in Java is a well-studied problem with several known solutions. For the second approach, there are several examples of declarative languages for digital TV, among the most significant are XHTML [21], SMIL [7], BML [2] and NCL [27]. All of them are XML applications [32].

Declarative languages are more abstract than their imperative counterparts, since it is not necessary an algorithmic description of the application, but rather the description of the author's final intention. Thus, development approaches for these languages also tend to be more abstract, using a conceptual model suitable for application authoring. Authoring tools for declarative languages also tend to reflect this feature, often resorting to common visual abstractions.

When designing an authoring tool for iTV applications, in general there is a need to provide users with a development environment that integrates a set of features that will guide them throughout the application development process. Thus, an IDE (Integrated Development Environment) is an environment that can provide both graphical abstractions for users who feel more comfortable with visual authoring, and useful features for textual authoring. In [23] a study is done on visual and textual authoring, explaining the advantages and disadvantages of each of these two approaches.

Regardless of the approach chosen, the authoring of hypermedia documents is essentially incremental. Thus it is likely that, while you are editing the application, only a small number of changes have been made between two consecutive code verifications. There are textual authoring tools, for example, that validate the code whenever the user stops typing, although it is possible that the difference between a check and another is just a character. In visual authoring, on the other hand, validation may be performed after the addition, editing or removal of a given visual component. It is noticeable that in both situations it is not strictly necessary to reconstruct the entire data structure representing that instance of code and validate it completely. This creates the opportunity to manage such a structure in memory and perform the validation only in the modified and affected parts of the document. This type of validation that checks only the pieces of code changed and those affected by the changes is commonly referred in the literature as **incremental validation** [20].

Intuitively we can see the influence of incremental validation in the conventional process of authoring, but this is not the only situation where such validation can offer performance gains. The fact that set-top boxes are environments with limited computing resources raises the need for validation techniques that perform minimal possible checking to ensure a significant performance gain in such a limited hardware. On the other hand, systems such as ISDB-Tb [28] allow broadcasters to send editing commands to applications while they are being displayed, allowing what is known as live editing of content. Before applying such edits it is necessary to first validate them in order to make sure that the editing commands will result in consistent, accurate and coherent documents. From the above discussion, we can notice the need for incremental validation mechanisms is present in various circumstances. The main contribution of this work is to define and implement a more efficient validation mechanism for NCL documents, which does not mandate the processing of the whole document but rather only the parts affected by certain changes made by the programmer.

NCL (Nested Context Language) is a declarative hypermedia language focused on the definition of synchronizing relationships between media objects. It is the standard language of ISDB-Tb for development of interactive applications and is also an international ITU-T recommendation for IPTV [17]. This work focuses on the definition of an incremental validation process for NCL documents and performs a study to identify the quantitative gain of incremental validation when compared to standard validation. The validation process described here is also generic, i.e., it can be tailored to different authoring environments, whether visual or textual, and is based on a componentized architecture, allowing such components to be exchanged for others with the same interface while keeping the same functionality.

Seeking to define and illustrate the proposed incremental validation process in NCL, this article is divided as follows. In Section 2, some related work is described. In Section 3, an overview of NCL is presented together with a metalanguage designed to tackle the difficulties of validating instances of code in NCL. Section 4 discusses the proposed incremental validation process. Section 5 presents and analyzes the results of quantitative tests comparing incremental validation and standard validation. Finally, Section 6 presents our conclusions and future work.

2. RELATED WORK

Several work found in the literature discuss the validation of XML-based languages. Among these, the most widespread techniques are based on the use of XML Schema [31] or DTD [13]. The fact that XML has become the de facto standard for storage and exchange of information in modern computer systems has increased the need for more efficient validation techniques of such documents. In [29] is proposed a validation approach based on an incremental data model called SXESP (Simplified XML Element Sequence Pattern) that checks whether a given XML document conforms to the rules expressed in XML Schema. The SXESP represents the XML tree through a sequence of elements using some operators to connect elements that have structural relations. In [4] is proposed an algorithm specialized in data storage applications that incrementally checks the structure of XML documents using either the DTD or XML Schema. Both approaches have in common the fact that they only carry out structural checks on the documents.

Thao and Munson [10] use the incremental idea to perform a three-way merge on XML documents. Each derived document is represented only by a delta (the changes between the original document and the derived one) and the merging algorithm creates a result document based on the original document and the deltas. This work carries out a performance evaluation of the proposed algorithm against commercial tools, proving the former to be faster, with lower memory utilization and more precise.

Although an XML language, the validation of NCL documents using the XML Schema or DTD is not enough, because this language has a number of characteristics that are not considered when using these metalanguages. Some of these special features regarding NCL are described in Section 3.2. Validating NCL using either of these techniques amounts to only validating the document structure, neglecting important contextual and referential aspects that provide semantics to applications.

In [9] is described a work that uses incremental validation to consistency checking for pervasive context. In this work, the approach employed is strongly coupled with the framework called xlinkit (a well recognized tool for consistency checking of distributed XML documents). One of the goals of this work is to be as much as possible independent of platform and technology in order to be easily tailored to different authoring and presentation environments.

In the context of authoring, the development of innovative and effective techniques to shorten and facilitate application development is a recurring problem in Computing. Such development drives many research projects that seek to improve the productivity of software creation. In recent years, the popularity of iTV applications has spurred several visual abstractions in hypermedia authoring tools specialized in this kind of application. Some examples of these abstractions are hypermedia temporal graph [11], timelines [18], WYSIWYG (What You See Is What You Get) [1].

SMIL Builder [5] is a visual authoring environment for SMIL that employs incremental validation techniques. As NCL, SMIL is a language focused on the definition of spatio-temporal synchronization relationships of media objects. SMIL Builder has a core that manages the SMIL document instance represented according to the H-SMIL-Net [6] data structure (a temporal extension of Petri nets [22]) that is updated as users interact with the graphical interface. For a change to take effect in the model, a validation is performed to check whether or not such a change has a temporal inconsistency. If the change is free of inconsistencies, it will be effected in the model, otherwise it will be rejected by the core. SMIL Builder validation tends to be facilitated given the graphic nature of the tool, since the interface can prevent the author from making some inconsistent operations, thus restraining the validation process to checking temporal inconsistencies.

In the context of textual authoring, a straightforward technique to validate XML documents is to convert them in a DOM tree [12] and iterate element-by-element performing the validation. A validation tool that employs this technique is the NCL Validator [19]. This library has been integrated in two of the most widely used NCL authoring tools: NCL Eclipse [3] and early versions of Composer [15]. In this tool, validation is divided into three steps: i) lexical validation, ii) structural validation, and iii) validation of contexts and references. Step i) validates aspects common to all XML-based languages. In step ii) the structure of the NCL document is checked (up to this point of validation, the use of XML Schema would be sufficient), and step iii) validates specific aspects of NCL.

NCL Validator does not manage the DOM tree dynamically concerning the document being edited. Therefore, the NCL document has to be continuously converted in this data structure. This implies in an additional computational cost during the validation process, given the DOM tree creation, which may compromise its utilization in environments with scarce computational resources. Considering that more elaborate iTV applications generate very large XML documents, it may become impractical to generate a DOM tree after each modification and then perform a complete validation. Thus, one downside of NCL Validator is its lack of support for incremental validation.

3. NCL VALIDATION

This section gives a brief description of NCL language and its conceptual data model NCM and highlights the special features that make it impractical to be validated using traditional techniques of XML validation.

3.1 NCL

NCL is a hypermedia declarative language based on XML standards. NCL adopts NCM (Nested Context Model) [26] as its conceptual data model. Although NCM defines relationships between media objects based on causal and constraint sentences, the NCL version adopted as ISDB-Tb and ITU-T standard for iTV applications development only makes use of causal sentences.

NCM is mainly based on four concepts, namely node, anchor, connector and link. Nodes can be divided into composite nodes and media nodes. Composite nodes are containers of other nodes and their relationships. In order to best organize the document, composite nodes encapsulate its internal structure, defining the perspective concept. Nodes can have relationships only with nodes present in the same perspective. Media nodes are entities that represent media files that comprise applications. In NCL we notice a clear distinction between the document that defines the application semantics and the media objects contents. This differs from HTML where the textual content is embedded within the document that defines hyperlinks. NCL anchors specify media object parts (content anchors, e.g. spatial or temporal anchors) or its presentation characteristics (property anchors, e.g. layout positioning in display devices). Each media object has at least an anchor declared by default representing the whole content and it is called lambda anchor.

Connectors are entities that define the relation to be played by nodes anchors. There is a clear distinction between relation and relationships in NCL. Thus, synchronism relations are present as a first order entity, independent from their relationships. Relations define causal sentences among roles. Casual sentences are expressed as a pair of conditions and actions roles so that a condition must be satisfied in order to trigger a related action. In order to define a relationship, links reuse the connector specification and relate the connector roles to nodes anchors. All nodes related through a link and the link itself must belong to the same perspective.

NCL document structure is divided into two main parts, header (**<head>** element) and body (**<body>** element). Some document bases are specified in the header and they can be reused in the same or distinct documents. Region bases (**<regionBase>**) define layout regions in display devices where media objects are shown (**<region>**). Descriptor bases (**<descriptorBase>**) define descriptors (**<descriptor>**) that specify the initial presentation characteristics of each media object. Rule bases (**<ruleBase>**) define rules (**<rule>**) that can be used in order to support content adaptation. Transition bases (**<transitionBase>**) can be used to apply start and end transitions effects in media objects presentation (these effects have been inherited from SMIL Transition Effects Module [24]). Connector bases (**<connectorBase>**) specify the causal connectors (**<causalConnector>**). Presentation structure and semantics are defined in document body mainly by composition of nodes and links present in the application specification.

3.2 NCL Particularities

NCL documents validation can be categorized in two types of approaches referred to as structural and referential. Structural validation deals with document structure. Some examples of this type of validation are attribute checking, elements cardinality and elements hierarchy. This kind of validation is accomplished using traditional XML validation techniques based on XML Schema. Nevertheless, referential validation cannot be performed in the same way, because NCL has several issues that cannot be described solely by XML Schema. The motivation to this subsection is to discuss some of those issues and propose a declarative metalanguage capable of expressing most of those NCL particular issues.

NCL has a scope based on perspectives. Thus, composite nodes define the scope in which relationships can be considered valid in the document. Two nodes can only be related by a link if both belong to the same composition. Composite nodes can participate in relationships found both in the perspective where they belong, and in the one they define.

NCL language has a conceptual model designed to provide a high level of reuse among its elements [25]. As an example, for layout reuse it is important that TV broadcasters keep a visual identity in all iTV applications. Thus, an NCL document imports a previously defined region base and its descriptors, through the **region** attribute. To assert the validity of such reference, it is not enough to simply analyze whether the **region** attribute of a **<descriptor>** element points to an **xsd:id** of some entity, but rather it is necessary to ensure that this entity is indeed a **<region>**. Another case of reuse occurs with the **refer** attribute, in which an element can reference another one of the same type, inheriting all its properties and anchors. Thus, if a B element makes a reference using the **refer** attribute to an A element, B inherits all properties of A. This reference type does not follow the perspective rule previously explained.

The above list of NCL validation issues does not intend to be exhaustive. The objective was rather to illustrate that conventional XML validation mechanisms are not enough to perform NCL validation in all its aspects. From this discussion, this paper employs a declarative metalanguage that we proposed in a previous work [8], as part of the NCL incremental validation method. This metalanguage has four basic primitives and corresponding arguments as described in Listing 1.

```
ELEMENT    (name, parent, cardinality,
            define_scope)

ATTRIBUTE  (element_name, name,
             is_required, datatype_id)

DATATYPE   (datatype_id, regex)

REFERENCE  (element_name, attr_name,
            ref_element_name,
            ref_attr_name, perspective)
```

Listing 1. Metalanguage proposed.

The ELEMENT primitive describes NCL elements with four arguments. The first argument defines the element name. The second specifies its parent element. The third argument is the element cardinality. The fourth argument is used to validate references according to element perspective. In NCL the element cardinality is defined by its parent element. The same element can be child of different elements, as happens to **<media>** element that can be child of **<body>**, **<context>** or **<switch>** elements. Thus, it is necessary to specify an ELEMENT primitive entry for each different pair of parent and child elements.

The ATTRIBUTE primitive specifies the attributes of all NCL elements. For each element attribute it is necessary a new ATTRIBUTE entry even if different elements have the same attribute. This is the case with the **id** attribute, shared by the majority of elements but that must have an entry for each element where it appears. The first argument of the ATTRIBUTE primitive is the attribute name. The second argument is the element name which this attribute belongs to. The third argument is a boolean value specifying if this attribute is mandatory. At last, the fourth attribute must be the identifier of one data type specified by the DATATYPE primitive.

The DATATYPE primitive defines data types for NCL attributes. This primitive has two arguments. The former is the identifier of the data type and the latter is a regular expression that can validate its value. In order to create a new data type (like boolean), we can create a DATATYPE entry with the identifier of this new data type (BOOLEAN) and a regular expression defining valid values for this data type (^(true|false)$).

Last but not least, there is the REFERENCE primitive. This primitive can express references that can be done among elements. In NCL, an element A referring to an element B has an attribute whose value is the B identifier. Some attributes identifying elements are **id**, **alias** and **name**. The REFERENCE primitive arguments are the element name that refers to another element, the attribute name whose value refers to an identifier of another element, the element name that is being referenced and the scope where the referred element must be found.

The method proposed in Section 4 for incremental validation is fully supported by the definition of NCL language in terms of the above metalanguage. The validator source code and NCL structure are loosely coupled. This happens because NCL is described in a proper metalanguage file that enables the adaptation of the validator to different versions of the language without editing and recompiling the validator source code. All that is needed is to choose a new metalanguage specification.

4. INCREMENTAL VALIDATION OF NCL DOCUMENTS

This section discusses the incremental validation of NCL documents and describes the approach proposed by this paper.

4.1 Incremental Validation

Incremental validation consists in validating only the parts of the document that need to be validated. It avoids the unnecessary checking of previously validated parts that have not been affected by recent modifications. We define incremental validation, based on the definition found in [29], as follows:

Definition 1 (incremental validation). Being μ the NCM data model and $S(\mu)$ the set of all NCL documents whose structure follows the rules and restrictions defined by μ, if α is a representation of an NCL document, a sequence of modifications U transforms α into $U(\alpha)$. Thus, considering $\alpha \in S(\mu)$, incremental validation consists in analyzing U and extracting from $U(\alpha)$ the subset of elements that needs to be validated so as to verify whether $U(\alpha) \in S(\mu)$.

According to Definition 1, the focus of incremental validation should be on checking small pieces of code rather than the whole document. Thus an important task to allow incremental validation is being able to infer, based on the set of document modifications, which segments of the document need to be further validated. In other words, we need to identify the parts of the document that have been modified since the latest validation and also those parts to be possibly affected by those modifications, thus eliminating the need for a complete rebuild of the NCL document representation and then perform a full validation on it, as is the case with the standard validation method.

Having identified the set of elements to be validated, it is necessary to decide which type of validation to apply in each case. Depending on the nature of the element and on the modification to be performed, it is quite possible that some elements may only need a structural or referential validation, thus discarding a thorough time-consuming document checking.

To better organize the process of identifying the type of validation suitable for each element, we divided NCL elements into four distinct groups: A) independent elements; B) referencing elements; C) referenced elements; and D) referencing and referenced elements. Figure 1 illustrates these categories.

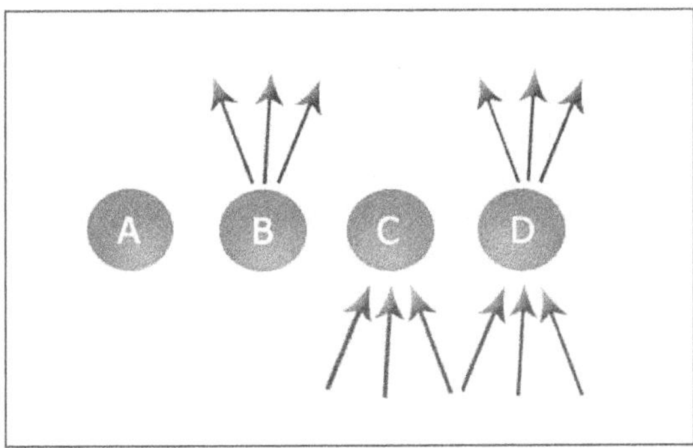

Figure 1. Classification of NCL elements according to their references to/from other elements.

Group A elements are those that do not reference any other element and are not referenced by any other one, the precise reason why they are named independent. When we need to validate a modification in an element of this kind, all that is required is the structural checking of the element itself and of the subtree it spawns. It is not necessary to perform a referential validation, as the example in Listing 2 shows: if an editing changes the value of attribute **comparator** from **"eq"** to **"lt"**, in element **<assessmentStatement>**, the validation merely needs to check if the new value of the attribute belongs to the set of possible values and then validate the structure of the subtree it generates, which in this case comprises only the elements **<attributeAssessment>** and **<valueAssessment>** as well as their corresponding attributes.

```
<causalConnector id="connector1">
   <connectorParam name="valueTest"/>
            . . .
      <assessmentStatement comparator="eq">
         <attributeAssessment role="test"
                eventType="attribution" />
         <valueAssessment
                         value="$valueTest"/>
      </assessmentStatement>
            . . .
</causalConnector>
```

Listing 2. Example validation of group A elements.

On the other hand, when elements of group B are modified, the validation is a bit more complicated. Since these elements make reference to other elements, it is necessary to perform a referential validation besides the structural validation, including both the element and its associated subtrees. Consider the case of the element **<link>** when referencing elements of the type **<causalConnector>**. According to Section 3, there should be as many **<bind>** elements as there are roles defined by the referenced connector. Thus if an editing in the document creates a link to a different connector, it is vital to verify whether the new connector does exist and the **<bind>** elements are consistent with the roles defined in its scope. Listing 3 presents an excerpt of code where validation becomes mandatory since attribute **xconnector** is now referencing a new connector named **"conn2"** instead of connector **"conn1"**.

```
<ncl>
  . . .
   <connectorBase>
      <causalConnector id="conn1">
         <simpleCondition role="onBegin"/>
         <simpleAction role="start"/>
      </causalConnector>
      <causalConnector id="conn2">
         <simpleCondition role="onEnd"/>
         <simpleAction role="stop"/>
      </causalConnector>
  . . .
<body>
  . . .
  <link xconnector="conn2">
      <bind role="onBegin" . . . />
      <bind role="start" . . . />
  </link>
  . . .
</ncl>
```

Listing 3. Example validation of group B elements.

We now discuss the validation of elements belonging to group C, i.e. elements referenced by others. When a member of this group is modified, the referencing elements also need to be checked. Two different types of validation are required in this case: the subtree generated by the modified element needs to be checked structurally, and the elements affected by the changes need to be checked referentially. Consider an element **<region>** being referenced by an element **<descriptor>**. If the element **<region>** **id** attribute with value **"rg1"** is modified, it is necessary to check if the new value of the **id** attribute is valid and it is also necessary to check whether the reference made by the **<descriptor>** element is still valid for this modification. Listing 4 shows the code snippet where the validation described applies.

```
<ncl>
  <head>
      . . .
     <regionBase>
        <region id="rg1" top="5%" />
        <region id="rg2" top="10%"
                              left="30%" />
     </regionBase>
     <descriptorBase>
        <descritor id="d1" region="rg1" />
     </descriptorBase>
  </head>
        . . .
</ncl>
```

Listing 4. Example validation of group C elements.

Finally, in group D are the elements that refer to other elements and are also referenced by other ones. The subtree generated from the modified element should be checked structurally and referentially, and the referencing elements should have their references checked also. Listing 5 shows an example of this type, in which a **<media>** element refers to a **<descriptor>** and is referred by an element **<bind>**. If a change occurs in **<media>**, it is necessary to check if the values of its attributes are correct and that the reference to the element **<descriptor>** and the reference from the element **<bind>** remain valid.

```
<ncl>
  <head>
     <descriptorBase>
        <descritor id="d1"  . . . />
     </descriptorBase>
  </head>
  <body>
        <media id="media1" src="sample.mp3"
                          descriptor="d1"/>

        <link xconnector="conn1">
           <bind component="media1" .../>
             . . .
        </link>
        . . .
  </body>
</ncl>
```

Listing 5. Example validation of group D elements.

From the discussion above, we conclude that the issue here is whether or not an element refers to other elements. In this case, whenever the referred element is edited, all the others that make reference to it must go through a reference validation as well. Structural validation, in its turn, is related to the fact that the element was directly modified and then needs to have its structure checked again.

4.2 Implementation

An incremental validation process, based on the method proposed in subsection 4.1 has been developed and integrated in the latest version of the Composer IDE in the form of a validation plugin.

Composer is an NCL authoring tool that has a microkernel extensible by plugins. The function of the microkernel is to maintain a representation of the NCL document being edited and manage all changes made to the code by sending messages to all plugins whenever some element of the model changes. Composer has an incremental microkernel, i.e., the changes that occur in the document are incrementally added to the data model. Thus, the incremental validation proposed in this work is consistent with the architecture of this IDE.

The process has been developed following a component-based architecture, facilitating the exchange of any one component with another implementation with the same API. In order to make the validator independent from the data model used by the IDE, the design pattern known as Adapter [14] was adopted. The validator has four main components: Model, Validation, Messages, and Interpreter. Figure 2 shows how these components interact.

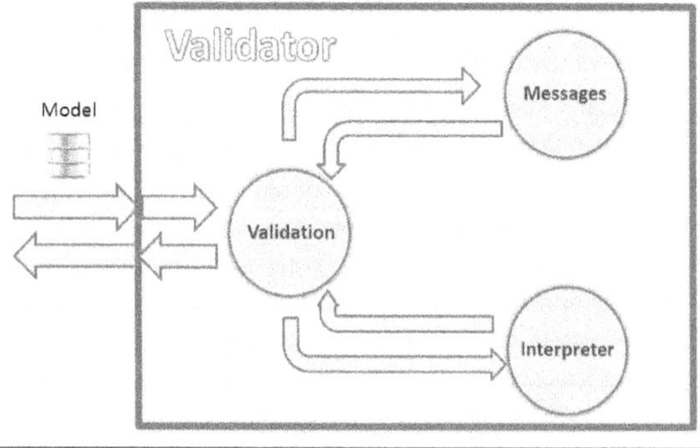

Figure 2. Proposed architecture.

The Interpreter component is responsible for keeping the structure and rules of the NCL language in order to support validation, according to what is defined by the metalanguage specification. The decision to componentize this feature intended to facilitate the adaptation of the validation process for different NCL versions or profiles. Consequently, only this module should be modified if we need to adapt the process to other versions of NCL. The Messages module instantiates a message for each type of error encountered and also manages the language in which error messages are displayed (currently Portuguese, English and Spanish).

The main component of the architecture is the Validation. It is responsible for receiving an instance of an NCL document and validating only those elements that have changed and those affected by these changes, according to the systematization presented in subsection 4.1. In order to check the structural and referential rules of NCL, the Validation can call the Interpreter and, whenever a contextual or referential error is found, the former instantiates a new message by calling the Messages component. At the end of the process a list of error messages is returned to the adapter that either delivers them to the IDE or prints the errors on the screen.

Finally, the Model component is the data structure that stores the representation of the NCL document being validated. This model has an API for inserting, editing and removing elements. In incremental validation, the Model plays an essential role, since this component is responsible for identifying the elements that were modified and not yet validated and also identify which elements are affected by these changes.

5. INCREMENTAL vs. STANDARD VALIDATION

This section presents a comparison between the methods of standard and incremental validation in terms of speed and responsiveness when applied to an NCL document according to the implementation described in earlier sections.

5.1 Experimental Design

As a scenario, it is considered an NCL document of a given size (namely, number of elements) which is being modified by a user/programmer/application and that is validated in the background by means of a standard or incremental method. The time spent to validate the document was chosen as response variable, i.e., the time necessary to examine the document (in whole or in part) and return control back to the programmer. As factors that may influence the outcome of the experiment, there are the number of elements in the document, the number of modifications between each validation (the step), and the type of validation process. For each factor two levels are defined resulting in a 2^3 Experimental Design as shown in Table 1. Regarding the number of elements, the choice of 100 and 1000 as levels for this factor (small and large applications, respectively) was influenced by a previous study performed in applications shared in Club NCL[1].

A program was developed that generates an NCL document of a certain size, introduces modifications in that document and submits it to validation. It then measures the time necessary to validate the modified document. Each experiment was repeated

[1] Club NCL is a public repository that shares iTV applications developed using NCL. (http://club.ncl.org.br/)

30 times and the means and 95% confidence intervals were calculated.

Table 1. A 2^3 experimental design

Factors	-1	1
# of elements (A)	100	1000
Step size (B)	5	15
Type of validation (C)	Incremental	Standard

The experiments were carried out in a desktop computer based on an Intel i5 processor with 4 GB of main memory running 32-bit Ubuntu 11.10.

5.2 Results

Figure 3 shows the result of a document of 100 elements validated by means of a standard or incremental method. The standard validation has to inspect the whole document and thus has an average time of 35 ms. For the incremental method, the step between validations is incremented by a factor of 5 elements each time and we observe the response time is dependent on the size of the step. This time can be even 7 times smaller than the time of the standard validation method, for a step of 5 elements, and grows as the interval between validations stretches. Smaller steps yield more responsiveness, as control is given back promptly to the IDE, however they can cause a certain performance penalty because of the frequent calls to the validation routine.

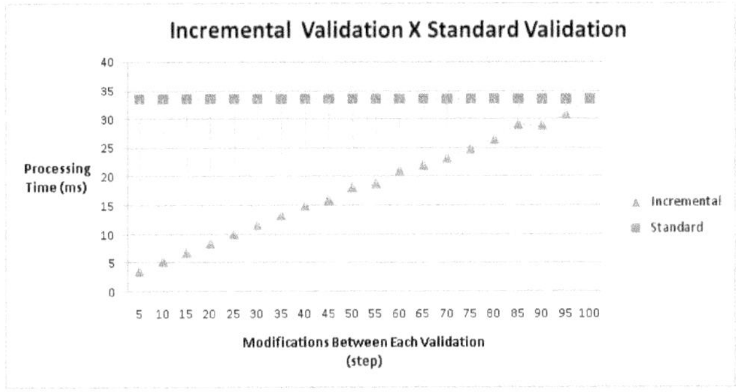

Figure 3. Comparison between the time necessary to validate the whole document and the time to validate the document in smaller parts (incrementally).

Table 2 summarizes the influence of each factor in the response variable. We notice that the type of validation method (A) and the number of elements in the document (C) were the two most influential factors alone, accounting respectively for 44.85% and 27.47% of the response variable. The combination of factors A and C also had an influence of 27.62%. The step size had a very small influence on the validation time.

5.3 Discussion

The experiments performed have shown that the incremental validation method is more advantageous than its standard counterpart. It is more intuitive, considering the nature of the declarative authoring process, consumes less processing time as it validates only the portion of the document that has been modified, and, although it could potentially impose a certain performance penalty when using small incremental validation steps, it has revealed in practice a negligible overhead. Overall the incremental validation is faster and more flexible than the standard method as our tests have demonstrated.

Although the 35 ms difference in the response time between the incremental and standard validation methods, for a step of 5 elements, may seem irrelevant for practical purposes, one should consider that the experiments were performed in a modern and powerful PC architecture, which is not the case in digital TV platforms. In a typical scenario, one would have a set-top box or smartphone with much more limited memory and computing power and thus those performance figures would be significantly different. Experimenting with such environments, however, is beyond the scope of this paper, as the intention here was to demonstrate the viability and usefulness of the proposed incremental method.

Table 2. Influence of different factors on document validation time.

Parameter	Estimated Average	Variation
q0	45.856	-
qA	31.7553	27.48%
qB	1.4081	0.005%
qC	40.5681	44.85%
qAB	-0.0461	0.00%
qAC	31.8378	27.62%
qABC	0.0618	0.00%

6. CONCLUSION

In the interactive digital TV (iTV) arena, application development and presentation usually occur in distinct places. The development phase is carried out at the broadcasters' and/or producers' premises whereas presentation occurs at viewers' households. In either case, there is a clear need to validate application code in order to guarantee it is in accordance with current standards. This not only allows applications to run on any manufacturers' equipment (as long as it adheres to the standard) but it can potentially avoid wasting scarce computational resources on set-top boxes trying to execute erroneous applications. Nowadays, with the advent of Social TV and similar applications, which gives the viewer the possibility to create and share his/her own content, the need for on-the-fly validation becomes more evident.

This work describes an incremental validation process for NCL, a declarative hypermedia language used for iTV applications development in Brazil, Argentina, Japan and several other countries. NCL is based in XML and is currently an ISDB-Tb standard and also an international ITU-T recommendation for IPTV.

The peculiarities of NCL have been discussed in the paper, especially those that make it particularly difficult or impractical to be validated by XML Schema or DTD, standards commonly used with other XML-based languages employed in iTV, such as SMIL, XHTML and BML. Given the incremental, almost interactive approach by which hypermedia documents are created, we believe that incremental validation, which is carried out gradually, as the user types a new line of code or adds a visual component in an IDE is more natural and efficient, besides consuming less computational resources.

The incremental validation process proposed and implemented in this paper is based on a categorization of NCL language elements that highlights which parts of code need to be validated further after the developer makes an editing on the document. Our proposal is organized into two distinct stages: firstly, it analyzes the local effects of a code modification and looks for any side effects that it may have triggered. Secondly, it selects the type of validation to be employed in order to guarantee document consistency. The determination of side effects is especially important, since NCL has elements, such as links and connectors, that semantically and syntactically bind elements distributed throughout the NCL document and which may not be so obviously correlated. This feature is accomplished through a metalanguage defined in our previous work, which provides a formal annotation of these relationships between elements and media objects in NCL documents. In order to adapt the incremental validation to other hypermedia languages, it should suffice to describe these languages in terms of the metalanguage proposed, since the whole validation process is supported by this description. The incremental method implemented here also allows the fine tuning of the interval between subsequent validations, given one may wish a more prompt system response (by validating each change) or a more conservative and efficient behavior (by validating a group of changes).

In order to verify the performance of the proposed method, comparative tests confronting standard and incremental validation have been carried out. It was chosen as factors the number of elements in the document, the interval between subsequent validations and the type of the validation method itself (incremental or standard) resulting in a 2^3 experimental design. The means, collected with a 95% confidence interval revealed that incremental validation, as proposed and implemented in this paper, can perform NCL document validation even seven times faster than the standard method, with negligible performance penalty due to the use of validation steps. It was also found that the type of validation and the number of elements in the document were the most prominent factors in the experiment, accounting for more than two thirds of the validation time.

As future work, it is our intention to perform comparative tests between the plug-in developed and tools already in use, such as in [19], considering factors as number of elements, service time, and amount of memory used. We also intend to experiment with hardware architectures such as set-top boxes and smartphones in order to assess how the proposed method would behave in a real-world scenario.

7. ACKNOWLEDGMENT

We would like to thank Brazilian foundation CAPES and Maranhão state foundation FAPEMA for the financial support to the development of this research.

8. REFERENCES

[1] Adobe Dreamweaver CS4 Professional. http://www.adobe.com/br/products/dreamweaver/

[2] ARIB B-24 XML-Based Multimedia Coding Scheme, ARIB Standard B-24 Data Coding and Transmission Specifications for Digital Broadcasting, version 4.0, February 2004.

[3] Azevedo, R. G. A., Soares Neto, C. S., Teixeira, M. M., Santos, R. C. M., and Gomes, T. A. 2011. Textual authoring of interactive digital TV applications. In *Proceddings of the 9th international interactive conference on Interactive television* (EuroITV '11, Lisbon, Portugal, July 1). DOI=http://doi.acm.org/10.1145/2000119.2000169

[4] Barbosa, D., Leighton, G., and Smith, A. Efficient Incremental Validation of XML Documents After Composite Updates. In *Proceedings of XSym*. 2006, 107-121.

[5] Bouyakoub, S. and Belkhir, A. 2011. *SMIL Builder: an incremental authoring tool for SMIL documents*. ACM Trans. Multimedia Comput. Commum. Appl. 7, 1, Article 2 (January 2011), 30 pages.

[6] Bouyakoub,S. and Belkhir, A. 2008. *H-SMIL-Net: A hierarchical Petri net model for SMIL documents*. In Proceedings of the 10th Conference on Computer Modeling and Simulation (UKSIM'08).

[7] Bulterman D. and et al. 2008. Synchronized Multimedia Integration Language (SMIL 3.0). http://www.w3c.org/TR/SMIL3/.

[8] Cerqueira Neto, J. R., Santos, R. C. M., Soares Neto, C. S., and Teixeira, M. A. M. 2011. Método de Validação Estrutural e Contextual de Documentos NCL. In *Proceedings of the 17th Brazilian Symposium on Multimedia Systems* (WebMedia'11, Florianópolis, Brazil, October 3 – 6, 2011).

[9] Chang Xu, S. C. Cheung, and W. K. Chan. 2006. Incremental consistency checking for pervasive context. In *Proceedings of the 28th international conference on Software engineering* (ICSE '06). ACM, New York, NY, USA, 292-301. DOI=10.1145/1134285.1134327 http://doi.acm.org/10.1145/1134285.1134327.

[10] Cheng Thao and Ethan V. Munson. 2010. Using versioned tree data structure, change detection and node identity for three-way XML merging. In *Proceedings of the 10th ACM symposium on Document engineering* (DocEng '10). ACM, New York, NY, USA, 77-86. DOI=10.1145/1860559.1860578 http://doi.acm.org/10.1145/1860559.1860578.

[11] Costa R.M.R, Moreno M.F., Soares L.F.G. 2008. Intermedia Synchronization Management in DTV Systems. In *Proceedings of ACM Symposium on Document Engineering* (Sao Paulo, Brazil, 2008). DocEng 2008, pp. 289-297. ISBN: 978-1-60558-081-4.

[12] Document Object Model (DOM) Level 1 Specification Version 1.0. http://www.w3.org/TR/1998/REC-DOM-Level-1-19981001/, 1998. W3C Recommendation.

[13] DTD. http://www.w3schools.com/DTD/

[14] Gamma, E. 1995. *Design Patterns: Elements of Reusable Object-Oriented Software*. Addison-Wesley.

[15] Guimarães, R. L., Costa, R. M. R. and Soares, L. F. G. 2008. *Composer: Authoring Tool for iTV Programs*. Changing Television Environments. Springer Berlin / Heidelberg, 2008.

[16] Hess, J., Ley, B., Ogonowski, C., Wan, L. and Wulf, V. 2011. Jumping between devices and services: towards an integrated concept for social tv. In *Proceddings of the 9th international interactive conference on Interactive television*

(EuroITV '11, Lisbon, Portugal, July 1). DOI=http://doi.acm.org/10.1145/2000119.2000122

[17] ITU - International Telecommunication Union (2009) *"Nested context language (NCL) and Ginga-NCL for IPTV services".*

[18] LimSee2 – SMIL Editor. http://limsee2.gforge.inria.fr

[19] NCL Validator. http://laws.deinf.ufma.br/nclvalidator

[20] Papakonstantinou, Y. and Vianu, V. 2003. *Incremental Validation of XML Documents.* Springer Berlin / Heidelberg.

[21] Pemberton, S. et al. 2000. XHTML 1.0: The extensible hypertext markup language. W3C Recommendation. http://www.w3c.org/TR/xhtml1.

[22] Peterson, J. L. 1981. *Petri Net Theory and the Modeling of Systems*, Prentice Hall PTR, Upper Saddle River, NJ.

[23] Petre, M. 1995. *Why Looking Isn't Always Seeing: Readership Skills and Graphical Programming.* Communication of the ACM – June 1995

[24] SMIL Transition Effects Module. http://www.w3.org/TR/2005/REC-SMIL2-20050107/smil-transitions.html

[25] Soares Neto, C. S., Soares, L. F. G. and Souza, C. S.2010. *The Nested Context Language reuse features.* Journal of the Brazilian Computer Society. DOI= DOI 10.1007/s13173-010-0017-z

[26] Soares, L.F.G and Rodrigues, R.F. *Nested Context Model 3.0: Part 1 - NCM Core*, Technical Report, Departamento de Informática PUC-Rio, May 2005, ISSN: 0103-9741

[27] Soares, L. F. G. and Rodrigues, R. F. 2006. *Nested Context Language 3.0.* Technical Report

[28] Soares, L. F. G., Rodrigues, R. F. and Moreno, M. F. 2007. *Ginga-NCL: the declarative environment of the Brazilian digital TV system.* J. Braz. Comp. Soc. 2007, vol.12, n.4, pp. 37-46. ISSN 0104-6500. http://dx.doi.org/10.1590/S0104-65002007000100005.

[29] Sun, B., Yuan, X., Kang, H., Huang X., and Guan, Y. 2010. Incremental Validation of XML Document Based on Simplified XML Element Sequence Pattern. In *Proceedings of the 2010 Seventh Web Information Systems and Applications Conference* . (WISA '10). IEEE Computer Society. DOI=http://dx.doi.org/10.1109/WISA.2010.28

[30] Viana, N. S. and Lucena Junior, V. F. 2009. A software model supporting the management of home network services through the brazilian iDTV. In *Proceedings of the seventh european conference on European interactive television conference* (EuroITV '09, Leuven, Belgium, June 4 – 5, 2009) DOI = http://doi.acm.org/10.1145/1542084.1542102.

[31] XML Schema Definition Language (XSD) 1.1 Part 1: Structures. 2009. http://www.w3.org/TR/xmlschema11-1/ W3C Recommendation.

[32] XML. Extensible Markup Language (XML) 1.0 (Fifth Edition). 2008. http://www.w3.org/TR/xml/ W3C Recommendation.

Digital TV Adopters and Non-adopters in the Context of the Analogue Terrestrial TV Switchover in Portugal

Célia Quico, Manuel José Damásio, Sara Henriques
Universidade Lusófona de Humanidades e Tecnologias (ULHT)
Centre for Research in Applied Communication, Culture, and New Technologies (CICANT)
Campo Grande, 376
1749-024 Lisboa, Portugal
+351 217515500

{celia.quico, mjdamasio, shenriques,} @ulusofona.pt

ABSTRACT

In this paper, we will present a selection of the main results of the research project ADOPT-DTV "Barriers to the adoption of digital television in the transition from analogue to digital television", which had as main goal to understand the most significant factors for adopting and rejecting digital TV by the Portuguese population. The focus of this research project was on the people who do not have the intention to adopt digital TV or who are doubtful about it. More precisely, our major goal was to understand and identify the main factors that explain these intentions, as well as their demographic and socioeconomic profile. The secondary goal was to propose recommendations that could be applied by the key stakeholders in Portugal, aiming to contribute effectively towards a more inclusive digital TV.

The determination of four profiles of adopters in accordance to their intention of using digital TV will be further detailed in this paper. Also here presented in detail are the tests of project's main hypothesis and secondary hypotheses, based on the *Unified Theory of Acceptance and Use of Technology* (UTAUT) model. In summary, the main and secondary hypothesis are confirmed: in the context of the transition from analogue terrestrial TV to digital TV in Portugal, the adoption of digital TV is considerably conditioned by factors such as performance expectation, effort expectation and social influence, with strong probability of significant rejection by older segments of the population, with lower education levels and special needs.

Categories and Subject Descriptors

K.4.0 Computers and Society; General

General Terms

Management, Economics, Human Factors, Theory

Keywords

Diffusion and adoption of innovation, digital TV, TV audiences

1. INTRODUCTION

To understand what are the most significant factors for adopting and rejecting digital TV by the Portuguese population in the context of the analogue terrestrial TV switchoff was the main goal of the project ADOPT-DTV conducted by Universidade Lusófona. This project focused on the people who receive free-to-air analogue terrestrial TV exclusively, particularly those who have no intention or are doubtful about adopting digital TV. The research project began in April 2010, and lasted for 18 months, being formally concluded in October 2011. The project combined quantitative and qualitative methods, in accordance with projects of a similar scope [10] [14] [15] – more details about methodology and theoretical framework on [16] and [17]:

1) Ethnographic study, which took place in the households of 30 Portuguese families with different characteristics, with the objective of exploring in context what are their attitudes regarding digital TV and what uses they give to television and other media, among other issues;
2) Interviews with stakeholders, to gather the views of major players in this specific field, namely, broadcasters, pay-TV operators, DTT operator, regulatory institutions, representatives of people with special needs, etc;
3) Quantitative survey, applied to a representative sample of the Portuguese population, with approximately 1.200 participants, with the overall objective to determine the main adoption and rejection factors of digital TV usage;
4) Usability study, with a sample of 20 users, with the objective of making a comparative analysis of the main digital TV systems in the Portugal in terms of ease of use and overall satisfaction.

Regarding the theoretical framework, the project followed the *Unified Theory of Acceptance and Use of Technology* (UTAUT) model [22], which considers that performance expectancy, effort expectancy, social influence and facilitating conditions are direct determinants of the usage intention and behavior in the adoption of innovations. The impact of these four constructs is mediated by age, gender, experience and voluntariness of use.

Therefore, the project main hypothesis was the following, adapted from the UTAUT model: in the context of the transition from analogue terrestrial TV to digital TV, the adoption of digital TV is considerably conditioned by factors such as performance expectation, effort expectation and social influence, with strong probability of significant rejection by older segments of the population, with lower education levels and with special needs. All these factors constitute heavy barriers to the adoption of technology.

2. CONTEXTUALIZATION

The digital terrestrial television (DTT) free-to-air service was launched in Portugal in April 2009, making it one of the countries with a more ambitious schedule – or risky, depending on the perspective - for the full transition from analogue to digital

EuroITV'12, July 4–6, 2012, Berlin, Germany.

terrestrial television. In Portugal, the first phase of the analogue terrestrial TV switchoff occurred on January 12, 2012, and the last phase took place April 26, 2012.

Yet, until early 2012, DTT viewers in Portugal have exactly the same number of channels offered by analogue terrestrial network – 4 channels in mainland Portugal and 5 channels in the islands of Azores and Madeira - and no public plans are known to increase the number of the free-to-air channels available to the population before - or after - the switchoff. A 5th free-to-air channel can be launched in the future, but its concession has been adjourned *sine die*, due to the exclusion of the only two contestants in a public tender promoted by the national media regulator Entidade Reguladora para a Comunicação Social – ERC [9]. The pay-TV DTT operation is also adjourned *sine die,* after the winner of the public tender for this operation Portugal Telecom (PT) decided to give up this license [4] [6], justifying it with the significant changes that occurred within the pay TV market, namely the increase of competition, which would reduce the competitive importance expected from the terrestrial platform. The telecommunications regulator Anacom - without ERC's support – accepted PT claim. At the moment, there are still no further plans regarding the pay-TV DTT service in Portugal.

Finally, the national communication campaign about the analogue TV switchoff began in mid March 2011, merely 10 months before the first phase for switching off the analogue terrestrial signal and just 13 months before the planned deadline for the switchover process. Also in March 2011, the telecom regulator and the company responsible to the DTT free-to-air operation (PT) announced that the maximum value for reimbursement for the DTT set-top was up to 50% of the total cost of the equipment, with a maximum of 22 Euros per device and per household. The groups who could benefit of this subsidy were people with special needs with 60% or more of disability degree, beneficiaries of "rendimento social de inserção" (social insertion subsidy) and retired people earning less than 500 Euros per month. Yet, until recently the average price of a DTT set-top box was about 40 to 50 Euros - and it could be necessary for a technician to go to the household to redirect the antenna, which also is an extra cost [8].

Yet, the DTT network will only covered about 87% of the population. Which means, in practical terms, the 13% of the Portuguese population who live in areas which are not covered by the DTT network (so called "shadow areas") will have more expenses in the case they wish to continue to have free-to-air TV, since they will have to install a satellite dish and set-top-box - receiving nonetheless the same 22 Euros of subsidy for buying and installing the necessary equipment.

This way, the Portuguese TV viewers continue to have the same offer on DTT as they currently have in analogue terrestrial TV, having to support in the vast majority of cases all or most of the costs and trouble to continue having free-to-air TV and, also, being warned with short notice about the mandatory TV switchover. In short, for the population there are almost no tangible benefits for migrating from analogue terrestrial TV to DTT, in which the choice is basically between the lesser of the two "evils": to pay for a decoder device or TV subscription to continue to have something now they have for free or, in alternative, to be left without television signal after the switchoff.

Next, we will present a selection of the main results of the research project, namely, a proposal of four profiles of adopters in accordance to their intention of use of digital TV and, also, the tests of project's main hypothesis and secondary hypothesis. The full final report and the partial reports of each empirical study are available at the project's web site: http://adoptdtv.ulusofona.pt/.

3. PROFILES OF DTV ADOPTERS

3.1. Pay-TV and no pay-TV viewers' profiles

As to better understand **the profiles of viewers with pay-TV and with no pay-TV in Portugal**, we now present the descriptive and inferential statistical analysis of some variables, based on the main survey of the ADOPT-DTV project, applied to a representative sample of the population.

The quantitative survey was applied to 1.205 individuals aged 18 to 92 years (average age 45.2), of which 48.9% were male (n=589) and 51.1% were female (n=616). Regarding the age distribution, 12% had 18 to 24 years, 21% had 25-34 years, 19.1%, were in the age group 35-44, 18.2% had 45-54 years, 13,3% had 55-64 years and, finally, 16.4% had 65 years and plus. Finally, regarding the nationality, 96.3% of the survey participants are Portuguese and the remaining respondents are from Brazil, Ukraine, Cape Verde and others. The participants were selected by a quota method, based on a matrix which crossed variables such as gender, age, education level, occupation, region and place of residence / size of the place of residence. Overall, the instrument was composed of a total of 33 questions and 22 characterization items and the market studies company GfK applied it during November 2010, at the participants' households by a total of 68 interviewers through a direct and personal interview. The data was analyzed with SPSS software.

Out of the 1.205 participants in the quantitative inquiry, 99.4% replied that they have at least one TV set at home (n=1.198). Of these 1,198 respondents, 54.7% have pay TV at home (n=655), which means that 45.3% of the total sample only received free-to-air TV at home (n=543). According to Anacom [5], the total number of subscribers to pay TV services reached 2.770.000 in December 2010. Anacom estimated a 48.5 penetration rate for pay TV subscribers per 100 households.

Regarding the inferential statistical analysis, it was conducted respecting a confidence level of 95% ($\alpha = 0.05$). The Chi-Square test was used since it proved to be the stronger and more adequate. When the premises of the Chi-Square were not verified we resorted to the use of Fisher's exact test.

About the **profiles of pay-TV viewers versus non-pay-TV or free-to-air TV viewers**, our analysis was performed specifically based on the genre, age, education level, status and visual, hearing and mobility impairment level variables. The results point out statistical significant differences between all variables refer to and the ownership of pay-TV ($\chi2$ $p<0,05$), indicating, generally, that individuals with pay-TV in Portugal are more likely to be young and middle-aged adults, more likely to have higher education levels and belong to higher status groups (A/ B/ C) and less likely to have any kind of disability (visual, hearing or motor). On the other hand, the individuals without pay-TV in Portugal are more likely to be over 55 years old, more likely to have lower education levels and lower *status* (D/ E) and, finally, to possess some sort of disability (hearing, visual or motor).

3.2. DTV adopters and non-adopters

Four profiles of adopters of digital TV in Portugal are proposed, considering possession of pay TV and the intention of using digital TV. These profiles were defined based on the ownership of pay-TV at home (Q.3) and on the intention of subscribing to a pay-TV service or to acquire equipment to receive digital TV (Q.28):

Group *Already Adopted*: which corresponds to those who have pay-TV (cable, DTH, IPTV, fibre optic and other technologies);
Group *Will Adopt:* free-to-air TV viewers who are considering buying a decoder or television set with integrated TDT or else subscribe to a pay TV service to continue watching television at home;
Group *Undecided*: free-to-air TV viewers who do not know or did not reply as to their intention regarding the purchase of digital TV;
Group *Won't Adopt:* free-to-air TV viewers who claim they have no intention of adopting digital TV.

Table 1: Profiles based on possession of pay-TV and the intention of using digital TV

Intention of using DTV		November 2010 (n=525)
***Will Adopt* group**	Buy new TV set with TDT	**23.4%**
	Buy TDT decoder	
	Subscribe cable pay-TV service	
	Subscribe satellite TV service:	
	Subscribe IPTV/ ADSL service	
	Subscribe fibre TV service	
***Won't Adopt* group**	None	**34.1%**
Undecided group	Do not know / Do not reply	**45.5%**

NB: respondents could choose more than one option.

So as to endeavour to analyse individuals' characteristics according to their intention of using digital TV – do they intend to adopt digital TV in the following 12 months (*Will Adopt*), have no intention of adopting digital TV in the following 12 months (*Won't Adopt*) and undecided as to adopting digital TV (*Undecided*) – an analysis was made of the variables gender, age, education, status and hearing, seeing and motor disabilities.

Table 2: Intention of adopting digital TV vs. Gender

Intention of using DTV		Gender		Total
		Male	Female	
Won't Adopt	N	90	89	179
	%	**50.3%**	**49.7%**	100.0%
Will Adopt	N	63	44	107
	%	**58.9%**	**41.1%**	100.0%
Undecided	N	102	137	239
	%	**42.7%**	**57.3%**	100.0%

Data indicates the existence of significant differences for a confidence level of 95% between female and male respondents for the variable intention of using DTV ($\chi2(2)=8.083$; $p=0.017$). We have found a higher percentage of male participants with the intention of adopting digital TV, very similar figures between the groups who say they have no intention of adopting digital TV and a higher percentage of female respondents in the group undecided about buying equipment or a subscription to access digital TV.

Regarding the variable age again significant differences were found between the groups ($\chi2(10)=46.380$; $p<0.001$). Analysing the following table it is possible to observe that the respondents who say they have no intention of adopting digital TV are mostly older people, aged 55 or older. On the contrary, individuals who claim they intend to adopt digital TV within 12 months are mostly younger respondents, with ages between 18 and 44 years.

Table 3: Intention of adopting digital TV vs. Age

Intention of using DTV		Age					
		18-24 years	25-34 years	35-44 years	45-54 years	55-64 years	Over 65 years
Won't Adopt	N	9	26	17	28	37	62
	%	**5.0%**	**14.5%**	**9.5%**	**15.6%**	**20.7%**	**34.6%**
Will Adopt	N	18	18	27	19	14	11
	%	**16.8%**	**16.8%**	**25.2%**	**17.8%**	**13.1%**	**10.3%**
Unde-cided	N	15	47	46	42	31	58
	%	**6.3%**	**19.7%**	**19.2%**	**17.6%**	**13.0%**	**24.3%**

Regarding education, significant differences can be observed between the groups and their respective intention of using digital TV ($\chi2(14)=40.219$; $p<0.001$). Thus, the group of individuals who intends to adopt digital TV is characterised by having a higher education level, whereas individuals who are undecided or claim they have no intention of adopting digital TV have a lower level of education – it should be noted that 60.9% of respondents with terrestrial analogue TV who claimed they had no intention of acquiring services or equipment to access digital TV only attended basic school or cannot read and write.

Table 4: Intention of adopting digital TV vs. Education

Intention of using DTV	***Won't Adopt***		***Will Adopt***		***Undecided***	
	N	%	N	%	N	%
University/ Master/PhD	5	**2.8%**	6	**5.6%**	4	**1.7%**
Polytechnic	1	**0.6%**	3	**2.8%**	1	**0.4%**
Attend university	1	**0.6%**	1	**0.9%**	3	**1.3%**
12th grade	24	**13.4%**	18	**16.8%**	33	**13.8%**
9th grade	18	**10.1%**	28	**26.2%**	39	**16.3%**
6th grade	21	**11.7%**	21	**19.6%**	37	**15.5%**
4th grade	74	**41.3%**	25	**23.4%**	87	**36.4%**
Incomplete 4th grade/ illiterate	35	**19.6%**	5	**4.7%**	35	**14.6%**

Concerning seeing, hearing or mobility disabilities, significant differences were found between the groups for the three situations (impaired sight $\chi2(6)=28.755$; $p<0.001$; impaired hearing $\chi2(8)=21.424$; $p=0.006$; impaired mobility $\chi2(8)=35.691$; $p<0.001$). Thus, we observe a higher percentage of people with some or high level of seeing, hearing or moving disability in the group of respondents who say they have no intention of adopting digital TV, as well as a higher percentage of these respondents who are undecided about adopting this technology, compared with the respondents who say they have little or no difficulty in seeing, hearing or moving.

Table 5: Intention of adopting DTV vs. Seeing disability

Intention of Using DTV		Q.34. Do you find it hard to see even when using glasses or contact lenses?			
		No difficulty	Little difficulty	Some difficulty	A lot of difficulty
Won't Adopt	N	78	32	50	19
	%	**43.6%**	**17.9%**	**27.9%**	**10.6%**
Will Adopt	N	79	13	12	3
	%	**73.8%**	**12.1%**	**11.2%**	**2.8%**
Undecided	N	136	37	54	12
	%	**56.9%**	**15.5%**	**22.6%**	**5.0%**

Table 6: Intention of adopting DTV vs. Hearing disability

Intention of Using DTV		Q.35. What about hearing? Do you find it difficult to hear even when using a hearing device?				
		No difficult-ty	Little difficult-ty	Some difficult-ty	A lot of difficult-ty	Cannot hear
Won't Adopt	N	113	24	31	10	1
	%	**63.1%**	**13.4%**	**17.3%**	**5.6%**	**0.6%**
Will Adopt	N	90	10	6	1	0
	%	**84.1%**	**9.3%**	**5.6%**	**0.9%**	**0.0%**
Undecided	N	176	33	24	6	0
	%	**73.6%**	**13.8%**	**10.0%**	**2.5%**	**0.0%**

Table 7: Intention of adopting DTV vs. Walking disability

Intention of Using DTV		Q.36. What about walking? Do you find it difficult to walk or to climb stairs? Would you say...				
		No difficul ty	Little difficult -ty	Some difficult -ty	A lot of difficult -ty	Cannot walk
Won't Adopt	N	96	30	32	19	2
	%	**53.6%**	**16.8%**	**17.9%**	**10.6%**	**1.1%**
Will Adopt	N	92	5	5	4	1
	%	**86.0%**	**4.7%**	**4.7%**	**3.7%**	**0.9%**
Undecided	N	164	32	29	14	0
	%	**68.6%**	**13.4%**	**12.1%**	**5.9%**	**0.0%**

To sum up, each of these groups can be characterised as follows:

Group *Will Adopt* (free-to-air TV viewers who are considering buying a decoder or a TV set with DTT or else subscribing to a pay-TV service to continue watching TV at home) are more likely to be men, aged between 18 and 44, to have higher education level and less likely to have some kind of disability (visual, hearing or mobility);

Group *Undecided* (free-to-air TV viewers who do not know or did not reply as to their intention of acquiring digital TV) these are more likely to be women, to have lower education level and a significant level of disability (visual, hearing or mobility);

Group *Won't Adopt* (free-to-air TV viewers who claim they have no intention of adopting digital TV) they are more likely to be over 55 years of age, to have a low education level (finished basic education or less) and to have a significant level of disability (visual, hearing or mobility).

4. MAIN HYPOTHESES

As it was mentioned in the introduction to this paper, the authors of the UTAUT model [16] defend that performance expectation, effort expectation, social influence and facilitating conditions are direct determinants of the intention of usage intention and behavior in the adoption of innovations, the impact of these four factors being mediated by age, gender, experience and voluntariness of use. Based on this theory the following research hypotheses were formulated for the research project ADOPT-DTV, with necessary adaptations for the realm of digital TV:

Main hypothesis - in the switchover context in Portugal, the adoption of the digital TV is significantly conditioned by factors of performance expectancy, effort expectancy, social influence, with a strong probability of rejection by older segments of the population, with lower education levels and with special needs.

H1. Performance expectations have an effect on the intention of using digital TV and its effect is stronger on young people and men.
H2. Effort expectations have an effect on the intention of using digital TV and its effect is stronger on older people, those with lower education level and on women.
H3. Social influence has an effect on the intention of using digital TV and its effect is stronger on older people, those with lower education level and on women.
H4. Facilitating conditions do not have a significant effect on the intention of using digital TV on most of the population, but have a significant effect on older people.
H5. a) Self-sufficiency in the use of technologies does not have significant influence in the intention of using digital TV; H5.b) Anxiety as regards the use of technologies does not have a significant effect on the intention of using digital TV; H5.c) Attitudes regarding the use of technologies do not have a significant influence on the intention of using digital TV.

The statistical analysis of these hypotheses was performed by two processes. The first part of the hypotheses was analysed by a variance analysis and the second part of the hypotheses by a multivariate ANOVA, intending to analyse the interaction of new factors in the intention of using digital TV for each dimension of the adapted scale of the UTAUT model. With a view of simplifying the reading of the analysis, we decided to mention briefly the designations used for each variable and the number of variables to be analysed. Thus, concerning the scale dimensions (adaptation of the UTAUT model – more details on 7. Annex in this document) used in the quantitative survey, seven dimensions are examined: performance expectation, effort expectation, social influence, facilitating conditions, self-efficacy, anxiety, and attitudes.

As regards the variable intention of using digital TV, three groups were formed, as previously mentioned: *Will Adopt* Group, *Undecided* Group: and *Won't Adopt* Group. In order to analyse whether the variable intention of using digital TV has an influence on the dimensions resulting from adapting the UTAUT model, a variance analysis was made by mean comparison, ANOVA One-

Way, after verification of its assumptions. Data indicate the existence of significant differences for a 95% level of confidence (α=0.05) in all variables of the mentioned model (Performance expectation F(2.417)=9.785; P<.001; Effort expectation F(2.317)=11.180; p<.001; Social influence F(2.416)=9.989; p<.001; Facilitating conditions F(2.400)=13.928; p<.001; Attitudes of use F(2.390)=10.184; p<.001; Self-sufficiency F(2.380)=5.064; p=.007; and Anxiety F(2.404)=6.438;p=0.002). Using Tuckey test, significant differences were found for the variable Performance expectations between the groups *Won't Adopt* vs. *Adopt* (p<0.001); *Adopt* vs. *Undecided* (p<0.001); for the variable Effort expectation between the groups *Won't Adopt* Vs *Adopt* (p<0.001); *Won't Adopt* vs. *Undecided* (p=0.01); for the variable Social influence between the groups *Won't Adopt* vs. *Adopt* (p=0.001); *Adopt* vs. *Undecided* (p<0.001); for the variable Facilitating Conditions between the groups *Won't adopt* vs. *Adopt* (p<0.001); *Adopt* vs. *Undecided* (p<0.001); for the variable Attitudes of Use between the groups *Won't adopt* vs. *Will adopt* (p<0.001) and *Will adopt* vs. *Undecided* (p<0.001); for the variable Self-Efficiency between the groups *Won't adopt* vs. *Will adopt* (p=0.005); and finally, for the variable Anxiety between the groups *Won't adopt* vs. *Will adopt* (p=0.001) and *Will adopt* vs. *Undecided* (p=0.028).

Table H. Means of variables of the UTAUT model and Intention of using DTV

		N	Mean	St. dev.	Min.	Max.
Performance Expectation	***Won't Adopt***	137	**8.18**	3.294	1	14
	Will Adopt	101	**9.79**	2.974	2	14
	Undecided	182	**8.25**	3.058	1	15
Effort Expectation	***Won't Adopt***	106	**7.52**	3.237	1	15
	Will Adopt	90	**9.54**	2.961	1	14
	Undecided	124	**8.69**	2.867	2	15
Social Influence	***Won't Adopt***	140	**7.59**	2.800	1	14
	Will Adopt	98	**8.95**	2.665	2	15
	Undecided	181	**7.42**	2.957	1	15
Facilitating Conditions	***Won't Adopt***	134	**5.87**	3.593	1	13
	Will Adopt	98	**8.20**	3.446	1	14
	Undecided	171	**6.22**	3.539	1	15
Attitudes of Use	***Won't Adopt***	129	**8.20**	3.355	2	15
	Will Adopt	99	**9.97**	2.844	1	15
	Undecided	165	**8.42**	3.197	1	15
Self-efficiency	***Won't Adopt***	121	**7.83**	2.848	1	15
	Will Adopt	100	**9.02**	3.104	2	15
	Undecided	162	**8.29**	2.516	2	14
Anxiety	***Won't Adopt***	128	**8.18**	3.281	1	15
	Will Adopt	100	**9.65**	3.079	2	15
	Undecided	179	**8.65**	2.993	2	15

The number of respondents per profile varies slightly per dimension since the "Do not know/do not answer" replies were eliminated from the calculations. According to the means of each group in each dimension, it is possible to observe that the group *Will Adopt* shows higher values in comparison with the other groups when significant differences were found. This data indicates that the different dimensions of the proposed model contribute positively to the intention of adopting digital TV. It should be noted that the dimension Anxiety was constructed in the negative, and for this reason the figures obtained on the scale were inverted to obtain the value of the variable and to further analyse – note that in this instrument we employed a 5-level Likert scale. Thus, it is necessary to conceptualise this very dimension in the negative – No anxiety, realising that the high values of the group *Adopt* in this dimension point the same (no anxiety) as having a positive effect on the intention of using digital TV.

So as to analyse the effect of the interaction, a multivariate ANOVA was conducted after verification of its assumptions in all variables (normality and homogeneity of the variance). Concerning the **first study hypothesis**, which probes the intention of using and its interaction with gender and age relative to the variable **performance expectations** (variable derived from the UTAUT model), we sought to understand if there is a positive effect on the intention of using, in other words, whether younger and male respondents in the sample are more likely to adopt digital TV. The following table (H1a) presents the means for the relation between the aforementioned variables.

Table H1a. Means: intention of using DTV and gender for the variable performance expectations

Performance Expectation				
Intention of using	Gender	Mean	Standard Deviation	N
Won't Adopt	Male	**8.65**	3.031	74
	Female	**7.62**	3.521	63
Will Adopt	Male	**9.98**	2.977	60
	Female	**9.51**	2.984	41
Undecided	Male	**8.46**	3.001	83
	Female	**8.08**	3.109	99

According to the data collected, there is no significant interaction effect between **intention of using DTV and gender** for the variable performance expectations (F(3.414)=0.461; p=0.631). The lack of interaction indicates that the difference in the intention of using digital TV between men and women is the same for respondents who intend to adopt, not to adopt or that are undecided as to adopting digital TV.

Nevertheless, as far as the main effects are concerned, we observe that there are considerable differences for intention of using digital TV (F(2.416)= 9.167; p<0.001) and for gender (F(1.416)= 4.041; p=0.045) in isolation. Using Benferroni's multiple comparisons test, differences can be found between male vs. female groups, as regards gender, and for the groups *Will Adopt* vs. *Won't Adopt* (p<0.001) and *Will Adopt* vs. *Undecided* (p<0.001). The male and the *Will Adopt* groups show higher means in both cases.

Data indicate thus that, although we could find no significant interaction between the gender factor and the intention of using digital TV factor for this dimension, there is a positive relation between the intention of adopting digital TV and gender as to performance expectations, and both groups, the male group and the group of those who intend to adopt digital TV, show higher figures when compared to the remaining groups.

Regarding age, likewise we sought to ascertain whether there is an interaction effect between **age and the intention of using DTV** for performance expectations. Data indicate that there is no interaction among the factors F(10.402)=0.310; p=0.978), although we can observe significant differences in the factors separately (intention of using: F(1.402)=5.333; p=0.005 and age F(5.402)=11.321; p<0.001). Analysing the values of the Bonferroni's test, the significant differences can be found between the groups *Will Adopt* vs. *Won't Adopt* (p<0.001) and *Will Adopt* vs. *Undecided* (p<0.001). Table H1b presents the descriptive data for the variables in question. Again, the group *Will Adopt* shows higher means when compared with the remaining groups. As regards the variable age, higher means could be observed in younger segments (from 18 to 24 years old, from 25 to 34 years old and also from 35 to 44 years old). Although there is no interaction among the factors, when analysed separately they indicate a positive relation between younger segments and the intention of adopting digital TV in the dimension performance expectation.

Table H1b. Means: intention to using DTV and age for the variable performance expectation

Intention of using DTV	Age	Mean	Standard deviation	N
Won't Adopt	18-24 years	**10.71**	1.496	7
	25-34 years	**9.70**	3.267	23
	35-44 years	**9.07**	2.764	15
	45-54 years	**8.91**	3.502	23
	55-64 years	**7.11**	3.059	28
	over 65 years	**6.88**	3.059	41
Will Adopt	18-24 years	**11.50**	2.036	18
	25-34 years	**10.78**	1.957	18
	35-44 years	**9.73**	2.933	26
	45-54 years	**9.71**	3.312	17
	55-64 years	**8.23**	3.086	13
	over 65 years	**7.00**	3.000	9
Undecided	18-24 years	**9.00**	1.871	13
	25-34 years	**9.32**	2.595	44
	35-44 years	**8.59**	3.219	37
	45-54 years	**8.42**	2.430	36
	55-64 years	**7.56**	3.468	18
	over 65 years	**6.41**	3.439	34

Concerning the **second theoretical hypothesis**, we question whether the variables age and gender have any effect on the intention of using, considering the **effort expectations** (variable of the UTAUT model). The analysis again resorted to multivariate ANOVA, looking for an interaction effect among the mentioned variables. Data indicate that the variable gender does not interact with the variable intention of using digital TV as regards effort expectations (F(2.314)=1.547; p=0.214). As far as the main effects of factors are concerned, we find significant differences for the variable intention of using DTV (F(2.314)=10.744; p<0.001) and gender (F(2.314)=10.742; p=0.001;) in male vs. female groups, *Will Adopt* vs. *Won't Adopt* (p<0.001) and *Will Adopt* vs. *Undecided* (p=0.009). Regarding the variable age, we could not find interaction among the factors either (F(10.302)=0.732; p=0.694), but there are statistically significant differences for the factors taken separately: Intention of using DTV (F(2.302)=6.003; p=0.003;) and age (F(5.302)=6.782; p<0.001). Differences were found between the male vs. female groups, and between the groups *Will Adopt* vs. *Won't Adopt* (p<0.001) and *Won't Adopt* vs. *Undecided* (p<0.009). The following tables (H2a. and H2b.) present the descriptive data for the variables of the second theoretical hypothesis.

Table H2a. Interaction between intention of using DTV and gender for the variable effort expectations

Intention of using DTV	Gender	Mean	Standard deviation	N
Won't Adopt	Male	**7.76**	3.344	59
	Female	**7.21**	3.106	47
Will Adopt	Male	**10.42**	2.658	50
	Female	**8.45**	2.987	40
Undecided	Male	**9.10**	2.721	59
	Female	**8.31**	2.963	65

Again, it is possible to observe that the male group shows higher means when compared, in isolation, with the female group, and that the younger segments show higher means when compared with the older segments. When we consider the groups of using DTV, the group *Will Adopt* shows higher means, followed by the group *Undecided* (see descriptive tables below). Thus, data confirm the theoretical hypothesis that we have raised: intention of using DTV has a relation with effort expectations, and the group of female respondents and older respondents have lower means.

Table H2b. Interaction between intention of using DTV and age for the variable effort expectations

Intention of using DTV	Age	Mean	Standard deviation	N
Won't Adopt	18-24 years	**8.43**	3.359	7
	25-34 years	**8.90**	2.844	21
	35-44 years	**8.62**	3.404	13
	45-54 years	**9.06**	3.255	16
	55-64 years	**6.41**	2.425	17
	over 65 years	**5.78**	2.904	32

(continues next page)

Table H2b. (continuation of previous page)

Intention of using DTV	Age	Mean	Standard deviation	N
Will Adopt	18-24 years	**10.00**	3.162	18
	25-34 years	**10.25**	2.082	16
	35-44 years	**9.04**	3.113	24
	45-54 years	**11.15**	1.994	13
	55-64 years	**8.18**	2.960	11
	over 65 years	**7.88**	3.643	8
Undecided	18-24 years	**9.18**	1.601	11
	25-34 years	**9.44**	1.795	34
	35-44 years	**9.14**	3.399	22
	45-54 years	**8.58**	2.928	26
	55-64 years	**8.40**	3.239	10
	over 65 years	**7.00**	3.464	21

As regards to the **third study hypothesis,** we argue that age and gender have an effect on the intention of using digital TV, as far as the variable **social influence** is concerned. According to the data collected, the interaction effect between these factors is inexistent, whether for age (F(2.413)=0.585; p=0.557) or for gender (F(2.413)=x, P=0.557), but once again when taken separately the factors show significant differences between the groups. Thus, when we consider intention of using DTV (F(2.413)=9.256; p<0.001) and age (F(1.313)=4.835; p=0.028) there are significant differences between the groups *Will Adopt* vs. *Won't Adopt* (p=0.001) and *Will Adopt* vs. *Undecided* (p<0.001); in both cases the group *Will Adopt* has the higher means (see descriptive tables H3a and H3b).

Table H3a. Interaction between intention of using DTV and gender for the variable social influence

Intention of using DTV	Gender	Mean	Standard deviation	N
Won't Adopt	Male	**8.07**	2.468	75
	Female	**7.05**	3.069	65
Will Adopt	Male	**9.18**	2.823	57
	Female	**8.63**	2.426	41
Undecided	Male	**7.60**	3.121	81
	Female	**7.27**	2.824	100

When we consider the interaction with the variable gender, again the isolated factors show significant differences between the groups, and the male group stands out with higher means. Therefore, data confirm the theoretical hypothesis formulated, intention of using digital TV has a relation with social influence, and the groups of female respondents and of older respondents show lower means.

Table H3b. Interaction between intention of using and age for the variable social influence

Intention of using	Age	Mean	Standard deviation	N
Won't Adopt	18-24 years	**7.25**	3.240	8
	25-34 years	**8.70**	2.183	23
	35-44 years	**8.00**	3.183	16
	45-54 years	**8.59**	2.282	22
	55-64 years	**7.63**	2.684	30
	over 65 years	**6.32**	2.832	41
Will Adopt	18-24 years	**9.33**	2.849	18
	25-34 years	**9.69**	2.330	16
	35-44 years	**9.08**	2.208	26
	45-54 years	**8.53**	3.484	17
	55-64 years	**8.83**	2.725	12
	over 65 years	**7.44**	2.128	9
Undecided	18-24 years	**7.31**	2.658	13
	25-34 years	**8.09**	2.662	43
	35-44 years	**7.62**	3.157	37
	45-54 years	**7.86**	2.631	36
	55-64 years	**6.48**	3.502	21
	over 65 years	**6.42**	2.986	31

Concerning the **fourth study hypothesis**, we argue that age has an effect on intention of using DTV in relation with the variable **facilitating conditions**. According to the data collected, there is no interaction between the age factor and the intention to use DTV factor (F(0.643;p=0.777); still, when considered separately, the factors show significant differences in their groups (intention to use: F(2.385)=9.306; p<0.001) and age (F(5.385)=4.925; p=0.000). Thus, based on the Bonferroni's test, differences were found between the groups *Will Adopt* vs. *Won't Adopt* (p<0.001) and *Will Adopt* vs. *Undecided* (p<0.001). The means are higher for the group of respondents who intend to adopt digital TV in the middle age and younger age segments.

Table H4a. Means: intention of using DTV and age for the variable facilitating conditions

Intention of using DTV	Age	Mean	Standard deviation	N
Won't Adopt	18-24 years	**5.50**	2.976	8
	25-34 years	**7.68**	3.286	22
	35-44 years	**6.33**	4.117	15
	45-54 years	**6.81**	3.027	21
	55-64 years	**5.26**	3.460	27
	over 65 years	**4.73**	3.668	41

(continues next page)

Table H4a. (continuation of previous page)

Will Adopt	18-24 years	**9.39**	2.593	18
	25-34 years	**8.72**	3.322	18
	35-44 years	**7.72**	3.814	25
	45-54 years	**8.31**	3.807	16
	55-64 years	**8.58**	2.811	12
	over 65 years	**5.44**	3.358	9
Undecided	18-24 year	**7.55**	3.532	11
	25-34 years	**7.37**	2.984	43
	35-44 years	**6.06**	3.626	34
	45-54 years	**5.91**	3.137	34
	55-64 years	**6.18**	4.433	17
	over 65 years	**4.72**	3.612	32

The fifth hypothesis of the study and its derivatives were answered using simple ANOVA, and the data indicated the existence of significant differences for a confidence level of 95% (alpha=0.05) in these variables of the mentioned model (Attitudes of use $F(2.390)=10.184$; $p<.001$; Self-efficiency $F(2.380)=5.064$; $p=.007$; Anxiety $F(2.404)=6.438$; $p=0.002$).

Therefore, the main hypothesis of the research project is confirmed: in the context of the transition from analogue terrestrial TV to digital TV, the adoption of digital TV is considerably conditioned by factors such as performance expectation, effort expectation and social influence, with strong probability of significant rejection by older segments of the population, with lower education levels and with special needs.

5. CONCLUSION

In this paper, we have presented a selection of the main results of the research project ADOPT-DTV, focusing on the presentation of profiles of DTV adopters in accordance to their intention of use of digital TV and, also, the exam of project's main hypothesis and secondary hypotheses.

It should be noted that in September 2011, the research team applied again a selection of questions in a new survey[1], conducted within the scope of the research project IDTV-Health, verifying that the reception of analogue terrestrial TV remained largely dominant with Portuguese people without pay-TV, and that the access to DTT has little expression: it was estimated that 38% of the population in mainland Portugal may be affected by the switchoff of the terrestrial analogue TV transmission system. In this latest survey on digital TV, 61.7% claimed to have pay-TV at home (n=742), which implies that 38.3% of those surveyed do not have pay-TV (n=460). Out of the 460 respondents who answered negatively to the question "do you have pay-TV" (total of respondents with TV =1,202), 92.4% claimed to receive analogue TV through the traditional antenna (n=425) and 3% indicated they have DTT (n=14), while 2.6% said they received TV free of charge through satellite dish and 2.6% do not know or did not reply to this question. In the previous survey (November 2010), from those polled who indicated they did not subscribe to pay-TV service, 96.7% claimed to have analogue terrestrial TV, whereas 1.8% said they received TV signal through satellite dish and 1.1% said they received DTT, with 0.7% choosing not to reply and 0.2% of those surveyed identifying another kind of access. Therefore, there was a slight increase in the percentage of those who said they had DTT, which went from 1.1% to 3% of those polled who did not have pay-TV. Naturally, some of these indicators altered after September 2011, as deadlines for the switch-off approached, yet it is still unknown up to what point – and to what cost for the Portuguese TV viewers, particularly the most vulnerable people such as the elderly, the poorest, the less educated and people with special needs.

These and other results and findings of this project are relevant to comprehend this process of transition, being further detailed in final report and partials reports already published on the project's web site, as well on other scientific publications [18] [19]. As part of the final report, the research team recommended that the postponing the switchoff date could be considered by those with responsibility in this matter, particularly considering the profile of the free-to-air TV viewers with access to analogue terrestrial TV, since it is estimated that there is a high risk of a substantial part of this population may no longer be able to watch TV after the switchoff - if the deadlines were to be maintained.

Also to backup this recommendation, it was also mentioned that in the USA the switchoff was postponed three times: from 2006 to December 31 2008, and then February 17 2009 and, finally, to June 12, 2009 [12] In January 2009, about one month before the switchoff deadline, the market research company Nielsen estimated that almost 7% of all the American households were not prepared for the end of the analogue terrestrial TV (7,8 million homes), since they did not have a TV set with an integrated DTT decoder or a DTT set-top box [11] This way, the recently elected president of the USA Barack Obama launched the proposal to postpone the switchoff, declaring that "millions of Americans, including those in our most vulnerable communities, would have been left in the dark if the conversion had gone on as planned" (cit. in Hart, 2011). Less than two weeks before the dead-line for the switchoff – set to February 17 2009 – the House of Representatives approved Obama's proposal to delay this date, a proposal previously approved by the Senate [21] In the perspective of the north-American researcher Jeffrey Hart [13] this decision to delay the switchoff from February to June 2009 helped to avoid serious disruptions in the daily live of many citizens.

Curiously, after the case for suspending or delaying switchoff was strongly refuted by the representative of Anacom in a special debate promoted on 4 January 2012 by news TV channel RTP Informação (from the public service broadcaster RTP), the telecom regulator would two days later on 6 January, announce an adjustment of the phased switch-off plan. Instead of terminating the analogue terrestrial broadcast in most of continental Portugal's littoral area on 12 January, the switch-off would be done progressively from 12 January until 23 February, in five sub-phases. The justification presented was that this switchoff fragmentation would "improve the possibility of intervening in the correction of eventual deficiencies and reducing the impact associated to operation in course" [1]. For the national consumers association DECO, this decision was a "turn of events" regarding the position taken so far by Anacom, which came after DECO had raised the alert about the inefficiency of the communication

[1] The survey fieldwork took place from 16 to 27 September 2011, with a representative sample of the Portuguese population over 18 years of age, constituted by 1.207 respondents, 1.202 of which claimed to have TV at home.

campaigns and the lack of preparation by the majority of the impacted population [7]. Another decision made public by Anacom [2] the same day related to the subsidies for the population in the DTT shadow zones: the satellite kit would cost 40 Euros, instead of 55 Euros, maintaining the same conditions previously defined (for instance, the subsidy is only for the first set-top box in each home, which means that this support does not apply to other TV sets the household might have).

Some members of the Parliament argued that these adjustments could not be enough to correct the course of action. The lack of information about DTT, how to access it and other practical issues provided the justification for a special debate on the DTT process by the Parliament Ethics Commission on 31 January 2012. Most of the political parties' representatives in this debate criticized the process, pointing to problems such as the coverage of the DTT network, misleading advertising and aggressive commercial practices [20].

If the lessons learned in countries such as USA - and other countries that already completed the switchover process - are being taken care into consideration by the responsible institutions in Portugal, for now this is not public knowledge. After April 26, 2012 it will be more clear how successful was the switchover in Portugal, particularly considering the impact on the most vulnerable populations in this process. As Jeffrey Hall observed [9] in the case of wealthy democratic countries "there will generally be a combination of governmental mandates and reliance on the market and consumer choices". On the other hand, in poorer countries, "authority may be more centralized in the government and consumer interests may be ignored" [9], in which the consumers have the burden of the transition, being forced to pay for services that they had for free, whether or not they can afford it. What is the case of Portugal - if any of these - it remains to be seen: the outcome of this process will surely shed some light about the quality of democracy in this country in the early XXI century, for the better or for the worse…

6. ACKNOWLEDGMENTS

The ADOPT-DTV project is funded by Fundação para a Ciência e Tecnologia – FCT (PTDC/CCI-COM/102576/2008), in partnership with ANACOM and OBERCOM.

7. ANNEX

- Items Used in Estimating UTAUT

UTAUT model original - Venkatesh Et Al. (2003)	*UTAUT adaptation for digital TV adoption - ADOPT-DTV project (2010)*
Performance expectancy	
U6: I would find the system useful in my job	Digital TV is a useful innovation
RA1: Using the system enables me to accomplish tasks more quickly.	Digital TV is better than analogue TV
RA5: Using the system increases my productivity.	Digital TV allows to improve TV viewing and my TV experience
Effort expectancy	
EOU5: It would be easy for me to become skilful at using the system.	Using digital TV does not seem to be complicated
EOU6: I would find the system easy to use.	I would find easy/ I find easy to learn how to use digital TV
EU4: Learning to operate the system is easy for me.	After learning, I believe I will not have/ I won't have difficulties in using DTV
Social influence	
SN2: People who are important to me think that I should use the system.	People who are important to me think that I should have and use digital TV
SF2: The senior management of this business has been helpful in the use of the system.	Whoever sells me digital TV services or equipments should help me to use it
SF4: In general, the organization has supported the use of the system.	The official communication campaigns convinced me to have digital TV
Facilitating conditions	
PBC2: I have the resources necessary to use the system.	I have the necessary resources and knowledge to use DTV
PBC3: I have the knowledge necessary to use the system.	
PBC5: The system is not compatible with other systems I use.	Digital TV is not compatible with other systems I have at home (TV sets, VCR, DVD)
FC3: A specific person (or group) is available for assistance with system difficulties.	I know that there are persons (or companies) available for assistance
Attitudes towards using technology	
A1: Using the system is a bad/good idea.	Using digital TV is a good idea
AF1: The system makes work more interesting.	Digital TV makes TV more interesting.
AF2: Working with the system is fun	Digital TV is fun
Self-efficacy I could complete a job or task using the system…	
SE1: If there was no one around to tell me what to do as I go.	I could/ I can use DTV if there is no one around to tell me what to do
SE6: If I had a lot of time to complete the job for which the software was provided	I could/ I can use digital TV in case I have enough time to learn by myself
SE7: If I had just the built-in help facility for assistance.	I could/ I can use DTV if I can call someone for help to install it and teach me who to use it
Anxiety	
ANX1: I feel apprehensive about using the system	I feel apprehensive about using digital TV
ANX2: It scares me to think that I could lose a lot of information using the system by hitting the wrong key.	I hesitate to use the system for fear of hitting some button and damage the TV set
ANX4: The system is somewhat intimidating to me	Digital TV is somewhat intimidating to me
Behavioural intention to use the system	
BI1: I intend to use the system in the next <n> months	I intend to have digital TV at home in the next 12 months

9. REFERENCES

[1] Anacom. 2012. Decision to adjust switch-off timetable for the 1st stage of the switch-off plan', http://www.anacom.pt/render.jsp?contentId=1113198

[2] Anacom. 2012. Change in value of complementary DTT kit (DTH) and clarification on subsidy programme', http://www.anacom.pt/render.jsp?contentId=1113205.

[3] Anacom. 2011. Fiber and alternative technologies drive subscription TV. Anacom. http://www.anacom.pt/render.jsp?contentId=1072790

[4] Anacom. 2010. Revocation of the rights of use of frequencies associated with Muxes B to F. Anacom. http://www.anacom.pt/render.jsp?contentId=1007377

[5] Anacom. 2010. 20% of new paid television customers use fibre. Anacom. http://www.anacom.pt/render.jsp?contentId=1027751

[6] Anacom .2009. TDT - Títulos do MUX B a F atribuídos à PTC. http://www.anacom.pt/render.jsp?contentId=957813

[7] DECO. 2012. TDT: apagão analógico faseado no litoral', http://www.deco.proteste.pt/dvd-tv-som/tdt-apagao-analogico-faseado-no-litoral-s674571.htm.

[8] DECO/ Proteste .2011. Descodificadores para televisão digital terrestre: poupe até 111 euros. http://www.deco.proteste.pt/dvd-tv-som/televisores-e-tdt-s669941.htm

[9] ERC .2009. Concurso Público do "5º Canal". http://www.erc.pt/pt/noticias/concurso-publico-do-5-canal

[10] Clarkson, P.J. and Keates, S. 2003. Digital TV For All: a report on usability and accessible design. Report for DTI.

[11] InformiTV. 2008. Calls to delay American analogue television switch off'. http://informitv.com/news/2009/01/11/callstodelay/

[12] Hart, J. 2011.The Transition to Digital Television in the United States: The Endgame'. *International Journal of Digital Television* 1 (1): 7–29.

[13] Hart, K. 2009. Congress Delays Troubled Switch To Digital TV'. http://www.washingtonpost.com/wp-dyn/content/article/2009/02/04/AR2009020402584.html?hpid=topnews&sid=ST2009020402856&s_pos

[14] Klein, J. Karger, S. and Sinclair, K. 2004. Attitudes to switchover: the impact of digital switchover on consumer adoption of digital television. Report for DTI.

[15] Klein, J. Karger, S. and Sinclair, K. 2004. Attitudes to digital television: preliminary findings on consumer adoption of digital television. Report for DTI.

[16] Quico, C. and Damásio, M.J. 2010. Understanding barrier to digital television adoption in the context of the digital switchover in Portugal. In Proceedings of *International Association for Media and Communication Research – IAMCR 2010*, 18–22 July, Universidade do Minho, Braga, Portugal.

[17] Quico, C., Damásio M. J., Henriques, S. and Veríssimo, I. 2011. Profiles of digital TV adopters in the switchover context in Portugal'. In Proceeding of *International Association for Media and Communication Research – IAMCR 2011*, 13–17 July, Kadir Has University, Istanbul, Turkey.

[18] Quico, C., Damásio, M. J., Henriques, S. and Veríssimo, I. 2012. Digital terrestrial TV switchover process in Portugal: viewers between a rock and a hard place" for Sousa, Helena & Denicoli, Sérgio (eds.) *Digital Communication Policies in the Information Society Promotion Stage*. eBook. Universidade do Minho. (to be published)

[19] Quico, C. 2012. Digital TV switchover in Portugal: what's in it for the viewer?. *International Journal of Digital Television*. 3, 2. (to be published)

[20] Sol . 2012. 'Partidos criticam processo de transição para a televisão digital'. http://sol.sapo.pt/inicio/Politica/Interior.aspx?content_id=40343

[21] Stelter, B. 2009.Switch to Digital TV Wins a Delay to June 12.http://www.nytimes.com/2009/02/05/business/media/05digital.html?adxnnl=1&adxnnlx=1319450480-3+OM5d74gbWgkmH1FcOpo

[22] Venkatesh, V., Morris, M. G., Davis, G. B. and Davis, F. D. 2003. User acceptance of information technology: Toward a unified view". *MIS Quarterly*, 27, 3, 425-478.

Story-Map: iPad Companion for Long Form TV Narratives

Janet H. Murray, Sergio Goldenberg, Kartik Agarwal, Tarun Chakravorty, Jonathan Cutrell, Abraham Doris-Down, Harish Kothandaraman
Georgia Institute of Technology
Digital Media Program
Atlanta GA 30308 USA
+1 404 894 6202
{jmurray,sergio.goldenberg,kagarwal9,tchakravorty3,jcutrell3,abraham,harish7}@gatech.edu

ABSTRACT

Long form TV narratives present multiple continuing characters and story arcs that last over multiple episodes and even over multiple seasons. Writers increasingly take pride in creating coherent and persistent story worlds with recurring characters and references to backstory. Since viewers may join the story at different points and different levels of commitment, they need support to orient them to the fictional world, to remind them of plot threads, and to allow them to review important story sequences across episodes. Using the affordances of the digital medium we can create navigation patterns and auxiliary information streams to minimize confusion and maximize immersion in the story world. In our application, the iPad is used as a secondary screen to create a character map synchronized with the TV content, and to support navigation of story threads across episodes.

Categories and Subject Descriptors

H.5.2 [**Information Interfaces and Presentation**]: User Interfaces - *Prototyping, Interaction styles, Graphical User Interfaces*. H.3.3 [**Information Storage and Retrieval**]: Information Search and Retrieval – *information filtering*

General Terms

Design, Experimentation, Human Factors, Standardization

Keywords

Interactive Television, Dual Device User Experience, Second Screen Application

1. INTRODUCTION

Serialized drama has long been one of the most critically acclaimed and popular forms of television, and plots have become more complex over the past decades [8]. The growth of digital formats has increased the consistency and continuity of television writing, by making the single season into a story-telling unit, and keeping events from past seasons current in viewer's minds, through distribution on DVDs and web-based fan activities. As a result, writers have incentives to create complex multi-character stories with plot-lines that arc across multiple episodes and even multiple seasons. But more complex plots and larger casts of recurring characters can leave viewers confused. Since the primary delivery is still one episode per week, new viewers need to be given contextual information about what has happened before, if a show is to gain viewership mid-season; and loyal viewers will also need reminders of characters or plot events that may be picked up from months before. There have been several attempts to provide this information, but they often risk "spoilers" that reveal plot points prematurely, or they provide information that is itself overwhelming and not completely relevant to the current scene. HBO GO for example, provides card-like information elements next to a streaming feed of a serial drama like Game of Thrones [5], and the last season of Lost was introduced by an annotated replay of key scenes with subtitles explaining lines of dialog that referenced previous events. Such attempts at simultaneous annotation show that viewers need additional guidance synchronized with the unfolding of the story. The limitations of existing applications make clear the design goals of increasing comprehension and immersion while minimizing distraction.

EuroITV'12, July 4–6, 2012, Berlin, Germany.

Since narrative is a fundamental human cognitive strategy [2] [12], and media like written books or recorded moving images increase our cognitive scope by allowing us to externalize memory functions [4], media forms that allow us to consume more complex narrative structures offer promise for increasing cultural expressivity and cognitive power. Therefore, applications that support comprehension and immersion in complex television dramas are a useful focus for digital invention.

The work at the eTV lab at Georgia Tech assumes an environment, which is rapidly becoming realized: television series available on-demand in multi-episode online archives; and multiscreen consumer configurations with all the affordances of computation fully integrated with television content. The Story-Map application is meant to run on a two-screen system in which digital television is available on a large browser-equipped screen and a smaller hand-held tablet that provides auxiliary information. We have implemented the system on both devices as web applications in HTML5. The application includes character maps, relationship iconography, and reviewing compendiums that access the content at scene-level granularity across multiple episodes.

2. RELATED WORK

StoryLines [11] explores a timeline-based method of navigating news and episodic television in the context of rich archival resources. Using Battlestar Galactica and news coverage of the Arab Spring as representative content, this prototyping project used a tablet computer as a navigation device. Users could identify individual story threads within a complex multi-threaded story environment by filtering the items on a composite timeline, which then split into multiple timelines. For example, viewers could follow the story of a romantic triangle across multiple episodes, and could see the component scenes in the order in which they were broadcast (which included some flashbacks) or in chronological order within the fictional time scheme. We identified such stories as "multisequential" because they could be experienced in multiple coherent sequences, which the timeline navigation organized and presented in relationship to one another. In addition the StoryLines project included an example of "multiform" story in which the same story beat existed in variant version, in this case a story of a date that could develop in multiple ways depending on choices such as whether coke or vodka was served. The tablet interface provided a way of replaying individual scenes and juxtaposing the variants without losing track of which prior choices led to which results.

Cesar et al. identify four major usages of the secondary screen in an interactive television environment, to control, enrich, share and transfer video content [3]. Our application builds on the concept of control as it allows users to navigate and select an episode from a list and presents real time enhanced information in the form of the character map about the selected episode. The concept of transfer is explored in relationships and thematic recaps, which the user can see even after moving away from the television screen. Motorola Mobility [1] prototyped a companion device experience that enhances TV viewing by providing auxiliary information and media on a second screen. The additional media is semantically related and synchronized, in terms of timeline, to the TV content. A three-week field trial in 11 households was conducted and the participants used the prototype as a companion to their TV shows, the overall feedback to the concept was quite positive with 10 out of 11 participants saying they enjoyed the experience. The researchers concluded that the prototype allowed participants to better connect with their TV shows and have an enriched social life around the TV by providing holistic infotainment.

The Game of Thrones character relationship tree infographic [9] created by a fan, Magdalena Maslowska symbolically represents characters, their relationships and their affiliation to houses. Due to the large number of characters, complex relationships and elaborate back-stories, it can be quite overwhelming for new viewers to start watching the series mid-way or for avid fans to keep track of these relationships in their head. The infographic does well to address these issues, but being a static representation of the relationship at a particular point of time, is unable to address the issue of evolving relationships (e.g. enemies turning into friends later on in the series). The viewing aid released by the producers for the computer-based one-screen HBO GO environment includes information synced with individual episodes [5] but some of it takes the viewer out of the frame of the fictional world by introducing production details. It provides additional information about some of the characters in an episode, but leaves a new viewer wondering about the many unexplained characters, relationships, and dialog references in this richly imagined fantasy world, without providing direct links to clarifying information.

In her 1997 book, *Hamlet on the Holodeck*, Janet Murray offers a prediction of a "hyperserial" that would grow out of the digital delivery of television content [10], predicting many of the applications such as virtual places and point of view information that have become staples of web sites associated with dramatic series and films. Henry Jenkins in *Convergence Culture* called attention to "transmedia storytelling" based around film and television properties, in which games and fan participation structures are not just marketing extentions but integrated parts of the canonical world [6]. In a web posting expanding upon his book, Jenkins identifies four characteristic functions of transmedia: offering back story, providing maps of the world, offering another character's perspective on the action, or deepening audience engagement through participation [7].

The Story-Map application builds upon earlier experiments with tablets used as secondary synchronized screens, and upon the concepts of the hyperserial and transmedia storytelling, by creating an application that is intended to foster the viewer's understanding and immersion in a complex story-world by making the component parts of the story structure apparent, and fostering multiple paths of coherent exploration.

3. SYSTEM DESCRIPTION

3.1 Setup

The system consists of two main components. The first is the Internet capable television, which displays the television show as streaming digital video and the second is the companion tablet (iPad) application that provides viewers with auxiliary information about the show. The television and tablet applications constantly communicate with each other through a common web server. The television sends information like season, episode and playtime to the iPad, which allows the companion application to display content, synchronized with what is appearing on the television screen.

3.2 Features

The companion app provides three features that augment the viewing experience: Character map, Relationship Recaps, and Thematic recaps (in this case, Shootings by the protagonist).

The prototype was developed based on content from the first season of the FX television series *Justified.* The show chronicles the adventures of U.S. Marshal Raylan Givens as he shoots bad guys, befriends his ex-wife, and struggles to maintain his integrity as a lawman while returning to his native Harlan County which is filled with family members and old friends who have varying degrees of criminality. The show is unusually consistent in creating a dense story world populated by well-differentiated and interconnected characters that appear in multiple episodes.

Figure 1. Real time character map

3.2.1 Character Map

The character map (see Figure 1) is a real time, updating graph of characters and relationships. When a character appears within the television show, their thumbnail image appears in real time on the companion iPad app and a connecting line with an icon represents their relationship with other characters on the screen and in the world of the series. A grayed out thumbnail represents characters that are only mentioned but who have not yet appeared in the series. Characters who have appeared before, but are not present in the scene appear in color but smaller than the characters in the current dramatic scene. The unit is not who is in the frame but who is present in the semantic dramatic unit, the scene which is generally based on a single location and continuous fictional time. In addition, characters are arranged semantically across the area of the tablet screen. In this case, there are three geographical areas that are referred to, the current location of Lexington Kentucky, the outlaw territory of Harlan County, and the organized crime headquarters of Miami. The main character, Raylan, has shot someone in Miami and therefore been reassigned to the Marshall's office in Lexington, where he has to come to terms with his ex-wife, working as a court recorder, and with his father and old friends who are outlaws back in Harlan County. The pilot episode introduces all these relationships, and so it serves as a good testbed for providing an auxiliary screen that supports viewing without distracting from the main focus, the television screen. Icons on the lines connecting characters indicate the nature of the relationships between them, such a gun for enemies, a handshake for friends and allies, and a whole or broken heart for romantic relationships. Touching the character thumbnail brings up a brief bio, which changes to reflect the unfolding dramatic revelations and events without exposing the viewer to "spoilers".

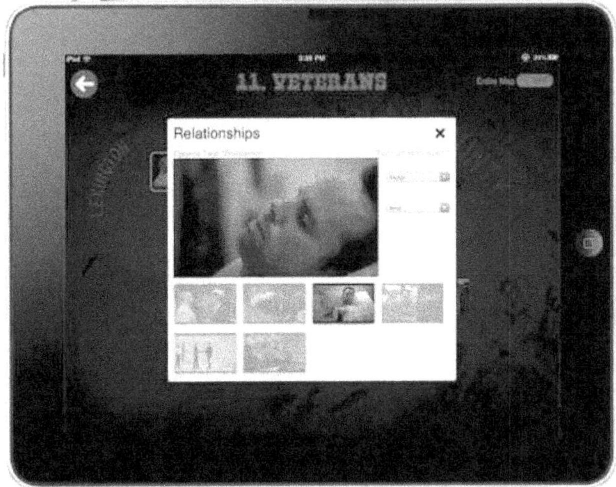

Figure 2. One story thread can be followed across multiple episodes through the Relationship Recap feature

3.2.2 Relationship Recap

The Relationship Recap (see Figure 2) is meant to be accessed from mid-season or late-season episodes to allow fans of the show to review key story threads, and to let viewers who join late in the development of the multi-episode story arc to catch up. The Recap feature is available from the top level of the tablet app, or during a viewing of an individual episode, by tapping on the relationship icon between two characters. Either access point brings up an overlay box that contains thumbnails linked to short video clips that summarize the plot thread concerning two key characters, such as Raylan and his father, Arlo or Raylan and his nemesis, Boyd Crowder. Two drop-downs within this box allow users to select different combinations of two characters to see the clips that summarize their relationship. The video clips play on the iPad without interfering with the television content and can be made to go full screen, so that a viewer may watch these clips independently of the single episode's continuous streaming on the television screen.

Figure 3. Video clips of shootings by the protagonist

3.2.3 Thematic Recap

The application also offers a thematic recap, in this case, all the iconic cowboy-style shoot out scenes featuring the quick draw hero (see Figure 3). Since these shoot outs are among the most exciting scenes in the series, viewers may want to revisit them after watching the entire season. The interface represents thumbnails of the villains in these scenes, arranged in a horizontally scrollable list in chronological order, with viewing space at the center of the iPad. Viewers tap any of the thumbnails to see the video clip on the iPad, with the option to go full screen. As with the Relationship Recaps, the excerpts are drawn from multiple episodes, but labeled with the episode number, name and a characteristic line of dialog that recalls the dramatic context. The recaps are to be seen when the show is not playing, this avoids simultaneous audio playback interference between the TV and the iPad.

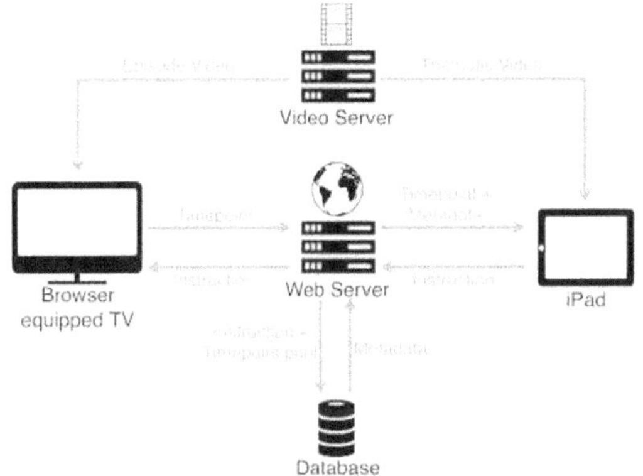

Figure 4. System Diagram

4. IMPLEMENTATION

4.1 Server

The server (see Figure 4) hosts the database that contains tables that keep track of the current timepoint (season, episode, playtime) of the video on the television, maintain a pool of instructions sent by the iPad (like play, pause) and store metadata for episodes, characters and their relationships. It also hosts the HTML, CSS and JavaScript files. The server returns the current timepoint and metadata to the iPad in response to an AJAX request and passes on instructions from the iPad to the TV. Other methods of synchronizing secondary screens like audio fingerprinting exist, but the purpose of this paper is not to explore such technologies, but to quickly develop prototypes that present the kinds of accompanying content that may be shown on a secondary screen in a two screen environment.

4.2 Video Player on a Television/Desktop Browser

The player is a web application that utilizes HTML, JavaScript and CSS. The HTML file contains the embedded flash player that displays the video streamed from a video server. The styling of the page like the background, images, color scheme is defined in the CSS file. JavaScript periodically checks the current timepoint of the video and sends an AJAX request to the server to save it into the database. The player also polls for instructions from the server to play/pause the video.

4.3 Companion App on the iPad

The companion app is a web application that also utilizes HTML, JavaScript and CSS. Being a web app, it can run on any tablet with a modern browser that supports HTML5. The building blocks of the application like the links, character images, relationship links, light-box (the pop up box that appears when a character or relationship is tapped) are specified in an HTML file. The styling of the application like the background, images, typeface, color scheme is defined in the CSS file. JavaScript periodically polls the server by an AJAX request and the server responds with the current timepoint of the video on the television. If the timepoint matches metadata that maps to appearances of characters, these characters and their relationships are shown on the iPad. The application also streams thematic video from the video server and sends instructions to play/pause the video.

5. CONCLUSION

As television series become more consistent and detailed in presenting complex story worlds and multi-episode story arcs, digital companion apps will become more useful in orienting new viewers and in reinforcing the immersive involvement of fans. This project offers an approach based on story structure to establish some conventions for making such aids helpful without creating unnecessary distractions from the viewing experience. User tests are being planned and will be reported on separately. Though developed for one series, *Justified*, the functionalities are presented abstractly so that they can be applied to the genre of television dramas. It will probably be necessary to create authoring templates to make such aids widely useful, including some that could be used by fans to make their own excerpted playlists based on a shared archive or common indexing convention for accessing series video at multiple levels of granularity.

6. ACKNOWLEDGMENTS

We thank eTV members Chethan Anil, Sarah Cooper, Paul Clifton, Thomas Barnwell, Hwajung Hong, Delisha Peterson, Don Fernandez, Tom Gibes, Ethiopia Hewitt, Christine Wu, Shannon Yao, Laurie Marion, Ali Tehrani, Pradyut Pokuri, Nachiketas Ramanujam, and Richard Shepherdson.

7. REFERENCES

[1] Basapur, S., Harboe, G., Mandalia, H., Novak, A., Vuong, V. AND Metcalf, C. 2011. Field trial of a dual device user experience for iTV. In *Proceddings of the 9th international interactive conference on Interactive television* (EuroITV '11). ACM, New York, NY, USA, 127-136. DOI=10.1145/2000119.2000145 http://doi.acm.org/10.1145/2000119.2000145

[2] Bruner, J. 1986. *Actual Minds, Possible Worlds.* Harvard University Press, Cambridge MA.

[3] Cesar, P., Bulterman, D.C.A. AND Jansen, A. J. 2008. Usages of the Secondary Screen in an Interactive Television Environment: Control, Enrich, Share, and Transfer Television Content. In *Proceedings of the 6th European conference on Changing Television Environments* (EUROITV '08), Manfred Tscheligi, Marianna Obrist, and Artur Lugmayr, Eds. Springer-Verlag, Berlin, Heidelberg, 168-177. DOI=10.1007/978-3-540-69478-6_22 http://dx.doi.org/10.1007/978-3-540-69478-6_22

[4] Donald, M. 1991. *Origins of the Modern Mind. Three Stages in the Evolution of Culture and Cognition.* Harvard University Press, Cambridge MA.

[5] HBO GO, 2011. Game of Thrones Interactive Experience. http://www.hbo.com/game-of-thrones/about/video/hbo-go-interactive-experience.html

[6] Jenkins, H. 2006. *Convergence Culture: Where Old and New Media Collide.* New York University Press, New York.

[7] Jenkins, H. 2011. Transmedia 202. http://henryjenkins.org/2011/08/defining_transmedia_further_re.html

[8] Johnson, S. 2005. *Everything Bad is Good for You: How Today's Popular Culture is Actually Making Us Smarter.* Riverhead Books, New York.

[9] Maslowska, M. 2011. Game of Thrones Fan Infographic. http://hauteslides.com/2011/05/game-of-thrones-infographic-illustrated-guide-to-houses-and-character-relationships/

[10] Murray, J.H. 1997. *Hamlet on the Holodeck: The Future of Narrative in Cyberspace.* Free Press, New York.

[11] Murray, J.H., Goldenberg, S., Agarwal, K., Doris-Down, A., Pokuri, P., Ramanujam, N. AND Chakravorty, T. 2011. StoryLines: an approach to navigating multisequential news and entertainment in a multiscreen framework. In *Proceedings of the 8th International Conference on Advances in Computer Entertainment Technology* (ACE '11), Teresa Romão, Nuno Correia, Masahiko Inami, Hirokasu Kato, Rui Prada, Tsutomu Terada, Eduardo Dias, and Teresa Chambel, Eds. ACM, New York, NY, USA, Article 92, 2 pages. DOI=10.1145/2071423.2071533 http://doi.acm.org/10.1145/2071423.2071533

[12] Oatley, K. 2011. *Such Stuff as Dreams: the Psychology of Fiction.* Wiley, Blackwell, Oxford UK.

Author Index